Lecture Notes in Computer Science   9219

Commenced Publication in 1973
Founding and Former Series Editors:
Gerhard Goos, Juris Hartmanis, and Jan van Leeuwen

More information about this series at http://www.springer.com/series/7412

Yu-Jin Zhang (Ed.)

Image
and Graphics

8th International Conference, ICIG 2015
Tianjin, China, August 13–16, 2015
Proceedings, Part III

 Springer

Editor
Yu-Jin Zhang
Department of Electronic Engineering
Tsinghua University
Beijing
China

ISSN 0302-9743 ISSN 1611-3349 (electronic)
Lecture Notes in Computer Science
ISBN 978-3-319-21968-4 ISBN 978-3-319-21969-1 (eBook)
DOI 10.1007/978-3-319-21969-1

Library of Congress Control Number: 2015944504

LNCS Sublibrary: SL6 – Image Processing, Computer Vision, Pattern Recognition, and Graphics

Springer Cham Heidelberg New York Dordrecht London

Printed on acid-free paper

Springer International Publishing AG Switzerland is part of Springer Science+Business Media
(www.springer.com)

Preface

These are the proceedings of the 8th International Conference on Image and Graphics (ICIG 2015), held in Tianjin, China, during August 13–16, 2015.

The China Society of Image and Graphics (CSIG) have organized this series of ICIG conferences since 2000. This time, Microsoft Research Asia was the co-organizer, and the Tianjin Society of Image and Graphics was again the host. Some information about the past seven conferences, as well as the current one, can be found in the following table:

Conference	Place	Date	Sub.	Proc.
First (ICIG 2000)	Tianjin, China	August 16–18	220	156
Second (ICIG 2002)	Hefei, China	August 15–18	280	166
Third (ICIG 2004)	Hong Kong, China	December 17–19	460	140
Fourth (ICIG 2007)	Chengdu, China	August 22–24	525	184
Fifth (ICIG 2009)	Xi'an, China	September 20–23	362	179
Sixth (ICIG 2011)	Hefei, China	August 12–15	329	183
Seventh (ICIG 2013)	Qingdao, China	July 26–28	346	181
Eighth (ICIG 2015)	Tianjin, China	August 13–16	345	170

This time, the proceedings are published by Springer in their LNCS series. The titles, abstracts, and biographies of the five invited speakers of plenary talks are presented first. To ease in the search of a required paper in these proceedings, the 164 regular papers have been arranged in alphabetical order according to their titles. Another six papers forming a special topic are included at the end.

Sincere thanks go to all the contributors (around 1,000), who came from around the world to present their advanced works at this event. Special thanks go to the members of Technical Program Committee (more than 100 with half from outside of mainland China) who carefully reviewed every single submission and made their valuable comments for improving the accepted papers.

The proceedings could not have been produced without the invaluable efforts of the publication chairs, the web chairs, and a number of active members of CSIG.

June 2015   Yu-Jin Zhang

Organizing Committee

(Alphabetical Listing)

Honorary Chairs

Thomas Huang   University of Illinois at Urbana-Champaign, USA
Yunhe Pan   Chinese Academy of Engineering, China
Guanhua Xu   Ministry of Science and Technology, China

General Chairs

Chang Wen Chen   State University of New York at Buffalo, USA
Wen Gao   Peking University, China
Yong Rui   Microsoft Research Asia, China

Program Committee Chairs

Ioannis Pitas   Aristotle University of Thessaloniki, Greece
Yu-Jin Zhang   Tsinghua University, China
Ce Zhu   University of Electronic Science and Technology, China

Publicity Chairs

Shuo Li   GE Healthcare, Canada
Hanzi Wang   Xiamen University, China

Publication Chairs

Yanwei Pang   Tianjin University, China
Lei Wang   University of Wollongong, Australia

Organizing Committee Chairs

Gang Cheng   Tianjin Jinhang Computing Technology Research Institute, China
Guohui Ding   Tianjin Jinhang Computing Technology Research Institute, China
Kailong Liu   China Society of Image and Graphics, China
Tao Mei   Microsoft Research Asia, China
Nenghai Yu   University of Science and Technology of China, China

Overseas Liaisons

Guobin Wu	Microsoft Research Asia, China
Lun Yu	Fuzhou University, China
David Zhang	Hong Kong Polytechnic University, Hong Kong, SAR China

Finance Chair

Boxia Xu	Tianjin Jinhang Computing Technology Research Institute, China

Exhibition Liaison

Xiaojuan Yu	China Society of Image and Graphics

Web Chairs

Yang Xu	Tianjin Society of Image and Graphics, China
Mandun Zhang	Hebei University of Technology, China

Local Arrangements Chair

Dianguo Zhang	Tianjin Jinhang Computing Technology Research Institute, China

Technical Program Committee

Ru An	Hohai University, China
Huihui Bai	Beijing Jiaotong University, China
Xiao Bai	Beihang University, China
Josep Blat	Universitat Pompeu Fabra, Spain
Zhanchuan Cai	Macau University of Science and Technology, Macau, SAR China
Huibin Chang	Tianjin Normal University, China
Chao Chen	Rutgers University, USA
Fuhua Chen	West Liberty University, USA
Jiansheng Chen	Tsinghua University, China
Jyh-Cheng Chen	National Yang Ming University, Taiwan, China
Wei Chen	UIUC, ECE, USA
Mingming Cheng	Nankai University, China
Wen-Huang Cheng	Academia Sinica, Taiwan, China
Casey Chow	University of Wollongong, Australia
Shen-Yang Dai	Google Inc., USA
Xiang Deng	GE Healthcare, China
Fuqing Duan	Beijing Normal University, China
Thomas Fevens	Concordia University, Canada

Pascal Frossard	École Polytechnique Fédérale de Lausanne, Switzerland
Shujun Fu	Shandong University, China
Fei Gao	Siemens, USA
Junbin Gao	Charles Sturt University, Australia
Yongying Gao	Beijing Huaxingvision Technologies Co., Ltd., China
Zexun Geng ˙	Information and Engineering University, PLA, China
Guodong Guo	West Virginia University, USA
Zhiqiang Hou	Air Force Engineering University, China
Dong Hu	Nanjing University of Posts and Telecommunications, China
Xuelong Hu	Yangzhou University, China
Fan Jiang	Facebook Inc., USA
Xiangwei Kong	Dalian University of Technology, China
Adam Krzyzak	Concordia University, Canada
Dengfeng Kuang	Nankai University, Tianjin, China
Chaofeng Li	Jiangnan University, China
Peihua Li	Dalian University of Technology, China
Shuai Li	University of Electronic Science and Technology, China
Xuelong Li	Chinese Academy of Science, China
Zhu Li	Samsung Telecomm America, USA
Haixia Liang	Xi'an Jiaotong-Liverpool University, China
Jianming Liang	University of Arizona, USA
Yawei Liang	Royal Military College of Canada, Canada
Shu Liao	Siemens Medical Solutions, USA
Baodi Liu	China University of Petroleum, China
Jun Liu	Beijing Normal University, China
Lingqia Liu	University of Adelaide, Australia
Wenyu Liu	Huazhong University of Science and Technology, China
Xiaofeng Liu	GE Global Research, USA
Xiao Min Liu	Hologic Inc., USA
Huimin Lu	Kyushu Institute of Technology, Japan
Le Lu	NIH, USA
Bin Luo	Anhui University, China
Xiongbiao Luo	University of Western Ontario, Canada
Jianhua Ma	Southern Medical University, China
Tao Mei	Microsoft Research Asia, China
Yanwei Pang	Tianjin University, China
Charley Paulus	Canal+ (French TV channel), France
Mingtao Pei	Beijing Institute of Technology, China
Son Lam Phung	University of Wollongong, Australia
Qiuqi Ruan	Beijing Jiaotong University, China
Bing Shen	Purdue University, USA
Shengli Sheng	University of Central Arkansas, USA
Yuying Shi	North China Electric Power University, China
Weidong Sun	Tsinghua University, China
Xue-Cheng Tai	University of Bergen, Norway
Huachun Tan	Beijing Institute of Technology, China

Jinshan Tang	Michigan Technological University, USA
Linmi Tao	Tsinghua University, China
Yun Tian	Beijing Normal University, China
Massimo Tistarelli	University of Sassari PolComing, Italy
Yan Tong	University of South Carolina, USA
Guanghui Wang	University of Kansas, USA
Guijin Wang	Tsinghua University, China
Hanzi Wang	Xiamen University, China
Jiening Wang	Civil Aviation University of China, China
Kai Wang	Nankai University, China
Lei Wang	University of Wollongong, Australia
Wei Wang	Tongji University, China
Yuanquan Wang	Tianjin University of Technology, China
Yu-Xiong Wang	Carnegie Mellon University, USA
Zhijie Wang	GE Healthcare, Canada
Chunlin Wu	Nankai University, China
Guobin Wu	Microsoft Research Asia, China
Jonathan Wu	University of Windsor, Canada
Liang Xiao	Nanjing University of Science and Technology, China
Zhitao Xiao	Tianjin Polytechnic University, China
Feng Xu	Samsung, USA
Jing Xu	Zhejiang Gongshang University, China
Ziyue Xu	NIH, USA
Jing-Hao Xue	University College London, UK
Fengbao Yang	North University of China, China
Jinfeng Yang	Civil Aviation University of China, China
Jufeng Yang	Nankai University, China
Jianhua Yao	NIH, USA
Hengyong Yu	Wake Forest University USA
Nenghai Yu	University of Science and Technology of China, China
Xin-Nan Yu	Google, Inc., USA
Tieyong Zeng	Hong Kong Baptist University, Hong Kong, SAR China
Yinwei Zhan	Guangdong University of Technology, China
Yiqiang Zhan	Siemens Medical Solution, USA
Yongzhao Zhan	Jiangsu University, China
Cha Zhang	Microsoft, USA
Lei Zhang	THALES, Hong Kong, SAR China
Qiang Zhang	Dalian University, China
Xuebo Zhang	Nankai University, China
Yu-Jin Zhang	Tsinghua University, China
Xi-Le Zhao	University of Electronic Science and Technology, China
Guoyan Zheng	University of Bern, Switzerland
Jun Zhou	Griffith University, Australia
Luping Zhou	University of Wollongong, Australia
Shoujun Zhou	Chinese Academy of Sciences, China
Xiangrong Zhou	Gifu University, Japan

Ce Zhu	University of Electronic Science and Technology, China
Xiao-Qin Zhu	Cisco Systems Inc., USA
Yong-Gui Zhu	Communication University of China, China
Xiahai Zhuang	Shanghai Jiao Tong University, China
Wangmeng Zuo	Harbin Institute of Technology, China

Plenary Talks

From Shape-from-Shading Through e-Heritage

Katsushi Ikeuchi

The University of Tokyo
http://www.cvl.iis.u-tokyo.ac.jp/~ki/katsu-index-j3.html

Abstract. This talk overviews my research activities from the shape-from-shading through the current e-Heritage project, which digitizes tangible and intangible heritage, analyzes such data for archaeological research and displays in the cloud computer for preservation and promotion.

I began my post-doctoral career at MIT working on shape-from-shading under BKP Horn. Later, I began a project at CMU, with Raj Reddy and Takeo Kanade, to obtain not only shape but also reflectance. This attempt later grew into image-based modeling. After returning to Japan, I applied these modeling and analyzing techniques for the preservation, analysis, and promotion of cultural heritage.

In this talk, I will not only cover current results but also overview the flow of research conducted along this line with emphasis on what were the motivations and how each research step moved into the next level of research; I will also try to extract key lessons learned through these activities.

This is an extended version of my distinguished researcher award talk at Barcelona ICCV with the addition of new archaeological findings obtained from the analysis of the e-Heritage data.

References

1. Ikeuchi, K., Horn, B.K.P: Numerical shape from shading with occluding boundaries. AIJ **17**, 141–184
2. Ikeuchi, K., Miyazaki, D.: Digitally Archiving Cultural Objects. Springer

Biography

Dr. Katsushi Ikeuchi is Professor at the University of Tokyo. He received a PhD degree in Information Engineering from the University of Tokyo in 1978. After working at the Massachusetts Institute of Technology's AI Lab for 2 years, at the Electro-technical Lab, Japan, for 5 years, and Carnegie Mellon University for 10 years, he joined Tokyo University in 1996. His research interest spans computer vision, robotics, and computer graphics. He was general/program chair of more than a dozen international conferences, including IROS 1995, CVPR 1996, ICCV 2003, ICRA 2009, and ICPR

2012. He is an EIC of International Journal of Computer Vision. He has received several awards, including the IEEE Marr Award, the IEEE RAS "most active distinguished lecturer" award, and the IEEE PAMI-TC Distinguished Researcher Award as well as ShijuHoushou (the Medal of Honor with purple ribbon) from the Emperor of Japan. He is a fellow of the IEEE, IEICE, IPSJ, and RSJ.

Tasking on the Natural Statistics of Pictures and Videos

Alan Conrad Bovik

Laboratory for Image and Video Engineering (LIVE)
The University of Texas at Austin

Abstract. I will discuss a variety of topics related to the statistics of pictures and videos of the real world, how they relate to visual perception, and most importantly how they can be used to accomplish perceptually relevant picture-processing and video-processing tasks. Underlying my talk is the thesis that pictures and videos of the real world obey lawful statistical behavior that can be modeled. These models supply useful statistical priors that can be used to define or regularize the solutions to a variety of visual problems. I will address the application of these models to such visual tasks as visual quality assessment, efficient video data delivery in rate-adaptive network environments, face detection in difficult environments, and depth estimation from a single image. I will describe the ongoing work in LIVE in these areas and pose some general problems to be solved in the future.

Biography

Al Bovik is the Curry/Cullen Trust Endowed Chair Professor at The University of Texas at Austin. He has received a number of major awards from the IEEE Signal Processing Society, including: the Society Award (2013); the Technical Achievement Award (2005); the Best Paper Award (2009); the Education Award (2007); the Magazine Best Paper Award (2013); the Distinguished Lecturer Award (2000); the Young Author Best Paper Award (2013); and the Meritorious Service Award (1998). He has also received the SPIE Technology Achievement Award in 2012, the IS&T Honorary Membership in 2014, and was named Imaging Scientist of the Year by IS&T/SPIE in 2011. He is the author/co-author of *The Handbook of Image and Video Processing*, *Modern Image Quality Assessment*, and two recent books, *The Essential Guides to Image and Video Processing*.

Al co-founded and was the longest-serving Editor-in-Chief of the *IEEE Transactions on Image Processing* (1996–2002), and created and served as the first General Chairman of the IEEE International Conference on Image Processing, held in Austin, Texas, in November, 1994.

Region of Interest Coding for Monitoring the Ground with an Unmanned Aerial Vehicle

Jörn Ostermann

Electrical Engineering and Communications Engineering
The University of Hannover and Imperial College London

Abstract. For the transmission of aerial surveillance videos taken from unmanned aerial vehicles, region-of-interest-based coding systems are of growing interest in order to cope with the limited channel capacities available. We present a fully automatic detection and coding system that is capable of transmitting HD-resolution aerial videos at bit rates below 1 Mbit/s. In order to achieve this goal, we extend the video coder HEVC by affine global motion compensation. Results of the computer vision algorithms control the extended HEVC encoder.

For detection of moving objects, we analyze the video and compare a motion-compensated previous image with the current image. Image segmentation based on superpixels helps to select entire moving objects. In order to achieve low false-positive rates and low data rates, we use different motion-compensation algorithms for video analysis and video coding. Depending on the size of the moving objects on the ground, we can save up to 90 % of the data rate of regular HEVC without loss of image quality and the additional benefit of providing a mosaic of the video with moving objects.

Biography

Jörn Ostermann studied Electrical Engineering and Communications Engineering at the University of Hannover and Imperial College London, respectively. He received Dipl.-Ing. and Dr.-Ing. degrees from the University of Hannover in 1988 and 1994, respectively. From 1988 to 1994, he worked as Research Assistant at the Institut für Theoretische Nachrichtentechnik conducting research in low bit-rate and object-based analysis-synthesis video coding. In 1994 and 1995 he worked in the Visual Communications Research Department at AT&T Bell Labs on video coding. He was a member of Image Processing and Technology Research within AT&T Labs–Research from 1996 to 2003. Since 2003 he is Full Professor and Head of the Institut für Informationsverarbeitung at the Leibniz Universität Hannover (LUH), Germany. From 2007 to 2011, he served as head of the Laboratory for Information Technology.

From 1993 to 1994, he chaired the European COST 211 sim group coordinating research in low bit-rate video coding. Within MPEG-4, he organized the evaluation of video tools to start defining the standard. He chaired the Ad Hoc Group on Coding of Arbitrarily Shaped Objects in MPEG-4 Video. Since 2008, he has been the Chair of the Requirements Group of MPEG (ISO/IEC JTC1 SC29 WG11). From 2011 to 2013, he served as Dean of the Faculty of Electrical Engineering and Computer Science at LUH.

Jörn was a scholar of the German National Foundation. In 1998, he received the AT&T Standards Recognition Award and the ISO award. He is a Fellow of the IEEE (class of 2005) and member of the IEEE Technical Committee on Multimedia Signal Processing and past chair of the IEEE CAS Visual Signal Processing and Communications (VSPC) Technical Committee. Jörn served as a Distinguished Lecturer of the IEEE CAS Society (2002/2003). He has published more than 100 research papers and book chapters. He is coauthor of a graduate-level textbook on video communications. He holds more than 30 patents.

His current research interests are video coding and streaming, computer vision, 3D modeling, face animation, and computer–human interfaces.

Big Data in Smart City

Deren Li

State Key Laboratory of Information Engineering in Surveying, Mapping,
and Remote Sensing,
Wuhan University, Wuhan 430079, China

Abstract. In this lecture, I will introduce the concept of smart city and summarize its development process. Then, I will describe the key technologies of smart cities and the proposed smart city infrastructure. Smart city is based on digital city, Internet of Things (IOT), and cloud computing, which will integrate the real world with the digital world. In order to achieve a comprehensive awareness and control of people and things, with intelligent service followed, smart city with mass sensors will continue to collect vast amounts of data, called big data. Typical types of big data such as geospatial image, graph and video data, are analyzed in my talk. The big data of smart city are not only a frontier, but also the driving force to promote the development of smart city, which will bring new opportunities and challenges. I will also propose a strategy for dealing with big data and will define the basic framework for a smart city big data operation center, which will eventually lead to a bright future for smart cities.

Keywords: Smart city; Big data; Digital city; IOT; Cloud computing; Intelligence service; Data mining; smart city big data operation center

Biography

Prof. Dr.-Ing Li Deren is a researcher in photogrammetry and remote sensing, and is a member of both the Chinese Academy of Sciences and the Chinese Academy of Engineering as well as the Euro-Asia International Academy of Science. He is a professor and PhD supervisor at Wuhan University, and is Vice-President of the Chinese Society of Geodesy, Photogrammetry and Cartography, and Chairman of the Academic Commission of Wuhan University and the National Laboratory for Information Engineering in Surveying, Mapping and Remote Sensing (LIESMARS). He has concentrated on research and education in spatial information science and technology represented by remote sensing (RS), global navigation satellite systems (GNSSs), and geographic information systems (GISs). His majors are analytic and digital photogrammetry, remote sensing, mathematical morphology and its application in spatial databases, theories of object-oriented GIS and spatial data mining in GIS, as well as mobile mapping systems, etc.

Professor Deren Li served as Comm. III and Comm. VI President of ISPRS in the periods 1988–1992 and 1992–1996, worked for CEOS during 2002–2004, and was president of the Asia GIS Association during 2003–2006. He received the title Dr.h.c. from ETH in 2008. In 2010 and 2012 he was elected ISPRS fellow and honorary member.

Computing Paradigms: Transformation and Opportunities

Thinking on Data Science and Machine Intelligence

Jinpeng Huai

President, Beihang University, China

Abstract. The arrival of the big data era is changing our traditional understanding and methodologies of computing. This includes, for example, the possibility of accessing enormous and statistically diversified data in their entirety, the shift from exactitude to inexactitude and from the pursuit of accuracy to quick forecasts of macro trends, and the possibility of extracting correlations across domains.

On the verge of this paradigm shift, we advocate three important features desirable in big data computation: inexactness, incrementalness, and inductiveness (3 *I*s). Firstly, finding inexact solutions with bounds shall substitute seeking exact solutions in the traditional regime. Secondly, incremental models and algorithms are desired to accommodate data that are being continuously and rapidly produced and updated.

Finally, correlations hidden among multiple data sources present greater demands for induction and pattern generalization. We will discuss relevant scientific problems exemplifying these three computing features.

Biography

Dr. Huai Jinpeng, born in December 1962, is Fellow of the Chinese Academy of Sciences and President of Beihang University (BUAA) in Beijing, China. He received his PhD in Computer Science from Beihang University.

Dr. Huai's research focus has been on computer science and software. His work has effectively broken through the limitations and difficulties of network resource sharing and utilization. He has established algebraic theories and algorithms for cryptographic protocol analyses, which greatly improved the security of critical information systems. He has also proposed a "zero-programming" model for process-oriented software developments, which significantly enhanced the automatic development of large-scale distributed applications. These works have benefited China's economic and social development.

Dr. Huai has won many prominent awards, including second prize in the National Award of Scientific and Technological Advancement (twice), second prize in the National Award of Technological Invention, the Scientific and Technological Advancement Award from the Ho Leung Ho Lee Fund, the 4th IET-Founder

University President Award, and the insignia of Knight of French National Order of the Legion of Honor. He has published more than 120 papers, owns more than 30 Chinese patents, has been invited to 14 international conferences as a keynote speaker, and has chaired conferences of considerable importance, such as WWW 2008 and SRDS 2007.

Dr. Huai has been Chief Scientist on the Steering Committees on the IT domain and advanced computing technology subject, both of the National High-Tech R&D Program (863 Program), since 2001. He is also Chair of the Steering Committee on Foundational Software for National Science and Technology Major Project and Deputy Chair of the China Computer Federation. He has made significant contributions to national strategic R&D planning and the industrialization of information technology, especially computing in China.

Contents – Part III

Special Topic: Edutainment and Application

Pan-Sharpening via Coupled Unitary Dictionary Learning

Shumiao Chen[1(✉)], Liang Xiao[1,2], Zhihui Wei[1], and Wei Huang[1]

[1] School of Computer Science and Engineering,
Nanjing University of Science and Technology,
Xiaolingwei Street 200, Nanjing 210094, Jiangsu, China
chenshumiao@126.com,
{xiaoliang,gswei}@mail.njust.edu.cn, hnhw235@163.com
[2] Key Lab of Intelligent Perception and Systems for High-Dimensional
Information of Ministry of Education,
Xiaolingwei Street 200, Nanjing 210094, Jiangsu, China

Abstract. In this paper, we propose a new pan-sharpening method by coupled unitary dictionary learning and clustered sparse representation. First, we randomly sample image patch pairs from the training images exclude the smooth patches, and divide these patch pairs into different groups by K-means clustering. Then, we learn sub-dictionaries offline from corresponding group patch pairs. Particularly, we use the principal component analysis (PCA) technique to learn sub-dictionaries. For a given LR MS patch, we adaptively select one sub-dictionary to reconstruct the HR MS patch online. Experiments show that the proposed method produces images with higher spectral resolution while maintaining the high-quality spatial resolution and gives better visual perception compared with the conventional methods.

Keywords: Pan-sharpening · Sparse representation · Sub-dictionaries learning · K-means clustering

1 Introduction

Many optical Earth observation satellites, such as QuickBird, Worldview2, and IKONOS, provide two types of images: high resolution panchromatic images (PAN) and low resolution multispectral (MS) images. The multispectral image lacks high spatial quality and the panchromatic image has low spectral quality. However, there are a number of applications in remote sensing that require images of both high spatial and high spectral resolutions, such as object detection, land-cover classification, map updating [1]. The fusion of PAN and MS images is called "pan-sharpening". It provides a solution to this by fusing a high spatial resolution MS image from the input LR MS image and the HR PAN image.

1.1 Related Work

Over the years, a large collection of pan-sharpening methods has been proposed, which usually consider physics of the remote sensing process and make some assumptions on

© Springer International Publishing Switzerland 2015
Y.-J. Zhang (Ed.): ICIG 2015, Part III, LNCS 9219, pp. 1–10, 2015.
DOI: 10.1007/978-3-319-21969-1_1

the original PAN and MS images. These fusion methods can be classified into three categories. First, projection-substitution methods assume that the PAN is equivalent to the structural component of the MS images when projected the MS images into a new space, for example, Intensity-Hue-Saturation Technique (IHS) [2] and its modifications such as the adaptive IHS (AIHS) [3], Principal Components Analysis (PCA) [4], Brovey transform [5]. Second, spatial details injection methods assume that the missing spatial information in the MS images can be obtained from the high frequencies of the PAN, such as wavelet-based fusion [6]. Third, the inverse-problem-based methods are used to restore the original high-resolution MS images from its degraded versions, i.e., the HR PAN and LR MS images.

Recently, Li and Zhu et al. proposed a novel pan-sharpening method using a compressed sensing technique and sparse representation [7, 8]. A critical issue in sparse representation modeling is the determination of dictionary. Li and Zhu generated the dictionary by randomly sampling or extracting all raw patches from the training image directly. In addition, analytically designed dictionaries, such as DCT, wavelet, curvelet, and contourlets, share the advantages of fast implementation. However, they lack the adaptivity to image local structures. There has been much effort in learning dictionaries from example image patches, such as K-SVD [9], leading to state-of-the-art results. These dictionary learning methods aim at learning a universal and over-complete dictionary to represent various image structures. However, the image contents can vary significantly across images. Sparse decomposition over a highly redundant dictionary is potentially unstable and tends to generate visual artifacts [10, 11]. One may argue that a well-learned over-complete dictionary can sparsely code all of the possible image structures; nonetheless, for each given image patch, such a "universal" dictionary is neither optimal nor efficient because many atoms in the dictionary are irrelevant to the given local patch. These irrelevant atoms will not only reduce the computational efficiency in sparse coding but also reduce the representation accuracy.

1.2   Our Contributions

In this paper, we propose an adaptive sparse domain selection scheme for sparse representation. A set of compact sub-dictionaries is learned from the PAN image patches, which are clustered into many clusters. Since each cluster consists of many patches with similar patterns, a compact sub-dictionary can be learned for each cluster. In particular, we use the PCA to learn each sub-dictionary for simplicity. For a LR MS image patch to be coded, the best sub-dictionary that is most relevant to the given patch is selected. Thus, the given patch can be better represented by the adaptively selected sub-dictionary. Therefore, the whole image can be more accurately reconstructed than using a universal dictionary, which will be validated by our experiments.

The rest of this paper is organized into four sections. Section 2 presents the proposed method. Numerical experiments and discussions are presented in Sect. 3. Conclusions are given in Sect. 4.

2 Proposed Work

Pan-sharpening requires a low-resolution multispectral (LR MS) image $\mathbf{Y}$ with N channels and a high-resolution panchromatic(HR PAN) image $\mathbf{X}_h$ and aims at increasing the spatial resolution of $\mathbf{Y}$ while keeping its spectral information, i.e., generating an HR MS image $\mathbf{X}$ utilizing both $\mathbf{Y}$ and $\mathbf{X}_h$ as inputs. While the SparseFI algorithm in Ref. [8] has achieved a very good pan-sharpening result compared with other conventional methods, there is still much room to improve this algorithm, especially in the dictionary training stage. In order to exploit the group similarity among image patch pairs, we propose coupled dictionary learning and clustered sparse representation method to improve the quality of the recovered HR MS image. The proposed method consists of three main steps: (1) coupled unitary sub-dictionaries learning; (2) sparse coefficients estimation; and (3) HR multispectral image reconstruction (see Fig. 1).

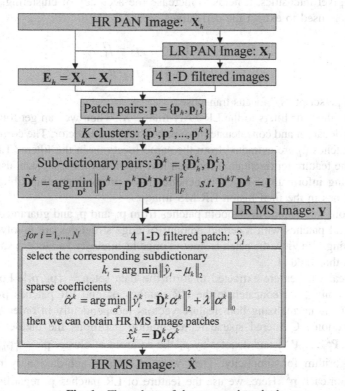

Fig. 1. Flow chart of the proposed method.

2.1 Coupled Unitary Sub-dictionaries Learning

The HR PAN image $\mathbf{X}_h$ is low-pass filtered and downsampled by a factor such that it has a final point spread function similar to a sampling grid identical to the multispectral channels, and then scaled-up by a bicubic interpolation operator that fills in the missing pixels to generate LR PAN image denoted by X_l. Thus, X_h and X_l have the same size so that can avoid the complexity caused by different size.

In order to learn a series of sub-dictionaries to code the various local image structures, we need to first construct a dataset of HR and LR image patches for training. The training HR image patches p_h are extracted from the difference image $E_h = X_h - X_l$, since we desire to focus the training on characterizing the relation between the LR patches and the edges and texture content within the corresponding HR ones [12]. In many literatures, people have suggested extracting different features for the LR image patch in order to boost the prediction accuracy. Freeman et al. [13] used a high-pass filter to extract the edge information from the LR input patches as the feature. Sun et al. [14] used a set of Gaussian derivative filters to extract the contours in the LR patches. Yang et al. [15] used the first-order and second-order gradients of the patches as the representation. In this paper, we also use the first-order and second-order derivatives as the feature for the LR patch due to its simplicity and effectiveness. It allows us to focus on the edges and structures of image patches without taking into account the pixel intensities. It helps to increase the accuracy of clustering. Here, the four 1-D filters used to extract the derivatives are:

$$f_1 = [-1, 0, 1], \qquad f_2 = f_1^T$$
$$f_3 = [1, 0, -2, 0, 1], \quad f_4 = f_3^T \tag{1}$$

where the superscript "T" means transpose.

We apply the four filters to the LR PAN image X_l. Then we can get four gradient maps at each location and concatenate them to be the feature vector. The corresponding LR image patches p_l are extracted from the same locations in the filtered LR images. Therefore, the feature representation for each low-resolution image patch also encodes its neighboring information, which is beneficial for promoting compatibility among adjacent patches in the final fusion HR MS image.

In addition, we exclude the smooth patches from p_h and p_l and guarantee that only the meaningful patches with a certain amount of edge structures are involved in dictionary learning. We view the patch is smooth once its intensity variance is smaller than a predefined threshold Δ.

Thus, local patches are extracted to form the data set $p = \{p_h, p_l\}$. For coupled dictionary learning, we concatenate the HR patches p_h and LR patches p_l into one single vector via normalizing both feature vectors independently in order to balance their contributions. Clustered sparse representation partitions the dataset p into K clusters $\{P^1, P^2, \ldots, P^K\}$ and denotes by μ_k the centroid of cluster $p^k = \{p_h^k, p_l^k\}$ with K-means algorithm for simplicity. Then we can learn a sub-dictionary pair $D^k = \{D_h^k, D_l^k\}$ from each p^k. Here, we use the feature of LR patches p_l regardless of HR patches p_h for clustering, since the LR patches are more reliable than the HR patches. In order to compute the sparse coefficients conveniently in stage two, we apply PCA to learn the sub-dictionary pair $\{D_h^k, D_l^k\}$ from each image patch pair $\{p_h^k, p_l^k\}$. PCA is a classical signal de-correlation and dimensionality reduction technique that is widely used in pattern recognition and statistical signal processing. In many literatures, PCA has been successfully used in spatially adaptive image denoising and super-resolution.

The purpose of PCA is to find an orthogonal transformation matrix minimizing the error of reconstruction. So, the learning model of each sub-dictionary can be mathematically written as follows:

$$\begin{cases} \hat{\mathbf{D}}_h^k = \arg\min_{\mathbf{D}_h^k} \left\| \mathbf{p}_h^k - \mathbf{p}_h^k \mathbf{D}_h^k \mathbf{D}_h^{kT} \right\|_F^2 \quad s.t. \ \mathbf{D}_h^{kT} \mathbf{D}_h^k = \mathbf{I} \\ \\ \hat{\mathbf{D}}_l^k = \arg\min_{\mathbf{D}_l^k} \left\| \mathbf{p}_l^k - \mathbf{p}_l^k \mathbf{D}_l^k \mathbf{D}_l^{kT} \right\|_F^2 \quad s.t. \ \mathbf{D}_l^{kT} \mathbf{D}_l^k = \mathbf{I} \end{cases}, k = 1, \ldots, K \quad (2)$$

where $\mathbf{p}_h^k$ denotes the k-th cluster of HR patches $\mathbf{p}_h$; $\mathbf{p}_l^k$ denotes the k-th cluster of LR patches $\mathbf{p}_l$. Equation (2) can be rewritten as follows:

$$\hat{\mathbf{D}}^k = \arg\min_{\mathbf{D}^k} \left\| \mathbf{p}^k - \mathbf{p}^k \mathbf{D}^k \mathbf{D}^{kT} \right\|_F^2 \quad s.t. \ \mathbf{D}^{kT} \mathbf{D}^k = \mathbf{I}$$

$$\text{Where } \hat{\mathbf{D}}^k = \begin{bmatrix} \hat{\mathbf{D}}_h^k \\ \hat{\mathbf{D}}_l^k \end{bmatrix}, \quad \mathbf{p}^k = \begin{bmatrix} \mathbf{P}_h^k \\ \mathbf{P}_l^k \end{bmatrix}, \quad k = 1, \ldots, K. \quad (3)$$

Denote by $\mathbf{\Omega}^k$ the co-variance matrix of sub-dataset $\mathbf{p}^k$. By applying PCA to $\mathbf{\Omega}^k$, an orthogonal transformation matrix can be obtained. We set the matrix as the sub-dictionary $\hat{\mathbf{D}}^k$.

2.2 Sparse Coefficients Estimation

For a given LR MS image $\mathbf{Y}$ corresponding to the HR PAN image $\mathbf{X}_h$ with N channels, $\mathbf{Y}$ are tiled into partially overlapping patches y_i, where φi stands for the i-th channel and $i = 1, \ldots, N$. As mentioned above, we have learned sub-dictionary pairs $\{\hat{\mathbf{D}}_h^k, \hat{\mathbf{D}}_l^k\}$ and obtained the centroid μ_k of each cluster. With regard to the observed LR MS image, we also extract the features $\mathbf{Y}$ using four 1-D filters in Eq. (1). Then, we select the corresponding sub-dictionary based on the minimum distance between $\hat{y}_i$ and the centroid μ_k by the following formula:

$$k_i = \arg\min \left\| \hat{y}_i - \mu_k \right\|_2 \quad (4)$$

By using Eq. (4), we can find the most similar patches $\hat{y}_i^k$ in the k_i-th cluster, which has sparse representation over the k_i-th sub-dictionary.

This step attempts to represent each LR MS patch $\hat{y}_i^k$ as a linear combination of the atoms of the dictionary $\hat{\mathbf{D}}_l^k$ with a coefficient vector denoted by α^k. We argue that it is very likely that the "best" solution is the one employing the least number of the atoms. Therefore, for each LR MS patch $\hat{y}_i^k$, a sparse coefficient vector α^k is estimated by the following formula:

$$\hat{\alpha}^k = \arg\min_{\alpha^k}\left\|\hat{y}_i^k - \hat{\mathbf{D}}_l^k\alpha^k\right\|_2^2, \quad s.t. \left\|\alpha^k\right\|_0 \leq L \tag{5}$$

where L denotes the sparsity threshold. Equation (5) can be rewritten as follows:

$$\hat{\alpha}^k = \arg\min_{\alpha^k}\left\|\hat{y}_i^k - \hat{\mathbf{D}}_l^k\alpha^k\right\|_2^2 + \lambda\left\|\alpha^k\right\|_0 \tag{6}$$

where λ is the standard Lagrangian multiplier, balancing the sparsity of the solution and the fidelity of the approximation to $\hat{y}_i^k$. Due to the orthogonality of $\hat{\mathbf{D}}_l^k$ and the L0 regularization of α^k, Eq. (4) can be solved by hard thresholding:

$$\alpha^k = H_\lambda\left(\hat{\mathbf{D}}_l^{kT}\hat{y}_i^k\right) \tag{7}$$

where H_λ is the threshold operator, i.e., $H_\lambda(\Theta) = \begin{cases} \Theta, & |\Theta| > \lambda \\ 0, & |\Theta| \leq \lambda \end{cases}$.

2.3   HR MS Image Reconstruction

Due to the fact that the sub-dictionaries are built up from the PAN image observing the same area and acquired at the same time as the multispectral channels, the LR MS image patches and their corresponding HR patches to be reconstructed are expected to have a sparse representation in this coupled unitary HR/LR dictionary pair. Furthermore, it is reasonable to assume that there exists a hidden mapping where the different resolutions images can be converted to each other. To keep the assumption simple, many literatures [7, 8, 15] supposed that the representation coefficients of the image pair should be equal. In this paper, we also assume that each of the HR image patches share the same sparse coefficients as the corresponding LR image patch in the dictionary pair, i.e., the coefficients of the corresponding k_i-th cluster HR MS image patches x_i^k in $\hat{\mathbf{D}}_h^k$ are identical to the coefficients of $\hat{y}_i^k$ in $\hat{\mathbf{D}}_l^k$. In the end, the final sharpened multispectral image patches $\hat{x}_i^k$ are reconstructed by

$$\hat{x}_i^k = \mathbf{D}_h^k\alpha^k \tag{8}$$

The tiling and summation of all patches in all individual channels finally give the desired pan-sharpened image $\hat{\mathbf{X}}$.

3   Experiments Results

3.1   Experiments on Worldview-2 Data Set

In this section, we evaluate our proposed method on Worldview-2 sensing image and both the sizes of PAN and up-sampled LR MS images are 512×512. The MS images have four bands, i.e., RGB and near infrared (NIR). In the sub-dictionaries learning stage, we randomly sample 100000 image patch pairs $\{\mathbf{p}_h, \mathbf{p}_l\}$ with the same size of 7×7. In addition, we set the threshold $\varDelta = 10$ to exclude the smooth patches and set the Lagrangian multiplier $\lambda = 0.15$. As a clustering-based method, an important issue is the selection of the number of classes. A too large or a too small number of the classes will make the learned sub-dictionaries less reliable. Based on the above considerations, we propose the following simple method to find a good number of classes: we first partition the training dataset into 200 clusters, and merge those classes that contain very few image patches (i.e., less than 300 patches) to their nearest neighboring classes. The original dual images are first downsampled to a lower resolution with bicubic interpolation (the downsampling factor is 1/2) and then fused back to the original resolution. Therefore, the HR MS image is available and the quality of the pan-sharpened images can be measured using full-reference image quality metrics.

We compare the performance with other existing fusion methods, namely, the adaptive IHS (AIHS) [3], the PCA method [4], Wavelet-based image fusion method [6], and SparseFI method [8]. Figures 2(a) and (b) show a Worldview-2 LR MS image (visualized using the color composite of red, green, and blue bands) and a PAN image, respectively. Figure 2(h) shows the reference HR MS image. Figures 2(c) and (g) show the pan-sharpened HR MS images obtained by five different methods.

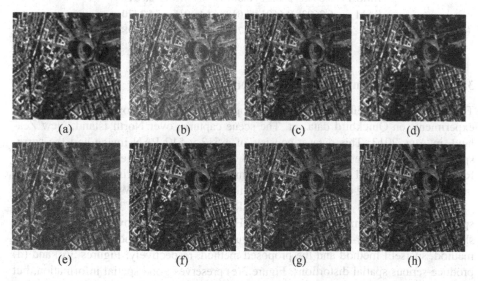

Fig. 2. Worldview-2 images and experimental results by different methods. (a) Resampled LR MS image. (b) PAN image. (c) AIHS method. (d) PCA method. (e) Wavelet-based method. (f) SparseFI method. (g) Proposed method. (h) Reference MS image.

Obviously, Fig. 2(c) produces halo artifacts around edges compared with the reference HR MS image. Figure 2(d) has poor visual perception due to its serious spatial distortions and spectral distortions. It can be seen that Fig. 2(e) generates good contrast, but it has an obvious chromatic aberration compared with the reference MS image, which reflects poor performance in preserving the spectral information. Figure 2(f) preserves the spectral properties better than the above methods, but it shows poor spatial results in details. By contrast, the proposed method in Fig. 2(g) can produce a pan-sharpened image looking very similar to the reference HR MS image. It can not only preserve the spectral information, but also show much finer details than all the methods.

In this paper, five widely used qualitative assessments, i.e., correlation coefficient (CC), root-mean squared error (RMSE), spectral angle mapper (SAM), error relative dimensionless global error in synthesis (ERGAS) and universal image quality indexes (Q4) are adopted. The objective qualitative assessments of fused images in Fig. 2 are shown in Table 1, in which the best results for each criterion are labeled in bold. It can be seen that the proposed method shows the best pan-sharpening performance in terms of all image quality indexes.

Table 1. Comparison of the proposed method with other methods on Worldview-2 data set

Method	AIHS	PCA	Wavelet	SparseFI	Proposed
CC	0.9291	0.8904	0.9184	0.9369	**0.9469**
ERGAS	4.9479	7.7581	5.1201	4.7095	**4.0633**
RMSE	0.0643	0.1027	0.0674	0.0613	**0.0519**
SAM	5.3603	8.6601	7.6128	4.4015	**4.2470**
Q4	0.7907	0.6221	0.7134	0.8236	**0.8498**

3.2 Experiments on Quickbird Data Set

To further verify the effectiveness of the proposed method, we move on to conduct the experiments on Quickbird data set. The scene captures over North Island, New Zealand, in Aug. 2012. This dataset consists of a 512×512 PAN image and the corresponding LR MS image with the size of 128×128. The MS image has four bands, i.e., RGB and near infrared (NIR). In this experiment, the size of PAN image, the number of image patch pairs, and other parameters are the same as those on Worldview-2 data set.

Figure 3(a) shows a resampled color LR MS image. Figure 3(b) gives the corresponding HR PAN image. The reference HR MS image is shown in Fig. 3(h). As shown in the Fig. 3(c)-(g), they are reconstructed by AIHS method, PCA method, WT method, sparseFI method and the proposed method, respectively. Figures 3(c) and (d) produce serious spatial distortions. Figure 3(e) preserves good spatial information, but suffers from significant spectral distortions. Figure 3(f) gains better performance on a tradeoff between the spatial and spectral information than Fig. 3(c) and (d), but it has great difference in spatial details compared with Fig. 3(h). On the whole, the proposed method shown in Fig. 3(g) outperforms other pan-sharpening methods, as well as the conclusions in Fig. 2.

The objective qualitative assessments of fused images in Fig. 3 are shown in Table 2, in which the best results for each criterion are labeled in bold. Similar to the Table 1, the proposed method performs best in all quality indexes. Therefore, the

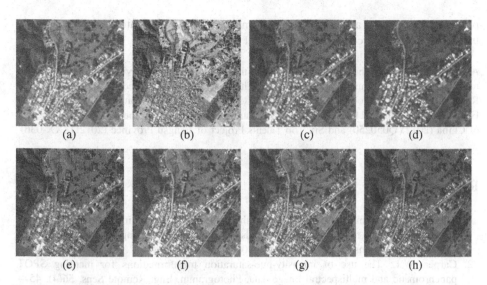

Fig. 3. Quickbird images and experimental results by different methods. (a) Resampled LR MS image. (b) PAN image. (c) AIHS method. (d) PCA method. (e) Wavelet-based method. (f) SparseFI method. (g) Proposed method. (h) Reference MS image.

Table 2. Comparison of the proposed method with other methods on Quickbird data set

Method	AIHS	PCA	Wavelet	SparseFI	Proposed
CC	0.9056	0.8510	0.8825	0.9065	**0.9112**
ERGAS	5.0827	6.4203	5.3053	4.6749	**3.6944**
RMSE	0.0412	0.0553	0.0387	0.0365	**0.0286**
SAM	5.9755	7.6028	8.1403	4.4015	**4.0232**
Q4	0.6808	0.6496	0.5790	0.6861	**0.7061**

proposed method produces the best fused results and performs the robustness for both the Worldview-2 and Quickbird data sets.

4 Conclusion

In this paper, we propose a new pan-sharpening method by coupled dictionary learning and clustered sparse representation for remote sensing image fusion problem. Sub-dictionaries learning overcome the drawback with those atoms which irrelevant to the given local patch in a universal dictionary. We use K-means algorithm and PCA technique to acquire the clusters and each corresponding sub-dictionary. After coupled unitary sub-dictionaries training, the proposed method will be able to reconstruct the HR MS image from the observed LR MS image, since we assume that each of the HR image patches share the same sparse coefficients as the corresponding LR image patch in the coupled HR/LR dictionary pair. Experimental results have demonstrated the proposed method can achieve better performance outperforms state-of-the-art methods in terms of visual perception and numerical measures.

Acknowledgement. The authors would like to thank the anonymous reviewers for their careful reading and useful comments on this paper. This research is supported by the Fundamental Research Funds for the Central Universities (30915012204), the National Nature Science Foundation of China (61171165, 11431015), National Scientific Equipment Developing Project of China (2012YQ050250) and Six Top Talents Project of Jiangsu Province (2012DZXX-036).

References

1. Thomas, C., Ranchin, T., Wald, L.: Synthesis of multispectral images to high spatial resolution: a critical review of fusion methods based on remote sensing physics. IEEE Trans. Geosci. Remote Sens. **46**(5), 1301–1312 (2008)
2. Carper, W.J.: The use of intensity-hue-saturation transformations for merging SPOT panchromatic and multispectral image data. Photogramm. Eng. Remote Sens. **56**(4), 457–467 (1990)
3. Rahmani, S., Strait, M., Merkurjev, D.: An adaptive IHS pan-sharpening method. IEEE Geosci. Remote Sens. Lett. **7**(4), 746–775 (2010)
4. Chen, M., Xuan, J.H., Li, D.R.: Image fusion algorithm based on independent component analysis. Opto-Electron. Eng. **34**(11), 82–84 (2007)
5. Zhang, Y.: Problems in the fusion of commercial high-resolution satelitte as well as Landsat 7 Images and Initial Solutions. Int. Arch. Photogrammetry Remote Sens. Spat. Inf. Sci. **34**(4), 587–592 (2002)
6. Otazu, X., González-Audícana, M., Fors, O.: Introduction of sensor spectral response into image fusion methods. IEEE Trans. Geosci. Remote Sens. **43**(10), 2376–2385 (2005)
7. Li, S., Yang, B.: A new pan-sharpening method using a compressed sensing technique. IEEE Trans. Geosci. Remote Sens. **49**(2), 738–746 (2011)
8. Zhu, X.X., Bamler, R.: A sparse image fusion algorithm with application to pan-sharpening. IEEE Trans. Geosci. Remote Sens. **51**(5), 2827–2836 (2013)
9. Aharon, M., Elad, M., Bruckstein, A.: K-SVD: an algorithm for designing overcomplete dictionaries for sparse representation. IEEE Trans. Sign. Process. **54**(11), 4311–4322 (2006)
10. Elad, M., Yavneh, I.: A plurality of sparse representations is better than the sparsest one alone. IEEE Trans. Inf. Theor. **55**(10), 4701–4714 (2009)
11. Protter, M., Yavneh, I., Elad, M.: Closed-form MMSE estimation for signal denoising under sparse representation modeling over a unitary dictionary. IEEE Trans. Sign. Process. **58**(7), 3471–3484 (2010)
12. Zeyde, R., Elad, M., Protter, M: On single image scale-up using sparse-representations. In: Proceedings of the 7th International Conference on Curves and Surfaces, pp. 711–730 (2010)
13. Freeman, W.T., Pasztor, E.C., Carmichael, O.T.: Learning low-level vision. Int. J. Comput. Vision **40**(1), 25–47 (2000)
14. Sun, J., Zheng, N.N., Tao, H., Shum, H.Y.: Image hallucination with primal sketch priors. Computer Society Conference on Computer Vision and Pattern Recognition, 2, pp. II-729 (2003)
15. Yang, J., Wright, J., Huang, T.S.: Image super-resolution via sparse representation. IEEE Trans. Image Process. **19**(11), 2861–2873 (2010)

Partial Differential Equation Inpainting Method Based on Image Characteristics

Fang Zhang[1], Ying Chen[1], Zhitao Xiao[1(✉)], Lei Geng[1], Jun Wu[1],
Tiejun Feng[1], Ping Liu[1], Yufei Tan[1], and Jinjiang Wang[2,3]

[1] School of Electronics and Information Engineering,
Tianjin Polytechnic University, Tianjin, China
xiaozhitao@tjpu.edu.cn
[2] Key Laboratory of Opto-Electronic Information Technology,
Ministry of Education (Tianjin University), Tianjin, China
[3] College of Precision Instrument and Opto-Electronics Engineering,
Tianjin University, Tianjin, China

Abstract. Inpainting is an image processing method to automatically restore the lost information according to the existing image information. Inpainting has great application on restoration of the lost information for photographs, text removal of image, and recovery for the loss coding of image, etc. Image restoration based on partial differential equation (PDE) is an important repair technology. To overcome the shortcomings of the existing PDEs in repair process, such as false edge, incomplete interpolation information, a new PDE for image restoration based on image characteristics is proposed. The new PDE applies different diffusion mode for image pixels with the different characteristics, which can effectively protect the edges, angular points, and other important characteristics of the image during the repair process. The experimental results in both gray images and color images show that our method can obviously improve the image visual effect after inpainting compared with different traditional diffusion models.

Keywords: Image inpainting · Partial differential equation · Edge · Corner

1 Introduction

Digital image inpainting is one of the fundamental problems in the field of digital image processing, which can be used for repairing the loss or damage part of an image. The inpainting process is filling-in the missing part in accordance with the information. The key of inpainting is to make the repaired image close to the original image in terms of visual effects and ensure the rationality of the repaired image. Image inpainting was required from the restoration for some medieval artworks since Renaissance Period, and it is a valuable technique. With the rapid development of computer science and technology, majority of artworks such as paintings, sculptures and many cultural relics are scanned into the computer and become digital images. Therefore, the formerly manual repair is transformed to inpainting on computer via variety of models, algorithm and software.

© Springer International Publishing Switzerland 2015
Y.-J. Zhang (Ed.): ICIG 2015, Part III, LNCS 9219, pp. 11–19, 2015.
DOI: 10.1007/978-3-319-21969-1_2

PDE-based image inpainting has been paid much attention in recent years [1]. It looks the gray value of each pixel upon heat, and take the image inpainting processing as heat diffusion. Therefore the lost gray information of some pixels can be supplemented through gray diffusion, which is achieved by a PDE. PDE for digital inpainting was first introduced by Bertalmio etc [2], who introduced BSCB (Bertalmio-Sapiro-Caselles-Ballester) model based on a third-order PDE. However, the model's speed is too slow, and it will blur the inpainted area, especially for the area with large loss information. TV (total variation) model [3] is better than BSCB in time, but its disadvantage is causing ladder-effect in the smooth regions. HCE (heat conduction equation) model was introduced by Adolf Fick, this model may obscure edge and lead poor visual effects after inpainting. PM (Perona-Malik) equation [4] is an improved model based on HCE, but it keeps traces of restoration due to excessive edge protection. To overcome the above shortcomings, a new PDE inpainting model is proposed based on image features in this paper, different interpolation strategies were adopted in the corresponding position according to the different characteristics of the image, which can protect the image features (such as edges and corners) better and have better visual effect.

2 Corner Detection

Corner is an important feature and is significant to various applications such as image matching, objective tracking, and image modeling. Corners must be protected in the process of inpainting in order to keep good visual effect and image quality.

The scatter matrix is used to detect corners, which is defined as:

$$J_\rho = \begin{vmatrix} j_{11} & j_{12} \\ j_{21} & j_{22} \end{vmatrix} = \begin{vmatrix} (\frac{\partial I_\sigma}{\partial x})^2 * G_\rho & (\frac{\partial I_\sigma}{\partial x} \frac{\partial I_\sigma}{\partial y}) * G_\rho \\ (\frac{\partial I_\sigma}{\partial x} \frac{\partial I_\sigma}{\partial y}) * G_\rho & (\frac{\partial I_\sigma}{\partial y})^2 * G_\rho \end{vmatrix} \tag{1}$$

where I_σ denotes the Gaussian smoothing image for the initial image I with the smoothing parameter σ, G_ρ is a Gaussian kernel with the parameter ρ, * is the convolution operator.

J_ρ has two eigenvectors $\omega^\perp$ and ω, which are calculated by:

$$\omega = (\cos\theta, \sin\theta)^T \quad \omega^\perp = (-\sin\theta, \cos\theta)^T \tag{2}$$

where ω denotes the gradient direction of image characteristic (such as edge or one side of corner) which is perpendicular to the direction of image edge or corner side; $\omega^\perp$ gives the coherence direction of the image edge or corner side, which is the tangent direction of the image edge or corner side; θ is the angle of ω with the horizontal axis, which can be calculated based on the scatter matrix:

$$\theta = \frac{1}{2}\arctan\frac{2j_{12}}{j_{11} - j_{22}} \tag{3}$$

Corner intensity C_I of image I can be evaluated based on Eqs. (1), (2) and (3):

$$C_I = \left| \nabla(\omega^\perp \omega^{\perp T})^T \cdot \nabla I \right| = \left| \nabla \begin{pmatrix} \sin^2 \theta & -\sin \theta \cos \theta \\ -\sin \theta \cos \theta & \cos^2 \theta \end{pmatrix} \cdot \nabla I \right| \qquad (4)$$

Figure 1 shows the corner detection results for the noiseless image, Gaussian fuzzy image and Gaussian noisy image, respectively. It can be seen that the corner detection based on the scattering matrix is robust for both Gaussian fuzzy and Gaussian noisy. This is because not only the gray value of current pixel is used, but also the gray information of the local neighborhood is applied when calculating Gaussian convolution of the initial image in Eq. (1) [6].

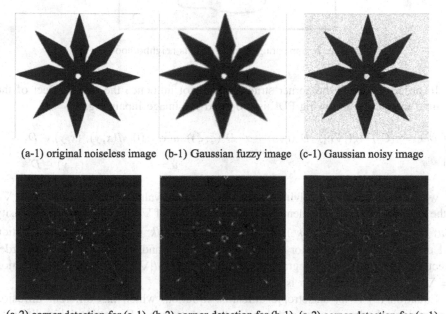

(a-1) original noiseless image   (b-1) Gaussian fuzzy image   (c-1) Gaussian noisy image

(a-2) corner detection for (a-1) (b-2) corner detection for (b-1) (c-2) corner detection for (c-1)

Fig. 1. Corner detection results

3 PDE Image Inpainting Method Based on Image Characteristics

3.1 PDE Image Inpainting Model

PDE image processing method considers the gray distribution of image as heat distribution, and regards the process of image evolution as heat conduction. By establishing and solving the corresponding PDE model to accomplish heat diffusion, image gray will be redistributed. PDE image inpainting method interpolates the missing image gray values for the initial image through gray diffusion [5–7].

As indicated in Fig. 2, assuming Ω as the entire domain of the initial image I, D is the inpainting domain, D^C is the complementation of D, E is the neighborhood out of the inpainting domain, Γ is the boundary of D. Let I represent a gray-level image to be processed, $I|_{D^C}$ denotes the known information, and u denote the repaired image [8].

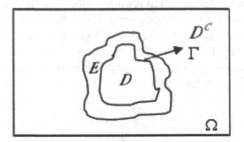

Fig. 2. Inpainting domain and its neighborhood

In order to protect the corner structure and not influence the visual effect of the repaired image, the following PDE is proposed for image inpainting.

$$\begin{cases} \partial_t u = g(C_u) \cdot (g(|\nabla u|) \cdot D^2(\eta,\eta) + \alpha \cdot D^2(\xi,\xi)), \ u(x,y,0){=}I(x,y), \ (x,y) \in D \\ \qquad\qquad\qquad u = I \qquad\qquad\qquad (x,y) \in D^C \end{cases} \tag{5}$$

where $u(x,y,t)$ is the evolving image, whose initial values is $u(x,y,0){=}I(x,y)$, ∇u is the gradient of u and $|\nabla u|$ denotes the module value of ∇u, C_u is the corner intensity of u; $g(|\nabla u|) = 1/(1 + |\nabla u|^2/k^2)$ and $g(C_u) = 1/(1 + C_u^2/k^2)$ are edge stopping function and corner protection operator respectively; $D^2(\eta,\eta)$ and $D^2(\xi,\xi)$ are second-order directional derivatives in the gradient direction $\eta = \nabla u/|\nabla u|$ and tangential direction $\xi = \nabla^\perp u/|\nabla u|$ respectively, α is a constant coefficient.

Equation (5) is an anisotropic diffusion equation, which has different diffusion degree along the image edge and through the image edge. By setting a big diffusion coefficient α for $D^2(\xi,\xi)$, the diffusion is strong along the tangential direction of image edge. While the diffusion along the gradient direction η is controlled by $g(|\nabla u|)$. The diffusion coefficient $g(|\nabla u|)$ is decided by the local image information, and is a reduction function of $|\nabla u|$. As $g(|\nabla u|)$ has small value on the edge of the image, diffusion is restricted along η but not completely forbidden, and mainly spreads along ξ, which can effectively remove the zigzag boundaries and obtain the inpainted image with smooth edge. Similarly, the corner protection operator $g(C_u)$ is a decreasing function of corner intensity and its value is small in corner, but the diffusion is not completely forbidden also, which can effectively avoid sudden change of corner grayscale in the inpainted results. Therefore, the diffusion equation can protect corner and edge features when inpainting, so that the processing results seem more natural.

3.2   Discrete Difference Form of the PDE

In order to solve Eq. (5) numerically, the equation has to be discretized. The images are represented by $M \times N$ matrices of intensity values. So, for any function (i.e., image) $u(x, y)$, we let $u_{i,j}$ denote $u(i, j)$ for $1 < i < M$, $1 < j < N$. The evolution equations give images at times $t_n = n \Delta t$. We denote $u(i, j, t_n)$ by $u_{i,j}^n$. The time derivative at (i, j, t_n) is approximated by the forward difference:

$$\partial_t u_{i,j}^n = \frac{u_{i,j}^{n+1} - u_{i,j}^n}{\Delta t} \tag{6}$$

where Δt is step-size in time.

The spatial derivatives are as follows:

$$(u_x)_{i,j}^n = u_{i+1,j}^n - u_{i,j}^n \tag{7}$$

$$(u_y)_{i,j}^n = u_{i,j+1}^n - u_{i,j}^n \tag{8}$$

$$(u_{xx})_{ij}^n = u_{i+1,j}^n + u_{i-1,j}^n - 2u_{i,j}^n \tag{9}$$

$$(u_{yy})_{i,j}^n = u_{i,j+1}^n + u_{i,j-1}^n - 2u_{i,j}^n \tag{10}$$

$$(u_{xy})_{i,j}^n = \left(u_{i+1,j+1}^n - u_{i,j+1}^n \right) - \left(u_{i+1,j}^n - u_{i,j}^n \right) \tag{11}$$

$$(u_{\eta\eta})_{i,j}^n = \frac{((u_x)_{i,j}^n)^2 \cdot (u_{xx})_{i,j}^n + ((u_y)_{i,j}^n)^2 \cdot (u_{yy})_{i,j}^n + 2(u_x)_{i,j}^n \cdot (u_y)_{i,j}^n \cdot (u_{xy})_{i,j}^n}{((u_x)_{i,j}^n)^2 + ((u_y)_{i,j}^n)^2} \tag{12}$$

$$(u_{\xi\xi})_{i,j}^n = \frac{((u_x)_{i,j}^n)^2 \cdot (u_{yy})_{i,j}^n + ((u_y)_{i,j}^n)^2 \cdot (u_{xx})_{i,j}^n - 2(u_x)_{i,j}^n \cdot (u_y)_{i,j}^n \cdot (u_{xy})_{i,j}^n}{((u_x)_{i,j}^n)^2 + ((u_y)_{i,j}^n)^2} \tag{13}$$

where u_x, u_y, u_{xx}, u_{yy}, u_{xy} are the first and second order spatial derivatives in the x and y direction, respectively. $u_{\eta\eta}$ and $u_{\xi\xi}$ are second-order derivatives in the gradient direction η and tangential direction ξ, respectively. Finally, we obtain PDE difference scheme based on the corner protect operator:

$$u_{i,j}^{n+1} = u_{i,j}^n + \Delta t \cdot \left(g\left((C_u)_{i,j}^n \right) \cdot \left(g\left(|\nabla u|_{i,j}^n \right) \cdot (u_{\eta\eta})_{i,j}^n + \alpha \cdot (u_{\xi\xi})_{i,j}^n \right) \right) \tag{14}$$

4   Image Inpainting Experiments and Discussion

In daily life, the inpainting images usually have no original undamaged image for comparison with the inpainted results. Inpainting effects evaluation cannot be determined with simple right or wrong, and should rely on visual perception, generally based on human visual habits and following four principles [5]:

(1) The goal of inpainting is to ensure the integrity and continuity of the original image;

(2) Important geometric features such as edge must be restored well, because human eyes have great interested in edge information;

(3) Repaired image regions are harmonic with the known information in visualization performance, and there isn't much unnatural things exist, including edge sharpness and zigzag effect, sharp degree of angle, and the ringing effect near the edge and the flat area;

(4) The method should be robust.

We used the proposed PDE for image inpainting. In addition we compared some typical PDEs with our method to illustrate the advantages of the proposed PDE model based on the above four principles.

Experiment 1: Test image was inpainted by the PDE image restoration method according to formula (14) based on image characteristics. Three classic PDE models including the heat conduction equation (HCE), PM equation, and the mean curvature flow equation (MCF) [7] were used to compare. Figure 3(a) is the original image, which includes structure of edges and corners. Figure 3(b) is the contaminated image, namely the image to be repaired. Figure 3(c) is the artificial calibration region of the damaged area, and Fig. 3(d) is the mask image that extracted from Fig. 3(c). The parameters of the experiment are chosen as $k = 20$, $\Delta t = 0.25$, $\alpha = 1$, $n = 250$. Figures 3(e) to (h) show the repaired results of the four methods respectively. HCE inpainted result given in Fig. 3(e) has obvious unrestored traces and blurred corners. Because PM equation and MCF equation focus on edge protection and ignore corner protection, when the difference of the gray values between the artificial calibration

(a)Original image; (b)Contaminated image; (c)Artificial calibration region; (d)Mask image;

(e)HCE inpainted result; (f)PM inpainted result; (g)MCF inpainted result; (h)Proposed method

Fig. 3. Comparison of different PDE inpainting methods for a test image

region and its surrounding pixel is great, these two PDEs will protect the artificial calibration region as image edge and lead to uncompleted repair (shown in Figs. 3(f) to (g)). Figure 3(h) shows inpainted result by the proposed method, which has the ability to protect the image characteristics (edges and corners), and repair the image more completely.

Experiment 2: A gray natural image was inpainted by the proposed PDE. The parameters in this experiment were used as: $k = 20$, $\Delta t = 0.25$, $\alpha = 1.5$, $n = 300$. Figures 4(d) to (f) show the repaired results of HCE, PM and MCF respectively. It is apparent that the edge of the hair excessively diffused and hairline blurred, especially in the HCE and PM inpainted images. Figure 4(g) is the result carried out by our proposed method. One can see that edge stop function and corner protection operator can well protect the edge of the hairline's border with background, and it avoids the loss of image detail.

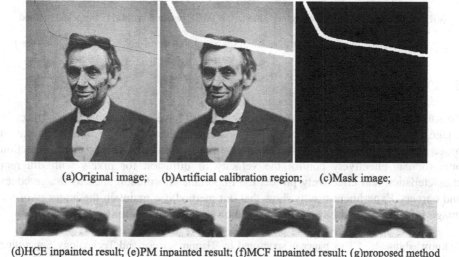

(a)Original image;   (b)Artificial calibration region;   (c)Mask image;

(d)HCE inpainted result; (e)PM inpainted result; (f)MCF inpainted result; (g)proposed method

Fig. 4. Comparison of different PDE inpainting methods for a gray natural image (part)

Experiment 3: A color natural image was inpainted by the proposed PDE. Three channels of color image of R, G, B are repaired respectively first, and then color image is composited by the three repaired images of the three channels after painting. In this experiment, $k = 20$, $\Delta t = 0.25$, $\alpha = 1.5$, $n = 300$. Figures 5(c) to (e) show the repaired results of HCE, PM, MCF models respectively. One can see that it exist different degrees of restoration traces in the three repaired results, especially the HCE and PM models, in which the marks of letters are very obvious. Figure 5(f) give the inpainted result used our method. There are no obvious traces of restoration in Fig. 5(f), and the method retains the integrity information of the original image.

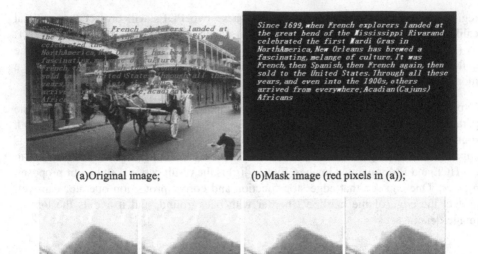

(a)Original image;   (b)Mask image (red pixels in (a));

(c)HCE inpainted result; (d)PM inpainted result; (e)MCF inpainted result; (f)proposed method

Fig. 5. Comparison of different PDE inpainting methods for a color natural image (part)

5 Conclusion

To solve the problems of the details missing or still have obvious unrestored traces in image inpainting, we present a new partial differential equation for image restoration based on image characteristics. The edge stopping function and corner protection operator can effectively control the velocity of diffusion for pixels with different characteristics, and effectively protect the important information such as image edges and corners. Experiment results show that our method can maintain the integrity of the image information and have great application on image inpainting.

Acknowledgments.   This paper is sponsored by Tianjin Science and Technology Supporting Projection under grant No. 14ZCZDGX00033, Tianjin Research Program of Application Foundation and Advanced Technology under grant No.15JCYBJC16600, and Open Foundation of Key laboratory of Opto-electronic Information Technology of Ministry of Education (Tianjin University).

References

1. Masnou, S.: Disocclusion: a variational approach using level lines. IEEE Trans. Image Process. **11**, 68–76 (2002)
2. Bertalmio, M., Sapiro, G., Caselles, V., Ballester, C.: Image inpainting. In: 27th International Conference on Computer Graphics and Interactive Techniques Conference, pp. 417–424. ACM Press, Los Angeles (2000)

3. Chan, T.F., Shen, J., Zhou, H.M.: Total variation wavelet inpainting. J. Math. Imaging Vis. **62**, 1019–1043 (2002)
4. Perona, P., Malik, J.: Scale-space and edge detection using anisotropic diffusion. IEEE Trans. Pattern Anal. Mach. Intell. **12**, 629–639 (1990)
5. Kang, Y.: Vatiational PDE-based image segmentation and inpainting with application in computer graphics. University of California, Los Angeles (2008)
6. Shao, W., Wei, Z.: Edge-and-corner preserving regularization for image interpolation and reconstruction. Image Vis. Comput. **26**, 1591–1606 (2008)
7. Catte, F., Lions, P.L., Morel, J.M., Coll, T.: Image selective smoothing and edge detection by nonlinear diffusion. SIAM J Numer Anal. **29**, 182–193 (1992)
8. Barcelos, Celia A., Zorzo, Batista: Marcos aurélio: image restoration using digital inpainting and noise removal. Image Vis. Comput. **25**, 61–69 (2007)

Patch-Based Visual Tracking with Two-Stage Multiple Kernel Learning

Heng Fan[1] and Jinhai Xiang[2]($\boxtimes$)

[1] College of Engineering, Huazhong Agricultural University,
Wuhan 430070, People's Republic of China
`hfan@webmail.hzau.edu.cn`
[2] College of Informatics, Huazhong Agricultural University,
Wuhan 430070, People's Republic of China
`jimmy_xiang@mail.hzau.edu.cn`

Abstract. In this paper a novel patch-based tracking algorithm is proposed by using two-stage multiple kernel learning. In the first stage, each object patch is represented with multiple features. Unlike simple feature combination, we utilize multiple kernel learning (MKL) method to obtain the optimal combination of multiple features and kernels, which assigns different weight to the features according to their discriminative power. In the second stage, we apply MKL to making full use of multiple patches of the target. This method can automatically distribute different weight to the object patches according to their importance, which improves the discriminative power of object patches as a whole. Within the Bayesian framework, we achieve object tracking by constructing a classifier, and the candidate with the maximum likelihood is chosen to be the target. Experiments demonstrate that the proposed tracking approach performs favorably against several state-of-the-art methods.

Keywords: Visual tracking · Multiple features · Patch-based tracking · Multiple kernel learning

1 Introduction

Visual tracking is one of the most important component of many applications in computer vision, such as surveillance, human-computer interaction, medical imaging and robotics [1]. For robust visual tracking, numerous methods have been presented. Despite reasonably good results from these approaches, some common challenges remain for tracking objects under complex scenes, e.g., when objects undergo significant pose changes or other severe deformations, i.e., object pose variations accompanied with object occlusions or object intersections. To address these problems, a wide range of appearance models for tracking have been proposed by researchers [2]. Roughly speaking, these models can be categorized into two types: discriminative-based model [5, 9–13, 18, 20, 21] and generative-based model [3, 4, 6–8, 14, 15, 19].

© Springer International Publishing Switzerland 2015
Y.-J. Zhang (Ed.): ICIG 2015, Part III, LNCS 9219, pp. 20–33, 2015.
DOI: 10.1007/978-3-319-21969-1_3

Recently multiple kernel learning (MKL) [22,27] has been applied in computer vision, such as object classification [23,24], object detection [25,26]. The MKL method aim to compute an optimal combination of weighted kernels in the supervised learning paradigm. Rather than using one single kernel, the MKL algorithms fuse different features and kernels in an optimal setting, which improves the discriminative power of multiple features.

Motivated by the MKL, we propose a novel patch-based tracking method based on two-stage multiple kernel learning. The patch-based methods utilize the local information of object and can effectively handle partial occlusion and deformation to some extend. However these trackers may cause drift problem because they do not consider the different importance of each patch when occlusion happens. In this work we combine patch-based method with MKL and present a patch-based tracking approach with two-stage MKL. In the first stage, each object patch is represented with multiple features. Unlike simple feature combination, we utilize MKL method to obtain the optimal combination of multiple features and kernels, which assigns different weight to the features according to their discriminative power. In the second stage, we apply MKL to making full use of multiple patches of the target. This method can automatically distribute different weight to the object patches according to their importance, which improves the discriminative power of object patches as a whole. Within the Bayesian framework, we achieve visual tracking by constructing a classifier, and the candidate with the maximum likelihood is selected to be the tracked result. Besides, an effective update method is adopted to help the proposed tracker adapt to the object appearance changes.

The rest of this paper is organized as follows. Section 2 briefly reviews the related works. Section 3 describes the multiple kernel learning method. The proposed two-stage multiple kernel learning is given in Sect. 4. Section 5 describes our tracking method. Experimental results are shown in Sect. 6, and Sect. 7 concludes this paper.

2   Related Work

General tracking approaches can be categorized into either discriminative or generative models [2]. The discriminative methods regard tracking as a classification problem which aims to best separate the object from the ever-changing background. These methods employ both the foreground and background information. Avidan [18] proposes an ensemble tracker which treats tracking as a pixel-based binary classification problem. This method can distinguish target from background, however the pixel-based representation needs more computational resources and thereby limits its performance. In [10], Grabner et al. present an online boosting tracker to update discriminative features and further in [20] a semi-online method is proposed to handle drifting problem. Kalal et al. [13] introduce a P-N learning algorithm to learn effective features from positive and negative samples for object tracking. This tracking method nevertheless is prone to induce drifting problem when object appearance varies. Fan et al. [15] suggest a weighted P-N learning algorithm and combine it with part-based framework for visual tracking. This method can improve the robustness of tracker in the presence of occlusion. Babenko et al. [9] utilize the multiple instance learning (MIL) method for visual tracking, which can alleviate drift to some extent. Whereas the MIL tracker may detect the positive sample that is less important because it does not consider the sample importance in its learning process. Further in [21], Zhang et al. propose the online weighted multiple instance learning (WMIL) by assigning weight to different samples in the process of training classifier. In [12], Zhang et al. propose a compressive tracker with an appearance model based on features extracted in the compressed domain. This tracker easily induce drift even failure since it is lack of an effective updating strategy in the presence of appearance variations.

On the contrary, the generative models formulate the tracking problem as searching for regions most similar to object. These methods are based on either subspace models or templates. To solve the problem of appearance variations caused by illumination or deformation, the appearance model is updated dynamically. In [3], the incremental visual tracking method suggests an online approach for efficiently learning and updating a low dimensional PCA subspace representation for the object. However, this PCA subspace based representation scheme is sensitive to partial occlusion. Adam et al. [4] present a fragment-based template model for visual tracking. This tracking method estimates the target based on voting map of each part via comparing its histogram with the templates. Nevertheless, static template with equal importance being assigned to each fragment obviously lowers the performance of tracker. Mei et al. [6] apply sparse representation to visual tracking, which can resist occlusion in some degree. However, this method is prone to cause drift because it does not have any update strategy. Jia et al. [8] propose a local structural spare appearance model for object tracking. This method adopts a online update mechanism to help the tracker adapt to appearance changes. Kwon et al. [14] decompose the appearance model into multiple basic observation models to cover a wide range of illumination and deformation.

Recently, MKL method has been widely used in image classification, object detection and recognition. In [23], Yang et al. present a group-sensitive MKL for object categorization. Jawanpuria et al. [24] utilize MKL for non-linear feature selection and apply it to classification. Vedaldi et al. [25] propose a novel three-stage classifier with MKL, which combines linear, quasi-linear, and non-linear kernel SVMs. Zhang et al. [26] proposes an E2LSH based clustering algorithm which combines the advantages of nonlinear multiple kernel combination methods, and use it for object detection.

The most related work to ours is [28], in which a multiple kernel boosting method with affinity constraints is proposed. This method boosts the multiple kernel learning process, thereby facilitating robust visual tracking in complex scenes effectively and efficiently. However, their method does not adopt patch-based representation and hence may be sensitive to partial occlusion. In our work, we segment object into multiple patches and combine it with a two-stage MKL method. Consequently, the proposed tracker is more adaptive to appearance variations.

3   Multiple Kernel Learning

Support vector machine (SVM) has been successfully applied to numerous classification and regression tasks. One of the most important problem in these tasks is to choose an appropriate data representation. In SVM-based approaches, the data representation is implicitly selected by the kernel function $K(x, x_i)$, where $K(\cdot, \cdot)$ is a function associated with a reproducing kernel Hilbert space [28]. Nevertheless, it is difficult for a single SVM classifier to select a good kernel function for the training set in some case. To address this issue, MKL algorithm is proposed. MKL is an extension of kernel learning method. By using different types of kernel to represent different properties of samples (e.g., feature and metric), MKL provides a unified framework for model combination and selection. One of the most popular multiple kernel learning methods is SimpleMKL (SMKL) [29] in which the kernel function is defined as a convex linear combination of kernels

$$K(x, x_i) = \sum_{m=1}^{M} \beta_m K_m(x, x_i), \ \sum_{m=1}^{M} \beta_m = 1, \beta_m \geq 0 \tag{1}$$

where $K(x, x_i)$ denotes the mth kernel and β_m is the corresponding weight. The SMKL is aimed to simultaneously obtain support vectors, support vector coefficients and kernel weights by solving the constrained optimization problem as follows

$$\min_{\beta} J(\beta) \quad s.t. \ \sum_{m=1}^{M} \beta_m = 1, \beta_m \geq 0 \tag{2}$$

where

$$J(\beta) = \min_{\{f\},b,\xi} \frac{1}{2} \sum_m \frac{1}{\beta_m} \|f_m\|_{\mathcal{H}_m}^2 + C \sum_i \xi_i$$
$$s.t. \ y_i \sum_m f_m(x_i) + y_i b \geq 1 - \xi_i, \xi_i \geq 0, \forall i \tag{3}$$

where x_i denotes the ith training sample, y_i is the class label for the ith sample, ξ_i and C represent its slack variable and penalty factor for slack variable respectively, $\mathcal{H}_m$ denotes the reproducing kernel Hilbert space (RKHS), and each function f_m belongs to a different RHSH $\mathcal{H}_m$ associated with a kernel K_m. The Formulation (3) can be solved by reduced gradient method [29], which computes simple differentiation of the dual function of Eq. (3) with respect to β_m

$$\frac{\partial J}{\partial \beta_m} = -\frac{1}{2} \sum_{i,j} \alpha_i \alpha_j y_i y_j K_m(x_i, x_j), \forall m \tag{4}$$

where α_i represents the dual coefficient of x_i. Then the decision function for binary classification is defined as

$$F(x) = \sum_i \alpha_i y_i \sum_m \beta_m K_m(x, x_i) + b \tag{5}$$

4   Patch-Based Two-Stage MKL

4.1   Object Segmentation

In this paper, we use multiple patches to represent the target, which utilizes the local information of object and can effectively handle partial occlusion and deformation to some extend. Different from [4], we adopt a overlapping slide window segmentation strategy as shown in Fig. 1. After segmentation, we can obtain a patch set $\mathcal{P} = \{p_1, p_2, \cdots, p_P\}$, where p_i is the ith patch and P is the number of patches.

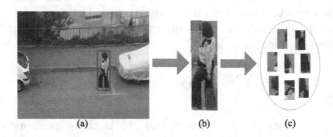

Fig. 1. Illustration of the overlapping slide window segmentation. Image (a) is the object, image (b) shows the segmentation method and image (c) is the set of object patches.

4.2   First-Stage Multiple Kernel Learning

In the first stage, we use multiple features (e.g., HIS histogram, HoG [16] and LBP [17] descriptors) to represent each object patch and apply MKL to the optimal combination for multiple features. For each ith patch, it can be represent with feature set $\{f_{i,1}, f_{i,2}, \cdots, f_{i,D}\}$, where $f_{i,j}$ denotes the $j^{th}(j = 1, 2, \cdots, D)$ feature and D is the number of features. Our goal is to find a strategy to integrate these multiple features to maximize the overall discriminative power. MKL has shown its potential in integrating multiple features in recent research. Therefore, for each ith patch, the output margin of first-stage MKL classifier can be written as the following

$$F_i'(f_i) = \sum_{l=1}^{L} \alpha_l' y_l' \sum_{d=1}^{D} \gamma_{i,d} K_d(f_i, f_{i,l}) + b_i' \tag{6}$$

where $F_i'(\cdot)$ denotes the classification function for the ith patch, $K_d(\cdot, \cdot)$ represent the dth kernel for the dth feature, L is the number of training samples, D stands for the number of features and $\gamma_{i,d}$ weights the discriminative power of the dth feature. Note that in the first stage, the MKL is only used to obtain the weight of each feature. Figure 2 gives a simple illustration about how we make use of MKL to obtain the weight of multiple features for each patch.

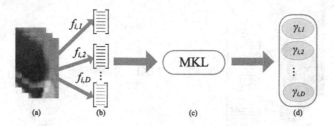

Fig. 2. We firstly collect the training samples for the ith patch in (a), and extract D features for it in (b). The MKL in (c) is then utilized to obtain the weight of multiple features for the patch i as shown in (d).

With the weight of different features, we can obtain the optimal combination of multiple features for the each patch. For the ith patch, we define $\mathcal{F}_i$ as its combined feature

$$\mathcal{F}_i = [\gamma_{i,1}f_{i,1}, \gamma_{i,2}f_{i,2}, \cdots, \gamma_{i,D}f_{i,D}], \ i = 1, 2, \cdots, P \tag{7}$$

4.3 Second-Stage Multiple Kernel Learning

In the second stage, we apply MKL to assigning different weight to the object patches according to their importance. In Sect. 4.1, the target is represented by a patch set $\mathcal{P} = \{p_1, p_2, \cdots, p_P\}$ in which p_i denotes the $i^{th}(i = 1, 2, \cdots, P)$ patch associated with a combination feature $\mathcal{F}_i$. Our goal is aimed to use MKL find an optimal combination for the patches in which the coefficient of each patch stands for the corresponding weight. Therefore, for the target, the output margin of MKL classifier can be written as follows

$$F^*(\mathcal{F}) = \sum_{q=1}^{N} \alpha_q^* y_q^* \sum_{i=1}^{P} \delta_i K_i(\mathcal{F}, \mathcal{F}_q) + b^* \tag{8}$$

where $F^*(\cdot)$ denotes the decision function , $K_i(\cdot, \cdot)$ represents the ith kernel for the ith patch, N is the number of training samples, P stands for the number of patches and δ_i weights the discriminative power of the ith patch. The process of weighing patches can be shown in Fig. 3.

After obtaining the weight of each patch, we can represent the object with a feature vector as follows

$$H = [\delta_1\mathcal{F}_1, \delta_2\mathcal{F}_2, \cdots, \delta_P\mathcal{F}_P] \tag{9}$$

where H denotes the feature of the target, δ_i and $\mathcal{F}_i$ are the weight and combined feature for the ith patch.

4.4 Classifier

In this section, a classifier is constructed to discriminative the object from the background. In the initial frame, we randomly sample bounding boxes around

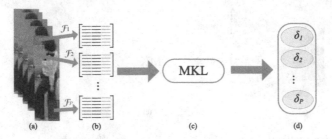

Fig. 3. To start with, we compute the combined features in (b) for all the training patches in (a). Then MKL in (c) is used to obtain the weight of each patch as shown in (d).

the tracked target as positive samples and far away from the target as negative samples. By controlling the distance from the tracked object, the negative samples contain pure background so that they are capable to differentiate from the target to the most extent. We use sets $S^+ = \{s_1^+, s_2^+, \cdots, s_{N+}^+\}$ and $S^- = \{s_1^-, s_2^-, \cdots, s_{N-}^-\}$ to denote the positive samples and the negative samples, where N^+ and N^- are the number of positive and negative samples. For each sample, it can be represented by a feature vector with Eq. (9) through two-stage MKL. Therefore, we use sets $\mathcal{H}^+ = \{H_1^+, H_2^+, \cdots, H_{N+}^+\}$ and $\mathcal{H}^- = \{H_1^-, H_2^-, \cdots, H_{N-}^-\}$ to represent the features of positive and negative samples. With these features, we can build a LIBSVM classifier G according to [30]. For a new sample s associated with the feature H_s, its classification error can be represented with $G(H_s)$. The smaller the classification error is, the more likely the sample belongs to the object.

5   The Proposed Tracking Method

5.1   Tracking Formulation

Our tracker is implemented via the Bayesian framework. Given the observation set of target $Y^t = \{y_1, y_2, \cdots, y_t\}$ up to the frame t, we can obtain estimation $\widehat{X}_t$ by computing the maximum a posterior via

$$\widehat{X}_t = \max_{X_t^i} p(X_t^i | Y^t) \tag{10}$$

where $\widehat{X}_t$ denotes the ith sample at the state of X_t. The posterior probability $p(X_t^i | Y^t)$ can be obtained by the Bayesian theorem recursively via

$$p(X_t | Y^t) \propto p(y_t | X_t) \int p(X_t | X_{t-1}) p(X_{t-1} | Y^{t-1}) dX_{t-1} \tag{11}$$

where $p(X_t | X_{t-1})$ and $p(X_{t-1} | Y^{t-1})$ represent the dynamic model and observation model respectively.

The dynamic model indicates the temporal correlation of the target state between consecutive frames. We apply affine transformation to model the target motion between two consecutive frames within the particle filter framework. The state transition can be formulated as

$$p(X_t|X_{t-1}) = \mathcal{N}(X_t; X_{t-1}, \Psi) \qquad (12)$$

where Ψ is a diagonal covariance matrix whose elements are the variance of affine parameters. The observation model $p(y_t|X_t)$ represents the probability of the observation y_t as state X_t. In this paper, the observation is designed by

$$p(y_t|X_t) \propto 1 - G(X_t) \qquad (13)$$

where $G(X_t)$ is the classification error of the tth candidate. Through Bayesian framework, we can determine the candidate sample with the smallest classification error as the tracking result.

5.2   Online Update

Due to the appearance variations of target, updating is essential. In this paper, an effective mechanism is proposed to update the classifier G. To start with, we design a set Φ. In each frame, after locating the target, we randomly sample bounding boxes around the tracked target as positive samples and far away from the target as negative samples. These samples are collected as a group, and added into the set Φ. When the set size v reaches a threshold V, we apply to the set Φ to updating the weight (both the feature weight and patch weight). Then we extract feature for each sample in Φ and train them for the classifier G, and empty Φ in the end. However, when accumulating elements into Φ, the tracking result may contain significant noise and thus is not reliable if the tracking result determined by our tracker has a high classification error which is greater than a threshold E. In this case, we skip this frame to avoid introducing noise into Φ.

So far, we have introduced the overall procedure of the proposed tracking algorithm as shown in Algorithm 1.

6   Experiments

In order to evaluate the performance of our tracking algorithm, we test our method on nine challenging image sequences and compare it with eight state-of-the-art trackers. These algorithms are Frag tracking [4], TLD tracking [13], ℓ_1 tracking [6], IVT tracking [3], MIL tracking [9], CT tracking [12] OAB tracking [10] and SPT tracking [5]. Some representative results are displayed in this section.

The proposed algorithm is implemented in MATLAB and runs at 1.6 frames on a 3.2 GHz Intel E3-1225 v3 Core PC with 8GB memory. We use three features (HSI histogram, HoG and LBP descriptors) and four types of kernels (linear, polynomial, RBF kernel, and sigmoid functions) to represent the target. The

---

Algorithm 1. Tracking Based on Proposed Method

Initialization:

1: Given initial state of the target, extract N^+ positive samples
   and N^- negative samples;

2: Segment each sample into P patches;

3: Extract D features for each patch, and apply MKL
   to obtaining the weights of multiple features;

4: Compute the combined feature for each patch, and apply
   MKL to obtaining the weights of patches;

5: Calculate the feature of each sample and utilize LIBSVM
   to train them for the classifier G;

Tracking:

6: **for** $t = 2$ to the end of the sequence **do**

7:    Generate N_c candidates $\{s_i\}_{i=1}^{N_c}$;

8:    **for** $n_c = 1$ to N_c **do**

9:        Compute the feature H_{n_c} for the n_c^{th} candidate;

10:       Calculate the classification error $G(H_{n_c})$;

11:   **end for**

12:   Select the smallest classification error and its index
      via $e = \min G(H_{n_c})$ and $\mathcal{K} = \min_{n_c} G(H_{n_c})$;

13:   The $\mathcal{K}^{th}$ candidate target is chosen to be the object;

14:   **if** $e \geq E$ **do**

15:       Skip this frame;

16:   **else**

17:       Extract samples as a group and add this group
          to set Φ;

18:       If the size of set Φ is equal V, update the weight
          and classifier, and then empty set Φ;

19:   **end if**

20:**end for**

End

---

parameters of the proposed tracker are fixed in all experiments. The number of particles in Bayesian framework is set to 300 to 500. The training frame N is 4 and the size of the set Φ in this work is set to 5. The parameter classification error threshold E is fixed to 0.4 to 0.6.

6.1   Quantitative Comparison

We evaluate the above mentioned trackers via center location error and overlapping rate [31], and the comparing results are shown in Tables 1 and 2. Figure 4 shows the center location error of the trackers on nine test sequences. Overall, the tracker proposed in this paper outperforms the state-of-the-art algorithms.

Table 1. Center location errors (in pixels). The best result is shown in **red** and the second best in **blue** fonts.

	ℓ_1	Frag	IVT	MIL	TLD	CT	OAB	SPT	Ours
Basketball	131.2	16.2	68.4	94.83	129.3	19.0	86.4	4.8	5.2
Bicycle	49.0	55.7	7.8	10.5	10.6	51.5	60.9	5.4	4.9
Bolt	361.7	100.6	374.9	365.4	87.8	348.0	-	6.8	6.6
Cup	2.9	7.0	1.8	40.60	3.1	25.13	4.45	-	2.8
Deer	91.7	93.4	222.5	214.0	47.8	235.9	27.6	97.0	9.8
Face	5.4	4.8	62.5	36.22	6.9	57.07	10.5	18.2	4.5
Jogging	14.5	9.3	130.0	146.1	7.2	124.7	-	-	10.2
Lemming	179.5	143.7	182.9	135.3	17.04	82.4	16.2	7.3	5.8
Woman	134.1	106.2	138.6	116.3	72.6	108.8	-	12.2	8.2
Average	101.3	56.2	114.7	119.2	38.4	116.9	34.1	19.9	6.4

Table 2. Overlapping rate. **Red** fonts indicate the best performance while the **blue** fonts indicate the second best.

	ℓ_1	Frag	IVT	MIL	TLD	CT	OAB	SPT	Ours
Basketball	0.03	0.55	0.41	0.21	0.09	0.61	0.16	0.83	0.81
Bicycle	0.31	0.25	0.33	0.43	0.39	0.29	0.24	0.55	0.72
Bolt	0.02	0.20	0.01	0.01	0.14	0.01	-	0.73	0.67
Cup	0.74	0.67	0.71	0.39	0.72	0.53	0.76	-	0.78
Deer	0.13	0.10	0.03	0.03	0.49	0.04	0.59	0.10	0.68
Face	0.85	0.86	0.36	0.55	0.77	0.38	0.79	0.74	0.88
Jogging	0.57	0.65	0.13	0.01	0.73	0.13	-	-	0.68
Lemming	0.14	0.13	0.12	0.12	0.30	0.33	0.61	0.65	0.81
Woman	0.06	0.19	0.16	0.13	0.29	0.16	-	0.60	0.62
Average	0.30	0.41	0.27	0.22	0.44	0.26	0.49	0.63	0.74

6.2 Qualitative Comparison

Heavy Occlusion: Deformation is a challenge for tracker, because the template features have completely changed when deformation occurs. As shown in Fig. 5, MIL, CT, IVT, OAB, TLD and ℓ_1 do not have good performances in the sequences *Bolt* and *Jogging*. Differently, Frag and SPT have relatively better tracking results in these sequences, because part-based trackers are less sensitive to structure variation than holistic appearance. Whereas, the lack of effective updating strategy still easily cause drifting away even failure. Our tracker have obvious advantage in handling structure deformation even in high frequency, since some local patches of the target remain the same in the presence of the deformation and with the help of effective updating mechanism, our tracking method robustly adapts to the deformation.

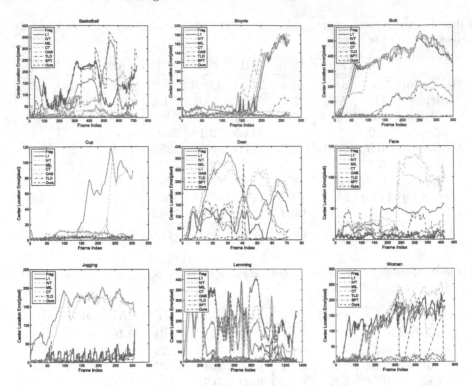

Fig. 4. Quantitative evaluation in terms of center location error (in pixel).

Motion Blur: Fig. 5 demonstrates experimental results on two challenging sequences (*Deer* and *Lemming*). Because the target undergoes fast and abrupt motion, it is more prone to cause blur, which causes drifting problem. It is worth noticing that the suggested approach in this paper performs better than other algorithms. When motion blur happens, our tracker can still effectively represent the target appearance. Besides, our updating mechanism can resist motion blur to some degree. Hence our tracker will not be undermined by the abrupt movement.

Deformation: Deformation is a challenge for tracker, because the template features have completely changed when deformation occurs. As shown in Fig. 5, MIL, CT, IVT, OAB, TLD and ℓ_1 do not have good performances in the sequences *Bolt* and *Jogging*. Differently, Frag and SPT have relatively better tracking results in these sequences, because part-based trackers are less sensitive to structure variation than holistic appearance. Whereas, the lack of effective updating strategy still easily cause drifting away even failure. Our tracker have obvious advantage in handling structure deformation even in high frequency, since some local patches of the target remain the same in the presence of the deformation and with the help of effective updating mechanism, our tracking method robustly adapts to the deformation.

(a) *Basketball*

(b) *Bicycle*

(c) *Bolt*

(d) *Cup*

(e) *Deer*

(f) *Face*

(g) *Jogging*

(h) *Lemming*

(i) *Woman*

Frag   L1   IVT   MIL   CT   OAB   TLD   SPT   Ours

Fig. 5. Screenshots of some sample tracking results.

Background Clutter: The sequences *Cup* and *Basketball* in Fig. 5 are challenging as the background cluttered and the target undergoes the scale variation. Our tracker performs well in this sequence as the target can be differentiated from the cluttered background with the use of our two-stage MKL method. In addition, the updating scheme is also robust to the complex background.

7   Conclusion

In this paper a novel patch-based tracking algorithm is proposed by using two-stage multiple kernel learning. Our method can automatically distribute different weight to the object patches according to their importance, which improves the discriminative power of object patches as a whole. Experiments on challenging image sequences demonstrate that our method performs favorably against several state-of-the-art methods.

Acknowledgement. This work was supported by the Fundamental Research Funds for the Central Universities (Program No. 2014BQ083) and National Training Programs of Innovation and Entrepreneurship for Undergraduates (Program No. 201510504116).

References

1. Wu, Y., Lim, J., Yang, M.H.: Online object tracking: a benchmark. In: 26th IEEE Conference on Computer Vision and Pattern Recognition, pp. 2411–2418. IEEE Press, Portland (2013)
2. Li, X., Hu, W., Shen, C., Zhang, Z., Dick, A.: A survey of appearance models in visual object tracking. ACM Trans. Intell. Syst. Technol. **4**(4), 2411–2418 (2013)
3. Ross, D.A., Lim, J., Lin, R.S., Yang, M.H.: Incremental learning for robust visual tracking. Int. J. Comput. Vision **77**(1–3), 125–141 (2008)
4. Adam, A., Rivlin, E., Shimshoni, I.: Robust fragments-based tracking using the integral histogram. In: 19th IEEE Conference on Computer Vision and Pattern Recognition, pp. 798–805. IEEE Press, New York (2006)
5. Yang, F., Lu, H.C., Yang, M.H.: Robust superpixel tracking. IEEE Trans. Image Process. **23**(4), 1639–1651 (2014)
6. Mei, X., Ling, H.B.: Robust visual tracking and vehicle classification via sparse representation. IEEE Trans. Pattern Anal. Mach. Intell. **33**(11), 2259–2272 (2011)
7. Xiao, Z.Y., Lu, H.C., Wang, D.: L2-RLS based object tracking. IEEE Trans. Circuits Syst. Video Technol. **24**(8), 1301–1308 (2014)
8. Jia, X., Lu, H. C., Yang, M. H.: Visual tracking via adaptive structural local sparse appearance model. In: 25th IEEE Conference on Computer Vision and Pattern Recognition, pp. 1822–1829. IEEE Press, Providence (2012)
9. Babenko, B., Yang, M.H., Belongie, S.: Robust object tracking with online multiple instance learning. IEEE Trans. Pattern Anal. Mach. Intell. **33**(8), 1619–1632 (2011)
10. Grabner, H., Grabner, M., Bischof, H.: Real-time tracking via on-line boosting. In: 17th British Machine Vision Conference, pp. 47–56. Edinburgh (2006)
11. Yang, F., Lu, H.C., Yang, M.H.: Learning structured visual dictionary for object tracking. Image Vis. Comput. **31**(12), 992–999 (2013)

12. Zhang, K.H., Zhang, L., Yang, M.H.: Fast compressive tracking. IEEE Trans. Pattern Anal. Mach. Intell. **36**(10), 2002–2015 (2014)
13. Kalal, Z., Mikolajczyk, K., Matas, J.: Tracking-learning-detection. IEEE Trans. Pattern Anal. Mach. Intell. **34**(7), 1409–1422 (2012)
14. Kwon, J, Lee, K. M.: Visual tracking decomposition. In: 23th IEEE Conference on Computer Vision and Pattern Recognition, pp. 1269–1276. IEEE Press, San Francisco (2010)
15. Fan, H., Xiang, J.H., Xu, J., Liao, H.H.: Part-based visual tracking via online weighted P-N learning. Sci. World J. pp. 13 (2014). Article ID 402158
16. Dalal, N., Triggs, B.: Histograms of oriented gradients for human detection. In: 18th IEEE Conference on Computer Vision and Pattern Recognition, pp. 886–893. IEEE Press, San Diego (2005)
17. Ojala, T., Pietikäinen, M., Mäenpää, T.: Multiresolution gray-scale and rotation invariant texture classification with local binary pattern. IEEE Trans. Pattern Anal. Mach. Intell. **24**(7), 971–987 (2002)
18. Avidan, S.: Ensemble tracking. IEEE Trans. Pattern Anal. Mach. Intell. **29**(2), 261–271 (2007)
19. Oron, S., Bar-Hillel, A., Levi, D., Avidan, S.: Locally orderless tracking. In: 25th IEEE Conference on Computer Vision and Pattern Recognition, pp. 1940–1947. IEEE Press, Providence (2012)
20. Grabner, H., Leistner, C., Bischof, H.: Semi-supervised on-line boosting for robust tracking. In: Forsyth, D., Torr, P., Zisserman, A. (eds.) ECCV 2008, Part I. LNCS, vol. 5302, pp. 234–247. Springer, Heidelberg (2008)
21. Zhang, K.H., Song, H.: Real-time visual tracking via online weighted multiple instance learning. Pattern recogn. **46**(1), 397–411 (2013)
22. Cortes, C., Mohri, M., Rostamizadeh, A.: Learning non-linear combinations of kernels. In: 23rd Advances in Neural Information Processing Systems, pp. 396–404. Vancouver (2009)
23. Yang, J., Li, Y., Tian, Y., Duan, L., Gao, W.: Group-sensitive multiple kernel learning for object categorization. In: 12th IEEE International Conference on Computer Vision pp. 436–443. IEEE Press, Kyoto (2009)
24. Jawanpuria, P., Varma, M., Nath, S.: On P-norm path following in multiple kernel learning for non-linear feature selection. In: 31st International Conference on Machine Learning, pp. 118–126. Beijing (2014)
25. Vedaldi, A., Gulshan, V., Varma, M., Zisserman, A.: Multiple kernels for object detection. In: 12th IEEE International Conference on Computer Vision, pp. 606–613. IEEE Press, Kyoto (2009)
26. Zhang, R., Wei, F., Li, B.: E2LSH based multiple kernel approach for object detection. Neurocomputing **124**, 105–110 (2014)
27. Sonnenburg, S., Ratsch, G., Schafer, C., Scholkopf, B.: Large scale multiple kernel learning. J. Mach. Learn. Res. **7**, 1531–1565 (2006)
28. Yang, F., Lu, H.C., Yang, M.H.: Robust visual tracking via multiple kernel boosting with affinity constraints. IEEE Trans. Circuits Syst. Video Technol. **24**(2), 242–254 (2014)
29. Rakotomamonjy, A., Bach, F., Canu, S., Grandvalet, Y.: SimpleMKL. J. Mach. Learn. Res. **9**, 2491–2521 (2008)
30. Chang, C.C., Lin, C.J.: LIBSVM: a library for support vector machines. ACM Trans. Intell. Syst. Technol. **2**(3), 27:1–27:27 (2011)
31. Everingham, M., Gool, L.V., Williams, C.K., Winn, J., Zisserman, A.: The Pascal visual object classes (VOC) challenge. Int. J. Comput. Vision **88**(2), 303–338 (2010)

Pattern Classification for Dermoscopic Images Based on Structure Textons and Bag-of-Features Model

Yang Li[1], Fengying Xie[1(✉)], Zhiguo Jiang[1], and Rusong Meng[2]

[1] Image Processing Center, School of Astronautics,
BeiHang University, Beijing 100191, China
oskorliyang@163.com, {xfy_73,jiangzg}@buaa.edu.cn
[2] General Hospital of the Air Force, PLA, 30 Fucheng Road, Beijing 100036, China
mrs5822@163.com

Abstract. An effective method of pattern classification for dermoscopic images based on structure textons and Bag-of-Features (BoFs) model is proposed in this paper. Firstly, the pattern structures of images were enhanced. Secondly, images with obvious directivity were rotated to align their principal directions with horizontal axis, and Otsu method was used to obtain interesting regions. The intensity values of each pixel in the interesting region and its neighborhood composed patch vector. For each pattern, patch vectors of training images were clustered to generate K structure textons and a dictionary with 5 K elements was obtained. Then BoFs model was applied to obtain texton histograms for training and testing images respectively. Finally, a nearest neighbor classifier with chi-square distance was adopted to classify. The experimental results shows that our enhancement method is beneficial to pattern classification and correct classification rate achieves 91.87 %.

Keywords: Dermoscopic image · Computer-aided diagnosis · Pattern classification · Texton

1 Introduction

As one of the most rapidly increasing cancers, especially in the United States, Australia and Japan with dry and sunny conditions, skin cancer has been getting more attentions [1]. In the last two decades, digital dermoscopy, a non-invasive skin imaging technique, has been widely used to collect dermoscopic images and many dermatologists turn to computerized analysis for dermoscopic images to improve the accuracy in the diagnosis of pigmented skin lesions (PSLs) [2,3]. Recently, computer-aided diagnosis (CAD) system based on image processing has been developed and become an active area of research, especially about melanoma which is a highly malignant skin cancer.

Now, although there are many algorithms based on computerized analysis to classify the benign and malignant melanoma objectively, the last diagnosis

© Springer International Publishing Switzerland 2015
Y.-J. Zhang (Ed.): ICIG 2015, Part III, LNCS 9219, pp. 34–45, 2015.
DOI: 10.1007/978-3-319-21969-1_4

results still need dermatologists to decide subjectively. Therefore, some objective indices such as color, shape and pattern types are more significant to assist dermatologists. Among these objective indices, pattern type is very important for dermatologists to diagnose melanoma using classic approaches like pattern analysis, Menzies method, 7-point checklist and CASH (color, architecture, symmetry, homogeneity). During the 2000 Consensus Net Meeting on Dermoscopy (CNMD), 7 principal patterns (global pattern) were related to the diagnosis of melanoma [4]. The 7 global patterns of the lesions are: Reticular Pattern, Globular Pattern, Cobblestone Pattern, Homogeneous Pattern, Parallel Pattern, Starburst Pattern and Multicomponent Pattern. Multicomponent pattern is with a combination of three or more above 6 patterns and highly suggestive of malignant melanoma [5]. An illustration of the first 6 patterns is presented in Fig. 1.

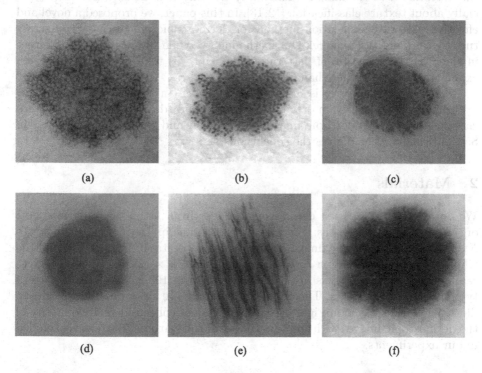

Fig. 1. An illustration of the six patterns in skin lesions. (a) Reticular pattern: it is the most common global pattern present in melanoma with net-like texture. (b) Globular pattern: it presents itself as small aggregated globules and may have different colors. (c) Cobblestone pattern: It is similar to Globular pattern but they are large and closely aggregated. (d) Homogeneous pattern: it presents uniform texture in the lesion. (e) Parallel pattern: it is found on the palms and soles due to the particular anatomy of these areas. (f) Starburst pattern: it is characterized by the presence of streaks in a radial arrangement (Color figure online) [5].

A few methods of pattern classification for dermoscopic images have been reported. In [6], Tanaka et.al. used 110 texture features to classify skin tumor into three patterns: homogeneous pattern, globular pattern and reticular pattern. Gola et. al. [7] also classified melanoma into the three patterns using a method based on edge detection, mathematical morphology and color analysis. Sadeghi et. al. [8] proposed a texton-based approach with the joint probability distribution of filter responses to detect five patterns. In [9], a pattern analysis by color and texture features is modeled by Markov random field. Sáez et.al. [10] improved this method and used Gaussian model, Gaussian mixture model and BoFs model to detect globular, homogeneous and reticular pattern for the whole lesion.

BoF is a feature extraction scheme used originally for text classifiers which was introduced to the imaging domain by treating textons as words [11], especially about texture classification [12,13]. In this paper, we proposed a novel and effective pattern classification method for dermoscopic images based on structure textons and BoFs model. Our methodology, while similar to [8], is different in that: (i) the structure of pattern is enhanced, (ii) texton is based on patch exemplars directly rather than filter banks.

The rest of the paper is organized as follows. In Sect. 2, the dataset for experiments is described in detail. In Sect. 3, we introduce the proposed pattern classification for dermoscopic images. Evaluation and results are presented in Sect. 4. Finally, Sect. 5 gives the conclusions.

2   Materials

We obtained 75 Caucasian dermoscopic images from http://www.dermoscopy. org/default.asp and https://dermoscopy.k.hosei.ac.jp/DermoPerl/, and 115 Xanthoderm dermoscopic images from General Hospital of the Air Force of the Chinese People's Liberation Army. A set of 128 pixels × 128 pixels lesion images representing the 5 patterns are extracted from the 190 images. Each pattern type has 50 lesion images. The details of database are shown in Table 1 and an illustration is displayed in Fig. 2. Because we cannot collect adequate quantity of the dermoscopic images with starburst pattern, the starburst pattern is excluded in our experiments.

Table 1. The details of database.

	Reticular	Globular	Cobblestone	Homogeneous	Parallel
Caucasian	13(12)[3]	20(18)	18(12)	24(21)	21(12)
Xanthoderm	37(25)	30(20)	32(24)	26(22)	29(24)
Total	50(37)	50(38)	50(36)	50(43)	50(36)

[3]Number of 128 × 128 lesion images (number of dermoscopic images)

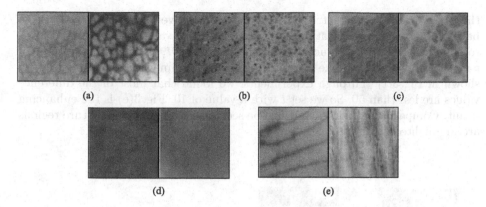

Fig. 2. 128 × 128 lesion image samples of each type of pattern(the left is Xanthoderm and the right is Caucasian). (a)∼(e) are reticular, globular, cobblestone, homogeneous, and parallel pattern respectively.

3   Pattern Classification Method

3.1   Enhancement of Lesion's Pattern Structure

From Fig. 2, it is not hard to find that, for one thing, the color belonging to the same pattern from different lesions has large differences, for another, similar color may exist in different pattern lesions. Therefore, color features are inappropriate for pattern classification. On the contrary, different patterns have huge disparities on the structure. Therefore, we tried to find features to represent the structure of each pattern. In order to avoid the influence of different contrasts in same pattern lesion, it is necessary to enhance the lesion's pattern structure.

For each lesion image, firstly grayscale image with 256 brightness levels (0 to 255) was obtained from the color image and then a median filter with size 3×3 was employed to remove the Gaussian white noise and impulse noise from the grayscale image. Secondly image I_g was yielded through inverting the grayscale image and a blurred image I_b was obtained from the image I_g through a 21×21 moving average filter. Then, a response function is defined to enhance the lesion's structure as follows:

$$I_e = \frac{2}{1 + exp(-\frac{max(0, I_g - I_b)}{t})} - 1 \qquad (1)$$

where t is a factor to determine overall steepness of the function.

There are two parameters: the size of average filter and t. As shown in Fig. 3, (a) is original grayscale image, (b) is the denoising result using median filter, (c) is the inverting result of (b). In order to reduce the brightness values of all pixels in pattern structure regions as far as possible, we changed the size of average filter and found that 21×21 can obtain satisfactory results. Fig. 3 (d) shows the blurred image converted from (c). We obtained the difference values between image (c) and image (d). It is easy to understand that the values of almost all the pixels in the pattern structure regions are positive and oppositely those in background region are negative. We set the negative values to 0 and used Eq. 1 to enhance the pattern structure. For the parameter t, the smaller the value of t is, the more threshold-like the function is and the image is over-enhanced, as shown in Fig. 3(f). Through experiments, we found that most of the difference values are less than 50. So we set t with a value of 10. Fig. 3(e) is the enhancing result. Comparing (e) with (a), it can be seen that the pattern structure regions are highlighted greatly.

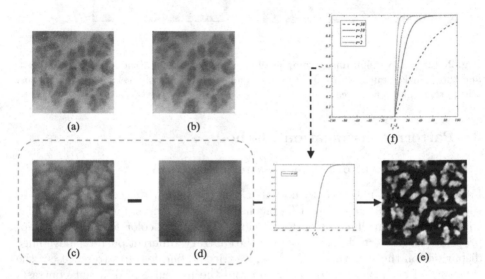

Fig. 3. Result of enhancing the lesion's pattern structure. (a) Grayscale image, (b) denoising result,(c) inverting result from (b), (d) blurred image, (e) enhancing result and (f) the curves of Eq. 1 with different t.

3.2   Creation of Texton Dictionary

Different patterns have different structures. We assume that different patterns are composed of different textons (local structure). Thus, for each pattern, we can densely extract local structure features pixel by pixel over the images, and then obtain the textons by simple clustering method. In a patch with $n \times n$ size, the brightness values of a central pixel and its neighborhood can directly represent the local structure. Before this, we do two steps as follows:

(1)Finding Principal Direction of the Texture Pattern

A good texture feature must have rotational invariance. However, the patch-based presentation method is not rotationally invariant [13]. In order to address this problem, we rotate the lesion image according to its the principal orientation.

The Fourier spectrum is ideally suited for describing the dominant direction for texture image [14]. For a grayscale image $I(x, y)$, its Fourier transform is defined as:

$$F(u,v) = \sum_{x=0}^{N-1} \sum_{y=0}^{N-1} I(x,y) exp(-\frac{j2\pi(ux+vy)}{N}), u, v = 0, 1, ..., N-1 \quad (2)$$

and its Fourier spectrum is defined as:

$$P(u,v) = F(u,v)\overline{F(u,v)} \quad (3)$$

where $\overline{F}$ is the conjugate complex of F. As shown in Fig. 4, (a) and (b) are two original grayscale lesion images with different patterns, (c) and (d) are the enhanced image of (a) and (b), (e) and (f) show the Fourier spectra of (c) and (d) respectively. It can be seen that the texture of image (c) has obvious directivity and in its spectra, the main energy is along the principal direction of image (c). But the energy distribution of the Fourier spectra for image (d) is uniform at each direction. In other words, the image (d) does not have principal direction.

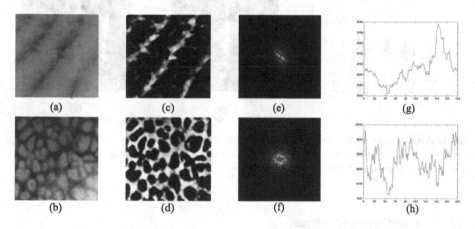

(a)   (c)   (e)   (g)

(b)   (d)   (f)   (h)

Fig. 4. Examples of Fourier spectrum for lesion images.(a) (b) lesion images. (c) (d) enhanced images. (e) (f) Fourier spectrum of (c) and (d). (g) (h) the $P(\theta)$ function curves of (e) and (f).

In order to describe this characteristic, we express the spectrum $P(u, v)$ in the polar coordinates $P(r, \theta)$, the original point of which locates at the center of spectra image. For each direction $\theta(\theta \in [0°, 1°, 2°, 3°, ..., 180°])$, we evaluate the integral $P(r, \theta)$ over r to obtain a 1-D function $P(\theta)$, which is defined as follows:

$$P(\theta) = \sum_{r=0}^{W} P(r, \theta) \quad (4)$$

where W is the radius of a circle centered at the origin. Fig. 4(g) and (f) are the $P(\theta)$ function curves for (e) and (f) respectively.

As mentioned above, not all texture images have obvious directivity. We only need to rotate the images with obvious directivity. We normalize $P(\theta)$ using following formula:

$$P_n(\theta) = \frac{P(\theta)}{\sum_\theta P(\theta)} \tag{5}$$

In fact, from Fig. 2, among the 5 patterns, only parallel pattern has obvious texture directivity. We calculate the maximum value of $P_n(\theta)$ for each enhanced lesion image in our database and find that the value for most of enhanced lesion images is less than 0.0077, except for the parallel pattern, as shown in Fig. 5(a). If the maximum value of $P_n(\theta)$ for an enhanced lesion image is more than 0.0077, the image is rotated θ_{max} (the value of θ corresponding to the maximum value of P_n) degree clockwise to align the principal direction of this image with horizontal direction. Fig. 5.(b) is the rotating result of Fig. 4(c).

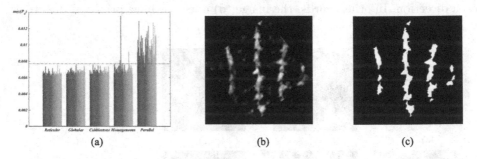

(a)   (b)   (c)

Fig. 5. An example of image rotation and interesting region extraction. (a) The maximum values of $P_n(\theta)$ for each enhanced lesion image. (b) The rotating result of Fig. 4(c). (c) The binary result of (b).

(2)Extracting Region of Interest

From Fig. 2, it can be seen that the texture for each pattern lesion image is non-homogeneous. The background regions of images after enhanced have very low intensities and the rotated images are also filled with 0 value. Therefore, if we use all of pixels in the image to generate textons, it would have a negative effect on the result. Because we are more concerned about the pattern structure, the enhanced images are binarized using Otsu method to extract the interesting region, as shown in Fig. 5(c). In addition, this operator can reduce the calculation time.

We create texton dictionary using the method proposed by Varma [13] in the interesting regions shown in Fig. 5(c). The process is illustrated in Fig. 6. For the training samples of each pattern, we extract the brightness values of a pixel located in interesting region and its neighborhood within the $n \times n$ window as

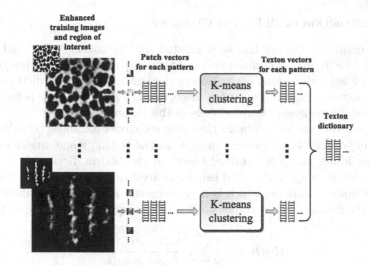

Fig. 6. Creation of texton dictionary.

a patch vector x. We normalize x via the Weber's law [13]:

$$x \leftarrow \frac{x}{\|x\|_2} log(1 + \frac{\|x\|_2}{0.03})$$ (6)

And then all patch vectors are clustered using K-means method to obtain K textons for each training pattern lesion images. At last, we can obtain 5 K textons in total. Fig. 7 is the visualization of texton dictionary, where the value of K for each pattern is 15 and the patch size is 13 × 13. It can be seen that there are disparities among the structure textons of the 5 patterns.

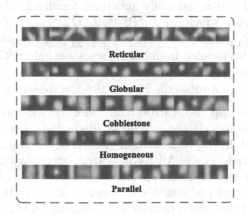

Fig. 7. The visualization of texton dictionary.

3.3   Construction of BoFs and Classifier

Now, the texton dictionary has been created and then the BoFs can be constructed by the frequency of occurrences of the textons. For a lesion image, each patch vector is labeled based on its closest element in the texton dictionary via Euclidean distance. The BoFs (texton histogram) of a lesion image is formed by counting the frequencies of texton labels of the lesion image.

In the learning stage, we obtain the category model database by calculating the BoFs of training lesion pattern images. In the testing stage, firstly the BoF of a testing lesion image is obtained based on the texton dictionary and then the testing lesion image is classified using a nearest neighbor classifier, where we use the chi-square statistic, which is a good metric in texture classification, to computer the distance between the two BoFs. The equation is defined as follows:

$$\chi^2(\boldsymbol{h}_t, \boldsymbol{h}_d) = \frac{1}{2} \sum_{k=1}^{5K} \frac{(h_t(k) - h_d(k))^2}{h_t(k) + h_d(k)} \tag{7}$$

4   Evaluation and Results

To evaluate the performance of our method, correct classification rate is computed. In addition, a 3-times 5-fold cross-validation is used. In a cross-validation, 40 images are randomly selected as training samples and the rest 10 images are as testing samples for each pattern. All steps of the proposed method were implemented using Matlab R2013a on the PC with 3.40 GHz Intel@ Core^T i7 processor and 8GB DDR3 SDRAM.

We compared our method with the state-of-the-art texton learning methods: LBP [15] and MR8 [12]. The experimental parameters of these two methods are given as follows:

LBP: We obtained the rotationally invariant, uniform LBP texton dictionary with 1 to 5 scales, which are $LBP^{riu2}_{8,1}$, $LBP^{riu2}_{8,1+12,1.5}$, $LBP^{riu2}_{8,1+12,1.5+16,2}$, $LBP^{riu2}_{8,1+12,1.5+16,2+20,3}$, and $LBP^{riu2}_{8,1+12,1.5+16,2+20,3+20,4}$ respectively. The Matlab code of LBP is downloaded from http://www.cse.oulu.fi/CMV/Downloads/LBPMatlab. The experiments are carried out on both original grayscale images and enhanced images (not rotated). The results are shown in Table 2;

MR8: The maximum response 8(MR8) filter bank also has rotationally invariant and multiscale characters. It consists of 38 filters but only maximum 8 filter responses were saved. In [12], this method yielded better results than any other filter bank. The Matlab code of MR8 comes from http://www.robots.ox.ac.uk/~vgg/research/texclass/with.html. The experiments are also carried out on both original grayscale images and enhanced images (not rotated). The filter size is 49×49(default) and the texton number for each pattern is 5, 10, 15 20, 25, 30, 35 respectively. The results are shown in Table 3.

From Tables 2 and 3, it can be seen that using the LBP method, the maximum average correct for grayscale images and enhanced images is respectively 86.27 %

Table 2. The average correct classification results(%) using LBP texton dictionary.

scale	1 scale	2 scale	3 scale	4 scale	5 scale
Gra.(Grayscale)	72.93 ± 0.92	80.27 ± 2.31	84.67 ± 1.97	**86.27±1.01**	85.87 ± 0.23
Enh.(Enhanced)	80.80 ± 0.00	85.73 ± 0.61	88.80 ± 1.06	**89.60±1.20**	89.33 ± 1.22

Table 3. The average correct classification results(%) using MR8 texton dictionary.

K	5	10	15	20	25	30	35
Gra.	67.87 ± 0.46	71.60 ± 2.08	73.60 ± 0.00	73.33±0.23	**76.53±0.46**	74.53 ± 1.85	76.00 ± 0.69
Enh.	87.07 ± 1.01	89.20 ± 0.69	89.60 ± 0.69	89.33±1.85	89.60 ± 1.83	90.40 ± 0.69	**90.93±0.92**

and 89.60 % at 4 scale and the method based on MR8 achieves 76.53 % maximum average correct for grayscale images and 90.93 % for enhanced images. In addition, we can find that the average classification results are obviously improved when using enhanced images to classify, especially for MR8. This shows that our enhanced method is beneficial to classify lesion images. For the proposed method, the texton number K for each pattern and the size of patch are two important parameters. In the experiments, the values of K are as the same as the values for MR8 and the patch size is set to 3×3, 5×5, 7×7, 9×9, 11×11 and 13×13 respectively. The results are shown in Table 4.

Table 4. The average correct classification results(%) using our method.

K	5	10	15	20	25	30	35
3×3	77.73 ± 1.51	81.07 ± 1.01	83.87 ± 1.97	83.73 ± 2.20	83.87 ± 0.23	85.07 ± 0.61	83.87 ± 0.61
5×5	84.13 ± 1.40	86.67 ± 1.40	87.73 ± 1.22	87.87 ± 1.15	88.67 ± 1.22	88.40 ± 0.69	90.13 ± 0.61
7×7	88.67 ± 0.83	89.33 ± 0.46	89.47 ± 1.01	90.13 ± 0.83	89.73 ± 0.92	90.53 ± 0.83	89.73 ± 0.23
9×9	89.33 ± 1.85	91.07 ± 1.01	91.33 ± 0.61	91.47 ± 1.40	90.67 ± 0.61	90.80 ± 0.00	90.80 ± 1.74
11×11	88.80 ± 1.06	90.93 ± 0.23	90.80 ± 1.06	91.33 ± 0.23	90.67 ± 0.23	91.60 ± 1.06	91.60 ± 0.40
13×13	89.87 ± 0.83	90.93 ± 1.01	**91.87±0.83**	91.33 ± 0.61	90.80 ± 0.40	91.47 ± 0.23	91.60 ± 1.06

From Table 4, it can be seen that in our experiments, the average correct is more than 90 % when the size of patch is more than 9×9 and the value of K is more than 10. Among those, there are 12 groups , the results of which are better than the best result of compared method (90.93 %). When K is 15 and patch size is 13×13, our method obtains best result (91.87 %). Besides, the best average accuracies of these three methods for each category of dermoscopic images are shown in Fig. 8. Clearly, in most cases our method is better than other methods. Especially for parallel pattern, the correct is more than other two methods 6 % and 14 % respectively, which shows that directly rotating lesion images to make them have same principal direction can get better result than the features including rotationally invariant.

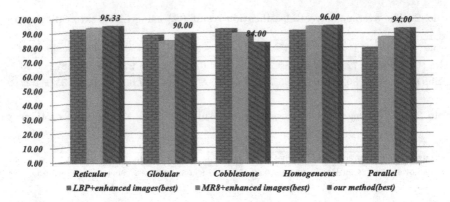

Fig. 8. The best average accuracies of these three methods for each category of dermoscopic images.

5   Conclusions and Future Works

In this paper, we presented an effective classification method based on textons and BoFs model to classify 5 patterns (reticular, globular, cobblestone, homogeneous, and parallel) for dermoscopic images. Firstly, a response function is defined to enhance the pattern structure. Secondly, the enhanced lesion images with obvious directivity are rotated to align principal directions with horizontal direction. Then we use Otsu method to extract interesting region and obtain patch vectors for each lesion image. For each pattern, the patch vectors of training lesion images are clustered to generate K structure textons and a texton dictionary with 5 K elements is obtained. We adopt the theory of BoFs to obtain texton histograms for training images and testing images respectively. At last, a nearest neighbor classifier with chi-square distance is adopted to classify. The experimental results show that our enhancement method is beneficial to lesion pattern classification and our classification method, which correct classification rate achieves 91.87 %, outperforms the LBP and MR8 methods.

In this paper, the 5 pattern lesion images with the size of 128×128 are manually extracted from dermoscopic images. So our future works mainly include two aspects: (i) designing an effective method to automatically segment dermoscopic images to obtain lesion region; (ii) adding starburst and multi-component pattern into the experiments to improve the abilities of assistant diagnoses. In addition, the recognition of malignant and benign lesions is also an important future work.

Acknowledgments. This work was supported by the National Natural Science Foundation of China (Grant nos. 61471016, 61371134 and 61271436).

References

1. Siegel, R., Ma, J., Zou, Z., et al.: Cancer statistics. CA Cancer J. Clin. **64**(1), 9–29 (2014)
2. Binder, M., Schwarz, M., Winkler, A., et al.: Epiluminescence microscopy: a useful tool for the diagnosis of pigmented skin lesions for formally trained dermatologists. Arch. Dermatol. **131**(3), 286–291 (1995)
3. Korotkov, K., Garcia, R.: Computerized analysis of pigmented skin lesions: a review. Artif. Intell. Med. **56**(2), 69–90 (2012)
4. Argenziano, G., Soyer, H.P., Chimenti, S., et al.: Dermoscopy of pigmented skin lesions: results of a consensus meeting via the Internet. J. Am. Acad. Dermatol. **48**(5), 679–693 (2003)
5. Argenziano, G., Soyer, H.P., Giorgi, V., Piccolo, D., Carli, P., et al.: Interactive Atlas of Dermoscopy. EDRA Medical Publishing, Milan (2000). www.dermoscopy.org
6. Tanaka, T., Torii, S., Kabuta, I., et al.: Pattern classification of nevus with texture analysis. IEEJ Trans. Electr. Electron. Eng. **3**(1), 143–150 (2008)
7. Isasi, A.G., Zapirain, B.G., Zorrilla, A.M.: Melanomas non-invasive diagnosis application based on the ABCD rule and pattern recognition image processing algorithms. Comput. Biol. Med. **41**(9), 742–755 (2011)
8. Sadeghi, M., Lee, T.K., McLean, D., et al.: Global pattern analysis and classification of dermoscopic images using textons. In: SPIE Medical Imaging. International Society for Optics and Photonics, pp. 83144X–83144X-6 (2012)
9. Serrano, C., Acha, B.: Pattern analysis of dermoscopic images based on Markov random fields. Pattern Recognit. **42**(6), 1052–1057 (2009)
10. Sáez, A., Serrano, C., Acha, B.: Model-based classification methods of global patterns in dermoscopic images. IEEE Trans. Med. Imaging **33**(5), 1137–1147 (2014)
11. Tsai, C.F.: Bag-of-words representation in image annotation: a review. Int. Sch. Res. Not. Artif. Intell. **2012**, 1–19 (2012)
12. Varma, M., Zisserman, A.: A statistical approach to texture classification from single images. Int. J. Comput. Vis. **62**(1–2), 61–81 (2005)
13. Varma, M., Zisserman, A.: A statistical approach to material classification using image patch exemplars. IEEE Trans. Pattern Anal. Mach. Intell. **31**(11), 2032–2047 (2009)
14. Gonzalez, R.C., Woods, R.E., Eddins, S.L.: Digital Image Processing Using MATLAB. Publishing house of electronics industry, Beijing (2005)
15. Ojala, T., Pietikainen, M., Maenpaa, T.: Multiresolution gray-scale and rotation invariant texture classification with local binary patterns. IEEE Trans. Pattern Anal. Mach. Intell. **24**(7), 971–987 (2002)

Performance-Driven Facial Expression Real-Time Animation Generation

Zhang Mandun$^{(\boxtimes)}$, Huo Jianglei, Na Shenruoyang,
and Huang Chunmeng

School of Computer Science and Engineering,
Hebei University of Technology, Tianjin, China
zhangmandun@126.com

Abstract. In view of the reality of facial expression animation and the efficiency of expression reconstruction, a novel method of real-time facial expression reconstruction is proposed. Our pipeline begins with the feature point capture of an actor's face using a Kinect device. A simple face model has been constructed. 38 feature points for control are manually chosen. Then we track the face of an actor in real-time and reconstruct target model with two different deformation algorithms. Experimental results show that our method can reconstruct facial expression efficiency in low-cost. The facial expression of target model is realistic and synchronizes with the actor.

Keywords: Kinect · Expression animation · Deformation algorithm · Facial reconstruction

1 Introduction

The research on facial expression animation [1] has been a hot field. Many breakthroughs have been made in the realistic simulation of face expression animation and many excellent researchers gathered in this field continuously, also many excellent systems come forth. Weise [2] presented a complete integrated system, in which a generic template mesh is built, fitted to a rigid reconstruction of the actor's face, is tracked offline in a training stage through a set of expression sequences. These sequences are used to build a person-specific linear face model. Ma [3] proposed an "analysis and synthesis" method, using motion capture markers to realize the synthesis of facial animation with captured data, and it performs well and the details are recorded completely. Zhang [4] employed synchronized video cameras and structured light projectors to capture streams of images from multiple viewpoints, a novel space-time stereo algorithm which could realize the reconstruction of high resolution face model is proposed in this paper. Liu [5] generated a model through an ordinary video camera, by specifying the semantic point in the video image and detecting corresponding relations among corner points, three-dimensional scattered points are obtained by stereoscopic vision technology to generate the 3D face models by fitting a linear class of human face geometries. Weise [6] provided a method of performance-driven real-time facial animation. The method obtained the depth information and image information of performer's head with Kinect, using the deformation model and the non-rigid registration

© Springer International Publishing Switzerland 2015
Y.-J. Zhang (Ed.): ICIG 2015, Part III, LNCS 9219, pp. 46–54, 2015.
DOI: 10.1007/978-3-319-21969-1_5

approach to generate the user-specific expression model, which is matched to the acquired 2D image and 3D depth map to obtain the blend shape weights that drive the digital avatar. Li [7] etc. proposed a self-adaptive PCA model frame, which used the blending shape and the deformation method of projection to self-adaptive space at the same time. Through the PCA learning, adjust the tracking results with corrective graphics constantly in the process of the performance.

On the basis of summarizing and analyzing the works of pioneer contributors, a novel real-time facial expression animation synthesis method is proposed, which uses relatively cheap data capture device combined with radial basis function (RBF) inter-polation deformation algorithm to synthesize realistic facial animation [8, 9], which achieves the aim of real-time interaction with performers, and be compared with the Laplace deformation algorithm on such basis [10, 11].

2   Expressions Reconstruction Algorithm

Experiments respectively adopt the deformation algorithm based on RBF interpolation algorithm and the deformation algorithm based on Laplace, and the specific applica-tions of the two algorithms are given respectively in the following.

2.1   Facial Expression Animation Based on the RBF Interpolation

In the experiment, the three-dimensional coordinates of the performer facial mesh vertices are regarded as the embedding space of the Radial basis function (RBF) to construct the interpolation function $f(x)$, Due to the RBF is a smooth interpolation function, meeting the conditions at the control points

$$V_k = f(x_k), 0 \leq k \leq L - 1 \tag{1}$$

Where V_k is the displacement of the control points, L is the quantity of the control points, the interpolation function employs

$$f(x_k) = \sum p_k \phi(\|x_k - x_l\|), 0 \leq k, l \leq L - 1 \tag{2}$$

Where $\|x_k - x_l\|$ is the Euclidean distance between x_k and x_l, $\phi(\|x_k - x_l\|)$ is the RBF, p_k is the corresponding weight of the control point x_k.

The corresponding weight of each control point can be calculated by solving the above equations. For the displacement V of the rest points, using the following formula to solve out

$$V = \sum p_k \varphi(\|x - x_k\|), 0 \leq k \leq L - 1 \tag{3}$$

Many choices can be made for RBF function, $\varphi(\|p - p_i\|) = e^{-\|p-p_i\|/64}$ is chosen in the experiment, this method is characterized by the better interpolation property, with direct analytical expressions for solving the interpolation, and the method is of high efficiency, which can reduce the complexity of the iteration and optimization, providing the foundation of the real-time processing. Deformation algorithm using RBF interpolation to realize the real-time process of facial expression animation is shown in Fig. 1.

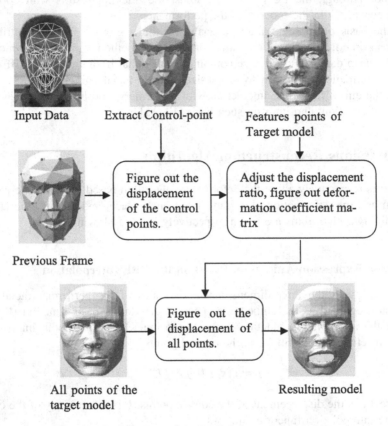

Fig. 1. The flowchart of the RBF deformation algorithm

2.2 Facial Expression Animation Based on the Laplacian Deformation Algorithm

The vertex $v_i(i = 1, 2, \ldots, n)$ is in Cartesian coordinates. Calculate the Laplace coordinate (differential coordinates) of vertex v_i

$$\delta_i = (\delta_i^x, \delta_i^y, \delta_i^z) = v_i - \frac{1}{d_i} \sum_{j \in N(i)} v_j \qquad (4)$$

$N(i)$ is the set of all adjacent points of vertices v_i, $d_i = |N(i)|$ is the quantity of the adjacent point of vertices i. (4) is expressed in the form of matrix, let diagonal matrix be D, where $D_{ii} = d_i$, let unit matrix be I, and let mesh adjacency matrix be A, so the transformation matrix comes to be:

$$L = I - D^{-1}A \tag{5}$$

The Laplace algorithm based on convex weights is employed in this article, calculating the contribution of each vertex:

$$w_{ij} = \frac{tan(\theta_{ij}^1/2) + tan(\theta_{ij}^2/2)}{||v_i - v_j||} \tag{6}$$

Feature points are chosen on the grid set C, taking V as the initial coordinates of the model, δ as the differential coordinate, w_j as the weight of vertex v_j, c_j as the j_{th} of the characteristic points. Transform differential coordinates by implicit methods, finally the least square method is used to solve all the points' coordinates of the model.

$$\tilde{V} = \underset{V}{argmin}(||LV - \delta||^2 + \sum_{j=1}^{m} w_j^2 |v_j - c_j|^2) \tag{7}$$

3 Data-Driven Facial Expression Animation

3.1 Feature Points on the Target Model

In order to realize the movement of the target model, the relationship between the performer and the target model must be set up; a simplified face mesh model is established based on the feature points of the performers' face captured by Kinect and 38 vertexes are selected as the control points, so 38 feature points are chosen on the target model too. The selected position is consistent with control point's position on the simplified facial mesh model which is shown in Fig. 2(a) and (b). These areas include three parts-top, middle, and bottom- as shown in Fig. 2(c).

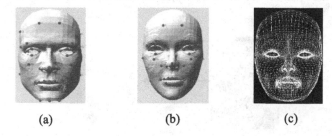

(a)   (b)   (c)

Fig. 2. Facial models, (a) male model, (b) female model, (c) model including 3 parts

3.2 Real-Time Facial Expression Acquisition and Data Processing

Proceed to real-time tracking human faces by Kinect is shown in Fig. 3(a); a simplified face mesh model is generated by using 121 feature points obtained from the tracking data as shown in Fig. 3(b). According to the Mpeg-4 standard [12], 38 vertices are chosen as control points on the simplified face mesh model as shown in Fig. 3(c). These control points will be real-time monitoring in the process of human face tracking.

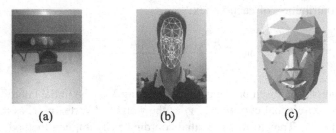

(a)　　　　　　　　(b)　　　　　　　　(c)

Fig. 3. Human face tracking, (a) Kinect, (b) face covered with mesh model, (c) selected 38 control-points

In the experiment, each frame is registered, and the previous frame of the captured data is saved to be compared with the current frame in order to obtain the displacement data of the marked control points. Due to the target model size is not consistent with the source model; the displacement data should be adjusted. Finally the displacement of the feature point on the target model is obtained.

4 Results and Discussions

This system is developed on Visual Studio 2010 platform, using C ++ as the development language, rendering with OpenGL. The computer configuration adopt in this experiment is Kinect for the XBOX 360, 3.2 GHz Intel (R) Core (TM) i5-3470 CPU, 4 GB memory.

It is found that when RBF algorithm is used for full face mesh deformation, there is almost no change in the displacement of the non-control points, which are located among the control points that are in the opposite directions, as shown in Fig. 4.

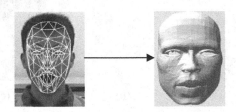

Fig. 4. Performer and a complete target model (RBF algorithm).

To solve this problem, the target model is divided into three parts - top, middle, and bottom - in the experiment, as shown in Fig. 2(c). Deform each part with RBF respectively, and then to integrate the three parts to get a complete target model. The pictures showed in Fig. 5 line 1 are the 6 frame data which is captured in the real-time facial animation process. The expression of male target model is obtained by the expression reconstruction of the male model with RBF algorithm and Laplace deformation algorithm as shown in line 2 and line 3. The female model obtained in the same process is shown in line 4 and line 5.

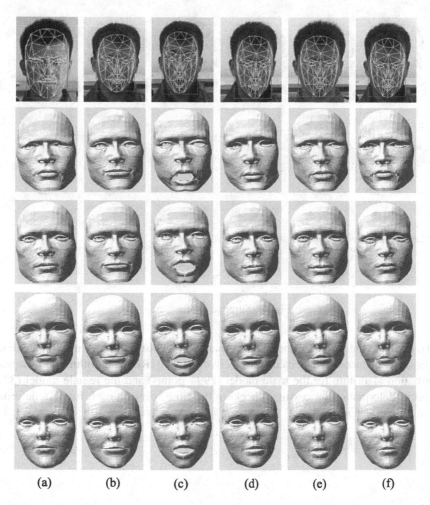

(a)   (b)   (c)   (d)   (e)   (f)

Fig. 5. Real-time facial animation, (a) disgust, (b) happy, (c) surprise, (d) sad, (e) fear, (f) anger.

Effect of deformation based on the Laplacian algorithm is compared to the one based on the RBF algorithm in this experiment. The real-time acquisition of the performer's facial expressions is shown in line 1. As the comparison between line 2 and line 3, line 4 and line 5, are shown in Fig. 5, the Laplace deformation algorithm is better than RBF deformation algorithm.

The performer's surprise expression is also captured continuously. The effect of the real-time reconstruction on target model based on the Laplacian algorithm and the RBF algorithm is given in this experiment too. The Laplacian algorithm performs better than

RBF algorithm in details as shown in Fig. 6. Line 1 shows the real-time capturing of performer's surprised expression, Line 2 shows the real-time reconstruction of female model using RBF deformation algorithm. Line 3 shows the real-time reconstruction of female model using Laplacian deformation algorithm.

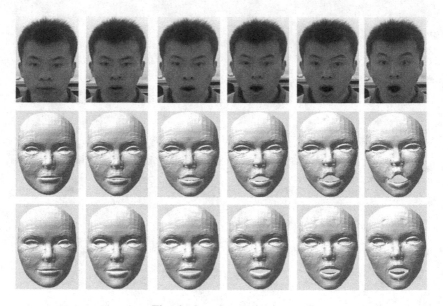

Fig. 6. Surprise expression.

To compare the two algorithms' performance in real-time, 100 frames of data in the animation sequence are selected. Respectively using RBF algorithm and Laplace deformation algorithm for the male model (2994 points) and the female model (3324 points) in deformation processing, checking the time spent on each frame's deformation as shown in Fig. 7.

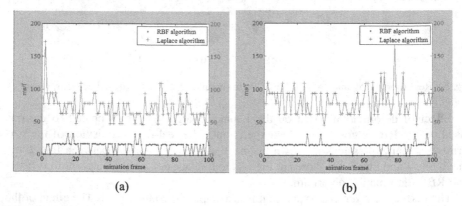

(a)   (b)

Fig. 7. The efficiency comparison, (a) The efficiency comparison on male model, (b) The efficiency comparison on female model.

5 Summary

As can be seen through the experiment, with the Kinect the depth data and RGB data can be outputted at a rate of about 30 FPS, we can position and track human faces accurately and output the characteristics of the facial feature points. The process of the facial expression animation algorithm proposed in this paper is simple and efficient. Just with the displacement of control points in the source model, the deformation algorithm can be used to control target model's real-time motion, without cumbersome steps of handling large amounts of data or extra overhead of computation in a large amount of data fitting. In addition, we use the RBF algorithm which has the advantage of fast calculation speed and good maintenance of physical structure after deformation. From the finally analysis results of the efficiency in real-time deformation, we can see the algorithms used in this experiment can fully meet the requirements of real-time capability, and the deformation results retain most of the features of the source model, the expression of generated target model is exquisite real.

As can be seen from the average time spending on the deformation, the deformation algorithm based on RBF algorithm is better than that based on Laplace in efficiency, but the Laplace deformation algorithm performs better in deformation effect in handling details. However, there are still some drawbacks in this experiment. After proceeding RBF deformation on each of the three parts, the synthesis of these parts shows some deficiency, leading to the imperfection in handling details. These problems will be solved in further works.

References

1. Yao, J.F., Chen, Q.: Survey on computer facial expression animation technology. J. Appl. Res. Comput. **25**(11), 3233–3237 (2008)
2. Weise, T., Li, H., Gool, L.V., Pauly, M.: Face/off: Live facial puppetry. In: Symposium on Computer Animation 2009 ACM SIGGRAPH/Eurographics Symposium, pp. 7–16 (2009)
3. Ma, W.C., Jones, A., Chiang, J.Y.: Facial performance synthesis using deformation driven polynomial displacement maps. ACM Trans. Graph. (ACM SIGGRAPH Asia) **27**(5), 121:1–121:10 (2008)
4. Zhang, L., Snavely, N., Curless, B., et al.: Spacetime faces: high resolution capture for modeling and animations. J. ACM Trans. Graph. **23**(3), 54–558 (2004)
5. Liu, Z.C., Zhang, Z.Y., Jacobs, C., et al.: Rapid modeling of animated faces from video. In: Proceedings of the Third International Conference on Visual Computing, pp. 58–67, Mexico (2000)
6. Weise, T., Li, H., Gool, L.V., Pauly, M.: Real-time performance-based facial animation. ACM Trans. Graph. Proc. SIGGRAPH 2011 **30**(4), 60:1–60:10 (2011)
7. Li, H., Yu, J., Ye, Y., Bregler, C.: Realtime facial animation with on-the-fly correctives. ACM Trans. Graph. **32**(4), 42:1–42:10 (2013)
8. Zhang, M.D., Yao, J., Ding, B., et al.: Fast individual face modeling and animation. In: Proceedings of the Second Australasian Conference on Interactive Entertainment, pp. 235-239. Creativity and Cognition Studios Press, Sydney (2005)

9. Wan, X.M., Jin, X.G.: Spacetime facial animation editing. J. Comput. Aided Des. Comput. Graph. **25**(8), 1183–1189 (2013)
10. Wan, X.M., Jin, X.G.: Data-driven facial expression synthesis via Laplacian deformation. J. Multimedia Tools Appl. **58**(1), 109–123 (2012)
11. Sorkine, O., Cohen-Or, D., Lipman, Y., et al.: Laplacian surface editing. In: Proceedings of 2004 Eurographics/ACM SIGGRAPH Symposium on Geometry Processing, pp. 175–184. ACM Press, New York (2004)
12. Zhang, Y.M., Ji, Q., Zhu, Z.W., et al.: Dynamic facial expression analysis and synthesis with MPEG-4 facial animation parameters. IEEE Trans. Circuits Syst. Video Technol. **18**(10), 1383–1396 (2008)

Person Re-identification with Density-Distance Unsupervised Salience Learning

Baoliang Zhou[1], Aihua Zheng[1(✉)], Bo Jiang[1], Chenglong Li[1], and Jin Tang[1,2]

[1] Key Laboratory of Intelligent Computing and Signal Processing of Ministry of Education, School of Computer Science and Technology, AnHui University, Hefei, China
zxzblwc@163.com, {ahzheng214,jiangbo}@ahu.edu.cn
lcl314@foxmail.com
[2] Key Laboratory of Industry Image Processing and Analysis in Anhui Province, Hefei, China
tj@ahu.edu.cn

Abstract. Human salience of pedestrians images is distinctive and has been shown importantly in person re-identification (or pedestrians identification) problem. Thus, how to obtain the salient area of pedestrian images is important for this salience based pedestrians identification problem. In this paper, we first show that this kind of salient area detection can be formulated as a kind of outlier detection problem, and then propose a novel unsupervised salience learning method using a local outlier-detection technique for person re-identification task. The main feature of the proposed salience computation method is that it exploits both distance and density information simultaneously. Experimental results on several datasets show the effectiveness of the proposed salience based person re-identification method.

Keywords: Salience learning · Person re-identification · Density-Distance · Head-priority

1 Introduction

Person re-identification is an important topic in computer vision area and has been widely used in video surveillance. The aim of person re-identification is to determine associations of the pedestrians in multi-camera networks in video surveillance. Here, we focus on the person re-identification (or pedestrian association problem) in non-overlapping camera networks.

Many works have been proposed for this problem. Generally, these works can be divided into two categories, *i.e.*, supervised and unsupervised methods. For supervised methods, distance metric learning is a classical method towards this problem [3,4,9,12,24]. Schwartz et al. [10] extracted high-dimensional features for metric learning. Porikli and Divakaran et al. [11] proposed a distance metric method and a non-parametric and non-linear model of color shift function based on color histogram. Li and Wang et al. [12] proposed a method which

© Springer International Publishing Switzerland 2015
Y.-J. Zhang (Ed.): ICIG 2015, Part III, LNCS 9219, pp. 55–67, 2015.
DOI: 10.1007/978-3-319-21969-1_6

learns different metrics for different camera image spaces. Chilgunde et al. [13] applied Kalman Filter to predict the person movement in blind areas of the monitoring cameras, and matched motion trail on Gaussian model. Similarly, Riccardo et al. [14] proposed Multi Social Force Model to predict the tracklets of pedestrians in blind regions. Javed et al. [15] used inter-camera space-time and appearance probabilities to find an object in different cameras by maximizing the conditional probability of the corresponding observations. For unsupervised methods, Ma et al. [20] modified the BiCov descriptor based on Gabor filters for person matching, and used the covariance descriptor to deal with illumination change and image misalignment. Farenzena et al. [17] proposed Symmetry-Driven Accumulation of Local Features to handle the change of camera viewpoint, as pedestrian images are symmetrical. Prosser et al. [1] formulated the person re-identification as a global optimum ranking problem, and utilized an ensemble of RankSVM to learn global feature weights. Liu et al. [9] adopted an attribute-based weighting scheme to find the unique appearance attribute. However, the most existing methods ignored some discriminative and simple features which are actually useful for person pairs matching in human images.

Recently, Zhao et al. [5] proposed a more effective unsupervised salience learning method with some distinct regions which are discriminative, reliable and useful for person matching. The main idea of this method is that it further detects and explores some human salient regions of pedestrian body in computing similarity scores between pedestrian images. Human salience of pedestrian images is distinctive and has been shown importantly in person re-identification problem. Thus, how to obtain the salient area of pedestrian images is important for this salience based pedestrians identification problem.

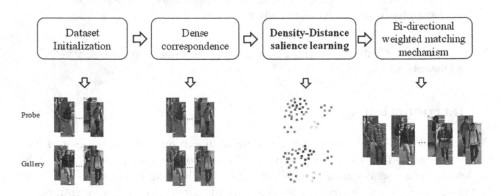

Fig. 1. The whole process of the proposed person re-identification algorithm.

Inspired by the work on salience leaning method in [5], in this paper, we first show that this kind of salient area detection can be formulated as a kind of general outlier detection problem. Then, we propose a novel unsupervised salience learning method, called Density-Distance salience learning, which aims to use a local outlier-detection technique for person re-identification problem.

The procedure of the whole algorithm has been shown in Fig. 1. The detailed algorithm is introduced in Sect. 3. One main feature of the proposed salience learning method is that it exploits both distance and density information simultaneously. Compared with traditional methods, the proposed salience detection method is simple and efficient for person re-identification problem. Promising experimental results on the widely used VIPeR and CUHK01 datasets demonstrate that the proposed salience-based person re-identification method is more effective and efficient than some recent methods.

2 Salience Learning with Density-Distance Outlier Detection

In this section, a novel salience learning method is proposed. As mentioned in work [5], the salient patches of pedestrian images generally have the following properties: (1) these patches are deviates markedly from others and thus provide some distinctive information for the pedestrian body image. (2) These patches are robust to the changes of camera viewpoint. Some examples of salient patches are shown in Fig. 2.

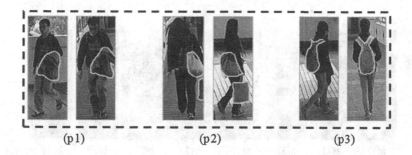

(p1)   (p2)   (p3)

Fig. 2. Illustration of person salience

Intuitively, this kind of salience definition can be regarded as the outlier patches in patch dataset. This motivates us to explore some outlier detection methods for salient patch detection. Outlier detection is a fundamental problem in data mining area. In outlier detection, an outlier is defined as an observation which deviates markedly from the other observations [29,30].

In the following, we first propose a local outlier detection based salience learning method, called Density-Distance salience learning, and then use this method for person re-identification problem. The core idea of the proposed Density-Distance salience learning method is to integrate both distance and density information for salience learning. Each human image is firstly densely segmented into some local patches, then the dLabSift features(details in Sect. 3.1) are extracted for each patch and denoted as $x_{A,i}(m,n)$, where (A,i) indicates the i-th person in camera A, and (m,n) is index denotes the patch located at the m-th row and the n-th column in the human image. The combined salience value is designed as:

$$Svalue_{DD}(x_{A,i}(m,n)) = \alpha \cdot Svalue_{density}(x_{A,i}(m,n)) \\ + (1-\alpha) \cdot Svalue_{distance}(x_{A,i}(m,n)) \tag{1}$$

where $Svalue_{density}(x_{A,i}(m,n))$ denotes the density salience values and similarly, $Svalue_{distance}(x_{A,i}(m,n))$ denotes the distance salience values. $\alpha(0 < \alpha < 1)$ is a balance parameter. In the following, we introduce the distance salience and density salience, respectively.

2.1 Distance Salience Learning

Each human image is densely segmented into some local patches, as shown in Fig. 3. The patches with discriminative property are called salient patches. Indeed, this kind of salient patches can be regarded as outliers in the patch set, as shown in Fig. 4. Byers et al. [21] proposed a method which uses the KNN distances and been demonstrated to be useful for outlier detection. In this paper, we use the mean value of KNN distance for salience learning.

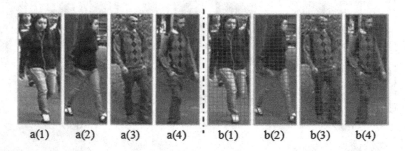

    a(1)   a(2)   a(3)   a(4)   b(1)   b(2)   b(3)   b(4)

Fig. 3. Examples of Dense Patches. a(1)–a(4) are human images, and b(1)–b(4) are illustrations of dense local patches. Each patch is dense and overlapping.

Before computing the average neighbor distance of each testing patch, the reference set initialization is needed. Let the number of the images in the reference set be R_n. After building the dense correspondences between a testing image and the images in reference set, each patch in the testing image will find an optimal matched patch in every image from the reference set, that is for each testing patch $x_{A,i}(m,n)$ there are R_n matched patches, or called neighbors from the reference set $X_{nn}(x_{A,i}(m,n))$.

$$X_{nn}(x_{A,i}(m,n)) = \{x | \arg\max s(x_{A,i}(m,n), \hat{x}), j = 1, 2, \ldots, R_n\}, \hat{x} \in S_{i,j} \tag{2}$$

$$S_{i,j} = S(x_{A,i}(m,n), x_{B,j}) \tag{3}$$

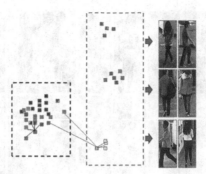

Fig. 4. Illustration of Salient Patches. The patches in the red and the black dotted boxes denote the salient patches and the general patches respectively.

More detailed introduction of Eq. (3) can refer to Sect. 3.1. Byers et al. [21] utilize the K nearest neighbor to find clutters. Instead of the k-th distance used in work [5], the average distance is calculated in our method, which is more reasonable and effective. The salience value can be computed as:

$$Svalue_{distance}(x_{A,i}(m,n)) = D_{average}\left(X_{nn}(x_{A,i}(m,n))\right) \tag{4}$$

where $D_{average}$ denotes the average distance to the R_n nearest neighbor. As we can see in Fig. 4, if the patch in the testing image is a salient patch then its $D_{average}$ will be larger than the average distance of general patch. In practice, it is not necessary to take all the R_n neighbors to achieve the global optimum. Therefore, the distance between the testing patch and all R_n neighbors are sorted and the intermediate $k(k = \beta R_n)$ neighbors are selected for computing, where $0 < \beta < 1$. Figure 5 shows the feature weighting map results of salience learning by our average distance strategy, and it is estimated by partial feast square (PLS)[10].

2.2 Density Salience Learning

As discussed in works [23,27,28], density information is also important for outlier detection, therefore it is also important for salience learning.

Similar to Sect. 2.1, each image in testing set is segmented into $M \times N$ dense patches. As mentioned above, each testing patch has R_n neighbors, *i.e.*, every image in testing set has a set of patches P^i:

$$P^i = \{X_{nn}(x_{A,i}(m,n))|m = 1, 2, \ldots, M; N = 1, 2, \ldots, N\} \tag{5}$$

Each neighbor has a matching distance to the testing patch. For each testing image, both maximum and minimum matching distances are used to compute the threshold d^i_{thr} for outliers, *i.e.*,

$$d_{max} = D_{max}(P^i) \tag{6}$$

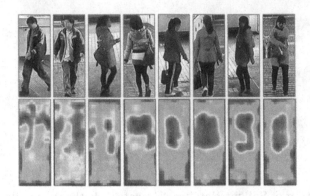

Fig. 5. Illustration of the feature weighting map of our average distance salience learning estimated by partial feast square (PLS) [10].

$$d_{min} = D_{min}(P^i) \tag{7}$$

$$d_{thr}^i = \mu(d_{max} - d_{min}) + d_{min} \tag{8}$$

where D_{max} and D_{min} are the maximum and minimum distances respectively in P^i set, $\mu(0 < \mu < 1)$ is a threshold parameter. For each testing patch, $Q^i(m, n)$ denotes the set of matching distances which are larger than d_{thr}^i:

$$Q^i(m, n) = \{D_k(X_{nn}(x_{A,i}(m, n))) | D_k(X_{nn}(x_{A,i}(m, n))) > d_{thr}^i, \\ k = 1, 2, \ldots, R_n\} \tag{9}$$

where D_k denotes the distance of the k-th nearest neighbor. The density factor can be defined as:

$$fa_{A,i}(m, n) = (R_n - |Q^i(m, n)|)/R_n \tag{10}$$

where $|Q^i(m, n)|$ is the number of element in $Q^i(m, n)$. Finally, the density salience value is obtained as follows:

$$Svalue_{density}(x_{A,i}(m, n)) = \exp(-fa_{A,i}(m, n)/2\sigma^2) \tag{11}$$

3   Person Re-identification Algorithm

The whole algorithm of our person re-identification is presented in Algorithm 1.

3.1   Dense Correspondence for Patches

In this section, the dense correspondence proposed in [5,9,19] is employed to achieve patch alignment.

Each human image is densely segmented into some local patches. Dense SIFT descriptor and a LAB color histogram, named as dLabSift features are extracted

Algorithm 1. Algorithm of person re-identification

Input:
    Probe person $x_{A,i}$ in Camera A
    Gallery person set x_B in Camera B
    Reference set R_n;
Output:
    Find the person x_{B,q^*} mostly matched with $x_{A,i}$
1: **For** each patch $x_{A,i}(m,n)$ in $x_{A,i}$ **do**
2:    Compute the salience value $Svalue_{DD}(x_{A,i}(m,n))$ using Eq. (3)
3: **Endfor**
4: **For** each person $x_{B,j}$ in x_B **do**
5:    **For** each patch $x_{B,j}(m,n)$ in $x_{B,j}$ **do**
6:       Compute the salience value $Svalue_{DD}(x_{B,j}(m,n))$ using Eq. (3)
7:    **Endfor**
8: **Endfor**
9: **For** each person $x_{B,j}$ in x_B **do**
10:    **For** each patch $x_{A,i}(m,n)$ in $x_{A,i}$ **do**
11:       Find the corresponding patch $x_{B,j}(m',n')$ in $x_{B,j}$ using Eq.(14)
12:       Compute the similarity score $s(x_{A,i}(m,n), x_{B,j}(m',n'))$ using Eq.(15)
13:    **Endfor**
14:    Compute the similarity score $Sim(x_{A,i}, x_{B,j})$ using Eq.(16) for $x_{A,i}$ and $x_{B,j}$
15: **Endfor**
16: Find the person x_{B,q^*} mostly matched with $x_{A,p}$ as

$$q^* = \arg \max_q Sim(x_{A,p}, x_{B,q})$$

17: **return** x_{B,q^*};

---

for each patch with the dimension of $32 \times 3 \times 3 + 128 \times 3 = 672$(more details can be found in [5]). Similar to work [5], for each image patch $x_{A,i}(m,n)$ in $x_{A,i}$, we first generate candidate patches in $x_{B,i}$ (shown in Fig. 6) as follows.

First, let $T_{A,i}(m)$ be the m-th row patches set of the i-th image of Camera A, $i.e.$,

$$T_{A,i}(m) = \{x_{A,i}(m,n) | n = 1, 2, \dots, N\} \tag{12}$$

Then, we obtain candidate patches in $x_{B,i}$, as

$$S(x_{A,i}(m,n), x_{B,j}) = \{T_{B,j}(a) | a \in \theta(m)\}, \forall x_{A,i}(m,n) \in T_{A,i}(m) \tag{13}$$

where $T_{B,j}(a)$ is the a-th row patches set of the j-th image of Camera B. $\theta(m)$ is the relaxation of adjacency search, as human images may have vertical misalignment.

After that, the optimal corresponding patch $x_{B,j}(m',n')$ is obtained from gallery, as

$$x_{B,j}(m',n') = \arg \max_{\bar{x} \in S_{i,j}} s(x_{A,i}(m,n), \bar{x}) \tag{14}$$

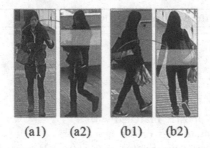

(a1)   (a2)   (b1)   (b2)

Fig. 6. Illustration of Adjacency Constrained Search. The green box region denotes search region of the patch in red box (Color figure online).

where $S_{ij} = S(x_{A,i}(m,n), x_{B,j})$, and $s(x,y)$ is computed as

$$s(x,y) = \exp\left(-\frac{\mathrm{d}(x,y)^2}{2\sigma^2}\right) \qquad (15)$$

where $\mathrm{d}(x,y)$ is Euclidean distance between x and y.

3.2 Similarity Computation

The testing human images always contain a large part of backgrounds, which are various around pedestrians especially due to the change of camera viewpoint. Therefore, it's unreasonable to take all the testing patches for salience learning.

In this paper, the statistical information of human head position is utilized to remove some background patches before computing the similarity scores. Since the backgrounds around human lower part are normally the similar pavement, only the statistics of human head position are produced to remove the backgrounds around human head.

For each image $x_{A,i}$ in the probe, the matching result is obtained as the image in the gallery with the maximal similarity score $x_{B,j}$, while the similarity score between two images is obtained by accumulating the score of their each patch pair which can be formulated as:

$$Sim(x_{A,i}, x_{B,j}) =$$
$$\sum_{m,n} \frac{Sa_{A,i}(m,n) \cdot s(x_{A,i}(m,n), x_{B,j}(m',n')) \cdot Sa_{B,j}(m',n')}{\varepsilon + |Sa_{A,i}(m,n) - Sa_{B,j}(m',n')|} \qquad (16)$$

where $x_{A,i}$ and $x_{B,j}$ are collection of patch features of the probe image and the gallery image. ε is a parameter controlling the salience difference, and,

$$Sa_{A,i}(m,n) = Svalue_{DD}(x_{A,i}(m,n)) \qquad (17)$$

$$Sa_{B,j}(m',n') = Svalue_{DD}(x_{B,j}(m',n')) \qquad (18)$$

4   Experiments

The proposed method is evaluated on two publicly available datasets, VIPeR dataset [22] and CUHK01 dataset [8]. Both reflect most challenging problems of person re-identification applications such as human pose variation, cameras viewpoint and illumination change, occlusions between persons.

Evaluation Protocol. Similar to the work [5], each dataset is randomly partitioned into two parts, 50 % for salience learning and 50 % for testing and the standard Cumulated Matching Characteristics (CMC) curve is mainly evaluated during experiments. Images from camera A are used as probe and other images from camera B are used as gallery. For each probe image the rank of matching scores to the images in gallery is obtained. Rank-k recognition rate is the expectation of correct match at rank-k, and the cumulated values of recognition rate at all ranks are recorded as one-trial CMC result. 10 trials of evaluation are executed to achieve stable statistics. Our Density-Distance salience learning method is denoted as DdSal. As mentioned above, before computing the similarity scores the position information of human head is utilized to remove some background patches, this process is denoted as heaPri. The combination of Density-Distance salience learning method and the process of heaPri is denoted as PriDd.

4.1   Evaluations on VIPeR Dataset

VIPeR dataset [22] is one of the most challenging person re-identification dataset and it is captured by two cameras in outdoor with two images for each person shot from different viewpoints. The persons have been accurately detected from

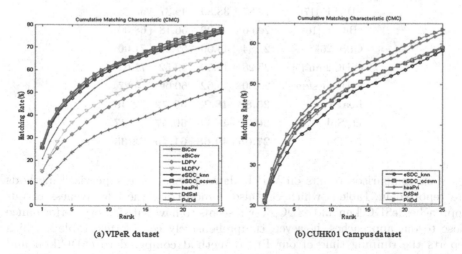

(a) VIPeR dataset   (b) CUHK01 Campus dataset

Fig. 7. CMC statistics on the VIPeR dataset and the CUHK01 Campus dataset. (a) On VIPeR dataset, our approach (heaPri, DdSal and PriDd) is compared with BiCov [16], eBiCov [16], LDFV [20], bLDFV [20], eSDC_knn [5] and eSDC_ocsvm [5]. (b) On CUHK01 Campus dataset, our method is compared with eSDC_knn and eSDC_ocsvm.

original videos. It contains 632 pedestrian pairs. Each person has two images from different cameras with different viewpoints, most of which are larger than 90 degree. All images are normalized to the same size of 128 × 48 [5].

On the VIPeR dataset, the results of DdSal, heaPri and PriDd are reported in Fig. 7(a), compared to several unsupervised methods including eSDC_knn [5], eSDC_ocsvm [5], BiCov [16], eBiCov [16], LDFV [20], bLDFV [20]. Generally speaking, (1) PriDd is slightly better than heaPri, DdSal which means both the Density-Distance salience information and the head background removal improve the matching results. (2) Our approaches and the eSDC-based methods outperform the other four methods. While our PriDd approach is slightly better than eSDC_knn salience learning approach and also slightly better than eSDC_ocsvm salience learning method from rank 1 to rank 15. It's worth mentioning that although eSDC_ocsvm slightly outperforms our approach after rank 15, it requires much higher computing cost.

Table 1. VIPeR dataset: top ranked matching rates in [%] with 316 persons.

Method	$r = 1$	$r = 5$	$r = 10$	$r = 20$
LMNN [4]	6.23	19.65	32.63	52.25
ITML [4]	11.61	31.39	45.76	63.86
PRDC [4]	15.66	38.42	53.86	70.09
PCCA [7]	19.27	48.89	64.91	80.28
BiCov [16]	9.08	23.58	33.59	45.97
ELF [25]	12.00	31.00	41.00	58.00
LDFV [20]	15.17	31.47	43.60	57.86
bLDFV [20]	15.39	36.77	47.93	61.43
SDALF [17]	19.87	38.89	49.37	65.73
eBiCov [16]	20.66	42.00	56.18	68.00
CPS [26]	21.84	44.00	57.21	71.00
eSDC_knn [5]	25.28	47.50	59.52	71.62
eSDC_ocsvm [5]	25.50	49.62	60.66	74.27
heaPri	**25.88**	**48.22**	**60.72**	**72.40**
DdSal	**26.32**	**48.73**	**60.57**	**72.37**
PriDd	**27.05**	**49.68**	**61.45**	**73.35**

More comparison results on VIPeR dataset with some supervised methods are reported in Table 1, which can also demonstrate the effectiveness of our approaches. eSDC_knn and eSDC_ocsvm seems to have satisfactory performance close to our approaches, however, comprehensively considering Table 2, which reports the running time of our PriDd method compared to eSDC_knn and eSDC_ocsvmon MATLAB (2013a), with 64-bit Win7, Intel core i7, 4.00 GHz CPU, our approaches can achieve better performance with acceptable computing complexity.

Table 2. VIPeR dataset: running time in [seconds] of three salience learning methods with 316 test persons.

Method	Trial1	Trial3	Trial5	Trial7	Trial9
eSDC_knn	0.601	0.578	0.600	0.588	0.597
eSDC_ocsvm	1196.959	1123.837	1260.092	1247.636	1219.456
PriDd	**4.694**	**4.694**	**4.866**	**4.862**	**4.840**

4.2   Evaluations on CUHK01 Dataset

The CUHK01 dataset [8] is also captured by two cameras in a campus environment with higher resolution compared to the VIPeR dataset. All the images are normalized to 160 × 60 for evaluation.

Table 3. CUHK01 dataset: top ranked matching rates in [%] with 316 persons.

Method	r = 1	r = 5	r = 10	r = 20
eSDC_knn	20.66	36.01	44.14	53.54
eSDC_ocsvm	21.20	37.91	45.91	55.16
heaPri	**21.62**	**38.98**	**48.32**	**57.94**
DdSal	**21.13**	**37.72**	**46.10**	**55.41**
PriDd	**22.53**	**40.06**	**49.59**	**59.52**

Table 4. CUHK01 dataset: running time in [seconds] of three salience learning methods with 316 test persons.

Method	Trial2	Trial4	Trial6	Trial8	Trial10
eSDC_knn	0.944	0.947	0.937	0.940	0.938
eSDC_ocsvm	2002.655	2061.217	1991.516	1972.510	2003.010
PriDd	**7.213**	**6.970**	**7.085**	**7.005**	**7.093**

For the concise presentation, only two outstanding methods, eSDC_knn and eSDC_ocsvm are implemented on CUHK01 dataset for comparison as shown in Fig. 7(b). From which we can see, our methods, especially PriDd method, have a significant improvement compared to eSDC_knn and eSDC_ocsvm. eSDC_ocsvm has almost identical performance as our DdSal method but much worse performance than our heaPri and PriDd methods, which means the background interference of human head has higher influence on CUHK01 dataset. More detailed comparison results on CUHK01 dataset are shown in Table 3. Same as the evaluation on VIPeR dataset, Table 4 reports the running time of our PriDd method compared to eSDC_knn and eSDC_ocsvm also on MATLAB (2013a), with 64-bit Win7, Intel core i7, 4.00 GHz CPU, which also can demonstrate that our approaches can achieve better performance with acceptable computing complexity.

5 Conclusion

A novel unsupervised salience learning method is proposed for person re-identification, where a Density-Distance is designed for salience learning. Meanwhile, the statistics of pedestrian's head position is learnt to relieve the background interference during similarity matching. The experimental results on widely used VIPeR dataset and CUHK01 dataset demonstrate the outperformance of our method which improves matching precision with acceptable computing complexity comparing with the state of art methods.

Acknowledgments. Our thanks to the support from 863 (2014AA015104), the National Nature Science Foundation of China (61472002), the Natural Science Foundation of Anhui Higher Education Institutions of China (KJ2014A015), the Natural Science Foundation of Anhui Province (1508085QF127) and the Doctoral Research Foundation of Anhui University (02303203/32030059).

References

1. Prosser, B., Zheng, W., Gong, S., Xiang, T., Mary, Q.: Person re-identification by support vector ranking. In: BMVC (2010)
2. Hirzer, M., Beleznai, C., Roth, P.M., Bischof, H.: Person re-identification by descriptive and discriminative classification. In: Heyden, A., Kahl, F. (eds.) SCIA 2011. LNCS, vol. 6688, pp. 91–102. Springer, Heidelberg (2011)
3. Dikmen, M., Akbas, E., Huang, T.S., Ahuja, N.: Pedestrian recognition with a learned metric. In: Kimmel, R., Klette, R., Sugimoto, A. (eds.) ACCV 2010, Part IV. LNCS, vol. 6495, pp. 501–512. Springer, Heidelberg (2011)
4. Zheng, W.-S., Gong, S., Xiang, T.: Person re-identification by probabilistic relative distance comparison. In: CVPR (2011)
5. Zhao, R., Ouyang, W., Wang, X.: Unsupervised salience learning for person re-identification. In: CVPR (2013)
6. Goferman, S., Zelnik-Manor, L., Tal, A.: Context-aware saliency detection. PAMI **34**(10), 1915–1926 (2012)
7. Mignon, A., Jurie, F.: Pcca: a new approach for distance learning from sparse pair wise constraints. In: CVPR (2012)
8. Li, W., Zhao, R., Wang, X.: Human reidentification with transferred metric learning. In: Lee, K.M., Matsushita, Y., Rehg, J.M., Hu, Z. (eds.) ACCV 2012, Part I. LNCS, vol. 7724, pp. 31–44. Springer, Heidelberg (2013)
9. Liu, C., Gong, S., Loy, C.C., Lin, X.: Person re-identification: what features are important? In: Fusiello, A., Murino, V., Cucchiara, R. (eds.) ECCV 2012 Ws/Demos, Part I. LNCS, vol. 7583, pp. 391–401. Springer, Heidelberg (2012)
10. Schwartz, W., Davis, L.: Learning discriminative appearance-based models using partial least squares. In: XXII Brazilian Symposium on Computer Graphics and Image Processing (SIBGRAPI) (2009)

11. Porikli F.: Inter-camera color calibration using cross-correlation model function. In: IEEE International Conference on Image Processing, pp. 133–136 (2003)
12. Li, W., Wang, X.: Locally aligned feature transforms across views. In: CVPR (2013)
13. Chilgunde, A., Kumar, P., Ranganath, S.: Multi-camera target tracking in blind regions of cameras with non-overlapping fields of view. In: British Machine Vision Conference, pp. 42.1–42.10 (2004)
14. Mazzon, R., Cavallaro, A.: Multi-camera tracking using a multi-goal social force model. Neurocomputing **100**, 41–50 (2013)
15. Javed, O., Rasheed, Z., Shafique, K., Shah, M.: Tracking across multiple cameras with disjoint views. In: Computer Vision (2003)
16. Ma, B., Su, Y., Jurie, F.: Bicov.: a novel image representation for person re-identification and face verification. In: British Machine Vision Conference (2012)
17. Farenzena, M., Bazzani, L., Perina, A., Murino, V., Cristani, M.: Person re-identification by symmetry-driven accumulation of local features. In: CVPR (2010)
18. Lu, Y., Lin, L., Zheng, W.-S.: Human re-identification by matching compositional template with cluster sampling. In: ICCV (2013)
19. Ma, K., Ben-Arie, J.: Vector array based multi-view face detection with compound exemplars. In: CVPR (2012)
20. Ma, B., Su, Y., Jurie, F.: Local descriptors encoded by fisher vectors for person re-identification. In: Fusiello, A., Murino, V., Cucchiara, R. (eds.) ECCV 2012 Ws/Demos, Part I. LNCS, vol. 7583, pp. 413–422. Springer, Heidelberg (2012)
21. Byers, S., Raftery, A.: Nearest-neighbor clutter removal for estimating features in spatial point processes. J. Am. Stat. Assoc. **93**, 577–584 (1998)
22. Gray, D., Brennan, S., Tao, H.: Evaluating appearance models for recognition, reacquisition, and tracking. In: IEEE International Workshop on Performance Evaluation for Tracking and Surveillance (PETS) (2007)
23. Papadimitriou, S., Kitagawa, H., Gibbons, P.B.: Loci: fast outlier detection using the local correlation integral. In: International Conference on Data Engineering, pp. 315–326. IEEE (2003)
24. Zhao, R., Ouyang, W., Wang, X.: Person Re-identification by Saliency Learning. arXiv preprint arXiv:1412.1908 (2014)
25. Gray, D., Tao, H.: Viewpoint invariant pedestrian recognition with an ensemble of localized features. In: Forsyth, D., Torr, P., Zisserman, A. (eds.) ECCV 2008, Part I. LNCS, vol. 5302, pp. 262–275. Springer, Heidelberg (2008)
26. Cheng, D., Cristani, M., Stoppa, M., Bazzani, L., Murino, V.: Custom pictorial structures for re-identification. In: BMVC (2011)
27. Hido, S., Tsuboi, Y., Kashima, H.: Statistical outlier detection using direct density ratio estimation. Knowl. Inf. Syst. **26**(2), 309–336 (2011)
28. Breunig, M.M., Kriegel, H.P., Ng, R.T.: LOF: identifying density-based local outliers. In: ACM Sigmod International Conference on Management of Data, pp. 93–104 (2000)
29. Chandola, V., Banerjee, A., Kumar, V.: Anomaly detection: a survey. ACM Comput. Surv. (CSUR) **41**(3), 15 (2009)
30. Kriegel, H.-P., Krger, P., Zimek, A.: Outlier detection techniques. In: Tutorial at the 13th Pacific-Asia Conference on Knowledge Discovery and Data Mining (2009)

Phase Unwrapping Method Based on Heterodyne Three Frequency Non-equal Step Phase Shift

Lei Geng, Yang Liu, Zhitao Xiao[✉], Jun Wu, Yang Zhang, Fei Yuan, Zhenjie Yang, Peng Gan, Jingjing Su, and Kun Ye

School of Electronics and Information Engineering, Tianjin Polytechnic University, Tianjin, China
xiaozhitao@tjpu.edu.cn

Abstract. This paper presents a phase unwrapping method of heterodyne three frequency non-equal step phase shift, to surmount disadvantages of needing dozens of images in 3-D measurement techniques of multi-frequency phase shift. The method selects three frequencies. Firstly, four-step phase-shifting algorithm is used to calculate wrapped phase and average intensity of the intermediate frequency. Then the wrapped phases of other frequencies are obtained utilizing two-step phase-shifting algorithm. Finally, the absolute phase is calculated using heterodyne method. In addition, the contour sine/cosine filter method is utilized to filter noise by the fringe orientation information. The 3-D points cloud of standard planar and calibration target are reconstructed experimentally. Then the planeness of standard planar is calculated. The centers of markers of calibration target are extracted to calculate distance between two adjacent circles. Experiments demonstrate that the proposed method reduces the number of fringe images, eliminates the effects of noise efficaciously.

Keywords: Non-equal step phase shift · Multi-frequency heterodyne · Phase unwrapping · Contour sine/cosine filter

1 Introduction

Grating Projection 3-D measurement technology is an accurate measurement method of three-dimensional profile using phase information. Phase shift method and Fourier transforming profilometry are the main methods to get phases at present. Phase shift method is widely used because of its high precision, resolution and less sensitivity to the surface reflectivity variations [1]. The method calculates wrapped phase values which include surface deformation information by collecting multiple phase-shift fringe patterns. Since the wrapped phase value is in the range of $[-\pi, \pi]$, in order to acquire continuous phase map, the wrapped phase needs to be unwrapped to get the absolute phase value [2]. Phase unwrapping methods can be divided into single-frequency-based and multiple-frequency-based method. Single-frequency-based method obtains only a set of wrapped phase values when measuring, so there are some deficiencies at unwrapping range, precision and error tolerance. While multiple-frequency-based method gets multiple sets of wrapped phase values, thus it increases the unwrapping range, precision

© Springer International Publishing Switzerland 2015
Y.-J. Zhang (Ed.): ICIG 2015, Part III, LNCS 9219, pp. 68–79, 2015.
DOI: 10.1007/978-3-319-21969-1_7

and reduces the error influence. Unwrapping method based on multi-frequency mainly includes Gray codes and multiple frequency phase shift method [3, 4]. Gray code method is more sensitive to light intensity and the surface shade of measured objects, which may lead to incorrect decoding of pixel boundaries, susceptible to noise, and also, the measurement range is restricted to the number of Gray code fringes. Multi-frequency phase-shift method improves the measurement accuracy and measurement range by adding fringes of different frequencies, thus its adaptability is enhanced. Currently, accuracy improvement by increasing the number of frequencies is an important tendency of multi-frequency phase shift method [5]. However, this method requires multiple images taken at different frequencies.

Generally speaking, the grayscale of encoding fringe pattern is cosine distribution in the Grating Projection 3-D measurement technology. However, amount of noise will be caused by the nonlinear output of projection system, electric noise and environmental noise. Errors would be produced in the phase recovery, which can influence the three-dimensional reconstruction of discontinuous object's surface. So phase error should be reduced by additional method. Firstly, nonlinear correction is used to reduce the phase error in the projection system, but it requires plenty of time and the gamma value of projector should be relatively fixed [6]. Secondly, the phase error should be compensated. Several methods are proposed [7–9]. However, the computation of spline fitting method [7] is rather complex. Look-up-table method [8] needs plenty of time and relatively stable environment. Image filter method [9] based on frequency domain or space domain can eliminate noise and reduce the phase error greatly, but the jump information of object boundary will be lost when the surface contains different height.

Our main contribution is that a method of heterodyne three frequency non-equal step phase shift combined with filter is proposed. Firstly, three frequency cosine waves are selected, and each cosine wave is shifted with different steps. Only by projecting eight fringe patterns, the phase map with rather high quality can be obtained. Secondly, the projection system is optimized by nonlinear correction. Thirdly, before the phase maps are unwrapped, the contour cosine filter method proposed by Fu [10] is used to reduce the noise caused by difference frequency superposition. The advantages of this method are that, accurate measurements can be realized by fewer projection pictures, inconsistent points on wrapped phase maps are filtered effectively by fringe orientation information.

2 Phase Unwrapping Theory of Three Frequency Non-equal Step Phase Shift

In this paper, eight fringe patterns of three different frequencies are projected (intermediate frequency f_2 is four step phase-shift fringes, frequency f_1 and f_3 is two step phase-shift fringes). Firstly, phase unwrapping theory of non-equal step phase shift is used to calculate light intensity of background and wrapped phase value $\Delta\varphi_2(x, y)$ of frequency f_2. The wrapped phase value $\Delta\varphi_1(x, y)$ and $\Delta\varphi_3(x, y)$ of f_1 and f_3 are obtained in the case that the background intensity is known. Then three wrapped phases should be carried on contour sine/cosine filter separately. According to the heterodyne theory, the phase function $\theta_{12}(x,y)$ of equivalent frequency f_{12} is obtained by superposing the difference frequency values of $\Delta\varphi_1(x,y)$ and $\Delta\varphi_2(x,y)$, and the phase function $\theta_{23}(x,y)$ of equivalent frequency f_{23} is obtained by $\Delta\varphi_2(x,y)$ and $\Delta\varphi_3(x,y)$. Then the phase functions should be performed sine/cosine filter respectively. The phase function $\theta_{123}(x,y)$ containing deformation information of object surface is calculated by double heterodyne. Finally, the point cloud data of object surface will be obtained by phase matching method based on binocular stereo vision. The flow chart is shown as Fig. 1.

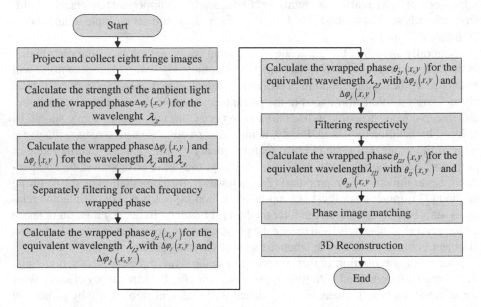

Fig. 1. The flowchart of the proposed method

2.1 Non-equal Step Phase Shift Method

In grating projection 3-D measurement system, cosine encoding fringes are projected to the surface of measured object and are modulated to be deformation fringes by object surface information. Assuming that the projection light intensity satisfies the standard cosine distribution, the light intensity distribution function of the deformation fringe patterns is:

$$I(x,y) = a(x,y) + b(x,y)\cos\left[2\pi fx + \Delta\varphi(x,y)\right] \tag{1}$$

Where, $I(x,y)$ indicates the light intensity of deformation fringe patterns; $a(x,y)$ is the intensity of background; $b(x,y)$ is the modulation amplitude; f is the frequency of fringes; and $\Delta\varphi(x,y)$ denotes the phase function to be solved. The formula contains three unknown quantities. Therefore, it requires at least three light intensity functions to solve phase value of one measured point.

Phase unwrapping method based on heterodyne three frequency non-equal step phase shift is using different steps phase shift algorithm to calculate wrapped phase values of fringes with three different frequencies respectively (the three frequencies are denoted as f_1, f_2 and f_3). The frequency f_2 adopts standard four-step phase shift fringes, the cosine gratings are moved four steps, and each step is $\alpha = \pi/2$. So that four images can be collected to obtain phase values of the object. Here, $I_n(x, y)$ represents light intensity of the n-th image, then

$$I_n(x, y) = a(x, y) + b(x, y) \cos \left[2\pi f_2 x + \Delta\varphi_2(x, y) + (n-1)\pi/2 \right], \ (n = 1, 2, 3, 4) \qquad (2)$$

The phase calculated by the four deformed fringe patterns is:

$$\Delta\varphi_2(x, y) = \arctan \left[\frac{I_4 - I_2}{I_1 - I_3} \right] - 2\pi f_2 x \qquad (3)$$

The surface reflection of the measured object is linear under the condition that cameras and projectors have a considerable depth of field. Then the average light intensity coefficient $a(x, y)$ of the same pixel point (i, j) is a constant value in these four images.

$$a(x, y) = \left(I_1(x, y) + I_2(x, y) + I_3(x, y) + I_4(x, y) \right) / 4 \qquad (4)$$

The frequency f_1 and f_3 adopt two-step phase shift method, each step is. In this way, both sine and cosine fringe pattern scan be collected, and the functions of light intensity are:

$$I_5(x, y) = a(x, y) + b(x, y) \sin \left(2\pi f_1 x + \Delta\varphi_1(x, y) \right) \qquad (5)$$

$$I_6(x, y) = a(x, y) + b(x, y) \cos \left(2\pi f_1 x + \Delta\varphi_1(x, y) \right) \qquad (6)$$

$$I_7(x, y) = a(x, y) + b(x, y) \sin \left(2\pi f_3 x + \Delta\varphi_3(x, y) \right) \qquad (7)$$

$$I_8(x, y) = a(x, y) + b(x, y) \cos \left(2\pi f_3 x + \Delta\varphi_3(x, y) \right) \qquad (8)$$

Therefore, $a(x, y)$ can be calculated by formula (4), and wrapped phase values $\Delta\varphi_1(x, y)$ and $\Delta\varphi_3(x, y)$ of deformed fringe patterns with f_1 and f_3 can be obtained by substituting $a(x, y)$ into formula (9) and (10).

$$\Delta\varphi_1(x, y) = \arctan \left[\frac{I_5(x, y) - a(x, y)}{I_6(x, y) - a(x, y)} \right] - 2\pi f_1 x \qquad (9)$$

$$\Delta\varphi_3(x, y) = \arctan \left[\frac{I_7(x, y) - a(x, y)}{I_8(x, y) - a(x, y)} \right] - 2\pi f_3 x \qquad (10)$$

In order to calculate the phase value of a measured point, it needs three light intensity functions at least. Namely, three steps phase shift at least are needed to get wrapped phases by the theory of phase shift method. In the phase unwrapping method using three frequency non-equal step phase shift, the wrapped phase value of intermediate frequency and the light intensity of background are calculated by four-step phase shift method.

Wrapped phase values of the other two frequencies can be obtained by two-step phase shift when light intensity of background is known. In this way, projection image scan be reduced. The phase map obtained containing three-dimensional morphologies information of object is in the range of $[-\pi, \pi]$. Therefore, the phase is unwrapped by heterodyne theory to recover the three-dimensional morphologies of the object.

2.2 Heterodyne Theory for Phase Unwrapping

Heterodyne theory [3] is to obtain a new phase function $\theta_{12}(x)$ of frequency f_{12} by superposing the difference frequencies of fringe phase function $\Delta\varphi_1(x)$ and $\Delta\varphi_2(x)$ with frequency f_1 and f_2. As is shown in Fig. 2, λ_1, λ_2 and λ_{12} are wavelengths corresponding to fringes of different frequencies f_1, f_2 and f_{12}.

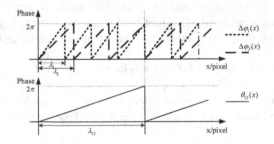

Fig. 2. Heterodyne principle

Then, the equivalent wavelength λ_{12} can be expressed as:

$$\lambda_{12} = \left| \frac{\lambda_1 \lambda_2}{\lambda_1 - \lambda_2} \right| \tag{11}$$

According to heterodyne theory, the continuous phase map in the whole range can be obtained by unwrapping the phase map wrapped within $[-\pi, \pi]$. Assuming that wavelengths corresponding to different frequencies are respectively λ_1, λ_2 and λ_3, the equivalent wavelength λ_{12} can be obtained by λ_1 and λ_2, λ_{23} is calculated by λ_2 and λ_3, and λ_{123} is gotten by λ_{12} and λ_{23}. In order to obtain the continuous absolute phase map in the whole range, the equivalent wavelength λ_{123} cannot be smaller than the number of rows pixels W of fringe image. That is, $\lambda_{123} \geq W$.

The unwrapping formula for the phases of fringes with different frequencies is:

$$\phi_i = 2\pi N_i + \Delta\varphi_i, \quad (i = 1, 2, 3) \tag{12}$$

Where, φ_i indicates the absolute phase, N_i is series of fringes.

The fringe wavelengths of the same point on the surface of measured object are λ_a and λ_b (a equals to 1, 2, 12, and b equals to 2, 3, 23 respectively). Phase function $\theta_{ab}(x)$ of λ_{ab} can be obtained by the following formula:

$\Delta\varphi_a > \Delta\varphi_b$:

$$\begin{cases} \theta_{12} = 2\pi + \Delta\varphi_1 - \Delta\varphi_2 \\ \theta_{23} = 2\pi + \Delta\varphi_2 - \Delta\varphi_3 \\ \theta_{123} = 2\pi + \Delta\varphi_{12} - \Delta\varphi_{23} \end{cases} \tag{13}$$

$\Delta\varphi_a \le \Delta\varphi_b$:

$$\begin{cases} \theta_{12} = \Delta\varphi_1 - \Delta\varphi_2 \\ \theta_{23} = \Delta\varphi_2 - \Delta\varphi_3 \\ \theta_{123} = \Delta\varphi_{12} - \Delta\varphi_{23} \end{cases} \tag{14}$$

Substituting it into formula (12), the absolute phase ϕ_2 of deformed fringe patterns with f_2 can be obtained by:

$$\phi_{2-12} = \Delta\varphi_2 + 2\pi \left(Round \left(\frac{\theta_{123}(x,y)}{2\pi} \times \frac{\lambda_{123}}{\lambda_{12}} \right) * \frac{\lambda_{12}}{\lambda_2} + Round \left(\frac{\theta_{12}(x,y)}{2\pi} \times \frac{\lambda_{12}}{\lambda_2} \right) \right) \tag{15}$$

$$\phi_{2-23} = \Delta\varphi_2 + 2\pi \left(Round \left(\frac{\theta_{123}(x,y)}{2\pi} \times \frac{\lambda_{123}}{\lambda_{23}} \right) * \frac{\lambda_{23}}{\lambda_2} + Round \left(\frac{\theta_{23}(x,y)}{2\pi} \times \frac{\lambda_{23}}{\lambda_2} \right) \right) \tag{16}$$

$$\varphi_2 = \left(\varphi_{2-12} + \varphi_{2-23} \right) / 2 \tag{17}$$

Where, ϕ_{2-12} indicates the absolute phase of deformation fringe pattern with frequency f_2 which is obtained by λ_{12} and $\theta_{12}(x,y)$, ϕ_{2-23} is the absolute phase of deformation

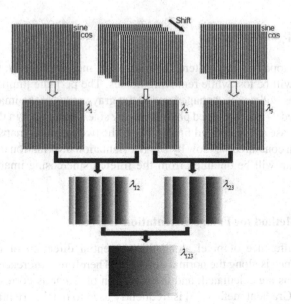

Fig. 3. Unwrapping algorithm based on three frequency non-equal step phase shift technology

fringe pattern with f_2 obtained by λ_{23} and $\theta_{23}(x, y)$. In order to reduce the error, the absolute phase ϕ_2 is the average of ϕ_{2-12} and ϕ_{2-23}.

Eight vertical fringes meeting coding scheme of three frequency non-equal step phase shift are generated by computer, whose corresponding wavelengths are $\lambda_1 = 7$, $\lambda_2 = 8$ and $\lambda_3 = 9$ (Unit: pixels/cycle). The process of phase unwrapping is shown as Fig. 3.

Phase unwrapping by three-frequency heterodyne is the method based on dual-frequency phase shift [4]. The equivalent wavelength λ_{12} is calculated by λ_1 and λ_2 with frequency f_1 and f_2. If wrapped phase of λ_1 and λ_2 contains noise, there will be noise of λ_{12} caused by superposition of difference frequency. As is shown in Fig. 4, there are plenty of noises in wrapped phase due to the system interference, environmental noise and other factors. Therefore, the wrapped phase maps need filtering.

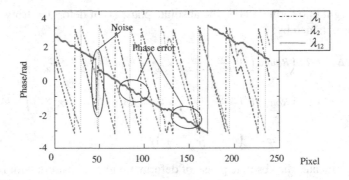

Fig. 4. Phase error and noise

3   Phase Map Filtering

If the absolute wrapped phase is filtered by traditional method directly, the jump information of phase will be lost while removing noises. The periodic jump information of sine/cosine images will not be damaged due to the gray values of the images are continuous. It is proposed to filter wrapped phase maps by sine/cosine filter in this paper. Sine/cosine maps of phase are calculated firstly. Then, the two resultant maps are conducted median filtering in contoured window by fringe orientation information to remove noise. Finally, phase map will be obtained from the filtered sine/cosine images by division operation.

3.1   Gradient Method for Fringe Orientation Images

The minimum difference of pixel along the tangential direction of fringe, and the maximum difference is along the normal direction. Therefore, differences of each point along all directions are calculated, and the direction of fringe is corresponding to the minimum value. Gradient method [5] is frequently used to obtain orientation of fringes defined as:

$$\theta\left(x,y\right)=\arctan\left[\frac{\partial\phi\left(x,y\right)}{\partial y}\bigg/\frac{\partial\phi\left(x,y\right)}{\partial x}\right]\pm\frac{\pi}{2} \tag{18}$$

Where, $\theta\left(x,y\right)$ is the orientation of fringes, $\phi\left(x,y\right)$ is the phase.

3.2   Determination of Fringes Contoured Windows

The purpose of calculating direction of fringes is to determine the contours and normal curves. Contours are locally parallel to current trend of fringes, and normal curves are partially perpendicular to current trend of fringes.

Here, $P_i\left(x_i,y_i\right)$ is set as the coordinates of a certain point of the image, the direction of fringe at this point is θ_i. The fringe orientation image shows that direction value θ is along the tangential direction of fringe contour. The fringe contour can be approximately replaced by tangential in the neighborhood of current point. The two adjacent points $P_{i+1}\left(x_{i+1},y_{i+1}\right)$ and $P_{i-1}\left(x_{i-1},y_{i-1}\right)$ of the current point on contour can be obtained according to the fringe orientation image:

$$\begin{cases} x_{i+1}=x_i+\cos\theta_i \\ y_{i+1}=y_i+\sin\theta_i \end{cases}, \quad \begin{cases} x_{i-1}=x_i-\cos\theta_i \\ y_{i-1}=y_i-\sin\theta_i \end{cases} \tag{19}$$

Similarly, $P_{i+2}\left(x_{i+2},y_{i+2}\right)$ and $P_{i-2}\left(x_{i-2},y_{i-2}\right)$ can be calculated. A curve through $P_i\left(x_i,y_i\right)$ and along the direction of fringe can thus be obtained, that is, fringe contour. Phase value of each point on the curve is equal to the phase value of point $P_i\left(x_i,y_i\right)$, namely, phase of fringe remains unchanged on the contour.

While the point $\left(x_i,y_i\right)$ obtained may not be integer. Fringe orientation value of point $\left(x_i,y_i\right)$ should be replaced by the linear interpolation of the four integer pixels adjacent to $\left(x_i,y_i\right)$. In this way, error caused by fringe orientation images only taking values on integer pixels will be reduced.

3.3   Sine/Cosine Filter Method

Since phase φ of wrapped phase map is discontinuous, current pixel point (i,j) satisfies: $-\pi\leq\varphi_{ij}\leq\pi$, $1\leq i\leq M$, $1\leq j\leq N$ where, $M\times N$ is the size of image. Sine/cosine components t_1,t_2 are set as $t_1=\sin\varphi$, $t_2=\cos\varphi$, and they are continuous. Namely, the discontinuous phase can be represented by its continuous vector $(\cos\varphi,\sin\varphi)$. After that, the sine/cosine images are conducted median filtering sequentially in contoured window. Finally, φ' can be obtained by T_1 and T_2:

$$\varphi'=\arctan\left(T_1\big/T_2\right) \tag{20}$$

Phase value φ' obtained by formula (20) is in the range of $\left[-\frac{\pi}{2},\frac{\pi}{2}\right]$, then quadrants of T_1,T_2 can be determined according to its plus-minus, and its range should be extended to $[-\pi,\pi]$.

The result of conducting contour sine/cosine filter to the wrapped phase map is shown in Fig. 5.

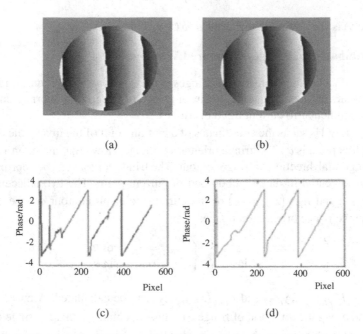

(a)   (b)

(c)   (d)

Fig. 5. The results of contour sine/cosine filter method in the contoured window. (a) Wrapped phase map. (b) Wrapped phase map after filtering. (c) A line data of wrapped phase map. (d) A line data of wrapped phase map after filtering.

3.4   Procedures and Results

(1) Calibration: The system is calibrated using the planar target proposed by Zhang [11], and calibration accuracy is evaluated by back-projection error. The calibration result shows that, the average errors of left, right cameras and the back-projection are 0.121 pixel, 0.110 pixel and 0.097 pixel. Distance between two pixels is calculated according to the calibration of parameters. The result is 0.47 mm, and the error of back-projection is 0.02 mm.

(2) Projection: Eight gray fringe patterns of three frequency non-equal step phase shift are generated by computer, and the wavelengths λ_1, λ_2 and λ_3 are 15,17 and 20 (Unit: pixels/cycle, the width of fringes is $W = 1020$ pixels). The eight fringe patterns are projected onto surface of the measured object, and the result is shown in Fig. 6(b).

(3) Phase Unwrapping: The fringe patterns are taken by the left and right cameras, and wrapped phase values φ_1, φ_2 and φ_3 of the three frequencies are calculated by non-equal step phase shift method respectively. Then φ_2 is unwrapped, and the absolute phase values of each point can be obtained. Simultaneously, phase values of the left and right cameras are set on a common benchmark. Unwrapping process of fringes captured by the left camera is shown in Fig. 6(a).

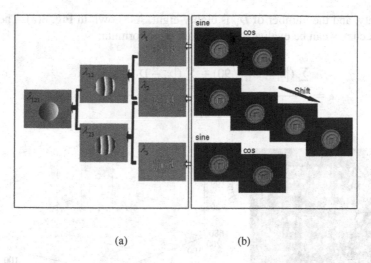

(a)   (b)

Fig. 6. Unwrapping process based on three frequency non-equal step phase shift. (a) Unwrapping phase. (b) Fringe patterns of non-equal step phase shift method.

(4) Matching: Geometry of binocular stereo vision is converted to standard geometry of binocular stereo by polar correction algorithm. Namely, the matching point on right image of arbitrary point on left image is on the polar with same row. Then matching of points on left and right images is realized according to the constraint of phase values.

(5) Point Cloud Reconstruction: After the matching points of left and right phases maps are obtained, internal and external parameters of the camera are used to restore the three-dimensional geometry information of objects based on binocular disparity theory. The result is shown in Fig. 7.

Fig. 7. The 3-D measurement result of the proposed method

A standard plate with size about 400 mm × 400 mm is measured to test the accuracy of the method proposed. Maximum absolute error of the planar is approximately 0.113 mm, and the standard deviation is 0.023 mm.

The planar target of 9 rows and 11 columns markers is placed on 10 different positions, and center distances of adjacent markers are measured. Assuming the horizontal distance between adjacent markers is D_H, vertical distance is D_V. The total number of

D_H is ninety, and the number of D_V is eighty-eight. As shown in Fig. 8(a). The measurement accuracy can be evaluated by the following formula:

$$e = \frac{\sum_{i=1}^{90}(|x_i - D_H|/90) + \sum_{j=1}^{88}(|x_j - D_V|/88)}{2} \tag{21}$$

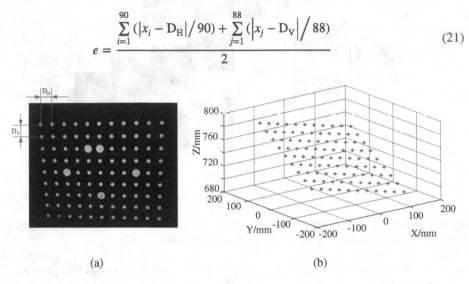

(a)   (b)

Fig. 8. The markers and measurement results. (a) Calibration target. (b) 3-D data of the markers.

Where, e is the standard deviation, x_i indicates the measured distance between two adjacent markers in horizontal direction, x_j is in vertical direction. Figure 8(b) shows the recovered three-dimensional diagram of all markers. The standard deviation is 0.047 mm.

4   Conclusion

Phase unwrapping method of heterodyne three frequency non-equal step phase shift is proposed in this paper. The absolute phase map with high quality can be obtained by only projecting eight fringe patterns. And it is easy to achieve three-dimensional surface restoration and three-dimensional accurate measurement of key points using a small number of fringe patterns. In addition, contour sine/cosine filter method based on the fringe orientation information is adopted to filter the absolute wrapped phases. The noise in wrapped phase maps are filtered out effectively, the amplification of fluctuation error is suppressed, and the blurring of 2π boundaries in wrapped phase maps is weakened. Experimental results show that, accurate measurement with fewer projection images can be realized by exploiting the method of heterodyne three frequency non-equal step phase shift combined with filter.

Acknowledgements. This work is supported by National Natural Science Foundation of China under grant No. 61302127, the key technologies R & D program of Tianjin under grant No. 14ZCZDGX00033, and research fund for the doctoral program of higher education of China under grant No. 20131201110001.

References

1. Pribanic, T., Obradovic, N., Salvi, J.: Stereo computation combining structured light and passive stereo matching. Opt. Commun. **285**, 1017–1022 (2012)
2. Zhong, K., Li, Z., Shi, Y., et al.: Fast phase measurement profilometry for arbitrary shape objects without phase unwrapping. Optics Lasers Eng. **51**(11), 1213–1222 (2013)
3. Song, L., Dong, X., Xi, J., Yu, Y., Yang, C.: A new phase unwrapping algorithm based on three wavelength phase shift profilometry method. Opt. Laser Technol. **45**, 319–329 (2013)
4. Ren, W., Su, X., Xiang, L.: 3-D surface shape restoration for breaking surface of dynamic process based on two-frequency grating. Opto-Electron. Eng. **37**, 144–150 (2010)
5. Cheng, Y.Y., Wyant, J.C.: Multiple-wavelength phase-shifting interferometry. Appl. Optics **24**, 804–807 (1985)
6. Ayubi, G.A., Di Martino, J.M., Alonso, J.R., et al.: Three-dimensional profiling with binaryfringes using phase-shifting interferometry algorithms. Appl. Optics **50**, 147–154 (2011)
7. Xiao, Y., Su, X., Zhang, Q., et al.: 3-D profilometry for the impact process with marked fringes tracking. Opto-Electron. Eng. **34**, 46–52 (2007)
8. Meneses, J., Gharbi, T., Humbert, P.: Phase-unwrapping algorithm for images with high noise content based on a local histogram. Appl. Optics **44**, 1207–1215 (2005)
9. Weng, J., Lu, Y.: Integration of robust filters and phase unwrapping algorithms for image reconstruction of objects containing height discontinuities. Opt. Express **20**, 10896–10920 (2012)
10. Fu, S., Lin, H., Yu, Q., et al.: Fringe-contoured-window sine/cosine filter for saw-tooth phase maps of electronic speckle pattern interferometry. Acta Optica Sinica **27**, 864–870 (2007)
11. Zheng, Z.: A flexible new technique for camera calibration. IEEE Trans. Pattern Anal. Mach. Intell. **22**, 1330–1334 (2000)

Photon Shooting with Programmable Scalar Contribution Function

Quan Zheng[1,2]($\boxtimes$) and Changwen Zheng[1]

[1] Science and Technology on Integrated Information System Laboratory,
Institute of Software, Chinese Academy of Sciences, Beijing 100190, China
`zhengquan12@iscas.ac.cn, cwzheng@ieee.org`
[2] University of Chinese Academy of Sciences, Beijing 100149, China

Abstract. This paper proposes a novel scalar contribution function for photon shooting to optimize the distribution of photons for scenes with complex lighting conditions. Normally, conventional particle tracing methods would become inefficient to render these scenes, where photons are poorly distributed due to occlusion. The new scalar contribution function combines the visual importance, the initial photon distribution and photon path visibility. Then adaptive Metropolis sampling on the function is implemented to shoot photons from the light source into the scene, effectively guiding more photons to critical area where the rendering error is prominent. Experimental results show that this approach can efficiently improve the photon distribution and produce images with less noise than state-of-the-art methods.

Keywords: Photon shooting · Scalar contribution function · Adaptive metropolis sampling · Global illumination

1 Introduction

Scenes with complex lighting conditions are commonly seen in the real life, movies and video games. Typical scenes are an interior room lit by moonlight through the dormer or a cave illuminated by sunlight through the entrance hole. Synthesizing images of these scenes with computer has long been an area of interest within computer graphics. Efficiently rendering the scenes, however, is still a challenging problem for existing rendering methods, because light paths which travel from the light source to visible area can hardly be sampled. Due to complex occlusion, most visible regions cannot receive direct lighting from the light source.

Take a dark room illuminated by an area light outside the door slit as an example. Most light paths are blocked outside and only a small portion of the light paths can go through the door slit. Classical rendering methods relying on light path sampling [1–3] will suffer from the difficult case, since they cannot efficiently find light-carrying paths which connect the viewpoint and the light source. Although particle tracing methods such as photon mapping [4], progressive photon mapping (PPM) [5] are popular for their robustness to handle

© Springer International Publishing Switzerland 2015
Y.-J. Zhang (Ed.): ICIG 2015, Part III, LNCS 9219, pp. 80–93, 2015.
DOI: 10.1007/978-3-319-21969-1_8

specular-diffuse-specular (SDS) paths in scenes, they also get inefficient for these scenes, because photons can hardly arrive at interior visible area.

To cope with this problem, Fan et al. [6] introduce Metropolis photon sampling method, which deposits photons according to complete light paths connecting the viewpoint and the light source in the path space. Recent studies [7,8] focus on designing special scalar contribution functions to improve the photon path sampling. Their scalar contribution functions consider either initial photon density [7] or photon path visibility [8]. Normally, another important knowledge from the scene, the visual importance, is neglected in these methods.

In this paper, we propose a photon shooting method for particle tracing to improve the photon distribution in visible and importance regions, which is referred to as critical regions. A novel scalar contribution function is introduced, which utilizes visual importance in addition to photon density and photon path visibility. Then photon paths are produced by implementing adaptive Metropolis sampling on the function to guide more photons to critical regions. Experimental results demonstrate that the ratio of visible paths that arrive at the critical regions are significantly increased. With more photons deposited at these regions, our method effectively improves the rendering efficiency for scenes with complex lighting settings. In addition, advice regarding the choice of rendering methods is also given based on the experiments.

2   Related Work

Most algorithms [1–3] based on Monte Carlo ray tracing have been proposed to solve the rendering equation [1] without any approximation. These approaches are unbiased and guaranteed to converge to the exact solution. Unfortunately, they are unable to sample SDS paths from extreme small light sources. Various forms of particle tracing methods [4,9] subsequently become popular for their robustness to handle caustics effects caused by SDS paths.

Hachisuka et al. [5] propose PPM to iteratively improve rendering results using infinite photons within limited memory, which is further extended to stochastic progressive photon mapping (SPPM) [10] by them to render distributed ray tracing effects. An alternative formulation of PPM has also been derived based on probability by Knaus et al. [11]. Kaplanyan et al. [12] further investigate α of PPM and propose to adjust α adaptively. These methods, however, become inefficient when rendering scenes with difficult visibility settings. In these cases, photons can hardly be traced to critical regions, resulting in a poor photon distribution.

Veach and Guibas [13] introduce Metropolis light transport (MLT) to address the same problem. MLT brings Metropolis sampling to rendering. While MLT is famous for finding difficult light paths, it is inefficient to sample SDS paths. Kelemen et al. [14] extend Metropolis sampling from the path space to the primary sample space. Hoberock and Hart [15] introduce multi-stage Metropolis light transport and demonstrate that the scalar contribution function can be modified and is not necessarily the path radiance. In this paper, a new scalar contribution function for photon shooting is designed. We also have verified that the function in the context of particle tracing can be carefully edited.

Fan et al. [6] introduce Metropolis sampling to photon mapping. Photons are stored along complete light paths. Since these paths are sampled using path tracing, SDS paths are usually missed. Chen et al. [7] propose a scalar contribution function based on the initial photon density. However, their mutation kernel cannot adapt to different scenes. RAPT [8] constructs a scalar contribution function using photon path visibility. In contrast, our method designs a novel scalar contribution function, which subsumes the available knowledge from the scene, including visual importance, initial photon density and photon path visibility. With more useful knowledge used, our method is able to effectively guide more photons to critical regions.

Visual importance emitted from the viewpoint measures the contribution of light paths to the final image. It has been used for different goals [16] in computer graphics. Peter et al. [17] implement a three-pass photon mapping method to emit importance particles from the viewpoint to construct a visual importance map. Recently, Bashford et al. [18] utilize visual importance to optimize the light path sampling for image based lighting. Vorba et al. [19] give an online learning method to reconstruct the distribution of visual importance. In this paper, the visual importance knowledge is utilized in the scalar contribution function for photon shooting.

3   Photon Shooting with New Scalar Contribution Function

Our method utilizes SPPM as the rendering algorithm. SPPM extends PPM to render distributed ray tracing effects. SPPM can progressively improve the rendering result with multiple iterations. There are two phases in each iteration: distributed ray tracing and photon tracing. In the first phase, camera rays are shot from the viewpoint to the scene, where hit points are stored on non-specular surfaces. In the second phase, photons are traced from the light source and deposited on diffuse surfaces. After the photon tracing phase, the statistics stored in hit points are updated as below:

$$N_{i+1}(S) = N_i(S) + \alpha M_i(x_i) \ , \tag{1}$$

$$R_{i+1}(S) = R_i(S)\sqrt{\frac{N_i(S) + \alpha M_i(x_i)}{N_i + M_i(x_i)}} \ , \tag{2}$$

$$\phi_i(x_i, \omega_i) = \sum_{p=1}^{M_i(x_i)} f_r(x_i, \omega_i, \omega_p)\phi_p(x_p, \omega_p) \ , \tag{3}$$

$$\tau_{i+1}(S) = (\tau_i(S) + \phi_i(x_i, \omega_i))\frac{R_{i+1}(S)^2}{R_i(S)^2} \ . \tag{4}$$

Here, i is the iteration count. $N_i(S)$ is the accumulated photon count within the shared area S. α is between 0 and 1. $R_i(S)$ is the shared radius in region S. $M_i(x_i)$ is the increment of photons within the radius. f_r is the BRDF. $\phi_p(x_p, \omega_p)$ is the flux of a photon p, whose incident direction is ω_p and position is x_p. $\phi_i(x_i, \omega_i)$ is the accumulated flux weighted by BSDF. $\tau_i(S)$ is the shared accumulated flux over S.

Note that the flux of a photon $\phi_p(x_p, \omega_p)$ in (3) has actually omitted the probability density function (p.d.f) $F(P)$ for sampling a photon path P. In other words, (3) should be rewritten as

$$\phi_i(x_i, \omega_i) = \sum_{p=1}^{M_i(x_i)} f_r(x_i, \omega_i, \omega_p) \frac{\phi_p(x_p, \omega_p)}{F(P)} . \tag{5}$$

Since SPPM uniformly shoots photons from the light source, its p.d.f is $F(P) = 1$, which is not shown in (3).

However, $F(P) = 1$, which follows the uniform random distribution, is not a suitable scalar contribution function for photon tracing. PPM and SPPM shoot photons using $F(P) = 1$ and thus they suffer from a slow convergence for rendering scenes with complex lighting conditions. In these scenes, most random photons are deposited at invisible area from the viewpoint, causing a low photon density in critical regions. Density estimation therefore requires a large bandwidth to smooth radiance noise, which introduces bias to the results.

In this paper, we propose a novel scalar contribution function for photon shooting. Normally, regions with large visual importance indicate that they are likely to contribute highly to the final image. In addition, regions with low photon density correspond to noisy area in the final image. Considering these facts, we design the function to combine the knowledge of visual importance, initial photon distribution and photon path visibility. Subsequently, we perform adaptive Markov chain sampling on the scalar contribution function to generate photon paths.

3.1   Visual Importance Map Construction

We compute visual importance in the eye pass of SPPM. Initially, we assign each eye ray with the same visual importance (we use 1 in this paper). Eye rays update visual importance value when they are scattered in the scene. If an eye ray hits a diffuse surface, it stores a hit point on the surface with visual importance value recorded. The visual importance computation for an eye ray can be expressed as:

$$I = \int_{\Omega} W_e(x_0 \rightarrow x_1) T(\overline{x'}) d\mu(\overline{x}) . \tag{6}$$

Here, Ω is the path space comprised of all eye rays. I stands for the visual importance emitted from the viewpoint. $\overline{x} = x_0 \cdots x_t$ is an eye path with t edges, and $\overline{x'} = x_1 \cdots x_t$ is an subpath of $\overline{x}$ with $t-1$ edges. x_0 is a point on the film and the rest vertexes of $\overline{x}$ are in the scene (see Fig. 1). $W_e(x_0 \rightarrow x_1)$ is the visual importance emitted from x_0 to x_1. $d\mu(\overline{x})$ is the differential product area measure. $T(\overline{x'})$ is the path throughput:

$$T(\overline{x'}) = \left[\prod_{i=1}^{t-1} f_r(x_{i-1} \to x_i \to x_{i+1})G(x_{i-1} \leftrightarrow x_i) \right] \cdot G(x_{t-1} \leftrightarrow x_t) , \qquad (7)$$

where $f_r(x_{i-1} \to x_i \to x_{i+1})$ is the BRDF at x_i, $G(x_i \leftrightarrow x_j)$ is the geometry term between x_i and x_j. For the practical purpose, we use a finite number of samples to estimate the visual importance (an eye ray per pixel in this paper). Each eye ray is traced in a way similar to path tracing. When an eye ray hits a diffuse surface, a hit point and its visual importance is stored. Otherwise, an eye ray is scattered along a new sampled direction. To avoid infinitely long eye rays, Russian Roulette is also applied to terminate eye rays with suitable probability.

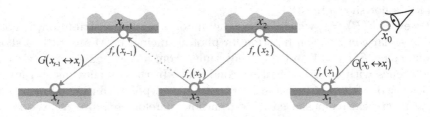

Fig. 1. An eye ray is emitted from the viewpoint x_0 and it is scattered in the scene. Russian Roulette is used to randomly terminate the path at x_t.

To remove the high frequency noise due to finite discrete samples, we transform the point density of visual importance to area density using density estimation. For each hit point, we search for its neighbour hit points within a radius d, which is set to the initial photon radius R_0. Then the visual importance at a point x is estimated as

$$I(x) = \frac{1}{\pi d^2} \sum_{j=1}^{K} I_j . \qquad (8)$$

Here K is the number of neighbour hit points. I_j is the visual importance of the jth neighbour.

Figure 2a depicts a visual importance map of the Door scene. In order to remove local extreme values, the original values in the map have been clamped between a new bound (we use 10–85 % of the original range). Then we further smooth the map with a low-pass median filter to eliminate local high frequency. The result is shown in Fig. 2b. The visual importance value is higher in regions which are close to the viewpoint. This is useful because these regions are distinctively indicated as important parts.

3.2   Scale Map Construction

We implement SPPM using uniform photon sampling (UPS) to trace photons from the light source into the scene and estimate a photon density map D. Initially, this step is implemented using several photon passes (e.g. 10 passes). As the accumulated photon count is stored within each hit point, the photon density can be directly visualized. The dynamic range of the visualization result, however, is usually much larger than the common displayable dynamic range between 0 and 255. We clamp the dynamic range using the power-law transformation (the exponent is 0.7). Afterwards, we employ a low-pass median filter to smooth it. (refer to Fig. 2c). As can be seen, the photon density in the innermost regions is rather low due to the complex occlusion in the scene.

To highlight the importance of the visible regions where photon density is low, we build a scale map S from the photon distribution map D. Regions with lower photon density are set to a larger scalar value, which indicates that they are more important. The element of S is estimated using:

$$s = \begin{cases} 1.0 & r > 1 \\ e^{1-r} & \delta < r \leq 1 \\ 1 + ke^{1-r} & r \leq \delta \end{cases}, \qquad (9)$$

where r is the ratio of the current density ρ and the average density ρ_{mid}, δ and k are user specified parameters. In this paper, we set $\delta = 0.3$ and $k = 4$. The equation is straightforward. If the photon density is higher than the average density, the scalar value equals 1.0 and it does not magnify the importance. If the ratio r is less than δ, the scalar factor is set to a large value. Otherwise, scalar factor is given an intermediate value when r is between δ and 1. We show a scale map in Fig. 2d.

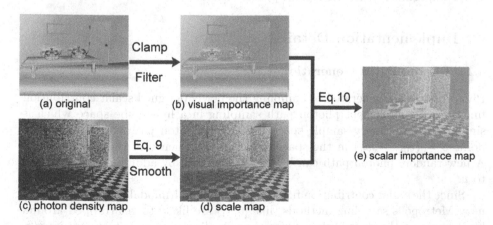

Fig. 2. The flow chart of building a scalar importance map for the door scene. The processing of the visual importance map and scale map are included.

3.3   Scalar Contribution Function

After the preprocessing of the above maps, a scalar importance map M is constructed according to the visual importance map V and the scale map S. An element of M is computed using

$$m_i = v_i + (v_{max} - v_i) * \frac{s_i - 1}{s_{max} - s_{min}} , \tag{10}$$

where m_i, v_i and s_i are the ith element of M, V, S respectively, s_{max} and s_{min} are the maximum and minimum values of S. v_{max} is the maximum value of V. This function reads as follows. The visual importance value v_i is magnified in regions with low photon density, where s_i will be a large value. Meanwhile, m_i is bounded in the dynamic range of V. Figure 2e depicts M, where critical regions are assigned with larger importance value. Importance sampling guided by this scalar importance map will efficiently pilot more paths to critical regions, which is desirable for reducing rendering error.

Finally, we define the new scalar contribution function as $F(p) = \frac{1}{f} \cdot M(p) \cdot U(p)$. Given a photon path p, $M(p)$ is the scalar importance value and $U(p)$ is its visibility. $U(p) = 1$ if p is visible from the viewpoint, and $U(p)$ is set to 0 otherwise. $f = \int_P F(p)dP$ is the normalization factor. We compute f in the first several iterations (10 iterations in this paper). The normalization factor is approximately estimated using

$$f = \int_P F(p)dP \approx \frac{1}{n} \sum_{i=1}^{n} F(p_i) , \tag{11}$$

where n is the number of uniform random photon paths. $F(p_i)$ is the maximum scalar importance of all the regions p_i has visited.

4   Implementation Details

4.1   Photon Paths Generation

Photon paths are generated by sampling the newly designed scalar contribution function. We implement photon path sampling in a hypercube space which is similar to the primary sample space [14]. Each photon path corresponds to a point $v = (v_0, \cdots, v_n)$ in the space, which is a sequence of random numbers. A new random photon path can be easily generated by adding a small offset ξ to v.

Since the scalar contribution function defines a multimodal distribution, ordinary Metropolis sampling methods (like [6,7]) are likely to get trapped around local peaks of the distribution. Once the sampling process is trapped, its efficiency quickly drops because the Markov chain cannot visit other parts of the sampling space. As a result, most areas of the sampling space are under-sampled, leading to much noise in the rendered image.

In order to efficiently take advantage of existing visible photon paths, we use the adaptive Metropolis sampling method to sample the new scalar contribution function. Adaptive Metropolis sampling [8] is good at locally exploring the sampling space. Its core idea is to automatically adjust the mutation parameter according to the historical acceptance rate of samples. A new photon path of the Markov chain is generated from a mutation of an existing photon path.

In addition, to avoid the path sampling getting trapped at local peaks, we use replica exchange Monte Carlo [20] to simultaneously run two Markov chains: a target Markov chain whose states distribute according to the target function and a companion Markov chain which follows the Uniform distribution. States of the two chains can be mutually exchanged without changing the original distribution of individual chains. Considering that new states can be easily generated from the Uniform distribution, we only perform unidirectional exchange from the companion chain to the target chain. In the context of photon shooting, paths from the assistant chain are swapped to the target chain if they are visible.

4.2 Acceptance Probability

Given a new path P' generated from a mutation of an existing photon path P, it is accepted with the probability:

$$a(P \to P') = \min\left(1, \frac{F(P')T(P' \to P)}{F(P)T(P \to P')}\right). \tag{12}$$

Because all photon paths are sampled in a hypercube space, the operation for generating a new path from the previous one is symmetric. Namely, the transition probabilities are equal: $T(P' \to P) = T(P \to P')$. We therefore estimate the acceptance probability as: $a(P \to P') = \min(1, \frac{F(P')}{F(P)})$. Then a random variable ε is employed to decide whether to accept P' as the current photon path. If ε is less than a, P' will be accepted as the current photon path. P is retained as the current photon path otherwise.

4.3 Radius Update

The consistency of SPPM relies on the gradually decreasing radii. Radii are progressively reduced using (2) in SPPM. In this paper, we update the radii in a simpler iterative way [11]:

$$R_{i+1} = R_i\sqrt{\frac{i + \alpha}{i + 1}}, \tag{13}$$

where $\alpha = 0.7$ and i is the iteration count.

Due to the decreasing shared radius, a visible photon path will become invisible if all its photons are outside of the shared area. Thus, The visibility function $V(p)$ is a dynamic function, which makes $F(p)$ a dynamic function. However, the convergence property for adaptive Metropolis sampling on dynamic target function has not been verified. Moreover, the pre-computed normalization factor f

does not match a dynamic target function. To avoid the problem, we use a fixed shared radius for visibility tests. The $F(p)$ is guaranteed to follow a stationary target distribution if $V(p)$ is a stationary function. In practice, the fixed radius is set to a 4-pixel width.

4.4   Algorithm Pseudocode

We summarised our method with pseudocode as below. $P_0, P_1, \cdots, P_N$ are photon paths of the target Markov chain, where N is the photon count of each pass. P' is a candidate photon path. We start by generating a visible initial photon path from the UPS. Then we perform adaptive Metropolis sampling to produce new photon paths.

Algorithm. adaptive photon shooting

Input: a scene descriptor file
Output: photon contributions of the current pass
Construct the scalar importance map M;
Estimate the normalization factor f;
P_0 := InitPhotonPath();
for i := 1 to N **do**
  P' := UniformSampling();
  $I(P')$:= TracePath();
  if IsVisble(P') **then**
    P_i := P'; $I(P_i)$:= $I(P')$;
  else
    P' := Mutate(P_{i-1});
    $I(P')$:= TracePath();
    a := AccpetProb();
    if $\varepsilon < a$ **then**
      P_i := P'; $I(P_i)$:= $I(P')$;
    else
      P_i := P_{i-1}; $I(P_i)$:= $I(P_{i-1})$;
    end if
    UpdateMutateSize();
  end if
  RecordContribution();
end for

5   Results and Discussion

All the images in this paper were rendered on a workstation with a dual quad-core 2.4 GHz Intel Xeon CPU E5-2609. Comparisons mainly focus on the most related methods, including UPS and RAPT. Our method and previous methods were implemented on LuxRender[1] using 4 threads (α is 0.7 for all methods).

---

[1] http://www.luxrender.net.

Three test scenes are used in this paper. The Door scene and the Dark Room scene are typical scenes with complex lighting conditions. The modified Cornell scene is an example with simple lighting settings to indicate the limitation. Parameters and rendering statistics for the tested scenes are listed in Table 1.

Table 1. It shows the parameters and rendering statistics for each test scene. The three columns on the right give the ratios of visible photon paths.

Scene	Resolution	Photons/Pass (K)	Time (min)	UPS	RAPT	Ours
Door	640×480	200	10	1.5 %	36.4 %	43.7 %
			60	1.2 %	30.5 %	41.6 %
Dark room	640×480	100	60	23.6 %	61.9 %	71.2 %
Cornell	512×512	50	30	72.1 %	84.7 %	83.2 %

5.1 Results

Figure 3 shows an interior scene which is illuminated by an area light through the door slit. We compare images rendered using UPS, RAPT and our method in the same rendering time of 10 and 60 min. The results of UPS are much noisier than other methods, since UPS shot photons without considering the viewpoint information. Thus only about 1.2 % of the photon paths can arrive at visible regions after 1 hour. With a well-designed scalar contribution function, our method significantly increase the percentage of visible photons to 43.7 % and adaptively pilots more photons to critical regions. Our method therefore can yield better results with less noise.

Note that, our method does not perform much better than RAPT at the beginning (10 min), because our method includes an initialization stage to construct the scalar importance map, which takes some time. Nevertheless, our method outperforms RAPT soon and generates visually smoother results.

The individual photon distribution after 60 min are given in the third row of Fig. 3. The whole photon density is low for UPS, since photons can hardly enter the room. Although RAPT raises the overall photon density, but the photon density is still rather low in the innermost area. In contrast, our method effectively optimizes the photon distribution and especially improves the photon density in critical regions.

The Dark Room scene in Fig. 4a is another challenging scene with complex lighting settings. In this case, our method raises the percentage of visible paths to 71.2 %, which is significantly higher than other methods. As a result, our method gives a better result (see the close-up views). Figure 4b depicts the RMSE (Root Mean Square Error) value of each method. Note that our method gives a slightly higher RMSE than RAPT in the early stage, because our method will perform a preprocessing to build the scalar importance map. However, our method exceeds RAPT later and gives lower RMSE.

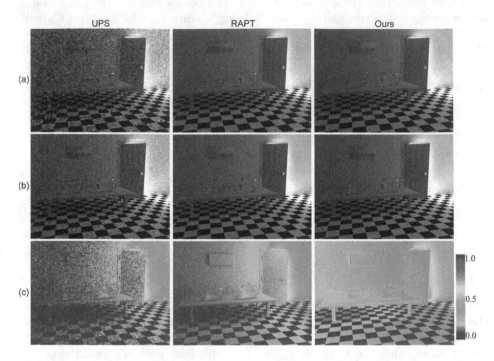

Fig. 3. Comparison of the door scene results of UPS (*left*), RAPT (*middle*) and our method (*right*) in the same rendering time: (a) 10 min and (b) 60 min. (c) Photon distribution of the three methods, where warm color indicates higher photon density and visa versa (color figure online).

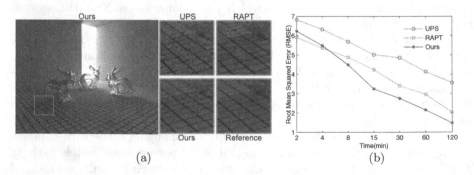

Fig. 4. (a) The dark room scene results in the same 60 min. The reference image is produced with PPM using 12 h. (b) The individual RMSE of rendering the scene with UPS, RAPT and our method.

Figure 5 is a variant of the classical Cornell Box scene, where the light source is directly visible and most photon paths hit visible regions. We compare our method with UPS and RAPT to show the limitation. In this case, the RMSE values are similar. Our method do not show additional advantage over UPS, while implementing less photon passes than others due to the preprocessing and scalar importance query for each photon path. The result is similar to the comparisons between RAPT and UPS in [8].

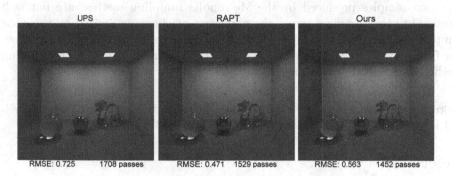

Fig. 5. The Cornell scene results of UPS (*left*), RAPT (*middle*) and our method (*right*) in 30 min.

5.2 Discussion

As stated in Sect. 4.3, we use a constant radius for the visibility test of photon paths, whereas the radii of hit points are normally updated using (13). A dynamic radius for the visibility test can be used, but the normalization factor f should be updated in a dynamical fashion rather than (11). A possible means is to progressively update the sum term and the photon count in (11) (refer to [8]).

Our new scalar contribution function utilizes more available knowledge from the scene, which makes the photon path sampling concentrating on critical regions. The construction of the scalar importance map introduces some user parameters (δ and k). The parameters can be easily tweaked by user to adapt to different scene features. Nevertheless, an inappropriate choice of these parameters also degrades the rendering efficiency. Automatically adjusting the parameters is an interesting problem for future work.

6 Conclusion and Future Work

We have presented a photon shooting method using a novel well-designed scalar contribution function. The function is introduced to define the target distribution. Then adaptive Markov sampling on the function is performed to generate photon paths which can reach critical regions. Experiments have validated that the scalar contribution function for photon shooting can be carefully designed to improve the photon distribution. Using the same rendering time, our method can effectively raise the photon density in critical regions, thus accelerating the convergence rate in these regions.

Our method has been tested on three scenes with various lighting conditions. According to the results, we provide a suggestion that when rendering scenes with difficult lighting conditions, our method is a strong candidate, while UPS may be considered for handling scenes with simple lighting conditions.

Since samples produced by the Metropolis sampling method are not well stratified in the sampling space, the rendering efficiency is limited by the poor sample stratification. Adaptive Metropolis sampling partly inherits the flaw. For future work, we therefore consider investigating new photon path sampling methods to generate well-stratified samples.

Acknowledgments. This work was partly supported by National High-Tech Research and Development Plan of China (Grant No. 2012AA011206).

References

1. Kajiya, J.T.: The rendering equation. In: Evans, D.C., Athay, R.J. (eds.) Proceedings of 13th Annual Conference on Computer Graphics and Interactive Techniques. ACM Press, New York (1986)
2. Lafortune, E.P., Willems, Y.D.: Bi-directional path tracing. In: Third International Conference on Computational Graphics and Visualization Techniques (Compugraphics 1993), pp. 145–153 (1993)
3. Veach, E., Guibas, L.J.: Optimally combining sampling techniques for monte carlo rendering. In: 22nd Annual Conference on Computer Graphics and Interactive Techniques. pp. 419–428. ACM Press, New York (1995)
4. Jensen, H.W.: Global illumination using photon maps. In: Pueyo, X., Schröder, P. (eds.) Rendering Techniques 1996. Eurographics, pp. 21–30. Springer, Heidelberg (1996)
5. Hachisuka, T., Ogaki, S., Jensen, H.W.: Progressive photon mapping. ACM Trans. Graph. (TOG) **27**(5), 130:1–130:8 (2008)
6. Fan, S., Chenney, S., Lai, Y.c., et al.: Metropolis photon sampling with optionaluser guidance. In: Rendering Techniques 5, pp. 127–138 (2005)
7. Chen, J., Wang, B., Yong, J.H.: Improved stochastic progressive photon mapping with metropolis sampling. Comput. Graph. Forum. **30**, 1205–1213 (2011)
8. Hachisuka, T., Jensen, H.W.: Robust adaptive photon tracing using photon path visibility. ACM Trans. Graph. (TOG) **30**(5), 114:1–114:11 (2011)
9. Arvo, J., Chelmsford, M.: Backward ray tracing. In: Developments in Ray Tracing, Computer Graphics, Proceedings of ACM SIGGRAPH 1986 Course Notes, pp. 259–263 (1986)
10. Hachisuka, T., Jensen, H.W.: Stochastic progressive photon mapping. ACM Trans. Graph. (TOG) **28**(5), 141:1–141:8 (2009)
11. Knaus, C., Zwicker, M.: Progressive photon mapping: a probabilistic approach. ACM Trans. Graph. (TOG) **30**(3), 25:1–25:13 (2011)
12. Kaplanyan, A.S., Dachsbacher, C.: Adaptive progressive photon mapping. ACM Trans. Graph. (TOG) **32**(2), 16:1–16:13 (2013)

13. Veach, E., Guibas, L.J.: Metropolis light transport. In: 24th annual conference on Computer graphics and interactive techniques. pp. 65–76. ACM Press, New York (1997)
14. Kelemen, C., Szirmay-Kalos, L., Antal, G., Csonka, F.: A simple and robust mutation strategy for the metropolis light transport algorithm. Comput. Graph. Forum. **21**, 531–540 (2002)
15. Hoberock, J., Hart, J.C.: Arbitrary importance functions for metropolis light transport. Comput. Graph. Forum. **29**, 1993–2003 (2010)
16. Christensen, P.H.: Adjoints and importance in rendering: an overview. IEEE Trans. Vis. Comput. Graph. **9**(3), 329–340 (2003)
17. Peter, I., Pietrek, G.: Importance driven construction of photon maps. In: 9th Eurographics Workshop on Rendering, pp. 269–280. Eurographics Association Press, Aire-la-Ville (1998)
18. Bashford-Rogers, T., Debattista, K., Chalmers, A.: Importance driven environment map sampling. IEEE Trans. Vis. Comput. Graph. **20**(6), 907–918 (2014)
19. Vorba, J., Karlík, O., Šik, M., Ritschel, T., Křivánek, J.: On-line learning of parametric mixture models for light transport simulation. ACM Trans. Graph. **33**(4), 101:1–101:11 (2014)
20. Kitaoka, S., Kitamura, Y., Kishino, F.: Replica exchange light transport. Comput. Graph. Forum **28**, 2330–2342 (2009)

Real-Time Locating Method for Palmvein Image Acquisition

Yaqin Liu[1(✉)], Yujia Zhou[1], Shirong Qiu[1], Jirui Qin[2],
and Yixiao Nie[3]

[1] School of Biomedical Engineering, Southern Medical University,
Guangzhou, China
liuyq@fimmu.com, zyj_shmily@sina.com, qiusrong@163.com
[2] Guangdong Wicrown Information Technology Co.. Ltd, Huizhou, China
qinjirui@wicrown.com
[3] Department of Electronical and Computer Engineering,
University of Illinois at Urbana-Champaign, Champaign, USA
nie4@illinois.edu

Abstract. Palmvein recognition has emerged as a promising alternative for human recognition because of its uniqueness, permanence, acceptability, live body identification, and resistance to fraud. Palmvein image acquisition is the premise of palmvein recognition, the position and posture of the hand above the camera directly determines the quality of palmvein image. Palmvein image-capture device mostly through manual adjustment, cannot meet the demands for the practicability and productization. This paper proposes a simple and practical real-time locating method. A locating electronic and optical circuit is designed to capture an image with four light-spots, and a locating algorithm is constructed to detect the appropriate position and posture of hands. The experimental results illustrate that the capture device with the proposed approach can realize palmvein image acquisition automatically and quickly as well as to guarantee the validity and consistency of the acquired palmvein images.

Keywords: Palmvein image acquisition · Capture device · Locating method · Validity · Consistency

1 Introduction

The development and popularity of the Internet and computers, particularly electronic commerce, have rendered biometric-based automated human identification important and indispensable [1]. Vein recognition is an automated human identification technology based on vein patterns, which is the vast network of blood vessels under the human hand skin [2–5]. Compared with other biometric technologies, such as that using fingerprints [6, 7], palmprints [8–11], and iris [12], palmvein recognition [5, 29, 30] has the advantages of uniqueness and abundance of identity information, live body identification, and counterfeiting difficulties. These advantages confirm palmvein recognition as a promising and effective technology with high accuracy and wide application range.

© Springer International Publishing Switzerland 2015
Y.-J. Zhang (Ed.): ICIG 2015, Part III, LNCS 9219, pp. 94–110, 2015.
DOI: 10.1007/978-3-319-21969-1_9

Palmvein recognition can be divided into the following steps: palmvein image acquisition from capture device, pre-processing of region-of-interest (ROI) and image enhancement, feature extraction, and matching. Among these steps, palmvein image acquisition is the premise. For example, during acquisition, the invalidation of palm range, poor quality, and inconsistency of the acquired palmvein images increase the complexity of the ROI and the feature extraction algorithm, and even causes the failure of palmvein recognition. Therefore, the quality [13, 14], validity, and consistency of the acquired palmvein image play an important role in palmvein recognition.

Existing literature on palmvein recognition mainly focuses on recognition algorithms, such as ROI extraction, image enhancement, feature extraction, and matching [15–30,41]. A few studies have focused on palmvein image capture device to improve the quality of palmvein image; the literature can be summarized into three research contents, namely, obtaining a palmvein image, designing the structure of the palmvein image-capture device, and choosing the near-infrared light source and image sensor [31–35]. All palmvein image capture devices have similar major structures, including near-infrared light source, camera, and circuit modules.

The capture mode of palmvein capture devices can be separated into two modes, namely, contact and contact-less. The contact mode usually constrains the hand of the user using a fixed peg or carrier frame. For example, the capture mode in the contact device [11] is as follows: a user is asked to place his/her hand on the platform, and several pegs serve as control points for the placement of the hand of the user. The device in [17] is based on the fact that the hand is on the support, which is approximately at 20 cm of the camera lens; this condition can help the persons positioning their hands and limit translations and rotations. The contact mode can only ensure that the hand is the focus of the camera, but it cannot ensure that the hand is flat and does not shift during image acquisition. Therefore, the validity and quality of the acquired palmvein image cannot be guaranteed. For the contact-less mode, no guidance peripheral exists to constrain the hand of the user, mostly through manual adjustment. In a contact-less device [19], the user needs to monitor whether the hand is properly displayed inside the working volume. The user is also asked to place his/her hand approximately 20 cm above the camera and decide whether the palmvein image on the monitor is clear to acquire a valid image [26]. The contact-less mode may spend several seconds to several minutes to adjust the placement of the hand, but it cannot ensure the consistency of the palmvein images from multiple acquisitions because of the different positions and postures of the hand. The following aspects are crucial: (1) how to automatically detect whether the placement of the hand is appropriate, and (2) when to shoot the palmvein image. However, no study has addressed these issues. Palmvein image-capture devices remain at the laboratory stage with a large size and cannot be commercially available products, except those of Fujitsu Co [36].

As mentioned, several problems should be studied with regard to the capture device of palmvein identification system, such as the validity and consistency of the acquired palmvein images, as well as the fast and automatic acquisition process of palmvein images. We elucidate the issues as follows:

(1) Validity of the acquired palmvein images. Regarding the validity of images, the acquired palmvein image has a good quality and the entire palm with all five finger root points should be acquired. When selecting the ROI area from the palm center, we need to extract the palm profile and find two critical points (root between the index and middle fingers and root between the ring and pinky fingers) [23, 26]. To ensure the validity of the acquired palmvein images, the position and posture of the hand above the camera must be appropriate, that is, (a) the position of the hand is at the center of the camera; (b) the hand should pose as flat as possible, not tilt; (c) the hand should be placed at the focus of the camera. If the hand is not placed at the center of the camera, which means that the left, right, forward, or backward shift is excessive, then the acquired palmvein image becomes incomplete; thus, the palmvein image ROI cannot be addressed and the palm cannot be identified. If the hand is not flat, which means that the hand tilts leftward, rightward, forward, or backward at a certain degree or the palm center is excessively concave or convex (see Fig. 12), then deformation of the acquired palmvein image becomes significant. This phenomenon increases the complexity of the subsequent algorithm and even causes the failure of recognition. If the hand is placed before or after the focus of the camera, then the acquired palmvein image is scaled up or down (see Fig. 12). This phenomenon increases the distortion and reduces the quality of image, which significantly affects the recognition results. Therefore, the position and posture of the hand above the camera directly determines the quality of the acquired palmvein image, which further affects the accuracy of palmvein recognition.

(2) Consistency of the acquired palmvein images. Consistency means that the acquired palmvein images have the same image quality and the same palm area when a palm is captured in the registration and identification processes at different acquisitions. The position and posture of the hand above the camera have to be the same at different capturing instants to ensure the consistency of palmvein imaging. If the same palm is placed inconsistently in the registration and recognition phases, then differences are generated in image quality and the ROI, which increase intra-class variances. Although some algorithms can deal with small deformations, including characteristic shift invariance and rotation invariance, they cannot deal well with large deformation. An inconsistent image increases the false rejection rate (FRR) and false acceptance rate (FAR), which decreases recognition accuracy.

(3) Fast and automatic acquisition. The acquisition time of a palmvein image is defined as follows: the time at which the hand of the user is placed above the camera to the time of capturing a valid palmvein image by adjusting the appropriate position and posture of the hand. In a practical palmvein identification system, the acquisition must be completed within 3 s; otherwise, it is not acceptable. If the process is controlled manually, several seconds to several minutes are needed to adjust the placement of the hand until appropriate depending on the experience of the user with the device. Moreover, palmvein image-capture device cannot be available products.

To develop a real-time palmvein identification system with a fast and automatic capture device and guarantee the validity and consistency of palmvein images, exploring a suitable locating method of hand is indispensable for palmvein image acquisition. Three key issues are considered in this study. First is how to detect whether the position and posture of the hand of the user above the camera is appropriate, and when the capture device automatically should capture a valid palmvein image. Second, in practical application, the intervals of identification and registration may be a few months or a few years. Thus, the issue is how to guarantee the same position and posture of the hand above the camera in the identification and registration processes. Third is how to guide the placement of the hand with appropriate position and posture quickly and capture palmvein images automatically only when appropriate.

To solve the aforementioned problems, this study proposes a real-time locating method that can guide a user on how to place his/her hand appropriately and quickly above the sensor and capture an palmvein image automatically when appropriate. The framework of the proposed method is illustrated in Fig. 1. First, four light-emitting diodes (LEDs) emit near-infrared light to the palm under the control of ARM. The near-infrared light reflected by the palm is captured by a complementary metal–oxide–semiconductor (CMOS) sensor. Therefore, the image includes four light-spots. Second, all edges of the four light-spots are found on the basis of Freeman Chain Code of Eight Directions (FCCE) after binarization, and the center coordinates of the four light-spots are obtained. Third, the length and angle of the quadrangle that consists of the four centers of the four light-spots are calculated, and the placement validity is determined according to the length and angle. Finally, ARM is informed to capture the palmvein image automatically when the length and angle are within a setup value, or the user is reminded to adjust the position and posture of his/her palm.

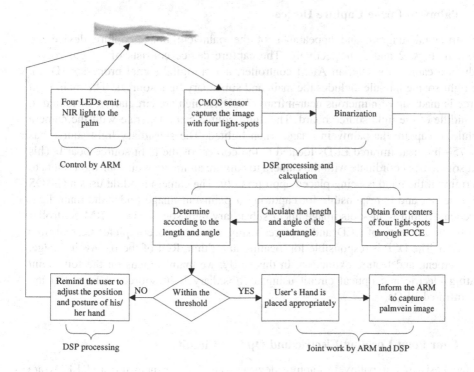

Fig. 1. Framework of the proposed method

The main contributions of this study are as follows:

(1) A simple and practical real-time locating method is proposed for the capture device of the palmvein identification system to realize palmvein image acquisition automatically and quickly as well as to guarantee the validity and consistency of the acquired palmvein images.
(2) A simple electric and optical circuit is designed and implemented to capture an image with four light-spots. This image is used as the input of the following locating algorithm.
(3) A locating algorithm is constructed to effectively detect whether the hand is being placed in an appropriate position and posture as well as to capture the palmvein image when appropriate.

The rest of this paper is organized as follows. Section 2 introduces the four-point locating electric and optical circuit based on a self-fabricated palmvein image capture device. Section 3 presents the proposed locating algorithm. Section 4 shows the experimental results. Section 5 summarizes this paper.

2 Four-Point Locating Electric and Optical Circuit

2.1 Palmvein Image Capture Device

The structural diagram and appearance of the palmvein image-capture device are shown in Figs. 2 and 3, respectively. The capture device consists of a light source module, a camera module, an ARM controller, and a digital signal processor (DSP). The light source module includes the main and subsidiary light sources. The main light source is made up of numerous near-infrared LEDs, which are circularly distributed in the middle of the light source board. This light source can cooperate with the camera module to capture the palmvein image when lighted. The subsidiary light source has four 750 nm near-infrared LEDs located at the corners of the light source board. This light source can coordinate with the camera to capture an image with four light-spots to determine if the hand is being placed appropriately. The camera module uses a CMOS image sensor and is responsible for capturing a palmvein image under the main light source and a four light-spots image under subsidiary light source. The ARM controller adjusts the intensity of LED and captures using a camera to complete the real-time collection. The DSP is responsible for locating algorithm, ROI of the palmvein image, enhancement, and feature extraction. In this study, we mainly focus on the four-point locating electric and optical circuit using a subsidiary light source of four 750 nm near-infrared LEDs.

2.2 Four-Point Locating Electric and Optical Circuit

On the basis of our palmvein capture device, four 750 nm near-infrared LEDs are placed on the corners of the light source board. The corresponding four-point locating circuit is shown in Fig. 4, which controls the lightening and intensity by ARM.

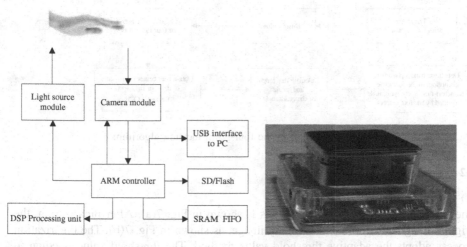

Fig. 2. Structural diagram of the capture device   **Fig. 3.** Appearance of the capture device

The four-point optical circuit is shown in Fig. 5, which consists of four LEDs, light pipe, and condensing lens. The near-infrared light emitted by LEDs are converged and amplified by the condensing lens through the light pipe to form four light-spots on the palm. A CMOS image sensor captures the reflection from the palm to generate an image under the control of ARM, as shown in Fig. 7(a).

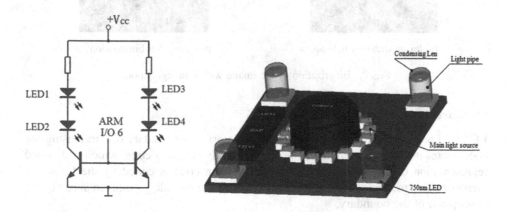

Fig. 4. Four-point locating electric circuit   **Fig. 5.** Four-point locating optical circuit

3   Four-Point Locating Algorithm

3.1   Flowchart of the Four-Point Locating Algorithm

When the image with four light-spots is acquired, it can be processed by the four-point locating algorithm, as shown in Fig. 6.

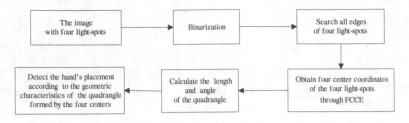

Fig. 6. Flowchart of the four-point locating algorithm

3.2   Four-Point Locating Algorithm

(1) Binarization

The original image with four light-spots is shown in Fig. 7(a). After binarization, the original image transforms into a binary image, as shown in Fig. 7(b). The binarization process adopts the adaptive threshold value method. The threshold value is equal to half of the maximum pixel values of the original BMP image.

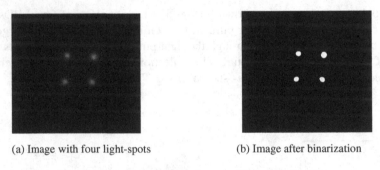

(a) Image with four light-spots   (b) Image after binarization

Fig. 7. Binarization of the image with four light-spots

(2) Searching the edge points using FCCE

FCCE. Freeman chain code is a method that describes a boundary or curve using the coordinates of the starting point of the curve and its direction code, which is a coded representation of the boundary. The Freeman chain code is coded by the boundary direction. This method is typically used to describe the boundary points to simplify the description of the boundary.

The Freeman chain code can be divided into Freeman Chain Code of Four Directions (FCCF) and FCCE based on the different numbers of adjacent directions of the center pixel. FCCF has four adjacent points in the directions of upper, lower, left, and right. Unlike FCCF, FCCE increases four adjacent points in the incline direction. FCCE fits in with the fact that each pixel has eight adjacent points in its neighborhood, which can precisely describe the information of the center point and its neighborhoods. Therefore, this study adopts FCCE to search the edge points (Fig. 8).

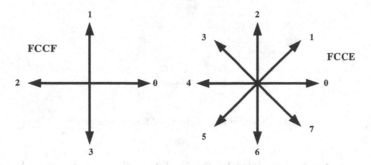

Fig. 8. FCCF and FCCE

Searching the edge points. We search the edge points of four light-spots in the entire binarized image. First, the image is split into four quadrants, as shown in Fig. 9(a). We adopt a traversal search for the edge points in the directions of upper left, upper right, lower left, and lower right of the original point using FCCE. The spot can be viewed as a closed image. If the edge point we searched is the first edge point, then the search process ends. If we have found all the edge points of one spot, then the search in this quadrant ends. When the search process ends, all edges of four light-spots can be obtained. We can draw four circles by the searched chain code of all edges, as shown in Fig. 9(b).

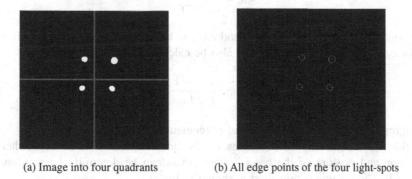

(a) Image into four quadrants   (b) All edge points of the four light-spots

Fig. 9. Searching for the edge points using FCCE

(3) Calculating the length and Angle
On the basis of the four circles, we can calculate the coordinates of their center points. A quadrangle can then be obtained using the center points of the four circles. Figure 10 shows the quadrangle that consists of four center points. The calculation procedure of the length and angle of the quadrangle is elucidated as follows:

We suppose that A,B,C, and D are the positions of the center points of the four circles. (x_1,y_1), (x_2,y_2), (x_3,y_3), and (x_4,y_4) are the coordinates of the four corresponding points. L_{AB}, L_{CD}, L_{AC}, and L_{BD} are the distances between two points, that is, the four side lengths of the quadrangle. α_1, α_2, α_3, and α_4 are the angles between two lines. The length of the

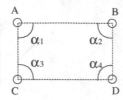

Fig. 10. Quadrangle consisting of four center points

side length L_{AB} can be calculated by the Euclidean distance of points A and B, as shown in Eq. 1. Similarly, the lengths of L_{CD}, L_{AC}, and L_{BD} can be calculated.

$$L_{AB} = \sqrt{(x_1 - x_2)^2 + (y_1 - y_2)^2} \tag{1}$$

k_{AB}, k_{CD}, k_{AC}, and k_{BD} represent the slopes of L_{AB}, L_{CD}, L_{AC}, and L_{BD}, respectively. k_{AB} and k_{AC} can be calculated using Eqs. (2) and (3). k_{CD} and k_{BD} can be calculated as well.

$$k_{AB} = \frac{y_2 - y_1}{x_2 - x_1} \tag{2}$$

$$k_{AC} = \frac{y_3 - y_1}{x_3 - x_1} \tag{3}$$

The angle α_1 between the lines AB and AC can be obtained using Eq. (4) (when α_1 does not equal 90°). α_2, α_3, and α_4 can also be calculated.

$$\alpha_1 = Arctg \frac{k_{AB} - k_{AC}}{1 + k_{AB}k_{AC}} \tag{4}$$

(4) Judging criteria for detecting hand placement
When the four lengths and four angles of the quadrangle are calculated, whether the position and posture of the hand is appropriate can be determined according to Eqs. (5)-(9). The detection flowchart is shown in Fig. 11.

$$L_{CD} - C_1 \leq L_{AB} \leq L_{CD} + C_1 \tag{5}$$

$$L_{BD} - C_2 \leq L_{AC} \leq L_{BD} + C_2 \tag{6}$$

$$Min\ (L_{AB}, L_{CD}, L_{AC}, L_{BD})\ > C_3 \tag{7}$$

$$Max(L_{AB}, L_{CD}, L_{AC}, L_{BD}) < C_4 \tag{8}$$

$$90° - \sigma \leq \alpha_i \leq 90° + \sigma (i = 1, 2, 3, 4) \tag{9}$$

where C_1, C_2, C_3, and C_4 are constants for pixels; σ is the constant for angle.

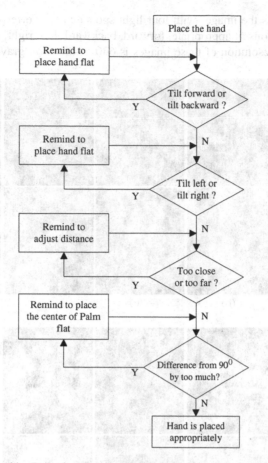

Fig. 11. Detection flowchart of determining hand placement

First, we should determine whether the palm inclines backward or forward according to Eq. (5). When $L_{CD} - C_1 > L_{AB}$, L_{AB} is short, and the front of the palm is far away from the camera, which indicate that the palm inclines forward. When $L_{CD} + C_1 < L_{AB}$, L_{AB} is long, and the rear of the palm is far away from the camera, which indicate that the palm inclines backward. Subsequently, we can determine whether the palm inclines left or right according to Eq. (6). When $L_{BD} - C_2 > L_{AC}$, the palm inclines to the left. When $L_{BD} + C_2 < L_{AC}$, the palm inclines to the right. When the quadrangle satisfies Eqs. (5) and (6), the palm is posed horizontally. However, the palm just being flat is not enough. The distance between the palm and the camera should be appropriate, which can be determined using Eqs. (7) and (8). When Eq. (7) is satisfied, the shortest side in the quadrangle is larger than the predefined threshold, and the distance between the palm and the camera is too small. When Eq. (8) is satisfied, the longest side in the quadrangle is smaller than the predefined threshold, and the distance between the palm and the camera is too large. Finally, the differences between the four angles in the quadrangle and 90° should be examined according to Eq. (9), that is, whether the palm is convex or concave.

Figure 12 shows the images with four light-spots and the corresponding palmvein images in the positions of appropriate, forward, backward, left, right, convex, concave, far and near. The resolution of these images is 640 × 480 8-bit gray-level BMP files.

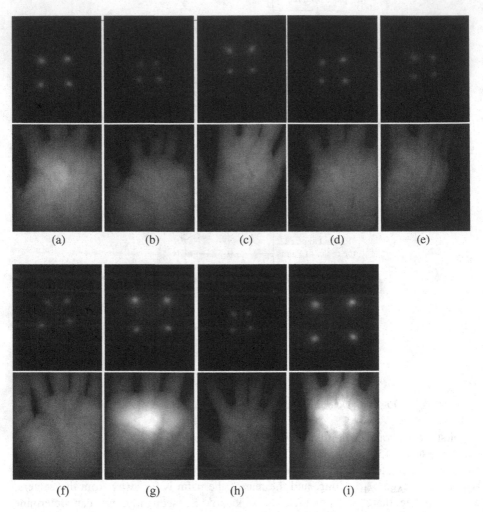

(a)   (b)   (c)   (d)   (e)

(f)   (g)   (h)   (i)

Fig. 12. Images with four light-spots and the corresponding palmvein images

4 Experiments and Discussion

Three experiments are conducted to prove the validity, consistency, and fast acquisition of the acquired palmvein images using the proposed method on the basis of recognition accuracy, matching score, and acquisition time of the palmvein image.

In this study, the proposed locating algorithm, ROI, and enhancement of palmvein image, as well as feature extraction are implemented using standard C in ARM (500 MHz) and DSP (240 MHz). Matching and the display program are developed using Visual Studio 2012 on a standard PC, which is equipped with a Core i5-3470 CPU 3.2 GHz and 4 GB RAM.

4.1 Palmvein Image Capture Steps

The palmvein image acquisition process based on the proposed method is described as follows. First, whether the hand of the user is above the camera is determined using four 750 nm near-infrared LEDs. Second, whether the position and posture of the hand are appropriate is detected using the proposed locating algorithm when the hand is placed above the camera. Third, the main illumination LEDs emit near-infrared light to the palm only when the hand is posed appropriately, and the palmvein image is captured by the camera. Fourth, the palmvein image is saved and transmitted for the subsequent identification process.

On the contrary, the steps without the proposed locating method are as follows. First, the main illumination LEDs always emit near-infrared light to the palm, and the camera continually takes shots to acquire a valid palmvein image. Second, the ROI process is performed on each palmvein image; the capture process is repeated if it fails to extract ROI from the palmvein image. Third, if the ROI is successfully extracted, then the capture process ends. Fourth, the palmvein image is saved and transmitted for the subsequent identification process.

4.2 Evaluation of Validity by Recognition Rate

The capture device based on the proposed method can acquire a palmvein image in contact or contact-less mode. The capture modes are shown in Fig. 13. The contact mode (see Fig. 13(a)) supports the hand using a bracket. A total of 1,224 images are acquired from 51 volunteers as self-built database. The images in this database are

(a) Contact mode   (b) Contact-less mode

Fig. 13. Capture modes of palmvein image in this study

captured in two sessions (six images in each session), with an average interval of 30 days between the sessions.

To demonstrate the validity of palmvein images in the self-built database, comparison experiments by recognition accuracy are performed between the self-built database and two open databases. One database is the PolyU Multispectral Palmprint Database (PolyU database) [37] in which all 6,000 images are acquired from 250 volunteers using a constrained device with finger-pegs in two sessions (six images in each session), with an average interval of nine days between the sessions. The other database is the CASIA Multi-Spectral Palmprint Database [38] in which all 1,200 images are acquired from 100 volunteers using a contact-less device in two sessions (three images in each session), with an average interval of one month between the two sessions.

The matching of the same session data tends to achieve better results than that of a different session because of small variations, thereby leading to an unreliable estimation. Therefore, the samples from the first session become the database samples, and the remaining images become the test samples. First, the input palmvein image should be extracted ROI and enhanced [39, 40], by which we can obtain a 128 × 128 enhanced palmvein ROI image. The ROI is then identified using the method in [39]. The identification experimental results are shown in Table 1. The recognition rate in the PolyU database is 99.83 % with an equal error rate (EER) of 0.14 %; the recognition rate in the CASIA database is 99.50 % with an EER of 0.67 %; and the recognition rate in the self-built database is 99.91 % with an EER of 0.09 %.

Table 1. The rank-1 identification rate and EER on three databases

Method	Self-built	PolyU	CASIA
EER	0.09 %	0.14 %	0.67 %
Rank one identification rate	99.91 %	99.83 %	99.50 %

Table 1 indicates that the self-built database can obtain a high recognition rate and a low EER. Thus, the validity of the palmvein image in the self-built database is good for the identification process.

4.3   Evaluation of Consistency by Matching Score

10 volunteers (with 20 palms; 10 men and 10 women) participate in the experiment. Two contact palmvein images are acquired under appropriate hand placements, and 10 contact-less palmvein images are acquired under appropriate (with 2 images), fore, back, left, right, far, near, convex, and concave hand placements. A total of 240 palmvein images are obtained, with 12 palmvein images for each palm. We use a contract palmvein image or a contract-less palmvein image under the appropriate placement as registration samples. The other 11 images serve as test samples. The matching score can be obtained by the methods in [39, 40], a part of them is shown in Table 2 (4 persons with 8 palms). This table indicates that the matching score

(including the comparisons between contact and contact, between contact and contact-less, and between contact-less and contact-less) is higher when the hand of the user is posed under the appropriate placement, and the matching score decreases significantly under other inappropriate placements. Therefore, the different positions and postures in the registration and identification phases affect the consistency of palmvein images, which leads to the decrease in the scores of intra-class palmvein images and the increment in FAR and FRR, that is, the recognition performance worsens.
- fail to extract ROI

Table 2. Matching score in different placements

Placements	Appropriate 1 (contact)	Appropriate 2 (contact)	Appropriate 1 (contact-less)	Appropriate 2 (contact-less)	Left	Right	Fore	Back	Far	Near	Convex	Concave
Appropriate1 (contact)	1.00	0.49	0.35	0.31	0.23	0.25	0.22	0.24	0.27	0.26	0.25	0.29
Appropriate1 (contact-less)	0.35	0.31	1.00	0.34	0.21	0.22	0.20	0.26	0.20	0.31	0.29	0.22
Appropriate 1 (contact)	1.00	0.57	0.38	0.32	0.19	0.24	0.22	0.29	0.23	-	0.24	0.28
Appropriate 1 (contact-less)	0.38	0.39	1.00	0.35	0.18	0.21	0.21	0.29	0.21	-	0.20	0.28
Appropriate1 (contact)	1.00	0.59	0.32	0.41	0.23	0.27	0.22	0.29	0.27	0.28	0.22	0.27
Appropriate1 (contact-less)	0.32	0.33	1.00	0.48	0.26	0.23	0.24	0.19	0.28	0.23	0.20	0.29
Appropriate1 (contact)	1.00	0.43	0.39	0.32	0.24	0.20	0.20	0.29	0.30	0.29	0.22	0.30
Appropriate1 (contact-less)	0.39	0.32	1.00	0.34	0.22	0.23	0.18	0.25	0.28	0.27	0.27	0.27
Appropriate1 (contact)	1.00	0.35	0.31	0.31	0.20	0.23	0.28	0.21	0.28	0.31	0.22	0.28
Appropriate1 (contact-less)	0.31	0.30	1.00	0.41	0.21	0.22	0.26	0.19	0.25	0.28	0.27	0.28
Appropriate1 (contact)	1.00	0.43	0.34	0.31	0.22	0.23	0.25	0.19	0.19	0.24	0.22	0.26
Appropriate1 (contact-less)	0.34	0.31	1.00	0.41	0.17	0.21	0.22	0.21	0.22	0.31	0.23	0.30
Appropriate1 (contact)	1.00	0.52	0.46	0.42	0.25	0.22	0.22	0.26	0.25	0.25	0.21	0.23
Appropriate1 (contact-less)	0.46	0.48	1.00	0.38	0.29	0.19	0.29	0.22	0.22	0.23	0.18	0.25
Appropriate1 (contact)	1.00	0.41	0.33	0.36	0.23	0.22	0.27	0.29	0.22	0.25	0.20	0.28
Appropriate1 (contact-less)	0.33	0.44	1.00	0.35	0.23	0.22	0.27	0.23	0.24	0.25	0.24	0.27

4.4   Evaluation of Acquisition Time

The acquisition time of a palmvein image is the time when the hand of the user is placed above the camera to the time that a valid palmvein image is captured by adjusting the appropriate position and posture of the hand. T_a and T'_a represent the acquisition times of a palmvein image with and without the proposed method, respectively; T_p, T_e, and T_m represent the response times of the pre-processing, feature extraction, and one-to-one matching, respectively. The consumed times for the registration and identification processes are determined as follows.

The registration time:

$$T_{registation} = T_a + T_p + T_e \text{ or } T_{registation} = T'_a + T_p + T_e \qquad (10)$$

The identification time:

$$T_{identification} = T_a + T_p + T_e + T_m \text{ or } T_{identification} = T'_a + T_p + T_e + T_m \qquad (11)$$

Given that T_p, T_e, and T_m do not depend on the proposed method, the registration time $T_{registration}$ and the identification time $T_{identification}$ are restricted by the acquisition times T_a and T'_a.

For the contact mode, considering that the user is asked to place his/her hand on the bracket, an insignificant difference exists between T_a and T'_a. For the contact-less mode, the acquisition time T_a is within 3 s in most cases, and T'_a is approximately 10 s to 120 s depending on the experience of the user.

Therefore, the proposed locating method not only shortens the acquisition time and realizes image capture automatically but also ensures the validity and consistency of the acquired palmvein image. The capture device cannot be productized without the proposed method because the judging experience of users cannot be embedded in the device.

5   Conclusion

To meet the demands for the practicability and productization of the capture device in the palmvein identification system, we propose a real-time detecting and locating method for palmvein image acquisition. The method ensures the validity and consistency of the acquired palmvein images and automatically captures the image fast. On the basis of a simple electric and optical circuit and a locating algorithm, we can detect whether the hand is placed in appropriate position and posture according to the acquired image with four light-spots. The palmvein image acquired by this method satisfies the requirements of subsequent processes, such as ROI, feature extraction, and matching. Experimental results show that the proposed method is practical and meets the demand for productization.

References

1. Jain, A.K., Ross, A., Prabhakar, S.: An introduction to biometric recognition. IEEE Trans. Circ. Syst. Video Technol. **14**, 4–20 (2004)
2. Wilson, C.: Vein Pattern Recognition: A Privacy-Enhancing Biometric. CRC Press, Boca Raton (2011)
3. Lu, Y., Xie, S.J., Sook, Y., Yang, J.C., Park, D.S.: Robust finger vein ROI localization based on flexible segmentation. Sens. **13**, 14339–14366 (2013)
4. Yang, L., Yang, G.P., Yin, Y.L., Xiao, R.Y.: Sliding window-based region of interest extraction for finger vein images. Sens. **13**, 3799–3815 (2013)

5. Watanabe, M., Endoh, T., Shiohara, M.: Palm vein authentication technology and its applications. In: Proceedings of the Biometric Consortium Conference, pp. 19–21 (2005)
6. Wang, Y., Hu, J.: Global ridge orientation modeling for partial fingerprint identification. IEEE Trans. Pattern Anal. Mach. Intell. **33**, 72–87 (2011)
7. Peralta, D., Triguero, I., Sanchez-Reillo, R., Herrera, F., Benítez, J.M.: Fast fingerprint identification for large databases. Pattern Recogn. **47**, 588–602 (2014)
8. Dai, J., Feng, J., Zhou, J.: Robust and efficient ridge-based palmprint matching. IEEE Trans. Pattern Anal. Mach. Intell. **34**, 1618–1632 (2012)
9. Kong, A., Zhang, D., Kamel, M.: A survey of palmprint recognition. Pattern Recogn. **42**, 1408–1418 (2009)
10. Zhang, D., Kong, W.K., You, J., Wong, M.: Online palmprint identification. IEEE Trans. Pattern Anal. Mach. Intell. **25**, 1041–1050 (2003)
11. Zhang, D., Guo, Z., Lu, G., Zuo, W.: An online system of multispectral palmprint verification. IEEE Trans. Instrum. Meas. **59**, 480–490 (2010)
12. Pillai, J.K., Patel, V.M., Chellappa, R., Ratha, N.K.: Secure and robust iris recognition using random projections and sparse representations. IEEE Trans. Pattern Anal. Mach. Intell. **33**, 1877–1893 (2011)
13. Cui, J.J., Wang, L.H., Chen, D.L.: On the vein image capturing system based on near-infrared image quality assessment. J. Northeast. Univ. Nat. Sci. **30**, 1099–1102 (2009)
14. Fuksis, R., Greitans, M., Nikisins, O.: Infrared imaging system for analysis of blood vessel structure. Electron. Electron. Eng. **1**, 45–48 (2010)
15. Zhou, Y.B., Kumar, A.: Human identification using palm-vein images. IEEE Trans. Inf. Forensics Secur. **6**, 1259–1274 (2011)
16. Wang, J.G., Yau, W.Y., Suwandy, A., Sung, E.: Person recognition by fusing palmprint and palm vein images based on "Laplacianpalm" representation. Pattern Recogn. **41**, 1514–1527 (2008)
17. Ladoux, P.O., Rosenberger, C., Dorizzi, B.: Palm vein verification system based on SIFT matching. In: Third International Conference Advances in Biometrics, pp. 1290–1298. Alghero, Italy (2009)
18. Xueyan, L., Shuxu, G., Fengli, G.: Vein pattern recognitions by moment invariants. In: The 1st International Conference on Bioinformatics and Biomedical Engineering, pp. 612–615. IEEE Press (2007)
19. Michael, G.K.O., Connie, T., Jin, A.T.B.: Design and implementation of a contactless palm print and palm vein sensor. In: 11th International Conference on Control, Automation, Robotics and Vision, pp. 1268–1273, Singapore (2010)
20. Mirmohamadsadeghi, L., Drygajlo, A.: Palm vein recognition with local binary patterns and local derivative patterns. In: 2011 International Joint Conference on Biometrics (IJCB), pp. 1–6. IEEE (2011)
21. Wu, K.S., Lee, J.C., Lo, T.M., Chang, K.C., Chang, C.P.: A secure palm vein recognition system. J. Syst. Softw. **86**, 2870–2876 (2013)
22. Hao, Y., Sun, Z., Tan, T.: Multispectral palm image fusion for accurate contact-free palmprint recognition. In: 15th IEEE International Conference on IEEE Image Processing, pp. 281–284, San Diego USA (2008)
23. Zhang, Y.-B., Li, Q., You, J., Bhattacharya, P.: Palm vein extraction and matching for personal authentication. In: Qiu, G., Leung, C., Xue, X.-Y., Laurini, R. (eds.) VISUAL 2007. LNCS, vol. 4781, pp. 154–164. Springer, Heidelberg (2007)
24. Chen, H., Lu, G.M., Wang, R.: A new palm vein matching method based on ICP algorithm. In: Proceedings of the 2nd International Conference on Interaction Sciences: Information Technology, pp. 1207–1211. Culture and Human, Seoul, Korea (2009)

25. Lee, J.C.: Palm vein feature extraction using 2-D gabor filters. Adv. Sci. Lett. **8**, 807–812 (2012)
26. Han, W.Y., Lee, J.C.: Palm vein recognition using adaptive gabor filter. Expert Syst. Appl. **39**, 13225–13234 (2012)
27. Lee, J.C.: A novel biometric system based on palm vein image. Pattern Recogn. Lett. **33**, 1520–1528 (2012)
28. Wang, R., Wang, G.Y., Chen, Z., Zeng, Z.G., Wang, Y.: A palm vein identification system based on Gabor wavelet features. Neural Comput. Appl. **24**, 161–168 (2014)
29. Kang, W.X., Liu, Y., Wu, Q.X., Yue, X.S.: Contact-free palm-vein recognition based on local invariant features. PloS ONE **9**, e97548 (2014)
30. Raut, S.D., Humbe, V.T.: Review of biometrics: palm vein recognition system. IBMRD's J. Manage. Res. **3**, 217–223 (2014)
31. Li, Q.: Theoretical and Experimental Research on Palm Vein Recognition Technology. Huazhong University of Science and Technology, Wuhan (2010)
32. Yuan, W.Q., Yang, G.T., Li, W.: Research on palm Vein acquisition system based on wavelength choice. Laser & Infrared 41, 234–239 (2011)
33. Wan, W.B.: Study on Palm-Vein Image Capture and Recognition System. Shenyang University of Technology, Shenyang (2009)
34. Zhang, H., Hu, D.W.: A palm vein recognition system. In: International Conference on Intelligent Computation Technology and Automation, pp. 285–288 (2010)
35. Zarina, M.N., Abdul, R.R., Marsyita, H., M, I. S.: Review on a palm vein infrared image acquisition systems. In: 2013 IEEE Student Conference on Research and Development (SCOReD), pp. 334–337. Putrajaya, Malaysia (2013)
36. Wu, W., Yuan, W.Q.: A survey of palm-vein image recognition. J. Image Graph. **18**, 1215–1224 (2013)
37. PolyU multispectral palmprint Database. http://www.comp.polyu.edu.hk/~biometrics/MultispectralPalmprint/MSP.htm
38. CASIA-MS-PalmprintV1. http://biometrics.idealtest.org/
39. Zhou, Y.J., Liu, Y.Q., Feng, Q.J., Yang, F., Huang, J.: Palm-vein classification based on principal orientation features. PLoS ONE **9**, e112429 (2014)
40. Zhou, Y.J., Liu, Y.Q., Yang, F., Huang, J.: Palm-vein recognition based on oriented features. J. Image Graph. **19**, 243–252 (2014)
41. Lee, Y.P.: Palm vein recognition based on a modified $(2D)^2LDA$. SIViP **9**, 229–242 (2015)

Real-Time Panoramic Image Mosaic
via Harris Corner Detection on FPGA

Lu Chen, Jing Han, Yi Zhang, and Lian-fa Bai[✉]

Jiangsu Key Laboratory of Spectral Imaging and Intelligent Sense,
Nanjing University of Science and Technology, Nanjing, China
mrblf@163.com

Abstract. To solve the problems such as low matching precision, high algorithm complexity and poor real-time in real-time panoramic image mosaic, this paper makes full use of the significance and parallelism of Harris corners as well as the invariance of feature describing methods in light intensity changes, translation and rotation, and proposes a real-time panoramic image mosaic algorithm which uses Harris corner detection and is logically implemented on FPGA. According to the basic features of classical algorithms and the properties of FPGA, several modules like feature point extraction, description and matching are optimized based on the logical implementation of FPGA. The optimized system realizes the high-precision matching in real time. The new algorithm collects images of 256×256 pixels by CCD camera on Spartan-6 hardware platform of Xilinx. After going through the algorithm, the mosaic images will finally be output on HD display in the form of DVI. The results show that the new algorithm based on FPGA has high precision, good real-time and robustness.

Keywords: Image mosaic · FPGA · Harris corner · Feature descriptor · Real-time

1 Introduction

Image mosaic has become an increasingly popular research field. It performs space matching of a series of images overlapping with each other in the same scene and presents a panorama containing image sequence information and a wide-angle view through image fusion. Currently, the research on static image mosaic algorithm has matured, but there are very few research and application of video mosaic. The key of video mosaic is the real-time of matching. Tsai Du-ming proposed a rapid cross-correlation algorithm of gray window [1], which effectively improves matching speed. But as it uses the matching method based on grayscale, the matching precision is greatly affected by huge image ratio differences and severe regional image deformation, as well as regions with little information. Lowe proposed the matching using SIFT feature descriptor [2, 3]. When conditions like contrast ratio, light intensity and rotation change, image features can still be extracted accurately. This method is widely used in image matching, but it is complex in computation and quite resource-consuming. Wei Zhiqiang and Huang Shuai found that Harris corners hold higher significance than SIFT feature points and are simple in computation [4, 5], effectively reducing resource consumption.

© Springer International Publishing Switzerland 2015
Y.-J. Zhang (Ed.): ICIG 2015, Part III, LNCS 9219, pp. 111–124, 2015.
DOI: 10.1007/978-3-319-21969-1_10

However, due to the limited software running speed, it takes nearly one second to perform feature point matching, which can not meet real-time demands. Yao Lifan optimized several modules of SIFT algorithm and tried to implement image matching through FPGA [6], but he only presented the logic implementation of FPGA in the main direction, rather than the whole matching process. V. Bonato carried out the implementation of FPGA based on SIFT algorithm [7], but due to high complexity of describing operation, this module was performed on FPGA's soft core. The system didn't realize real-time because of the limited running speed of the soft core.

In order to satisfy the demand for real-time in mosaic system, many designers prefer to use FPGA as it holds parallel structures, a large number of logic arrays and fast signal processing. Harris corner detection, which has good parallelism, can perform real-time detection on FPGA and accurately extract corners when images rotate or grayscale changes [8]. The point feature describing method used in SIFT algorithm can provide the matching with highly multi-faceted information of feature points and improve matching precision. This paper uses Harris corner detection to extract feature points and introduces the point feature describing method to match those points on Spartan-6 hardware platform of Xilinx. With its properties and precision invariable, the algorithm is reasonably optimized to run on hardware, which realizes real-time, and acquires panoramic video mosaic images with high precision and stability.

2   The Video Mosaic Algorithm and Its Optimization

2.1   Overlapping Region Estimate

According to the image-forming principle of cameras, the angular transformation of the camera in the horizontal direction is in proportion to the horizontally moving distance of the video image. The formula is as follows:

$$\frac{\Delta\theta}{\theta} \approx \frac{\Delta X}{X} \tag{1}$$

Where $\Delta\theta$ represents the angular transformation of the camera in the horizontal direction. θ means visual angle, which is generally 12 degrees. Smaller object distance makes bigger visual angle. ΔX means the horizontally moving distance of the video image, and X means the width of the video image. The length of the overlapping region of two sequential images is $X-\Delta X$.

Assuming the horizontally rotating speed of the camera is less than 30 degrees per second, and the frame rate is 25 frames per second, then the angular transformation between two frames will be less than 1.2 degrees. It can be roughly estimated that the horizontally moving distance of the video image is less than 10 % of the image width. Subject to hardware conditions, the highest matching precision is acquired when the size of the overlapping region is 50 % of the image size. Hence this paper only perform matching on the half part of the image region. Compared with the matching on the full image, this matching mode can improve matching precision because of the centralized distribution of the feature points, which can also enhance computing speed effectively and save resources.

2.2 Determination of Significant Feature Points

SIFT algorithm can extract 200–800 feature points from an image of 256 × 256. By contrast, Harris operator can extract highly significant and stable corners and the calculation is very simple. Harris corners don't perform very well when scales change, but they are still chosen as the significant feature points of the images as scales have little influence on the matching process in video mosaic. Subsequently SIFT feature vector describing method is used to do describing calculation. The time for feature description is in direct proportion to the number of feature points, which thus must be restricted to ensure the real-time of the algorithm. Here the threshold value of CRF set in Non-Maximum Suppression is used to realize adaptive extraction of feature points. The formula to calculate the threshold value of CRF is as follows:

$$CRF_t = CRF_{max}/n \tag{2}$$

Where CRF is the value from the response function of the pixels, judging whether the Harris corner. CRF_{max} represents the maximum value of CRF, changing when scenes change. n is threshold coefficient. If the number of feature points goes beyond the limit, this paper can change the threshold value of CRF by changing the value of n to control the number of feature points.

2.3 Optimization of Feature Point Description

Classical SIFT feature vector describing method performs calculation of Gaussian pyramid images. As Gaussian pyramid is not used in the new algorithm, it is necessary to optimize the classical method. Specific procedures are as follows:

(1) Main direction extraction. Lowe's SIFT performs calculation of Gaussian-filtered images to get the gradient whose module value m(x,y) will be processed by Gaussian distribution, where the parameter σ satisfies the formula σ' = 1.5 σ, and the radius of the window is 3 × 1.5 σ. But this algorithm compute the histogram of the gradient of the 3 × 3 region around the feature point of the original image. There is no need to do Gaussian distribution processing to module values, which greatly reduces the calculation amount.

(2) The calculated region of the descriptor. Divide the neighbor region around the feature point into 4 × 4 subregions, and the scale of each subregion equals the region used in the calculation of the corner's main direction, which is 3 × 3. Taking bilinear interpolation and coordinate axis rotation into account, the radius of the calculated region should be set as:

$$r = \frac{3 \times \sqrt{2} \times (d + 1)}{2} \tag{3}$$

Calculated results are rounded to integers. As it is very complex to implement circular neighbor regions in FPGA, this paper choose square neighbor regions to simplify the calculation. And there should be a large number of sampling points, so this paper choose a feature point-centered region with the scale of 21 × 21 for calculation.

(3) The calculation of the coordinates and module values in the descriptor. Due to the change of the calculated regions in the descriptor, the formula used to calculate coordinates and module values should be altered accordingly. The coordinate values of the sampling points in subregions are as follows:

$$\begin{pmatrix} x' \\ y' \end{pmatrix} = \begin{pmatrix} \cos\theta & -\sin\theta \\ \sin\theta & \cos\theta \end{pmatrix} \begin{pmatrix} x \\ y \end{pmatrix}, \ x, y \in [-r, r] \tag{4}$$

$$\begin{pmatrix} x'' \\ y'' \end{pmatrix} = \frac{1}{3} \begin{pmatrix} x' \\ y' \end{pmatrix} + \frac{d}{2} \tag{5}$$

Where (x,y) represents pixel coordinate, θ means the main direction of the feature point, (x',y') means the rotated coordinate.

Use a weighted Gaussian($\sigma = d/2$) to process the module values of the gradients in subregions and do additions according to corresponding directions:

$$w = m(x,y)\exp(-\frac{(x'/3)^2 + (y'/3)^2}{2 \times (d/2)^2}) \tag{6}$$

$$weight = w \cdot dr^k \cdot (1-dr)^{1-k} \cdot dc^m \cdot (1-dc)^{1-m} \cdot do^n \cdot (1-do)^{1-n} \tag{7}$$

where $m(x,y)$ is the gradient magnitude of the pixel. dr and dc respectively represent the contribution pixels make to neighbor seed points in rows and columns. do represents the contribution pixels make to neighbor directions. k, m and n are set as 0 or 1.

2.4   Determination of the Best Matching Points

After the descriptor matching which uses Euclidean distance, one simple and efficient method is used to choose the best matching point in the proposed algorithm. Assuming n pairs of matching points are got through feature point matching and the coordinate values of the ith pair in I_1 and I_2 are (x_{i1},y_{i1}) and (x_{i2},y_{i2}) respectively, then calculate the coordinate offsets between them:

$$\Delta x_i = x_{i2} - x_{i1}; \ \Delta y_i = y_{i2} - y_{i1} \tag{8}$$

Calculate the number of the matched point pairs with the same Δx and Δy. The Δx and Δy of which the number is the largest are considered as the offsets in direction x and direction y of the two images. If none of the matching points has the same Δx and Δy, then the matching is unsuccessful and the mosaic will not be performed.

3   The Hardware Implementation of the Video Mosaic System

For the real-time video mosaic algorithm based on FPGA in this paper, its logic implementation on hardware is mainly made up of three parts, namely adaptive Harris corner detection, feature description and feature matching. The specific procedures are shown as Fig. 1.

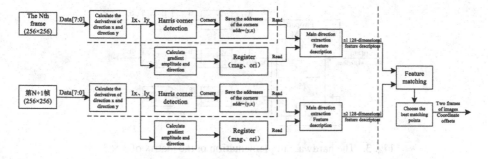

Fig. 1. The block diagram of the hardware implementation of the panoramic video mosaic algorithm

3.1 Significant Feature Point Extraction

This module which makes full use of the design concept of the FPGA pipelining can simultanenously store images and use Harris corner detection to finish the feature point extraction of each image in video streaming, and then store the coordinate values of the feature points. The implementation of Harris corner detection is shown as Fig. 2.

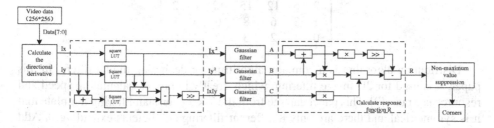

Fig. 2. The hardware implementation of Harris corner extraction

(1) The calculation of directional derivatives. To calculate the gradients of the pixels in direction x and direction y, the gradient convolution template is integrated as:

$$\begin{bmatrix} a_{11} & a_{12} & a_{13} \\ a_{21} & a_{22} & a_{23} \\ a_{31} & a_{32} & a_{33} \end{bmatrix} = \begin{bmatrix} 0 & -1 & 0 \\ -1 & 0 & 1 \\ 0 & 1 & 0 \end{bmatrix} \tag{9}$$

In the implementation of the 3×3-pixel window, in order to save resources, this paper replaces FIFO IP with a twoport RAM whose depth is 512 datum for the function of automatic line delay of the images. To realize first-in first-out, just like FIFO, this paper only need to set RAM to the mode read first, which will at least reduce half of the resources. The hardware implementation of the matrix of 3×3 is shown as Fig. 3.

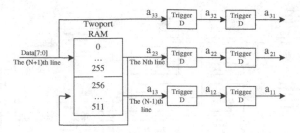

Fig. 3. The hardware implementation of the matrix of 3×3

(2) Distributed Gaussian filter. To realize the Gaussian filter of I_x^2, I_y^2 and I_xI_y, the 7×7 filter template whose scale meets $\sigma = 1.5$ is used in this paper. The implementation of the 7×7 window is similar to that of the 3×3, but the former one needs three RAMs. With the premise that the effect of corner detection is ensured, the filter coefficients generated by Matlab are quantificat, thus the adopted filter template is as follows:

$$
G = \frac{1}{255}
\begin{bmatrix}
0 & 1 & 2 & 3 & 2 & 1 & 0 \\
1 & 3 & 6 & 8 & 6 & 3 & 1 \\
2 & 6 & 12 & 15 & 12 & 6 & 2 \\
3 & 8 & 15 & 19 & 15 & 8 & 3 \\
2 & 6 & 12 & 15 & 12 & 6 & 2 \\
1 & 3 & 6 & 8 & 6 & 3 & 1 \\
0 & 1 & 2 & 3 & 2 & 1 & 0
\end{bmatrix}
\tag{10}
$$

Distribution algorithm is a common algorithm for designing digital filters. In this paper, it is used for 2D image filtering, which greatly improves calculating speed and resource use ratio [9]. This paper can see from the 7×7 Gaussian filtering template that it is symmetrical and there are only 8 different filtering coefficients excluding 0. Add the values with the same coefficients in the image window and filter the eight values. Make lookup tables with the size of 2^8 and store the adding results of the products of the ith place of the eight values and their responding Gaussian template coefficients. Make an eight-bit address of lookup table with the ith place of each figure, then output the ith place of the figure having been processed by Gaussian filter. Do shifting operation to restore the output figures and add them to get the Gaussian filtered values of the 7×7 image window. The parallel structure of the distributed filter is shown as Fig. 4.

3.2   Feature Point Description

In order to make the corners possess distinct characteristics which are useful to image matching, this paper performs quantitative description of the gray features of the corners and the regions around them to generate the corner descriptor, which is the key and difficult point in the hardware implementation. As shown in Fig. 5, this part is mainly made up of the calculation of image gradient amplitude and direction, main direction extraction and descriptor generation.

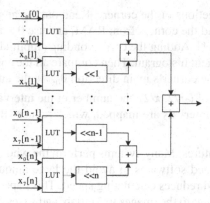

Fig. 4. The parallel structure of the distributed filtering

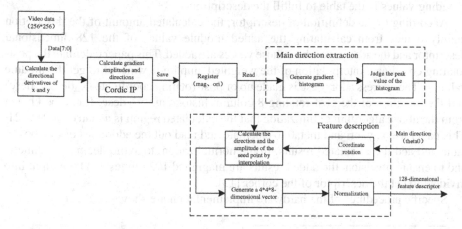

Fig. 5. The hardware implementation of the main direction and feature description

(1) Calculate gradient amplitude and direction. To ensure real-time, when extracting Harris corners, this paper uses the results of the derivatives in direction x and direction y, to calculate the gradient amplitudes and directions of image pixels:

$$\begin{cases} m(x,y) = \sqrt{(I(x+1,y) - I(x-1,y))^2 + (I(x,y+1) - I(x,y-1))^2} \\ \theta(x,y) = \tan^{-1} \dfrac{I(x,y+1) - I(x,y-1)}{I(x+1,y) - I(x-1,y)} \end{cases} \tag{11}$$

As it is not easy to realize rooting and trigonometric function on FPGA, this paper uses Cordic algorithm to carry out the operations and saves the calculated results of the amplitudes and directions in RAM for future use [10]. In the calculation, it is very convenient to carry out the hardware implementation of these complex no-linear functions, in that Cordic only uses shift and addition. To enhance system stability, this paper directly invoke Xilinx's build-in core, Cordic IP, to do the calculation.

(2) Extract the main directions of the corners. Read out the amplitudes and directions of the 3×3 region around the corners from RAM, and use $\theta \times \pi/180$ to judge whether the angles are integers [11]. Adding the corresponding amplitudes of the same integral directions to get the gradient histogram. Then compare all the columns of the histogram in pairs and finally get the corner's main direction θ_0. As the angle calculated through $\tan^{-1}$ is within the range of $(-\pi/2, \pi/2)$, the number of the intervals, 36, will be reduced to 18 after the direction intervals are mapped, which reduces the comparing time and resource consumption.

(3) Describe corners' features. Many systems perform the whole description in DSP or FPGA's build-in embedded softwares to avoid the large amount of calculation [12], which increases costs and reduces calculating speed. This paper skillfully transfers the calculation that is irrelevant to the images to Matlab, and saves the calculated results in the form of lookup tables into registers. This paper only need to read out the corresponding values in the table to fulfill the description.

According to the definition of descriptor, the calculated amount of the description mainly comes from calculating the added module values of the 128-dimensional descriptor and the addresses where those values are added. This paper calculate the post-rotating coordinate interpolation of the weighted amplitude wincoef to get the module value w. The address addr_desc is made up of post-rotating coordinate (x_desc,y_desc) and the direction of the post-rotating 8-column histogram, ori_desc. It can be known from the above algorithm optimization that the calculated region is a matrix of 21×21. This paper use x, y, ori and theta0 to calculate and read out the addresses of the lookup table and add the calculated results. In the normalization, to avoid decimal arithmetic and to ensure precision, the added results are magnified 1024 times and then input into dividers to get the descriptor of the corner [13].

Specific procedures of the hardware implementation are shown as Fig. 6.

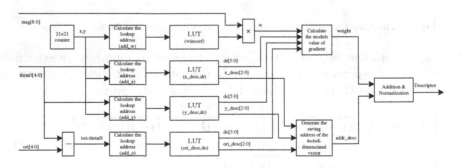

Fig. 6. The hardware implementation of the description of corners' features

3.3 Feature Point Matching

This module is made up of initial feature point matching and the determination of the best matching point pair. The matching relationship of the feature points is got from feature point matching and the coordinate offsets of the images are calculated through the determination of the best matching point pair.

(1) Initial feature point matching. The Euclidean distance used in Classical SIFT matching involves square and root operation, which is not suitable for the implementation on FPGA. In this paper, the sum of absolute differences is used to replace Euclidean distance:

$$D(L_a, L_b') = \sum_{i=1}^{128} |l_{ai} - l_{bi}'|$$
(12)

Where $D(L_a, L_b')$ is the sum of absolute differences. l_a and l_b represent the corresponding feature vector.

When the state machine detects the rising edge of signal desc_all_end in the initial state, it starts the matching made up of two loop nestings. The main procedure of image matching is performed by a state machine, as shown in Fig. 7.

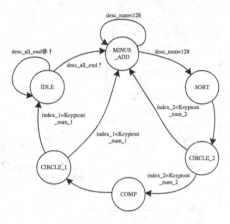

Fig. 7. The state machine of matching

First successively calculate the sums of absolute differences between the descriptor of corner 1 in the Nth frame and the descriptor of each corner in the N + 1th frame, and then sort the results. If the minimum value is less than 75 % of the sub-minimum value, then the two corners are considered as matching points and save the coordinate values of them into registers; If not, then the two corners are not matching points. Continue the calculation of the matching situations between corner 2 in the Nth frame and each corner in the N + 1th frame, and so on. If all the corners in the Nth frame have been detected, the state machine jumps back to the initial state and waits for the starting signal of the next matching process.

(2) The determination of the best matching point pair. After receiving the finishing signal of the feature point matching, match_end_flag, this paper read out the coordinate values of the matching point pairs in the register and calculate the coordinate differences:

$$diff_i = \{y_{i2} - y_{i1}, x_{i2} - x_{i1}\}$$
(13)

(1) Sort the results of diff$_i$. This paper uses a brand new comparison sort algorithm in parallel, which is a sort algorithm using the method of time-for-space [14]. This algorithm needs many defined logic variables, but it can fulfill the sort in several clock cycles. Compare the values of diff$_i$ with each other and get the quantized comparing results (1 for greater-than, 0 for less-than). Add the results of comparing one figure with all the other figures, and the sum is the sorting value of this figure in the sequence. Finally, set this sorting value as the address of RAM and save diff$_i$ into RAM in order. When the sort is finished, set sort_end as 1.

(2) Count the numbers of the different values of diff$_i$. The value corresponding to the largest number is the coordinate offset of the images. Introduce three variables, num, num_max, and diff_best. num represents the number of the value appearing frequently; num_max and diff_best respectively represent the number of the value appearing most frequently and the corresponding coordinate offset. The procedures are shown an Fig. 8.

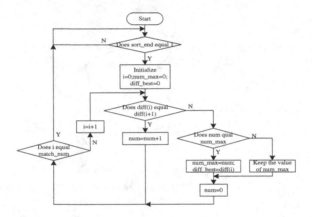

Fig. 8. The flowchart of the statistic of the coordinate absolute differences

4   Results and Analysis of the Experiments

The image mosaic algorithm in this paper is implemented on Xilinx's Spartan-6 hardware platform. ISE 13.1 and Verilog are used to write programs. The mosaic images of 256×256 pixels are output in the form of DVI. The experimental results are shown as Fig. 9.

4.1   Accuracy Analysis

Take indoor scenes for example, MATLAB is used to simulate the mosaic process of two sequential static images with the classical Harris matching algorithm, classical SIFT matching algorithm, the new matching algorithm in this paper and its adapted version for hardware platform respectively, as shown in Fig. 10 and Table 1. Table 1 shows the

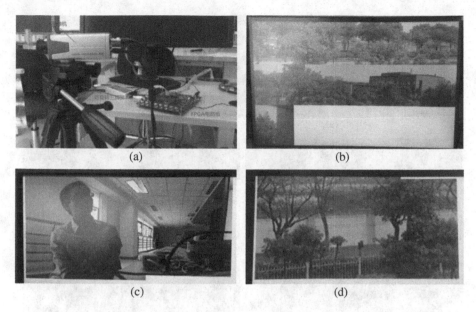

Fig. 9. The experimental results of the system: (a) Experimental equipment; (b) Panoramic mosaic; (c) Indoor scene mosaic; (d) Outdoor scene mosaic.

simulating data acquired by using different algorithms to mosaic the image in Fig. 10(a). This paper can see from the data that, compared with classical algorithms, the new algorithm can extract feature points of higher significance and holds higher matching precision. And its adapted version for hardware keeps excellent matching effect without reducing matching precision.

Table 1. The simulating data of outdoor scenes acquired by using different algorithms

	Feature Points of the left image	Feature points of the right image	Matching pairs	Mismatching pairs
Classical Harris matching algorithm	91	81	9	1
Classical SIFT matching algorithm	206	135	16	3
The new algorithm	39	41	5	0
Adapted version of the new algorithm for hardware	40	39	2	0

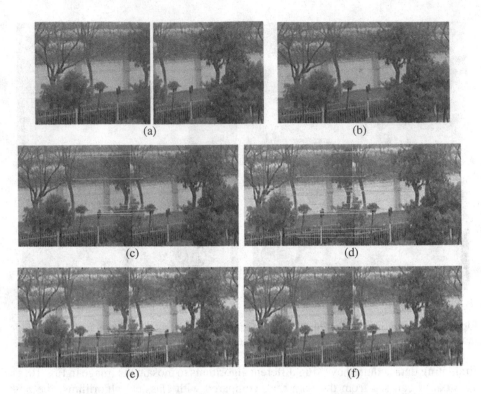

Fig. 10. The matching results of different algorithms: (a) The original images; (b) The mosaic image; (c) The classical Harris matching algorithm; (d) The classical SIFT matching algorithm; (e) The new matching algorithm in this paper; (f) The adapted version for hardware

4.2   Real-Time Analysis

To test the real-time effect of the new algorithm on FPGA, this paper compares the running time of each procedure on hardware platform with that on computer, as shown in Table 2. On FPGA, the module of feature point extraction uses the pixel clock input by the video which is acquired and coded by using SAA7113. The frame rate is 25 frames per second and the pixel clock is 24.576 MHz. The other three modules use FPGA's main clock, which is 100 MHz. From Table 2 we can see the total running time of the mosaic algorithm on FPGA is 10 ms, far less than that on Intel CPU with a dominant frequency of 2.5 GHz. And it takes 40 ms to receive a frame of video image, thus the algorithm can satisfy the demand for real-time mosaic.

4.3   Consumption of FPGA's Resources

Spartan-6 XC6SLX150T abounds with logic and storage resources. As shown in Table 3, the algorithm consumes comparatively few logic resources but a great many resources of on-chip RAM. This is because in the implementation most of the complex operations are stored in on-chip RAM with the form of lookup tables, which reduces logic resource consumption and enhances the algorithm's running speed. Meanwhile, the video image data for storage and display is saved in off-chip register DDR3 to reduce the consumption of on-chip RAM's resources.

Table 2. Comparison of the running time needed respectively on FPGA and Intel CPU

	S6-XC6SLX150T-3(ms)	Intel-Core i5 2.5 GHz (ms)
Significant feature point extraction	2.687	1505
Main direction extraction	0.036	16
Feature point description	3.716	406
Image matching	5.464	218
Total time	10.904	2145

Table 3. FPGA Resource consumption

FPGA resources	Used	Available	Utilization
Slice registers	16134	184304	8 %
Slice LUTs	28712	92152	31 %
Multipliers (DSP48A1 s)	14	180	7 %
RAMs	185	268	69 %
Bonded IOBs	16134	184304	8 %

5 Conclusion

This paper, which explores the implementing process of the image mosaic algorithm on FPGA, makes full use of the invariance of feature describing methods of SIFT in light intensity changes, translation and rotation, and applies the property to image matching based on Harris corners. The new algorithm is also optimized according to the features of the hardware. The performance test results of the application of the image mosaic system to video images of 256×256 show that implementing the algorithm on FPGA is of very good real-time and satisfies the demand for high matching precision of sequential images. But due to the limitation of the hardware, how to realize highly precise matching in conditions like huge image scale changes or severe image distortion still needs further research.

Acknowledgment. This work was financially supported by the National Natural Science Foundation of China (61231014).

References

1. Tsai, D., Lin, C.: Fast normalized cross correlation for defect detection. J. Pattern Recogn. Lett. **24**, 2625–2631 (2003)
2. Lowe, D.G.: Object recognition from local scale-invariant features. C. In: Proceedings of the International Conference on Computer Vision vol. 9, pp. 1150–1157(1999)
3. Lowe, D.G.: Distinctive image features from scale- invariant keypoints. J. Int. J. Comput. Vis. **60**, 91–110 (2004)
4. Wei, Z., Huang, L., Ji, X.: Research on sequence image matching based on point feature. J. J. Image Graph. **14**, 525–530 (2009)
5. Shuai, H., Ke-wei, W., Ling, S.: An image matching algorithm based on Harris scale invariant feature. J. J. Hefei Univ. Technol. **34**, 379–382 (2011)
6. Yao, L., Feng, H., Zhu, Y., et al.: An architecture of optimised SIFT feature detection for an FPGA implementation of an image matcher. J. Int. Conf. Field programmable Technol. (FPT), 30–37 (2010)
7. Bonato, V., Marques, E., Constantinides, G.A.: A parallel hardware architecture for scale and rotation invariant feature detection. J IEEE Trans. Circ. Syst. Video Technol. **18**, 1703–1712 (2008)
8. Amaricai, A., Gavriliu, C., Boncalo, O.: An FPGA sliding window-based architecture harris corner detector. C. In: 2014 24th International Conference on IEEE Field Programmable Logic and Applications (FPL), pp. 1–4 (2014)
9. Li, H., Tian, K.: A design of distributed FIR digital filter based on FPGA. J. Audio Eng. **36**, 28–32 (2012)
10. Volder, J.E.: The CORDIC trigonometric computing technique. J. IRE Trans. Electron. Comput. **EC-8**, 330–334 (1959)
11. Agrawal, K., Chowdhury, S.R.: FPGA based accelerated orientation calculation in SIFT using luts. C. In: 2013 IEEE Asia Pacific Conference on Postgraduate Research in Microelectronics and Electronics (PrimeAsia), pp. 225–227. IEEE (2013)
12. Xiao, H., He, W., Yuan, K., et al.: Real-time scene recognition on embedded system with SIFT keypoints and a new descriptor. C. In: 2013 IEEE International Conference on Mechatronics and Automation (ICMA), pp. 1317–1324. IEEE (2013)
13. Leyva, P., Domenech-Asensi, G., Garrigos, J., et al.: Simplification and hardware implementation of the feature descriptor vector calculation in the SIFT algorithm. C. In: 2014 24th International Conference on Field Programmable Logic and Applications (FPL), pp. 1–4. IEEE (2014)
14. Shi, T., Jin, C.: The comparison sort algorithm in parallel based on FPGA. J. Digit. Technol. Appl. **10**, 126–127 (2013)

Real-Time Robust Video Stabilization Based on Empirical Mode Decomposition and Multiple Evaluation Criteria

Jun Yu[✉], Chang-wei Luo, Chen Jiang, Rui Li, Ling-yan Li, and Zeng-fu Wang

Deptartment of Automation, University of Science and Technology of China, Hefei 230026, China
{harrtjun, zfwang}@ustc.edu.cn

Abstract. A real-time robust video stabilization system is proposed. Firstly, SIFT feature points are extracted and matched between the reference frame and current frame, and then global motion parameters are obtained by fitting the feature matches with random sample consensus algorithm. Secondly, multiple evaluation criteria, i.e., global motion parameters and location errors of corresponding feature matches, are fused by empirical mode decomposition to smooth global motion for obtaining correction vector. Thirdly, motion compensation is applied to the current frame by using correction vector. Finally, stabilized video is obtained after each frame is completed by combining the texture synthesis method and the spatio-temporal information of video. By comparing the jittered video and stabilized video, the experimental results demonstrate the system can increase the average peak signal-to-noise ratio around 7.2 dB, the identification ability and perceptive comfort on video content.

Keywords: Global motion estimation · Motion filtering and compensation · Video completion

1 Introduction

Video enhancement has been gaining in importance with the increasing prevalence of digital media. One of the most important enhancements is video stabilization [1]. Often, home videos suffer from an amount of unexpected image motion caused by unintentional shake of a human hand. The goal of video stabilization is to generate a new compensated video sequence where undesirable image motion is removed [2, 3].

1.1 Related Works

There are several major stages constituting a video stabilization process: global motion estimation [4], motion filtering and compensation [5], video completion [6].

Global motion estimation is achieved by estimating the interframe motion of adjacent frames [7]. In [8], global motion estimation using local motion vectors of

© Springer International Publishing Switzerland 2015
Y.-J. Zhang (Ed.): ICIG 2015, Part III, LNCS 9219, pp. 125–136, 2015.
DOI: 10.1007/978-3-319-21969-1_11

subimages obtained by block-matching was presented. Motion estimation based on edge pattern matching was demonstrated in [9]. An iterative, multi-resolution motion estimation scheme that estimates affine motion parameters between levels of the Laplacian pyramid was described in [10, 11]. Fast motion estimation based on bit-plane matching was demonstrated in [12, 13]. A robust approach for phase correlation-based global motion estimation was demonstrated in [14]. Feature-based algorithms estimate interframe motion using extracted feature locations and robust filters [15, 16], these methods have gained larger consensus for their good performances [7, 17, 18].

In motion filtering, the estimated motion is evaluated to recognize intentional movement. Several techniques, such as DFT filtered frame position smoothing [14], Kalman filtering [19] and motion vector integration [20], were proposed and modified to correct translational and rotational jitters [21, 22] according to real systems constraints. After motion filtering, the jitter is obtained, then the image frames are spatially displaced inversely to jitter. This process is referred to as the motion compensation, and the compensation amount of each frame is referred to as the correction vector.

Filling in missing image areas in a video is called video completion [23]. In [24], mosaicing is used to fill up the missing image areas in the context of video stabilization. Wexler et al. [25] filled in the holes in a video by sampling spatio-temporal volume patches from different portions of the same video. Jia et al. [26] and Cheung et al. [27] proposed an approach by segmenting the video into a moving object layer and a static background layer. Cheung et al. [28] showed an effective video fill-in result in their video epitomes framework. Matsushita et al. [29] conduct the video completion based on the local motion estimation of missing image areas. Criminisi et al. [30] and Tang et al. [31] proposed a texture synthesis method. The most similar texture patch is searched around the missing image area to replace the unknown part in the original texture patch. It can achieve good result if enough similar information are available.

1.2 Paper Contribution

This paper proposes a real-time robust video stabilization system. Our work has following advantages: (1) Global motion is estimated by random sample consensus (RANSAC) fitting on the matched scale invariant feature transform (SIFT) features. (2) The advantage of empirical mode decomposition (EMD) is firstly verified in the video stabilization community, and a satisfying motion filtering result is obtained. (3) Multiple evaluation criteria are fused to increase the robustness of motion filtering and compensation, and thus the correction vector, especially the rotation component, can be obtained accurately in the motion filtering process, and used accurately in the motion compensation process. (4) Different from the single image, there are plenty of interframe similar information among the adjacent frames of video, Therefore, the image texture synthesis method in [30] is combined with the spatio-tempral information of video to carry out the video completion.

2 Framework

Figure 1 is the framework of the proposed system. Firstly, when input jittered video, SIFT keypoints are extracted from two consecutive frames, and these two sets of features are matched and then fitted to obtain global motion parameters by the RANSAC algorithm. Secondly, by fusing multiple evaluation criteria, EMD is used to filter global motion for obtaining correction vector. Thirdly, according to evaluation criteria, motion compensation is applied to the current frame by using correction vector. Finally, missing image areas in each frame is completed by combining the texture synthesis method and the spatio-temporal information of video.

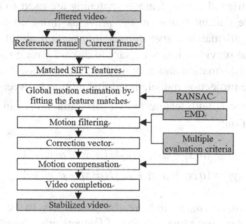

Fig. 1. Framework.

3 Image Matching

SIFT is designed for extracting highly distinctive invariant features from images [32, 33], which can be used to perform reliable matching of the same object between different images. SIFT algorithm has several free parameters, so our implementation is designed to make features more suitable for video stabilization. The first stage is building the scale-space pyramid. Two successive Gaussians are separated by a factor of $\sqrt{2}$ and 5 images per octave are computed, resulting in 4 Difference-of-Gaussian images and therefore extrema are searched on two different images. When keypoints are located, each of them is interpolated, evaluated for contrast and then passed through a Harris edge detector. Avoiding unstable features is very important in video stabilization. In order to obtain better features, original thresholds used in the SIFT algorithm for keypoints validation are hardened to discard a larger number of features. After orientation assignment has been fulfilled, a 128-element feature vector is derived and bilinear interpolation is successfully used to increase descriptor robustness and invariance. The final output is therefore a set of keypoints with their descriptors.

The keypoint matching is performed using Euclidean distance between descriptors' vectors and a distance ratio, namely ratio of closest neighbor distance to that of the second-closest one, that can be checked against a threshold to discard false matches. In fact, correct matches should have lower ratios while wrong ones should have ratios closer to one. We investigated correlation between distance ratio and correctness of matches and found that using a value of 0.6 as threshold performs well in discarding wrong matches. The result of this matching process is a list of keypoints pairs that can be easily used as input of the feature-based motion estimation algorithm.

4   Global Motion Estimation

The set of features retrieved during features matching are used to estimate the motion needed to overlay the current frame on the previous frame to minimize the visible motion. Because not all matches give correct information about how the frame has moved relatively to the previous, it is necessary to discard wrong matches that do not fit into the estimated transformation and may mislead the process. Assuming the imaging model is a perspective projection model, the global motion between frames, associating feature $(x_i, y_i)^T$ in frame I_n with feature $(x_j, y_j)^T$ in frame I_{n+1}, can be described by the following transformation:

$$
\begin{aligned}
x_j &= (a_1 x_i + a_2 y_i + a_3)/(a_7 x_i + a_8 y_i + 1) \\
y_j &= (a_4 x_i + a_5 y_i + a_6)/(a_7 x_i + a_8 y_i + 1)
\end{aligned}
\tag{1}
$$

Where $(a_1, a_2, a_3, a_4, a_5, a_6, a_7, a_8)$ are the parameters to be solved. In order to estimate eight parameters, only four couples of features are needed. However, features may be affected by noise, so it is useful to apply a Levenberg-Marquardt (LM) method on a set of redundant equations.

The whole set of feature matches does not contain useful information for effective motion compensation, as probably it includes wrong matches or correct matches that indeed belong to self-moving objects in the filmed scene. Obviously there are some correct pairs that do represent real camera shakes but several points simply do not relate to such information. Here we use RANSAC [34] to deal with this problem. RANSAC is an iterative method to estimate parameters of a mathematical model from a set of observed data which contains outliers.

Firstly, six couples of features are selected randomly from the feature set $P = \left\{ \left((x_i, y_i)^T; (x_j, y_j)^T \right) \right\}, i,j = 1 \cdots n$. These features are comprised of a subset S_1 of P, and a solution M_1 is obtained from S_1. Then a new subset S_1^* of P is obtained by

$$
S_1^* = \left\{ \left((x_i, y_i)^T; (x_j, y_j)^T \right) \left\| \begin{matrix} x_j - (a_1 x_i + a_2 y_i + a_3)/(a_7 x_i + a_8 y_i + 1) \\ y_j - (a_4 x_i + a_5 y_i + a_6)/(a_7 x_i + a_8 y_i + 1) \end{matrix} \right\| \leq T \right\}, T \text{ is a}
$$

given threshold.

Secondly, above process is repeated K times, and the S_k^* with the most elements is selected. K is determined according to the criterion in [18].

Finally, LM method is applied on S_k^* to obtain the final solution M.

5 Motion Filtering and Compensation

EMD and multiple evaluation criteria are used in the motion filtering, and then multiple evaluation criteria are also used in the motion compensation.

5.1 Motion Filtering

The EMD method [35] can decompose any complicated data set into a finite and often small number of components. These components form a complete and nearly orthogonal basis for the original signal. Essentially, It is a multi-level de-noising process for signal, and can be described as intrinsic mode functions (IMF). Without leaving the time domain, EMD is adaptive and highly efficient. Since the decomposition is based on the local characteristic time scale of the data, it can be applied to nonlinear and nonstationary processes. Because the excellent de-noising characteristics, EMD has been widely used in the signal de-noising, is also used for motion filtering here.

Firstly, the estimated global motion parameters M is chosen as one criterion to evaluate the video jitter. EMD is applied on M, and the smoothing components are set as the motion filtering result. However, we found the motion filtering result of M is not satisfying when the jitter has very frequent tiny rotation component. The reason is: when the rotation component is very tiny, the filtering result is almost same to the original value, thus the compensation effect is very limited, and the human visual system still feel jittery when watching the compensated result. To alleviate this problem, an additional criterion should be chosen. Here we use the Euclidean distance of matched keypoints (EDMK) between adjacent frames as the second criterion, and the EMD is also used to smooth the x component and y component of EDMK.

Finally, the average of the filtering results by both criteria is set as the final result.

5.2 Motion Compensation

Firstly, the correction vector for the first criterion is obtained by computing the difference between original parameters M and filtering parameters $\hat{M}$. Then the motion compensation is applied by the correction vector as follows:

$$
\begin{aligned}
x_j &= (a_{1c}x_i + a_{2c}y_i + a_{3c})/(a_{7c}x_i + a_{8c}y_i + 1) \\
y_j &= (a_{4c}x_i + a_{5c}y_i + a_{6c})/(a_{7c}x_i + a_{8c}y_i + 1)
\end{aligned}
\tag{2}
$$

Where $(a_{1c}, a_{2c}, a_{3c}, a_{4c}, a_{5c}, a_{6c}, a_{7c}, a_{8c})$ is the correction vector, (x_i, y_i) is the pixel position before compensation, (x_j, y_j) is the pixel position after compensation.

Secondly, the correction vector for the second criterion is obtained by computing the difference between original EDMK and filtering EDMK. Then the motion compensation is applied by the correction vector as follows:

$$x_j = x_i + x_c \qquad y_j = y_i + y_c \tag{3}$$

Where (x_c, y_c) is the correction vector, (x_i, y_i) is the pixel position before compensation, (x_j, y_j) is the pixel position after compensation.

Finally, the coordinates of pixels are set as the average coordinates of the pixels compensated by the first evaluation criterion and the pixels compensated by the second evaluation criterion.

In addition, when features are tracked through consecutive frames, the relative error is cumulated, and the compensation process would drift by the cumulative error. To solve this problem, a re-initialization control strategy is adopted. The cumulative error of original image sequence updated to current frame (*cumulative error 1*) and the cumulative error of stabilized image sequence updated to current frame (*cumulative error 2*) are computed respectively. If the absolute difference between *cumulative error 1* and *cumulative error 2* is below a given threshold, the previous frame of stabilized image sequence is used as the reference frame, otherwise, the previous frame of original image sequence is used as the reference frame.

6 Video Completion

As stated before, the texture synthesis method [30, 31] searches the most similar texture patch around the missing image area to replace the unknown part in the original texture patch. However, because the similar information in the single image is usually not enough, it is hard to obtain satisfying result only by this method. In other word, there are plenty of interframe similar information among the adjacent frames of video. Therefore, the texture synthesis method can be improved if the interframe information is introduced. The way of combining them is: the most similar texture patch of an original texture patch A in the current frame is searched in the adjacent frames by the texture synthesis method [30]. If it is found, and the found texture patch is B in the adjacent frames, the neighbor texture patch of B will have the high priority to be the most similar texture patch of the neighbor texture patch of A during searching. If it is not found, it is searched in the current frame by the texture synthesis method [30].

7 Experiments

Experiments are conducted using a workstation with AMD Athlon (tm) II X4 640 3.01G, memory 2G, NVIDIA GT200 and CUDA 1.3. Two jittered videos are captured. The first is the video without moving object, and has 2476 frames, while the second is the video with moving object, and has 3124 frames.

As a special graphical processor, the computation performance and video memory bandwidth of GPU can be 10 times those of CPU. Therefore, the GPU+CPU framework [36] is used to achieve the real-time ability. Because the global motion estimation, motion filtering and compensation need large computation, they are implemented in GPU, while other parts are implemented in CPU. In addition, the GPU implement of SIFT [37] is used to accelerate the feature extraction.

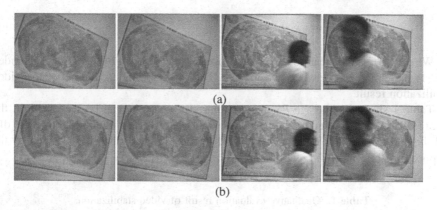

Fig. 2. (a) Current frames before video stabilization. (b) current frames after video stabilization.

Figure 2 shows the video stabilization results on the captured videos.

A video stabilization video can be downloaded from: http://staff.ustc.edu.cn/ ~harryjun/links/Video_Stabilization_1.avi. In addition, the real-time running process can be downloaded from: http://staff.ustc.edu.cn/ ~harryjun/links/Video_Stabilization_ 2.exe.

Figure 3 is the motion filtering results of M by EMD. They show the smoothing effect of EMD.

An index, peak signal-to-noise ratio ($PSNR$) between the reference frame S_0 and current frame S_1, is defined to evaluate the stabilization quality:

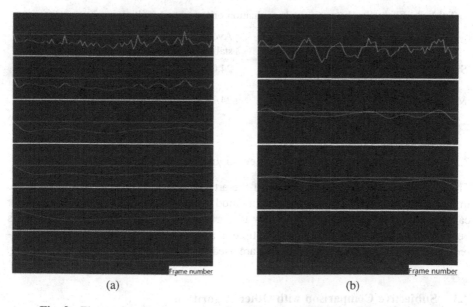

Fig. 3. The motion filtering results of a_3: (a) and a_6: (b) under different scales.

$$PSNR(S_1, S_0) = 10 \cdot \log_{10}^{255^2/MSE(S_1,S_0)} \tag{4}$$

Where *MSE* is the mean square error of pixel value between two images. This index reflects the coherence between two images. The large the index, the better the video stabilization result.

Table 1 show the average *PSNR* on captured videos. As can be seen from it, the average *PSNR* is increased by the proposed video stabilization method around 7.2 dB, and the real-time ability is also achieved. Therefore, jittered video is stabilized by the proposed method nicely in real-time.

Table 1. Qualitative evaluation result of video stabilization.

	Average *PSNR* of original videos	Average *PSNR* of stabilized videos	Average time each frame takes
Captured video	25.35	32.53	0.045 s

7.1 Using Single Evaluation Criterion Vs. Fusing Multiple Evaluation Criteria

The effect of fusing multiple evaluation criteria is verified on a video clip, in which some very frequent tiny rotation component is added. From Table 2, we can see the superiority of fusing multiple evaluation criteria.

Table 2. Evaluation between single evaluation criterion and multiple evaluation criteria.

	Average *PSNR* of original videos	Average *PSNR* of stabilized videos	Average time each frame takes
Single evaluation criterion	18.56	24.04	0.037 s
Multiple evaluation criteria	18.56	24.79	0.045 s

7.2 Objective Comparison with Other Algorithm

The method in [29] is one of the state-of-the-art video stabilization methods. We have implemented it, then it and the proposed method are tested on the above video clip. We can see the proposed method is superior to the method in [29] from Table 3. This is because the proposed method fuses multiple evaluation criteria to conduct motion filtering by EMD, and stable SIFT features are used to match the adjacent frames robustly.

7.3 Subjective Comparison with Other Algorithm

The problem with an objective evaluation is that the absolute truth of camera motion is not known. However, it is less problematic for the subjective evaluation since the

Table 3. Evaluation of several video stabilization algorithms.

	Average *PSNR* of original videos	Average *PSNR* of stabilized videos	Average time each frame takes
The proposed method	18.56	24.79	0.045 s
The method in [29]	18.56	24.21	0.053 s

human visual system is very sensitive to the video jitter. The video stabilization system is developed as Fig. 4 shows. The original video is displayed in the upper-left window, while the stabilized video is displayed in the upper-right window. Afterwards, user's reactions interacting with this system are evaluated.

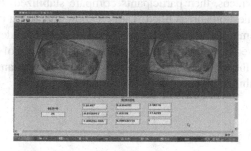

Fig. 4. Video stabilization system.

The participants in Table 4 are used. The goal of the evaluation is to decide if the system can remove the discomfort on human visual system, and if the objects in the stabilized video can be identified easily.

Table 4. Distributions of participants.

Construct	Profiles	Distribution
Age	1. Younger than 20. 2. Between 20 and 30. 3. Older than 30.	8/18/8
Gender	1. Male. 2. Female.	20/14
Dialect background	1. Northeastern. 2. Beijing. 3. Zhongyuan. 4. Southwestern. 5. Xiang. 6. Gan. 7. Minnan. 8. Cantonese. 9. Jilu. 10. Guiliu Pian. 11. Wu.	2/3/7/3/2/3/ 2/4/3/1/4

In the first stage, the questionnaire is chosen for participants. Table 5 shows the constructs and questions of the survey related to the system performance. The answers to these questions are given from 'disagree' to 'agree' on a ten point scale. A Cronbach's alpha test [38] is carried out to determine if these constructs refer to the same topic. Typically, an alpha of 0.7 or greater is considered acceptable in psychological experiments. As Table 5 shows, all the alpha values obtained are greater than 0.7, indicating that the questionnaire is suitable for the evaluation in this paper.

Table 5. Cronbach's alpha results of questionnaire and mean scores after evaluation.

Construct	Question	Cronbach's alpha	Mean score of the proposed method	Mean score of the method in [29]
Smoothness	If the stabilized video is smooth and coherent.	0.743	7.87	6.73
Identification	If objects in the stabilized video can be identified easily.	0.811	7.83	6.48

In the second stage, the developed system and the method in [29] perform stabilization on captured videos, then participants compare stabilized videos with original videos. Finally, the questionnaire is filled. Table 5 shows the result of mean scores after evaluation. The maximum is 10, while the minimum is 0. For the developed system, all the scores obtained are greater than 7.5, and are higher than those of the method in [29], indicating that it has the ability to remove the discomfort on human visual system, and the objects in the stabilized video can be identified easily.

8   Conclusion

A real-time robust video stabilization system is proposed. The stable SIFT features are used to match the adjacent frames robustly. Global motion parameters are obtained by RANSAC to exclude wrong matches or correct matches that indeed belong to self-moving objects in the filmed scene effectively. Multiple evaluation criteria are fused to conduct motion filtering by EMD. The spatio-temporal information are combined with the texture synthesis method to obtain a complete video.

In future, the accuracy of global motion estimation will be further improved.

Acknowledgements. This work was supported by the National Natural Science Foundation of China (No. 61303150), the Open Project Program of the State Key Lab of CAD&CG (No. A1501), Zhejiang University.

References

1. Ejaz, N., Wonil, K., Soon II, K., et al.: Video stabilization by detecting intentional and unintentional camera motions. In: International Conference on Intelligent Systems, Modelling and Simulation, pp. 312–316. IEEE Press, New York (2012)
2. Chen, C.H., Chen, C.Y., Chen, C.H., et al.: Real-time video stabilization based on vibration compensation by using feature block. Int. J. Innovative Comput. Inf. Control **7**, 5285–5298 (2011)
3. Seok-Jae, K., Tae-Shick, W., Dae-Hwan, K., et al.: Video stabilization based on motion segmentation. In: IEEE International Conference on Consumer Electronics, pp. 416–417. IEEE Press, New York (2012)

4. Dung, T.V., Lertrattanapanich, S., Cao, B.T., et al.: Real time video stabilization with reduced temporal mismatch and low frame buffer. In: IEEE International Conference on Consumer Electronics, pp. 61–62. IEEE Press, New York (2012)
5. Puglisi, G., Battiato, S.: A robust image alignment algorithm for video stabilization purposes. IEEE Trans. Circuits Syst. Video Technol. **21**, 1390–1400 (2011)
6. Puglisi, G., Battiato, S.: Robust video stabilization approach based on a voting strategy. In: IEEE International Conference on Image Processing, pp. 629–632. IEEE Press, New York (2011)
7. Abraham, S.C., Thomas, M.R., Basheer, R., et al.: A novel approach for video stabilization. In: IEEE Recent Advances in Intelligent Computational Systems, vol. 1, pp. 134-137 (2011)
8. Uomori, K., Morimura, A., Ishii, H.: Electronic image stabilization system for video cameras and VCRs. J. Soc. Motion Picture Telev. Eng. **101**, 66–75 (1992)
9. Pail, J.K., Park, Y.C., Kim, D.W.: An adaptive motion decision system for digital image stabilizer based on edge pattern matching. IEEE Trans. Consum. Electron. **38**, 607–615 (1992)
10. Burt, A., Anandan, P.: Image stabilization by registration to a reference mosaic. In: Proceedings of ARPA Image Understanding Workshop, pp. 425–434. IEEE Press, New York (1994)
11. Morimoto, C., Chellappa, R.: Fast electronic digital image stabilization for off-road navigation. Real-Time Imaging **2**, 285–296 (1996)
12. Ko, S.J., Lee, S.H., Lee, K.H.: Digital image stabilizing algorithms based on bit-plane matching. IEEE Trans. Consum. Electron. **44**, 617–622 (1998)
13. Ko, S.J., Lee, S.H., Jeon, S.W., Kang, E.S.: Fast digital image stabilizer based on gray-coded bit-plane matching. IEEE Trans. Consum. Electron. **45**, 598–603 (1999)
14. Erturk, S., Dennis, T.J.: Image sequence stabilization based on DFT filtering. IEE Proc. Image Vision Signal Proc. **127**, 95–102 (2000)
15. Bosco, A., Bruna, A., Battiato, S., Bella, G.D.: Video stabilization through dynamic analysis of frames signatures. In: IEEE International Conference on Consumer Electronics, pp. 312–316. IEEE Press, New York (2006)
16. Censi, A., Fusiello, A., Roberto, V.: Image stabilization by features tracking. In: International Conference on Image Analysis and Processing, pp. 2354–2361. IEEE Press, New York (1999)
17. Veon, K.L., Mahoor, M.H., Voyles, R.M.: Video stabilization using SIFT-ME features and fuzzy clustering. In: IEEE/RSJ International Conference on Intelligent Robots and Systems, pp. 2377–2382. IEEE Press, New York (2011)
18. Windau, J., Itti, L.: Multilayer real-time video image stabilization. IEEE/RSJ International Conference on Intelligent Robots and Systems, pp. 2397–2402. IEEE Press, New York (2011)
19. Erturk, S.: Image sequence stabilization based on kalman filtering of frame positions. Electron. Lett. **37**, 95–102 (2001)
20. Paik, P.: An adaptive motion decision system for digital image stabilizer based on edge pattern matching. In: Consumer Electronics, Digest of Technical Papers (1992)
21. Auberger, S., Miro, C.: Digital video stabilization architecture for low cost devices. In: Proceedings of the 4th International Symposium on Image and Signal Processing and Analysis, pp. 474-483. IEEE Press, New York (2005)
22. Tico, M., Vehvilainen, M.: Constraint translational and rotational motion filtering for video stabilization. In: Proceedings of the 13th European Signal Processing Conference, pp. 1474-1483. IEEE Press, New York (2005)

23. Zhiyong, H., Fazhi H., Xiantao C., et al.: A 2D-3D hybrid approach to video stabilization. In: International Conference on Computer-Aided Design and Computer Graphics, pp. 146–150. IEEE Press, New York (2011)

24. Litvin, A., Konrad, J., Karl, W.: Probabilistic video stabilization using kalman filtering and mosaicking. In: Proceedings of IS&T/SPIE Symposium Electronic Imaging, Image, and Video Communications, pp. 663–674. IEEE Press, New York (2003)

25. Wexler, Y., Shechtman, E., Irani, M.: Space-time video completion. In: Proceedings of IEEE Conference on Computer Vision and Pattern Recognition, pp. 120–127. IEEE Press, New York (2004)

26. Jia, J., Wu, T., Tai, Y., Tang, C.: Video repairing: inference of foreground and background under severe occlusion. Proceedings of IEEE Conference on Computer Vision and Pattern Recognition, pp. 364–371. IEEE Press, New York (2004)

27. Cheung, S.C.S., Zhao, J., Venkatesh M.V.: Efficient object-based video in painting. In: IEEE International Conference on Image Processing, pp. 705–708. IEEE Press, New York (2006)

28. Cheung, V., Frey, B.J., Jojic, N.: Video Epitomes. In: Proceedings of IEEE Conference on Computer Vision and Pattern Recognition, pp. 42–49. IEEE Press, New York (2005)

29. Matsushita, Y., Ofek, E., Ge, W.N., et al.: Full-frame video stabilization with motion inpainting. IEEE Trans. Pattern Anal. Machine Intelligence. **28**, 1150–1163 (2006)

30. Criminisi, A., Perez, P., Toyama, K.: Region filling and object removal by exemplar-based image inpainting. IEEE Trans. Image Process. **13**, 1200–1212 (2004)

31. Tang, F., Ying, Y.T., Wang, J., et al.: A novel texture synthesis based algorithm for object removal in photographs. In: Proceedings of 9th Asian Computing Science Conference, pp. 248-258. IEEE Press, New York (2005)

32. Battiato, S., Gallo, G., Puglisi, G., Scellato, S.: SIFT features tracking for video stabilization. In: International Conference on Image Analysis and Processing, pp. 2255–2258. IEEE Press, New York (2007)

33. Lowe, D.: Distinctive image features from scale-invariant keypoints. Int. J. Comput. Vision **60**, 91–110 (2004)

34. Hoper, P.J.: Robust statistical procedures. SIAM, Philadelphia (1996)

35. Huang, N.E., Shen, Z., Long, S.R., et al.: The empirical mode decomposition and the Hilbert spectrum for nun-linear and non-stationary time series analysis. Proc. R. Soc. Lond. A **454**, 903–995 (1998)

36. Juang, C., Chen, T., Cheng, W.: Speedup of implementing fuzzy neural networks with high-dimensional inputs through parallel processing on graphic processing units. IEEE Trans. Fuzzy Syst. **19**, 717–728 (2011)

37. http://cs.unc.edu/~ccwu/siftgpu/

38. Marcosa, S., Gómez-García-Bermejob, J., Zalama, E.: A realistic, virtual head for human-computer interaction. Interact. Comput. **22**, 176–192 (2010)

Real-Time Underwater Image Contrast Enhancement Through Guided Filtering

Huimin Lu[1,2]($\boxtimes$), Yujie Li[1,2], Xuelong Hu[2], Shiyuan Yang[1],
and Seiichi Serikawa[1]

[1] Kyushu Institute of Technology, Kitakyushu, Japan
rikukeibin@gmail.com
[2] Yangzhou University, Yangzhou, China

Abstract. Absorption, scattering, and color distortion are three major issues in underwater optical imaging. In this paper, we propose a novel underwater imaging model that compensates for the attenuation discrepancy along the propagation path. In addition, we develop a fast weighted guided filtering algorithm for enhancing underwater optical transmission map. The final enhanced images are characterized by a reduced noised level, better exposure in dark regions, and improved global contrast, by which the finest details and edges are enhanced significantly. Our experiments show that with the use of our proposed algorithm, the peak signal-to-noise ratio is improved by at least 2 dB compared to existing state-of-the-art methods. The structural similarity index is improved by about 0.01.

1 Introduction

With the development of exploring the ocean by unmanned underwater vehicles (UUVs), the recognition of underwater objects is known as a major issue. That is, how to acquire a clear underwater image is a question. In the past years, sonar has been widely used for the detection and recognition of objects in underwater environment. Because of acoustic imaging principle, the sonar images have the shortcomings of low signal to ratio, low resolution et al. Consequently, optical vision sensors must be used instead for short-range identification because of the low quality of images restored by sonar imaging [1].

In contrast to common photographs, underwater optical images suffer from poor visibility owing to the medium, which causes scattering, color distortion, and absorption. Large suspended particles cause scattering similar to the scattering of light in fog or turbid water that contain many suspended particles. Color distortion occurs because different wavelengths are attenuated to different degrees in water; consequently, images of ambient underwater environments are dominated by a bluish tone, because higher wavelengths are attenuated more quickly. Absorption of light in water substantially reduces its intensity. The random attenuation of light causes a hazy appearance as the light backscattered by water along the line of sight considerably degrades image contrast. In particular, objects at a distance of more than 10 m from the observation point are

© Springer International Publishing Switzerland 2015
Y.-J. Zhang (Ed.): ICIG 2015, Part III, LNCS 9219, pp. 137–147, 2015.
DOI: 10.1007/978-3-319-21969-1_12

almost indistinguishable because colors are faded as characteristic wavelengths are filtered according to the distance traveled by light in water [2].

Many researchers have developed techniques to restore and enhance underwater images. Most of the recent approaches can enhance the image contrast, they have several drawbacks that reduce their practical applicability. First, the imaging equipment is difficult to use in practice (e.g., a range-gated laser imaging system, which is rarely applied in practice [3,4]). Second, multiple input images are required [5] (e.g., different polarization images or different exposed images) for fusing a high-quality image. Third, the image processing approaches are not suitable for underwater images [6–8] as they ignore the imaging environment, in addition to being time consuming. Fourth, manual operation is needed in processing, which leads to lack of intelligence [9].

Instead of multiple input images, we focus on enhancement methods which use a single optical image. Fattal [9] estimated the scene radiance and derived the transmission image using a single image. However, this method cannot be used for sufficiently process images with heavy haze. It also needs manual operation, which limits the application scope. He et al. [7] analyzed abundant natural sky images, found that it contains a dark channel in most color images, and proposed a scene-depth-information-based dark channel prior dehazing algorithm. However, this algorithm requires significant computation time with a complexity of $O(N2)$, and the processed images may have artificial halos in some cases. To overcome this disadvantage, He et al. also proposed a guided image filter [10], which used the foggy image as a reference image. However, this method leads to incomplete haze removal and does not meet the requirements for real-time processing. Ancuti et al. [11] compared Laplacian contrast, contrast, saliency, and exposedness features between a white-balanced image and color-corrected image. Then, they utilized the exposure fusion algorithm to obtain the final result. However, this method has two main disadvantages: images are obtained with dark corners and processing parameters are difficult to set, which is problematic because the exposure blending algorithm used is sensitive to the parameters set. In Serikawa's work [12], we proposed a guided trigonometric filter to refine the depth map. The optimization algorithm can achieve better results with a peak signal-to-noise ratio (PSNR) improved by 1 dB compared to traditional methods. However, this method does not take the wavelength into account.

In an underwater environment, the captured images are significantly influenced by inherent optical properties (e.g., wavelength, scatter, and absorption). Inspired by Chiang's work [13], in the present paper, we propose a novel shallow-ocean optical imaging model and a corresponding enhancement algorithm. We first estimate the depth map through dark channels. Second, considering the positions of the lighting lamp, camera, and imaging plane, we develop a rational imaging model. The effects of scattering are removed by using a guided weighted median filter (GWMF). Finally, color correction is performed by spectral properties. In our experiments conducted for verifying our proposed model and algorithm, we used a commercial RGB camera and natural underwater light. The performance of the proposed method is evaluated both analytically and experimentally.

2 Shallow Water Imaging Model

Artificial light and atmospheric light traveling through the water are the sources of illumination in a shallow ocean environment. The amount of radiation light $W(x)$ formed after wavelength attenuation can be formulated according to the energy attenuation model as follows [13],

$$E_\lambda^W(x) = E_\lambda^A(x) \cdot Nrer(\lambda)^{D(x)} + E_\lambda^I(x) \cdot Nrer(\lambda)^{L(x)},$$
$$\lambda \in \{r, g, b\} \tag{1}$$

At the scene point x, the artificial light reflected again travels distance $L(x)$ to the camera forming pixel $I_\lambda(x)$, $\lambda \in \{r, g, b\}$. $D(x)$ is the scene depth underwater. The color distortion (absorption) and scattering are occurred in this process. We suppose the absorption and scattering rate is $\rho(x)$, artificial light $J_\lambda(x)$ emanated from point x is equal to the amount of illuminating ambient light $E_\lambda^\omega(x)$ reflected,

$$E_\lambda^\omega(x) = \left(E_\lambda^A(x) \cdot Nrer(\lambda)^{D(x)} + E_\lambda^I(x) \cdot Nrer(\lambda)^{L(x)}\right) \cdot \rho_\lambda(x),$$
$$\lambda \in \{r, g, b\} \tag{2}$$

By following the underwater dehazing model [14], the image $I_\lambda(x)$ formed at the camera can be formulated as follows:

$$I_\lambda(x) = \left[\left(E_\lambda^A(x) \cdot Nrer(\lambda)^{D(x)} + E_\lambda^I(x) \cdot Nrer(\lambda)^{L(x)}\right) \cdot \rho_\lambda(x)\right] \cdot t_\lambda(x)$$
$$+ (1 - t_\lambda(x)) \cdot B_\lambda, \quad \lambda \in \{r, g, b\} \tag{3}$$

where the background B_λ represents the part of the object reflected light J_λ and ambient light E_λ^W scattered toward the camera by particles in the water. The residual energy ratio $t_\lambda(x)$ can be represented alternatively as the energy of a light beam with wavelength λ before and after traveling distance $d(x)$ within the water $E_\lambda^{residual}(x)$ and $E_\lambda^{initial}(x)$, respectively, as follows:

$$t_\lambda(x) = \frac{E_\lambda^{residual}(x)}{E_\lambda^{initial}(x)} = 10^{-\beta(\lambda)d(x)} = Nrer(\lambda)^{d(x)} \tag{4}$$

where $Nrer$ is the normalized residual energy ratio [12], in the Ocean Type I, it follows:

$$Nrer(\lambda) = \begin{cases} 0.8 \sim 0.85 & if \ \lambda = 650 \sim 750 \ \mu m (red) \\ 0.93 \sim 0.97 & if \ \lambda = 490 \sim 550 \ \mu m (green) \\ 0.95 \sim 0.99 & if \ \lambda = 400 \sim 490 \ \mu m (blue) \end{cases} \tag{5}$$

Consequently, subscribing the Eq. (3) and (4), we can obtain:

$$I_\lambda(x) = \left[\left(E_\lambda^A(x) \cdot Nrer(\lambda)^{D(x)} + E_\lambda^I(x) \cdot Nrer(\lambda)^{L(x)}\right) \cdot \rho_\lambda(x)\right]$$
$$\cdot Nrer(\lambda)^{d(x)} + \left(1 - Nrer(\lambda)^{d(x)}\right) \cdot B_\lambda, \quad \lambda \in \{r, g, b\} \tag{6}$$

The above equation incorporates light scattering during the course of propagation from object to the camera $d(x)$, and the wavelength attenuation along both the light-object path $L(x)$, scene depth $D(x)$ and object-camera path $d(x)$. Once the light-object distance $L(x)$, scene depth $D(x)$ and object-camera distance $d(x)$ is known, the final clean image will be recovered. Figure 1 shows the diagrammatic sketch of the proposed model.

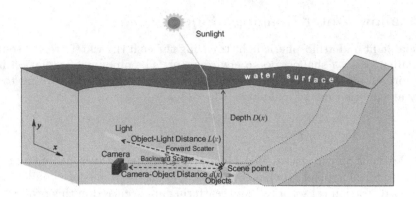

Fig. 1. Diagram of shallow ocean optical imaging model

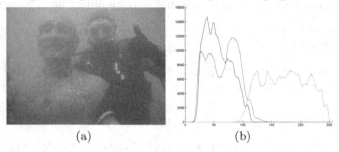

(a)   (b)

Fig. 2. RGB histogram of Underwater Image. (a) Underwater image. (b) RGB Histogram

3   Underwater Scene Reconstruction

3.1   Camera-Object Distance Estimation

In [13], the author found the red color channel is the dark channel of underwater images. During our experiments, we found that the lowest channel of RGB channels in turbidly water is not always the red color channel; the blue color channel is also very significant. The reason is that we usually take the artificial light in imaging. Although the red wavelength absorbed easily through traveling in water, the distance between the camera and object is not enough to absorb the red wavelength significantly (See Fig. 2). The blue channel may be the lowest. Consequently, in this paper, we take the minimum pixel value as the rough depth map.

As mentioned in Eq. (6), light $J_\lambda(x)$ reflected from point x is

$$J_\lambda(x) = \left(E_\lambda^A(x) \cdot Nrer(\lambda)^{D(x)} + E_\lambda^I(x) \cdot Nrer(\lambda)^{L(x)} \right) \cdot \rho_\lambda(x),$$
$$\lambda \in \{r, b\} \tag{7}$$

We define the minimum pixel channel $J_{dark}(x)$ for the underwater image $J_\lambda(x)$ as

$$J_{dark}(x) = \min_\lambda \min_{y \in \Omega(x)} J_\lambda(y), \lambda \in \{r, b\} \tag{8}$$

If point x belongs to a part of the foreground object, the value of the minimum pixel channel is very small. Taking the min operation in the local patch $\Omega(x)$ on the hazy image $I_\lambda(x)$ in Eq. (6), we have

$$
\min_{y\in\Omega(x)} (I_\lambda(y)) = \min_{y\in\Omega(x)} \left\{ J_\lambda(y)\cdot Nrer(\lambda)^{d(y)} + \left(1 - Nrer(\lambda)^{d(y)}\right)\cdot B_\lambda \right\},
$$
$$
\lambda \in \{r,b\} \tag{9}
$$

Since B_λ is the homogeneous background light and the residual energy ratio $Nrer(\lambda)^{d(y)}$ on the small local patch $\Omega(x)$ surrounding point x is essentially a constant $Nrer(\lambda)^{d(x)}$, the min value on the second term of Eq. (9) can be subsequently removed as

$$
\min_{y\in\Omega(x)} (I_\lambda(y)) = \min_{y\in\Omega(x)} \left\{ J_\lambda(y)\cdot Nrer(\lambda)^{d(x)} + \left(1 - Nrer(\lambda)^{d(x)}\right)\cdot B_\lambda \right\},
$$
$$
\lambda \in \{r,b\} \tag{10}
$$

We rearrange the above equation and perform on more min operation among red color channel and blue channel as follows:

$$
\min_\lambda \left\{ \frac{\min_{y\in\Omega(x)}(I_\lambda(y))}{B_\lambda} \right\} = \min_\lambda \left\{ \frac{\min\limits_{y\in\Omega(x)} J_\lambda(y)}{B_\lambda} \cdot Nrer(\lambda)^{d(x)} \right\}
$$
$$
+ \min_\lambda \left(1 - Nrer(\lambda)^{d(x)}\right), \lambda \in \{r,b\} \tag{11}
$$

Therefore, the second term of the above equation is dark channel equal to 0. Consequently, the estimated depth map is

$$
\min_\lambda \left(Nrer(\lambda)^{d(x)} \right) = 1 - \min_\lambda \left\{ \frac{\min_{y\in\Omega(x)} (I_\lambda(y))}{B_\lambda} \right\}, \lambda \in \{r,b\} \tag{12}
$$

3.2   Depth Map Refinement by GWMF

In the above subsection, we roughly estimated the camera-object distance $d(x)$. This distance depth contains mosaic effects and produces less accurately. Consequently, we need to use the proposed guided weighted median filter to reduce the mosaicking. In this section, we introduce our constant time algorithm for weighted guided median filter at first.

The traditional median filter has been considered as an effective way of removing "outliers". The traditional median filter usually leads to morphological artifacts like rounding sharp corners. To address this problem, the weighted median filter [15] has been proposed. The weighted median filter is defined as

$$
h(\mathbf{x},i) = \sum_{y\in N(\mathbf{x})} W(\mathbf{x},\mathbf{y})\delta(V(\mathbf{y}) - i) \tag{13}
$$

where $W(\mathbf{x},\mathbf{y})$ corresponds to the weight assigned to a pixel $\mathbf{y}$ inside a local region centered at pixel x, the weight $W(\mathbf{x},\mathbf{y})$ depends on the image d that can be different from V. $N(\mathbf{x})$ is a local window near pixel $\mathbf{x}$. i is the discrete bin index, and δ is the Kronecker delta function, δ is 1 when the argument is 0, and is 0 otherwise.

Then the compute the refined depth map by guided weighted median filter is defined as:

$$I_x^{WG} = \frac{\sum_{y \in N(x)} f_S(x,y) f_R(I_x, I_y) I_y W_y}{\sum_{y \in N(x)} f_S(x,y) f_R(I_x, I_y) W_y} \tag{14}$$

where y is a pixel in the neighborhood $N(x)$ of pixel x. Note that kernels other than Gaussian kernels are not excluded.

$$f_S(x,y) = \upsilon(x-y) = \tfrac{1}{2} e^{-\frac{(x-y)(x-y)}{2\sigma_D^2}} \tag{15}$$

where x and y denote pixel spatial positions. The spatial scale is set by σ_D. The range filter weights pixels based on the photometric difference,

$$f_R(I_x, I_y) = w(f(x) - f(y)) = \frac{1}{2} e^{-\frac{(f(x)-f(y))(f(x)-f(y))}{2\sigma_R^2}} \tag{16}$$

where $f(\bullet)$ is image tonal values. The degree of tonal filter is set by σ_R. W_y is the weight map, which is defined as:

$$W_y = \sum_{y \in N(x)} f_s(y,q) f_R(y,q) e^{-(\|I_y - I_q\|_2)/2\sigma_R} \tag{17}$$

where q is the coordinate of support pixel centered around pixel y. The final refined depth map is produced by:

$$h(\tilde{d}(x), i) = \sum_{\mathbf{y} \in N(\mathbf{x})} I_x^{WG}(d(x), x) \delta(V(x) - i) \tag{18}$$

This filters images, preserving edges and filters noise based on a dimensionality reduction strategy, having high quality results, while achieving significant speedups over existing techniques, such as bilateral filter [10], guided filter [14], trilateral filter [16] and weighted bilateral median filter [15]. The refined depth image is shown in Fig. 3.

3.3   De-scattering

From above subsection, we obtained the refined depth map $d(x)$. In order to remove the scatter, we also need to solve the reflectivity $\rho_\lambda (x)$. We take the least squares solution for achieving this by

$$\rho_\lambda(x) = \left(J_\lambda(x)^T \cdot J_\lambda(x)\right)^{-1} \cdot J_\lambda(x)^T$$
$$\cdot \left(E_\lambda^A(x) \cdot Nrer(\lambda)^{D(x)} + E_\lambda^I(x) \cdot Nrer(\lambda)^{L(x)}\right), \quad \lambda \in \{r, g, b\} \tag{19}$$

After removing the artificial light, the Eq. (6) can be written as

$$I_\lambda(x) = E_\lambda^A(x) \cdot Nrer(\lambda)^{D(x)} \cdot \rho_\lambda(x) \cdot Nrer(\lambda)^{d(x)}$$
$$+ \left(1 - Nrer(\lambda)^{d(x)}\right) \cdot B_\lambda, \quad \lambda \in \{r, g, b\} \tag{20}$$

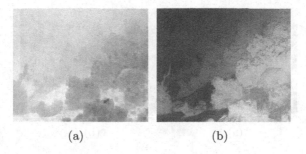

(a)   (b)

Fig. 3. Depth map refinement by weighted normalized convolution domain filter. (a) Input course depth image. (b) Refined depth image.

According to dehazing model, we can obtain the descattered image by

$$\tilde{J}_\lambda(x) = \frac{I_\lambda(x) - \left(1 - Nrer(\lambda)^{d(x)}\right) \cdot B_\lambda}{Nrer(\lambda)^{d(x)}}$$
$$= E_\lambda^A(x) \cdot Nrer(\lambda)^{D(x)} \cdot \rho_\lambda(x) \cdot Nrer(\lambda)^{d(x)}, \quad \lambda \in \{r, g, b\} \tag{21}$$

In this paper, we assume the light for imaging is uniform. Consequently, we need not to correct the vignetting effects here (Fig. 4).

(a)   (b)

Fig. 4. De-scattered result. (a) Input image. (b) De-scattered image.

3.4   Color Correction

In [13], the author simply corrected the scene color by the attenuation of water depth. However, in practice, the spectral response function of a camera maps the relative sensitivity of the camera imaging system as a function of the wavelength of the light. We take the chromatic transfer function τ for weighting the light from the surface to a given depth of objects as

$$\tau_\lambda = \frac{E_\lambda^{surface}}{E_\lambda^{object}} \tag{22}$$

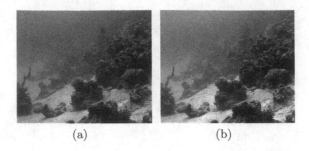

(a)   (b)

Fig. 5. Color correction result. (a) Input image. (b) Color corrected image

where the transfer function τ at wavelength λ is derived from the irradiance of surface $E_\lambda^{surface}$ by the irradiance of the object E_λ^{object}. Based on the spectral response of RGB camera, we convert the transfer function to RGB domain:

$$\tau_{RGB} = \sum^{k} \tau_\lambda \cdot C_c(\lambda) \tag{23}$$

where the weighted RGB transfer function is τ_{RGB}, $C_c(\lambda)$ is the underwater spectral characteristic function for color band c, $c \in \{r, g, b\}$. k is the number of discrete bands of the camera spectral characteristic function.

Finally, the corrected image as gathered from the weighted RGB transfer function by

$$J_\lambda(x) = \hat{J}_\lambda(x) \cdot \tau_{RGB} \tag{24}$$

where $J_\lambda(x)$ and $\hat{J}_\lambda(x)$ are the color corrected and uncorrected images respectively. Figure 6 shows the color corrected result.

4   Experiments and Discussions

The performance of the proposed algorithm is evaluated both objectively and subjectively, utilizing ground-truth color patches. We also compare the proposed method with the state-of-the-art methods. Both results demonstrate superior haze removal and color balancing capabilities of the proposed method over the others.

In simulation experiment, Fig. 5 shows the results, and Table 1 shows the quantitative analysis results. In the simulation, we take OLYMPUS Tough TG-2 underwater camera, the water depth $D(x)$ is 0.3 m, camera-object distance $d(x)$ is 0.8 m, light-object distance $L(x)$ is 0.5 m. Firstly, we take the shallow scene in clean water. Then, we captured the noisy image by adding some turbid liquid in the tank. The computer used is equipped with Windows XP and an Intel Core 2 (2.0 GHz) with 2 GB RAM. The size of the images is 416 × 512 pixels.

Bazeille's method simply used image processing technologies, which ignored the physical model of underwater, distorted the image seriously. While Fattal's

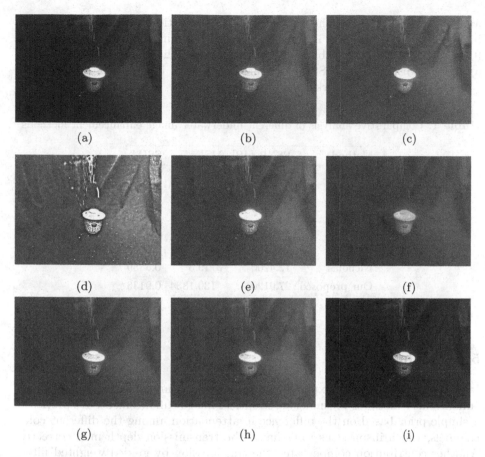

Fig. 6. Simulation results by different algorithms. (a) Noise-free image. (b) Noisy image. (c) Ancuti's result. (d) Bazeille's result. (e) Chiang's result. (f) Fattal's result. (g) He's result. (h) Nicholas's result. (i) Our result.

approach performs well, however, it needed manually operation for determine the background and objects. The algorithms proposed by Nicholas and He are very time consuming, with the computation complex over $O(N^2)$. Ancuti et al. took the high dynamic range imaging ideas for underwater enhancement. The enhanced image relays on the pre-processed white balance image and color corrected image, which may be based on a wrong assumption. Chiang et al. firstly recommend the effects of wavelength is highly influence the underwater images. However, the Laplacian matting for depth map refinement is time consuming, and also neglected the fact that color distortion is corrected to the scene depth, camera spectral properties, and inherent optical properties. The processing time of our method is 15.4 ms, and the result also superior than the others.

In addition to the visual analysis mentioned above, we conducted quantitative analysis, mainly from the perspective of mathematical statistics and the statistical parameters for the images (see Table 1). This analysis includes PSNR, and SSIM. PSNR means the peak signal to noise ratio (values are over 0, the higher the best), and SSIM is named as structural similarity (values are between 0 (worst) to 1 (best)). Table 1 displays the values that have been filtered by applying MSE,PSNR and SSIM measured on several images. The results indicate that our approach works well for haze removal.

Table 1. Comparative analysis of different underwater image enhancement methods

Methods	PSNR [dB]	MSE	SSIM
Ancuti	10.7715	5444.2	0.5530
Bazeille	9.5787	7164.9	0.4330
Chiang	11.7472	4348.7	0.5198
Fattal	13.9595	2612.9	0.6338
He	14.3188	2400.5	0.6653
Nicholas	12.4260	3719.5	0.5859
Our proposed	27.0120	130.1834	0.9136

5   Conclusions

In this paper, we have explored and successfully implemented novel image enhancement methods for underwater optical image enhancement. We proposed a simple prior based on the difference in attenuation among the different color channels, which inspired us to estimate the transmission depth map correctly. Another contribution compensated the transmission by guided weighted filter, which has the benefits of edge-preserving, noise removing, and a reduction in the computation time. Moreover, the proposed spectral-based underwater image color correction method successfully recover the underwater distorted images. Furthermore, the proposed method had solved the limitation of the influence of possible artificial light sources. Abundant experiments present the proposed method is suitable for underwater imaging, and solve the major problem of underwater optical imaging.

Acknowledgement. This work was partially supported by Grant in Aid for Japan Society for the Promotion of Science (No.15F15077), Research Fund of State Key Laboratory of Ocean Engineering in Shanghai Jiaotong University (OEK1315), Research Fund of State Key Laboratory of Marine Geology in Tongji University (MGK1407), and Grant in Aid for Japan Society for the Promotion of Science (No.13J10713).

References

1. Kocak, D.M., Dalglcish, F.R., Caimi, F.M., Yoav, S.: A focus on recent developments and trends in underwater imaging. Mar. Technol. Soc. J. **42**, 52–67 (2008)

2. Schettini, R., Corchs, S.: Underwater image processing: state of the art of restoration and image enhancement methods. EURASIP J. Adv. Signal Process. **2010**, 1–14 (2010)
3. Hou, W., Gray, D.J., Weidemann, A.D., Fournier, G.R., Forand, J.L.: Automated underwater image restoration and retrieval of related optical properties. In: Proceedings of IEEE International Symposium of Geoscience and Remote Sensing, pp. 1889–1892 (2007)
4. Ouyang, B., Dalgleish, F.R., Caimi, F.M., Vuorenkoski, A.K., Giddings, T.E., Shirron, J.J.: Image enhancement for underwater pulsed laser line scan imaging system. In: Proceedings of SPIE 8372, pp. 83720R1-83720R8 (2012)
5. Schechner, Y.Y., Karpel, N.: Recovery of underwater visibility and structure by polarization analysis. IEEE J. Ocean. Eng. **30**, 570–587 (2005)
6. Bazeille, S., Quidu, I., Jaulin, L., Malkasse, J.P. : Automatic underwater image pre-processing. In: Proceedings of Caracterisation Du Milieu Marin (CMM06), pp. 1–8 (2006)
7. He, K., Sun, J., Tang, X.: Single image haze removal using dark channel prior. IEEE Trans. Pattern Anal. Mach. Intell. **33**(2), 2341–2353 (2011)
8. C.B. Nicholas, M. Anush, R.E.: Initial results in underwater single image dehazing. In: Proceedings of IEEE OCEANS 2010, pp. 1–8 (2010)
9. Fattal, R.: Single image dehazing. ACM Trans. Graph. **27**, 1–8 (2008)
10. Tomasi, C., Manduchi, R.: Bilateral filtering for gray and color images. In: Proceeding of the IEEE International Conference on Computer Vision(ICCV 1998), pp. 839–846 (1998)
11. Ancuti, C., Ancuti, C.O., Haber, T., Bekaert, P.: Enhancing underwater images and videos by fusion. In: Proceedings of IEEE Conference on Computer Vision and Pattern Recognition (CVPR 2012), pp. 81–88 (2012)
12. Serikawa, S., Lu, H.: Underwater image dehazing using joint trilateral filter. Comput. Electr. Eng. **40**, 41–50 (2014)
13. Chiang, J., Chen, Y.: Underwater image enhancement by wavelength compensation and dehazing. IEEE Trans. Image Process. **21**, 1756–1769 (2012)
14. He, K., Sun, J., Tang, X.: Guided image filtering. IEEE Trans. Pattern Anal. Mach. Intell. **35**, 1397–1409 (2013)
15. Yang, Q., Ahuja, N., Yang, R., Tan, K.H., Davis, J., Culbertson, B., Wang, G.: Fusion of median and bilateral filtering for range image upsampling. IEEE Trans. Image Process. **22**(12), 4841–4852 (2013)
16. Lu, H., Li, Y., Serikawa, S.: Underwater image enhancement using guided trigonometric bilateral filter and fast automation color correction. In: Proceedings of 20th IEEE International Conference on Image Processing (ICIP2013), pp. 3412–3416 (2013)

Recent Progress of Structural Variations Detection Algorithms Based on Next-Generation Sequencing: A Survey

Zhen-Le Wei[✉]

Bio-Computing Research Center, Shenzhen Graduate School,
Harbin Institute of Technology, Harbin, China
weizhenle013@foxmail.com

Abstract. Structural variations (SVs) are one of the genetic markers in the human genome and detecting them by using ultra high-throughput genome sequencing techniques has vital significance for genetic and evolutionary studies. In recent decades, bioinformatics techniques based on next-generation sequencing (NGS) have become a research focus owing to its high resolution and accuracy. Moreover, NGS devices are becoming cheaper. In this survey, we will summarize current methods based on next-generation sequencing algorithms for SVs detection and discuss the impacts of them. We also analyze the problems and give an outlook for the future research directions.

Keywords: Next-generation sequencing · Structural variations · Bioinformatics algorithm

1 Introduction

In recent years, studies have shown that a diverse array of genetic variation occur in the human genome. Studies on these variations will not only help to reveal a large number of complex diseases and to find the genetic mechanism associated with individuals but also speed up the pace of personalized medicine. The genetic variation is simply classified into two kinds: single nucleotide polymorphism (SNP) and structural variation (SV). Since the last quarter of the twentieth century, SNP has long been regarded as the most common genetic variation in human genomic and widely studied [1], and identified by traditional PCR-based methods. On the other hand, several types of genetic variations, including insertions or deletions and copy number variations (CNVs) are also widespread in human genomes [2], which have more significance in several areas of biology such as the studies of obesity diseases [3], cancer genome [4–6], and molecular evolution [7, 8]. Especially, the discovery of CNVs, present in the human genome, has changed dramatically our focus on structural variations and phenotype association with diseases. Recent review has revealed that SVs, especially CNVs have extended along over 1000 genes; in addition to, CNVs often encompass a large proportion of the genome, to a great extent than SNPs, ranging from $\sim 12\%$ of the human reference genome [9, 10]. This proves that CNVs is more responsible for genetic diversity and evolution between human populations. CNVs are just one class of

© Springer International Publishing Switzerland 2015
Y.-J. Zhang (Ed.): ICIG 2015, Part III, LNCS 9219, pp. 148–159, 2015.
DOI: 10.1007/978-3-319-21969-1_13

SVs, which are defined in terms of the size of insertions and deletions (> 1 kb). The recognized types of SVs (are shown in Fig. 1) contain indels, inversions, copy-number variations (CNVs) and translocations. Term "indels" means that the amount of inserted or deleted genes is smaller than 1 kb. If the amount is larger than 1 kb, these types of structural variations are referred to as copy number variations, that is, the large genomic segment of duplications or deletions.

Until recently, the methods used to detect SVs mainly have microarray-based technology [11], the fluorescent hybrid technology [12], Multiple PCR technology [13] and Sequencing-based technology [14]. The earliest methods are based on micro-array platforms such as the oligonucleotide-based microarray comparative genomic hybridization (array-CGH) [15] and bacterial artificial chromosome (BAC) [16]. Although these computational approaches based on array data, were successfully used to identify CNVs and other types of SVs like translocations. They also have some limitations. For example, Array-CGH method cannot detect chromosomal translocations or inversions owing to a limited dynamic range; furthermore, the prediction of breakpoint resolution is controlled by the density of the array. Sequencing-based method is emerging recently like Sanger sequencing, which was in place to identify genomic variants in the human genome, while the objectionable feature of Sanger sequencing is too expensive and time-consuming. Compared with the conventional microarray-based method and Sanger sequencing, NGS has an overriding strength on cost-effective and high-throughput. It has driven the development of NGS-based technologies for detecting genetic variations in the human genome.

There are many NGS-based detection algorithms for SVs springing up, have enabled extensive SVs detection. It basically contains the following mainstream algorithms: PEM-based method, read-depth method, split-read method and sequence assembly method. The split-read method generally was combined with PEM-based method and used in various detecting SVs tools. In general, the identification and detecting for SVs involve these steps: Firstly, aligning the short sequencing reads to a given reference genome; then finding the interest regions that different from the reference which is likely being a potential SV; finally, verifying these variations by some strategies.

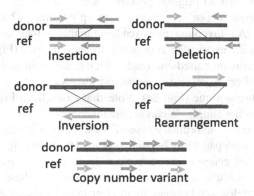

Fig. 1. Several types of structural variations [17].

In this survey, we will describe currently algorithms for detecting SVs by using next-generation sequencing, which have roughly classified into three types. And then, we will discuss the strength and the weakness of these methods, lastly we will provide an outlook for the future research development and make a summary of this article.

2   Algorithms for Structural Variations Detection

Paired-end reads, and mate-pair reads are two distinct reads generated by sequencing-based technologies and two disparate strategies at a known distance. The difference between them is that the length of fragments of the paired-end reads is shorter than those of mate pairs. The length of these read is restricted by the space of the slide, so we can distinguish according to the length of them. The first strategy is the circularization of the DNA segments within the sequencing process; the generated reads with a long insert size are better for detecting a large SV. Another way is obtained from both ends of a segment of DNA, whose sizes are approximately known; that is, the insert size. This method can obtain a high resolution during detecting a small SV. In this survey, these two reads are called "pairs-read" unified.

PEM-based methods identify SV breakpoints by aligning the short paired-end reads to the reference genome to find the 'discordant' with the reference genome, which is probably being one class of SVs. The paired-end reads comes from a sequencing library which contains plenty of fragments with a known length. The 'discordant' paired-end reads are either the expected distance or orientation divergence. In the aligning or the examining strategy, a mapping signature can be produced, which indicate the presence of SVs. So we should discuss the mapping signature first.

2.1   Signatures Based on PEM

The earliest two signatures were insertions and deletions (Fig. 2a and b). Figure 2 shows two types of read signatures; one is the paired-end reads, and the other is split-reads. Since most of the current methods use the fusion of these two reads to detect SVs, we simplify to categorize it into the PEM-based methods.

Term "ref" means that an original genome. A ref case often is used as a control genome; similarly, term "donor" represents a group genome, which comes from the sequencing process. An inversion pairs-read, spanning either of breakpoint of an inversion, will map with an orientation opposite to the reference (Fig. 2c). Figure 2d is the most obvious discordant paired-end read, which occurs within a chromosome. In a case that two mapped reads beyond its expected distance, and the other read of both appear on another chromosome (Fig. 2e). Note that cases from Fig. 2e to Fig. 2i are more complicate than the simple deletions and insertions.

Tandem duplication is the ordinary case of SVs; these pairs-read were linked from the end of the duplication part to its beginning (Fig. 2f). A linking case is that the two distant reads of the ref genome are very close lying on the donor, in other words, comparing with the ref the orientation and the order of these pairs-read remain un-changed, while the distance between them after mapping is fewer than the distance

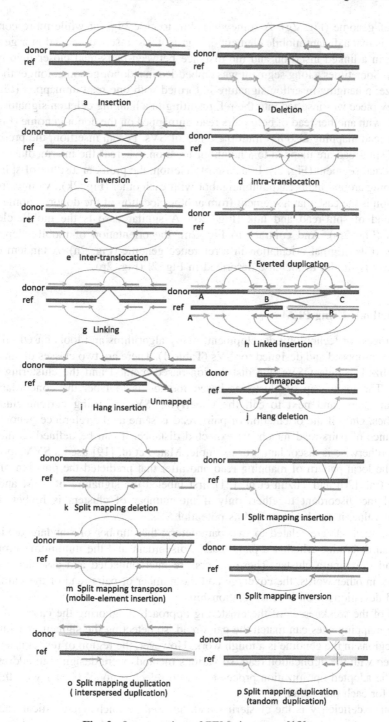

Fig. 2. Interpretation of PEM signatures [18].

on the ref genome (Fig. 2g). A somewhat akin to case Fig. 2g while more complex situation is that a distant mobile element or segment was inserted into a donor genome, resulting in a linked insertion and the distance between pairs-read closer than before (Fig. 2h). Sometimes a long segment was embedded in a donor genome, longer than the insert size; a hanging insertion signature is formed with one read unmapped (Fig. 2i). A lengthy piece was inserted into the ref, resulting in a hanging deletion signature akin to Fig. 2i with another read of both pairs read unmapped on the donor genome (Fig. 2j).

Split-read mapping also has multiple types of SVs. For an insertion, the prefix and suffix of split-read are mapped to a neighbor location, whereas the intermediate region is an inserted segment (Fig. 2l). In a case of deletion, the prefix and suffix of split-read are mapping around the breakpoint neighbor with each other (Fig. 2k). An interspersed duplication is the case that a segment from another location of the donor genome shifts to one end of split-read and link (Fig. 2o). A similar case is the mobile-element insertion (Fig. 2m). And contrary to Fig. 2m, the orientation of mobile-element is opposite to its original orientation in a reference genome (Fig. 2n). A tandem duplication case is similar to the case described in Fig. 2f (Fig. 2p).

2.2   Methods Using PEM

In the process of technology development, many algorithms and tools based-on PEM have been proposed and designed for SVs (Table 1). There are two classes of strategies were utilized to detect SVs, the distribution-based method and the clustering-based method. The main step of clustering-based method is to label the concordant and discordant pairs, and next to call the underlying SVs by using current clustering approaches. Only if the orientation of pairs-read is same as the reference genome and the distance of pairs-read match the expected distance, it can be defined as the concordant, otherwise is discordant. For example, Mateo et al. [19] used a SVM model to cluster the local pattern of mapping read and after that predicted the position of SVs. Korbel et al. [20] and Tuzun et al. [21] first labeled the signature of PEM and then clustered the discordant together, only if the number of clusters is higher than a specified value, it can be identified as potential SVs.

These methods are related to two parameters: the number of standard deviations which can determine whether a pairs-read is discordant and the minimum number of pairs-read to define a cluster. These factors are interconnected and associated to the coverage, in other words, the coverage and the number of pairs-read or the number of standard deviations is an inverse relationship.

One of the weaknesses of the clustering approach is ignoring the case that many multiple mapping sites can match the pairs-read, so detecting the signatures within the repeat regions in the genome is a tough work. However, the region of repeat is strongly associated with the duplication read, so various methods were designed to address this issue. The adopted optimization processes are to select a 'good' cluster with the max support for each pairs-read.

Another deficiency is the clustering method used an unchanged critical value for the number of standard deviations after a signature of PEM is considered as a discordant. When the threshold of discordance changes mapped distance of PEM

Table 1. Tools of PEM-based method [16]

Tool	Type of detection	Sever	Reference
VariationHunter	Insertion, Deletion, Inversion, Everted duplication;	http://compbio.cs.sfu.ca/strvat.htm	[23]
BreakDancer	Insertion, Deletion, Inversion, Hang insertion;	http://breakdancer.sourceforge.net	[24]
MoDIL	Insertion, Deletion;	http://compbio.cs.toronto.edu/modil	[22]
PEMer	Insertion, Deletion, Inversion, Linking, Linked insertion;	http://sv.gersteinlab.org/pemer	[20]
SVDetect	Larger insertions-deletions, Inversions ,Duplications,Balanced or unbalanced inter-chromosomal translocations	http://svdetect.sourceforge.net/	[25]
commonLAW	Mobile element insertions, Medium and large-size deletions	http://compbio.cs.sfu.ca/strvar.htm	[26]
genomeSTRiP	Mobile-element insertion, Deletion;	http://www.broadinstitute.org/	[27]
InGAP-sv	Large insertion	http://ingap.sourceforge.net/	[28]
SVseq	Deletion	http://www.engr.uconn.edu/~jiz08001/svseq.html	[29]
Pindel	Split mapping insertion, Split mapping deletion;	http://www.ebi.ac.uk/~kye/pindel/	[30]

signatures from 2 s.d to 1 s.d, spanning the same breakpoint, there are no clusters be set up. While Lee et al. [22] successfully solves this problem by proposing a distribution-based method, which allows the distribution of all the map-ping around a known breakpoint to be visualizing. If the mapping distribution corresponds with the distribution of expected insert size, while the orientation is opposite, then an indel cluster was set up. Despite this method is good at detecting much smaller indels than the clustering-based method, it also leads to other problems such as the rare variants appeared between homozygous and heterozygous, the power of detecting is not always reliable.

2.3 Signatures Based on Depth of Coverage

Unlike the signature of PEM, there are only two cases happened on the based-depth of coverage. One case is the copy-number duplication; that is, the frequency of read fragment in the donor in some region is higher than in the ref genome; another situation is the copy-number deletion. The density in this region is lower than in the ref. These two cases are shown in the Fig. 3.

2.4 Methods Using Read-Depth

Most of read-depth methods usually partition a genome into the tag count windows and non-overlapping windows. The general procedure of these methods is to determine the region which tags counts are notably different from the normal counts in the genome. These strategies have got an admirable accuracy in detecting large CNVs. Despite the strength of sensitivity and specificity of these methods arising with the size of CNVs,

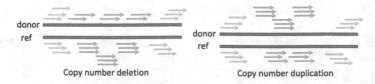

Copy number deletion   Copy number duplication

Fig. 3. The illustrations of DOC signatures [31]

they only customized for the dosage changing SVs; in other words, the range of these methods can be detected not include translocations and inversions, just CNVs and indels.

There are numerous investigations on the based-depth of coverage, and a number of tools have been developed (Table 2). For instance, Xie et al. [32] proposed one method to segregate the genome of a small fixed size window and then find out that the window of the case genome which notably distinct from the reference genome. The resolution of these methods is related to the size of the window. That is to say, too small will weaken the detecting power; too large may lose the resolution.

Table 2. Tools of read-depth-based method [17]

Tool	Case-control	Strategy	Sever	Reference
SeqSeq	Yes	Local change-point analysis	http://www.broadinstitute.org	[33]
ReadDepth	No	Negative binomial model	http://rdxplorer.sourceforge.net/	[34]
RDXplorer	No	Clustering based on Event-wise testing and windowing	http://rdxplorer.sourceforge.net/	[35]
CONTRA	Yes	Base-level log-ratios method	http://contra-cnv.sourceforge.net/	[36]
AB-CNV	No	Variable-length windowing based on HMM and clustering	http://solidsoftwaretools.com/gf/project/cnv/	[37]
CNVnator	No	Mean-shift technology	http://sv.gersteinlab.org/	[38]
CNV-seq	Yes	Fixed-size windowing	http://tiger.dbs.nus.edu.sg/cnv-seq/	[32]

The deficiency of these methods is the factor resulting in abnormal tag count is uncertainty. For instance, the sequencing error rate of NGS such as the poor or rich region of GC is lower than the average GC; it may cause a potential loss or gain of read; moreover, a read mapped by mistake will make the discovery of signature of DOC more complicate.

2.5 Methods Using Sequence Assembly

As the signatures are more and more complicate, people are attaching much importance to the local de novo. Recently, local de novo has been rapid development, just as its name implies, it just finds out the local region which differs from the reference genome, and then will be cut out to reassemble from the set of reads. Comparing the de novo assembly by using all the reads, local de novo methods have enabled the computational time reduced greatly. There also have been several types of SVs, and we will give an illustration in the following (Fig. 4).

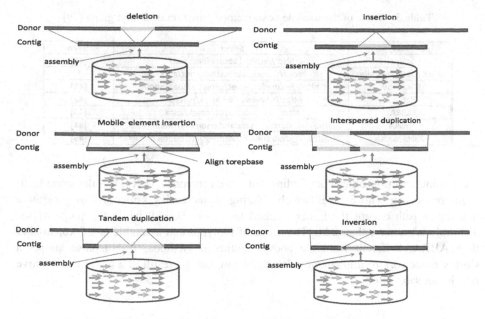

Fig. 4. The illustrations of assembly signature [31]

Given a case that a larger insertion reads lies on the donor genome, the number of matching bases is fewer, or a larger deletion occurs on the donor genome, the mapping signature will more complicate as we described on the signature of PEM. As we point out, PEM-based method is difficult in detecting these cases, since the matched bases are fewer and no enough evidence to use for detecting. Although in later some "soft clip" of PEM-based methods can tackle with this problem, but result is inefficient. So we should consider another alternative way to recover them for detecting. With the development of next-generation sequencing, some reassembly methods for variation detection are emerging to become a popular alternative method such as the micro-assembly methods. Its main idea is that to perform localized de novo, to detect the region encompasses potential SVs and perform assembly, finally to remap a contig, created by assembly from the reads set, to the reference genome. Table 3 shows the recent developed tools that based on local de novo. In this table, signal '*' means that there are no published literature about this tool, but we can learn more detail on its website on guide section.

These methods are roughly similar to each other except the way to handle the cycle in the graph. For example, Scalpel has a high accuracy in detecting repeat region via utilizing a self-tuning k-mer size approach, and a deeper analysis of the rich repeat region used by Scalpel can avoid the cycle path generated. GATK Haplotype-Caller is akin to Scalpel to improve the accuracy of indels detection through larger the k-mer size gradually, while the detected accuracy is weaker than Scalpel on account of ignoring the approximately matching repeat sequences. SOAPindel uses another strategy to form a non-cycle path from unused reads by reducing k-mer sizes. The k-mer size of TIGRA can be specified by the user, and this tool is just designed for

Table 3. Tools of the local de novo method based on de Bruijn graph [39]

Tool	Sever	Reference
Scalpel	http://scalpel.sourceforge.net/	[40]
GATK HaplotypeCaller	http://www.broadinstitute.org/gatk/	*
SOAPindel	http://sourceforge.net/projects/soapindel/	[41]
Platypus	http://www.well.ox.ac.uk/platypus	[42]
ABRA	https://github.com/mozack/abra.	[43]
TIGRA	http://bioinformatics.mdanderson.org/main/TIGRA	[44]
Bubbleparse	https://github.com/richarmleggett/bubbleparse	[45]

breakpoint detection other than finding out repeat regions. ABRA has the same technique processing with Scalpel, which utilizing an increasing k-mer size to generate a non-repeat path except the k-mer reached the upper bound, while the scope of the assembly is no more than 2 kb. The scope of Platypus can assemble is 1.5 kb, smaller than ABRA. Different from the above-mentioned methods, Bubbleparse adopts a Cortex framework to implement indels detection, but the result of a high false-positive rate is not satisfactory.

3 Discussion

Recent studies have shown that SVs are prevalent as SNPs in the genome. SV has become a hot area of biomedical researchers, and the precise identification of SV will accelerate the research of mechanisms related to human genetics or complex diseases. It is virtually certain that some new algorithms and experimental schemes for detecting SV will continuously arise in the future. The NGS-based method has provided numerous opportunities to mutation detection. Although these methods described above have some strength, they also have their scope of application. For instance, read-depth methods can achieve good accuracy in detecting CNVs and indels, but the power of detecting dosage-unchanged mutation is poor. PEM-based methods may be difficult in looking for the precise position of breakpoint; furthermore, its performance is dependent on the completeness of the pairs-read. For example, if a larger insertion or deletion emerges around the breakpoint and the matched bases are fewer, the accuracy of SVs detection will decrease. The PEM-based method and read-depth method have their respective strengths, so the combination of them may have a more satisfactory result. So we can consider the fusion of multiple methods or strategies, because a single method or strategy is too plain for detecting composite variation, and the fusion can utilize more information. Now some tools also comprehensively use two or more strategies such as algorithm in BreakDancer which has combined clustering-based strategy and distribution-based method, and SVseq has been fused with the PEM-based method and split-read method. Integrating various detection algorithms is becoming a popular strand for SVs.

Another difficulty of SV detection is that the optimal value of the parameter is hard to ascertain. For instance, the PEM-based method has two parameters, the standard deviation to determine whether the pairs-read is discordant and the minimum number of the pairs-read. The first parameter is associated with the distance mean, which is a fixed value and too reliant on the experience. It is vital that to make the parameter self-tuning based on some adaptive technology.

With the development of sequencing techniques, the structural variation algorithm is suffering from the problem that how to adapt to the new characteristics of the sequenced data. Regardless of the fact that short data generated by NGS-based technology can well be utilized for detecting SVs, some large insertions or deletions cases also happen in the genome. Moreover, other technologies such as Sanger and Roche have generated a long read data. To use a long read is becoming a feasible strategy on many platforms in the future. So the related research is also required.

Acknowledgements. This work was supported by Shenzhen Municipal Science and Technology Innovation Council (Grant No. CXZZ20140904154910774, Grant No.JCYJ20140417172417174, Grant No.JCYJ20140904154645958, Grant No.JCYJ20130329151843309) and China Postdoctoral Science Foundation funded project (Grant No.2014M560264).

References

1. Altshuler, D.: A haplotype map of the human genome. J. Nat. **437**, 1299–1320 (2005)
2. Check, E.: Human genome: patchwork people. J. Nat. **437**, 1084–1086 (2005)
3. McCarroll, S.A., Altshuler, D.M.: Copy-number variation and association studies of human disease. J. Nat. Genet. **39**, S37 (2007)
4. Parkin, D.M., Bray, F., Ferlay, J., Pisani, P.: Global Cancer Statistics, 2002. J CA: A Cancer J. Clin. **55**, 74–108 (2005)
5. Parkin, D.M., Pisani, P., Ferlay, J.: Global cancer statistics. J CA: A Cancer J. Clin. **49**, 33–64 (1999)
6. Jemal, A., Siegel, R., Ward, E., Murray, T., Xu, J., Smigal, C., Thun, M.J.: Cancer statistics 2006. J CA: A Cancer J. Clin. **56**, 106–130 (2006)
7. Dover, G.A., Linares, A.R., Bowen, T., Hancock, J.M.: Detection and quantification of concerted evolution and molecular drive. J. Methods Enzymol. **224**, 525–541 (1993)
8. Nei, M.: Human evolution at the molecular level. J. Popul. Genet. Mol. Evol. (Mishima, 1984), pp. 41–64 (1985)
9. Stankiewicz, P., Lupski, J.R.: Structural variation in the human genome and its role in disease. J. Annu. Rev. Med. **61**, 437–455 (2010)
10. Bickhart, D.M., Liu, G.E.: The challenges and importance of structural variation detection in livestock. J. Front. Genet. **5**, 37 (2014)
11. Durbin, R.M., Abecasis, G.R., Altshuler, D.L., Auton, A., Brooks, L.D., Gibbs, R.A., Hurles, M.E., McVean, G.A.: A map of human genome variation from population-scale sequencing. J. Nat. **467**, 1061–1073 (2010)
12. Bauman, J.G.J., Wiegant, J., Borst, P., van Duijn, P.: A new method for fluorescence microscopical localization of specific DNA sequences by in situ hybridization of fluorochromelabelled RNA. J. Exp Cell Res. **128**, 485–490 (1980)
13. Cheng, Z., Sharp, A.J., Eichler, E.E.: Structural variation of the human genome. J Annu. Rev. Genomics Hum. Genet. **7**, 477 (2006)
14. Redon, R., Ishikawa, S., Fitch, K.R., Feuk, L., Perry, G.H., Andrews, T.D., Fiegler, H., Shapero, M.H., Carson, A.R., Chen, W.: Global variation in copy number in the human genome. J. Nat. **444**, 444–454 (2006)

15. Carter, N.P.: Methods and strategies for analyzing copy number variation using DNA microarrays. J. Nat. Genet. **39**, S16–S21 (2007)
16. Ylstra, B., van den, IJssel, P., Carvalho, B., Brakenhoff, R.H., Meijer, G.A.: BAC to the future! or oligonucleotides: a perspective for micro array comparative genomic hybridization (array CGH). J Nucleic Acids Res. **34**, 445–450 (2006)
17. Yong, L: Survey on structural variants detection algorithms for next generation sequencing technology. J. Appl. Res. Comput. **31**(2), 328–332 (2014)
18. Medvedev, P., Stanciu, M., Brudno, M.: Computational methods for discovering structural variation with next-generation sequencing. J. Nat Meth. **6**, S13–S20 (2009)
19. Chiara, M., Horner, D.S., Pesole, G., Chiara, M., Horner, D.S.: SVM2: an improved paired-end-based tool for the detection of small genomic structural variations using high-throughput single-genome resequencing data. J. Nucleic Acids Res. **40**, 727–739 (2012)
20. Korbel, J.O., Abyzov, A., Mu, X.J., Carriero, N., Cayting, P., Zhang, Z., Snyder, M., Gerstein, M.B.: PEMer: a computational framework with simulation-based error models for inferring genomic structural variants from massive paired-end sequencing data. J. Genome Biol. **10**, R23–R23 (2009)
21. Tuzun, E., Sharp, A.J., Bailey, J.A., Kaul, R., Morrison, V.A., Pertz, L.M., Haugen, E., Hayden, H., Albertson, D., Pinkel, D.: Fine-scale structural variation of the human genome. J. Nat. Genet. **37**, 727–732 (2005)
22. Lee, S., Hormozdiari, F., Alkan, C., Brudno, M.: MoDIL: detecting small indels from clone-end sequencing with mixtures of distributions. J. Nat. Methods. **6**, 473–474 (2009)
23. Hormozdiari, F., Hajirasouliha, I., Dao, P., Hach, F., Yorukoglu, D., Alkan, C., Eichler, E.E., Sahinalp, S.C.: Next-generation variationHunter: combinatorial algorithms for transposon insertion discovery. J. Bioinform. **26**, i350–i357 (2010)
24. Chen, K., Wallis, J.W., McLellan, M.D., Larson, D.E., Kalicki, J.M., Pohl, C.S., McGrath, S.D., Wendl, M.C., Zhang, Q., Locke, D.P.: BreakDancer: an algorithm for high-resolution mapping of genomic structural variation. J. Nat Methods. **6**, 677–681 (2009)
25. Zeitouni, B., Boeva, V., Janoueix-Lerosey, I., Loeillet, S., Legoix-né, P., Nicolas, A., Delattre, O., Barillot, E.: SVDetect: a tool to identify genomic structural variations from paired-end and mate-pair sequencing data. J. Bioinform. **26**, 1895–1896 (2010)
26. Hormozdiari, F., Hajirasouliha, I., McPherson, A., Eichler, E.E., Sahinalp, S.C.: Simultaneous structural variation discovery among multiple paired-end sequenced genomes. J. Genome Res. **21**, 2203–2212 (2011)
27. Handsaker, R.E., Korn, J.M., Nemesh, J., McCarroll, S.A.: Discovery and genotyping of genome structural polymorphism by sequencing on a population scale. J. Nat. Genet. **43**, 269–276 (2011)
28. Qi, J., Zhao, F.: inGAP-sv: a novel scheme to identify and visualize structural variation from paired end mapping data. J. Nucleic Acids Res. **39**, W567–W575 (2011)
29. Zhang, J., Wu, Y.: SVseq: an approach for detecting exact breakpoints of deletions with low-coverage sequence data. J. Bioinform. **27**, 3228–3234 (2011)
30. Ye, K., Schulz, M.H., Long, Q., Apweiler, R., Ning, Z.: Pindel: a pattern growth approach to detect break points of large deletions and medium sized insertions from paired-end short reads. J. Bioinform. **25**, 2865–2871 (2009)
31. Public Library of Bioinformatics. http://www.plob.org/2014/03/08/6794.html
32. Xie, C.: Martti T Tammi: CNV-seq, a new method to detect copy number variation using high-throughput sequencing. J. BMC Bioinform. **10**, 883–890 (2009)
33. Chiang, D.Y., Getz, G., Jaffe, D.B., O'Kelly, M.J., Zhao, X., Carter, S.L., Russ, C., Nusbaum, C., Meyerson, M., Lander, E.S.: High-resolution mapping of copy-number alterations with massively parallel sequencing. J. Nat Methods. **6**, 99–103 (2009)

34. Miller, C.A., Hampton, O., Coarfa, C., Milosavljevic, A.: readdepth: a parallel r package for detecting copy number alterations from short sequencing reads. J. PLOS ONE. **6**, e16327 (2011)

35. Yoon, S., Xuan, Z., Makarov, V., Ye, K., Sebat, J.: Sensitive and accurate detection of copy number variants using read depth of coverage. J. Genome Res. **19**, 1586–1592 (2009)

36. Li, J., Lupat, R., Amarasinghe, K.C., Thompson, E.R., Doyle, M.A., Ryland, G.L., Tothill, R.W., Halgamuge, S.K., Campbell, I.G., Gorringe, K.L.: CONTRA: copy number analysis for targeted resequencing. J. Bioinform. **28**(7), 1307–1313 (2012)

37. McKernan, K.J., Peckham, H.E., Costa, G.L., McLaughlin, S.F., Fu, Y., Tsung, E.F., Clouser, C.R., Duncan, C., Ichikawa, J.K., Lee, C.C.: Sequence and structural variation in a human genome uncovered by short-read, massively parallel ligation sequencing using two-base encoding. J. Genome Res. **19**, 1527–1541 (2009)

38. Abyzov, A., Urban, A.E., Snyder, M., Gerstein, M.: CNVnator: an approach to discover, genotype, and characterize typical and atypical CNVs from family and population genome sequencing. J. Genome Res. **21**, 974–984 (2011)

39. Narzisi, G., Schatz, M.C.: The challenge of small-scale repeats for indel discovery. J. Front Bioeng Biotechnol. **3**, 8 (2015)

40. Narzisi, G., O'Rawe, J.A., Iossifov, I., Fang, H., Lee, Y.H., Wang, Z., Wu, Y., Lyon, G.J., Wigler, M., Schatz, M.C.: Accurate de novo and transmitted indel detection in exome-capture data using microassembly. J. Nat Methods **11**, 1033–1036 (2014)

41. Li, S., Li, R., Li, H., Lu, J., Li, Y., Bolund, L., Schierup, M.H., Wang, J.: SOAPindel: efficient identification of indels from short paired reads. J. Genome Res. **23**, 195–200 (2013)

42. Rimmer, A., Phan, H., Mathieson, I., Iqbal, Z., Twigg, S.R., Consortium, W.G.S., Wilkie, A.O., McVean, G.: Integrating mapping-, assembly- and haplotype-based approaches for calling variants in clinical sequencing applications. J. Nat Genet. **46**, 912–918 (2014)

43. Mose, L.E., Wilkerson, M.D., Hayes, D.N., Perou, C.M., Parker, J.S.: ABRA: improved coding indel detection via assembly based re-alignment. J. Bioinform. **30**, 2813–2815 (2014)

44. Chen, K., Chen, L., Fan, X., Wallis, J., Ding, L., Weinstock, G.: TIGRA: a targeted iterative graph routing assembler for breakpoint assembly. J. Genome Res. **24**, 310–317 (2014)

45. Leggett, R.M., MacLean, D.: Reference-free SNP detection: dealing with the data deluge. J. BMC Genomics. **15**, 246–253 (2014)

Recognition of In-air Handwritten Chinese Character Based on Leap Motion Controller

Ning Xu, Weiqiang Wang$^{(\boxtimes)}$, and Xiwen Qu

School of Computer and Control Engineering,
University of Chinese Academy of Sciences, Beijing, China
wqwang@ict.ac.cn

Abstract. The three-dimensional interaction has been widely used as a natural and direct way in Human-Computer Interaction (HCI). In this paper, we propose a novel 3D interaction method by recognizing Chinese character written in the air. Firstly, the moving trajectory of fingertip is precisely captured using the Leap Motion Controller. Then, we describe the trajectory by combining the directional feature and direction-change feature. We construct a dataset called IAHCC-UCAS2014, which contains 3755 classes of Chinese characters and each character class has 65 samples. In the evaluation experiments, the proposed method shows promising recognition performance with little increase in computational cost.

Keywords: In-air handwritten Chinese character recognition · Directional feature · Leap Motion Controller

1 Introduction

To achieve high recognition accuracy and system efficiency in online handwritten character recognition (OHCCR) systems, many features and classifiers have been proposed [1], and some satisfying experimental results have been obtained on the existing datasets [2,3]. Recent technologies in vision sensors are capable of capturing 3D finger positions and movements. To chase a more friendly experience of writing, the conception of in-air writing has been proposed and several writing-in-the-air systems [4–6] have been developed, which brings people's writing behavior to the 3D space now.

Feng et al. [4] proposed a finger-writing character recognition system based on the Kinect sensor. By using the depth information and clustering algorithms, the fingertip is located and then the fingertip's trajectory is captured. This approach has gained high tracking accuracy in the dataset including digits and some Chinese characters. In [5], the algorithms for fingertips' detection and tracking are further improved. Jin et al. [6] proposed a digit string recognition method, where the trajectory captured by Kinect is first over-segmented and then recognized by a path-searching algorithm.

The Leap Motion controller is a new generation of 3D interaction sensor which focuses on the interaction by human hands. It can accurately track the

© Springer International Publishing Switzerland 2015
Y.-J. Zhang (Ed.): ICIG 2015, Part III, LNCS 9219, pp. 160–168, 2015.
DOI: 10.1007/978-3-319-21969-1_14

movement of hands and fingertips in a three-dimensional space [7] and it provides application programming interfaces (API) for related interaction. The Leap Motion Controller has been applied into many fields [8–10] and these applications demonstrate the high performance and practical value of it. In our work, we apply the Leap Motion Controller to provide precise and real-time fingertip positions in its 3D workspace. Actually, writing with the Leap Motion Controller is very user-friendly owing to its excellent performance for fingertip detection. In the proposed system to recognize handwritten characters in the air, users can write a Chinese character in the air by moving their fingers relatively fast and fluently.

Compared with traditional OHCCR, in-air handwritten character recognition (IAHCCR) is technically more difficult due to two reasons: First, in-air writing behavior is more likely to be casual which can result in great variation and distortion of the character's structure. Second, there is no pen-up or pen-down information when writing in the air, because the whole character is written by one single stroke. Examples of the handwritten SCUT-COUCH2009 dataset [2] and some in-air written samples from our IAHCC-UCAS2014 dataset are shown in Fig. 1.

To overcome the challenges in in-air handwritten Chinese character recognition, a more robust feature is needed. We exploit the 8-directional feature [11] widely used in online handwritten Chinese character recognition, since the two problems have a lot in common. The 8-directional feature can reflect writing direction for the input Chinese character, and is relatively robust. In [12], a similar directional feature is introduced and in [13] the 8-directional feature is improved. In [14,15] the direction-change feature is proposed and combined with the 4-directional feature. The direction-change feature reflects the direction variation during the writing process. This paper combines the 8-directional feature with the direction-change feature into our recognition system for IAHCCR.

(a) handwritten data for Chinese "Shi".   (b) in-air handwritten data for "Shi".

Fig. 1. Examples of handwritten and in-air handwritten Chinese characters

The rest of this paper is organized as follows: First, we introduce how the trajectory was captured using the Leap Motion Controller. Second, we describe our combined feature using 8-directional feature and direction-change feature. Third, the framework of our recognition system is introduced. Finally, we test the proposed feature on our IAHCC-UCAS2014 dataset and compare the performance with 8-directional feature and the origin direction-change feature.

2 Writing Trajectory Capturing

In our system, by using the Leap Motion Controller, users can move their fingers casually in a customized 3D space. Compared with the Kinect sensor, the Leap Motion Controller has a higher tracking accuracy for fingertips. So the proposed method makes it possible for users to just write by their fingertips with little body movement. Also, owing to the real-time performance of the Leap Motion Controller, users can write relatively fast and naturally, which is hard to achieve in systems based on Kinect sensors. The writing progress by our system can be seen from Fig. 2, where the user is writing the Chinese character of "Shi".

Fig. 2. A user writing a Chinese character "Shi" using our writing-in-the-air system

The 3D writing trajectory can be captured by tracing the movement of the writing fingertip based on the APIs of the Leap Motion Controller. Further, the 2D writing trajectory is obtained by projecting the 3D trajectory onto a screen plane. By adjusting the parameters of Leap Motion Controller, the stability and accuracy of writing trajectory can be guaranteed.

In practice, we find the detection accuracy of the Leap Motion is so high that a slight shake of fingertip can cause apparent structure jitter in the 2D trajectory. So we apply the classic Kalman Filter to smooth the obtained 2D tracking trajectory to reduce the distortion caused by slight shake.

In OHCCR, the imaginary stroke refers to manual straight lines between the end point of one stroke and the start point of its next stroke. In our writing-in-the-air system, the character is always written by one single stroke, so the imaginary stroke is already there for recognition. It should be also noted that the sampling points are usually dense in OHCCR problem, but in our system they can be sparse, since some users can write really fast. So we join the sampling points using Bresenham's line algorithm to construct the final 2D trajectory.

3 Combined Directional Feature

3.1 8-Directional Feature

After several pre-processing steps, each testing sample is normalized into a fixed size of 64×64, and then the 8-directional feature is extracted. Concretely, for a given point $P_j = (x_j, y_j)$ in the the sequence of sampling points $P_j, j = 1, 2, \cdots$, let $\boldsymbol{V}_j$ denote its direction vector, $\boldsymbol{V}_j$ is defined as follows:

$$\boldsymbol{V}_j = \begin{cases} \overrightarrow{P_j P_{j+1}} & \text{If } P_j \text{ is a start point} \\ \overrightarrow{P_{j-1} P_{j+1}} & \text{If } P_j \text{ is a non-end point} \\ \overrightarrow{P_{j-1} P_j} & \text{If } P_j \text{ is an end point} \end{cases} \tag{1}$$

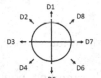

(a) Eight direction axes for 8-directional feature.

(b) An mapping example of the direction vector.

Fig. 3. Axes and mapping example of the direction vector

Then its normalized $\boldsymbol{V}_j / \|\boldsymbol{V}_j\|$ is projected to two directions from eight directions as shown in Fig. 3(a). One is from the direction set $\{D1, D3, D5, D7\}$ and denoted by d_j^1, and the other is from set $\{D2, D4, D6, D8\}$ and denoted by d_j^2. Figure 3(b) shows an example, where $d_j^1 = D1$ and $d_j^2 = D8$ for the highlighted sampling point. The corresponding mapping values a_j^1 and a_j^2 for directions d_j^1 and d_j^2 is computed by

$$a_j^1 = \frac{|d_x - d_y|}{s},$$
$$a_j^2 = \frac{\sqrt{2} \cdot \min(d_x, d_y)}{s}, \tag{2}$$

where $d_x = |x_{j+1} - x_{j-1}|$, $d_y = |y_{j+1} - y_{j-1}|$, and $s = \sqrt{d_x^2 + d_y^2}$ for a non-end point. Further, eight directional pattern images $\{B_d = [f_d(x, y)], x, y = 1, \cdots, 64, d = D1, \cdots, D8\}$ are generated by setting $f_{d_j^1}(x_j, y_j) = a_j^1$ and $f_{d_j^2}(x_j, y_j) = a_j^2$. All the remaining values for $f_d(x, y)$ are set as 0s. The eight directional pattern images are thickened by a maximum filter and then smoothed by a Gaussian filter $G(x, y) = \frac{4}{\lambda^2} \exp[-\frac{2(x^2 + y^2)}{\lambda^2}]$, where λ is the wavelength of the plane wave of the original Gabor filter.

Finally, each directional pattern image is divided uniformly into 8×8 grids. In each grid, the values are summed up to get a feature value. Since we have 8 images and each image has 64 grids, we obtain $8 \times 64 = 512$ dimensional feature vector. A nonlinear transformation (the square root function) is applied to form the final 8-directional feature vector.

3.2   Direction-Change Feature

The direction-change degree and the directions after direction change are obtained from the normalized on-line data by using the direction-change feature. For each sampling point P_j, the direction-change degree is measured by the absolute value of the difference in direction from direction vector $\overrightarrow{P_{j-1}P_j}$ to the next direction vector $\overrightarrow{P_jP_{j+1}}$. The direction-change feature's degree (Fdc), is calculated by

$$Fdc = \frac{|D\theta|}{60} + 1 \tag{3}$$

where $D\theta$ ($-180° \leq D\theta \leq 180°$) is the angle of the direction change between $\overrightarrow{P_{j-1}P_j}$ and $\overrightarrow{P_jP_{j+1}}$.

Just as the 8-directional feature, the Fdc of each sampling point is also mapped to eight directions as Fig. 3(a). However, in direction-change feature, each Fdc is mapped to only one direction d_j^m from $D1, D2, \ldots, D8$. Concretely, it is the direction which the greater value between a_j^1 and a_j^2 corresponds to. Similarly, 8 direction-change pattern images $\{\dot{B}_d = [\dot{f}_d(x,y)], x, y = 1, 2, \ldots, 64, d = D1, \ldots D8\}$ are generated by setting $\dot{f}_{d_j^m}(x_j, y_j) = \max(a_j^1, a_j^2)$ and the remaining values as 0s. Then, the same computation is carried out on the generated direction-change pattern images to obtain the 512-dimensional direction-change feature vector.

We combine it with the 8-direction feature to form 1024-dimensional combined feature vector. Figure 4 shows 16 pattern images extracted from the Chinese character "Shi", where the first row represents the eight directional pattern images and the second row represents the direction-change pattern images.

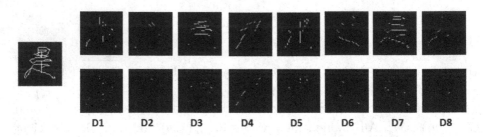

D1   D2   D3   D4   D5   D6   D7   D8

Fig. 4. Examples of pattern images for the directional and direction-change feature

4   Framework of Our Recognition System

We have implemented an recognition system for the in-air handwritten characters. Our system contains the following three stages of computations.

(1) Pre-processing. A series of pre-processing steps are used to reduce the noise and normalize the trajectory shapes of input characters to make the samples easier to recognize. First, we normalize the X-coordinates and Y-coordinates of the sampling points to a fixed size of 64 by 64 by linear mapping. Then, the coordinates of each sampling point are smoothed by computing the average of its neighbors, and we remove some redundant points to ensure that only one point left in the same position of the trajectory. Further, we exploit the dot density shape normalization method [16] to adjust the trajectory shape of the input Chinese character. Finally, the re-sampling step is carried out to generate a sequence of equidistance points.

(2) Feature Extraction. After the preprocessing step, we can extract the 1024-dimensional combined features. The related computational details have been presented in Subsects. 3.1 and 3.2.

(3) Two-Level Classifier. To make the classification more efficient, we exploit the Linear Discriminant Analysis (LDA) to learn a projection subspace so as to project the feature vector to a low-dimensional subspace. The projection axis learned by LDA helps to make prototypes more separable in the subspace. In LDA, we define within-class and between-class scatter matrices by S_W and S_B respectively and also define the optimal projection axis (discriminant vector) by $\mathbf{w}$. We then estimate $\mathbf{w}$ by maximizing the Fisher criterion:

$$J(\mathbf{w}) = tr((\mathbf{w}^T S_w \mathbf{w})^{-1}(\mathbf{w}^T S_B \mathbf{w})) \tag{4}$$

where $tr(\cdot)$ denotes the trace of matrix. This criterion considers the within-class and between-class scatter matrices and helps to make the data separable in the projected subspace. It can be shown that $\mathbf{w}$ is the solution to the generalized eigenvector problem $S_B w_i = \lambda_i S_W w_i, i = 1, 2, \ldots$ where w_i denotes the eigenvector for the ith eigenvalue λ_i. By using LDA, the dimension of the feature space is reduced while different classes are separated. Also, the dimension reduction makes the following computation cost of training process decrease.

In our system, we design a two-level classifier to achieve both accuracy and efficiency. Our classifier is based on the Nearest Prototype Classifier (NPC) rule. For each unknown pattern, we label it by the class of the nearest prototype. The metric we use between samples and the prototypes is the the Euclidean distance. The first-level classier is the coarse classifier which aims to remove most impossible candidate classes with low computation cost. In the first level classifier, the combined feature vector is projected to 20-dimensional, and the nearest 450 prototypes are retained. Afterwards, in the second level classifier, we project the combined feature vector to 160 dimensional subspace, and then the distances are computed between the testing sample and prototypes retained by the first-level classifier. Finally, we sort these prototypes by the corresponding distances and generate the candidate label list.

5   Experimental Results

We evaluate the performance of the proposed feature on the IAHCC-UCAS2014 dataset which is constructed by ourself, since there is no related dataset publicly available. The dataset includes 3755 classes of Chinese characters, and each of them has 65 samples. The 3755 classes include all Chinese characters in GB2312-80 level-1 set, which makes our dataset challenging since works of other researchers [4,5] only cover limited number of classes in Chinese characters. Some of the samples in our dataset are shown in Fig. 5. As described in the previous section, it can be seen from Fig. 5 that the IAHCCR is technically difficult due to great variation of character's structure.

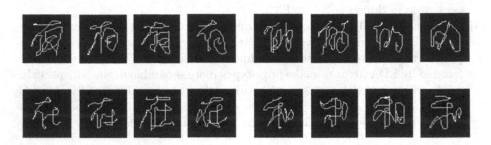

Fig. 5. Some in-air handwritten chinese characters from our IAHCC-UCAS2014 dataset

To evaluate the classification performance, the recognition accuracy on the testing data is of primary interest. We compare our recognition result with the other two features. The 8-directional feature refers to the method in [11] and the direction-change feature refers to the feature in [14]. The recognition accuracy is calculated by

$$R_k = N_k/N \qquad (5)$$

where R_k denotes the top-k recognition accuracy of the system. For each testing sample, we generate a candidate label list for it by the two-level classifier. The top-k metric means we check candidate label list and find out if the right label is included in the top k label of the list. The N_k denotes the number of testing samples whose labels are properly included in the top-k candidate labels, while the N denotes the total number of the testing samples. We compare the accuracy of top 1, top 5, and top10, which are metrics widely used to compare Chinese character recognition performance. In our experiments, we randomly select 10 samples from each class as the testing samples and the remaining samples are used for training. The experimental results are summarized in Table 1.

It can be seen from the table that the proposed feature obtained better performance compared with the other two features according to top 1/5/10 metrics. It is also worth noting that the framework of our recognition system achieves 90.6 % accuracy on the top 1 metrics when dealing with the OHCCR

Table 1. Recognition accuracy comparison of three features on our in-air handwritten Chinese character dataset

Methods	Top1	Top5	Top10
direction-change	66.68 %	83.36 %	87.42 %
8-directional	68.81 %	84.80 %	88.52 %
Combined (Ours)	69.67 %	85.36 %	89.08 %

using dataset of SCUT-COUCH2009 [2]. The relatively low accuracy on the IAHCC-UCAS2014 dataset indicates that the IAHCCR is very challenging and it needs more research efforts in the future.

Compared with the 8-directional feature, the proposed method seems to bring more computational cost owing to combining the two features together. In practice, we apply the same pre-processing steps and direction vector extraction process to the two features in our recognition system so that the time cost can be reduced. We compare the time consumption (millisecond) during the feature extraction step and the recognition step. The experiments are performed on a desktop computer with 2.40 GHz CPU, and the recognition system is implemented using MATLAB. It can been seen from Table 2 that our combined feature results in little time consumption. Regarding the applied background of the IAHCCR, the increase of time consumption is negligible.

Table 2. Comparison of time consumption (millisecond) vs. 8-directional feature

Methods	Extraction	Recognition	Total
8-directional	96.5	10.7	107.2
Combined (Ours)	128.6	10.8	139.4

6   Conclusions

In this paper, we present a novel HCI interface for writing interaction. The writing behavior can be conducted in a 3D space and in a more natural and user-friendly way by using the Leap Motion Controller. We then propose a combined feature based on the 8-directional feature and the direction-change feature, and apply them to our in-air handwritten character recognition system. The performance of the combined feature is evaluated on our IAHCC-UCAS2014 dataset and the experimental results show that the combined feature can achieve better performance with reasonable computational cost.

Acknowledgments. This work is supported by the National Science Foundation of China (NSFC) under Grant No. 61232013, No. 61271434 and No. 61175115.

References

1. Liu, C.-L., Jaeger, S., Nakagawa, M.: Online recognition of Chinese characters: the state-of-the-art. IEEE Trans Pattern Anal. Mach. Intell. **26**(2), 198–213 (2004)
2. Jin, L., Gao, Y., Liu, G., Li, Y., Ding, K.: SCUT-COUCH2009-a comprehensive online unconstrained Chinese handwriting database and benchmark evaluation. Int. J. Doc. Anal. Recogn. **14**(1), 53–64 (2011)
3. Liu, C.-L., Yin, F., Wang, D.-H., Wang, Q.-F.: Online and offline handwritten Chinese character recognition: benchmarking on new databases. Pattern Recognit. **46**(1), 155–162 (2013)
4. Feng, Z., Xu, S., Jin, L., Ye, Z., Yang, W.: Real-time fingertip tracking and detection using Kinect depth sensor for a new writing-in-the-air system. In: Proceedings of the 4th International Conference on Internet Multimedia Computing and Service, pp. 70–74 (2012)
5. Ye, Z., Zhang, X., Jin, L., Feng, Z., Shaojie, X.: A new writing experience: finger writing in the air using a kinect sensor. IEEE Trans. Multimed. **20**(4), 85–93 (2013)
6. Jin, X.-J., Wang, Q.-F., Liu, C.-L.: Visual gesture character string recognition by classification based segmentation with stroke deletion. In: Proceedings of 2nd IAPR Asian Conference on Pattern Recognition, pp. 120–124 (2013)
7. Hodson, H.: Leap motion hacks show potential of new gesture tech. New Sci. **218**(2911), 21 (2013)
8. Sutton, J.: Air painting with Corel Painter Freestyle and the leap motion controller: a revolutionary new way to paint. In: ACM SIGGRAPH 2013 Studio Talks, no. 21 (2013)
9. Hantrakul, L., Kaczmarek, K.: Implementations of the Leap Motion device in sound synthesis and interactive live performance. In: Proceedings of the 2014 International Workshop on Movement and Computing, pp. 142 (2014)
10. Khademi, M., Hondori, H.M., McKenzie, A.: Free-hand interaction with leap motion controller for stroke rehabilitation. In: CHI 14 Extended Abstracts on Human Factors in Computing Systems, pp. 1663–1668 (2014)
11. Bai, Z.-L., Huo, Q.: A study on the use of 8-directional features for online handwritten Chinese character recognition. In: Proceedings of the 8th International Conference on Document Analysis and Recognition, pp. 262–266 (2005)
12. Liu, C.-L., Zhou, X.-D.: Online Japanese character recognition using trajectory-based normalization and direction feature extraction. In: Proceedings of 10th International Workshop on Frontiers in Handwriting Recognition, pp. 217–222. Suvisoft (2006)
13. Ding, K., Deng, G., Jin, L.: An investigation of imaginary stroke technique for cursive online handwriting Chinese character recognition. In: Proceedings of the 10th ICDAR, pp. 531–535. Barcelona, Spain (2009)
14. Masayoshi, O., Yamamoto, K.: On-line handwriting character recognition using direction-change features that consider imaginary strokes. Pattern Recognit. **32**(7), 1115–1128 (1999)
15. Okamoto, M., Yamamoto, K.: On-line handwritten character recognition method using directional features and clockwise/counter-clockwise direction-change features. In: Proceedings of 5th International Conference on Document Analysis and Recognition, pp. 491–494 (1999)
16. Bai, Z.-L., Huo, Q.: A study of nonlinear shape normalization for online handwritten Chinese character recognition: dot density vs. line density equalization. In: Proceedings of 18th International Conference on Pattern Recognition, pp. 921–924 (2006)

Relations Between Minkowski-Reduced Basis and θ-orthogonal Basis of Lattice

Yuyun Chen[1]($^{\boxtimes}$), Gengran Hu[2], Renzhang Liu[2], Yanbin Pan[2], and Shikui Shang[3]

[1] College of Science, National University of Defense Technology, Changsha 410073, China
kasineya@sina.com
[2] Key Laboratory of Mathematics Mechanization, NCMIS, Academy of Mathematics and Systems Science, Chinese Academy of Sciences, Beijing 100190, China
[3] Department of Mathematics, University of Science and Technology of China, Hefei 230026, China

Abstract. We prove that the angle between any two Minkowski-reduced basis vectors is more than $\pi/3$; if the orthogonal defect of 3-dimension lattice is less than $2/\sqrt{3}$, the Minkowski-reduced basis of the lattice is $\pi/3$-orthogonal; if a weakly θ-orthogonal basis for a lattice with $\theta \geqslant \pi/3$ has been ordered by the Euclidean norm of the vectors, and the minimum length ratio maximum length is more than $2\cos\theta$, the basis is Minkowski reduced. We improve an algorithm used in JPEG CHEst by changing it from heuristic one to deterministic one, furthermore we add a constraint to reduce the number of unimodular matrix that need to determine. *abstract* environment.

Keywords: Lattice · Minkowski-reduced basis · Orthogonal defect · Greedy algorithm · θ-orthogonal

1 Introduction

The theory of reduction of positive definite quadratic forms was introduced by Hermann Minkowski in 1905 [1]. This theory is one of the essential foundations of the geometry of numbers, while another is the lattice theory. The structure of lattice is widely studied. In [2], the authors study the lattices of A and E styles. In [3], the authors study the covering dimension for the class of the finite lattices. A lattice is a discrete additive subgroup of $\mathbb{R}^n$. Any lattice has a lattice basis, i.e., a set $\{b_1, \cdots, b_m\}$ of linearly independent vectors such that the lattice is the set of all integer linear combinations of the b_i's:

$$\mathcal{L}(b_1, \cdots, b_m) = \{\sum_{i=1}^{m} x_i b_i | x_i \in \mathbb{Z}, 1 \leq i \leq m\}.$$

© Springer International Publishing Switzerland 2015
Y.-J. Zhang (Ed.): ICIG 2015, Part III, LNCS 9219, pp. 169–179, 2015.
DOI: 10.1007/978-3-319-21969-1_15

In lattice theory, an important thing is lattice basis reduction. Roughly speaking, a reduced basis is a basis made of almost orthogonal vectors which are reasonably short. This problem is known as lattice reduction and can intuitively be viewed as a vectorial generalization of gcd computation [4]. There exist many different notions of reduction, such as those of Hermite, Minkowski, Hermite-Korkine-Zolotarev, Lenstra-Lenstra-Lovsz. Among these, the most intuitive one is perhaps Minkowskis, and up to dimension four it is arguably optimal compared to all other known reductions, because it reaches all the so-called successive minima of a lattice [4]. Finding good reduced bases has been proved to be important in many fields of computer science and mathematics.

In [5], Neelamani, Dash and Baraniuk define a lattice basis to be θ-orthogonal if the angle between any basis vector and the linear subspace spanned by the remaining basis vectors is at least θ, and if θ is at least $\frac{\pi}{3}$-radians, they call the θ-orthogonal basis "nearly orthogonal" [6]. Because they have proved that a shortest non-zero lattice vector is always contained in a $\frac{\pi}{3}$-orthogonal basis, then SVP for a given $\pi/3$-orthogonal basis is trivial. In [6], Dash, Neelamani, and Sorkin prove additional properties of $\frac{\pi}{3}$-orthogonal bases. They show that the basis is Minkowski reduced for some ordering of the vectors, if all vectors of a θ-orthogonal $\left(\theta > \frac{\pi}{3}\right)$ basis have lengths no more than $\frac{2}{\cos\theta}$ times the length of the shortest basis vector. In this point, we find that if the weakly θ-orthogonal basis vectors rather than θ-orthogonal basis for a lattice $\mathcal{L}$ with $\theta \geqslant \frac{\pi}{3}$ are ordered by their lengths, the shortest vector length ratios the maximum vector length is more than $2\cos\theta$, then the basis is Minkowski reduced. We also find that the angle between any two Minkowski-reduced basis vectors is more than $\frac{\pi}{3}$. In 3-dimension lattice, we find that if the orthogonal defect is less than $\frac{2}{\sqrt{3}}$, the Minkowski-reduced basis is $\frac{\pi}{3}$-orthogonal. We also find some intuitive relations between Minkowski-reduced basis and orthogonal defect of lattice.

The settings used during the previous JPEG compression and decompression, such as the color transformation matrix, and the quantization table will be stored in the JPEG compressed file format and be discarded after decompression. We refer to such previous JPEG compression settings as the images JPEG compression history [5]. The compression history is lost during operations such as conversion from JPEG format to BMP or TIFF format, while it can be used for JPEG recompression, for covert message passing, or to uncover the compression settings used inside digital cameras [7]. In [5], Neelamani, Dash, and Baraniuk give a heuristic algorithm which solved the JPEG CHEst. We find that all the color-transform matrices orthogonal defect which were tested in [5] are less than $\frac{2}{\sqrt{3}}$, and the Minkowski-reduced bases of the lattices spanned by them are $\frac{\pi}{3}$-orthogonal. We use the greedy algorithm [4] to find the Minkowski-reduced bases, and add a constraint when enumerating the unimodular matrix. The improved algorithm is deterministic algorithm.

The paper is organized as follows. Section 2 provides some basic definitions and well-known results about nearly orthogonal basis, formally states our result on Minkowski-reduced basis and orthogonal defect. Section 3 describe the improvement of algorithm. Section 4 is the conclusion.

2   The Relations Between Minkowski-Reduced Basis and Nearly Orthogonal Basis

2.1   Some Definitions

Consider an m-dimensional lattice in $\mathbb{R}^n$, $m \leqslant n$. By an ordered basis of $\mathcal{L}$, we mean a basis with a certain ordering of the basis vector, we use the brace $(.,.)$ for ordered sets and $\{.,.\}$ otherwise, just like Neelamani, Dash and Baraniuk have done in [5]. For vectors $u, v \in \mathbb{R}^n$, we use $\langle u, v \rangle$ to denote the inner product and $\|v\|$ to denote the Euclidean norm of a vector v. Let B_1 and B_2 (when treated as $n \times m$ matrices) be any two bases of $\mathcal{L}$, there exists a unimodular matrix U (i.e., a $m \times m$ matrix with integer entries and determinant ± 1) such that $B_1 = B_2 U$.

The shortest vector problem (SVP) and the closest vector problem (CVP) [8] are most important computational problems of lattice problems. An appealing class of problems involves finding closest and shortest vectors in lattices. The shortest vector problem (SVP) is to find a shortest nonzero vector in $\mathcal{L}$ and the closet vector problem(CVP) is that given a vector $t \in \mathbb{R}^n$ not in $\mathcal{L}$, find a vector in $\mathcal{L}$ that is closest to t. The general CVP is known to be NP-hard and the SVP is NP-hard under a randomized reduction hypothesis.

Neelamani et al. define a lattice basis to be weakly θ-orthogonal, θ-orthogonal and nearly orthogonal [5]. Minkowski gave the notion of Minkowski reduction in 1896. Minkowski reduction is the most intuitive one among all known reduction, and up to dimension four it is arguably optimal, because it reaches all the so-called successive minima of a lattice [4]. We revisit the definitions and give the relations between them.

Definition 1. *(Weak θ-orthogonality) [5]. An ordered set of vectors $(b_1, b_2, \cdots, b_m)$ is weakly θ-orthogonal if for $i = 2, 3, \cdots, m$, the angle between b_i and the subspace spanned by $\{b_1, b_2, \cdots, b_{i-1}\}$ lies in the range $[\theta, \frac{\pi}{2}]$. That is,*

$$\cos^{-1}\left(\frac{|\langle b_i, \sum_{j=1}^{i-1} \alpha_i b_i \rangle|}{\|b_i\| \cdot \|\sum_{j=1}^{i-1} \alpha_i b_i\|} \right) \geq \theta,$$

for all $\alpha_j \in \mathbb{R}$ with $\sum_j |\alpha_j| > 0$.

If a basis is a weakly θ-orthogonal basis, at first, it is ordered, secondly, the angle between any two basis vectors is more than θ.

Definition 2. *(θ-orthogonality) [5]. A set of vectors $\{b_1, b_2, \cdots, b_m\}$ is θ-orthogonal if every ordering of the vectors yields a weakly θ-orthogonal set.*

Definition 3. *(Nearly orthogonal) [5]. A θ-orthogonal basis is deemed to be nearly orthogonal if θ is at least $\frac{\pi}{3}$ radians.*

We do not expect all rational lattices to have such bases because this would imply that NP=co-NP [5]. For example, the basis:

$$B = \begin{bmatrix} 1 & 0 & \frac{1}{2} \\ 0 & 1 & \frac{1}{2} \\ 0 & 0 & \frac{1}{\sqrt{2}} \end{bmatrix}$$

span the lattice $\mathcal{L}$, but $\mathcal{L}$ does not have any weakly $\frac{\pi}{3}$-orthogonal basis.

Definition 4. *(Successive minimum) [9]. Let $\mathcal{L}$ be a lattice of rank m. For $i \in \{1, \cdots, m\}$, we define the ith successive minimum as:*

$$\lambda_i(\mathcal{L}) = inf\left\{r \,\middle|\, dim(span(\mathcal{L} \cap \overline{B}(0, r))) \geq i\right\},$$

where

$$\overline{B}(0, r) = \left\{x \in \mathbb{R}^n \,\middle|\, \|x\| \leqslant r\right\}$$

is the closed ball of radius r around 0.

Definition 5. *(Orthogonal Defect) [10]. The orthogonal defect of a latticxe basis $\{b_1, b_2, \cdots, b_m\}$ is*

$$\frac{\prod_{i=1}^m \|b_i\|}{|det([b_1, b_2, \cdots, b_m])|},$$

with det denoting determinant.

Definition 6. *(OD-r-orthogonality). Let $r \in \mathbb{R}$, a set of vectors $\{b_1, b_2, \cdots, b_m\}$ is OD-r-orthogonal if the orthogonal defect is at most r.*

Definition 7. *(Minkowski reduced) [6]. An ordered basis $(b_1, b_2, \cdots, b_m)$ is Minkowski reduced if b_1 is a shortest lattice vector, and for $i \in \{2, 3, \cdots, m\}$, b_i is a shortest vector among all the lattice vectors $\tilde{b}_i$ s.t. $\{b_1, b_2, \cdots, b_{i-1}, \tilde{b}_i\}$ can be extended to a complete lattice basis.*

A basis of a m-dimensional lattice that reaches the m minima must be Minkowski reduced, but a Minkowski-reduced basis may not reach all the minima, except the first four ones: if $(b_1, b_2, \cdots, b_m)$ is a Minkowski-reduced basis, then we have

$$\|b_i\| = \lambda_i(\mathcal{L}), 1 \leqslant i \leqslant min(d, 4),$$

but the best theoretical upper bound known for $\|b_d\|/\lambda_d(\mathcal{L})$ grows exponentially in d. Therefore, a Minkowski-reduced basis is optimal in a natural sense up to dimension four. There is a classical result states that the orthogonal defect of a Minkowski-reduced basis can be upper-bounded by a constant that only depends on the lattice dimension.

2.2   Some Results

Theorem 1. *[5] Let $B = (b_1, b_2, \cdots, b_m)$ be an ordered basis of a lattice $\mathcal{L}$. If B is weakly $\left(\frac{\pi}{3} + \epsilon\right)$-orthogonal, for $0 \leqslant \epsilon \leqslant \frac{\pi}{6}$, then a shortest vector in B is a shortest non-zero vector in $\mathcal{L}$. More generally,*

$$min_{j \in \{1, 2, \cdots, m\}} \|b_j\| \leqslant \|\sum_{i=1}^m u_i b_i\|,$$

for all $u_i \in \mathbb{Z}$ with $\sum_{i=1}^m |u_i| \geqslant 1$, with equality possible only if $\epsilon = 0$ or $\sum_{i=1}^m |u_i| = 1$.

From Theorem 1, we conclude that if $\theta \geqslant \frac{\pi}{3}$, the weakly θ-orthogonal lattice basis contain a shortest lattice vector, so, it is not easier to find a weakly θ-orthogonal lattice basis $\left(\theta \geqslant \frac{\pi}{3}\right)$ than to find the shortest vector.

Corollary 1. *[5] If $0 < \epsilon \leqslant \frac{\pi}{6}$, then a weakly $\left(\frac{\pi}{3} + \epsilon\right)$-orthogonal basis contains every shortest non-zero lattice vector(up to multiplication by ± 1).*

Theorem 2. *[5] Let $B = (b_1, b_2, \cdots, b_m)$ be a weakly θ-orthogonal basis for a lattice $\mathcal{L}$ with $\theta > \frac{\pi}{3}$. For all $i \in \{1, 2, \cdots, m\}$, if*

$$\|b_i\| < \eta(\theta) \min_{j \in \{1,2,\cdots,m\}} \|b_j\|,$$

with

$$\eta(\theta) = \frac{\sqrt{3}}{\sin\theta + \sqrt{3}\cos\theta},$$

then any $\frac{\pi}{3}$-orthogonal basis comprises the vectors in B multiplied by ± 1.

This means that when the lengths of its basis vectors are almost equal, a nearly orthogonal basis is essentially unique.

Theorem 3. *[5] Let $B = (b_1, b_2, \cdots, b_m)$ and $\widetilde{B}$ be two weakly θ-orthogonal bases for a lattice $\mathcal{L}$, where $\theta > \frac{\pi}{3}$. Let $U = (u_{ij})$ be a unimodular matrix such that $B = \widetilde{B}U$.*

$$\kappa(B) = \left(\frac{2}{\sqrt{3}}\right)^{m-1} \times \frac{\max_{i \in \{1,\ldots,m\}} \|b_i\|}{\min_{i \in \{1,\ldots,m\}} \|b_i\|},$$

then $|u_{ij}| \leqslant \kappa(B)$, for all i and j.

From Theorem 3, we know that if a weakly $\frac{\pi}{3}$-orthogonal basis vectors transform into another weakly orthogonal basis by a unimodular matrix, the coefficient of unimodular matrix will be small.

Theorem 4. *[6] Let $B = b_1, b_2, \cdots, b_m$ be a θ-orthogonal basis for a lattice $\mathcal{L}$ with $\theta \geqslant \frac{\pi}{3}$. Further, suppose that*

$$\frac{min_i \|b_i\|}{max_i \|b_i\|} \geqslant 2\cos\theta.$$

Then some ordering of the basis is Minkowski reduced.

The proof of Theorem 4 is omitted, the detail can be found in [6]. From Theorem 4, we can quickly get the Theorem 5 whose conditions are not harder than Theorem 4.

Theorem 5. *Let $B = (b_1, b_2, \cdots, b_m)$ be a weakly θ-orthogonal basis for a lattice $\mathcal{L}$ with $\theta \geqslant \frac{\pi}{3}$, and it has been ordered by the Euclidean norm of the vectors, if*

$$\frac{min_i \|b_i\|}{max_i \|b_i\|} \geqslant 2\cos\theta,$$

then $B = (b_1, b_2, \cdots, b_m)$ is Minkowski reduced.

Theorem 6. *Let $B = (b_1, b_2, \cdots, b_m)$ be a Minkowski-reduced basis for a lattice $\mathcal{L}$, the angle between b_i and b_j is θ_{ij}, for all $i, j \in \{1, 2, \cdots, m\}$, $i \neq j$, then $|cos\theta_{ij}| \leqslant \frac{1}{2}$.*

Proof. By the definition of Minkowski-reduced basis, we have

$$\|b_1\| \leqslant \|b_2\| \leqslant \cdots \leqslant \|b_m\|.$$

For any $i < j$, we have

$$\|b_j\| \leqslant \|b_i + b_j\|,$$

$$\|b_j\|^2 \leqslant \|b_i + b_j\|^2 = \|b_i\|^2 + \|b_j\|^2 + 2\langle b_i, b_j \rangle.$$

Delete the $\|b_j\|^2$ from two sides of inequality, we have

$$\|b_i\|^2 + 2\langle b_i, b_j \rangle \geqslant 0,$$

then

$$\left| \frac{\langle b_i, b_j \rangle}{\|b_i\| \cdot \|b_j\|} \right| \leqslant \left| \frac{\langle b_i, b_j \rangle}{\|b_i\|^2} \right| \leqslant \frac{1}{2}.$$

Theorem 7. *If the orthogonal defect of 3-dimension lattice $\mathcal{L}$ is less than $\frac{2}{\sqrt{3}}$, then there exits $\epsilon > 0$ such that the Minkowski-reduced basis of the lattice is $\left(\frac{\pi}{3} + \epsilon\right)$-orthogonal.*

Proof. Let $B = \{b_1, b_2, b_3\}$ be the basis whose orthogonal defect is smaller than $\frac{2}{\sqrt{3}}$. Let us define the angle between b_1 and b_2 is θ_{12}, the angle between b_3 and the subspace spanned by $\{b_1, b_2\}$ is θ_{3-12}. Because

$$det(\mathcal{L}) = \|b_1\| \cdot \|b_2\| \cdot \|b_3\| \cdot \sin \theta_{12} \cdot \sin \theta_{3-12},$$

we can get that

$$\frac{\|b_1\| \cdot \|b_2\| \cdot \|b_3\|}{det(\mathcal{L})} = \frac{1}{\sin \theta_{12} \cdot \sin \theta_{3-12}} < \frac{2}{\sqrt{3}},$$

i.e.

$$\sin \theta_{12} \cdot \sin \theta_{3-12} > \frac{\sqrt{3}}{2}.$$

Let $\{m_1, m_2, m_3\}$ be the Minkowski-reduced basis of the lattice $\mathcal{L}$, from the definition of Minkwoski-reduced basis, we have that

$$\|m_1\| = \lambda_1(\mathcal{L}), \|m_2\| = \lambda_2(\mathcal{L}), \|m_3\| = \lambda_3(\mathcal{L}).$$

Let the angle between m_1 and m_2 be φ_{12}, and the angle between m_3 and the subspace spanned by $\{m_1, m_2\}$ be φ_{3-12}. The same as above,

$$\|m_1\| \cdot \|m_2\| \cdot \|m_3\| \cdot \sin \varphi_{12} \cdot \sin \varphi_{3-12} = det(\mathcal{L}).$$

Because

$$\|m_1\| \cdot \|m_2\| \cdot \|m_3\| \leqslant \|b_1\| \cdot \|b_2\| \cdot \|b_3\|,$$

then

$$\sin \varphi_{12} \cdot \sin \varphi_{3-12} \geqslant \sin \theta_{12} \cdot \sin \theta_{3-12} > \frac{\sqrt{3}}{2}.$$

Obviously,

$$\sin \varphi_{12} \neq \frac{\sqrt{3}}{2},$$

otherwise,

$$\sin \varphi_{3-12} > 1,$$

thus

$$\sin \varphi_{12} > \frac{\sqrt{3}}{2}.$$

At the same time, $\sin \varphi_{12} \leqslant 1$, we have

$$\sin \varphi_{3-12} > \frac{\sqrt{3}}{2},$$

i.e.

$$\varphi_{3-12} > \frac{\pi}{3}.$$

Thus the Minkowski-reduced basis is weakly $\left(\frac{\pi}{3} + \epsilon\right)$-orthogonal. Because during the period of comparing the size of $\|m_1\| \cdot \|m_2\| \cdot \|m_3\|$ and $\|b_1\| \cdot \|b_2\| \cdot \|b_3\|$, we need not consider the order of the basis, thus we can conclude that the Minkowski-reduced basis is $\left(\frac{\pi}{3} + \epsilon\right)$-orthogonal.

We have known of some properties of the weakly θ-orthogonality, θ-orthogonality, nearly orthogonality, orthogonal defect and the Minkowski-reduced basis. It is easy to induce the relations between them:

(i) Let $B = (b_1, b_2, \cdots, b_m)$ be a weakly θ-orthogonal basis for a lattice $\mathcal{L}$, then B is $(\sin \theta)^{1-n}$-orthogonal basis.

(ii) Changing the ordering of the basis vectors will change the weakly θ-orthogonality , but will not change the OD-r-orthogonality.

(iii) Let $B = (b_1, b_2, \cdots, b_m)$ be a OD-r-orthogonal basis for a lattice $\mathcal{L}$, then B is $\arcsin \frac{1}{r}$-orthogonal basis.

3   JPEG Compression History Estimation (CHEst)

In this section, we briefly describe the JPEG CHEst problem firstly; secondly, we describe the algorithm that Neelamani et al. gives in [5]; thirdly, we apply the properties of orthogonal defect of color-transform matrix and give a Deterministic algorithm.

3.1   JPEG CHEst Problem Statement

In [5,11], the authors discussed the JPEG CHEst problem as follows:
Given a decompressed image

$$P_d = \{CQ_1P_{c,1}, CQ_2P_{c,2}, \cdots, CQ_kP_{c,k}\}, C \in \mathbb{R}^{3\times3}$$

which is a color-transform matrix, the columns of C form a different basis for the color space spanned by the R, G and B vectors. P is the image and is mapped to $C^{-1}P$. Choose a diagonal, positive and integer quantization matrix Q, then compute the quantized compressed image as

$$p_c = \lceil Q^{-1}C^{-1}P \rfloor$$

where $\lceil \cdot \rfloor$ means rounding to the nearest integer. JPEG decompression constructs

$$P_d = CQP_c = CQ\lceil Q^{-1}C^{-1}P \rfloor.$$

In fact, during compression, the image matrix P is decomposed into different frequency components $P = \{P_1, P_2, \cdots, P_k\}$, $k > 1$. Then the same C and different quantization matrix Q_i are applied to the sub-matrices P_i, $i = 1, \cdots, k$. The compressed image is

$$P_c = \{P_{c,1}, P_{c,2}, \cdots, P_{c,k}\} = \{\lceil Q_1^{-1}C^{-1}P_1 \rfloor \lceil Q_2^{-1}C^{-1}P_2 \rfloor, \cdots, \lceil Q_kC^{-1}P_k \rfloor\},$$

and the decompressed image is

$$P_d = \{CQ_1P_{c,1}, CQ_2P_{c,2}, \cdots, CQ_kP_{c,k}\}.$$

The JPEG compressed file format stores the C and the matrices Q_i with P_c. When decompressing the JPEG image, we will use the stored matrices and discarded them afterward. We call the set $\{C, Q_1, Q_2, \cdots, Q_k\}$ the compression history of the image.

3.2   Neelamani, Dash and Baraniuk's Contributions [5] Revisited

Neelamani, Dash and Baraniuk's contributions [5] are a heuristic algorithm to solve the following question: given a decompressed image

$$P_d = \{CQ_1P_{c,1}, \cdots, CQ_kP_{c,k}\}$$

and some information about the structure of C and the Q_i's, how can we find the color transform C and the quantization matrices Q_i's.

We can see the columns of $CQ_iP_{c,i}$ lie on a 3-D lattice basis with basis CQ_i, because $P_{c,i}$ are integer matrices. The estimation of CQ_is comprise the main step in JPEG CHEst. What Neelamani et al. have done is exploiting the near-orthogonality of C to estimate the products CQ_i. Neelamani et al. use the LLL algorithm to compute LLL-reduced bases B_i for each $\mathcal{L}$ spanned by CQ_i, but such B_i are not guaranteed to be weakly $(\frac{\pi}{3} + \epsilon)$-orthogonal. Because B_i and

CQ_i are the bases of the same lattice $\mathcal{L}_i$, there exist some unimodular matrix U_i, such that

$$B_i = CQ_iU_i,$$

then estimating CQ_i is equivalent to estimating the respective U_i. Using the theorems above, Neelamani et al. list the constraints that the correct U_is must satisfied at first, secondly, they enumerate a lot of U_i satisfying Theorems 1 and 3, then test constraints that Neelamani et al. list in [5]. At last, by a four-step heuristic algorithm, they can find the solution. Neelamani et al. believe that the solution can be non-unique only if the Q_is are chosen carefully, but JPEG employ Q_is that are not related in any special way. Therefore, they believe that for most practical cases JPEG CHEst has a unique solution. For clarity, the correct U_is should satisfy some constraints as follows [5]:

1. The U_i's are such that $B_iU_i^{-1}$ is weakly $\left(\frac{\pi}{3} + \epsilon\right)$-orthogonal.
2. The product $U_iB_i^{-1}B_jU_j^{-1}$ is diagonal with positive entries for any $i, j \in \{1, 2, \cdots, k\}$.
3. The columns of U_i corresponding to the shortest columns of B_i are the standard unit vectors times ± 1.
4. All entries of U_i are $\leqslant \kappa(B_i)$ in magnitude.

Neelamani, Dash and Baraniuks heuristic algorithm [5] is as follows:

(i) Obtain bases B_i for the lattices $\mathcal{L}_i$, $i = 1, 2, \cdots, k$. Construct a weakly $\left(\frac{\pi}{3} + \epsilon\right)$-orthogonal basis B_i for at least one lattice $\mathcal{L}_i$, $i \in \{1, 2, \cdots, k\}$.
(ii) Compute $\kappa(B_i)$.
(iii) For every unimodular matrix U_i satisfying constraints 1,3 and 4, go to step (iv).
(iv) For chosen in step (iii), test if there exit unimodular matrices U_j for each $j = 1, 2, \cdots, k$, $j \neq l$ that satisfy constraint 2. If such collection of matrices exists, then return this collection; otherwise go to step (iii).

3.3   Our Improvement

What we want to do is to improve the algorithm that Neelamani, Dash and Baraniuk [5] solved the JPEG CHEst problem. The algorithm used in [5] is heuristic, because in the step (i), constructing a weakly $\left(\frac{\pi}{3} + \epsilon\right)$-orthogonal basis B_i for at least one lattice $\mathcal{L}_i$, $i \in \{1, 2, \cdots, k\}$ is uncertain. Using the property of orthogonal defect of the color-transform matrix C, we can exactly construct a $\left(\frac{\pi}{3} + \epsilon\right)$-orthogonal basis B_i for every lattice $\mathcal{L}_i$, $i \in \{1, 2, \cdots, k\}$.

Neelamani, Dash and Baraniuk [5] have verified that all C's used in practice are weakly $\left(\frac{\pi}{3} + \epsilon\right)$-orthogonal, with $0 < \epsilon \leqslant \frac{\pi}{6}$, while we have verified that all C's used in practice whose orthogonal defect is less than $\frac{2}{\sqrt{3}}$. By Theorem 6, we find that the Minkowski-reduced basis of lattice spanned by all C's used in practice is $\left(\frac{\pi}{3} + \epsilon\right)$-orthogonal. We can use the greedy algorithm to find the Minkowski-reduced basis of the lattice. From now on, the algorithm becomes a deterministic algorithm. And because C's used in practice whose orthogonal defect is less than $\frac{2}{\sqrt{3}}$, we can change constraint 1 as follows: the U_i's are such that $B_i U_i^{-1}$'s orthogonal defect is less than $\frac{2}{\sqrt{3}}$. In step (iii) of the algorithm in [5], besides satisfy the constraint 3 and constraint 4 at first, every unimodular matrix U_{ij} should satisfy the following constraint: every unimodular matrix U_{ij} by B_i is some basis M_i of lattice $\mathcal{L}_i$, if M_is orthogonal defect is less than $\frac{2}{\sqrt{3}}$, then go on to test the other constraints, otherwise discard the U_{ij}. Add the constraint, we will greatly reduce the number of the unimodular matrix tested.

4   Conclusion

In this paper, we derived some interesting relations among Minkowski-reduced basis, orthogonal defect and nearly orthogonal lattice basis. We prove that the angle between Minkowski-reduced basis vectors is in $\left[\frac{\pi}{3}, \frac{2\pi}{3}\right]$, and if the orthogonal defect of 3-dimension lattice $\mathcal{L}$ is less than $\frac{2}{\sqrt{3}}$, the Minkowski-reduced basis of the lattice is $\frac{\pi}{3}$-orthogonal. We use the property of the Minkowski-reduced basis to improve the algorithm in [5] by removing the heuristic hypothesis, thus our algorithm is deterministic. We also use the orthogonal defect to constraint the unimodular matrix to greatly reduce the number of the unimodular matrix that should be tested next.

Acknowledgment. This work was supported by the grants from the Student Research Innovation Scholarship of Hunan Province (Grant No. CX2014B010) and the National Natural Science Foundation of China (Grant No. 61304119).

References

1. Donaldson, J.L.: Minkowski reduction of integral matrices. Math. Comput. **33**(145), 201–216 (1979)
2. Dube, T., Georgiou, D.N., Megaritis, A.C., Moshokoa, S.P.: A study of covering dimension for the class of finite lattices. Discrete Math. **338**(7), 1096–1110 (2015)
3. Jorge, G.C., de Andrade, A.A., Costa, S.I., Strapasson, J.E.: Algebraic constructions of densest lattices. J. Algebra **429**, 218–235 (2015)
4. Nguyên, P.Q., Stehlé, D.: Low-dimensional lattice basis reduction revisited. In: Buell, D.A. (ed.) ANTS 2004. LNCS, vol. 3076, pp. 338–357. Springer, Heidelberg (2004)
5. Neelamani, R., Dash, S., Baraniuk, R.G.: On nearly orthogonal lattice bases and random lattices. SIAM J. Discrete Math. **21**(1), 199–219 (2007)
6. Dash, R.S., Sorkin, G.: On nearly orthogonal lattice bases and minkowski reduction, IBM Research Report RC (24696)
7. Neelamani, R.: Inverse Problems in Image Processing. Rice University, Houston, Texas (2003)
8. Agrell, E., Eriksson, T., Vardy, A., Zeger, K.: Closest point search in lattices. IEEE Trans. Inf. Theory **48**(8), 2201–2214 (2002)
9. Wang, Y., Shang, S., Gao, F., Huang, M.: Some sufficient conditions of the equivalence between successive minimal independent vectors and minkowski-reduced basis in lattices. Sci. Sinica (Math.) **8**, 001 (2010)

10. Lenstra, A.K., Lenstra, H.W., Lovász, L.: Factoring polynomials with rational coefficients. Math. Ann. **261**(4), 515–534 (1982)
11. Bauschke, H.H., Hamilton, C.H., Macklem, M.S., McMichael, J.S., Swart, N.R.: Recompression of JPEG images by requantization. IEEE Trans. Image Process. **12**(7), 843–849 (2003)

Research on Image Quality Assessment in Foggy Conditions

Wenjun Lu[✉], Congli Li, Xiaoning Sun, and Song Xue

Army Officer Academy, Mailbox 081 in Huangshan Road No. 451, Hefei AP, China
{Wenjun.lu2013,sunxiaoning0117}@gmail.com, lcliqa@163.com,
xs_xs6688@sina.com

Abstract. Recently, no-reference image quality assessment has been followed with interest by researchers, but no-reference quality assessment of foggy images is rarely reported. This paper proposes a no-reference quality assessment of foggy images based on codebooks. Proposed method aims to be consistent with human subjective perception. The Technical roadmap of the method is from feature extraction to quality metric model. The features need to reflect characteristics of foggy images exactly. Then codebook is built by the features and used to acquire feature vectors of training images by encoding. At last, regression is introduced to quality model construction by feature vectors and subjective ratings. The method is tested in simulation library of foggy images. Results show that Pearson Linear Correlation Coefficient (PLCC) and Spearman rank Order Correlation Coefficient (SROCC) are both above 0.99. And compared with state-of-art algorithms, our method perceives higher performance, and it can be a good predictor of subjective perception of foggy images.

Keywords: Foggy images · Image quality assessment (IQA) · Codebook · No-reference IQA

1 Introduction

In National Standard of China GB/T 27964-2011 [1], fog is classified to five grades. Mist is a weather phenomenon of visibility above 1 km. Visibility of fog is from 500 m to 1 km. Visibility of heavy fog is from 200 m to 500 m. Visibility of strong fog is from 50 m to 200 m. Visibility of ultra strong fog is below 50 m.

Currently researches on foggy images processing have focused on image defog and enhancement, quality assessment of image in foggy conditions has focused on image defog [2, 3], the result of assessment is used to determine defog effect. Research on quality assessment of foggy image has rarely been reported. How to evaluate quality grades of foggy image has important significance to real-time forecasting of fog, defog algorithms and foggy image enhancement.

It is difficult to obtain a reference image, only no-reference method can be used to evaluate quality of foggy image. No-reference IQA can be divided into two categories, distortion specific method and non distortion specific method.

© Springer International Publishing Switzerland 2015
Y.-J. Zhang (Ed.): ICIG 2015, Part III, LNCS 9219, pp. 180–187, 2015.
DOI: 10.1007/978-3-319-21969-1_16

Distortion specific method refers distortion to evaluate is known. For example, Zhou Wang [4] proposed algorithm to evaluate JPEG distortion. Sheikh [5] proposed an algorithm based on NSS to evaluate JP2 K distortion. But in most cases, type of distortion is unknown, and it is difficult to determine which no-reference algorithm to use. This limits the application of these algorithms.

Non-distortion specific method refers to unknown distortion, which is a general no-reference IQA algorithm. We can also divide it into two categories, OA-DU (Opinion Aware- Distortion Unknown) and OU-DU (Opinion Unaware- Distortion Unknown). OA-DU is the algorithms of requiring subjective score in training process, such as BIQI [6], BRISQUE [7], CBIQ [8], CORNIA [9] and so on. OU-DU is the kind of algorithm which does not require subjective score. For example, in QAC [10] algorithm, subjective score does not be used directly. But in training process full-reference IQA algorithm was used to acquire 'subjective rating'. And the benefit of the algorithm does not require classical image databases to train, so that the scope of the training images was larger. NIQE [11] algorithm aims to require the reference by training, which is equivalent to construct a 'reference image'. It may not select training images from classical databases. The benefit is not dependent on the database and has adaptability.

Quality assessment of foggy image is also a kind of distortion specific method. However, fog is not only unlike any known distortion, but also is not included in classical image databases.

Figure 1 shows quality assessment results of foggy image by new presented no reference algorithms of NIQE and CORNIA. X-axis is 20 fog densities which gradually rise, y-axis is quality score. In figure, we can see that the two no-reference algorithms cannot evaluate quality of foggy image in accordance with subjective perception.

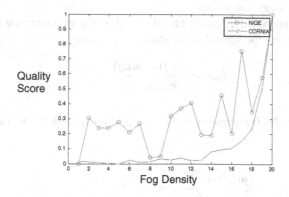

Fig. 1. Quality assessment curves of foggy image by different algorithms (Results of the two methods are normalized)

This paper is to propose a no-reference IQA method of foggy specific, the results of its evaluation is consistent with human subjective perception.

The remainder of this paper is organized as follows. Section 2 analyzes features of foggy image. Section 3 presents structure of algorithm design. Section 4 reports the experimental results and Sect. 5 concludes the paper.

2   Feature Ananlysis of Foggy Images

Influence on image quality in foggy weather contains three aspects. Firstly, fog breaks structure information of image. Secondly, existence of fog adds several channel information as a mask, and it enhances overall luminance. Lastly, new multiplicative information is derived from fog, it makes image blur and degrades contrast.

Figure 2 shows that contrast and gradient of the image apparently decrease with the increase of fog density.

Fig. 2. Contrast, gradient map (1st row is original image, 2nd row is contrast map, and 3rd row is gradient map. Every row is from mist to ultra strong fog)

Although contrast and gradient can well reflect the characteristics of foggy image, in order to get a better quality mapping, natural scene statistics (NSS) are used to learn image features in foggy conditions.

In BRISQUE proposed by Anish Mittal [7], MSCN coefficients are first used in the algorithm to represent the natural scene statistics of images.

$$\hat{I}(i,j) = \frac{I(i,j) - \mu(i,j)}{\sigma(i,j) + c} \tag{1}$$

In formula (1), $I(i,j)$ represents the image, and $\hat{I}(i,j)$ are MSCN coefficients. $c = 1$ is a stable parameter.

$$\mu(i,j) = \sum_{k=-K}^{K} \sum_{l=-L}^{L} W_{k,l} I_{k,l}(i,j) \tag{2}$$

$$\sigma(i,j) = \sqrt{\sum_{k=-K}^{K} \sum_{l=-L}^{L} W_{k,l}(I_{k,l}(i,j) - \mu(i,j))^2} \tag{3}$$

Here $W_{k,l} | k = -K \ldots K, l = -L \ldots L$ is two-dimensional Gaussian weighting function of $K \times L$ block size, here we take $K = L = 3$.

Previous researches on the natural scene statistics show that generalized Gaussian distribution (GGD) can effectively obtain coefficients changes in natural images and their distorted images.

$$f(x;\alpha,\beta) = \frac{\alpha}{2\beta\Gamma(1/\alpha)}\exp(-(\frac{|x|}{\beta})^\alpha) \tag{4}$$

$$\Gamma(a) = \int_0^\infty t^{a-1}e^{-t}dt \quad a > 0 \tag{5}$$

(α, β) of generalized Gaussian distribution can be effectively estimated [12]. In formula (1), there is a relatively regular distribution, but the distortion changed this distribution, and this change can be calculated by the product of four directions of adjacent coefficients, which can be fitted by adjacent asymmetric generalized Gaussian distribution (AGGD).

$$f(x;\gamma,\beta_l,\beta_r) = \begin{cases} \frac{\gamma}{(\beta_l+\beta_r)\Gamma(\frac{1}{\gamma})}\exp(-(\frac{-x}{\beta_l})^\gamma)\forall x\leq 0 \\ \frac{\gamma}{(\beta_l+\beta_r)\Gamma(\frac{1}{\gamma})}\exp(-(\frac{x}{\beta_r})^\gamma)\forall x\geq 0 \end{cases} \tag{6}$$

AGGD parameters $(\gamma, \beta_l, \beta_r)$ can also be effectively estimated [13].
Mean of the distribution is one of the parameters.

$$\eta = (\beta_r - \beta_l)\frac{\Gamma(\frac{2}{\gamma})}{\Gamma(\frac{1}{\gamma})} \tag{7}$$

18 parameters are extracted in one scale, but extracted information will not produce significant changes. So two scales are selected, one is scale of the original image, and another scale is after the next sample image. On each scale a 18-dimensional feature extraction, feature vector to form a total of 36 dimensions. Add up to luminance, contrast, and gradient magnitude, dimension of features is 39.

3 Structure of Proposed Algorithm

Figure 3 shows structure of the algorithm design, which contains feature extraction, codebook construction and encoding, feature training of support vector regression. Codebook construction follows the CORNIA Algorithm [9].

3.1 Local Feature Extraction

In this paper, an image is divided into B × B size of blocks. In each block, NSS are extracted to forms local features vector x_i.

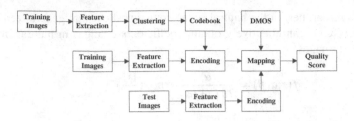

Fig. 3. Flow chart of proposed algorithm

3.2 Codebook Construction

When features extraction of all the training images complete, extracted features are clustered by K-mean. Then codebook is built. Codebook is represented by $D_{[d \times K]} = [D_1, D_2 \dots D_K]$. Code word $D_{i(i=1,2\dots K)}$ is cluster centers. Here none of the training images have labels. And a general codebook not sparse is used in this paper because that encoding is more important than codebook construction [14].

3.3 Coding Local Features

A soft-assignment encoding is used to calculate distance between code words and the local features. Denotes $s(i,j) = x_i \cdot D_j$ as a partial similarity between local features vector x_i and code word D_j. Local features x_i are represented by

$$x_i = [\max(s_{i1}, 0), \dots, \max(s_{ik}, 0),$$
$$\max(-s_{i1}, 0)], \dots, \max(-s_{ik}, 0) \tag{8}$$

Similarity has positive and negative components, it will increase the degree of recognition.

3.4 Features Pooling

A coefficient matrix $C_{2K \times N} = [c_1, c_2 \dots c_n]$ is used in encoding, and $c_i = [c_{i,1}, c_{i,2} \dots c_{i,2k}]^T$. In order to support vector regression, a fixed-length feature vectors are needed. A lot of image quality assessment algorithms [15, 16], the percentage of pooling have been adopted. The worst image region of image affects perception greatest. In image classification, the maximum pooling proved to have classification results. This paper uses the maximum pooling, which can be considered as a special percentage pooling. Max pooling is

$$\hat{\beta} = \psi_{\max}(C) \tag{9}$$

Here we define $\psi_{\max}$ as the maximum value of each row.

$$\hat{\beta}_i = \max\{c_{1i}, c_{2i} \dots c_{Ni}\} \tag{10}$$

$\hat{\beta}_i$ will be used to regression training.

4   Experiments Results and Analysis

4.1   Database of Foggy Images

There is no established databases of foggy image, in order verify the proposed we have set up foggy image database. 29 reference images are selected in LIVE database. For each image, we plus fog from 0 % to 95 % density by Photoshop software in accordance with interval of 5 % density. Each group of images contains a reference image and 19 foggy images. The entire image database contains 29 images and 551 foggy images. Fog density of each image is used as DMOS. In this paper, 80 % images of database are used for training, and 20 % for test.

4.2   Experimental Results

In experiment, block size is 96×96, and the size of codebook is 500. In order to evaluate performance of algorithm, two correlation coefficients of SROCC and PLCC are introduced. SROCC is monotonic measurement, and PLCC is consistency measurement. Table 1 shows the evaluation results.

Table 1. Comparison to four no-reference IQA algorithms

No-reference IQA	SROCC	PLCC
CORNIA	0.6845	0.7828
DIIVINE	0.7533	0.8064
BRISQUE	0.7695	0.8406
NIQE	0.7997	0.8660
Paper	**0.9529**	**0.9620**

4.3   Experimental Analysis

From Table 1, it is clear that our algorithm is superior to CORNIA and NIQE. It mainly because that the two classical algorithms are both based on existing image quality assessment database, but fog distortion is not involved, so evaluation results are not good. The proposed algorithm aims to appropriate features, and it is based on foggy image database, so the evaluation results are better.

4.3.1   Selection of Codebook Size

We change codebook size of 50, 100, 200, 300, 400, 500, 1000, the performance is shown in Fig. 4. When the size of the codebook reaches 500, the performance is no more increase. Therefore, we determine codebook size as 500.

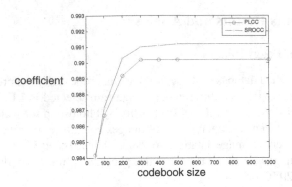

Fig. 4. Effect of codebook size

4.3.2 Effect Encoding

Codebook encoding impacts larger on the final quality score. Here we select three encoding pattern to comprise, which are hard-assignment encoding, LLC-assignment encoding [17], and soft-assignment encoding. The indexes of comparison are SROCC, PLCC, and algorithm time. The comparison is selected codebook size of 500 as in Table 2.

Table 2. Comparison to different encoding

Encoding pattern	SROCC	PLCC	Algorithm time
hard	0.9705	0.9744	0.6333 s/i
SC	0.8745	0.9037	0.7250 s/i
LLC	0.9346	0.9633	0.7333 s/i
Soft	0.9902	0.9912	0.7250 s/i

In Table 2, Soft-assignment may be the best encoding pattern.

5   Conclusions

This paper presents an efficient codebook-based no-reference quality assessment algorithm of foggy image, which performance is higher than some classical algorithms. The algorithm selects the best codebook size and the optimal codebook encoding. This algorithm obtains a better linearity and consistency with foggy image database. The proposed method gives a good solution to the problem of image quality assessment in conditions and provides a reference to solve foggy weather forecasting. The next step will be further looking for features to reflect foggy image quality well, and more accurate image quality assessment of foggy image.

References

1. Guiming, Y., Jian, L., Zhiping, Z.: National Standard of China. GB/T 27964 (2011)
2. Guo, F., Cai, Z.: Objective assessment method for the clearness effect of image defogging algorithm. Acta Automatica Sin. **38**, 1410–1419 (2012)
3. Li, D., Yu, J., Xiao, C.: No-reference image quality assessment method for defogged images. J. Image Graph. **16**, 1753–1757 (2011)
4. Wang, Z., Sheikh, H.R., Bovik, A.C.: No-reference perceptual quality assessment of JPEG compressed images. In: Proceedings of 2002 International Conference on Image Processing, pp. 22–25. IEEE, New York (2002)
5. Sheikh, H.R., Bovik, A.C., Cormack, L.: No-reference quality assessment using natural scene statistics: JPEG2000. IEEE Trans. IP **14**, 1918–1927 (2005)
6. Moorthy, A.K., Bovik, A.C.: A two-step framework for constructing blind image quality indice. IEEE Signal Process. Lett. **17**, 513–516 (2010)
7. Mittal, A., Moorthy, A.K., Bovik, A.C.: No-reference image quality assessment in the spatial domain. IEEE Trans. IP **21**, 4695–4708 (2012)
8. Ye, P., Doermann, D.: No-reference image quality assessment using visual codebook. In: Proceedings of 2011 International Conference on Image Processing, pp. 3150–3153. IEEE, Brussels (2011)
9. Ye, P., Kumar, J., Kang, L., Doermann, D.: Unsupervised feature learning framework for no-reference image quality assessment. In: Proceedings of 2012 International Conference on Computer Vision and Pattern Recognition, pp. 1098–1105. IEEE, Providence (2012)
10. Xue, W., Zhang, L., Mou, X.: Learning without human scores for blind image quality assessment. In: Proceedings of 2013 International Conference on Computer Vision and Pattern Recognition, pp. 995–1002. IEEE, Portland (2013)
11. Mittal, A., Soundararajan, R., Bovik, A.C.: Making a 'completely blind' image quality analyzer. IEEE Signal Process. Lett. **3**, 209–212 (2013)
12. Sharifi, K., Leon-Garcia, A.: Estimation of shape parameter for generalized Gaussian distributions in subband decompositions of video. IEEE Trans. Circ. Syst. Video Technol. **5**, 52–56 (1995)
13. Lasmar, N. E., Stitou, Y., Berthoumieu, Y.: Multiscale skewed heavy tailed model for texture analysis. In: Proceedings of 2009 International Conference on Image processing, pp. 2281–2284. IEEE, Cairo (2009)
14. Coates, A., Ng, A.Y.: The importance of encoding versus training with sparse coding and vector quantization. In: Proceedings of 2011 International Conference on Machine Learning, pp. 921–928. Springer, Bellevue (2011)
15. Liu, L., Wang, L., Liu, X.: In defense of soft-assignment coding. In: ICCV 2011, pp. 1794–1801 (2011)
16. Yang, J., Yu, K., Gong, Y., Huang, T.: Linear spatial pyramid matching using sparse coding for image classification. In: Proceedings of 2009 International Conference on Computer Vision and Pattern Recognition, pp. 1794 –1801. IEEE, Miami (2009)
17. Wang, J., Yang, J., Yu, K., Lv, F., Huang, T., Gong, Y.: Locality-constrained Linear Coding for Image Classification. In: Proceedings of 2010 International Conference on Computer Vision and Pattern Recognition, pp. 3360–3367. IEEE, Maryland (2010)

Research on Vehicle Type Classification Based on Spatial Pyramid Representation and BP Neural Network

Shaoyue Song[⊠] and Zhenjiang Miao

Institute of Information Science, Beijing Jiaotong University, Beijing, China
{14112060,zjmiao}@bjtu.edu.cn

Abstract. This paper presents a method of the vehicle type classification based on spatial pyramid representation and BP neural network. We extract feature vectors of each vehicle image by using the spatial pyramid representation method. By this way, we can use different size of pictures instead of changing the picture into a fixed size avoiding the deformation of the target images when cropping or warping and so on. We choose BP neural network to train our classifier and have a good performance on car, bus and truck classification.

Keywords: Vehicle type classification · Spatial pyramid representation · BP neural network

1 Introduction

With the growth in the volume of our country's car ownership, it's important for us to establish and improve an intelligent transportation system. The vehicle type classification is an important part of intelligent transport system and has a wide application prospect in the future. There are many methods on classifying vehicle type. Usually we can divide them into several categories: by contour scanning, by changing magnetic field and by the image-based method. [1] Compared with the other two methods, the method which based on images is simple, fast and effective.

As is known to us, feature extraction is the key task of target classification. Some researchers [2–5] get length, roof length and height of the vehicle through pictures and use them to classify the vehicle. This kind of methods are geometric-based methods that some geometric measurements are needed. Because of the diversity of the vehicle and the change of vehicle's attitude in the image, it's difficult to meet the requirement of accuracy and fast classification.

Another common approach is appearance-based method. In this kind of methods, vehicle images are usually represented as vectors in some high-dimensional space. [6] Weixin Kang et al. [7] combine Harris corner and SIFT feature to classify the vehicle. In the research of Fuqing Zhu et al. [8], the image features they used are based on the

---

Supported by "The Fundamental Research Funds for the Central Universities".

Y.-J. Zhang (Ed.): ICIG 2015, Part III, LNCS 9219, pp. 188–196, 2015.
DOI: 10.1007/978-3-319-21969-1_17

histogram of the image local feature sparse coding. They use a SVM method to train the classifier and achieve accuracy of more than 90 % over six categories.

The algorithm artificial neural network is one of the most popular research directions in object recognition and classification based on images. [9, 10] BP neural network is the most intensively studied and the most widely applied model in artificial neural network. [11] In some studies of the BP network, the images need to be changed into a fixed size before classification. But after the size normalization, there usually will be some problems like image deletion or geometric distortion. This will reduce the performance of the classification of the vehicle. In [9], the authors present a spatial pyramid representation method which can remove the fixed-size constrain of the method by using the SPP (Spatial pyramid pooling) model. The CNNs networks method in [9] usually needs a period of time to train. We want to find out an easier way to achieve our classification task, so a simple BP neural network is used in our experiment.

In this paper, we extract the feature vector via SPR model presented in [12] and train our classifier using a three-layer BP neural network. Details on the algorithm are discussed in later sections. The images we used in the experiment are captured from traffic video which is collected in the real life scenarios. We train a three-type classifier of vehicle and the classification accuracy rate can reach 91.0 %.

2   Method

We combine spatial pyramid representation and BP neural network to design the vehicle type classifier. Any size of pictures can be directly inputted into our classifier instead of being transformed into the same size.

2.1   BP Neural Network

BP (back-propagation) neural network is a multi-layer feed-forward neural network. Most of the ANN models use BP neural network or its changing forms. [13] A BP neural network consists of an input layer, a number of hidden layers and one output layer and realizes the whole connection between each layer. But there is no connection between each layer's neuron units themselves.

The basic idea of the BP neural network algorithm is the learning process that propagating the signal forward and propagating the error backward. This is one of the reasons for the BP neural networks named. Figure 1 shows a basic structure of the BP neural network. In Fig. 1, w means weight and b represents bias item, and each layer has a threshold. In the forward propagation, data is inputted via input layer and sequentially processed in each hidden layer until reach the output layer. If the output is not expected, the error between the real output and the expected output will be propagated backward as adjustment signal. The network will adjust its weight and threshold according to the error repeatedly until the output is come to the expectancy or the number of iterations or other settings has reach to a limit and so on.

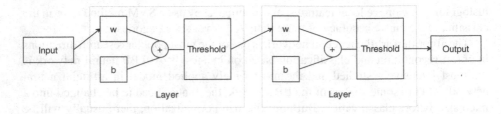

Fig. 1. The structure of BP neural network.

Robert Hecht-Nielsen [14] has proven that a three layers BP neural network which including one hidden layer can approximate any kind of continuous function effectively. So in this paper, we choose a simple three layers BP neural network to train our classifier. The number of input units is the dimensionality of each image's feature vector and the output number is the number of the vehicle type.

The selection of hidden layer units' number is a very important but complicated problem. It's usually directly connected with the number of input and output units. If the number is too small, it would be difficult for the network to get enough information to solve the classification problem; while if the number is too large, it would not only increase the training time, but may not get the best performance and cause the problem of over-fitting which may cause the test error increases and lead to generalization ability of the classifier drop. Therefore the reasonable choice of the number of hidden layer units is very important.

Usually the designers choose the number of the hidden layers by experience and many times experiments. This paper takes the empirical formula presented in [4] as a reference.

$$h = \sqrt{n + m} + \alpha \qquad (1)$$

In Eq. (1), h is the number of the hidden layer units, and n is the number of the input units; m is the number of output units and α is a constant between 1 and 10.

We set the number of the hidden layer units mainly according to Eq. (1) and at the same time we also adjust the number of the layer to improve the performance.

2.2 Spatial Pyramid Representation

In this part, we will introduce the Spatial Pyramid Representation (SPR). SPR is a widely used method in image recognition for embedding spatial information into a feature vector. [15] Lazebnik et al. [12] present the SPM method and get a significantly improved result on the recognition tasks. We use the same Spatial Pyramid Representation method as [12].

The images we used in the task of classification usually in different sizes or in different scales. It is important for us to find a standard in term of the size of image to avoid reduce the performance. In some works, the images are simply cut or resized into a fixed size before object classification. But these kinds of size normalization usually result geometric distortion, or change the content of the image. This will reduce the performance of the classification. Besides, the appearance of vehicle are usually similar to each other, normalizing the size of the images simply may make the feature less obviously, so is not a very suitable choice for the vehicle type classification. The spatial pyramid representation model [9, 12, 15] is an effective way for us to solve the problem.

The structure of the spatial pyramid shows as the Fig. 2. It's a spatial pyramid with three levels. The spatial pyramid can also be viewed as expansion of the BoW (Bag of Words or Bag of Keypoints) [16], and a 0 level spatial pyramid is a simple BoW representation.

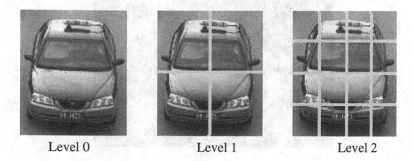

| Level 0 | Level 1 | Level 2 |

Fig. 2. The three-level spatial pyramid used in this paper.

We divide the images into three different levels of resolution and count dense SIFT feature descriptors in each spatial cell. The SPR defined the number of cells at level L as Eq. (2), and divided each cell into four cells at the next level of the pyramid which shows in Fig. 1. As the number of levels increases, the feature vector becomes large, so the SPR is usually used up to three levels (L = 2) [15], and it is the reason why we choose a three-level spatial pyramid. We calculate the histogram of the number of the dense SIFT features that fall in each spatial bin by the k-means method, and then we normalize all histograms by all features in the image like [12]. For a k cluster centers used in calculate the histogram, the dimensionality D in L level is counted like Eq. (3). We don't use the pyramid match kernel [17], but we put the same weight on our SPR model as [12] and then connect the vector with weight of each level together directly. The whole dimensionality of the SPR vector is come to a total of M (Eq. (4)).

$$c(l) = 4^l \tag{2}$$

$$D(l) = kc(l) = k4^l \tag{3}$$

$$M = \sum_{l=0}^{L} D(l) = \sum_{l=0}^{L} k4^l \tag{4}$$

3   Vehicle Dataset

In this section, we will introduce the vehicle dataset we used in the experiment. In order to imitate the realistic scenario in our life we collect a set of vehicle dataset from the video of a real life vehicle scene. (Figure 3) We use the same dataset as [18]. The images are divided into three types and tags are put on them. The three types of vehicle are car, bus and truck which are common to see in our life. The vehicle images we used are as the Fig. 4 shows, and we divide them into three types.

Fig. 3. The screenshot of the video we used in the experiment.

Fig. 4. Some examples from the dataset we collected. The vehicle images are captured by hand and collected in different time and illumination.

We choose the most common types of vehicle appearing in the video. Figure 3 shows a screenshot in the video. The videos are collected in the same angel and a certain spot but different in time. It is not difficult for us to think of that, the illumination may vary in different time of a day or even in the close time of different days the illumination may be different. So it's important to find a proper method to reduce the influence of the light of the classification and the SIFT descriptor is a good choice. [12, 16]

Another challenge of the classification is the various scales of the vehicle images. We cut out the vehicle images by hand and it's really a tough task to make the vehicle images are in a similar scale.

We use a 900 images dataset which include 300 images per type.

4   Experimental Evaluation

In order to compare our multi-size vehicle classification method with the fix-size method, we divide our experiment into two parts: one is experiment with multi-size images, and the other is the experiment with fixed-size images. In these two kinds of experiment, we use the method we mentioned before. The three-fold cross validation method is used in our experiment.

The number of input layer units is the dimensionality of each image's feature vector and the output unit's number is the number of the vehicle types.

Experiment with Multi-size Images. This time, we use the original size of images directly. In order to get a common vector representation of each images, we extract dense SIFT descriptors of each image and make the feature vectors in the representation of the SPR model.

We choose a different number of k-means method's cluster centers, and set the hidden layer unit's number at 40 to get a compromise between the performance and the training time. We get the performance like the Table 1 shows.

Table 1. Performance with multi-size images.

Cluster center numbers	40	80	120	160	200	300
Performance	79.3 %	86.7 %	88.3 %	89.3 %	90.7 %	91.0 %

We compare our method to the methods which are used in [18]. Table 2 shows the performance in [18].

Table 2. Performance in [18].

Feature types	SIFT	Surf	Eigenface	SIFT + Surf	SIFT + Eigenface	Surf + Eigenface	SIFT + Surf + Eigenface
performance	73.7 %	70.9 %	67.0 %	77.3 %	81.7 %	80.7 %	89.3 %

From Table 1 and Table 2, we can know that our method achieve better performance on the classification of the vehicle type than the methods in [18].

Experiment with Fixed-Size Images. In this part, we simply resize the vehicle images into a same size, and find the connection between image size and the performance. Obviously, there are some deformations of the vehicle (Fig. 5) after resizing. We take the whole picture as a vector to train the classifier. The performance shows in the Table 3. The number of BP neural network's input units is the dimensionality of each image. We also set 40 units of the hidden layer to compare with the multi-size experiment.

Table 3. Performance with fixed-size images.

Size	32*32	64*64	128*128
Performance	41.29 %	72.73 %	76.52 %

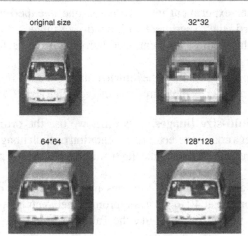

Fig. 5. A car which are resized into different size. The 32*32 means to resizing the picture into 32 × 32 pixels.

From Table 3, we can find that the larger the size of the images is the better performance will be. But in the experiment we also find that as the size improved, the training time are increased at the same time.

The dimensionality of feature vector in the fixed-size is 4096 at the 64*64 size. And when the cluster center numbers is 200 the feature vector is 4200. At a similar dimensionality level, the multi-size method gets better performance than the fixed-size one.

5   Conclusion

As we said above, the SPR method is easier to implement than those geometric-based methods. And it gets better performance than the fixed-size image method. By combining the SPR and the BP neural network method, we implement an effective method in the field of vehicle type classification in a real life scenario. The dataset in our experiment is a little small. So we will enlarge our dataset and improve the performance of our algorithm in the future.

References

1. Ma, B.: Vehicle Identification Technology In Video surveillance. D. Xidian University, Xi'an (2010) (in Chinese)(马蓓: 车型识别技术在视频监控中的应用. 硕士学位论文. 西安电子科技大学, 西安 (2010))

2. Zhou, X.: A recognition of automobile types method based on the BP neural network. J. Microelectron. Comput. **20**(4), 39–41 (2003). (in Chinese) 周红晓: 基于 BP 神经网络的汽车车型识别方法. J. 微电子学与计算机. 20(4), 39-41 (2003))

3. Hu, F., Jian, Q., Zhang, X.: The classifier of car type using BP neural networks. J. Xianan Univ. **32**(3), 439–442 (2005). (in Chinese) (胡方明, 简琴, 张秀君: 基于 BP 神经网络的车型分类器. 西安电子科技大学学报. J. 32(3), 439-442 (2005))

4. Wu, Z.: Research on vehicle type recognition based on BP neural network. J. Mod. Comput. **2**, 38–41 (2013). (in Chinese) (吴志攀: 基于 BP 神经网络的车型识别研究. J. 现代计算机 2, 38-41 (2013))

5. Du, H.: Implementation of BP algorithm using matlab based on vehicle type recognition. J. Comput. Modernization. **5**, 20–22 (2012). (in Chinese) (杜华英: 基于车型识别的 BP 算法 Matlab 实现. J. 计算机与现代化.5, 20-22 (2012))

6. Ghada, S.M.: Vehicle type classification with geometric and appearance attributes. Int. J. Civil Architectural Sci. Eng. **8**(3), 273–278 (2014)

7. Kang, W., Cao, Y., Sheng, Z., Li, P., Jiang, P.: Harris corner and SI FT Feature of vehicle and type recognition. J. Harbin Univ. Sci. Technol. **17**(3), 69–73 (2012). (in Chinese) (康维新, 曹宇亭, 盛卓, 李鹏, 姜澎: 车辆的 Harris 与 SIFT 特征及车型识别. J. 哈尔滨理工大学学报. 17(3), 69-73 (2012))

8. Zhu, F., Jia, J., Mi, X.: Vehicle Image Classification Based on Sparse Coding. J. Video Eng. **37**(11), 198–202 (2013). (in Chinese) (朱福庆, 贾世杰, 米晓莉: 基于稀疏编码的车型图像分类研究. J. 电视技术.37(11), 198-202 (2013))

9. He, K. et al.: Spatial pyramid pooling in deep convolutional networks for visual recognition. arXiv preprint arXiv:1406.4729 (2014)

10. Gan, J., Youwei, Z.: Face recognition based on BP neural network systems. Eng. Electron. **25**(1), 113–115 (2003). (in Chinese) (甘俊英, 张有为: 基于 BP 神经网络的人脸识别. 系统工程与电子技术.25(1), 113-115 (2003))

11. Shao, H., Xu, Q., Cui, C.: Research of Human Face Recognition Method Based on BP Neural Network. J. Shenyang Univ. Technol. **22**(4), 346–348 (2000). (in Chinese) (邵虹, 徐全生, 崔文成: 基于 BP 神经网络的人脸图像识别方法的研究. J. 沈阳工业大学学报. 22 (4), 346-348 (2000))

12. Lazebnik, S., Cordelia S., Jean P.: Beyond bags of features: Spatial pyramid matching for recognizing natural scene categories. In: 2006 IEEE Computer Society Conference on Computer Vision and Pattern Recognition, vol. 2. IEEE (2006)

13. Huichao, Q., Hongping, H., Yanping, B.: BP neural network classification on passenger vehicle type based on GA of feature selection. J. Meas. Sci. Instrum. **3**(3), 251–254 (2012)

14. Hecht-Nielsen, R.: Theory of the backpropagation neural network. In: International Joint Conference on Neural Networks, 1989 IJCNN. IEEE (1989)

15. Tatsuya, H., et al.: Discriminative spatial pyramid. In: 2011 IEEE Conference on Computer Vision and Pattern Recognition (CVPR), IEEE (2011)

16. Gabriella, C., et al.: Visual categorization with bags of keypoints. In: Workshop on Statistical Learning in Computer Vision, ECCV. Vol. 1, pp. 1–22 (2004)

17. Kristen, G., Darrell, T.: The pyramid match kernel: discriminative classification with sets of image features. In: Tenth IEEE International Conference on Computer Vision, 2005, ICCV 2005, vol. 2, IEEE (2005)

18. Ma, W.: Vehicle Classification Methods Research Based on Multi-feature Fusion. D. Beijing Jiaotong University, Beijing (2014). (in Chinese) (马文华: 基于多特征融合的车型分类方法研究. 硕士学位论文. 北京交通大学, 北京 (2014))

RGB-D Sensors Calibration for Service Robots SLAM

Yue Sun[1,2], Jingtai Liu[1,2(✉)], and Lei Sun[1,2]

[1] Institute of Robotics and Automatic Information System, Nankai University,
Tianjin 300071, China
[2] Tianjin Key Laboratory of Intelligent Robotics, Tianjin 300071, China
liujt@nankai.edu.cn

Abstract. One of the major research directions in robotic vision focuses on SLAM using RGB-D sensors. The information can be used for decision making of robots and other areas that require precise position as a feature. This paper presents a novel algorithm to calibrate the RGB-D sensors for service robots SLAM. The distortions of the RGB and depth images are calibrated before the sensor is used as a measuring device for robot navigation. The calibration procedure includes the correction of the RGB and depth image as well as alignment of the RGB lens with the depth lens. The key advances in this paper are: a new method for RDB-D sensors calibration, and use of a depth distortion correcting model to help improve measurement precision. We experimentally verify our algorithm using varies of methods. The results show that, typically, our approach provides accurate calibration and the RGB-D sensors could provide reliable measurement information for robots navigating in unknown environments.

Keywords: RGB-D sensors · Camera calibration · Robot SLAM · Depth distortion correcting

1 Introduction

When a robot is navigating in an unknown environment, it relies on sensors to recognize the outside world and estimate the state of the robot itself to achieve the task of autonomous navigation. RGB-D sensors as low cost Kinect are widely used in robotics applications. Obstacle Avoidance (OA), Augmented Reality (AR), Simultaneous Localization and Mapping (SLAM), Mobile Object Tracking (MOT) all are needed accurate information about the position of objects in the environment.

Depth information is an important cue for robot SLAM and any other scenes in a real world. In all of the depth needed applications, it's very important to gain robust and accurate depth image of the relevant RGB image. Different kinds of RGB-D sensors can provide real time depth estimation at each pixel, which give us 3D information. The depth information has generally been acquired using stereo cameras or other expensive hardware such as laser range scanner or Time of Flight cameras. But most of them are too expensive to be extensively used or capture only two-dimensional images without depth information of environmental objects. This study uses Microsoft

© Springer International Publishing Switzerland 2015
Y.-J. Zhang (Ed.): ICIG 2015, Part III, LNCS 9219, pp. 197–211, 2015.
DOI: 10.1007/978-3-319-21969-1_18

Kinect as the RGB-D sensor to capture color and depth images as environmental information for service robots SLAM because of its functions and low price.

The distortions of color images and depth images need to be calibrated before the RGB-D sensor is applied as a measuring device. The calibration includes internal calibration of color and depth camera as well as relative pose calibration between the camera pair. Many procedures have been developed to calibrate the color image by determining the camera intrinsic parameters [1, 2]. However, such earlier methods are fail to produce an answer in depth sensor calibration. On the other hand, the distortion of the depth image is due to the relative pose between the RGB sensor and the depth sensor. In the literature, Herrera [3, 4], Khoshelham [5] proposed calibration algorithm for structured light depth sensor. Zhang [6] adopt the method of depth camera calibration from depth images. Smisek [7] analyzed the measurement error of depth camera calibration from infrared projected light. Raposo [8] proposed several modifications to the work of Herrera [4] that improved runtime using less images. Nakayama [9] propose an alignment method which is based on line segments to improve the camera pose accuracy. However, all these methods are either not robust, or produce a result which is not accurate enough for real applications, or require relatively complex processing procedure. So there is no popular method to transfer and align the depth image with the RGB image.

In this paper, the proposed a novel method uses algorithm based on distortion for RGB-D sensors calibration. We choose the origin of the RGB sensor as the reference frame and transform the depth sensor to align with the RGB sensor frame. Depth information is used to distorting the disparity error. The method was validated in the experiments by performing SLAM tasks using a RGB-D sensor as the only sensing device. The contribution of this paper is to solve the problem of aligning the depth sensor with the RGB sensor as well as calibrate the RGB-D sensor.

The rest of the paper is structured as follows: Sect. 2 studies the principle of RGB-D sensors like Kinect and introduces the background of camera calibration. Section 3 presents a novel calibration method of typical RGB-D sensors and depth distortion algorithm proposed by this paper. In addition, we use image processing technology to locate landmark and measure its distance in the coordinate system of the robot. In Sect. 4 the experimental setups are detailed and the results are discussed. This paper ends with conclusion and future work in Sect. 5.

2 Overview of RGB-D Sensors and Background

2.1 RGB-D Sensors

This section will provide brief introduction to the RGB-D sensors and how they work. There are two kinds of RGB-D sensors, one is structured light depth sensor such as Kinect 1, Xtion Pro live, Creative Senze3D and so on. The Kinect1's depth camera is not a real camera; it's a virtual camera, created by combining images from the real IR camera with light patterns projected by the IR emitter. But for Kinect 2, the technology for the depth estimation changes from structured light to time of flight (ToF), another type of method to sense depth. In a time-of-flight depth camera, the depth camera is a real camera, with every pixel containing a real depth measurement.

The Kinect has two cameras and a laser-based IR projector. Figure 1 shows their placement on the device. The sensors are able to produce two images: a color image from RGB camera and a depth image from the couple of IR projector and camera. The depth in a depth image is the perpendicular distance from the object to the sensor plane rather than the actual distance from the object to the sensor as shown in the Fig. 2.

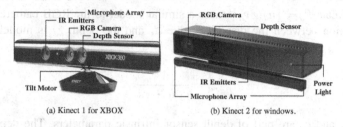

(a) Kinect 1 for XBOX   (b) Kinect 2 for windows.

Fig. 1. RGB-D sensor Kinect.

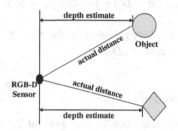

Fig. 2. Depth distance vs actual distance.

2.2 RGB Camera Model

In this work, we use a similar intrinsic model of the color camera as Heikkila [10]. Let $X_c = [x_c \ \ y_c \ \ z_c]^T$ be a point in RGB camera coordinates while $P_c = [u_c \ \ v_c]^T$ be a point in color image coordinates. The point is normalized by $X_n = [x_n \ \ y_n]^T = [x_c/z_c \ \ y_c/z_c]^T$. Distortion is performed:

$$X_g = \begin{bmatrix} 2k_3 x_n y_n + k_4 \left(r^2 + 2x_n^2\right) \\ k_3 \left(r^2 + 2y_n^2\right) + 2k_4 x_n y_n \end{bmatrix} \tag{1}$$

$$X_k = \left(1 + k_1 r^2 + k_2 r^4 + k_5 r^6\right) X_n + X_g \tag{2}$$

where $k_c = [k_1 \ \ k_2 \ \ k_3 \ \ k_4 \ \ k_5]$ is a vector containing the distortion coefficients. The image coordinates are obtained:

$$\begin{bmatrix} u_c \\ v_c \end{bmatrix} = \begin{bmatrix} f_{cx} & 0 \\ 0 & f_{cy} \end{bmatrix} \begin{bmatrix} x_k \\ y_k \end{bmatrix} + \begin{bmatrix} u_{0c} \\ v_{0c} \end{bmatrix} \tag{3}$$

where $f_c = [f_{cx} \quad f_{cy}]$ are the focal lengths and $p_{0c} = [u_{0c} \quad v_{0c}]$ is the principal point. The model for RGB camera is described by $L_c = \{f_c, p_{0c}, k_c\}$.

2.3 Depth Camera Model

The transformation between depth camera coordinates $X_d = [x_d \quad y_d \quad z_d]^T$ and depth image coordinate $P_d = [u_d \quad v_d]^T$ uses a similar model to the RGB camera.

The relation between the disparity value d_k and the depth z_d is modeled by the equation:

$$z_d = \frac{1}{c_1 d_k + c_0} \tag{4}$$

where c_1 and c_0 are part of depth sensor intrinsic parameters. The depth camera presents a depth distortion which has been modeled by Herrera [4]:

$$d_k = d + D_\delta(u, v) \cdot \exp(\alpha_0 - \alpha_1 d) \tag{5}$$

where d is the distorted disparity returned by the Kinect. The depth camera model is described by $L_d = \{f_d, p_{0d}, k_d, c_0, c_1, D_\delta, \alpha\}$.

2.4 Extrinsic and Relative Pose

Figure 3 shows the different reference frames present in a scene. The relative pose between the sensors can be denoted by $T = \{R, t\}$, where R is a rotation and t is a translation.

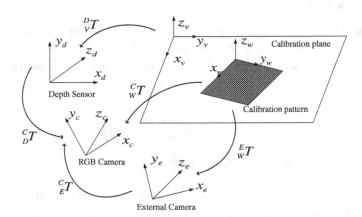

Fig. 3. The relative pose between different sensors. {C}, {D} and {E} are the RGB, depth and external cameras. {W} and {V} are the calibration pattern and calibration plane.

3 Calibration of RGB-D Sensors

In this study, we develop an algorithm to calibrate the RGB-D sensor based on depth distortion corrected. All the calibrations done below are based on RGB and infrared images of chessboard patterns, as well as depth images returned from RGB-D sensor. The concept and procedures are described in the following subsections.

3.1 Calibration Principle and Method

Figure 4 shows the structure of depth visual and the calibration principle of RGB-D sensor in both front view and side view.

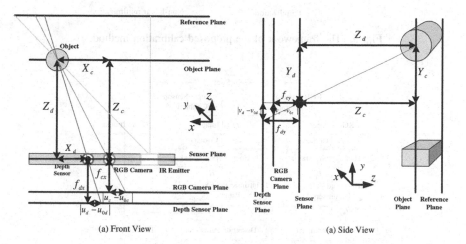

(a) Front View   (a) Side View

Fig. 4. The structure of depth visual.

In this work, we compare our method with the work of Herrera [4] that uses image-disparity map pairs of planes to accurately calibrate a RGB-D sensor. The method relies on the steps of calibration and the format of images. So we propose several modifications to this pipeline that improve applicability and stability, as show in Fig. 5. We collect depth images by OpenNI and convert them into disparity images instead of catching disparity images directly so that we can finish calibration in real time. But the edges and corners of the depth images are not obvious leading to low precision. So this paper proposes a new calibration method that calibrate depth camera with infrared image and increase a depth distortion correcting model.

The calibration model described below will be used to retrieve the intrinsic and extrinsic parameters of the RGB-D sensors. As show in Fig. 6, a block diagram of our calibration method is presented. We consider that the intrinsic matrices of RGB camera and depth sensor can be obtained using calibration toolbox for Matlab [11]. While the extrinsic parameters which are the translational and rotational displacements between the RGB camera and the depth sensor providing the depth image will be estimated.

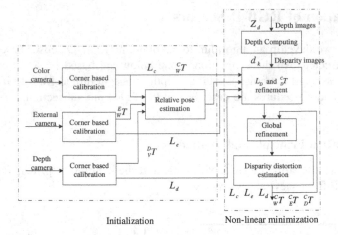

Fig. 5. The framework of the proposed calibration method.

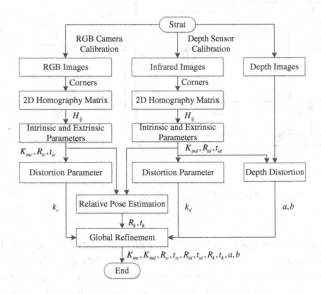

Fig. 6. Calibration algorithm.

After calibrating the intrinsic and extrinsic parameters, the model will be nonlinear optimized by a global cost function:

$$\min\{L_c + L_i + \alpha L_d\} \tag{6}$$

where α is ratio to optimize the relationship between depth distortion correction and image reprojection error.

The reprojection error of color camera and infrared camera, as well as the deviation of depth distortion for the cost function can be obtained by the equations:

$$L_c = \sum_{i=1}^{n} \sum_{j=1}^{m} \left\| \hat{m}_{ijc}\left(K_{inc}, R_{ic}, t_{ic}, M_{ij}\right) - m_{ijc}\left(K_{inc}, k_c\right) \right\|^2 \tag{7}$$

$$L_i = \sum_{i=1}^{n} \sum_{j=1}^{m} \left\| \hat{m}_{ijc}\left(K_{ind}, R_{id}, t_{id}, M_{ij}\right) - m_{ijd}\left(K_{ind}, k_d\right) \right\|^2 \tag{8}$$

$$L_d = \sum_{i=1}^{n} \sum_{j=1}^{m} \left\| \hat{d}_{ijd}\left(R_{ic}, t_{ic}, M_{ij}\right) - d_{ijd} \right\|^2 \tag{9}$$

which can be solved by Newton iteration solver or the Levenberg-Marquardt algorithm.

3.2 Depth Distortion Correcting Algorithm

Using the calibration results obtained with data sets acquired by RGB-D sensor, we estimate the depth distortion correcting model with different images of a plane at different depths. We get the measured distance read from depth image and the real distance after calibration and fitted the linear relationship between them as shown in Fig. 7. It can be seen that the measured value and the true value are on the whole close but there are some deviations between them. And experimental data (Fig. 8) shows that the farther the distance of the target object, the greater the depth error of measurement.

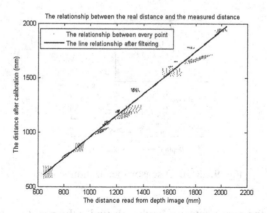

Fig. 7. The relationship between true value and measured value.

The linear relationship between the measured depth and the real depth can be established by:

$$d_c = ad_0 + b \tag{10}$$

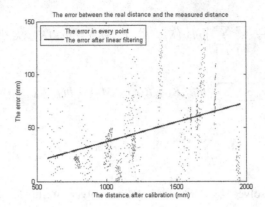

Fig. 8. The depth error between true value and measured value.

where d_0 is distance read from depth image and d_c is true distance. The coefficients a and b are varied along with different RGB-D sensors.

3.3   Robot SLAM Calibration

When a robot performs SLAM tasks, the states of robot and landmarks in the environment are estimated on the basis of measurement information. The observed image feature can be initialized using 3D coordinates in the world frame as shown in Fig. 9.

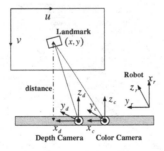

Fig. 9. RGB-D sensor localization system.

For calculating the coordinates of landmark under the robot coordinate system, we need to calibrate the relative pose between robot system and RGB-D sensor system by transformation matrix as follow:

$$_c^r T = \begin{bmatrix} R & t \\ 0 & 1 \end{bmatrix} \tag{11}$$

Suppose that the coordinates of landmark under RGB-D sensor system can be described as $X_c = [\begin{array}{ccc} x_c & y_c & z_c \end{array}]$ while the coordinates of landmark under robot system can be described as $X_r = [\begin{array}{ccc} x_r & y_r & z_r \end{array}]$.

1. Distortion correction for RGB and depth images with calibration results.
2. Calculate the depth of each pixel in RGB image by:

$$s \begin{bmatrix} u_c \\ v_c \\ 1 \end{bmatrix} = K_{inc} \left(Z_d R_k \begin{bmatrix} \frac{u_d - u_{0d}}{f_{dx}} \\ \frac{v_d - v_{0d}}{f_{dy}} \\ 1 \end{bmatrix} + t_k \right) \tag{12}$$

3. Do a binary morphology operation on registration RGB image to get the connected domain of landmark.
4. Get the coordinates of landmark under robot system from the center of landmark on RGB image by:

$$X_r = R^{-1}(X_c - t) \tag{13}$$

5. Remove the glitter according to the position relationship between center and corners of landmark.

4   Experiments and Results

In this section the methods to test and verify the robust and accuracy of RGB-D sensors calibration will be discussed. The calibration results for different RGB-D sensors will be given in the first part and two experiments including ground truth and robot SLAM are carried out to validate the proposed algorithm.

4.1   Calibration

Two sets of experiments were conducted in order to prove the accuracy of our calibration method. The first one uses the data set acquired by Kinect1 (Fig. 10) while the second set uses images acquired by Kinect2 (Fig. 11), in order to further validate the results. For each set, the captured images were divided into calibration and validation images. All results presented here were obtained from the validation images.

The calibration results and average RMS reprojection errors for two sets are shown in Table 1. It can be seen that the model was corrected since the reprojection errors significantly decreased from 0.4 to 0.1. Our method, on the other hand, yields good results with both Kinect1 and Kinect2.

4.2   Ground Truth

To test the performance of robot SLAM using the RGB-D sensor, the sensor is carried to follow a track with each landmark at a distance of one meter, as shown in Fig. 12.

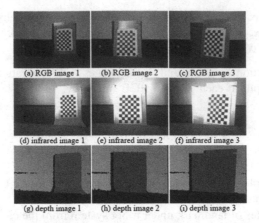

Fig. 10. Images used for calibration from Kinect1.

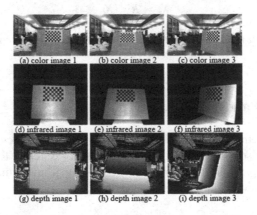

Fig. 11. Images used for calibration from Kinect2.

The experimental results of ground truth are listed in Table 2. The coordinates in the table are localization errors that the difference between estimated locations and ground truth locations of each landmark. The four columns of the table are acquired with the parameters of manufacturer calibration, uncorrected calibration, Herrera's calibration [4] and our calibration. As shown in the table, the localization results are successfully estimated to be much more close to the true coordinate of the real world using the algorithm proposed in our paper. Results clearly show that under the same conditions, our method achieves a better accuracy. This can be confirmed in Figs. 13 and 14 where the average localization errors obtained in each landmark for different images are shown. It can be seen that after applying the distortion correction, the depth errors significantly decrease from 56 mm to 21 mm on average.

Table 1. Kinect calibration result

Intrinsic parameters of RGB camera					
Coefficients f_{cx}	f_{cx}	u_{c0}	v_{c0}	e_{cx}	e_{cy}
Kinect1	530.77	530.64	295.66	253.79	0.1096	0.1104
Kinect2	1132.22	1125.53	959.50	539.50	0.1895	0.1895
Coefficients k_1	k_2	k_3	k_4	k_5	
Kinect1	0.2116	-0.4111	-0.0031	-0.0054	0.0000	
Kinect2	-0.0242	0.8815	0.0042	0.0055	0.0000	
Intrinsic parameters of depth sensor					
Coefficients f_{dx}	f_{dy}	u_{d0}	v_{d0}	e_{dx}	e_{dy}
Kinect1	600.13	596.84	301.98	241.65	0.1217	0.1182
Kinect2	401.27	393.84	221.68	186.14	0.2132	0.1981
Coefficients k_1	k_2	k_3	k_4	k_5	
Kinect1	-0.0904	0.2373	-0.0008	-0.0081	0.0000	
Kinect2	0.2889	-0.3514	-0.0131	-0.0664	0.0000	
Extrinsic parameters (position of RGB camera wrt depth sensor)					
Coefficients R_x	R_y	R_z	T_x	T_y	T_z
Kinect1	-0.0011	0.0042	-0.0001	23.755	0.1001	-3.9342
Kinect2	0.0289	-0.0942	-0.0157	40.883	-0.6866	-16.368

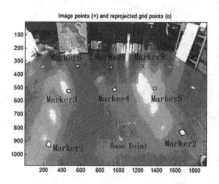

Fig. 12. Trajectory of ground truth.

4.3 Robot SLAM

This paper also testify the accuracy of calibration by reconstructing a scene. The fully calibrated system can be used to obtain a colored point cloud [12] in metric coordinates. For illustration purposes, Fig. 15 shows an example scene and a reconstruction from a different view point. Applying distortion correction leads to a more accurate reconstruction in our experiment. To reconstruct and interact with a 3D environment, we also testified our method by using KinectFusion [13] as shown in Fig. 16.

Table 2. Localization result

Error	Uncalibration (mm)	Uncorrected (mm)	Herrera's method (mm)	Our method (mm)
Mark1	(-39,-71,-41)	(-66,-7,-26)	(-59,-7,-33)	(-45,-12,-3)
Mark2	(-21,-130,-37)	(-82,-23,-60)	(-76,-48,-39)	(-41,-32,-16)
Mark3	(-15,-125,-35)	(-89,-5,-59)	(-81,-19,-33)	(-43,-15,-9)
Mark4	(-37,-110,-51)	(-100,-24,-52)	(-89,12,-36)	(-49,-35,2)
Mark5	(-25,-172,-42)	(-127,-26,-85)	(-139,-54,-50)	(-61,-40,-14)
Mark6	(-37,-156,-62)	(-183,10,-115)	(-81,-30,-26)	(-111,-5,-37)
Mark7	(27,-70,-29)	(1,-4,-14)	(8,-5,-20)	(20,-9,7)
Mark8	(-36,-83,-74)	(-54,39,-68)	(-70,3,-62)	(-17,29,-25)
Mark9	(48,-67,-42)	(-16,51,-66)	(-1,33,-35)	(24,40,-17)
Mark10	(92,-78,-31)	(49,24,-37)	(48,27,-1)	(94,12,15)
Mark11	(-84,-81,-114)	(-160,73,-147)	(-209,17,-118)	(-99,57,-73)
Mark12	(5,-47,-87)	(-81,109,-123)	(-88,89,-90)	(-16,91,-45)

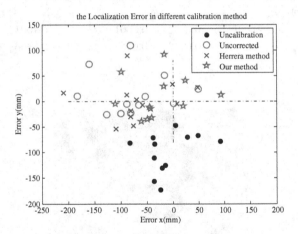

Fig. 13. Localization error in different calibration method.

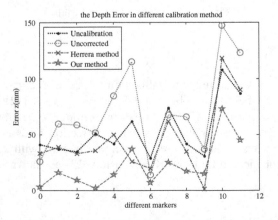

Fig. 14. Depth error in different calibration method.

(a) RGB image   (b) infrared image

(c) depth image   (d) disparity image

(e) 2D point cloud   (f) 3D point cloud

Fig. 15. Sample scene.

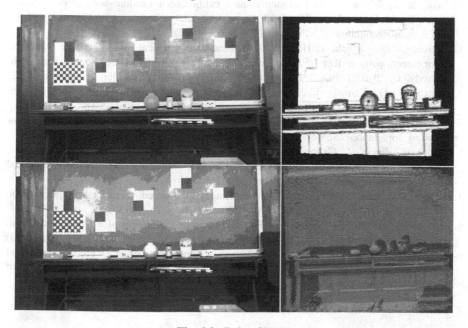

Fig. 16. Robot SLAM.

5 Conclusion

Depth measurement equipment based on structured light or TOF made great progress in recent years, which promoted the progress of depth perception technology such as 3D reconstruction, object detection, human tracking and so on.

In this paper we analyzed the imaging principle and realized the calibration method of RGB-D sensors. What's more, we compared the results with different calibration methods and completed the registration between depth image and color image. The experiments show that our method is able to accomplish better accuracy to [4], using for not only structured light camera but also time-of-flight camera.

Future work will be devoted to: (1) improve the calibration algorithm we presented for different RGB-D sensors in different kinds of surrounding environment, thereby it will be more fast and robust; (2) design a human-robot interactive system based on RGB-D information to replace sensors previously used for indoor service robotics platforms, such as stereo cameras and laser range finders, while increasing the precision and reducing the required computational burden for robotics applications.

Acknowledgements. This work was supported by National Natural Science Foundation of China (Grant No.61375087), National High Technology Research and Development Program (863 Program) of China under Grant 2012AA041403.

References

1. Zhang, Z.: A flexible new technique for camera calibration. IEEE Trans. Pattern Anal. Mach. Intell. **22**(11), 1330–1334 (2000)
2. Heikkilä, J., Silven, O.: A four-step camera calibration procedure with implicit image correction. In: Proceedings of the IEEE Computer Society Conference on Computer Vision and Pattern Recognition (CVPR), pp. 1106–1112 (1997)
3. Herrera C., D., Kannala, J., Heikkilä, J.: Accurate and practical calibration of a depth and color camera pair. In: Real, P., Diaz-Pernil, D., Molina-Abril, H., Berciano, A., Kropatsch, W. (eds.) CAIP 2011, Part II. LNCS, vol. 6855, pp. 437–445. Springer, Heidelberg (2011)
4. Herrera C., D., Kannala, J., Heikkilä, J.: Joint depth and color camera calibration with distortion correction. IEEE Trans. Pattern Anal. Mach. Intell. **34**(10), 2058–2064 (2012)
5. Khoshelham, K., Elberink, S.O.: Accuracy and resolution of Kinect depth data for indoor mapping applications. Sensors **12**(2), 1437–1454 (2012)
6. Zhang, C., Zhang, Z.: Calibration between depth and color sensors for commodity depth cameras. In: Proceedings of the Springer International Publishing on Computer Vision and Machine Learning with RGB-D Sensors, pp. 47–64 (2014)
7. Smisek, J., Jancosek, M., Pajdla, T.: 3D with Kinect. In: Proceedings of the Springer London on Consumer Depth Cameras for Computer Vision, pp. 3–25 (2013)
8. Raposo, C., Barreto, J.P., Nunes, U.: Fast and accurate calibration of a Kinect sensor. In: Proceedings of the IEEE International Conference on 3D Vision-3DV, pp. 342–349 (2013)
9. Nakayama, Y., Honda, T., Saito, H.: Accurate camera pose estimation for kinectfusion based on line segment matching by LEHF. In: Proceedings of the IEEE International Conference on Pattern Recognition (ICPR), pp. 2149–2154 (2014)

10. Heikkila, J.: Geometric camera calibration using circular control points. IEEE Trans. Pattern Anal. Mach. Intell. **22**(10), 1066–1077 (2000)
11. Bouguet, J.Y.: Camera Calibration Toolbox for Matlab. http://www.vision.caltech.edu/bouguetj/calib_doc/
12. Rusu, R.B., Cousins, S.: 3D is here: Point cloud library (PCL). In: Proceedings of the IEEE International Conference on Robotics and Automation (ICRA), pp. 1–4 (2011)
13. Newcombe, R.A., Izadi, S., Hilliges, O., et al.: KinectFusion: real-time dense surface mapping and tracking. In: Proceedings of the IEEE International Symposium on Mixed and Augmented Reality (ISMAR), pp. 127–136 (2011)

Road Detection Based on Image Boundary Prior

Huan Wang[✉], Yan Gong, Yangyang Hou, and Ting Cao

School of Computer Science and Engineering,
Nanjing University of Science and Technology, Nanjing, China
{wanghuanphd,113106000700,renmingwu}@njust.edu.cn,
wangchao234@163.com

Abstract. As for vision based road detection, most of color based methods use a center-lower region as a "safe" road region to model road appearance. However, this region heavily relies on the pose of ego-vehicle. Color models trained by using samples from this region often yield biased results when some non-road regions are included. In this paper, we proposed a novel color based road detection method which can overcome this problem. It is based on an image boundary prior, which infers a road region by measuring the extent of the region connecting to the bottom boundary of an image. This prior is more robust than the center-lower prior. Moreover, we use illumination invariance color space for the distance metric of two neighboring regions in order to make our approach robust to shadows. Experiments demonstrate that the proposed method is superior to both the Gaussian mixture model based method and illumination invariance based method.

Keywords: Road detection · Image boundary prior · Illumination invariance space

1 Introduction

Vision based road detection refers to the accurate detection of the free road surface ahead of a vehicle, it is a key module of advanced driver assistance systems and robot vision navigation systems. A large number of road detection methods have been proposed in last decades. These methods can be categorize to appearance based [1–6], structure from motion based [7, 8] and stereo vision based [9]. Among these methods, appearance based methods have been extensively investigated, where color and texture are two main appearances. Lu [1] directly use RGB color and Gaussian Mixture model (GMM) to obtain a road probability distribution map, Rotaru [2] and Wang [3] respectively use Hue-Saturation-Intensity and CIE-Lab color space to model road pattern, and Christopher [4] combines color and texture cues to improve the road detection. Alvarez [5] comprehensively compares the performance of different color space for road detection. In order to overcome shadows in the road, Alvarez [6] also consider the physics behind color formation and design an illuminant-invariant image, which is a shadow free image converted from RGB image.

In order to capture road appearance online in lack of other road information, the above methods all assume a region localized in the center-lower part of a road image to

Y.-J. Zhang (Ed.): ICIG 2015, Part III, LNCS 9219, pp. 212–222, 2015.
DOI: 10.1007/978-3-319-21969-1_19

be a confident road region and use it to train their road appearance models. However, for one thing, this region is sometimes reservative, which may lose important appearance information when multiple road materials exist; For another, this assumption is hold when the host-vehicle is moving along a road with regular pose, it might be violated when the pose of the host-vehicle undergoes serve variances, for instance, in the scenarios of turning and avoiding obstacles, where the center-lower region often incorporates many non-road pixels, which may affect the performance of these appearance models. In this paper, we propose a more sensible assumption, that is, the true road region is always connect to the image bottom boundary, and the boundary of a road region should take up large common part with the image bottom boundary due to the perspective effect. With this new assumption, a road region can be identified by measuring the extent of the road region connecting to the bottom boundary of a road image. Therefore, the road region can be more accurately inferred which is insensitive to the pose variations and road surface with multiple materials. This idea is motivated by Zhu's work [9], which is originally proposed for the saliency object detection base on background prior. Different from [9], we use the idea of boundary prior to road detection problem, and we rather than use all the image boundary, but only use the bottom boundary. We also consider embedding illumination invariance space to remove the disturbance of shadows.

2 Related Work

Over the years, the most popular road detection approaches might be appearance based. Since modeling the appearance of non-road regions is very difficult due to its diversity, most of methods try to model road appearance only. These methods usually incorporate the assumption that road appears in the lower part of the road image, and road samples can be used to learn an appearance model. Then the model is used to identify other regions of the image. The appearance can be well modeled by one-class classifiers, such as GMM, Nearest Neighboring and so on. Color and texture [1–6] are the most popular features for this one-class learning. Unfortunately, the center-lower part assumption does not belong to the road in some scenarios, such as the pose variance of ego-vehicle and turning. Moreover, the samples in the center-lower part may be insufficient for modeling the whole road appearance, for example, shadows and non-uniform road surface.

With available training road images, a binary or multiple classifiers can also be learned to classify the appearance of road and non-road region. Reference [2] use support vector machine to identify road and non-road regions with an online incremental learning strategy. In Ref. [4], convolution neural network is trained offline to classify road scene into sky, vertical and road region. Reference [3] applied Adaboost classifier is trained offline first and then adapt to the specific scene by online updating.

In this paper, we proposed an appearance based road detection method based on road image boundary prior. It can deal with road detection in the scenarios of irregular vehicle pose, surfaces with multiple materials and shadows to some extent. The rest of this paper is organized as follows: In section two, the related work on road detection is reviewed firstly, then the image boundary prior based road detection method is introduced in section three, and we report our experimental results and draw a conclusion in section four and five respectively.

3 Method

3.1 Image Boundary Prior

Common road detection methods assume that the central–lower part of a road image belongs to the confident road surface. For example, Ref. [1] define a "safe" window in a road image which is depicted as the red region in Fig. 1(a), and in Ref. [4], nine patches with a size of 10×10 are uniformly located in the center-bottom to modal construction, see the green patches in Fig. 1(a). However, their assumption has a main drawback since that area does not always belong to the road surface, such as overtaking, left/right turn, see Fig. 1(b). Fortunately, we observe that the road image boundary can provide more accurate road/non-road information. For instance, road regions are much more connected to the image bottom boundary since the perspective projection effect, and non-road regions (sky, trees and building et al.) are much less connected to image bottom boundary, but are much more connected to the image top boundary and the left and right boundaries. Motivated by this, we relax the center-lower part assumption to a more generate one, that is, road region might take large common boundary with the bottom boundary of a road image over the perimeter of the road region. Therefore the non-road region marked with green in Fig. 1(d) can be excluded since it has large boundary but only a few of them is common with the bottom boundary of the image. Therefore, we consider this as bottom boundary prior. By considering the whole bottom boundary, we not only can include more confident road region than center lower or limited seeds patch assumption when multiple materials exists, but also it is insensitive to the effect of including non-road regions due to the pose variance of the vehicle by considering the extent of a region connecting to the bottom boundary.

(a)   (b)   (c)   (d)

Fig. 1. Traditional "safe" road region or seeds (a) used by researchers may be affected by the including of non-road regions when the pose of the vehicle changes (b). The image boundary prior overcome this problem and can classify road and non-road regions accurately, as (c) and (d).

To measure the extent of a region connecting to the bottom boundary, we initially over-segment a road image into non-overlapping patches. Here we use uniform square patches for simplicity, i.e., if N patches are needed, then the length of each patch's side L equals to $\sqrt{\frac{w \cdot h}{N}}$, where w and h are the width and height of input images. Note that some more accurate over-segmentation methods, such as the super-pixel method [31], can also be used. Afterwards, an indirection graph is constructed as shown in Fig. 2, where each node denotes an image patch. Let p denotes one of the patches and all the patches are denoted by the set $L = \{p_i\}_{i=1}^{N}$. We define the geodesic distance $d_{geo}(p, p_i)$ as the distance of the shortest path from p_i to each p_i:

$$d_{geo}(p, q) = \min_{r_1, r_2, \cdots r_N \in \{p - > q\}} \sum_{i=1}^{N-1} d_{pair}(p_i, p_{i+1}) \tag{1}$$

where the pair-wise distance $d_{pair}(p_i, p_{i+1})$ represents the Euclidean distance of mean colors of the adjacent patches p_i and p_{i+1}. We choose the CIE-Lab color space to calculate the distance since it is perceptually linear, meaning that similar differences between two color vectors in this color space are considered about equally important color changes to human. Therefore, it is an appropriate choice for measuring with Euclidean distance. In the Eq. (2), the symbol $\{p \to q\}$ represents the set of all paths from p to q, e.g. in Fig. 2, the red, blue and green paths are three different paths. If a path from $\{p \to q\}$ is denoted by $r_1, r_2, \cdots, r_N$, then the geodesic distance $d_{geo}(p, q)$ is defined as the shortest path of all from p to q on the graph, where the calculation of the shortest path can be realized efficiently by Johnson's algorithm [32]. If all distance on all edges of the graph in Fig. 2 are assumed to be equal, the shortest path from p to q is $p \to a \to q$, in this case,$d_{geo}(p, q)$ equals to $d_{app}(p, a) + d_{app}(a, p)$.

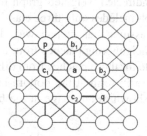

Fig. 2. An illustration of the geodesic distance from p to q on the graph. The red, blue and green paths are three candidate paths from p to q, where the red one with the shortest path of all the geodesic distances from p to q (Color figure online).

Then all the distance can be turned into a similarity between p and p_i by using the $\exp(\cdot)$ function as following.

$$sim(p, p_i) = \exp(-\frac{d_{geo}^2(p, p_i)}{2\sigma_1^2}) \tag{2}$$

Where σ_1 is a factor to control the smoothness of the distance $d_{geo}(p, q)$. We sum up all the similarity to obtain the contribution from all patches.

$$A(p) = \sum_{i=1}^{N} sim(p, p_i) \tag{3}$$

And we also sum up the similarity of those patches which are on the image bottom boundary.

$$B(p) = \sum_{i=1}^{N} sim(p,p_i) \cdot \delta(B(p_i) = 1) \tag{4}$$

Where $B(p_i) = 1$ represents that p_i is on the image bottom boundary. $\delta(\cdot)$ is an indication function, which returns 1 if p_i exactly lies in the bottom boundary of the road image and 0 otherwise.

So far, $A(p)$ and $B(p)$ are calculated, where $B(p)$ can be view as the sharing length of p with the bottom boundary and $A(p)$ is an area but not the region's perimeter. Since the shape of the region is arbitrary, we assume the region is a circle in shape. And the perimeter can be estimated by $A(p)$, that is $\sqrt{4\pi A(p)}$. By neglecting the constant $\sqrt{4\pi}$, we formulate the bottom boundary prior as:

$$\alpha(p) = \frac{B(p)}{\sqrt{A(p)}} \tag{5}$$

where $\alpha(p)$ reflects the extent of p connecting with the image bottom boundary, which can well used to identify the road.

Figure 3 gives a simple undirected weighted graph to illustrate the process of the inference of the road. The graph includes only three class, sky, tree and road, which are shown in different colors. We assume that the pair-wise distance $d_{pair}(p,p_i)$ associated with the edge connecting two neighboring patches from the same class equals to 0, and that the distance is set to infinite for those patches from different classes, The $\alpha(p)$ value of all nodes are shown in a matrix form at the bottom left of Fig. 3. The normalized version of this matrix is also shown as an image at the bottom right of Fig. 3.

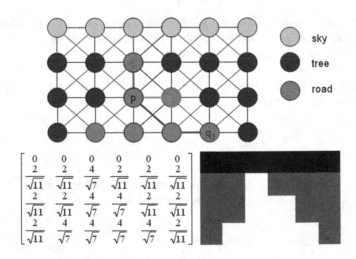

Fig. 3. Illustration of the road inference based on image boundary prior

The $\alpha(p)$ values of all patches can provide us a probability map Pb using Eq. (4), where σ_2 is a smoothness factor which is empirically set to 1.

$$Pb(p) = 1 - \exp(-\frac{\alpha^2(p)}{2\sigma_2^2}) \qquad (6)$$

3.2 Embedding Illumination Invariance Space

From Fig. 3, we can see clearly that the bottom boundary prior can infer road pretty good if small color distance is assigned to the inner region of the road while high distance is assigned to the boundary between road and non-road regions. However, road region often exits high color distance due to shadows. In practice, Shadows are one of main challenges to road detection. Under different illumination condition, shadows might cast on the road with random shapes and locations, and with different extent from shallow shadows to heavy ones. The Lab color space we used above is not photometrically invariant. Big changes of the intensity due to shadows can influence all three coordinates. In [11], Shannon's entropy is applied to find and distinguish the intrinsic quality of surfaces's spectral properties. In [4], the authors proposed an illumination invariant color space to suppress shadows in the road based on the work of [11]. They find the intrinsic feature of an RGB road image to obtain an illumination invariance space, the road and shadows on it looks more similar in this space. Specifically, for an RGB road image, the 3-D dara are transformed to a 2-D log chromaticity space (ρ_1, ρ_2), where $\rho_1 = \log\frac{R}{B}$, $\rho_2 = \log\frac{G}{B}$, the pixels on the same surface under different illumination form a straight line in this space. The 1-D space I_θ is obtained by projecting the point in the (ρ_1, ρ_2) space with a line l_θ, which makes an angle θ with the horizontal axis, as Eq. (5).

$$I_\theta = (\rho_1, \rho_2) \cdot (\cos\theta, \sin\theta)^T \qquad (7)$$

Finally, the angle with minimum Shannon entropy θ' is the best projection direction, and $I_{\theta'}$ is the illumination invariance space (IIS).

$$\theta' = \min_\theta \left\{ -\sum_j P_j(I_\theta) \log(P_j(I_\theta)) \right\} \qquad (8)$$

However, we observed from our experiments that this space lost some discrimination between road and non-road, and we can obtain better performance if we combine it with Lab color space. Therefore, we linearly weight the distance of the average color vector in *Lab* color space and illumination invariant space I in the computation of the color distance of arbitrary patches according to Eq. (5), here γ is a constant aiming to balance the importance of two distances. Therefore, image bottom prior can combine with Lab, IIS and both Lab and IIS to obtain three methods which denoted by IBP-Lab, IBP-IIS and IBP-Lab-IIS, respectively in the following.

$$d_{app}(p_i, q) = \sqrt{(L_p - L_q)^2 + (a_p - a_q)^2 + (b_p - b_q)^2} + \gamma|I_p - I_q| \qquad (9)$$

The final result of road detection is realized by the segmentation of the probability map using a simple adaptive threshold $T = u + \alpha \cdot \sigma$, where u and σ are the mean and standard deviation of the probability map, α is a constant which can take the value in the interval [1, 3]. However, we directly use the probability map for experimental comparison since it is the core of both our approach and the methods exploit for comparison.

4 Experiments

The proposed approach and the methods used for comparison have been implemented in Matlab on a PC with 2 Duo CPU (2.4 GHz) and 2 GB memory without any code optimization.

We evaluate our approach using BCN-2 open datasets and a dataset collected by ourselves, detailed description of the two datasets are listed in Table 1. They contain many challenging and complicated scenarios. Example images from these dataset are shown in Figs. 3 and 4. We compare our method with GMM based method [3] and illumination invariance based method [4]. We apply Maximum F1-measure (MaxF), Average Precision (AP), Precision(PRE), Recall(REC), False Positive Rate (FPR) and False Negative Rate(FNR) to show the comparison result as [10] and [12].

Table 1. Description of used datasets

Name	Number of images	Resolution	Description
BCN-2	481 + 219	convert 640 × 480 to 320 × 240	After-Rain and Sunny-Shadows
NUST	500	348 × 258	Rural, campus and inner-city scene

4.1 Result on Irregular Vehicle Pose and Multiple Materials Surface

Our approach is first assessed using NUST dataset, which include some adverse conditions due to irregular vehicle pose and non-uniform road surface. Figure 4 gives five sampled images from NUST dataset, and their detection results are also shown. It is observed that the GMM and IIS methods are dependent on the pose of the vehicle, they often don't work when non-road pixels are dominant in their "safe" road regions. Moreover, in non-uniform road surface scenarios, GMM based method often causes false negative result since road samples are not adequate in lower center region, while IIS often cause false positive if the bottom boundary include both road and non-road regions. However, our method is robust to these problems since we consider all the patches on the bottom boundary as road reference region and improve road discriminative ability by measuring the connection extent with the bottom boundary, which is insensitive to the incidence of non-road regions. Result of performance comparison on the whole dataset is shown in Table 2. Three IBP-X based methods are all superior to both GMM and IIS, where IBP-IIS yields the best result.

Fig. 4. Sampled detection results in NUST dataset. The original images are shown in the first row, Ground-Truth are shown in the second row. For three to seven row, detection results are corresponds to GMM-HSV, IIS, IBP-Lab, IBP-IIS and IBP-Lab-IIS respectively.

4.2 Result in Shadows Scenarios and Non-Uniform Road Surface

Our approach is also assessed using the BCN-2 dataset, which includes two sub-datasets, one is sunny shadow scenario and the other is after rain scenario, the two often lead to non-uniform road surface. Figure 5 give some illustrative detection

Table 2. Performance comparison on NUST dataset (%)

	Fmax	AP	PRE	REC	FPR	FNR
GMM-HSV	54.41	60.00	63.45	65.66	18.19	13.46
IIS	68.62	58.28	60.25	84.39	15.37	3.80
IBP-Lab	80.90	78.90	81.68	82.72	4.32	6.03
IBP-IIS	**85.26**	**80.26**	81.58	**91.24**	5.08	**3.23**
IBP-Lab-IIS	83.90	82.03	**85.51**	85.12	**3.63**	6.04

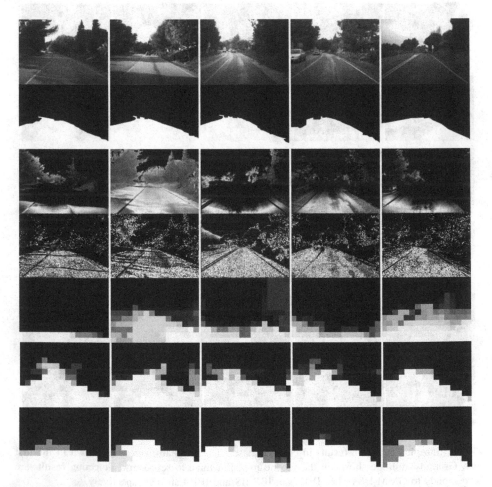

Fig. 5. Sampled detection results in BCN-2 dataset. The original images are shown in the first row, the first two frames are sunny shadow scenario (the frame 105 and 153) and the last three are after-rain scenario (the frame 47, 107 and 475). Ground-Truths are shown in the second row. From the third to seventh row, detection results are corresponds to GMM-HSV, IIS, IBP-Lab, IBP-IIS and IBP-Lab-IIS respectively.

results, and Tables 3 and 4 show their quantitative results respectively. We find that IBP-IIS yield best in the sunny shadow scenario and IBP-Lab-IIS performs best in the after rain scenario.

Table 3. Performance comparison on the sunny shadows dataset of BCN-2 (%)

	Fmax	AP	PRE	REC	FPR	FNR
GMM-HSV	81.45	71.78	80.56	84.72	9.82	5.63
IIS	83.61	73.79	77.58	91.00	10.21	3.39
IBP-Lab	80.17	76.36	85.30	77.85	5.93	8.28
IBP-IIS	93.75	86.09	92.93	**94.65**	2.71	**2.00**
IBP-Lab-IIS	**94.30**	**88.46**	**97.24**	91.69	**1.00**	3.14

Table 4. Performance comparison on the after rain dataset of BCN-2 (%)

	Fmax	AP	PRE	REC	FPR	FNR
GMM-HSV	81.89	72.31	80.07	84.41	8.07	5.89
IIS	83.34	74.87	77.12	91.03	10.50	3.39
IBP-Lab	82.30	79.78	83.55	83.55	7.27	6.18
IBP-IIS	94.52	87.45	94.13	**94.97**	2.25	**1.88**
IBP-Lab-IIS	**95.47**	**89.42**	**96.53**	94.47	**1.28**	2.07

4.3   Parameter Sensitivity and Time Cost Analysis

We also conduct parameter selection and sensitivity test. In our method, γ is a key parameter. We change γ within the range [0,50] and we find that $\gamma = [2, 8]$ always yields the similar good performance. So we set $\gamma = 5$ in all experiments. Finally, we compute the time cost of these methods (Table 5).

Table 5. Comparison of average time cost (s)

	GMM-HSV	IIS	IBP-Lab	IBP-IIS	IBP-Lab-IIS
NUST	6.75	1.90	1.17	2.15	2.34
BCN-2	6.10	0.87	0.10	1.47	1.55

5   Conclusion

Road detection is a key technique of ADAS, robot vision navigation and other applications. Road detection in arbitrary road scene is still an open problem. In this paper, we proposed an image boundary prior to infer road region, which can deal with the problem of pose variance of host-vehicles and exists of non-uniform road surface and shadows. Experiments demonstrate that the probability map generated based on image boundary prior is superior to GMM and IIS based ones. The IBP with illumi-nation invariance space and with the combination of IIS and Lab color space always yield the best performance on the used datasets, and the performance can also be improved if superpixel segmentation is used instead of rectangle patches, however, this may increase time complexity. Moreover, our method can be applied to flexibly locate the "safe" road region so as to boost many appearance based road detection methods.

References

1. Lu, K., Li, J., An, X., He, H.: A hierarchical approach for road detection. In: IEEE International conference on Robotics and Automation(ICRA), Hong Kong (2014)
2. Rotaru, C., Graf, T., Zhang, J.: Color image segmentation in HIS space for automotive applications. J. Real-time Image Proc. **3**, 311–322 (2008)
3. Wang, H., Gong, Y., Liu, Y., Ren, M.: Road detection via superpixels and interactive image segmentation. In: IEEE 4th Annual International Conference on Cyber Technology in Automation, Control and Intelligent Systems (2014)
4. Alvarez, J.M., Gevers, T., Lopez, A.M.: Evaluating color representations for on-line road detection
5. Alvarez, J.M., Lopez, A.M.: Road detection based on illuminant invariance. IEEE Trans. Intell. Transp. Syst. **12**, 184–193 (2011)
6. Lookingbill, A., Rogers, J., Lieb, D., Curry, J., Thrun, S.: Reverse optical flow for self-supervised adaptive autonomous robot navigation. Int. J. Comput. Vision **74**(3), 287–302 (2007)
7. Darms, M., Komar, M., LueKe, S.: Map-based road boundary estimation. In: Proceedings of the IEEE Intelligent Vehicels Symposium, pp. 609–641 (2010)
8. Gallup, D., frahm, J.M., Pollefeys, M.: Picecwise planar and non-plannar stereo for unban scene reconstruction. In: IEEE Conference on Computer Vision and Pattern Recognition (CVPR), pp. 1418–1425 (2010)
9. Zhu, W.J., Liang, S., Wei, Y.C., Sun, J.: Saliency optimization from robust background detection. In: IEEE Conference on Computer Vision and Pattern Recognition (CVPR) (2014)
10. Wang, B., Fremout, V., Rodriguez, S.A.: Color-based road detection and its evaluation on the KITTI road benchmark. In: IEEE Intelligent Vehicles Symposium (2014)
11. Finlayson, G.D., Drew, M.S., Lu, C.: Intrinsic Images by Entropy Minimization. In: Pajdla, T., Matas, J. (eds.) ECCV 2004. LNCS, vol. 3023, pp. 582–595. Springer, Heidelberg (2004)
12. Frisch, J., Kuhnl, T., Geiger, A.: A new performance measure and evaluation benchmark for road detection algorithms. In: IEEE Intelligent Vehicels Symposium (2012)

Robust and Real-Time Lane Marking Detection for Embedded System

Yueting Guo[1], Yongjun Zhang[2], Sha Liu[1], Jun Liu[1],
and Yong zhao[1(⊠)]

[1] School of Electronic and Computer Engineering,
Shenzhen Graduate School of Peking University, Shenzhen, China
{guoyueting,liusha,liujun}@sz.pku.edu.cn,
zhaoyong@pkusz.edu.cn
[2] College of Computer Science and Technology,
Guizhou University, Guiyang 550025, China
zyj6667@126.com

Abstract. Lane marking detection is part of most advanced driver assistance systems (ADAS) as an important component of computer vision. This paper presents a lane detection system based on a novel lane feature extraction approach. The robustness and real-time of algorithm enable different configurations of embedded solutions. The system is divided into three phases. Firstly, using the Prewitt operator we can get the rich useful details and using Shen Jun operator we can get step edge, on the other hand Shen Jun operator is the best filter to detect the symmetrical markings according to the maximum signal noise ratio (SNR) criterion. So we introduce the best compromise method between noise smoothing and edge locating that combining the Prewitt operator with Shen Jun operator to extract lane markings. Then a fast Hough transform based on image pyramid is applied to get the lane lines. The posterior algorithm of reasonably refining the Lane lines angle is introduced to correct to error caused by Hough transform. Finally, robust detection of vehicle's departure warning is also discussed. Experiment results on real road will be presented to prove the robustness and effectiveness of the proposed lane detection algorithm.

Keywords: Shen Jun operator · Fast Hough transform · Warning of lane departure

1 Introduction

Traffic accidents have become one of the most serious problems in our live today because of driver careless negligence, languor and distraction. Therefore many woks have been done to investigate improved ways of driving-assistance system to enhance vehicle driving safety. Driver assistance system (DAS) being capable of detecting the lane markings and warning the driver when the vehicle begins to move out of its lane is desperately needed to eliminate these accidents.

Throughout the last two decades, different approaches for lane analysis were proposed, demonstrated and improved. This topic can be separated into three essential blocks: lane marking detection, lane tracking and lane departure warning. For the lane

© Springer International Publishing Switzerland 2015
Y.-J. Zhang (Ed.): ICIG 2015, Part III, LNCS 9219, pp. 223–235, 2015.
DOI: 10.1007/978-3-319-21969-1_20

marking detection algorithm, the existing solutions can be classified as feature-based [1, 3, 4], model-based [2, 5] and region-based [1, 6] methods. Among these methods, different feature-based methods for Lane detection are still the most popular and commonly used ways which contribute to its efficiency in multiple algorithms. There are many related research works on the lane detection methods. Firstly, the determination of the region of interest (ROI) can reduce the complexity and the unnecessary information caused by noises. Isolating the ROI from other region before the computation [6] can reduce processing time while keeping a good performance. The fixed size of ROI may not work well, so some adaptive road ROI determination algorithms are proposed to detect the road region using the positional information of a vanishing point [7] or the position of the heading vehicles [4]. Secondly, extraction algorithms of the lane features have been widely studied based on color [9], template matching [13] or edge features [8, 12, 13]. Edge-based techniques not only work well with solid and segmented lines but also can compensate for circular reflectors. However, many of the proposed methods are not suitable for the accurate lane marking points extraction in the situations that contain many extraneous lines. Thirdly, various shapes of mathematical models such as parabolas [2, 14, 15] or splines [10, 11] have been used to match the lane lines. While road modeling can eliminate false positions via outlier removal, they might not be a suitable choice for variety of road conditions. Not to mention the fact that a stable control system only require approximate 10-m lookahead, making a linear road model satisfactory. Then, a sensing system [1] such as GPS or other sensors may be used to gather information about the vehicle's environment or augment lane-position estimates. In this paper, we only focus on the camera to get the images of lane information. Finally, various of tracking methods such as kalman filter [8, 12], particle filter [16, 17] have been used to track the lane line.

However, many of theses algorithms do not work well in realtime and robustness or the results are shown on a limited scenarios with no obstacles present. Considering that DAS are implemented on battery powered embedded platforms inside a car, we present a robust and real-time lane detection system which shows robust results in a variety of road conditions.

Following the introduction, the algorithm used to detection lane marking is detailed organized as follows. Section 2 presents the image preprocessing method including selection of ROI and image gray-enhancing conversion method. Section 3 proposes lane feature extraction algorithm. Section 4 illustrates the lane lines detection algorithm and vehicle's Departure warning algorithm. Section 5 describes some experimental results under various illumination conditions to confirm the robustness of the proposed algorithm. Section 6 concludes the paper and discusses future works.

2   The Preprocessing of Image

The selection of ROI minimizes the detection of extraneous objects while maximizing the likelihood of detecting lane markers. Both the speed and the accuracy can be improved by cropping and shrinking the original image. At present, a portion of the image that is above the hood of the vehicle and below the vanishing point is selected as the ROI. In order to reduce the compute time we just choose the G channel of the RGB to get the gray image. This method save much time but has no influence to the final result of experiment. Then histogram equalization is applied After getting the gray scale image to enhance the contrast of image. The images are obtained by applying Histogram equalization as illustrated in Fig. 1. Then shrinking the region of interest to half of the original ROI by taking the maximum value of each four-pixel box as the current pixel value. Trough shrinking the ROI, we find that the accuracy of detection does not decrease in the final experimental results, but the detection time reduces.

Fig. 1. The ROI of original gray image and histogram equalization image. (a, b, c) Are ROI gray imges, (d, e, f) are histogram equalization images.

3   Lane Marking Points Extraction

Road lane points extraction is one of the key steps in real-time lane analysis, which decides the accuracy of the entire lane analysis system. The robustness, and hence the efficiency, of these points extraction step is dependent on vehicle surround conditions such as road types, shadows, road surface etc. Figure 2 shows the framework of lane points extraction. Firstly, the input image (Orgimg) is smoothed with a 5 × 5 Prewitt operator to remove background noises and get image (Grandimg). In order to eliminate the influence of illumination, a adaptive threshold is used on the smoothed image to get image (Mskimg). Image (ShunJunimg) that got by Shun Jun edge operator is used to restrict the threshold image (Mskimg) and get image (Laneimg). The following sections are the detail component of this improved system.

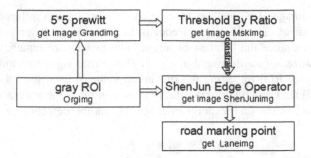

Fig. 2. Framework of lane points extraction.

3.1 Prewitt Operator and Adaptive Threshold

A 5 × 5 Prewitt operator is used to smooth the gray image and find initial edge pixels inside the ROI. Then the adaptive threshold is used to extract the lane marking points. In order to reduce the shadows influence, before the adaptive threshold, we segment the smoothed image Grandimg into six small blocks whose width is the three-fifth of the length of ROI width and height is one-third of the length of ROI height. (x1, y1) and (x2, y2) are one block's starting coordinates and end coordinates, as shown in Fig. 3(b). we propose the adaptive threshold method shown in Algorithm 1.

Algorithm1 Adaptive Threshold

```
1: read input image Grandimg block
2: get the 256-level gray histogram
3: Histogram[i]=the pixel count of the i level
4: P0=pixel value after threshold
5: Count = 0; i = 255
6:If (i > 0) then
7: Count = count + histogram[i]
8: If (count>sum) then
9:   Threshold = i ;break
10:else
11: i=i-1
12:end if
13:end if
14:For(each pixel) then
15: If (the pixel value>threshold ) then
16: Po=255
17: else
18: P0=0
19: end if
20: end for
```

---

where sum $= (x2 - x1)(y2 - y1) \times R$, R is the ratio of the number of possible road lane points unit area. This value can be got through experiment.

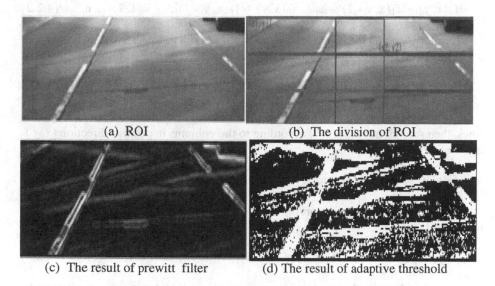

(a) ROI

(b) The division of ROI

(c) The result of prewitt filter

(d) The result of adaptive threshold

Fig. 3. The division of image and the result of threshold.

3.2 Shen Jun Edge Operator

Shen Jun edge operator is similar to LoG edge operator which smooths the image first, then find the second derivative of the zero-crossing points. But the difference is that the LoG operator selects a two-dimensional Gaussian low-pass function to smooth image, while Shen Jun edge detection operator uses symmetric exponential function to smooth image. Shen Jun edge detection operator is proved to be the best symmetrical exponential filter for step edge with noise according to the maximum SNR criterion. Shen Jun edge operator only need one parameter, the details of the image will have a great change when we adjust this parameter. So if the appropriate parameter is selected, the rich useful details can be got. The function of symmetrical exponential filter as follows:

$$h(\mathrm{x}, \mathrm{y}) = C_1^2 + C_2^{|x|+|y|} \qquad (4.2.1)$$

$$\text{where } C_1 = \frac{a_0}{2 - a_0}, C_2 = 1 - a_0, a_0 \in (0, 1)$$

a_0 is the only parameter. When a_0 is closer to 1, the $h(\mathrm{x}, \mathrm{y})$ becomes narrower, at the same time the filter will be less resistant, but the edge position will be more accurate.

Shen Jun proved that Using (4.2.1) function to smooth the image $f_0(\mathrm{x}, \mathrm{y})$ which can be implemented through recursive smoothing the image in positive and negative direction according to the rows and columns. The detail smoothing function as follows:

Firstly, smooth the image $f_0(x, y)$ according to rows in positive direction ($y = 1$, 2, ..., n).

$$f_1(x, y) = f_1(x, y - 1) + a_0 \times [f_0(x, y) - f_1(x, y - 1)], \quad y = 1, 2, ..., n \qquad (4.2.2)$$

Secondly, smooth the image $f_1(x, y)$ according to rows in negative direction ($y = n$, n - 1, ... 1).

$$f_2(x, y) = f_1(x, y + 1) + a_0 \times [f_1(x, y) - f_1(x, y + 1)], \quad y = n, n - 1, ..., 1 \qquad (4.2.3)$$

$f_2(x, y)$ is the smoothing output in positive and negative directions according to the rows, then smooth image $f_2(x, y)$ according to the columns in positive direction ($x = 1$, 2, ... n).

$$f_3(x, y) = f_3(x - 1, y) + a_0 \times [f_2(x, y) - f_3(x - 1, y)], \quad x = 1, 2, ..., n \qquad (4.2.4)$$

Finally, smooth image according to the columns in negative direction ($x = n$, n - 1, ... 1).

$$f_4(x, y) = f_4(x + 1, y) + a_0 \times [f_3(x, y) - f_4(x + 1, y)], \quad x = n, n - 1, ..., 1 \qquad (4.2.5)$$

$f_4(x, y)$ is the smoothing output in positive and negative directions according to the columns, using $f_4(x, y)$ substract $f_0(x, y)$ to get the difference image. The final output of the filter is the threshold image of the difference image, as shown in Fig. 6(a).

3.3   The Constraint Between Prewitt and Shen Jun Edge Detection

After get the edge points from Shen jun edge detection, we can restrict the edge points based on edge points from Prewitt edge detection in order to eliminate the inaccurate points and noise points.

Firstly, in a starting row (near the top) of the image, a search is conducted to find edge pixel positions x1 and x2. Figure 4 are two illustrations of possible edge position. According to the possible width of the lane markings, the width between x1 and x2 is set bigger than minRL (which is set 2 pixel width) smaller than maxRL (which is set 35 pixel width). a, b are the pixel values bigger than 0.

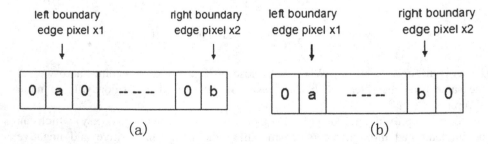

Fig. 4. x1 and x2 in (a, b) are illustrations of the edge points

The constraint algorithm is composed of three major steps: gratitude and gray value restriction, elimination of holes caused by Shen Jun edge detection and removing of wider continuous horizontal lines than lane markings. The flowchart is shown in Fig. 5.

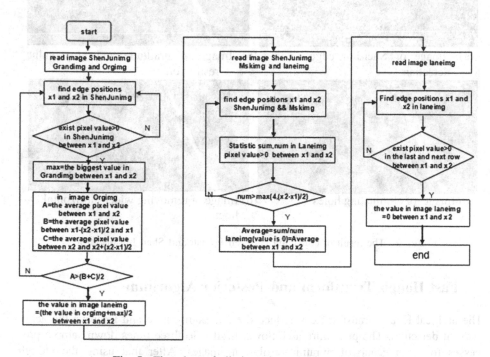

Fig. 5. Flowchart of eliminate incorrect lane markings

At first, when the edge points are found in ShenJunimg, a comparison is carried out in the same position of image Orgimg. If the average gray value in the both sides of the edge positions is bigger than the average gray value in middle of the edge positions, we can make the value in image Laneimg equal to the pixel value in Orgimg plus the maximum of gratitude in image Grandimg, which is shown in Fig. 6(b).

Then, after Shen Jun edge detection, there are some holes whose pixel-values are zero in image ShenJunimg. In order to fill the holes that belong to lane markings, the edge points that not only belong to image ShenJunimg but also belong to image Mskimg are found. When the distance between the edge points satisfy the threshold, the value in image Laneimg which are zero can be replaced by the average value in image Laneimg between edge points, the result is shown in Fig. 6(c).

Finally, sometimes there are some wider continuous horizontal lines than the actual width of the lane marking. We eliminate these continuous horizontal lines through making their pixel-values to be zero value, the image Laneimg is shown in Fig. 6(d).

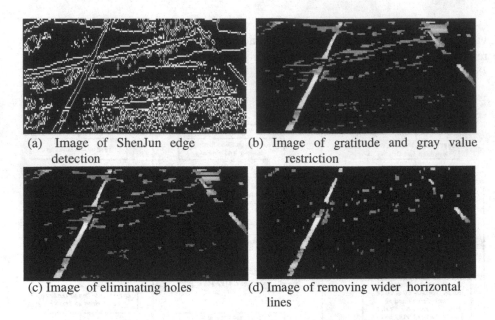

(a) Image of ShenJun edge   (b) Image of gratitude and gray value
     detection   restriction

(c) Image of eliminating holes   (d) Image of removing wider horizontal
                                           lines

Fig. 6. The result of constraint between Prewitt and Shen Jun operator

4 Fast Hough Transform and Posterior Algorithm

Hierarchical Hough transform can reduce the computing time and improve the accuracy of detection. The procedure as follows: firstly, do three times down-sample processes to get a group of pyramid-resolution images. After that using the Hough transform at the lowest-resolution image to get the rough lean angle. Through Refining the lean angel at a higher-resolution image to get more accurate lane lines. At last, the most accurate lane lines can be got in the original image. As can be seen from the above process, the overall calculation is not big because of the pyramid-resolution Hough transform, but we can get higher precision. Suitable down-sample process also helps to improve the ability to resist noise.

After Hough transform, we can find several candidate lines at the left and right half of the image. The posterior algorithm removing the incorrect lane lines is carried out according to the following two steps. Firstly, each of the candidate lines is sampled at the equal interval sampling rows. At each sampled points, the average pixel value the middle rectangular window is compared with the each left and right area around the middle window. If the difference between them bigger than the threshold, the sample window is qualified. Only when the rate of the qualified sample window is large enough, the lane line will be reserved. Secondly, After two fittest lines are found in ROI, as shown in Fig. 7(a). Posterior algorithm of road marking lines is carried out to refine the lane angel. Firstly, each of the lines is sampled at the equal interval sampling rows, as shown in Fig. 7(b). The corresponding sampled points are then found, the intensity values which have a transition from dark to light to dark near the sampled point along the row would produce a rectangular pulse. An adjustable template [12] is used to find the middle of the lane markings near the sampled points, as shown in Fig. 7 (c). Best lane markings estimation using the new middle points is shown in blue line in Fig. 7(d).

(a)   (b)

(c)   (d)

Fig. 7. The images in posterior algorithm of road marking lines

After the lane markings are detected and the vehicle's lateral position are calculated, the departure warning system must interact with the driver to prevent road departure. A measure of roadway departure based on the vehicle's lateral displacement and lateral velocity can works well. The vehicle's lateral displacement is usually small because of the corrective driving, as shown in Fig. 8. To computer lateral velocity, we uses the lateral position of recent 1/2 s equal to fifteen frames. The function is as follows:

$$TTC = distance/averagespeed \qquad (4.1)$$

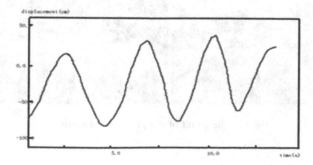

Fig. 8. The illustration of vehicle's displacement from the road center

Fig. 9. The result of the proposed algorithm

$$\text{Averagespeed} = (\text{Speed}\,1 + \text{speed}\,2 + \ldots + \text{speed}\,m)/m \qquad (4.2)$$

$$\text{Speedm} = (\text{leftPoint}[m + 8] - \text{leftPoint}[m])/\text{dTm}(m + 8) \qquad (4.3)$$

Where leftPoint[m] is the vehicle's displacement from the road center in the frame m, dTab is the time difference between frame a and b.

5 Experimental Result

Our test vehicle equipped with a camera installed under the rear-view mirror is used to recorded videos of the roadways. Videos are recorded resolution at 30 frames/s. The algorithm has been implement in visual studio 2010. For images the resolution is 640 × 480, ROI is 640 × 240 resolution, shrinking the ROI to 320 × 120 resolution. Although images down-sampling will cause edge pixels loss, this does not affect the accuracy of the detection algorithm very much, as edge pixels can be restored by using the constraint between Shen Jun edge detection and Prewitt operator edge detection. The algorithm can achieve an average speed of 20 frames per second on an Intel Core2 2.53 GHZ processor.

We tested our algorithm for many different marked roads. It fast and successfully detected road lane even under conditions including different shadows. Figure 9 Shows the result of the proposed algorithm under various illumination conditions to confirm the robustness of the proposed algorithm. Where the green lines is the lane lines found by the Hough Transform, the blue lines represent the results of posterior algorithm, the green blocks at the upper of the images represent there no lane departure warnings,

The red characters at the below of the images such as TTC time 6.0303 represent the collision time.

6 Conclusion and Future Work

In this paper, a robust and real-time lane markings detection system is presented. The major part of the system is the lane points extraction module based on the constraint between Prewitt and Shen Jun operator. Compared with other model-based lane detection methods, the proposed algorithm simplifies the modeling process so that it satisfies real-time detection. At constraint step, Shen Jun edge detection images are checked to select edge points which belong to the images of Prewitt operator detection. Most noises can be removed at this step, only edge points which belong to lane markings are used to Hough transform. Additionally, in the proposed algorithm, there are no special requirements for background models, camera parameters, or any other road surface models. This makes the algorithm more adaptive to different road environment.

For future works, we will develop the fast tracking algorithm. Now this algorithm has a real-time and robust detection of road markings every frame. So a tracking algorithm will be need to reduce the detection time and enhance the detection robustness, so that it can be carried out in a embedded system.

Acknowledgment. This work was supported by the Joint Fund of Department of Science and Technology of Guizhou Province and guizhou university under Grant: LH [2014] 7635. We would like to thank our colleagues for helping to this paper and the anonymous reviewers and the associate editor for their valuable suggestions.

References

1. McCall, J.C., Trivedi, M.M.: Video-based lane estimation and tracking for driver assistance: survey, system, and evaluation. IEEE Trans. Intell. Transp. Syst. **7**, 20–37 (2006). doi:10.1109/TITS.2006.869595
2. Zhou, S., Jiang, Y., Xi, J., et al.: A novel lane detection based on geometrical model and Gabor filter. In: IEEE Intelligent Vehicles Symposium (2010)
3. Liu, W., Zhang, H., Duan, B., et al.: Vision-based real-time lane marking detection and tracking. In: IEEE Transactions on Intelligent Transportation Systems, pp. 49–54 (2008)
4. Satzoda, R.K., Trivedi, M.M.: Efficient lane and vehicle detection with integrated synergies (ELVIS). In: IEEE Conference on Computer Vision and Pattern Recognition Workshops, pp. 708–713 (2014)
5. Satzoda, R.K., Trivedi, M.M.: Vision-based lane analysis: exploration of issues and approaches for embedded realization. In: Kisačanin, B., Gelautz, M. (eds.) Advances in Embedded Computer Vision, pp. 217–235. Springer International Publishing, Switzerland (2014)
6. Lin, Q., Han, Y., Han, H.: Real-time lane departure detection based on extended edge-linking algorithm. In: Second International Conference Computer Research and Development, pp. 725–730. IEEE (2010)
7. Ding, D., Lee, C., Lee, K.: An adaptive road ROI determination algorithm for lane detection. In: TENCON 2013–2013 IEEE Region 10 Conference (31194), pp. 1–4. IEEE (2013)
8. Li, W., Gong, X., Wang, Y., et al.: A lane marking detection and tracking algorithm based on sub-regions. In: International Conference on Informative and Cybernetics for Computational Social Systems (ICCSS), pp. 68–73. IEEE (2014)
9. Grisman, J.D., Thorpe, C.E.: SCARF, A color vision system that tracks roads and intersections. IEEE Trans. Robot. Autom. **9**, 49–58 (1993)
10. Wang, Y., Teoh, E.K., Shen, D.: Lane detection and tracking using B-Snake. Image Vis. Comput. **22**(4), 269–280 (2004)
11. Ruyi, J., Reinhard, K., Tobi, V., et al.: Lane detection and tracking using a new lane model and distance transform. Mach. Vis. Appl. **22**(4), 721–737 (2011)
12. Borkar, A., Hayes, M., Smith, M.T.: A novel lane detection system with efficient ground truth generation. IEEE Trans. Intell. Transp. Syst. **13**(1), 365–374 (2012)
13. Chen, M., Jochem, T., Pomerleau, D.: AURORA, A vision-based roadway departure warning system. In: 1995 IEEE/RSJ International Conference on Intelligent Robots and Systems 95, Human Robot Interaction and Cooperative Robots, Proceedings, vol. 1, pp. 243–248. IEEE (1995)
14. Lu, W., Rodriguez, F., Sergio, A., et al.: Monocular multi-kernel based lane marking detection. In: 2014 IEEE 4th Annual International Conference on Cyber Technology in Automation, Control, and Intelligent Systems (CYBER), pp. 123–128. IEEE (2014)
15. Kluge, K., Lakshmanan, S.: A deformable-template approach to lane detection. In: Proceedings of the Intelligent Vehicles 1995 Symposium, pp. 54–59. IEEE (1995)

16. Álvarez, J.M., Lopez, A.: Novel index for objective evaluation of road detection algorithms. In: 11th International IEEE Conference on Intelligent Transportation Systems, ITSC 2008, pp. 815–820. IEEE (2008)
17. Kim, Z.: Realtime lane tracking of curved local road. In: Intelligent Transportation Systems Conference, ITSC 2006, pp. 1149–1155. IEEE (2006)

Robust Contour Tracking via Constrained Separate Tracking of Location and Shape

Huijun Di[1(✉)], Linmi Tao[2], and Guangyou Xu[2]

[1] Beijing Key Laboratory of Intelligent Information Technology,
School of Computer Science, Beijing Institute of Technology,
Beijing 100081, People's Republic of China
ajon@bit.edu.cn
[2] Key Laboratory of Pervasive Computing, Ministry of Education,
Department of Computer Science and Technology, Tsinghua University,
Beijing 100084, People's Republic of China
{linmi,xgy-dcs}@tsinghua.edu.cn

Abstract. In traditional contour tracker, object's location and shape are usually bound together to form the system state. Such approaches suffer from the problem that most sampled states cannot match the object's boundary exactly when the boundary cannot be captured by the shape model. To overcome such drawbacks, Constrained Separate Tracking of Location and Shape (CSTLS) is proposed. In CSTLS, location and shape are tracked by separate tracker, L-Tracker and S-Tracker, with the constraints enforced by the global contour tracking. The likelihood measurement for each sample in L-Tracker/S-Tracker is calculated by taking multiple shape/location hypotheses into consideration, which help to improve the robustness of tracking. The relationships of L-Tracker and S-Tracker with original problem are established under Sequential Mean Field Monte Carlo method. Experiments demonstrate the effectiveness of the CSTLS.

Keywords: Contour tracking · Mean field

1 Introduction

Contour tracking is an active and challenging topic in computer vision. The tracking methods based on Monte Carlo technique [1–5] are focused on in this paper. The goal of contour tracking through an image sequence is to estimate of the target object's location and shape in every frame of that sequence. In traditional contour tracking methods [1–3, 12, 13], the object's location and shape are usually bound together to form an entire system state of the tracker (see Fig. 1a). Such a binding approach suffers from the problem that most sampled states cannot match the object's boundary exactly when the boundary cannot be captured by the learnt shape model, or shape dynamics

This research was supported in part by the National Natural Science Foundation of China under Grant No. 61003098.

Y.-J. Zhang (Ed.): ICIG 2015, Part III, LNCS 9219, pp. 236–246, 2015.
DOI: 10.1007/978-3-319-21969-1_21

cannot follow the dramatic change of the boundary. As a result, the likelihood measurement will be insufficient. Since the likelihood measurement of contour tracking is often peaked, insufficient measurement may cause the loss of tracking.

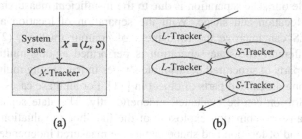

(a)   (b)

Fig. 1. The difference between traditional contour tracking and CSTLS: (a) traditional L-S binding approach, (b) our CSTLS.

To overcome the drawbacks of traditional L-S binding approach, this paper proposes a novel approach to contour tracking: Constrained Separate Tracking of Location and Shape (CSTLS). In the CSTLS, location and shape are tracked by the separate tracker, L-Tracker and S-Tracker (see Fig. 1b), with the constraints enforced by the global contour tracking. In the L-Tracker, the likelihood measurement is calculated by taking multiple shape hypotheses into consideration, which helps to track the location more robustly. Especially when the object's boundary cannot be captured by the learnt shape model, a combination of exist shapes can achieve a better shape representation of the object, and can give more sufficient likelihood measurement. While in the S-Tracker, the likelihood measurement is calculated by taking multiple location hypotheses into consideration, which also helps to track the shape more robustly. Especially when the sampled shape can only partially match the object's boundary, by considering different locations, the likelihood measurement of S-Tracker can account for multiple possible matches, and thus giving more reliable measurement. Consequently, owing to the above collaborations between L-Tracker and S-Tracker, the CSTLS can improve the robustness of contour tracking.

In the CSTLS, the relationships of L-Tracker and S-Tracker with original problem of contour tracking are established under Sequential Mean Field Monte Carlo (SMFMC) method [6]. However, it is infeasible to directly apply SMFMC. The likelihood measurement of contour tracking is in a form of P(observation | location, shape), i.e., the location and shape cannot be measured independently. This factor results in sample-level interdependence of L-Tracker and S-Tracker, and will cause combination explosion when the number of samples of each tracker is large. For example, one will need to evaluate the likelihood 1000×1000 times, if the number of samples of each tracker is 1000. To tackle this problem, we propose two novel notions: integral shape and integral observation, which can help to decouple the sample-level interdependence of location and shape, and can achieve linear complexity of likelihood evaluations w.r.t. the sample numbers.

The idea of state separation is not new, which is already used in existing work [6, 9–11]. In those work, the complete state of the target problem is also divided into some partitions, each of which maintains an individual set of weighted samples. Neverthe-less, the proposed CSTLS is different with those work in two following aspects: (1) The purpose is different. The state separation in those work is due to the curse of dimen-sionality. With state separation, the original problem can be solved more efficiently and effectively. While our state separation is due to the insufficient measurement caused by the binding of location and shape. With the separation of location and shape, the proposed CSTLS can improve the robustness of contour tracking. (2) The case of separation is different. The state separation is performed among multiple correlated de-formable subparts of structured deformable shapes in [6], among multiple objects in [9, 10], and among articulated parts of object in [11]. For all these cases, the likelihood of each state partition can be evaluated independently. The state separation in these cases will not cause combination explosion of the likelihood evaluation. While in our case, the likelihood of location and shape cannot be measured independently. Tackling the combination explosion via integral shape and integral observation is the key con-tribution of our work, which makes the separation of location and shape possible.

This paper is organized as following. The outline of our approach is given in Sect. 2. The formal derivation of the CSTLS is presented in Sect. 3. Experiments on contour tracking of person as well as the performance comparisons of different trackers are discussed in Sect. 4. Finally, conclusion and future work are elaborated.

2 Outline of Our Approach

Exemplar based tracking method [3] is used as an example to discuss the CSTLS. However, the CSTLS can be straightforwardly integrated into the tracking methods based on other type of shape representation. In the exemplar based tracker, a set of contour exemplars $\{E: E_k; k = 1, 2, ..., M\}$ are used as primitives to represent object's contour. E_k can be raw contour points (e.g., see Fig. 4), i.e., $E_k = \{E_k^q \equiv (x_k^q, y_k^q), q = 1, 2, ..., m_k\}$. The contour of target object is represented by $T_a \cdot E_k$ (i.e., a transformed version of the k-th contour exemplar), where $1 \leq k \leq M$, and T_a a geo-metric transformation with parameter a. In the case of Euclidean similarity, $a = (x, y, \theta, s)$ and row vectors transform as $T_a \cdot V = (x, y) + s \cdot V \cdot R(\theta)$. The traditional system state of tracking at frame t is defined as $X_t = (k, a)_t$. Given the observation Z_t, the likelihood measurement is defined as

$$P(Z_t|X_t) \propto \exp(-\lambda \rho(Z_t, T_{a_t} \cdot E_{k_t})) \tag{1}$$

where ρ is chamfer distance [7]. The dynamics is calculated as $P(X_t|X_{t-1}) = P(a_t|a_{t-1})P(k_t|k_{t-1})$, where $P(a_t|a_{t-1})$ is the ARP model of the parameter a, and $P(k_t|k_{t-1})$ is the index transition of the exemplars. The ultimate goal of tracking is the calculation of posterior $P(X_t|Z_{1:t})$.

In the CSTLS, the entire system state is divided into two parts: location state $L_t = (x, y)_t$, and shape state $S_t = (k, \theta, s)_t$. Location and shape are tracked by the separate tracker, L-Tracker and S-Tracker, with the constraints enforced by the global contour tracking. The relationships of L-Tracker and S-Tracker with original problem of con-tour tracking are established under SMFMC in Sect. 3.1, where the posterior $P(X_t|Z_{1:t})$

is approximated by $Q(L_t) \cdot Q(S_t)$. And the found optimal distributions $Q(L_t)$ and $Q(S_t)$ will give the final tracking results of the CSTLS.

However, since the likelihood measurement is in a form of $P(Z_t | L_t, S_t)$, it cannot be calculated with only L_t or S_t. Therefore, the calculation of $Q(L_t)$ or $Q(S_t)$ will involve an integral of the likelihood over another one. Since the major computation of tracking comes from the evaluation of the likelihood, such a combinational calculation of the likelihood will be infeasible. Suppose the number of samples of L-Tracker is N_L and the number of samples of S-Tracker is N_S, we will need evaluate the likelihood $N_L \cdot N_S$ times for each tracker. It will be computational infeasible when N_L and N_S are large (say 1000). In Sect. 3.2, we will introduce two notions: integral shape and integral observation, which can achieve $N_L \cdot N_S$ likelihood evaluations equivalently with only $(N_L + N_S)$ complexity.

3 Constrained Separate Tracking of Location and Shape

3.1 Problem Formulation Under SMFMC

In the CSTLS, two sub-trackers, L-Tracker and S-Tracker, will collaborate with each other to achieve a complete contour tracking. We employ a variational mean field method to established the relationships of these two trackers with original contour tracking problem, where the posterior $P(L_t, S_t | Z_{1:t})$ is approximated by

$$P(L_t, S_t | Z_{1:t}) \sim Q(L_t) Q(S_t) \tag{2}$$

where $Q(L_t)$ and $Q(S_t)$ are independent approximate distributions of $P(L_t | Z_{1:t})$ and $P(S_t | Z_{1:t})$, respectively. The goodness of the approximation is measured by Gibbs free energy [8].

$$F(Q, P) = \int_{L_t, S_t} Q(L_t) Q(S_t) \ln(Q(L_t) Q(S_t)) / P(L_t, S_t | Z_{1:t}). \tag{3}$$

The optimal $Q(L_t)$ and $Q(S_t)$ can be obtained by maximizing the free energy $F(Q, P)$, which are

$$Q(L_t) \propto \exp\left(\int_{S_t} Q(S_t) \ln P(Z_t | L_t, S_t) \right) \int_{L_{t-1}} P(L_t | L_{t-1}) Q(L_{t-1}) \tag{4}$$

$$Q(S_t) \propto \exp\left(\int_{L_t} Q(L_t) \ln P(Z_t | L_t, S_t) \right) \int_{S_{t-1}} P(S_t | S_{t-1}) Q(S_{t-1}) \tag{5}$$

Sequential Monte Carlo technique is subsequently applied to calculate the $Q(L_t)$ and $Q(S_t)$, where two sets of weighted samples are used to represent them, i.e.,

$$Q(L_t) \sim \{u_t^i, \pi_t^i; i = 1, 2, \ldots, N_L\} \tag{6}$$

$$Q(S_t) \sim \{v_t^j, \eta_t^j; j = 1, 2, \ldots, N_S\} \tag{7}$$

This leads to the Sequential Mean Field Monte Carlo (SMFMC) algorithm.

However, the weight calculations of $Q(L_t)$ and $Q(S_t)$ are not independent. For example, for one sample u of $Q(L_t)$, when it is sampled from a proposal distribution g, its weight is calculated by

$$\begin{aligned}
\pi &= Q(u)/g(u) \\
&= \prod_{j=1}^{N_S} P(Z_t | L_t = u, S_t = v_t^j)^{\eta_t^j} \sum_{i=1}^{N_L} w_{t-1}^i P(L_t = u | L_{t-1} = u_{t-1}^i)/g(u),
\end{aligned} \tag{8}$$

which depends on the samples of $Q(S_t)$, and involves N_S likelihood evaluations. Therefore, there will have $N_L \cdot N_S$ likelihood evaluations for $Q(L_t)$. This is computational infeasible. The next subsection will give an efficient approach to weight calculation of $Q(L_t)$ and $Q(S_t)$.

3.2   Integral Shape and Integral Observation

Based on the definition of chamfer distance [7], we have

$$\ln P(Z_t | L_t, S_t = (k_t, \theta_t, s_t)) \propto -\frac{\lambda}{m_{k_t}} \sum_{q=1}^{m_{k_t}} D_t \big(C_q(S_t) + L_t \big) \tag{9}$$

where m_{k_t} is the number of points in the k_t-th contour exemplar, D_t is Distance Transform (DT) image of the edge map detected from input image Z_t, $C_q(S_t)$ is defined as

$$C_q(S_t) = s_t \cdot E_{k_t}^q \cdot R(\theta_t), \tag{10}$$

which is the q-th point of the similarity-transformed k_t-th contour exemplar. Define a contour mask

$$\mathfrak{M}(ROI|S_t) = \begin{cases} 1, \ (x, y) \ locates \ on \ C(S_t) \\ \qquad\qquad\qquad\qquad\qquad , \ (x, y) \in ROI, \\ 0, \ otherwise \end{cases} \tag{11}$$

where $C(S_t) = \{C_q(S_t), q = 1, 2, \ldots, m_{k_t}\}$, and the ROI is a bounding rectangle of $C(S_t)$. Equation (9) can be rewritten as a 2D convolution

$$\ln P(Z_t | L_t, S_t) \propto -\lambda/m_{k_t} \cdot D_t(ROI + L_t) * \mathfrak{M}(ROI|S_t), \tag{12}$$

where '$*$' is the operation of convolution. Subsequently, the likelihood related terms in (4) and (5) can be written as

$$\int_{S_t} Q(S_t) \ln P(Z_t|L_t, S_t) = -\lambda \left[\int_{S_t} Q(S_t) \mathfrak{M}(ROI|S_t)/m_{k_t} \right] * D_t(ROI + L_t)$$

$$= -\lambda \bar{C}_{Int}^t * D_t(ROI + L_t),$$

$$(13)$$

$$\int_{L_t} Q(L_t) \ln P(Z_t|L_t, S_t) = -\lambda/m_{k_t} \cdot \mathfrak{M}(ROI|S_t) * \left[\int_{L_t} Q(L_t) \cdot D_t(ROI + L_t) \right]$$

$$= -\lambda/m_{k_t} \cdot \mathfrak{M}(ROI|S_t) * \bar{D}_{Int}^t,$$

$$(14)$$

where $\bar{C}_{Int}^t$ and $\bar{D}_{Int}^t$ are named as integral shape and integral observation, respectively. Based on the sample representations of $Q(L_t)$ and $Q(S_t)$, integral shape and integral observation can be calculated numerically. The derivations of (13) and (14) use the exchangeable property between convolution and integral. With the notions of integral shape and integral observation, (4) and (5) can be rewritten as:

$$Q(L_t) \propto \exp\left(-\lambda \bar{C}_{Int}^t * D_t(ROI + L_t)\right) \int_{L_{t-1}} P(L_t|L_{t-1})Q(L_{t-1}) \qquad (15)$$

$$Q(S_t) \propto \exp\left(-\lambda/m_{k_t} \cdot \mathfrak{M}(ROI|S_t) * \bar{D}_{Int}^t\right) \int_{S_{t-1}} P(S_t|S_{t-1})Q(S_{t-1}) \qquad (16)$$

Generate $\{u_t^i, \pi_t^i; i = 1, 2, ..., N_L\}$, $\{v_t^j, \eta_t^j; j = 1, 2, ..., N_S\}$ from $\{u_{t-1}^i, \pi_{t-1}^i; i = 1, 2, ..., N_L\}$, $\{v_{t-1}^j, \eta_{t-1}^j; j = 1, 2, ..., N_S\}$:

1. Calculate DT image D_t from input image Z_t.

2. Predict the samples at frame t-1 of the S-Tracker according to the dynamics, and obtain $\{\hat{v}_{t-1}^j, \eta_{t-1}^j; j = 1, 2, ..., N_S\}$.

3. Calculate integral shape $\bar{C}_{Int}^t$ from $\{\hat{v}_{t-1}^j, \eta_{t-1}^j; j = 1, 2, ..., N_S\}$.

4. Mean filed iteration h=1:H

4.1. L-Tracker (input: integral shape $\bar{C}_{Int}^t$ and observation D_t)

4.1.1. Importance sampling: sample $\{u_t^i; i = 1, 2, ..., N_L\}$ based on importance function $I_L(u)$.

4.1.2. Likelihood measurement: calculate $\pi_t^i = Q(L_t = u_t^i)/I_L(u_t^i)$, where $Q(L_t = u_t^i)$ can be calculated efficiently based on $\bar{C}_{Int}^t$ and D_t, according to (15).

4.1.3. Normalize weight π_t^i, then we get $\{u_t^i, \pi_t^i; i = 1, 2, ..., N_L\}$.

4.2. Calculate integral observation $\bar{D}_{Int}^t$ from $\{u_t^i, \pi_t^i; i = 1, 2, ..., N_L\}$.

4.3. S-Tracker (input: integral observation $\bar{D}_{Int}^t$)

4.3.1. Importance sampling: sample $\{v_t^j; j = 1, 2, ..., N_S\}$ based on importance function $I_S(v)$.

4.3.2. Likelihood measurement: calculate $\eta_t^j = Q(S_t = v_t^j)/I_S(v_t^j)$, where $Q(S_t = v_t^j)$ can be calculated efficiently based on $\bar{D}_{Int}^t$, according to (16).

4.3.3. Normalize weight η_t^j, then we get $\{v_t^j, \eta_t^j; j = 1, 2, ..., N_S\}$.

4.4. Calculate integral shape $\bar{C}_{Int}^t$ from $\{v_t^j, \eta_t^j; j = 1, 2, ..., N_S\}$.

Fig. 2. The Algorithm of CSTLS

The complete algorithm is shown in Fig. 2, where the sample weights of $Q(L_t)$ and $Q(S_t)$ can be calculated efficiently based on integral shape and integral observation. Therefore, the sample-level interdependence between location and shape are decoupled via integral shape and integral observation. We can achieve $N_L \cdot N_S$ likelihood evaluations equivalently with only $(N_L + N_S)$ complexity.

4 Experiment

4.1 Method Comparisons and Data Set

To demonstrate the effectiveness of the CSTLS algorithm, we integrated it into the exemplar-based tracker [3], and compare the performance of the tracker with CSTLS and the tracker without CSTLS. The tracking of human body's contour is considered. Two ballet videos with size of 352×288 are used, one for training and another one for testing. The training video consists of 300 frames, of which 103 frames are labeled to learn the exemplars of object's contour as well as related dynamics. A handful of exemplars are shown in Fig. 3. The dramatic change of the object's contour can be seen, which will introduce the difficulties in tracking. Section 4.2 will give the experiments on the test video, where superior performance of the tracker with CSTLS is shown.

Fig. 3. Some exemplars of object's contour.

The entire state of contour tracking is defined as a 5 dimensional vector: (x, y, k, s_x, s_y), where (x, y) is the location, k is the index of contour exemplars, and s_x and s_y are the scale along x and y axis, respectively. Rotation is not considered, which has been reflected into the exemplars (i.e., no rotation alignment is considered during the learning of exemplars). In the CSTLS, the location state is defined as (x, y), and the shape state is defined as (k, s_x, s_y).

The typical configurations for the tracker with CSTLS are: the numbers of samples are chosen as 300×300 (i.e., 300 for L-Tracker and 300 for S-Tracker), and the number of mean field iterations is set as 2. These configurations are used in all the experiments. The typical number of samples for the tracker without CSTLS is 1000, which is used in all the experiments, except the quantitative analysis in Sect. 4.2 where different numbers of samples are tried but all give poor performance.

All the experiments run on a PC with 2.9 GHz CPU. The code is programmed with C++ and no special code optimization is performed. The processing frame rate of the tracker with CSTLS is 2.1 fps, 1.1 fps, and 0.6 fps, if the numbers of samples are set as 300×300, 600×600, and 1200×1200, respectively. Therefore, the CSTLS do have linear complexity w.r.t. the sample numbers, just as we have expected. The processing frame rate of the tracker without CSTLS is 10.1 fps, 6.3 fps, 3.8 fps, and 1.7 fps, if the number of samples is set as 300, 600, 1200, and 2400, respectively.

4.2   Contour Tracking on Testing Video

The intermediate results of the CSTLS are shown in Fig. 4. Figure 4b shows the integral shape, where the lighter of the red color, the higher probability that the pixel represents the object's boundary. To give more clear view of the integral shape, Fig. 4c shows the region representation of integral shape (i.e., the integral is carried out on the interior of contours), from which we can observe that the multiple shape hypotheses are accounted. In the L-Tracker, based on such integral shape, when likelihood is measured on the DT observation (see Fig. 4e), it can take multiple shape hypotheses into consideration, which help to track the location more robustly. Especially when the object's boundary cannot be captured by the learnt shape model, a combination of exist shapes can achieve a better shape representation of the object, and can give more sufficient likelihood measurement.

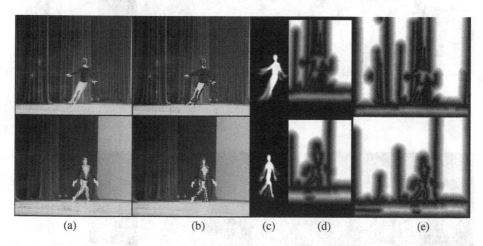

Fig. 4. Intermediate results of CSTLS: (a) original image superimposed with tracked contour, (b) original image superimposed with integral shape, (c) the region representation of integral shape, (d) integral observation, (e) DT image. Top row: Frame 84, Bottom row: Frame 115.

Figure 4d shows the integral observation. If compared with the DT observation in Fig. 4e, it is blurred. This is due to the integral carried out over possible locations. But, this is not just a normal blur process. When the uncertainty of the location is low (i.e. the discriminability of the likelihood measurement is strong), then the integral observation will be less blurred, which means the likelihood measurement of S-Tracker will be more precise, and thus helping to maintain accurate contour. When the uncertainty of location is high (i.e., the discriminability of the likelihood measurement is weak), then the integral observation will be more blurred, which means the likelihood measurement of S-Tracker will be more relaxed, and thus giving more opportunities to maintain multiple shape hypotheses to improve the robustness of L-Tracker.

Therefore, from above discussions of integral shape and integral observation, the L-Tracker and S-Tracker can collaborate with each other in a smart way. The complete tracking results on the video sequence by the tracker with CTLS are shown in Fig. 5. If we compare with the tracking results achieved by the tracker without CTLS (see Fig. 6), the effectiveness of the CSTLS can be proved. The tracker with CSTLS can track the object's contour on entire sequence, while the tracker without CSTLS lost the shape tracking after frame 161, and totally lost the object near the end.

Frame 1   Frame 53   Frame 99   Frame 127

Frame 161   Frame 173   Frame 201   Frame 256

Fig. 5. Contour tracking achieved by exemplar-based tracker with CSTLS.

Frame 99   Frame 161   Frame 256   Frame 298

Fig. 6. Contour tracking achieved by exemplar-based tracker without CSTLS.

By comparing the labeled contours with the contours tracked by different trackers, quantitative analysis can be obtained, which is shown in Fig. 7. The distance values shown in Fig. 7 are calculated based chamfer distance of two contours. Since the chamfer distance is asymmetric, the distance of two contours C_1 and C_2 is calculated as: $dist(C_1, C_2) = \max(chamfer(C_1, C_2), chamfer(C_2, C_1))$. For the tracker without

CSTLS, as the tracking performance is poor, different choices of sample numbers are tested, i.e., 300, 600, 1200, 2400, 4800. But, as shown in Fig. 7, none of them gives good tracking performance. While for the tracker with CSTLS, the distance is much smaller, except some ones are great than 5 pixels, which are similar with the case at frame 173 shown in Fig. 5. The quantitative analysis is obtained by running every tracker 5 times and mean distance over different runs are calculated.

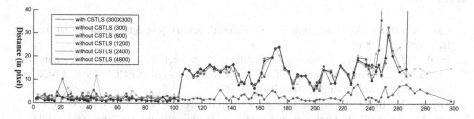

Fig. 7. Quantitative analysis of the performance of different trackers.

5   Conclusion

This paper proposes a novel CSTLS algorithm for contour tracking. Different with the traditional contour tracking methods in which the object's location and shape are bound together to form an entire system state, in the CSTLS, location and shape are tracked by the separate tracker, L-Tracker and S-Tracker, with the constraints enforced by the global contour tracking. The relationships of the L-Tracker and S-Tracker with original problem of contour tracking are established under SMFMC method. However, directly applying SMFMC will cause combination explosion. Two novel notions, integral shape and integral observation, are subsequently proposed to give a feasible algorithm of the CSTLS.

Proved by the experiments on contour tracking, the CSTLS can overcome the drawbacks of traditional L-S binding approach. This is owing to the function of integral shape and integral observation, and the collaboration between L-Tracker and S-Tracker.

The integral shape takes multiple shape hypotheses into consideration, which can achieve a better shape representation of the object. With the integral shape, the L-Tracker can match more parts of the object, and thus improving the robustness. The integral observation is calculated over possible locations, which is blurred than original DT observation. With more blurred integral observation, more shape hypotheses in the S-Tracker can be maintained, which help to improve the robustness. With less blurred integral observation, the likelihood measurement of S-Tracker will be more precise, and thus helping to maintain accurate contour. The blur of the integral observation is affected by the uncertainty of the location, which give a smart balance between the accuracy and robustness.

Although exemplar based tracking method is used to demonstrate the effectiveness of the CSTLS, the CSTLS can also be integrated straightforwardly into the contour tracking methods based on other type of shape representation. Our future work includes applying CSTLS to other contour tracking methods and digging more functions of integral shape and integral observation. For example, with the integral observation at hand, techniques of shape retrieval can be applied to give importance shape function for S-Tracker.

References

1. Isard, M., Blake, A.: Condensation – conditional density propagation for visual tracking. IJCV **28**(1), 5–28 (1998)
2. Isard, M., Blake, A.: Icondensation: unifying low-level and high-level tracking in a stochastic framework. In: Burkhardt, H.-J., Neumann, B. (eds.) ECCV 1998. LNCS, vol. 1406, pp. 893–908. Springer, Heidelberg (1998)
3. Toyama, K., Blake, A.: Probabilistic tracking in a metric space. In: ICCV (2001)
4. Liu, J.S.: Monte Carlo Strategies in Scientific Computing. Springer, New York (1994)
5. Doucet, A., de Freitas, N., Gordon, N.: Sequential Monte Carlo Methods in Practice. Springer, New York (2001)
6. Hua, G., Wu, Y.: Sequential mean field variational analysis of structured deformable shapes. CVIU **101**(2), 87–99 (2006)
7. Gavrila, D., Philomin, V.: Real-time object detection for smart vehicles. In: ICCV (1999)
8. Frey, B., Jojic, N.: A comparison of algorithms for inference and learning in probabilistic graphical models. PAMI **27**(9), 1392–1416 (2005)
9. Jin, Y., Mokhtarian, F.: Variational particle filter for multi-object tracking. In: ICCV (2007)
10. MacCormick, J., Blake, A.: A probabilistic exclusion principle for tracking multiple objects. In: ICCV (1999)
11. MacCormick, J., Isard, M.: Partitioned sampling, articulated objects, and interface-quality hand tracking. In: Vernon, D. (ed.) ECCV 2000. LNCS, vol. 1843, pp. 3–19. Springer, Heidelberg (2000)
12. Hu, W.M., Zhou, X., Li, W., Luo, W.H., Zhang, X.Q., Maybank, S.: Active contour-based visual tracking by integrating colors, shapes, and motions. TIP **22**(5), 1778–1792 (2013)
13. Siew, W.C., Seng, K.P., Ang, L.M.: Lips contour detection and tracking using watershed region-based active contour model and modified H$_\infty$. TCSVT **22**(6), 869–874 (2012)

Robust Face Hallucination via Similarity Selection and Representation

Feng Liu[✉], Ruoxuan Yin, Zongliang Gan, Changhong Chen,
and Guijin Tang

Jiangsu Provincial Key Lab of Image Processing and Image Communication,
Nanjing University of Posts and Telecommunications, Nanjing 210003, China
{liuf,13010614,ganzl,chenchh,tanggj}@njupt.edu.cn

Abstract. Face image super resolution, also referred to as face hallucination, is aiming to estimate the high-resolution (HR) face image from its low-resolution (LR) version. In this paper, a novel two-layer face hallucination method is proposed. Different from the previous SR methods, by applying global similarity selecting, the proposed approach can narrow the scope of samples and boost the reconstruction speed. And the local similarity representation step make the method have better ability to suppress noise for applications under severe condition. As a general framework, other useful algorithms can also be incorporated into it conveniently. Experiments on commonly used face database demonstrate our scheme has better performance, especially for noise face image.

Keywords: Face hallucination · Eigen face · Global similarity selection · Local similarity representation

1 Introduction

Rapid development of video and image services call for high resolution face images. But existing condition of image and video equipment often can't meet the requirement. Therefore, many single image super-resolution researches, targeting on sensitive regions such as vehicle plates and faces, attract much attention. Face hallucination refers to the technique of reconstructing the latent high-resolution (HR) face from a single low-resolution (LR) face. Recent state-of-the-art face hallucination methods are mostly learning-based. These learning-based methods [1] utilize HR and LR dictionary pair to obtain the similar local geometry between HR and LR samples, and achieve satisfactory result under stationary condition.

Freeman et al. [2] firstly proposed a patch-based Markov network to model the local geometry relationship between LR patches and their HR counterparts which is time consuming. Baker and Kanade [4] employed a Bayesian model to estimate the

This research was supported in part by the National Nature Science Foundation, P. R. China. (No. 61071166, 61172118, 61071091, 61471201), Jiangsu Province Universities Natural Science Research Key Grant Project (No. 13KJA510004), Natural Science Foundation of Jiangsu Province (BK20130867), the Six Kinds Peak Talents Plan Project of Jiangsu Province(2014-DZXX-008), and the "1311" Talent Plan of NUPT.

Y.-J. Zhang (Ed.): ICIG 2015, Part III, LNCS 9219, pp. 247–259, 2015.
DOI: 10.1007/978-3-319-21969-1_22

latent high-frequency components. Inspired by locally linear embedding (LLE), Chang et al. [7] obtained high-resolution image through neighbor embedding (NE) method, but the fixed number of neighbors is unstable and difficult to estimate. Considering that face images have stable structure, Ma et al. [8] took it as prior and proposed a position-patch based method, which only use the patches in the same position. But when the number of training faces is much larger than the LR patch's dimension, unconstrained least square estimation (LSE) [8, 9] will lead to inaccurate solutions. Yang et al. [12] and Jung et al. [13] introduced sparse representation (SR) method and convex optimization to address this problem, respectively. Although these SR based methods have achieved good results, their performance are strictly limited by the noise level and degradation process. Figure 1 shows the framework of these typical position-patch based methods. To better adapt to real situation, constrained SR methods are proposed. By affixing similarity constrained factor to optimization coefficients [15, 16], adding illumination compensation for constrained factor [17], and introducing adaptive ℓ-q norm to sparse representation [18], these constrained SR methods improved the ability to resist noise. But the computational load of the commonly used SLEP toolbox [23] which solves the optimization problem is significant.

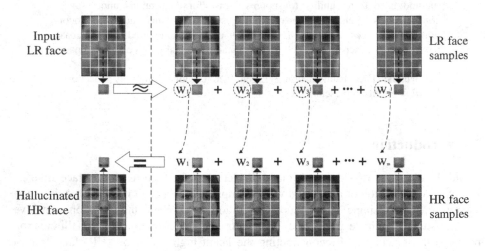

Fig. 1. Outline of the traditional position-patch based face hallucination framework.

In this paper, we prove that the common face database used to face hallucination is over-complete and not all the samples are necessary. We also establish a novel two-layer framework which has a natural parallel structure to infer HR patch. Inspired by the constrained sparse representation methods, we think part of the samples in training set are very different from the input face, which corresponding to the nearly-zero coefficients during optimization. These faces are less important and can even be directly ignored to improve robustness and also reduce computation. We find that reducing the number of trained samples according to their similarities with the input LR face hardly affect the result but save a lot of time, which proves our assumption above. So a sample selection strategy is needed. Considering that the samples in database are all well-aligned faces and almost under the same condition, we intuitively choose eigenface to present the sample reducing operation. Finally, by using global similarity selection via eigenface to speed up the reconstruction process, and using local similarity representation between the same position patches and neighbor patches to synthesize HR patch, our proposed similarity selection and representation (SSR) method get better performance when the input image is corrupted by noise and different blur kernels. As a general framework, the global comparison and local representation algorithm can also be replaced by other useful face recognition and representation methods conveniently. The proposed method has the following features.

- When the surrounding (neighbor) patches are considered to improve robustness against face position changing, about ten times of calculation will be increased. Our two-layer parallel framework can boost the reconstruction speed.
- By excluding insignificant or dissimilar samples in the training set before reconstruction, the algorithm is further accelerated with no decrease on the quality.
- Using constrained exponential distance as coefficients can guarantee good structure similarities between patches, and meanwhile solve the over-fitting problem caused by noise in sparse representation, which make the method very robust to noise and blur kernel changing in real scenarios.

2   Existing Position-Patch Based Approaches

Let N be the dimension of a patch (usually a patch with size $\sqrt{N} \times \sqrt{N}$) and M be the number of samples in the training set. Given a test patch $\mathbf{x} \in R^{N \times 1}$, the patches at the same position in LR training set is represented as $\mathbf{Y} \in R^{N \times M}$, with mth column $\mathbf{Y}^m$ ($m = 1, \ldots M$) being the patch in sample m. Then the input patch can be represented by the sample patches as:

$$\mathbf{x} = \mathbf{Yw} + \mathbf{e} \tag{1}$$

where $\mathbf{w} \in R^{M \times 1}$ is the coefficients vector with entry w_m and $\mathbf{e}$ is the reconstruction error vector.

Obviously, solving the coefficients $\mathbf{w}$ is the key problem in patch-based methods. In [7–9], reconstruction coefficients are solved by constrained least square estimation (LSE) as

$$\mathbf{w}^* = \arg \min_{\mathbf{w}} \|\mathbf{x} - \mathbf{Yw}\|_2^2 \text{ s.t. } \sum_{m=1}^{M} w_m = 1 \tag{2}$$

This least square problem's closed-form solution can be solved with the help of Gram matrix, but it becomes unstable when the number of samples M is much bigger than the patch dimension N. Jung et al. [13] introduce sparse representation into face hallucination and convert (2) into a standard SR problem:

$$\min_{\mathbf{w}} \|\mathbf{w}\|_0 \text{s.t.} \|\mathbf{x} - \mathbf{Y}\mathbf{w}\|_2^2 \leq \varepsilon \tag{3}$$

where ℓ_0 norm counts the non-zero entries number in $\mathbf{w}$ and ε is error tolerance. Yang et al. [12] and Zhang et al. [14] respectively use squared ℓ_2 norm $\|\mathbf{w}\|_2^2$ and ℓ_1 norm $\|\mathbf{w}\|_1$ to replace ℓ_0 norm, which means the statistics of coefficients are constrained by Gaussian and Laplacian distribution.

Similarity constrained SR methods proposed in [15–18] can be formulated as

$$\mathbf{w}^* = \arg\min_{\mathbf{w}} \left\{ \|\mathbf{x} - \mathbf{Y}\mathbf{w}\|_2^2 + \lambda \|\mathbf{D}\mathbf{w}\|_q \right\},$$

$$d_{mn} = \|g\mathbf{x} - \mathbf{Y}^m\|_2, 1 \leq m \leq M \tag{4}$$

where $\mathbf{D} \in R^{M \times M}$ is the diagonal matrix which controls the similarity constrains placed on coefficients. The entries d_{mn} on the main diagonal of $\mathbf{D}$ represent the Euclidean distance with gain factor g. Furthermore, in [15–17], q is set to 1 and 2 respectively. In [18], an adaptively selected ℓ_q norm scheme is introduced to improve its robustness against different conditions.

After the coefficients are obtained, the reconstructed HR test patch $\mathbf{x}_H$ can be represented as

$$\mathbf{x}_H = \mathbf{Y}_H \mathbf{w} \tag{5}$$

with coefficients being directly mapped to the patches of HR samples $\mathbf{Y}_H$.

3 Proposed Method

The methods introduced in Sect. 2 have shown impressive results for experimental noise free faces. But when the noise level, blur kernel and degradation process change, the performance will drop dramatically. It's mainly due to the under-sparse nature of noise, and the local geometry between the high dimension and the low dimension manifolds are no longer coherent since the degradation process has changed. To overcome this problem, we propose global similarity selection and local similarity representation to improve its robustness.

3.1 Global Similarity Selection

In SR based methods, a test LR patch is represented by a large number of LR sample patches through coefficients with sparse. Therefore, heavy calculation is cost on the coefficients with sparsity even the corrupted face is not sparse. So we think not all the samples in the over-complete face database are necessary. Some faces in training set are very different from the input face, which corresponding to very tiny weights during optimization. These faces are not worth occupying so much calculation because they have very limited impact on the results.

Therefore, for the noise corrupted faces, we no longer look for the representation with sparsity but use similarity representation to represent LR patch directly. In order to exclude the dissimilar samples which corresponding to the nearly-zero coefficients, a similarity comparison strategy is needed. And we choose global similarity selection scheme, instead of local (patch) similarity comparison before the reconstruction. This is mainly because the face databases we used are all same size, well aligned and under same lighting condition, global comparison can be reliable enough and very fast.

We intuitively apply Turk and Pentlad's [10] eigenface method, which projects the test face image into the eigenface space, and selects the most similar M faces according to Euclidean distance. Given the LR face database $\mathbf{F}$, with mth column being sample $\mathbf{F}^m$. After being normalized by subtracting its mean value, the covariance matrix $\mathbf{C}$ can be obtained by (6), where M is the number of samples in $\mathbf{F}$. Then the eigenface $\mathbf{P}$ is easy to compute by singular value decomposition, and the projected database $\mathbf{F}'$ is given in (7). Before reconstruction, the input LR face $\mathbf{x}$ is firstly projected to the eigenface space by (8), and the similar faces can be selected between the samples and $\mathbf{x}$ through Euclidean distance, according to $\mathbf{F}'_m - \mathbf{x}'^2_2$.

$$\mathbf{C} = \frac{1}{M}\mathbf{F}_{norm}\mathbf{F}_{norm}^T, \; \mathbf{F}_{norm} = \mathbf{F} - mean(\mathbf{F}). \tag{6}$$

$$\mathbf{F}' = \mathbf{F}_{norm}^T\mathbf{P}. \tag{7}$$

$$\mathbf{x}' = [\mathbf{x} - mean(\mathbf{F})]^T\mathbf{P}. \tag{8}$$

Results shown in Fig. 3 in Sect. 4 demonstrate our assumption perfectly. This global similarity selection method have saved about half of the traditional method's calculation before reconstruction.

3.2 Local Similarity Representation

After picking out the similar faces we need from the entire training set. To make full use of the information in neighbor patches, we establish a framework with parallel two-layer structure which integrates the information of patches surrounding the test LR patch, as shown in Fig. 2. Instead of using all the sample patches at the same position to estimate the test patch (as in Fig. 1), we change the traditional structure into a two layer mode which every sample outputs a middle-layer HR patch before synthesizing the final HR patch.

In Fig. 2, we can notice that the test LR patch's neighbor patches in training samples are marked with dark lines. Let M be the number of samples we picked out and S (S is 9 in Fig. 2) be the number of neighbor patches we used surrounding the center patch. The test LR patch is still $\mathbf{x} \in R^{N \times 1}$, and all its neighbor patches in sample m ($m = 1,...M$) is represented as $\mathbf{Y}_m^S \in R^{N \times S}$ with sth column being $\mathbf{Y}_m^s$ ($s = 1,...S$).

For every sample in the LR training set, a weight vector $\mathbf{w}_m \in R^{S \times 1}$ which represents the similarity between the test patch and its neighbor patches is obtained, the entries $\mathbf{w}_m^s$ are computed as

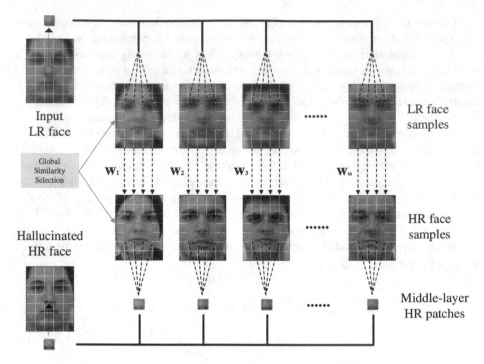

Fig. 2. Proposed parallel two-layer face hallucination framework

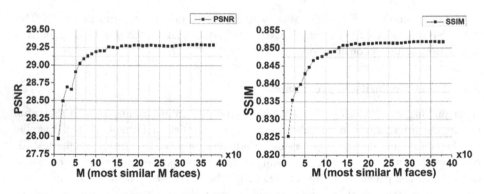

Fig. 3. Average PSNR and SSIM with the number of the similar faces M changes

$$w_m^s = exp\left(\left\|\mathbf{x} - \mathbf{Y}_m^s\right\|_2 + \left\|D(s) - D(\mathbf{x})\right\|_2\right), 1 \le s \le S. \qquad (9)$$

The function $D(\cdot)$ calculates the patch distance from the current patch to the center patch. Then the middle-layer HR patch of sample m can be represented as

$$\mathbf{x}_{H1m} = \frac{1}{G_m} \mathbf{Y}_m^S \mathbf{w}_m,$$

$$G_m = \sum_{s=1}^{S} w_m^s \tag{10}$$

After every sample output its corresponding middle-layer HR patch, the final HR patch can be synthesized simply by

$$x_{H2} = \frac{1}{\sum_{m=1}^{M} G_m} \sum_{m=1}^{M} G_m x_{H1m}. \tag{11}$$

Finally, by assembling all reconstructed HR patches to the corresponding position and averaging the pixels in overlapped regions. The estimated HR face is obtained. The entire similarity selection and representation face hallucination method is summarized as following steps.

Face Hallucination via SSR

---

1. **Input:** HR and LR training set with M' samples, LR test face x_L, number of neighbors S, *patchsize, overlap.*
2. Project LR test face into the eigenface space, and pick out the most M similar samples according to Euclidean distance.
3. Divide the input test face and the picked out M training samples into UV patches according to *patchsize* and *overlap.*
4. **For** $i = 1$ to U **do**
5. **For** $j = 1$ to V **do**
6. **For** $m = 1$ to M **do**
   (a) Calculate similarity weights w_m between test patch $x_L(i,j)$ and its neighbors in sample m.

   $$w_m^s = exp(\|x - Y_m^s\|_2 + \|D(x) - D(s)\|_2), \ 1 \leq s \leq S$$

   (b) Synthesize middle-layer HR patch over LR neighbor patches Y_m^S

   $$x_{H1m}(i,j) = \frac{1}{G_m} Y_m^S w_m, \ G_m = \sum_{s=1}^{S} w_m^s.$$

7. **End for**
8. Synthesize final HR patch at position (i,j)

   $$x_{H2}(i,j) = \frac{1}{\sum_{m=1}^{M} G_m} \sum_{m=1}^{M} G_m x_{H1m}(i,j).$$

9. **End for**
10. **End for**
11. Integrate all the reconstructed HR patches to their corresponding position and averaging the pixel values in the overlapped regions.
12. **Output:** HR hallucinated face x_H.

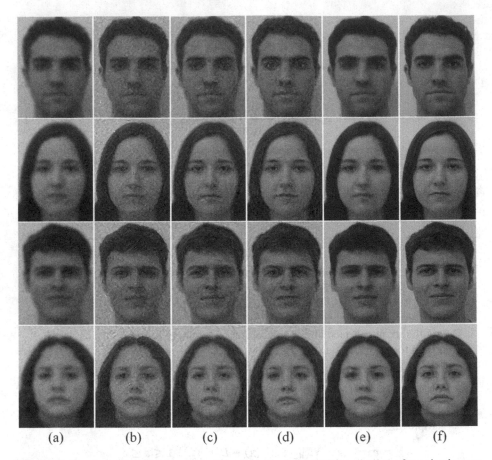

| (a) | (b) | (c) | (d) | (e) | (f) |

Fig. 4. Comparison of results based on different methods on FEI face database for noisy images ($\sigma = 5$). (a) Bicubic. (b) Chang's NE [7]. (c) Ma's LSR [8]. (d) Jiang's LcR [15]. (e) Proposed SSR. (f) Original HR faces.

4   Experiments and Results

In this section, we conduct face hallucination experiments on the proposed SSR method to testify its performance under inconsistent degradation conditions between the test face image and training face images. The face database we apply is FEI face database [24], which contains 400 faces from 200 adults (100 men and 100 women). Among them, we randomly select 380 faces for training and the rest 20 faces for testing. All the samples are well-aligned and in the same size 360×260. The LR samples are smoothed and down-sampled with factor of 4. The LR patch size is set to 3×3 pixels with overlap of 1 pixel and the HR patch size is 12×12 pixels with 4 overlapped pixels. The smooth kernel we use in the training phase is fixed by 20×20 Gaussian lowpass filter with standard deviation of 4.

In Fig. 3, we show how the number of similar faces M in the global similarity selection stage affect the quality of reconstruction. We can see that the second half of

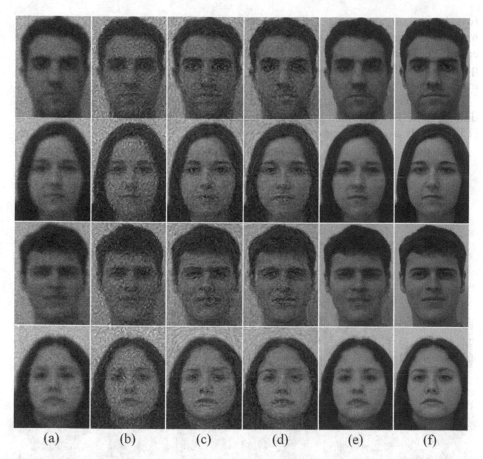

(a)   (b)   (c)   (d)   (e)   (f)

Fig. 5. Comparison of results based on different methods on FEI face database for noisy images ($\sigma = 10$). (a) Bicubic. (b) Chang's NE [7]. (c) Ma's LSR [8]. (d) Jiang's LcR [15]. (e) Proposed SSR. (f) Original HR faces.

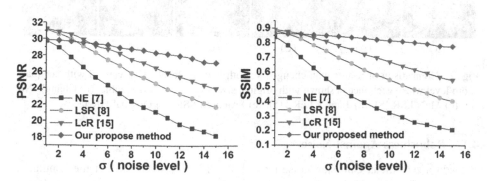

Fig. 6. Comparison of different methods: Average PSNR and SSIM with the noise level σ grows.

two curves are almost flat, which means the reconstruction quality is basically unchanged even the number of faces we use to reconstruct is reduced to half of the entire set. Therefore, we set M to 190 (half of the entire set) without affecting the quality in the following tests, while other methods still use the entire set with 380 training faces.

We conduct the following experiments under two unconformity degradation conditions: noise corrupted and smoothed by different kernels. NE [7], LSR [8] and LcR [15] methods are tested for better comparison.

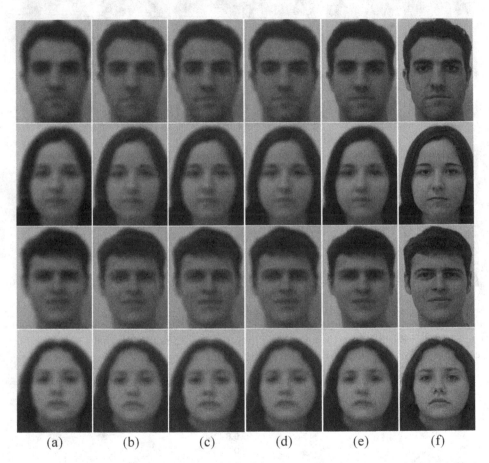

(a)   (b)   (c)   (d)   (e)   (f)

Fig. 7. Comparison of results with changed smooth kernel (Results best viewed with adequate zoom level where each face is shown with original size 360 × 260). (a) Bicubic. (b) Chang's NE [7]. (c) Ma's LSR [8]. (d) Jiang's LcR [15]. (e) Proposed SSR. (f) Original HR faces.

4.1   Robustness Against Noise

We add a zero-mean Gaussian noise ($\sigma = 1, 2 \ldots 15$) to test face to get the simulated noisy face. The smooth kernel is the same with the one in the training phase. Some randomly selected objects' results are shown in Figs. 4 and 5 when σ is set to 5 and 10.

The corresponding average PSNR and SSIM values are listed in Table 1. We can see that with the increase of noise level, the input face is no longer sparse. So the traditional SR methods can't distinguish the noise component from original images, the performance drop dramatically, and there are many artificial texture due to gaussian noise. But our SSR method is much less affected by noise and is able to restore a much clearer face. Relative to the second best LcR, PSNR gains of SSR approach 0.23 dB and 1.83 dB respectively for noise level 5 and 10. More results under different noise levels are shown in Fig. 6. As we can see, with the noise level continues to grow, SSR method will continue to widen the gap with the traditional methods.

Table 1. PSNR and SSIM comparison of different methods

Images	Metrics	NE [7]	LSR [8]	LcR [15]	Proposed SSR
$\sigma = 5$ Gaussian	PSNR	25.31	28.32	29.17	**29.40**
	SSIM	0.5549	0.7447	0.8102	**0.8502**
$\sigma = 10$ Gaussian	PSNR	21.13	24.61	26.50	**28.33**
	SSIM	0.3229	0.5489	0.6722	**0.8162**
Kernel changed	PSNR	27.86	28.93	**29.30**	28.45
	SSIM	0.8446	0.8570	**0.8587**	0.8414

4.2 Robustness Against Kernel Changes

We find the performance of SR methods decrease significantly even the kernel in reconstruction phase is slightly changed, compared to the one in training phase. However, this situation is the most common one in practical applications. Therefore, we decide to test different methods under the condition of inconformity kernels in training and reconstruction phase. As mentioned above, a fixed 20×20 gaussian lowpass filter with standard deviation of 4 is used in training phase. We change the standard deviation to 8 from 4 to make the input face more blurred than the faces in LR set.

According to Table 1, despite SSR method can't beat LSR and LcR in PSNR and SSIM values, results in Fig. 7 intuitively demonstrate that SSR method can create more details and sharper edges than others, which is more valuable in practical use. Performances of the first three methods are influenced a lot due to the different kernel, only the eye's region is artificially enhanced while other region is basically the same blurred as input face. But SSR can generate much clear facial edges like eyes, nose and facial contours, which proves its superiority in subjective visual quality.

5 Conclusion

In this paper, we have proposed a general parallel two-layer face hallucination framework to boost reconstruction speed and improve robustness against noise. Our method can exclude the unnecessary samples from over-complete training set using global similarity selection without quality loss. Then the local similarity representation stage can make the method output satisfactory result under severe conditions. Experiments on FEI face database demonstrate this method can achieve better results under heavy noise conditions and gain good visual quality when the degradation process is changed. As a general framework, many other existing face hallucination schemes can also be incorporated into SSR method conveniently.

References

1. Wang, N., Tao, D., Gao, X., Li, X., Li, J.: A comprehensive survey to face hallucination. Int. J. Comput. Vis. **106**, 9–30 (2014)
2. Freeman, W., Pasztor, E., Carmichael, O.: Learning low-level vision. Int. J. Computer. Vis. **40**(1), 25–47 (2000)
3. William, T.F., Thouis, R.J., Egon, C.P.: Example-based super-resolution. IEEE Comput. Graph. Appl. **22**(2), 56–65 (2002)
4. Baker, S., Kanade, T.: Limits on super-resolution and how to break them. IEEE Trans. Pattern Anal. Mach. Intell. **24**(9), 1167–1183 (2002)
5. Dalley, G., Freeman, B., Marks, J.: Single-frame text super-resolution: a bayesian approach. In: Proceedings of IEEE Conference on Image Processing, vol. 5, pp. 3295–3298 (2004)
6. Yang, C., Liu, S., Yang, M.: Structured face hallucination. In: Proceedings of IEEE Conference on Computer Vision and Pattern Recognition, pp. 1099–1106 (2013)
7. Chang, H., Yeung, D., Xiong, Y.: Super-resolution through neighbor embedding. In: Proceedings of IEEE Conference on Computer Vision and Pattern Recognition, pp. 275–282 (2004)
8. Ma, X., Zhang, J., Qi, C.: Position-based face hallucination method. In: Proceedings of IEEE Conference on Multimedia and Expo, pp. 290–293 (2009)
9. Ma, X., Zhang, J., Qi, C.: Hallucinating face by position-patch. Pattern Recogn. **43**(6), 3178–3194 (2010)
10. Matthew, A.T., Alex P.P.: Face recognition using eigenfaces. In: Proceedings of IEEE Conference on Computer Vision and Pattern Recognition, pp. 586–591 (1991)
11. Wright, J., Yang, A.Y., Ganesh, A., Shankar Sastry, S., Ma, Y.: Robust face recognition via sparse representation. IEEE Trans. PAMI. **31**(2), 210–227 (2009)
12. Yang, J., Tang, H., Ma, Y., Huang, T.: Image super-resolution via sparse representation. IEEE Trans. Image Process. **19**(11), 2861–2873 (2010)
13. Jung, C., Jiao, L., Liu, B., Gong, M.: Position-patch based face hallucination using convex optimization. IEEE Signal Process. Lett. **18**(6), 367–370 (2011)
14. Zhang, J., Zhao, C., Xiong, R., Ma, S., Zhao, D.: Image super-resolution via dual-dictionary learning and sparse representation. In: Proceedings of IEEE International Symposium on Circuits Systems, pp. 1688–1691 (2012)
15. Jiang, J., Hu, R., Han, Z., Lu, T., Huang, K.: Position-patch based face hallucination via locality-constrained representation. In: Proceedings of IEEE International Conference on Multimedia and Expo (ICME), pp. 212–217 (2012)
16. Jiang, J., Hu, R., Wang, Z., Han, Z.: Noise robust face hallucination via locality-constrained representation. IEEE Trans. Multimedia **16**, 1268–1281 (2014)
17. Wang, Z., Jiang, J., Xiong, Z., Hu, R., Shao, Z.: Face hallucination via weighted sparse representation. In: Proceedings of the IEEE International Conference on Acoustics, Speech and Signal Processing, pp. 2198–2201 (2013)

18. Wang, Z., Hu, R., Wang, S., Jiang, J.: Face hallucination via weighted adaptive sparse regularization. IEEE Trans. Circ. Syst. Video Technol. **24**, 802–813 (2013)
19. Weiss, Y., Freeman, W.T.: What makes a good model of natural images? In: Proceedings of IEEE Conference on Computer Vision and Pattern Recognition, pp. 1–8 (2007)
20. Roth, S., Black, M.J.: Fields of experts. Int. J. Comput. Vis. **82**(2), 205–229 (2009)
21. Schmidt, U., Gao, Q., Roth, S.: A generative perspective on MRFs in low-level vision. In: Proceedings of IEEE Conference on Computer Vision and Pattern Recognition, pp. 1751–1758 (2010)
22. Zhang, H., Zhang, Y., Li, H., Huang, T.S.: Generative bayesian image super resolution with natural image prior. IEEE Trans. Image Process. **21**(9), 4054–4067 (2012)
23. Liu, J., Ji, S., Ye, J.: SLEP: sparse learning with efficient projections (2010). http://www.public.asu.edu/jye02/Software/SLEP
24. FEI face database. http://fei.edu.br/cet/facedatabase.html

Robust Face Recognition
with Locality-Sensitive Sparsity and Group
Sparsity Constraints

Xi Sun, Wentao Chan, and Lei Qu[✉]

Key Laboratory of Intelligent Computing and Signal Processing,
Anhui University, Hefei 230039, China
qulei@ahu.edu.cn

Abstract. In this paper, we present a robust face recognition method with combined locality-sensitive sparsity and group sparsity constraint. The group sparsity constraint is designed to utilize the grouped structure information embedded in the training data. Its key idea is to try representing the test image with training images from fewer individuals. We show that, by further integrating the local similarity information between the test image and training images, the embedded group structure information can be better utilized, and as result, the recognition performance can be significantly improved. Experimental results on the ORL, AR and Extended Yale B database verify the superiority of our proposed method under different pose, illumination, expression variations and different dimension reduction settings.

Keywords: Face recognition · Sparse representation · Locality-sensitive · Group sparsity

1 Introduction

Face recognition is one of the most challenging research topics in the field of pattern recognition and computer vision. It has many applications in business and law enforcement besides its scientific significance, for instance, supervision, security, communication, human-computer interaction, etc. After 30 years of research, Numerous face recognition methods have been proposed by researchers and scientists. However, robust face recognition is still an open problem due to the complexity arising from expressions, hairstyle, post, illumination variations and the similarity of the facial organ distribution among different peoples.

In the past few years, due to the rising of Compressive Sensing, especially the core technology of sparse representation which can not only reduce the cost of data analysis and processing, but also improve the efficiency of data compression. Method based on sparse representation received extensive attention because of its excellent performance and robustness to noise and occlusion. In 2009, Wright et. al. [1] introduced sparse representation to solve the face recognition problem successfully and proposed Sparse Representation Classification (SRC) method. SRC looks for the sparsest representation of a test sample in the dictionary which composed of all training data, and can be

© Springer International Publishing Switzerland 2015
Y.-J. Zhang (Ed.): ICIG 2015, Part III, LNCS 9219, pp. 260–270, 2015.
DOI: 10.1007/978-3-319-21969-1_23

solved efficiently via l_1-norm minimization. SRC is effective and robust in the classification, but the interior structure information of the training data dictionary has not been considered. Yang and Zhang [2] proposed a Gabor-feature based SRC (GSRC) scheme in 2010, which uses the image local Gabor features for SRC. The significant superiority of GSRC is its compact occlusion dictionary, which can greatly reduce the computational cost of sparse coding. Although GSRC has much better performance than SRC, the interior structure information has not been taking into account either. Yuan et al. [3] proposed the group lasso which could solve the convex optimization problem at the group level. In 2011, Elhamifar et al. [4] proposed a more robust classification method that using group sparse representation, which searching a representation that uses the minimum number of blocks. It overcomes the drawback of SRC, however, group sparse representation loses to capture the locality structure of data. Friedman et al. [5, 6] proposed an idea of "A sparse-group lasso", which includes both individual and group sparse representation classification. When the groups consist of linearly independent data, this method can well solve face recognition problem. In recent years some initial efforts have been devoted to develop kernel sparse representation classification (KSRC) [7, 8]. It integrates the kernel method and the SRC method, so that KSRC has been successfully applied for image classification and face recognition, but it is not able to capture the locality structure information. Shrivastava et al. [9] proposed a multiple kernel learning (MKL) algorithm, which is based on the SRC method. It makes full use of the nonlinear kernel SRC in efficiently representing the nonlinearities in the high dimensional feature space, but still could not obtain the locality structure of data. In 2014, Zhang and Zhao [10] integrate KSRC with data locality in the kernel feature space, and develop an extension of KSRC, called locality-sensitive kernel sparse representation classification (LS-KSRC). Due to integrating the data locality, it can preserve the similarity between the test sample and its neighboring training data when searching sparse representation coefficients. This is good property for classification.

In this paper, inspired by the cogitation of LS-KSRC [10], we introduce a new method which combined the locality-sensitive sparsity with the group sparsity constraint. It not only takes account of the grouped structure information of the training data dictionary, but also integrates the data locality. The proposed method aims to learn both group sparsity and data locality at the same time, and achieve improved classification.

The rest of this paper is organized as follows. In Sect. 2, we review the sparse representation classification method and the group sparsity classification method in brief. Section 3 provides the method that we proposed in detail. Experimental results and analysis are presented in Sect. 4. Section 5 conclusions this paper with a summary.

2 Sparse Representation

2.1 Sparse Representation-Based Classification

The SRC method can be seen as a process that converts the input test image into the sparsest linear combination of training images with illumination, expression, etc.

variations. Suppose we have n classes, the ith class has n_i training samples, $a_{i,j} \in R^{D \times 1}$ as the image feature vector of the jth image in the ith class, D denotes dimension of the image feature vector, $A_i = [a_{i,1}, a_{i,2}, \ldots, a_{i,n_i}] \in R^{D \times n_i}$ contains training images of the ith class. Let $A = [A_1, A_2, \ldots, A_n]$ be the entire training set, y denotes an input test image. To avoid the NP-hard problem result from the l_0-norm, practically, the SRC often refers to solving the following l_1-norm minimization problem,

$$\min_{x \in R^D} \|x\|_1 \quad s.t. \quad \|y - Ax\|_2 < \varepsilon, \tag{1}$$

where x is the sparse coefficient vector, ε is associated with a noise term with bounded energy. The optimal solution is denoted by $x^{*T} = [x_1^{*T}, x_2^{*T}, \ldots, x_n^{*T}]$, x_i contains the coefficients associated with the ith class.

2.2 Group Sparsity Classification

Although great success can be obtained by the SRC, one potential problem of this method is that the test image may be represented by the training images from different individuals. For the task of face recognition, this problem may result in ambiguous or even wrong recognition. Ideally, the test image should be only represented by the training images from only one individual which corresponding to the correct classification. Based on this idea, Elhamifar et al. proposed a more robust grouped sparse representation based classification method [4] which tries to represent the test image by the training images from as fewer individuals as possible. To implement this constraint, the training data dictionary is divided into groups where each group is form by the training images from the same individual. Then, the recognition is realized by searching a representation that uses the minimum number of group. This is equivalent to convert the classification problem to a structural sparse recovery problem.

Given a test image y, the following convex problem is considered to derive the sparse coefficient x of y, which minimizes the number of nonzero groups x_i from the dictionary,

$$P_1 : \quad \min_{x \in R^D} \sum_{i=1}^{n} \|x_i\|_2 \quad s.t. \quad \|y - Ax\|_2 < \varepsilon, \tag{2}$$

where x_i represents the coefficients associated with the ith class, ε is associated with a noise term with bounded energy, $A = [A_1, A_2, \ldots, A_n]$ is denoted as the entire training set.

In addition to minimize the number of nonzero groups, one alternative method is to minimizes the number of nonzero reconstructed vectors $A_i x_i$,

$$P_2 : \quad \min_{x \in R^D} \sum_{i=1}^{n} \|A_i x_i\|_2 \quad s.t. \quad \|y - Ax\|_2 < \varepsilon, \tag{3}$$

where $A_i = [a_{i,1}, a_{i,2}, \ldots, a_{i,n_i}] \in R^{D \times n_i}$ denotes the ith training sample.

From the Eqs. (2) and (3), we note that they are equivalent only if the groups consist of linearly independent data. Because of the similarity of the facial organ distribution among different people, it is very easy to appear linearly dependent data in face recognition application.

3   The Proposed Method

Nowadays in many pattern recognition problems, data locality has been widely used, such as K-nearest neighbor (KNN) classifier [11], data clustering [12], and image classification [13] et al. And it has been pointed out in [14], which data locality is more essential than sparsity for sparse coding. As mentioned in the introduction, group sparse representation loses to capture the locality structure of data. To overcome this drawback, now we propose a more advanced method which combined the locality-sensitive sparsity with the group sparsity constraint.

First, we consider one type of group sparse representation in our method, which minimizes the number of nonzero groups from the dictionary. By means of enforcing data locality in the kernel feature space to the l_1-norm minimization problem in LS-KSRC [10], the l_1-norm minimization problem in our proposed method is formulated as follows,

$$P3: \quad \min_{x \in R^D} \lambda \|p \bullet x\|_2 + \beta \sum_{i=1}^{n} \|x_i\|_2 \quad s.t. \quad \|y - Ax\|_2 < \varepsilon \tag{4}$$

where λ is the regularization parameter, the symbol $\bullet$ represents element-wise multiplication, x denotes the sparse coefficient vector, β weights the group sparsity regularizer, $A = [A_1, A_2, \ldots, A_n]$ is the concatenation of training samples from all the classes, y denotes a test sample, ε is associated with a noise term with bounded energy, x_i is the representation coefficient associated with the ith training sample. p is the locality adaptor, and we use the following exponential locality adaptor like the LS-KSRC [10] in our method,

$$p = \sqrt{\exp\left(\frac{d(y_i, y_j)}{\eta}\right)} \tag{5}$$

where η is a positive constant, y_i denotes a test sample, y_j denotes a neighboring training sample of y_i, and $d(y_i, y_j)$ induced by a l_2-norm is defined as,

$$d(y_i, y_j) = \|y_i - y_j\|_2 \tag{6}$$

where $d(y_i, y_j)$ denotes the Euclidean distance.

In Eq. (4), the vector p is used to measure the distance between a test sample and each column of training sample. In another word, the vector p can be seen as a dissimilarity vector, and is applied to constrain the corresponding sparse coefficient. It should be noted that since the solutions only have few significant values whereas most coefficients are zero, the resulting coefficients of Eq. (4) is regarded to be still sparse in the sense of l_1-norm, but not sparse in the sense of l_2-norm. Thus minimizing the problem in Eq. (4) means to encode the test sample with its neighboring training samples, and make the proposed method integrates both group sparsity and data locality structure while obtaining the optimal sparse coefficients. This guarantees our method with a good ability of learning discriminating sparse representation coefficients for classification.

Then, similarly, we consider another way to optimize the group sparse representation in our proposed method, which minimizes the number of nonzero reconstructed vectors. And the l_1-norm minimization problem in our proposed method is formulated as follows,

$$P4: \quad \min_{x \in R^D} \lambda \|p \bullet x\|_2 + \beta \sum_{i=1}^{n} \|A_i x_i\|_2 \quad s.t. \quad \|y - Ax\|_2 < \varepsilon \quad \quad (7)$$

where $A_i \in R^{D \times n_i}$ is the subset of the training samples from class i.

It is worth pointing out that in Eqs. (4) and (7), the first term constraints the data locality, it can preserve the similarity between the test sample and its neighboring training data, and give sparse representation coefficients with discriminating information. The second term constraints group sparsity, it takes account of the grouped structure information embedded in the training data. As a result, our method integrates group sparsity constraints and data locality structure at the same time. Our method which combines locality-sensitive sparsity with group sparsity constraints is summarized in Algorithm 1.

Algorithm 1. The proposed method

---

(1) Input: the matrix of all training samples A, and a test sample y

(2) Calculate the dissimilarity vector between a test sample and each training sample by using the exponential locality adaptor p

(3) Solve the l_1-norm minimization problem

(4) Compute the residuals by using the samples associated with the ith class by

$$r_i(y) = \min_{i=1,2..n} \left(\left\| y - A_i x_i^{*T} \right\|_2 \right)$$

(5) Output: the class label y of the given test sample

$$class(y) = \arg\min_{i=1,2..n} r_i(y)$$

---

where $x_i^{*T} = [x_1^{*T}, x_2^{*T}, \ldots, x_n^{*T}]$ denotes the optimal solution, which contains the coefficients associated with the ith class.

4 Experiments

In this section, we evaluate the performance of our proposed method on several commonly used face databases, including ORL [15], AR [16], and the Extended Yale B [17]. Figure 1 shows some sample images from three benchmarking face databases, where various pose, expression and illumination variations can be observed. To illustrate the superiority of our method, the recognition performance of several closely related sparse representation based face recognition methods [1, 4, 10] are investigated and compared.

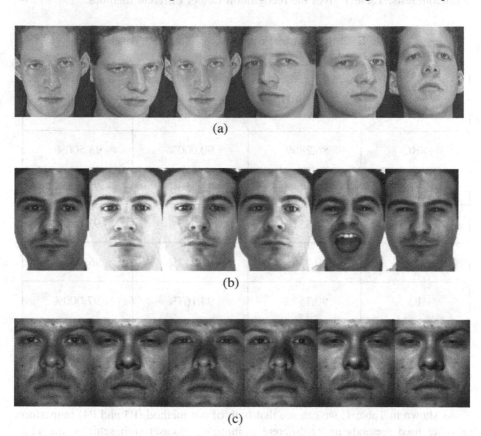

(a)

(b)

(c)

Fig. 1. Sample images from three face databases: (a) the ORL database, (b) the AR database and (c) the extended Yale B database.

For all experiment, the Principal Component Analysis (PCA) [18] is used to reduce the feature dimension before classification is performed, and the CVX toolbox is employed to solve the l_1-norm minimization problem. We choose $\varepsilon=0.05$, $\eta = 0.5$ for all experiments. Since for different methods and databases, the best performance was achieved with different λ and β settings. To conduct a fair comparison, we tested different λ and β combination for all methods, only their best performances were recorded and compared.

4.1 Experiments on ORL Database

In this experiment, we tested the performance of different methods under different training/test split settings on the ORL database. The ORL database contains 400 face images from 40 subjects (10 different images per subject) with variations in poses, illuminations and facial expressions. For each test, we randomly select a subset with L (L = 3, 4, 5) images per subject to form the training set, and the rest images was taken as testing set. The recognition accuracy is calculated as the average recognition rate of 30 random tests. Table 1 gives the recognition rate of different methods.

Table 1. The performance comparisons on the ORL database.

method L (PCA)	3 (40)	4 (40)	5 (40)
SRC	86.286%	90.000%	93.500%
LS-KSRC	89.643%	92.750%	95.500%
P1	87.857%	89.167%	93.000%
P2	89.286%	92.917%	96.500%
P3	90.357%	94.167%	97.000%
P4	94.286%	95.417%	98.000%

As shown in Table 1, we can see that both of our method (P3 and P4) outperform the other used methods under different training/test dataset split settings, including SRC, LS-KSRC and two types of group sparsity. P3 method obtains the best recognition performance with an accuracy of 90.357 % for 3 Train, 94.167 % for 4 Train, and 97.000 % for 5 Train, and our P4 method obtains the best recognition performance with an accuracy of 94.286 % for 3 Train, 95.417 % for 4 Train, and 98.000 % for 5 Train. And we can also note that in each setting, the highest recognition accuracy was always obtained by the P4 method. For instance, in the case of L = 3, the performance of P4 method is about 8 % better than SRC, 4.643 % better than LS-KSRC, 6.429 % better than P1, 5 % better than P2, and even 3.929 % better than our P3 method. These indicate that our method is a more effective classification method for face recognition in comparison with the other used methods.

4.2   Experiments on AR Database

In this experiment, the performance of different methods was evaluated on the AR database under different PCA feature dimension reduction settings. The AR database contains 3276 face images from 126 subjects with various poses, expressions, and illuminations. The original size of images is 165 * 120. We choose a subset of 1400 images from 100 subjects (50 male and 50 female), to ensure that for each subject, there are 14 frontal face images. In each test, we randomly select 7 images per subject to form the training dataset, and the rest is use as test dataset. Same as the experiments on the ORL database, the recognition accuracy is calculated as the average recognition rate of 30 random tests. Table 2 gives the best recognition rate of different methods under different PCA feature dimension reduction settings.

Table 2. The performance comparisons on the AR database.

reduced dimension / method	36	54	130
SRC	73.104%	79.828%	86.266%
LS-KSRC	73.247%	80.687%	87.554%
P1	72.818%	81.402%	86.981%
P2	74.678%	81.545%	88.698%
P3	75.393%	81.688%	87.838%
P4	78.112%	82.546%	89.557%

As shown in Table 2, both our method (P3 and P4) show their superiority over other methods under different PCA dimension reduction settings. The highest recognition accuracy obtained by P3 is 75.393 % for 36 dimension, 81.688 % for 54 dimension, and 87.838 % for 130 dimension. Our P4 method shows better recognition performance than the P3 with an accuracy of 78.112 % for 36 dimension, 82.546 % for 54 dimension, and 89.557 % for 130 dimension. These demonstrate the advantage of our method as a classifier for face recognition again, especially in the low dimension cases. When the reduced dimension is 36, the P3 method can achieve 2.289 % improvement over SRC, 2.146 % over LS-KSRC, and 2.575 % over P1, the P4 method can achieve 5.008 % improvement over SRC, 4.865 % over LS-KSRC, and 3.434 % over P2.

4.3   Experiments on Extended Yale B Database

The Extended Yale B database is composed of 2414 cropped frontal face images from 38 subjects. For each subject, there are about 64 face images of size 192 * 168 with different illuminations. We select a subset with 32 images per individual for training, and the rest images are used for testing. Table 3 gives the best recognition accuracy of different methods under different PCA dimension reduction settings.

Table 3. The performance comparisons on the extended Yale B database.

reduced dimension / method	36	54	130
SRC	87.572%	89.877%	94.897%
LS-KSRC	88.230%	89.959%	95.073%
P1	80.412%	90.123%	94.815%
P2	82.469%	92.827%	95.556%
P3	89.043%	91.275%	95.274%
P4	90.041%	93.004%	96.626%

As can be seen from the results in Table 3, the proposed methods (P3 and P4) still outperform others methods. The P3 method obtains the best recognition performance with an accuracy of 89.043 % for 36 dimension, 91.275 % for 54 dimension, and 95.274 % for 130 dimension. In the low dimension cases, our method shows much better performance than other methods. This is consistent with the previous experimental results on the AR database. For instance, when the feature dimension is reduced to 36, the P4 method obtains the best recognition performance with an accuracy of 90.041%. This performance is about 2.469 % better than SRC, 1.811 % better than LS-KSRC, 9.629 % better than P1, and 7.572 % better than P2. The P4 method obtains the highest performance (96.626 %) when the feature dimension is setting to 130.

5 Conclusions

In this paper, we propose a novel classification method with locality-sensitive sparsity and group sparsity constraints for robust face recognition. This method learns group sparsity and data locality at the same time. It not only takes into account the grouped structure information of the training data dictionary, but also integrates the data locality, thus can learn more discriminating sparse representation coefficients for face recognition. To testify the effectiveness of the method that we proposed, we perform experiments for face recognition on the ORL, AR, and Extended Yale B databases and demonstrate the power of our algorithm compared to some other methods. Experimental results show that our method achieves very promising recognition results on these datasets.

Acknowledgements. This work was supported by Chinese Natural Science Foundation Project (No. 61201396, 61301296, 61377006, U1201255); Anhui Provincial Natural Science Foundation (No. 1508085MF120); Scientific Research Foundation for the Returned Overseas Chinese Scholars, State Education Ministry; Technology Foundation for Selected Overseas Chinese Scholar, Ministry of Personnel of China.

References

1. Wright, J., Yang, A.Y., Ganesh, A., et al.: Robust face recognition via sparse representation. IEEE Trans. Pattern Anal. Mach. Intell. **31**(2), 210–227 (2009)
2. Yang, M., Zhang, L.: Gabor feature based sparse representation for face recognition with Gabor occlusion dictionary. In: Daniilidis, K., Maragos, P., Paragios, N. (eds.) ECCV 2010, Part VI. LNCS, vol. 6316, pp. 448–461. Springer, Heidelberg (2010)
3. Yuan, M., Lin, Y.: Model selection and estimation in regression with grouped varables. J. Roy. Stat. Soc. B (Stat. Methodol.) **68**(1), 49–67 (2006)
4. Elhamifar, E., Vidal, R.: Robust classification using structured sparse representation. In: 2011 IEEE Conference on Computer Vision and Pattern Recognition (CVPR), pp. 1873–1879. IEEE (2011)
5. Friedman, J., Hastie, T., Tibshirani, R.: A note on the group lasso and a sparse group lasso. arXiv preprint arXiv:1001.0736 (2010)
6. Simon, N., Friedman, J., Hastie, T., et al.: A sparse-group lasso. J. Comput. Graph. Stat. **22**(2), 231–245 (2013)
7. Zhang, L., Zhou, W.-D., Chang, P.-C., Liu, J., Yan, Z., Wang, T., Li, F.-Z.: Kernel sparse representation-based classifier. IEEE Trans. Signal Process. **60**, 1684–1695 (2012)
8. Zhou, Y., Gao, J., Barner, K.E.: An enhanced sparse representation strategy for signal classification. In: SPIE 8365, Compressive Sensing, Baltimore, p. 83650H (2012)

9. Shrivastava, A., Patel, V., Chellappa, R.: Multiple kernel learning for sparse representation-based classification. IEEE Trans. Image Process. **23**(7), 3013–3024 (2014)
10. Zhang, S., Zhao, X.: Locality-sensitive kernel sparse representation classification for face recognition. J. Vis. Commun. Image Represent. **25**, 1878–1885 (2014)
11. Cover, T., Hart, P.: Nearest neighbor pattern classification. IEEE Trans. Inf. Theor. **13**, 21–27 (1967)
12. Cai, D., He, X., Han, J.: Document clustering using locality preserving indexing. IEEE Trans. Knowl. Data Eng. **17**, 1624–1637 (2005)
13. Wang, J., Yang, J., Yu, K., Lv, F., et al.: Locality-constrained linear coding for image classification. In: 2010 IEEE Conference on Computer Vision and Pattern Recognition (CVPR 2010), San Francisco, pp. 3360–3367 (2010)
14. Yu, K., Zhang, T., Gong, Y.: Nonlinear learning using local coordinate coding. Adv. Neural Inf. Process. Syst. **22**, 2223–2231 (2009)
15. Samaria, F.S., Harter, A.C.: Parameterisation of a stochastic model for human face identification. In: The Second IEEE Workshop on Applications of Computer Vision, Sarasota, pp. 138–142 (1994)
16. Martinez, A.M.: The AR face database. CVC technical report, p. 24 (1998)
17. Georghiades, A.S., Belhumeur, P.N., Kriegman, D.J.: From few to many: illumination cone models for face recognition under variable lighting and pose. IEEE Trans. Pattern Anal. Mach. Intell. **23**, 643–660 (2001)
18. Jolliffe, I.T.: Principal Component Analysis. Springer, New York (1986)

Robust Salient Object Detection and Segmentation

Hong Li$^{(\boxtimes)}$, Wen Wu, and Enhua Wu

Department of Computer and Information Science,
University of Macau, Macau 999078, China
{yb27441,wenwu,ehwu}@umac.mo

Abstract. Background prior has been widely used in many salient object detection models with promising results. These methods assume that the image boundary is all background. Then, color feature based methods are used to extract the salient object. However, such assumption may be inaccurate when the salient object is partially cropped by the image boundary. Besides, using only color feature is also insufficient. We present a novel salient object detection model based on background selection and multi-features. Firstly, we present a simple but effective method to pick out more reliable background seeds. Secondly, we utilize multi-features enhanced graph-based manifold ranking to get the saliency maps. Finally, we also present the salient object segmentation via computed saliency map. Qualitative and quantitative evaluation results on three widely used data sets demonstrate significant appeal and advantages of our technique compared with many state-of-the art models.

Keywords: Salient object detection · Graph-based manifold ranking · Multi features · Salient object segmentation

1 Introduction

Salient object detection aims to detect the most salient attention-grabbing object in a scene and the great value of it mainly lies in kinds of applications such as object detection and recognition [1,2], image and video compression [3,4], object content aware image retargeting [5,6], to name a few. Therefore, numerous salient object detection models have been developed in recent years [7,8]. All these models can be categorized as either bottom-up or top-down approaches. Bottom-up saliency models are based on some pre-assumed priors (e.g., contrast prior, central bias prior, background prior and so on). On the other side, top-down models usually use high-level information to guide the detection. We only focus on bottom-up models in this work.

For bottom-up salient object detection models, the priors play a critical role. The most widely used is the contrast prior and often measured with respect to local [9–11] or the global fashion [12–14]. Motivated by the early primate vision, Itti et al. [11] regard the visual attention as the local center-surround

© Springer International Publishing Switzerland 2015
Y.-J. Zhang (Ed.): ICIG 2015, Part III, LNCS 9219, pp. 271–284, 2015.
DOI: 10.1007/978-3-319-21969-1_24

difference and present a pioneer saliency model based on multi-scales image features. Goferman et al. [9] take advantage of multi-clues including local low-level features, high-level features, and global considerations to segment out the salient objects along with their contexts. In [10], Jiang et al. utilize the shape information to find the regions of distinct color by computing the difference between the color histogram of a region and its adjacent regions. Due to the lack of higher-level information about the object, all these local contrast based models tend to produce higher saliency values near edges instead of uniformly highlighting the whole salient object.

On the other side, global contrast based methods take holistic rarity over the complete image into account. The model of Achanta et al. [12] works on a per-pixel basis through computing color dissimilarities to the mean image color and achieves globally consistent results. They also use Gaussian blur to decrease the influence of noise and high frequency patterns. Cheng et al. [13] define a regional contrast-based method by generating 3D histograms and using segmentation, which evaluates not only global contrast differences but also spatial coherence. Model [14] measures global contrast-based saliency based on spatially weighted feature dissimilarities. However, global contrast-based methods may highlight background regions as salient because they do not account for any spatial relationship inside the image.

The central-bias prior is based on a well-known fact that when humans take photos they often frame the interested objects near the center of the image. So Judd et al. [15] present a saliency model via computing the distance between each pixel and the coordinate center of the image. Their model presents a better prediction of the salient object than many previous saliency models. Later, both Goferman et al. [9] and Jiang et al. [10] enhance the intermediate saliency map with weight implemented via a 2D Gaussian fallof positioned at the center of the image. This prior usually improves the saliency performance of the most the natural images. However, the certral-bias prior is not always true when the photographer faces a big scene or the objects of interest cannot be located near the center of image.

Besides above two commonly used priors, several recent models also utilize the background prior, i.e., image boundary should be treated as background, to perform saliency detection. Wei et al. [16] propose a novel saliency measure called geodesic saliency, which use two priors about common backgrounds in natural images, namely boundary and connectivity priors, to help removing background clutters and in turn lead to better salient object detection. Later, Yang et al. [17] utilize this background prior and graph-based manifold ranking to detect the salient object and get promising results. However, they assume that all the four image sides are background. This is not always true when the image is cropped. Recently, Zhu et al. [18] propose a novel and reliable background measure, called boundary connectivity, and a principled optimization framework to integrate multiple low level cues. They do not treat all the image boundaries as background.However, their method is too complicated. Unlike all these afore-mentioned methods, our model not only adaptively treat the image boundaries as background or non-background, but also is very easy to be implemented. Figure 1 gives an overview of our framework.

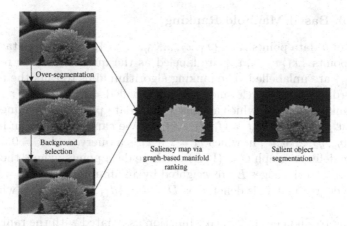

Fig. 1. Overview of our model. Given input image, we first over-segment the image into superpixels. Then we adaptively select the background superpixels and compute the saliency via multi-features enhanced graph-based manifold ranking. Finally we present the salient object segmentation.

The contributions of this paper are three-fold:

- We adaptively treat the four image boundaries as background. A simple but effective method is proposed to adaptively treat the boundary pixels as background and non-background pixels.
- We not only use the color information, but also utilize the variance and histogram features in multi color spaces (LAB and RGB) to enhance the detection performance.
- We present a simple but effective salient object segmentation via computed saliency map.

The rest of this paper is organized as follows. In Sect. 2, we first give a detailed description of graph-based manifold ranking, and then present our proposed model. Then, in Sect. 3, we provide a qualitative and quantitative comparison with previous methods. We will present application of salient object detection: salient object segmentation in Sect. 4. Finally, we conclude with a short summary and discussion in Sect. 5.

2 Robust Salient Object Detection

In 2004, Zhou et al. [19,20] propose a graph-based manifold ranking model, a method that can exploit the intrinsic manifold structure of data. It can be regarded as a kind of semi-supervised learning problem. We present a robust salient object detection method via adaptive background selection and multi-features enhancement. We first give a brief introduction to the graph-based manifold ranking, and then present the details of our proposed method.

2.1   Graph-Based Manifold Ranking

Given a set of n data points $X = \{x_1, x_2, ..., x_q, ..., x_n\}$, with each data $x_i \in R^m$, the first q points $\{x_1, x_2, ..., x_q\}$ are labeled as the queries and the rest points $\{x_{q+1}, ..., x_n\}$ are unlabelled. The ranking algorithm aims to rank the remaining points according to their relevances to the labelled queries. Let $f: X \rightarrow R^n$ denotes a ranking function which assigns to each data point x_i a ranking value f_i. We can treat f as a vector $f = [f_1, f_2, ..., f_n]^T$. We can also define an indication vector $y = [y_1, y_2, ..., y_n]^T$, in which $y_i = 1$ if x_i is a query, and $y_i = 0$ otherwise.

Next, we define a graph $G = (V, E)$ on these data points, where the nodes V are dataset X and the edges E are weighted by an affinity matrix $W = [w_{ij}]_{n \times n}$. Give G, the degree matrix is denoted as $D = diag\{d_{11}, d_{22}, ..., d_{nn}\}$, where $d_{ii} = \sum_{j=1}^{n} w_{ij}$.

According to Zhou et al. [20], cost function associated with the ranking function f is defined to be

$$Q(f) = \frac{1}{2}(\sum_{i,j=1}^{n} w_{ij}\|\frac{1}{\sqrt{d_{ii}}}f_i - \frac{1}{\sqrt{d_{jj}}}f_j\|^2 + \mu\sum_{i=1}^{n}\|f_i - y_i\|^2) \qquad (1)$$

where the regularization parameter $\mu > 0$ controls the balance of the first term (smoothness constraint) and the second term (fitting constraint, containing labelled as well as unlabelled data.). Then the optimal ranking f^* of queries is computed by solving the following optimization problem:

$$f^* = \arg\min_f Q(f) \qquad (2)$$

The trade-off between these two competing constraints is captured by a positive parameter μ and usually set to be 0.99 to put more emphasis on the label consistency. The solution of Eq. (2) can be denoted as

$$f^* = (I - \alpha S)^{-1}y \qquad (3)$$

where I is an identity matrix, and $S = D^{-\frac{1}{2}}WD^{-\frac{1}{2}}$ is the normalized Laplacian matrix, $\alpha = 1/(1 + \mu)$. The detailed derivation can be found in [20].

This ranking algorithm indicates that the salient object detection model should consist of two parts: graph construction and ranking with queries. In Sect. 2.2, we present our multi-features enhanced graph construction and then in Sect. 2.3, we give the details of our adaptive background selection and saliency ranking.

2.2   Multi-Features Enhanced Graph Construction

To better exploit the intrinsic relationship between data points, there are two aspects should be carefully treated in graph construction: graph structure and edge weights. We over-segment input image into small homogeneous regions using SLIC algorithm [21] and regard each superpixel as a node in the graph G.

Fig. 2. An illustration of graph construction.

For graph structure, we take into account the local smoothness cue (i.e., local neighboring superpixels are more likely to belong to the same object) and follow two rules. Firstly, each node is not only connected with its direct adjacent neighboring nodes, but also is connected with those nodes sharing common boundaries with its neighboring nodes. Secondly, the nodes on the four image sides should be connected together. Figure 2 gives an illustration of graph construction.

After modelling the graph structure, the very core problem is how to get the edge weight between any pairwise nodes given input data. The color information has been shown to be effective in saliency detection [7,12]. So most models only adopt color information to generate the edge weights. However, there are other features can be utilized to improve the performance. We employ more features: color, variance and histogram feature. We denote the edge weight as following

$$w_{ij} = e^{-(\frac{c_c(r_i,r_j)}{\sigma_c^2} + \frac{c_v(r_i,r_j)}{\sigma_v^2} + \frac{c_h(r_i,r_j)}{\sigma_h^2})} \tag{4}$$

where r_i and r_j denote the superpixel region i and j respectively. $c_c(r_i,r_j)$, $c_v(r_i,r_j)$ and $c_h(r_i,r_j)$ represent the corresponding color, variance and histogram feature difference between region r_i and r_j respectively. σ_c, σ_v and σ_h are feature parameters controlling the strength of the corresponding weight and we take 5, 2 and 2 in all experiments. The color feature is defined as

$$c_c(r_i,r_j) = \|c_c(r_i) - c_c(r_j)\|^2 \tag{5}$$

where $c_c(r_i)$ and $c_c(r_j)$ denote the mean of region r_i and r_j respectively in *Lab* color space.

Generally speaking, the color distributions of image regions are independent of each other with different variances, so we should also take advantage of the variance information. We define the variance feature difference as

$$c_v(r_i,r_j) = \frac{\|c_c(r_i) - c_c(r_j)\|^2}{\sqrt{\frac{\sigma_v^2(r_i)}{n(r_i)} + \frac{\sigma_v^2(r_j)}{n(r_j)} + \epsilon}} \tag{6}$$

where $\sigma_v(r_i)$ and $\sigma_v(r_j)$ are corresponding computed regional variance. $n(r_i)$ and $n(r_j)$ are number of pixels in the regions r_i and r_j respectively. ϵ is a small

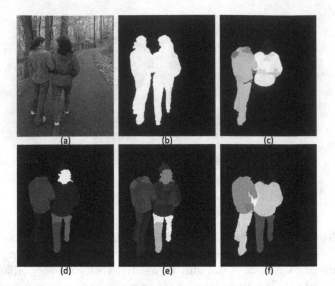

Fig. 3. An illustration of the effectiveness of multi features. (a) Input image, (b) Ground-truth, (c) Result of GMR [17], (d) Result with color and histogram features, (e) Result with color and variance features, (f) Our result with all three features.

number to avoid arithmetic error. Note that we also take the region size into account. This is performed in RGB color space.

For histogram feature, we utilize χ^2 distance instead of simple Euclidean distance to define the disparity between two histograms as suggested in [22]. The histogram feature is defined by

$$c_h(r_i, r_j) = \frac{1}{2} \sum_{k=1}^{d} \frac{(h_k(r_i) - h_k(r_j))^2}{(h_k(r_i) + h_k(r_j))^2} \tag{7}$$

where $h_k(r_i)$ denotes the k-th component of the color histogram of region r_i, d denotes the number of component in the histogram, we take $d = 256$ in this work for simpleness, however, d can be much more smaller in order to improve the computational efficiency. This is also performed in RGB color space.

All these three features are normalized to $[0, 1]$[1]. We keep all other parameters unchanged, and add feature(s) to compute the saliency map and give an comparative example in Fig. 3. We can see that these two additional features can both improve the saliency detection performance.

2.3 Saliency Ranking via Adaptive Background Selection

Most background prior based models treat all the four image sides as background by assuming that photographers will not crop salient objects along the view

---

[1] For different channels in LAB and RGB color spaces, we perform the calculation separately and add the results together to get the corresponding feature descriptor.

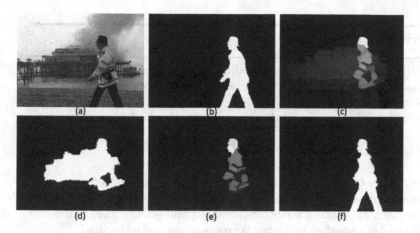

Fig. 4. Visual comparison. (a) Input image, (b) Ground-truth, (c) Saliency map of GMR [17], (d) Bi-segmentation of (c), (e) Our saliency map, (f) Bi-segmentation of (e). Note that our saliency map is more robust than that of GMR [17].

frame. However, this is not always true. Figure 4 shows a special case and the visual comparison of our model and [17]. We can see that when the salient object touches the image border, the detection result of [17] is not so robust anymore. While our proposed method can handle this drawback. See Algorithm 1 and Algorithm 2 for our adaptive background selection and saliency ranking respectively.

Algorithm 1. Contrast based adaptive background selection

Input: All the n superpixels located on the image boundary
1: Concatenate the superpixels along four image sides into one vector.
2: Compute the contrast between one superpixel and all other superpixels as following :
$$Contrast(r_i) = \sum_{j=1}^{n}(c_c(r_i) - c_c(r_j))^2$$
where $c(r_i)$ and $c_c(r_j)$ denote the mean of superpixel region r_i and r_j respectively in LAB color space.
3: Take the superpixels whose contrast is smaller than adaptive threshold ς as background. We take
$$\varsigma = 0.5 * \overline{Contrast(r_1, r_2, ..., r_n)},$$
i.e., half mean of all contrast.
Output: Selected background superpxiels.

Algorithm 2. Robust salient object detection

Input: An image and its corresponding superpixel image
1: Construct the graph with each superpixel as a node and compute
its weight matrix by Eq. 4.
2: Form the indicator y according to our adaptive background selection.
3: Compute the saliency map by Eq. 3 for each side and integrate
them into one single map according to
$$S_{back} = S_t \times S_b \times S_l \times S_r$$
where S_t denotes the complementary saliency map computed by taking
top image side as query. Others are defined the same way.
4: Bi-sement S_{back} using adaptive threshold and get the foreground
queries to form another indicator vector and compute the final
saliency map by Eq. 3.
Output: Final saliency map.

---

3   Experiments

In this section, we extensively evaluate our model and make quantitative evaluation and qualitative evaluation on three widely used datasets SOD [23], ECSSD [24] and ASD [12].

We compare our approaches with twenty state-of-the-art salient object models on these three widely used datasets. These twenty models are: CA [9], CB [10], CHM [25], FES [26], FT [12], GMR [17], GS [16], HDCT [27], HS [24], MC [28], MSS [29], PCA [30], SF [31], SVO [32], SWD [14], BM [33], LRMR [34], GB [35], SR [36], IT [11].

3.1   Quantitative Evaluation

For quantitative evaluation, we evaluate the performance using three commonly used metrics including the PR (precision-recall) curve, F-Measure and MAE (mean absolute error).

PR curve is based on the overlapping area between pixel-wise annotation and saliency prediction. F-Measure, jointly considers recall and precision. We also introduce the mean absolute error (MAE) into the evaluation because the PR curves are limited in that they only consider whether the object saliency is higher than the background saliency. MAE is the average per-pixel difference between the pixel-wise annotation and the computed saliency map. It directly measures how close a saliency map is to the ground truth and is more meaningful and complementary to PR curves.

Figures 5, 6 and 7 show the PR curves, F-Measures and MAEs of all compared and our models on these three data sets. We note that the PR curve of proposed method outperforms PR curves of all other methods on SOD dataset. On ECSSD

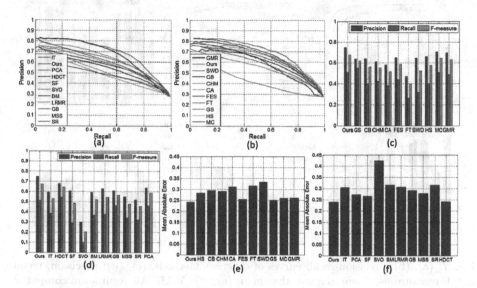

Fig. 5. (a), (b): precision-recall curves of different methods. (c), (d): precision, recall and F-measure using an adaptive threshold. (e), (f): MAE. All results are computed on the SOD dataset. The proposed method performs well in all these metrics.

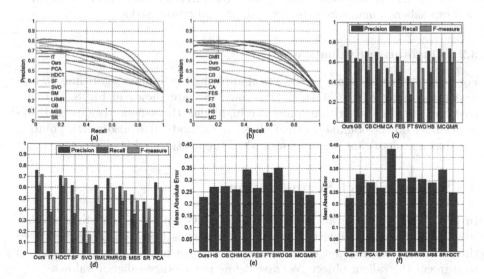

Fig. 6. (a), (b): precision-recall curves of different methods. (c), (d): precision, recall and F-measure using an adaptive threshold. (e), (f): MAE. All results are computed on the ECSSD dataset. The proposed method performs well for all these metrics.

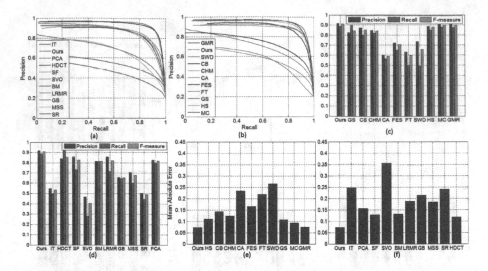

Fig. 7. (a), (b): precision-recall curves of different methods. (c), (d): precision, recall and F-measure using an adaptive threshold. (e), (f): MAE. All results are computed on the ASD dataset. The proposed method performs very well.

and ASD data sets, our model is among the best performance models. For F-Measure, our model gets the best performance on all data sets. And for MAE, our model has the smallest value on all these three data set and this indicates that our saliency maps are closest to the ground truth masks.

3.2 Qualitative Evaluation

For qualitative evaluation, the results of applying the various algorithms to representative images from SOD, ECSSD and ASD are shown in Fig. 8. We note that the proposed algorithm uniformly highlights the salient regions and preserves finer object boundaries than all other methods. It is also worth pointing out that our algorithm performs well when the background is cluttered.

4 Salient Object Segmentation

In [37], Cheng propose an iterative version of GrabCut, named SaliencyCut, to cut out the salient object. However, their work is based on predefined fixed threshold and is a little bit time consuming. We just use the adaptive threshold to segment the salient object. We first define the average saliency value as

$$sal_{mean} = \frac{1}{mn} \sum_{i=1}^{m} \sum_{j=1}^{n} S(i,j) \tag{8}$$

Fig. 8. Visual comparison of proposed model and twenty other methods. From top to bottom and left to right are input, ground truth and results of BM [33], CA [9], CB [10], CHM [25], FES [26], FT [12], GB [35], GMR [17], GS [16], HDCT [27], HS [24], IT [11], LRMR [34], MC [28], MSS [29], PCA [30], SF [31], SR [36], SVO [32], SWD [14] and ours.

where m and n denote image rows and columns respectively. Then the salient object mask is denoted as

$$Sal_{mask}(i,j) = \begin{cases} 1, & S(i,j) >= sal_{mean} \\ 0, & S(i,j) < sal_{mean} \end{cases} \qquad (9)$$

The final segmented salient object is defined as

$$S_{obj} = I.*Sal_{mask} \qquad (10)$$

where .* denotes pixel-wise multiplication. See Fig. 9 for some segmentation examples.

Fig. 9. Examples of salient object segmentation. (a) input images, (b) saliency maps, (c) segmented salient objects.

5   Conclusion

In this paper, we address the salient object detection problem using a semi-supervised method. We tackle the failure case when the salient object touches the image border by adaptive background selection. We also take more features into account to better exploit the intrinsic relationship between image pixels. We evaluate our model on large datasets and demonstrate promising results with comparisons to twenty state-of-the-art methods. Finally, we present a simple but effective salient object segmentation method.

Acknowledgments. The authors would like to thank the editor and anonymous reviews for their valued suggestions which helped a lot to improve the manuscript. This work was supported in part by the Research Committee at University of Macau under Grant MYRG2014-00139-FST.

References

1. Rutishauser, U., Walther, D., Koch, C., Perona, P.: Is bottom-up attention useful for object recognition?. In: IEEE CVPR, pp. II-37–II-44 (2004)
2. Ren, Z., Gao, S., Chia, L.-T., Tsang, I.: Region-based saliency detection and its application in object recognition. IEEE TCSVT **24**(5), 769–779 (2013)
3. Guo, C., Zhang, L.: A novel multi resolution spatiotemporal saliency detection model and its applications in image and video compression. IEEE TIP **19**(1), 185–198 (2010)
4. Itti, L.: Automatic foveation for video compression using a neurobiological model of visual attention. IEEE TIP **13**(10), 1304–1318 (2004)
5. Ding, Y., Xiao, J., Yu, J.: Importance filtering for image retargeting. In: IEEE CVPR, pp. 89–96 (2011)
6. Sun, J., Ling, H.: Scale and object aware image retargeting for thumbnail browsing. In: ICCV, pp. 1511–1518 (2011)
7. Borji, A., Sihite, D.N., Itti, L.: Salient object detection: a benchmark. In: Fitzgibbon, A., Lazebnik, S., Perona, P., Sato, Y., Schmid, C. (eds.) ECCV 2012, Part II. LNCS, vol. 7573, pp. 414–429. Springer, Heidelberg (2012)
8. Borji, A., Cheng, M.M., Jiang, H. Z., Li, J.: Salient object detection: a survey. CORR, abs/1411.5878 (2014)
9. Goferman, S., Zelnik-Manor, L., Tal, A.: Context-aware saliency detection. IEEE Trans. Patt. Anal. Mach. Intell. **32**(10), 1915–1925 (2012)
10. Jiang, H., Wang, J., Yuan, Z., Liu, T., Zheng, N., Li, S.: Automatic salient object segmentation based on context and shape prior. In: BMVC, pp. 110.1–110.12 (2011)
11. Itti, L., Koch, C., Niebur, E.: A model of saliency-based visual attention for rapid scene analysis. IEEE Trans. Patt. Anal. Mach. Intell. **20**(11), 1254–1259 (1998)
12. Achanta, R., Hemami, S., Estrada, F., Susstrunk, S.: Frequency Tuned salient region detection. In: IEEE CVPR, pp. 1597–1604 (2009)
13. Cheng, M., Zhang, G.X., Mitra, N.J. Huang, X., Hu, S.M.: Global contrast based salient region detection. In: IEEE CVPR, pp. 409–416 (2011)
14. Duan, L., Wu, C., Miao, J., Qing, L., Fu, Y.: Visual saliency detection by spatially weighted dissimilarity. In: IEEE CVPR, pp. 473–480 (2011)
15. Judd, T., Ehinger, K., Durand, F., Torralba, A.: Learning to predict where humans look. In: International Conference on Computer Vision, pp. 2106–2113 (2009)
16. Wei, Y., Wen, F., Zhu, W., Sun, J.: Geodesic saliency using background priors. In: Fitzgibbon, A., Lazebnik, S., Perona, P., Sato, Y., Schmid, C. (eds.) ECCV 2012, Part III. LNCS, vol. 7574, pp. 29–42. Springer, Heidelberg (2012)
17. Yang, C., Zhang, L., Lu, H., Ruan, X., Yang, M.H.: Saliency detection via graph-based manifold ranking. In: IEEE CVPR, pp. 3166–3173 (2013)
18. Zhu, W., Liang, S., Wei, Y., Sun, J.: Saliency optimization from robust background detection. In: IEEE CVPR, pp. 2814–2821 (2014)
19. Zhou, D., Weston, J., Gretton, A., Bousquet, O., Scholkopf, B.: Ranking on data manifolds. In: NIPS (2004)
20. Zhou, D., Bousquet, O., Lal, T.N., Weston, J., Scholkopf, B.: Learning with local and global consistency. In: NIPS, pp. 321–328 (2004)
21. Achanta, R., Shaji, A., Smith, K., Lucchi, A., Fua, P., Susstrunk, S.: SLIC superpixels compared to state-of-the-art superpixel methods. IEEE Trans. Patt. Anal. Mach. Intell. **34**(11), 2274–2282 (2012)
22. Gorisse, D., Cord, M., Precioso, F.: Locality-sensitive hashing for chi2 distance. IEEE Trans. Patt. Anal. Mach. Intell. **34**(2), 402–409 (2012)

23. Movahedi, V., Elder, J.: Design and perceptual validation of performance measures for salient object segmentation. In: IEEE CVPRW, pp. 49–56 (2010)
24. Yan, Q., Xu, L., Shi, J., Jia, J.: Hierarchical saliency detection. In: IEEE CVPR, pp. 1155–1162 (2013)
25. Li, X., Li, Y., Shen, C., Dick, A., Hengel, A.: Contextual hypergraph modelling for salient object detection. In: IEEE ICCV, pp. 3328–3335 (2013)
26. Rezazadegan Tavakoli, H., Rahtu, E., Heikkilä, J.: Fast and efficient saliency detection using sparse sampling and kernel density estimation. In: Heyden, A., Kahl, F. (eds.) SCIA 2011. LNCS, vol. 6688, pp. 666–675. Springer, Heidelberg (2011)
27. Kim, J., Han, D., Tai, Y.W., Kim, J.: Salient region detection via high-dimensional color transform. In: IEEE CVPR, pp. 883–890 (2014)
28. Jiang, B., Zhang, L., Lu, H., Yang, C.: Saliency detection via absorbing markov chain. In: IEEE ICCV, pp. 1665–1672 (2013)
29. Achanta, R., Susstrunk, S.: Saliency detection using maximum symmetric surround. In: IEEE ICIP, pp. 2653–2656 (2010)
30. Margolin, R., Tal, A., Manor, L.: What makes a patch distinct?. In: IEEE CVPR, pp. 1139–1146 (2013)
31. Perazzi, F., Krahenbuhl, P., Pritch, Y., Hornung, A.: Saliency filters: contrast based filtering for salient region detection. In: IEEE CVPR, pp. 733–740 (2012)
32. Chang, K., Liu, T, Chen, H., Lai, S.: Fusing generic objectness and visual saliency for salient object detection. In: IEEE ICCV, pp. 914–921 (2011)
33. Xie, Y., Lu, L.: Visual saliency detection based on bayesian model. In: IEEE ICIP, pp. 645–648 (2011)
34. Shen, X., Wu, Y.: A unified approach to salient object detection via low rank matrix recovery. In: IEEE CVPR, pp. 853–860 (2012)
35. Harel, J., Koch, C., Perona, P.: Graph-based visual saliency. In: NIPS, pp. 545–552 (2006)
36. Hou, X., Zhang, L.: Saliency detection: a spectral residual approach. In: IEEE CVPR, pp. 1–8 (2007)
37. Cheng, M.M., Mitra, N.J., Huang, X.L., Torr, P.H.S., Hu, S.M.: Salient object detection and segmentation. doi:10.1109/TPAMI.2014.2345401

Rough Lane Marking Locating Based on Adaboost

Wuwen Jin[✉] and Mingwu Ren

Nanjing University of Science and Technology, Nanjing, China
ww_jin@yeah.net, renmingwu@njust.edu.cn

Abstract. Lane marking detection is a basic task of Driver Assistance Systems (DAS) and Autonomous Land Vehicle (ALV). In order to improve the accuracy of lane marking detection, we design a rough lane marking locating method based on predecessors' work. Considering the characteristic of lane markings, we extract Haar-like features of lane marking regions and train a strong cascade classifier by Adaboost Algorithm. The classifier is simple in principle and can fast locate the possible areas of lane markings accurately. Experimental results show that our method performs well.

Keywords: Lane marking locating · Adaboost algorithm · Haar-like features

1 Introduction

With the rapid development of science and technology, driving assistance systems (DAS) gradually enter people's daily life. It can not only raise an alarm when the vehicle is at risk, but also take driving permission to control the vehicle to void dangers, to prevent accidents. At the same time, as a typical representative of wheeled robot, autonomous land vehicle (ALV) senses environment information, and control the vehicle's steering and speed, relying on on-board camera or other sensors. It must ensure the vehicle run safety and reliably on the road without manual intervention.

Such intelligent transportation systems are developing towards to sense more complex environment and challenge more complicated tasks. The bottleneck of the development lies in the accurate perception of the environment [1]. This refers to two principal problems. One is road and lane marking detection, the other is obstacle detection. The lane marking is one of the key technologies for visual navigation. In this paper, we will focus on this problem.

Like human's driving, semi-autonomous or autonomous vehicles running on the road also rely on main perceptual cues such as road color and texture, road boundaries, lane markings and so on. Lane markings are identifications of road information and it can make vehicles driver orderly on the road. However, due to the complex and changeable of the traffic environment, and the high robust and real-time demands, fast and accurately detection of the lane markings is a difficulty and emphasis in the study of intelligent transportation [2].

The structure of this paper is as follows: in the next section we will introduce the current research situation on lane marking detection and put forward our method. In Sects. 3, 4, 5 we will introduce the work of our method particularly. Section 6 presents

© Springer International Publishing Switzerland 2015
Y.-J. Zhang (Ed.): ICIG 2015, Part III, LNCS 9219, pp. 285–296, 2015.
DOI: 10.1007/978-3-319-21969-1_25

the experiments on lane marking locating. Section 7 concludes the paper with a summary and directions for future work.

2 Related Work

The research on lane marking detection has been going on for decades. According to different detection methods, we can simply divide all these methods into three flavors, respectively based on models, based on regions and based on features [3]. Methods based on models firstly establish the models of roads. They obtain the lane markings after calculating the parameters related to these models. Common road models include line models and curve models, etc. These methods can satisfy all sorts of changeable environment of highways and the real time demand of the task. They can detect the lane markings fast and simply, but they are sensitive to noise [4]. Methods based on regions are only suitable for structured road. When the environment becomes complex, or road marking is blurred, the detection accuracy fell sharply [5]. Methods based on features using the color or texture features of the roads. They are simple but easy influenced by shadows, climate, illumination and so on. The detection accuracy is low [6]. So some scholars put forward the combination of other features such as geometric or shape features [7–9]. The fusion of such features indeed increases the accuracy, but increase the time cost as well. Considering Hough transform is not sensitive to the noise, many researchers apply it into the lane marking detection [10, 11]. But the computational complexity is high, so the applied range is limited [5].

In recent years, some scholars put forward the lane marking detection algorithms based on classifiers. They use neural network, Bayesian classification algorithm, k-Nearest Neighbor to establish classifiers for lane markings and obtain ideal results [12–14].

Based on predecessors' work, we proposed a new method to get the possible areas of lane marking by training a lane marking classifier. The process is presented in Fig. 1.

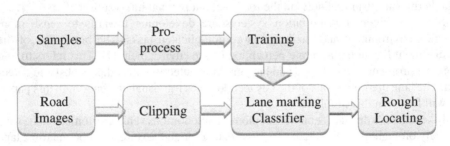

Fig. 1. Our method's processes

3 Image Pretreatment

Before training a classifier, we design the image pretreatment process to enhance the features of lane marking regions to make training and detecting stages faster and more accurate, including ROI clipping, image grayed and image enhancement.

3.1 ROI Clipping

Images captured by an on-board camera have broad vision, high resolution in complicated environment. As far as lane marking detection concerned, we do not have too much time and cost to focus on surroundings outside the road. Hence, before detection we need to clip the image to obtain the region of interest (ROI). After considering the structure characteristics of lane markings as well as speed and effect demands of our task, we clip the original image to get 4/5 part of regions near the bottom under the lane markings vanish point as our ROI. After that, we obtain a new road image in which the lane markings are approximate to straight lines and relatively clear shown as Fig. 2.

Fig. 2. ROI clipping

3.2 Graying

As we consider the structure features but not color features while detecting the lane markings, we convert the color images to grayscale images while considering the performance of the classifier and detection speed. Common methods to gray an image include component method, maximum method, average method and weighted average method. As we human eyes are highest sensitive to green and lowest to blue, we calculate the sum of three components by different weights. And then we get the average value. The proportions of R, G, B are 0.30, 0.59, 0.11. For an RGB image, the corresponding grayed image F can be expressed as:

$$F_{ij} = 0.30\,R_{ij} + 0.59\,G_{ij} + 0.11\,B_{ij} \tag{1}$$

3.3 Image Enhancement

Considering the nature of the positive sample images, that is, there are only two types of objects we concerned, we process these samples after a gray-scale transformation. In order to enhance the lane markings regions, we need to strengthen the gray level which is greater than a certain value and suppress it when it is lower than the value. Therefore, it is a difficult problem to choose a suitable threshold. Obviously, it is not a good way to choose a fixed threshold for all samples.

As we know, lane markings in these positive samples are easy to distinguish from the road regions. OTUS may take this problem easily.

OTSU was proposed for image binarization by a Japan scholar named Otsu in 1979. Through the way of traversing all gray level, it selects a gray value which makes the variance between different classes greatest as the threshold of the whole image. For simple reasons, we choose this method to obtain an optimal threshold T for each positive sample image F_{ij}. We use T to stretch the positive sample by piecewise linear method and obtain a new grayed image G_{ij}. Figure 3 shows the graying and enhancement steps.

$$G_{ij} = \begin{cases} \min\left(1.2 * F_{ij}, 255\right), & \text{if } G_{ij} > T \\ 0.7 * F_{ij}, & \text{if } G_{ij} \leq T \end{cases} \tag{2}$$

Fig. 3. Graying and stretching process

4   Feature Extraction

We firstly need to choose some simple features for training if we want to obtain a lane marking classifier. These features should have to easily distinguish lane markings and non-lane markings. We use extended Haar features proposed by Rainer and Lienhart in [15]. They added several features with 45° rotating Angle based on original Haar features [16]. The extended features include four types: edge, linear, central, diagonal shown by Fig. 4.

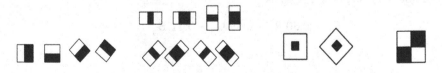

Fig. 4. Haar-like features

Haar eigenvalue is defined as the integral of the pixel gray value in the rectangular region. Black region has a negative weight and white region has a positive one. Actually, the eigenvalue reflects the information of gray scale changes. Some characteristics of lane marking regions can be described with Haar-like features. For example, color of regions on both sides of lane markings are deeper than lane marking itself.

5 Adaboost Algorithm

Adaboost is an adaptive boosting algorithm [17]. It combines multiple weak learning algorithms into a strong learning algorithm. This algorithm was proposed by Rreund and Robert in 1995 [18]. Its basic idea is using a large number of weak classifiers to establish a strong classifier with well classification capacity. Theoretically as long as classification capacity of each weak classifier is better than random guesses, the stronger one will obtain very low error rate close to zero.

At the beginning of training the first weak classifier H_0, each sample in the training set S_0 is evenly distributed. We reduce its distribution probability if it is classified exactly and we increase the probability when it is classified falsely. Then we obtain a new training set S_1 which is mainly for the samples difficult to classify. After T iterations, we obtain T weak classifiers. If the accuracy of a classifier is high, its weight is high followed.

Adaboost classifier is based on cascade classification model. This model can be presented as Fig. 5.

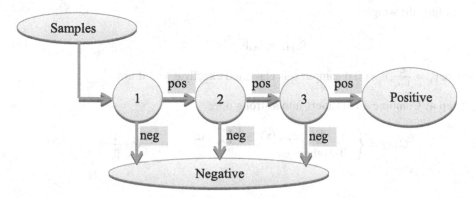

Fig. 5. Cascade classifier model

The procedure is presented as follows.

Step 1: For a given training set $S\left\{(x_1,y_1),(x_2,y_2),\ldots,(x_n,y_n)\right\}$, while $y_i = 0$ means negative and $y_i = 1$ means positive, n is the total number of training samples.

Step 2: Initialize the weights:

$$w_{1,i} = \left\{ \begin{array}{c} \frac{1}{2m} \\ \frac{1}{2l} \end{array} \right. \tag{3}$$

where m, n are numbers of negative samples and positive samples respectively.

Step 3: While $t = 1, 2, \ldots, T$, t is times of iterations:
First, normalize the weights:

$$q_{t,i} = \frac{w_{t,i}}{\sum_{j=1}^{n} w_{t,i}} \tag{4}$$

Then we train a weak classifier $h(x, f, p, \theta)$ for each feature. The weak classifier for j_{th} feature is presented as:

$$h_j(x) = \begin{cases} 1, & p_j f_j(x) < p_j \theta_j \\ 0, & \text{otherwise} \end{cases} \tag{5}$$

The weak classifier is decided by a threshold θ_j and an offset p_j. p_j decides the direction of the inequality and $p_j = \pm 1$.

We calculate weighted error rate of all weak classifiers respectively and take the lowest one. Then the corresponding classifier is the best one:

$$\varepsilon_t = \min_{f,p,\theta} \sum_i q_i \cdot \left| h\left(x_i, f, p, \theta\right) - y_i \right| \tag{6}$$

Adjust the weights:

$$q_{t+1,i} = q_{t,i} \beta_t^{1-e_i} \tag{7}$$

where $\beta_t = \frac{\varepsilon_t}{1-\varepsilon_t}$, $e_i = 0$ if sample x_i is classified exactly, $e_i = 1$ if not.

Step 4: Combine T classifiers into a strong one:

$$C(x) = \begin{cases} 1 & \sum_{t=1}^{T} \alpha_t h_t(x) \geq \frac{1}{2} \sum_{t=1}^{T} \alpha_t \\ 0 & \text{otherwise} \end{cases}, \quad \alpha_t = \log \frac{1}{\beta_t} \tag{8}$$

6   Experiment

We collect large numbers of images by an on-board camera and establish a small lane marking database including common kinds of lane markings. Parts of the database are shown as follow (Fig. 6).

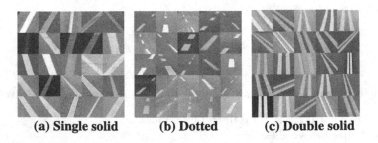

(a) Single solid   (b) Dotted   (c) Double solid

Fig. 6. Three different samples sets

We pro-process positive samples before training and normalize them to fixed size and then train a lane marking classifier. We use the classifier to detect possible regions of lane markings in some real images' ROIs. Based on enough experiments, we compare and analyze the results.

6.1 Training Time

Training process will last a long time, and the specific time is related to several factors.

Number of Samples. Time cost will increases as the number of training samples increasing. We find that when the number of samples is between 100 and 200, the training process will finish in 1 h. But if the number adds up to 900–1000, the process will last as long as 6 h.

Layers of Classifier. It will cost longer time when the layers of cascade classifier become higher. Before training a classifier, we can set this training parameter manually. The experimental results show that when we set a small one, the capacity of the classifier is weak. But a larger one will lead to larger time cost. That is an annoying problem. In experiments we let the classifier to decide the layers itself. When the training process achieve a stable state or reach the maximum false-alarm rate (FA) we set before training, it will ends the training process.

Experimental Platform. Training platform also determines the time consumption of training process. Our experiment platform is a laptop with Windows 7(64 bits), carrying Intel i5 CPU and 4 GB memory.

6.2 Detection Effect

The stand or fall of the lane marking locating effect is directly influenced by the trained classifier's capacity. We design some contrast experiments among different combinations of sample sets, different pretreatment methods and different size normalization scales.

Different Combinations of Sample Sets. Choice of sample elements, different combinations of sample sets lead to different capacity of classifiers. We train different classifiers using different types of lane marking sets and their hybrid. The results are shown as Fig. 7.

In Figs. 7(a), (b) and (c) are detected by classifiers trained by single solid lane marking set, mixture of single solid lane marking set and dotted lane marking set, mixture of single, double solid lane marking set and dotted lane marking set. We train other classifiers trained by dotted lane set and double lane set alone or mixed as well. It is proved that classifier trained by mixed sample set performs well than single sample set. From all results of all kinds of combinations, we find the classifier trained by three kinds of lane markings performs best. Hence, we chose this kind of mixture samples as our training set at last.

(a) Solid lane marking set

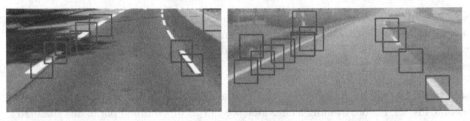

(b) Mixture of single solid lane marking set and dotted lane marking set

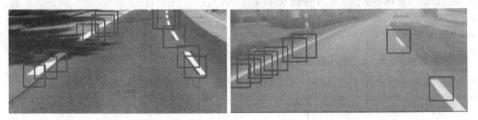

(c) Mixture of single, double solid lane and dotted lane marking set

Fig. 7. Locating results of classifiers trained by different combinations of samples sets

Different Pretreatment Methods. Different pretreatment methods for samples before training will lead to different capacity of classifiers. We process the samples through three different ways before training. The results are show as Fig. 8.

In Fig. 8(a), (b) and (c) are detected by classifiers trained by samples which are pre-processed by different ways including non-processing, binarization and linear grayscale stretching. Threshold in latter two methods is obtained by OTSU. From the results it is easy to find that if we do nothing for samples before training, although most lane marking regions are located, other regions without any lane markings are located as well, because these regions have similar features as lane marking regions due to road texture, shadows or illumination. Classifier trained by samples after binarization does better than the former but worse than the latter in which classifier is trained by stretched samples as the latter method reserves more information of the road. We now maintain the training set and pretreatment method to continue our experiment and study how the different size normalization scales affect our classifiers.

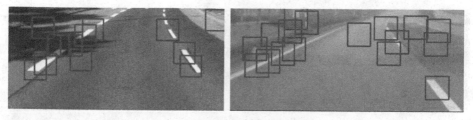

(a) Original samples

(b) Samples after binarization

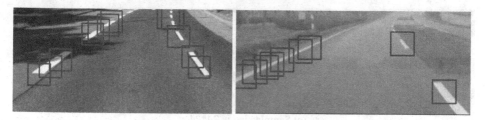

(c) Samples after linear grayscale stretching

Fig. 8. Locating results of classifiers trained by different processed samples

Different Size Normalization Scales. Different size normalization scales lead to different results of lane marking detection. We normalize all samples to different sizes and then train the classifiers. The results are shown as Fig. 9.

In Fig. 9(a), (b) and (c) are detected by classifiers trained by samples with different sizes of 20*20, 24*20, 24*24 pixels respectively. We find the effects of different lane marking locating are similar because these three size scales of samples are all close to real lane marking regions' size.

We mix three types of samples together, totally 996 positive samples. After grayscale stretching, we normalize all these samples into 24*24 pixels. A 13 layers classifier is achieved at last. We select several images from on-board camera and opened database and then detect the possible regions contain lane markings through this classifier. Figure 10 shows the results.

As Fig. 10 shows, Fig. 10(a) is detection on normal road regions. Figure 10(b) shows lane markings interfered by shadows and vehicles. In Fig. 10(c), there are some instructional markings on roads. Figure 10(d) shows the results in bad weather.

We then test this strong classifier on several road data sets who are collected from daily life and network. The result is shown as Table 1.

(a) Sample size is 20*20

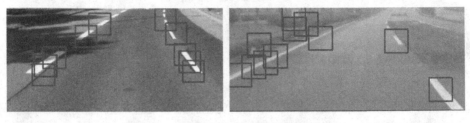

(b) Sample size is 24*20

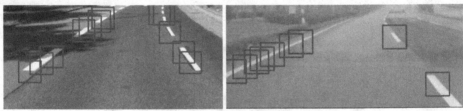

(c) Sample size is 24*24

Fig. 9. Locating results of classifiers trained by samples with different size normalization scales

Set 1 and Set 2 are collected from the internet and road in images are in usual environment in the daytime. Set 3 is an opened road database from KITTI and it is a challenging task to detect the road markings because of the complicated road environment. We collect a large number of road data from on-board cameras. Then we select road images in bad weather and ban illumination condition and construct Set 4 and Set 5.

Table 1. The result on different road data sets

Set name	Image size	Number of images	Accuracy	Average time
Set 1	320*105	324	98.72 %	152.16 ms
Set 2	320*105	334	88.98 %	46.92 ms
Set 3	1392*262	908	71.04 %	1024.12 ms
Set 4	736 *200	1543	92.56 %	592.40 ms
Set 5	736 *200	1070	93.22 %	461.35 ms

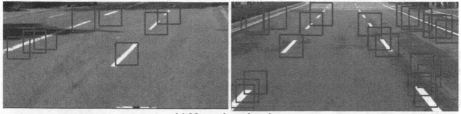

(a) Normal road regions

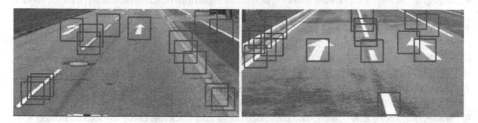

(b) Lane markings interfered by shadows and vehicles

(c) Instructional markings on roads

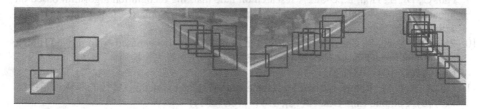

(d) Detections in bad weather

Fig. 10. Locating results in different environments

All the results show that our method can locate most possible lane marking regions in complicated surroundings although there are some noise regions and take a not ideal time.

7   Conclusion and Future Work

This paper designs a rough lane marking locating method based on Adaboost algorithm. Through extracting Haar-like features of lane marking regions, this method trains a cascade classifier and locates the possible regions which contain lane markings. The experimental results show that this method is robust and accurate.

Our work will continue. First we will enrich the lane marking database and process the results which this paper has gained to get the precise lane markings. Second we will adjust several key details to short the detection time. At the same time, we will focus on lane marking tracking algorithm among frames. Our final aim is to establish a system which from image acquisition to exactly detecting and tracking the lane markings on the road.

References

1. Thorpe, C., Hebert, M., Kanade, T., Shafer, S.: Toward autonomous driving: the CMU Navlab. Part I: perception. IEEE Expert **6**, 31–42 (1991)
2. Li, S., Shen, H.: Lane marking detection in structured road based on monocular vision method (结构化道路中车道线的弹幕视觉检测方法). Chin. J. Sci. Instrum. **31**(2), 397–403 (2010)
3. Jung C.R., C., R'Kellber, C.R.: Lane following and lane departure using a linear–parabolic model. Image Vis. Comput. **23**, 1192–1202 (2005)
4. Wang, X., Wang, Y.: The lane marking detection algorithm based on linear hyperbolic model (基于线性双曲线模型的车道线检测算法). J. Hangzhou Dianzi Univ. **30**(6), 64–67 (2010)
5. Ju, Q., Ying, R.: A fast lane marking recognition based on machine vision (基于机器视觉的快速车道线识别). Appl. Res. Comput. **30**(5), 1544–1546 (2013)
6. Hu, X., Li, S., Wu, J., et al.: The lane marking detection algorithm based on feature colors (基于特征颜色的车道线检测算法). Comput. Simul. **28**(10), 344–348 (2011)
7. Shen, Y., Luo, W.: A new and fast lane marking recognition algorithm (一种新的车道线快速识别算法). Appl. Res. Comput. **28**(4), 1544–1546, 1550 (2011)
8. Wang, Y., Teoh, E.K., Shen, D.: Lane detection and tracking using B-Snake. Image Vis. Comput. **22**(4), 269–280 (2004)
9. Fan, C., Di, S., Hou, L., et al.: A research on lane marking recognition algorithm based on linear model (一种基于直线模型的车道线识别算法研究). Appl. Res. Comput. **29**(1), 326–328 (2012)
10. Zhao, Y., Wang, S., Chen, B.: Fast detection of lines on highway based on improved Hough transformation method (基于改进 Hough 变换的公路车道线快速检测算法). J. China Agric. Univ. **11**(3), 104–108 (2006)
11. Cai, A., Ren, M.: Robust method for vehicle lane marking extraction (鲁棒的车辆行道线提取方法). Comput. Eng. Des. **32**(12), 4164–4168 (2011)
12. Zhang, H., Lai, H., Tan, X.: Lane marking detection method based on wavelet analysis and minimum variance in the class (基于小波分析与类内最小方差法的车道线检测). Laser J. **35**(3), 31–32 (2014)
13. Kim, Z.: Robust lane detection and tracking in challenging scenarios. IEEE Trans. Intell. Transp. Syst. **9**(1), 16–26 (2008)
14. Huang, C.L., Wang, C.J.: A GA-based feature selection and parameters optimization for support vector machines. Expert Syst. Appl. **31**(2), 231–240 (2011)
15. Lienhart, R., Maydt, J.: An Extended set of haar-like features for rapid object detection. In: IEEE ICIP 2002, vol. 1, pp. 900–903 (2002)
16. Viola, P., Jones, M.J.: Robust real-time face detection. Int. J. Comput. Vis. **57**, 137–154 (2004)
17. Valicant, L.G.: A theory of the learnable. Commun. ACM **27**(11), 1134–1142 (1984)
18. Freund, Y., Schapire, R.E.: A decision-theoretic generalization of on-line learning and an application to boosting. J. Comput. Syst. Sci. **55**, 119–139 (1997)

S-box: L-L Cascade Chaotic Map and Line Map

Ye Tian[1,2(✉)] and Zhimao Lu[1,3]

[1] College of Information and Communication Engineering,
Harbin Engineering University, Harbin 150001, People's Republic of China
hsdtianye@126.com, lzm@dlut.edu.cn
[2] Key Laboratory of Photonic and Electronic Bandgap Materials,
Ministry of Education, School of Physics and Electronic Engineering,
Harbin Normal University, Harbin 150025, People's Republic of China
[3] Faculty of Electronic Information and Electrical Engineering,
Dalian University of Technology, Dalian 116024, People's Republic of China

Abstract. Being as an important nonlinear component of block ciphers, Substitution box (S-box) directly affect the security of the cryptographic systems. It is important and difficult to design cryptographically strong S-box that simultaneously meet with multiple cryptographic criteria such as bijection, non-linearity, strict avalanche criterion (SAC), bits independence criterion (BIC), differential probability (DP) and linear probability (LP). To address the issue, an S-box generation approach based on L-L cascade Chaotic Map and Line Map (LLCMLM) is proposed in this paper. L-L cascade chaotic map is used to generate an integer sequence ranging 0–255, and line map is applied to scramble the position of the integer sequence. A series of experiments have been conducted to compare multiple cryptographic criteria of LLCMLM with other algorithms. Simulation results indicate that LLCMLM meets well with the design criteria of the S-box.

Keywords: Substitution box (S-box) · Multiple cryptographic criteria · L-L cascade chaotic map · Line map

1 Introduction

With dynamic developments in the multimedia industry and internet, a large amount of worry has been brought up regarding the security of digital images transmitted over open or stored channels [1–3]. How to protect digital images from being unauthorized handled is becoming extremely crucial. As a branch of modern cryptography, digital images encryption is one of the most useful techniques for images security [4]. Block cipher algorithm is an important research direction in modern cryptography, which has the features of high speed, ease of standardization and software and hardware implementation, therefore it is an effective mean of digital images encryption. In block cipher algorithm, Substitution box (S-box) is the only one nonlinear component of cryptographic algorithm [5], providing the block cipher system with necessary confusing and

© Springer International Publishing Switzerland 2015
Y.-J. Zhang (Ed.): ICIG 2015, Part III, LNCS 9219, pp. 297–309, 2015.
DOI: 10.1007/978-3-319-21969-1_26

scrambling effect against attacks. And its cryptography security features directly determine the safety of the entire cipher performance [1]. Mathematically, a $n \times n$ size of S-box is a non-linear mapping $S : \{0, 1\}^n \rightarrow \{0, 1\}^n$, here $\{0, 1\}^n$ represents the vector spaces of n elements from GF(2), we set $n = 8$ in this paper.

S-box has the following main design criteria [6–8]: Nonlinearity, strict avalanche criterion (SAC), bits independence criterion (BIC), differential probability (DP) and linear probability (LP). The construction methods of S-box can be divided into two categories: one is based on the structure of mathematical functions including logarithmic functions, exponential functions, inverse map of finite fields and power function of finite fields. The other is a random selection method of construction, i.e., selecting better performance S-box from some randomly generated S-boxes [9]. There exist, however, two main disadvantages in these approaches, poor performance S-box and large amounts of computing resources consumption.

In recent years, most secure systems generate the S-box by chaotic scheme as it has some advantages such as ergodicity, pseudo-randomness and unpredictability. Literature [9] proposed a four-steps method of generating chaotic S-box based on discrete Logistic map. Literature [10] improved the work in [9] by means of bit extraction and Baker map. Furthermore, literature [11] proposed an S-box design approach based on iteration discrete chaotic. Literature [12] developed an S-box generating method using three-dimensional chaotic Baker map.

These algorithms have a common characteristic that they have strong S-boxes using the chaotic maps' random distribution property. However, the performance gap between the some of these chaotic S-boxes and classic ones still exists, for example, few chaos based S-boxes can achieve the high performance like the one used in advanced encryption standard (AES) [13].

To tackle this issue, researchers have attempted to design the S-boxes in the way of incorporating the advantages of the chaotic S-boxes and the genetic algorithms [13]. For example, literature [14] developed a new way of constructing S-box, that is combing chaotic maps and simulated annealing, thus resulting good performance. However, such schemes choose only one criterion, for example, the nonlinearity, for optimization in the process of designing the S-boxes [13].

Later, some literatures applied the chaotic system to the construction of S-boxes. Literature [15] used the continuous-time Lorenz system to design S-box. Literature [16] proposed to generate S-box by means of Rössler and Lorenz chaotic system. Moreover, Literature [17] presented an S-box design method based on Duffing chaotic system. For more S-box design approaches base on chaotic system, readers can refer to literatures [18–20].

Although we can obtain some S-boxes of good cryptography performance using the chaotic model, the non-linearity and differential uniformity of these S-boxes are still not ideal. And the generation of some superior performance S-boxes still has some difficulties. For example, output sequence constructed by the single chaotic system can not reach the theoretical random completely, due to the limited precision of computer, thus resulting the cyclical issues of the pseudo-random sequence [21].

Researchers have shown that multi-chaotic system and more complex chaotic systems can be applied to enhance security and produce pseudo-random sequences of excellent statistical properties. In this paper, we propose an S-box generation approach based on L-L cascade Chaotic Map and Line Map (LLCMLM). L-L cascade chaotic map is used to construct an integer sequence ranging 0–255, and line map is applied to scramble the position of the integer sequence. The experimental results show that LLCMLM meets well with the design criteria of S-box.

2 Cascade Chaotic Map and Line Map

2.1 Cascade Chaotic Map

We represent the cascade of two Logistic maps as L-L cascade [22]. Logistic map is,

$$x_{n+1} = \mu x_n (1 - x_n) \tag{1}$$

where μ is the system parameter, $\mu \in [0, 4]$, x is the initial value, $x \in [0, 1]$. Because of its simple structure and complex behavior, it has been widely studied and applied. However, the chaotic map range of the Logistic system is small, that is, it is full map at the unit interval [0, 1] and can present strong chaotic characteristics only when $\mu = 4$. Figure 1(a), (b) depict the bifurcation diagram of the Logistic system and Lyapunov exponent. A smaller range chaotic map may have closer iteration values and may be easier to appear shorter cycle and kinetics degradation when performing quantization in a digital system.

In order to improve the dynamics of Logistic map, we process to cascade and observe* its dynamics performance improvement. Logistic map cascade of two parameters μ_1 and μ_2 can be expressed as,

$$x_{n+1} = \mu_1 [\mu_2 x_n (1 - x_n)] \{1 - [\mu_2 x_n (1 - x_n)]\} \tag{2}$$

where, $\mu_1, \mu_2 \in [0, 4]$, x is the initial value [0, 1]. To extend the range of the full map and enhance chaotic characteristics, we set $\mu_1 = 4$, μ_2 be the bifurcation parameter. Figure 1(c), (d) show the bifurcation diagram of L-L cascade system and Lyapunov exponents.

The parameter range of L-L cascade system chaotic map expands larger than that of the Logistic chaotic map. And larger chaotic map parameter range provided a larger key space (with initial values and system parameters as the key), thus can enhancing the difficulty of deciphering and improving security. Comparing with non-full map, full map corresponds to the strength of strong chaos whose iteration value range is large. The latter iteration values may difficultly approximate to the previous iteration values, so we can extend the period of the chaotic sequence of numbers to improve the kinetics degradation of the chaotic sequence. Lyapunov exponents of the L-L cascade system is greater than that of the Logistic system in the chaotic region. The increase of Lyapunov exponent may enhance its initial sensitivity, thus improving its power.

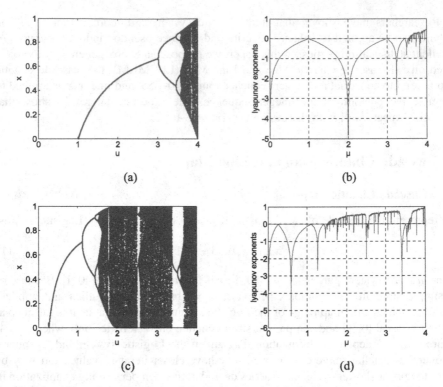

Fig. 1. The bifurcation diagrams of Logistic map and L-L cascade map and Lyapunov exponents (a) the bifurcation diagram of Logistic map, (b) the Lyapunov exponents of Logistic map, (c) the bifurcation diagram of L-L cascade map (d) the Lyapunov exponents of L-L cascade map ($\mu_1 = 4$)

2.2   Line-Map

The main idea of Line-Map [23] is that we insert the line of pixels in the diagonal direction of the image pixel matrix into an adjacent row of pixels to be finally stretched into one-dimensional series, and then folded into the same size of the original image matrix. This can give the original adjacent pixels, not in the original position, high efficiency of scrambling. According to the direction of diagonal, we divide it into left and right line maps. The map transform patterns are shown in Fig. 2.

The Left Line Map. We assume that $A(i,j)$, $i,j = 0, 1, \ldots, N - 1$ is any point in the image. $L(i)$, $i,j = 0, 1, \ldots, N^2 - 1$ is the dimensional vector after stretching $A(i,j)$.

$$L(\sum_{k=0}^{i-1} (4k - 1) + j + 1) = A(floor(\frac{4i - j + 1}{2}), floor(\frac{j + 1}{2})) \tag{3}$$

where $j = 1, 2, \ldots, 4i - 1$, $i = 1, 2, \ldots, floor(N/2)$.

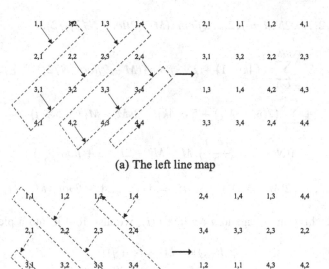

(a) The left line map

(b)The right line map

Fig. 2. The process of line maps

$$L\left(\sum_{k=1}^{floor(N/2)}(4k-1)+\sum_{k=floor(N/2)}^{i-1}(4N+1-4k)-4floor(\frac{N+1}{2})-1+j\right)$$

$$=A\left(floor(\frac{2N+2-j}{2}),2i-N+floor(\frac{j}{2})\right)$$ (4)

where $j=1,2,\ldots,4N+1-4i$, $i=floor(N/2)+1,floor(N/2)+2,\ldots,N$

The Right Line Map. We assume that $A(i,j)$, $i,j=0,1,\ldots,N-1$ is any point in the image. $L(i)$, $i,j=0,1,\ldots,N^2-1$ is the dimensional vector after stretching $A(i,j)$.

$$L\left(\sum_{k=0}^{i-1}(4k-1)+j+1\right)=A\left(floor(\frac{4i-j+1}{2}),M+1-floor(\frac{j+1}{2})\right)$$ (5)

where $j=1,2,\ldots,4i-1$, $i=1,2,\ldots,floor(N/2)$.

$$L\left(\sum_{k=1}^{floor(N/2)}(4k-1)+2N(i-1)+j\right)$$ (6)

$$=A\left(floor(\frac{2N+2-j}{2}),M-2i+2+\bmod(N,2)-floor(\frac{j+2}{2})\right)$$

where $j = 1, 2, \ldots, 2N$, $i = 1, 2, \ldots, floor((M - 2floor(N/2))/2)$.

$$L(\sum_{k=1}^{floor(N/2)} (4k - 1) + 2N \cdot floor((M - 2floor(N/2))/2))$$

$$+ \sum_{k=0}^{i-1} (2(M - M_1) + 5 - 4k) - 2(M - M_1) - 5 + j) \tag{7}$$

$$= A(N - floor(\frac{j-1}{2}), M - M_1 - 2i + 3 + floor(\frac{j}{2}))$$

where $j = 1, 2, \ldots, 2(M - M_1) + 5 - 4i$; $i = 1, 2, \ldots, 1 + floor((M - M_1)/2)$.

After stretching the image to a N^2 line $L(i)$, we also fold it into a picture,

$$B(i,j) = L(i \times N + j) \tag{8}$$

where $i = 0, 1, \ldots, N - 1$, $j = 0, 1, \ldots, N - 1$.

3 Algorithm Description

In summary, we can conclude the proposed algorithm as follows.

Step 1. The initial value x_0 is substituted into Eq. (1), iterate N_0 times to obtain x_1, and define a length of 256 integer array.
Step 2. With x_1 as the initial value, we begin to value from $N_0 + 1$, the real value of the resulting sequences is denoted by $x_i, i = 1, 2, \ldots$.
Step 3. Substitute x_i into Eq. (9) to obtain an integer Q_i in range [0, 255].

$$Q_i = \mod(floor(x_i \times 10^3, 256)) \tag{9}$$

Step 4. If Q_i has appeared in the array S, abandon Q_i, otherwise, deposit Q_i into S. When the array is filled in, the S-box is generated.
Step 5. The sequence of integers S is arranged in a 16×16 table to construct an initial prototype S-box.
Step 6. Use left line map to perform S-box m times and right line map n times, and fold the addressed S-box.

4 S-box Evaluation Criteria

In order to obtain the S-box of desired cryptography properties, many scholars designed many criteria to test S-box, among which Bijectivity, nonlinearity, Strict avalanche criterion, Bit independent criterion, Differential approximation probability, Linear approximation probability are widely accepted and adopted. In this paper, the evaluation of S-boxes will also use these criteria.

4.1 Bijectivity

Adamas C and Tavares S defined that f is bijective for a $n \times n$ S-box, if the sum of linear operation of Boolean functions of each component is 2^{n-1} [7],

$$\text{wt}(\sum_{i=1}^{n} a_i f_i) = 2^{n-1} \tag{10}$$

where $a_i \in \{0, 1\}$, $(a_1, a_2, \ldots, a_n) \neq (0, 0, \ldots, 0)$, $wt()$ represents Hamming Weight.

The reversibility of S-box is usually required, especially in a displacement of the network S-box.

4.2 Nonlinearity

Definition 1. Let $f(x) : F_2^n \to F_2$ is an n Boolean function, the non-linearity of $f(x)$ can take the form,

$$N_f = \min_{l \in L_n} d_H(f, l) \tag{11}$$

where, L_n is a set of all linear and affine functions, $d_H(f, l)$ represents the Hamming distance between f and l.

The non-linearity represented by Walsh spectrum can take a different form,

$$N_f = 2^{-n}(1 - \max_{\omega \in GF(2^n)} |S_{<f>}(\omega)|) \tag{12}$$

The cyclic spectrum of $f(x)$ is,

$$S_{<f>}(\omega) = 2^{-n} \sum_{x \in GF(2^n)} (-1)^{f(x) \oplus x \cdot \omega} \tag{13}$$

where, $\omega \in GF(2^n)$, $x \cdot \omega$ represents the dot product of x and w.

The larger the nonlinearity N_f of the function f, the stronger the ability of its resisting to the linear attacks, and vice versa.

4.3 Strict Avalanche Criterion

Webster A F and Tavares S E proposed strict avalanche criterion. Strict avalanche criterion describes this fact that when one bit in the input of Boolean function changes, the changing probability of every bit in its output should be 1/2. In practical application, a correlation matrix, the construction method of which can be found in literature [6], is always constructed to test SAC property of the Boolean function.

4.4   Bit Independent Criterion

Adams C and Tavares S proposed Bit independent criterion [7]. For the given Boolean function $f_j, f_k (j \neq k)$ is a two bits output of an S-box, if $f_j \oplus f_k$ is highly nonlinear and meets the SAC, it is possible to ensure that the correlation coefficient of each output bit pair is close to 0 when one input bit is inversed. Therefore, we can check the BIC of the S-box by verifying whether $f_j \oplus f_k (j \neq k)$ of any two output bits of the S-box meets the nonlinearity and SAC.

4.5   Differential Approximation Probability

The Differential probability DP_f is used to reflect the XOR distribution of the input and output of the Boolean function [9], i.e., maximum likelihood of outputting Δy, when the input is Δx,

$$DP_f = \max_{\Delta x \neq 0, \Delta y} \left(\frac{\neq \{x \in X | f(x) \oplus f(x \oplus \Delta x) = \Delta y\}}{2^n} \right) \tag{14}$$

where, X represents the set of all possible inputs, 2^n is the number of elements in the set.

The smaller the DP_f, the stronger the ability of the S-box for fighting against differential cryptanalysis attacks, vice versa.

4.6   Linear Approximation Probability

Under the condition of randomly selecting two masks Γx and Γy, we use Γx to calculate the mask of all possible values of input x, and use Γy to calculate the mask of the output values $S(x)$ of the corresponding S-box. Mask the input and the output, and the maximum number of the same results is called the maximum linear approximation [24], which can be computed by the following equation,

$$LP = \max_{\Gamma x, \Gamma x \neq 0} \left| \frac{\neq \{x | x \cdot \Gamma x = S(x) \cdot \Gamma y\}}{2^n} - \frac{1}{2} \right| \tag{15}$$

where, Γx and Γy are the mask values of the input and output, respectively, X is a set of all possible input values of x, the elements of which is 2^n.

The smaller the LP, the stronger the ability of the S-box for fighting against linear cryptanalysis attacks, and vice versa.

5   S-box Performance Analysis

To validate the LLCMLM, we compare it with the algorithms in literatures [9–12, 14–20], respectively. And our experimental environment is Inter Core i3 CPU 540 3.07 GHz, memory 2.00 GHz. The program runs in Matlab2012b version. Set initial values of L-L cascaded chaotic map, $x_0 = 0.1, N_0 = 500$, parameters $\mu_1 = 4, \mu_2 = 2, m = 7, n = 1$, thus resulting a 8 × 8 S-box, as shown in Table 1. Next, we test the S-box according to the above design criteria.

5.1   Bijectivity of the S-box of LLCMLM

According to the formula (13), we compute the bijectivity of the generated S-box. The computed value of S-box is just the desired value 128. This indicates that S-box of the LLCMLM meets the bijectivity.

5.2   Nonlinearity of the S-box of LLCMLM

Using (16) to calculate the non-linearity of the S-box of LLCMLM, the results are shown in Table 2. The minimum degree of a non-linear design of S-box 8 Boolean functions is 104 and a maximum of 108, with an average of 106.25. Comparing with the algorithms in literatures [9–12, 14–20], LLCMLM has a larger nonlinearity, shown in the nonlinearity column of Table 6. The results showed that the S-boxes are non-linear, and have the ability to resist linear cryptanalysis.

5.3   Strict Avalanche Criterion of the S-box of LLCMLM

The testing results are shown in Table 2, the maximum strict avalanche criterion of the generated S-box is 0.5625, the minimum is 0.3906, the average is close to the ideal value of 0.5. Comparing with the results of the literatures [9–12, 14–20], shown in the SAC column of Table 6, the S-box of LLCMLM can better meet the strict avalanche criterion.

Table 1. The S-box generated by LLCMLM

0	147	10	22	208	68	188	242	233	16	116	241	43	1	227	182
105	106	206	198	73	187	61	215	110	59	79	246	77	234	135	139
129	71	186	175	250	237	42	176	168	153	60	252	39	177	80	54
136	18	253	224	138	123	149	248	19	115	38	56	178	58	230	190
118	87	120	209	83	254	167	27	25	194	229	51	99	217	90	69
97	239	236	172	199	23	212	13	197	146	180	185	75	200	70	96
53	109	222	148	95	103	31	181	207	243	169	111	98	160	66	48
36	3	72	192	164	174	245	24	32	184	204	155	251	128	12	121
228	162	202	45	195	193	26	100	49	158	232	157	142	82	30	44
37	113	189	240	88	165	94	104	14	34	171	74	170	108	143	140
76	137	225	28	11	50	216	203	151	201	119	102	35	226	214	20
41	57	131	107	247	150	84	156	213	9	17	47	89	166	211	55
114	117	46	6	130	145	205	122	63	255	196	67	29	78	163	124
125	144	159	81	52	220	219	92	238	101	244	93	85	231	134	141
191	62	210	33	91	65	183	112	152	4	249	8	218	5	64	40
173	132	21	126	235	154	133	223	15	161	86	221	127	2	179	7

Table 2. The dependence matrix of the S-box of LLCMLM

0.5000	0.5000	0.4844	0.5156	0.5000	0.4375	0.5000	0.5156
0.5156	0.4219	0.5000	0.5000	0.4531	0.5469	0.5156	0.5625
0.5000	0.4844	0.4063	0.4531	0.4688	0.5313	0.5469	0.5625
0.5312	0.5000	0.5000	0.5000	0.5469	0.4375	0.5313	0.4688
0.5625	0.4688	0.5469	0.4375	0.5000	0.4844	0.4844	0.4844
0.5000	0.4531	0.3906	0.5469	0.4219	0.5313	0.4844	0.5000
0.5156	0.5156	0.4531	0.4375	0.4531	0.5156	0.4688	0.5156
0.5469	0.5469	0.5469	0.4688	0.5156	0.5000	0.4844	0.4531

Table 3. BIC-nonlinearity criterion for the S-box of LLCMLM

0	96	100	104	106	100	102	102
96	0	106	106	106	108	104	102
100	106	0	108	106	104	102	100
104	106	108	0	106	106	108	106
106	106	106	106	0	104	104	102
100	108	104	106	104	0	98	104
102	104	102	108	104	98	0	102
102	102	100	106	102	104	102	0

Table 4. BIC-SAC criterion for the S-box of LLCMLM

0	0.5020	0.5078	0.4844	0.5117	0.5156	0.5039	0.4941
0.5020	0	0.5215	0.4902	0.5156	0.5137	0.5215	0.4805
0.5078	0.5215	0	0.5059	0.4805	0.5176	0.5020	0.4727
0.4844	0.4902	0.5059	0	0.4824	0.5215	0.4902	0.4844
0.5117	0.5156	0.4805	0.4824	0	0.5156	0.4824	0.5215
0.5156	0.5137	0.5176	0.5215	0.5156	0	0.4941	0.5020
0.5039	0.5215	0.5020	0.4902	0.4824	0.4941	0	0.4844
0.49415	0.4805	0.4727	0.4844	0.5215	0.5020	0.4844	0

5.4   Bit Independent Criterion of the S-box of LLCMLM

The results of the testing are shown in Tables 3 and 4. The average value of non-linearity of the S-box of LLCMLM is 103.64, The average value of correlation matrix is 0.5007, which is close to the ideal value of 0.5. Comparing with the results of literatures [9–12, 14–20], shown in BIC column of Table 6, S-box has a better bit independent criterion.

5.5   Differential Approximation Probability of the S-box of LLCMLM

We use Eq. (17) to calculate differential approximation probability of the generated S-box, shown in Table 5. And comparing with the results of literatures [9–12, 14–20], shown in the DP column of Table 6, the results show that the maximum value of differential approximation probability of the S-box of LLCMLM is only 10, the minimum is 4, which means that the generated S-box has a good ability to resist differential cryptanalysis.

Table 5. Differential approximation probability of the S-box of LLCMLM

6	6	8	8	6	6	6	8	8	8	6	6	8	6	6	6
8	6	6	8	6	8	8	8	8	4	6	6	8	8	6	8
6	8	6	6	8	6	6	6	6	8	6	8	6	8	6	6
8	6	6	8	6	6	6	6	8	6	6	8	8	6	6	6
6	6	6	8	8	6	6	8	6	8	8	6	8	6	6	6
8	6	8	6	6	8	10	6	8	8	8	6	6	8	8	6
6	8	8	8	6	6	8	8	6	6	6	6	6	6	8	6
8	8	6	6	6	6	6	6	6	10	6	6	6	6	6	6
8	8	8	4	6	6	6	6	6	8	8	8	8	6	6	8
8	6	6	8	6	6	8	6	6	8	6	8	6	6	10	8
4	6	6	6	6	6	6	6	6	6	8	8	8	6	6	6
8	8	8	6	8	6	8	6	4	6	8	6	6	6	6	6
6	8	8	6	4	6	6	6	6	8	8	6	6	6	8	6
6	8	6	8	10	6	6	10	6	6	6	8	8	8	8	6
6	6	6	6	8	8	6	6	8	6	10	8	8	6	6	6
6	6	8	6	10	8	8	6	6	6	6	8	6	6	8	0

Table 6. Cryptanalysis comparison results of S-boxes

S-boxes	Nonlinearity			SAC			BIC-SAC	BIC	DP	LP
	Min	Max	Avg.	Min	Max	Avg.				
LLCMLM	104	108	106.25	0.3906	0.5625	0.4949	103.64	0.5007	0.03906	0.140625
Ref. [9]	100	108	103.250	0.3750	0.5938	0.5059	104.29	0.5031	0.04688	0.125000
Ref. [10]	103	109	104.875	0.3984	0.5703	0.4966	102.96	0.5044	0.03906	0.132813
Ref. [11]	101	108	103.875	0.3906	0.5781	0.5059	102.68	0.4958	0.03906	0.132813
Ref. [12]	100	106	103	0.4219	0.6094	0.5000	103.14	0.5024	0.05469	0.132813
Ref. [14]	102	106	104	0.3750	0.6094	0.4980	103.29	0.4971	0.03906	0.148438
Ref. [15]	96	106	103	0.3906	0.6250	0.5039	100.36	0.5010	0.03906	0.148438
Ref. [16]	98	108	103	0.4063	0.5938	0.5012	104.07	0.4989	0.04688	0.148438
Ref. [17]	100	106	104	0.3750	0.6250	0.4946	103.21	0.5019	0.03906	0.132813
Ref. [18]	103	109	105.125	0.4141	0.6094	0.5061	103.68	0.4983	0.03906	0.156250
Ref. [19]	102	108	105.250	0.4063	0.5781	0.5059	104.29	0.5029	0.04688	0.125000
Ref. [20]	100	108	104.5	0.4219	0.6094	0.4978	103.64	0.5010	0.04688	0.140625

5.6 Linear Approximation Probability of the S-box of LLCMLM

In this subsection, we use (18) to calculate Linear approximation probability of the generated S-box and compare LLCMLM with other algorithms proposed in literatures [9–12, 14–20]. The experimental results are shown in the right column of Table 6. For LLCMLM, it obtains a greater LP, 0.140625. And the remaining columns are the nonlinearity, SAC, BIC-SAC and BIC results of the comparison algorithms. Table 6 indicates that all of the chaotic based comparison algorithms can generate S-boxes with good performance, however, LLCMLM may obtain an S-box that has a better performance of resisting modern cryptanalysis attacks such as differential and linear cryptanalysis attacks.

6 Conclusion

An S-box generation approach based on L-L cascade Chaotic Map and Line Map (LLCMLM) is designed in this paper. LLCMLM uses L-L cascade chaotic map to generate an integer sequence ranging 0–255, and applies line map to scramble the position of the integer sequence. A series of experiments have been conducted to compare multiple cryptographic criteria of LLCMLM with other algorithms. The experimental results show that the S-box of the CSABC has some good cryptography features such as Bijectivity, Non-linearity, strict avalanche criterion (SAC), bit independent criterion (BIC), differential probability (DP) and linear probability (LP), and it can effectively resist to some attacks. Though LLCMLM can be used to find the S-box with good Cryptography performance, it is still hard to find some S-boxes with very good Cryptography performance. In the future, we will further clarify the relationship between chaos and cryptography, and research how to set chaos parameters to find the S-box with excellent performance.

References

1. Wang, X., Wang, Q.: A novel image encryption algorithm based on dynamic S-boxes constructed by chaos. Nonlinear Dyn. **75**(3), 567–576 (2014)
2. Hussain, I., Shah, T., Gondal, M.A.: Application of S-box and chaoticmap for image encryption. Math. Comput. Model. **57**(9), 2576–2579 (2013)
3. Zhang, X., Mao, Y., Zhao, Z.: An efficient chaotic image encryption based on alternate circular S-boxes. Nonlinear Dyn. **78**(1), 359–369 (2014)
4. Hussain, I., Gondal, M.A.: An extended image encryption using chaotic coupled map and S-box transformation. Nonlinear Dyn. **76**(2), 1355–1363 (2014)
5. Liu, H., Kadir, A., Niu, Y.: Chaos-based color image block encryption scheme using S-box. AEU Int. J. Electron. Commun. **68**(7), 676–686 (2014)
6. Webster, A.F., Tavares, S.: On the design of S-boxes. In: Williams, H.C. (ed.) CRYPTO 1985. LNCS, vol. 218, pp. 523–534. Springer, Heidelberg (1986)
7. Adams, C.M., Tavares, S.: Good S-boxes are easy to find. In: Brassard, G. (ed.) CRYPTO 1989. LNCS, vol. 435, pp. 612–615. Springer, Heidelberg (1990)

8. Dawson, M.H., Tavares, S.: An expanded set of S-box design criteria based on information theory and its relation to differential-like attacks. In: Davies, D.W. (ed.) EUROCRYPT 1991. LNCS, vol. 547, pp. 352–367. Springer, Heidelberg (1991)
9. Jakimoski, G., Kocarev, L.: Chaos and cryptography: block encryption ciphers based on chaotic maps. IEEE Trans. Circ. Syst. I: Fundam. Theor. Appl. 48(2), 163–169 (2001)
10. Tang, G., Liao, X., Chen, Y.: A novel method for designing S-boxes based on chaotic maps. Chaos, Solitons Fractals 23(2), 413–419 (2005)
11. Tang, G., Liao, X.: A method for designing dynamical S-boxes based on discretized chaotic map. Chaos, Solitons Fractals 23(5), 1901–1909 (2005)
12. Chen, G., Chen, Y., Liao, X.: An extended method for obtaining S-boxes based on three-dimensional chaotic baker maps. Chaos, Solitons Fractals 31(3), 571–579 (2007)
13. Wang, Y., Wong, K.W., Li, C.B., Li, Y.: A novel method to design S-box based on chaotic map and genetic algorithm. Phys. Lett. A 376(6), 827–833 (2012)
14. Chen, G.: A novel heuristic method for obtaining S-boxes. Chaos, Solitons Fractals 36(4), 1028–1036 (2008)
15. Khan, M., Shah, T., Mahmood, H., Gondal, M.A., Hussain, I.: A novel technique for the construction of strong S-boxes based on chaotic lorenz systems. Nonlinear Dyn. 70(3), 2303–2311 (2012)
16. Khan, M., Shah, T., Mahmood, H., Gondal, M.A.: An efficient method for the construction of block cipher with multi-chaotic systems. Nonlinear Dyn. 71(3), 489–492 (2013)
17. Khan, M., Shah, T.: A construction of novel chaos base nonlinear component of block cipher. Nonlinear Dyn. 76(1), 377–382 (2014)
18. Özkaynak, F., Yavuz, S.: Designing chaotic S-boxes based on time-delay chaotic system. Nonlinear Dyn. 74(3), 551–557 (2013)
19. Hussain, I., Shah, T., Gondal, M.A., Mahmood, H.: A novel method for designing nonlinear component for block cipher based on TD-ERCS chaotic sequence. Nonlinear Dyn. 73(1–2), 633–637 (2013)
20. Khan, M., Shah, T.: An Efficient construction of substitution box with fractional chaotic system. SIViP 1–4 (2013)
21. Liu, X.C., Feng, D.G.: Construction of S-boxes with some cryptographic properties. J. Softw. 11(10), 1299–1302 (2000)
22. Wang, G.Y., Yuan, F.: Cascade Chaos and Its Dynamic Characteristics. Acta Phys. Sin. 62(2), 2–10 (2013). 020506
23. Feng, Y., Li, L., Huang, F.: A symmetric image encryption approach based on line maps. In: 1st International Symposium on Systems and Control in Aerospace and Astronautics, pp. 1362–1367. IEEE Press (2006)
24. Matsui, M.: Linear cryptanalysis method for DES cipher. In: Helleseth, T. (ed.) EUROCRYPT 1993. LNCS, vol. 765, pp. 386–397. Springer, Heidelberg (1994)

Scene Character and Text Recognition: The State-of-the-Art

Chongmu Chen[1], Da-Han Wang[2], and Hanzi Wang[1(✉)]

[1] Fujian Key Laboratory of Sensing and Computing for Smart City,
School of Information Science and Engineering,
Xiamen University, Xiamen, Fujian, China
Chongmu.chen@gmail.com, hanzi.wang@xmu.edu.cn
[2] School of Computer and Information Engineering,
Xiamen University of Technology, Xiamen, Fujian, China
wangdh@xmut.edu.cn

Abstract. Scene text recognition is gaining renewed interest owing to the increase of scene image based applications and new intelligent devices. Unlike recognition of printed text, scene text recognition is challenging due to the complexity of scene images. To provide an overview of the techniques and inspire future research, this paper reviews the advances in scene character and text recognition, with emphasize on character feature representation methods and word recognition models. The papers published in the most recent conferences ECCV 2014, ACCV 2014, ICIP 2014, and ICPR 2014 are also reviewed in this paper to provide the state-of-the-art of scene character and text recognition. The state-of-the-art performance is provided to show the achieved performance so far and demonstrate the potential of deep learning based methods.

Keywords: Scene character recognition · Scene text recognition · Character feature representation · Word recognition models

1 Introduction

Scene text recognition has attracted renewed interests in recent years due to the wide use of intelligent devices such as smart phones. In a typical application, for example, one needs to recognize text in an image captured by a mobile phones and translate text into other languages. As a result, numerous researchers devoted to the research of scene text recognition [1].

However, scene text recognition is a challenging problem due to the complexity of scene images such as background clutter, illumination changes, and the variation of text position, size, font, color and line orientation. Figure 1 shows some scene images that contain text. We can see that unlike the recognition of text in printed documents (this is also called Optical Character Recognition, OCR), which contain clean and well-formatted text, scene text detection and recognition is a more challenging problem.

© Springer International Publishing Switzerland 2015
Y.-J. Zhang (Ed.): ICIG 2015, Part III, LNCS 9219, pp. 310–320, 2015.
DOI: 10.1007/978-3-319-21969-1_27

Fig. 1. Some scene images that contain text.

In scene text recognition, there are four main problems: (1) text detection, (2) text recognition, (3) full image word recognition, and (4) isolated scene character recognition. Text detection is to locate text regions in an image; while text recognition, given text regions, is usually referred to as cropped word recognition. Full image word recognition usually includes both text detection and text recognition in an end-to-end scene text recognition system. Isolated character recognition is usually a basic component of a scene text recognition system. Hence the problem of isolated scene character recognition is also a fundamental problem and has attracted increasing attentions recently.

Numerous methods have been proposed for these problems, and have achieved great progresses in the past decade. Ten years ago two papers [2] and [3] addressed these problems and provided comprehensive surveys on text information extraction and camera-based document analysis. Recently, Zhang et al. [4] reviewed the text detection problem. More recently, Ye et al. [1] presented more general and extensive discussions on all the problems in scene text recognition.

However, we notice that, there are still some issues remained to be addressed. First, athough in [1] the achieved progresses of scene word recognition and end-to-end recognition are surveyed, the state-of-the-art of scene character recognition is ignored. Second, the papers published in some recent literature such as ECCV 2014, ACCV 2014, ICIP 2014, and ICPR 2014 are not included in [1]. In fact, some papers in these conferences have renewed the state-of-the-art. Third, the paper [1] describes the problems of scene word recognition and end-to-end recognition briefly while the methods proposed for these problems are not categorized in details.

In this paper, we focus on the problems of scene character recognition and scene text recognition (mainly in the context of cropped word recognition), and present the state-of-the-art of these problems. We do not review the text detection problem and end-to-end recognition problem due to the space limitation. We review the most recently published papers on scene text recognition in ECCV 2014, ACCV 2014, ICIP 2014, and ICPR 2014. Specifically, we review the papers in two aspects: character feature representation and word recognition model, which are two important issues in scene text recognition.

The rest of the paper is organized as follows. In Sect. 2, we first review some public databases used for scene character and text recognition. In Sect. 3, we then introduce scene character recognition methods, focusing on the issue of character feature representation, and provide the state-of-the-art performance achieved so far. In Sect. 4, we review the problems of scene word recognition, focusing on the multiple information integration methods, and provide the state-of-the-art performance achieved so far. In Sect. 5, we conclude the paper with some discussion.

2   The Databases for Scene Character and Text Recognition

In this subsection, we summarize some publicly available datasets that are commonly used for scene character and text recognition. The most widely used datasets for scene character and/or text recognition include the ICDAR2003 dataset [5], the ICDAR2011 dataset [6], the Chars74K dataset [7], the Street View Text (SVT) dataset [8], and the III5K-Word dataset [9]. Among them, the ICDAR2003 and ICDAR2011 datasets are used for the "Robust OCR", "Robust Reading and Text Locating", and "Robust Word Recognition" competitions organized jointly with the ICDAR main conference. Hence the ICDAR2003 and ICDAR2011 datasets contain natural scene images, from which words and character samples can be cropped. The original SVT dataset contains natural scene images and cropped words only. Later, Mishra et al. provided the character level annotations of the test set of the SVT dataset [9]. The III5K-Word dataset is composed of word images, and character level annotations are provided by the authors. The Chars74K dataset is composed of isolated scene character samples.

Besides the datasets mentioned above, there are also some other datesets for research of scene text detection and recognition (see [1] for a brief review). Since this paper focuses on the state-of-the-art of scene character and text recognition, we only introduce the commonly used datasets for evaluation of scene character and text recognition.

The ICDAR2003 dataset contains 507 natural scene images including 258 training images and 249 test images in total. There are totally 1,156 words (including 6,185 character samples) cropped from the training set of the ICDAR2003 dataset, and 1,107 words (including 5,379 character samples) cropped from the test set of the ICDAR2003 dataset. The ICDAR2011 dataset contains 229 images for training (including 846 words) and 255 images for test (including 1,189 words). The SVT dataset is composed of 100 training images (including 258 words) and 249 test images (including 647 words that contains 3,796 character samples). For the ICDAR2011 dataset, only the words in the images can be cropped because the images are annotated at word level only. The IIIT5K-Word dataset is the largest and most challenging dataset for word recognition so far. This dataset includes 5000 word images, where 2000 images are used for training and 3000 images for test. The Chars74K dataset contains nearly 74 thousand scene character samples.

In summary, for evaluating scene character recognition methods, the ICDAR2003 and Chars74K datasets are commonly used. For evaluating scene text recognition methods, the ICDAR2003, ICDAR2011, SVT, and III5K-Word datasets are usually used.

3   The State-of-the-Art Scene Character Recognition Methods

For scene character recognition, two important issues may affect the performance of scene character recognition: character feature representation methods and character classification methods. Whereas, much more attentions are paid to feature representation. For the character classification methods, the support vector machine (SVM) classifier (with a linear kernel or RBF or chi-square kernel) is one of the most popular one. Some other classifiers such as the random ferns classifier (FERNS) [8], the nearest neighbor (NN) classifier [8], random forest [10] and the convolutional neural network classifier (CNN) [11] have been adopted.

Since much more attentions are paid to character feature representation methods, in the following we mainly review the papers related to feature representation. We categorize the existing methods in three main kinds: HOG and its variants, mid-level character structural features, and deep learning based methods. Table 1 shows the state-of-the-art performance achieved so far. From the results, we can see that, the deep learning based feature learning methods achieve the highest performance.

3.1   HOG and Its Variants

The Histograms of Oriented Gradients (HOG) features have been shown to be effective and have been used in object detection [24], and for scene character feature representation [8,25]. Although HOG is very simple and is effective in describing local features (such as edges), HOG ignores the spatial and structural information. Hence some methods are proposed to improve HOG. For example, Yi et al. [22] improve the HOG features by global sampling (called GHOG) or local sampling (called LHOG) to better model character structures. Tian et al. [20] propose the Co-occurrence of Histogram of Oriented Gradients (called CoHOG) features, which capture the spatial distribution of neighboring orientation pairs instead of only a single gradient orientation, for scene text recognition. The CoHOG method improves HOG significantly in scene character recognition. Later, the authors of [20] propose the pyramid of HOG (called

Table 1. The state-of-the-art methods and their results for scene character recognition(%).

Method	Chars74K-15	ICDAR03-CH	SVT-CHAR	III5K
Deep CNN [12]	–	91.0	80.3	–
Maxout+Hybrid HMMs [13]	–	89.8	–	–
Feature learning (CNN) [14]	–	81.7	–	–
ConvCoHOG+Linear SVM [15]	–	81	75	–
CoStrokes [16]	67.5	82.7	–	–
PHOG+Chi-Square SVM [17]	–	79.0	74.7	75.8
Stroke Bank [18]	65.9	79.8		
Feature Pooling+L2 SVM [19]	64	79	–	–
CoHOG + Linear SVM [20]	–	79.4	75.4	–
HOG+AT+Linear SVM [21]	**68**	73	–	–
GHOG+Chi-Square SVM [22]	62	76	–	–
LHOG+Chi-Square SVM [22]	58	75	–	–
MSER [23]	-	67	–	–
HOG+NN [8]	58	52	–	–
MKL [7]	55	-	–	–
HOG+FERNS [8]	54	64	–	–
GB+RBF SVM [7]	53	-	–	–
ABBYY [7]	31	21	–	–

PHOG) [17] to encode the relative spatial layout of the character parts, and propose the convolutional CoHOG (called ConvCoHOG) to extract richer character features. These methods effectively improve the performance of scene character recognition.

3.2 Mid-level Character Structural Features

Character structure information is important to character representation and has been exploited in [10, 19, 26–28, 30]. In [26–28], the authors propose to use part-based tree-structured features, which are originally designed for face detection [29] for representing character features. The part-based tree-structured features are designed directly according to the shape and structure of each character class. Yao et al. [10] propose to use a set of mid-level detectable primitives (called strokelets), which capture substructures of characters, for character representation. The strokelets are used in conjunction with the HOG features for character description, as supplementary features to the HOG features. In [19], a discriminative feature pooling method that automatically learns the most informative sub-regions of each scene character is proposed for character feature representation. Zhang et al. [30] propose to use sparse coding based features for capturing character structures. The basis idea of [30] is to learn common structures with sparse coding and to capture character structures using histograms of sparse codes.

Recently, Gao et al. [18] propose a stroke bank based character representation method. The basic idea is to design a stroke detector for scene character recognition. In [16], Gao et al. propose to learn co-occurrence of local strokes by using a spatiality embedded dictionary, which is used to introduce more precise spatial information for character recognition. The results demonstrate the effectiveness of the two methods.

It is interesting to find that, some character feature representation methods mentioned above explore the mid-level features to describe character structures. Such as strokelets extracted in Yao et al. [10], the sub-regions learned by [19], and the stoke bank designed in [18], and the sub-structures learned by [30], they are all mid-level features. These learned mid-level features have shown their effectiveness in scene characeter/text recognition.

3.3 Deep Learning Based Methods

The deep learning methods have also been adopted for feature learning of scene characters. Coates et al. [14] propose a unsupervised feature learning method using convolutional neural networks (CNN) for scene character recognition. Recently, in ECCV 2014, Jaderberg et al. [12] develop a CNN classifier that can be used for both text detection and recognition. The CNN classifier has a novel architecture that enables efficient feature sharing using a number of layers in common for character recognition. The performance achieved by Jaderberg et al. [12] on both scene character recognition and text recognition is pretty high and is the best among the existing methods so far (see Sect. 4 for the performance of text recognition achieved by [12]).

4 The State-of-the-Art Scene Text Recognition Methods

Since the scene text recognition methods in end-to-end recognition systems are similar to those in cropped word recognition. In this paper, we mainly focus on the state-of-the-art of cropped word recognition. In the following, we review the methods in cropped word recognition methods.

4.1 A Typical Word Recognition Procedure

In a typical word recognition system, there are mainly two steps. The first step is character detection, which aims to simultaneously detect and recognize characters. In this step, a 63-class (10 digits, 52 English letters, and the outlier/backgound class) classifier is used to obtain character candidates and classify them. For generating character candidates, two strategies have been used: one is the sliding window strategy (such the work in [8,11,30], etc.), and one is to detect character candidates using the character detector/classifier directly (such as the work in [10, 26], etc.). In this step, the character feature representation methods play an important role in scene text recognition, and the performance of character classification highly affects the performance of scene text recognition.

The second step is the word formation step, which aims to combine character candidates to yield the word recognition result. In this step, multiple information can be integrated to help improve the performance of scene text recognition. An information integration model or a word recognition model can be used to integrate multiple information, which raises another important issue in scene text recognition. In the next subsection, we will briefly review the word recognition model (or score function or object function) in the literature. Figure 2 shows the scene text recognition procedure presented in [26], showing the results of the two steps.

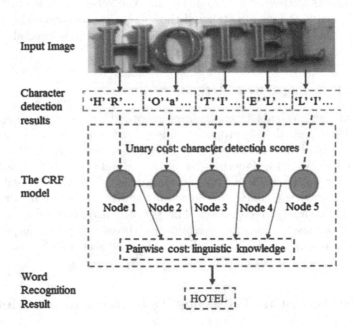

Fig. 2. A typical scene text recognition procedure. The images are referred to paper [26]. In this paper, a CRF model is used as the information integration model.

4.2   Information Integration Model/Word Recognition Model

Regarding the word recognition model for yielding word recognition results, Wang et al. [8] apply a lexicon-driven pictorial structures model to combine character detection scores and geometric constraints. Mishra et al. [25] build a conditional random field (CRF) model to integrate bottom-up cues (character detection scores) with top-down cues (lexicon prior). Similarly, Shi et al. [26] use a CRF model to get final word recognition results. In [11, 12, 31–33], heuristic integration models (summation of character detection scores) are used to integrate character detection result. In [28], a probabilistic model is proposed to combine the character detection scores and a language model from the Bayesian decision view. In those works, the parameters of the word recognition model are set empirically.

In [30], Zhang et al. apply the lexicon-driven pictorial structures model similar to that in [8] for word recognition. However, they improve it by taking into account the influence of the word length (i.e., the number of characters in the word) to word recognition results. Moreover, they propose to learn parameters using the Minimum Classification Error (MCE) training method [34] to optimize scene text recognition. For searching the optimal word as the recognition result, the dynamic programming algorithm is commonly used, such as the work in [8,12,30], etc.

4.3   Word Spotting Based Methods Versus Open Vocabulary Based Methods

For cropped word recognition, the existing scene text recognition methods can be categorized into two kinds: word spotting based methods [8,11,12,30,32,35] and open vocabulary based methods [9,10,19,25,26,31,36–39]. For word spotting based methods, a lexicon is provided for each cropped word image, and the optimal word is the one yielding the maximum matching score. This is similar to a word spotting procedure. For open vocabulary based methods, language prior or language model is obtained using a general larger corpus, from which the language prior or language model can be estimated.

Since the work of Wang et al. [8], most papers on scene text recognition report results using lexicons consisting of a list of words (which can be 50 words containing the ground truth word or the words created from all the words in the test set, called Full lexicons). That is, for open vocabulary based methods, one needs to retrieve the word with the smallest edit distance in the lexicon as the recognition result, such as [25,26], etc.

4.4   The State-of-the-art Performance of Scene Text Recognition

We show the state-of-the-art performance of scene text recognition in Table 2. In the table, SVT, I03, I11, and III5K denotes the SVT, ICDAR2003, ICDAR2011, and III5K-Word dataset, respectively. In the end of each name of the dataset, the number "50" means using the lexicon consisting of 50 words; the word "Full" means using the lexicons created from words of the test set; and the word "Med" means using the Medium lexicon provided by the authors of [9].

From the table, we can see that the PhotoOCR method presented in [33] report the highest performance on SVT-50, achieving accuracy of 90.3 % on SVT-50. On I03-50 and I03-Full, the method proposed in [12] performs the best, achieving accuracy of 96.2 % and 91.5 % on I03-50 and I03-Full, respectively. It is worth noting that both [33] and [12] adopt deep learning based methods. This demonstrates the potential advantages of the deep learning based methods. Only a few works report performance on I11-50, I11-Full, III5K-50 and III5K-Med. On I11-50 and I11-Full, Shi et al. [28] report promising performance, achieving

Table 2. The state-of-the-Art performance of scene text recognition. (%)

Method	SVT-50	I03-50	I03-Full	I11-50	I11-Full	III5K-50	III5K-Med
K. Wang et al. [8]	57	76	62	–	–	–	–
Mishra et al. [25]	73.26	81.78	–	–	–	68.25	55.50
Mishra et al. [9]	73.57	80.28	–	–	–	66	57.5
Novikova et al. [39]	72.9	82.8	–	–	–	–	–
T. Wang et al. [11]	70	90	84	–	–	–	–
Yildirim et al. [37]	–	85.70	–	–	–	–	–
Shi et al. [26]	73.51	87.44	79.30	87.04	82.87	–	–
Goel et al. [35]	77.28	89.69	–	–	–	–	–
Weinmann et al. [40]	78.05	–	–	–	–	–	–
Shi et al. [27]	74.65	84.52	79.98	–	–	–	–
Shi et al. [28]	73.67	87.83	79.58	87.22	83.21	–	–
Zhang et al. [30]	74.34	88.24	80.56	–	–	–	–
Yao et al. [10]	75.89	88.48	80.33	–	–	80.2	69.3
Lee et al. [19]	80	88	76	88	77	–	–
Bissacco et al. [33]	90.3	–	–	–	–	–	–
Su et al. [32]	83	92	82	91	83	–	–
Alsharif et al. [13]	74.3	93.1	88.6	–	–	–	–
Jaderberg et al. [12]	86.1	96.2	91.5	–	–	–	–

accuracy of 87.22 % and 83.21 % on I11-50 and I11-Full, respectively. On III5K-50 and III5K-Med, Yao et al. [10] report promising results, achieving accuracy of 80.2 % and 69.3 % on III5K-50 and III5K-Med, respectively.

5   Conclusions

This paper reviews the state-of-the-art of scene character and text recognition, with emphasize on character feature representation and word recognition models. The performance of scene character recognition and text recognition obtained by the recently proposed methods on both scene character recognition and text recognition are reviewed, including the most recent papers in ECCV 2014, ACCV 2014, ICIP 2014, and ICPR 2014. From the reported results, we can see that the deep learning based methods achieve the highest performance, indicating that this type of methods open a new direction for scene character and text recognition. Character feature representation, as a basic component of scene character and text recognition systems, will also be an important research direction in the future.

Acknowledgment. This work was supported by the National Natural Science Foundation of China under Grants 61305004 and 61472334, by the Specialized Research Fund for the Doctoral Program of Higher Education of China under Grant 20110121110033, and by the Fundamental Research Funds for the Central Universities under Grant 20720130720.

References

1. Ye, Q., Doermann, D.: Text detection and recognition in imagery: a survey, IEEE. Trans. Pattern Anal. Mach. Intell. **37**(7), 1480–1500 (2015)
2. Jung, K., Kim, K.I., Jain, A.K.: Text information extraction in images and video: a survey. Pattern Recognit. **37**(5), 977–997 (2004)
3. Liang, J., Doermann, D., Li, H.: Camera-based analysis of text and documents: a survey. Int. J. Doc. Anal. Recognit. **7**(2–3), 84–104 (2005)
4. Zhang, H., Zhao, K., Song, Y.-Z., Guo, J.: Text extraction from natural scene image: a survey. Neurocomputing **122**, 310–323 (2013)
5. Lucas, S.M., Panaretos, A., Sosa, L., Tang, A., Wong, S., Young, R.: ICDAR 2003 robust reading competitions. In: Proceedings of International Conference on Document Analysis and Recognition (2003)
6. Shahab, A., Shafait, F., Dengel, A.: ICDAR 2011 robust reading competition challenge 2: reading text in scene images. In: Proceedings ICDAR, pp. 1491–1496 (2011)
7. de Campos, T.E., Babu, B.R., Varma, M.: Character recognition in natural images. In: Proceedings of International Conference on Computer Vision Theory and Applications, Lisbon (2009)
8. Wang, K., Babenko, B., Belongie, S.: End-to-end scene text recognition. In: Proceedings ICCV, pp. 1457–1464 (2011)
9. Mishra, A., Alahari, K., Jawahar, C.V.: Scene text recognition using higher order language priors. In: Proceedings BMVC, pp. 1–11 (2012)
10. Yao, C., Bai, X., Shi, B., Liu, W.: Strokelets: a learned multi-scale representation for scene text recognition. In: Proceedings CVPR (2014)
11. Wang, T., Wu, D.J., Coates, A., Ng, A.Y.: End-to-end text recognition with convolutional neural networks. In: Proceedings ICPR, pp. 3304–3308 (2012)
12. Jaderberg, M., Vedaldi, A., Zisserman, A.: Deep features for text spotting. In: Fleet, D., Pajdla, T., Schiele, B., Tuytelaars, T. (eds.) ECCV 2014, Part IV. LNCS, vol. 8692, pp. 512–528. Springer, Heidelberg (2014)
13. Alsharif, O., Pineau, J.: End-to-end text recognition with hybrid HMM maxout models. In: International Conference on Learning Representations (2014)
14. Coates, A., Carpenter, B., Case, C., Satheesh, S., Suresh, B., Wang, T., Wu, D.J., Ng, A.Y.: Text detection and character recognition in scene images with unsupervised feature learning. In: Proceedings ICDAR, pp. 440–445 (2011)
15. Su, B., Lu, S., Tian, S. , Lim, J.-H., Tan, C.L.: Character recognition in natural scenes using convolutional co-occurrence HOG. In: Proceedings ICPR, pp. 2926–2931 (2014)
16. Gao, S., Wang, C., Xiao, B., Shi, C., Zhou, W., Zhang, Z.: Learning co-occurrence strokes for scene character recognition based on spatiality embedded dictionary. In: Proceedings ICIP, pp. 5956–5960 (2014)
17. Tan, Z.R., Tian, S., Tan, C.L.: Using pyramid of histogram of oriented gradients on natural scene text recognition. In: Proceedings ICIP, pp. 2629–2633 (2014)
18. Gao, S., Wang, C., Xiao, B., Shi, C., Zhang, Z.: Stroke bank: a high-level representation for scene character recognition. In: Proceedings ICPR, pp. 2909–2913 (2014)
19. Lee, C.-Y., Bhardwaj, A., Di, W., Jagadeesh, V., Piramuthu, R.: Region-based discriminative feature pooling for scene text recognition. In: Proceedings CVPR, pp. 4050–4057 (2014)
20. Tian, S., Lu, S., Su, B., Tan, C.L.: Scene text recognition using co-occurrence of histogram of oriented gradients. In: Proceedings ICDAR, pp. 912–916 (2013)

21. Mishra, A., Alahari, K., Jawahar, C.V.: Image retrieval using textual cues. In: Proceedings ICCV, pp. 3040–3047 (2013)
22. Yi, C., Yang, X., Tian, Y.: Feature representations for scene text character recognition: a comparative study. In: Proceedings ICDAR, pp. 907–911 (2013)
23. Neumann, L., Matas, J.: A method for text localization and recognition in real-world images. In: Kimmel, R., Klette, R., Sugimoto, A. (eds.) ACCV 2010, Part III. LNCS, vol. 6494, pp. 770–783. Springer, Heidelberg (2011)
24. Dalal, N., Triggs, B.: Histograms of oriented gradients for human detection. In: Proceedings CVPR, pp. 886–893 (2005)
25. Mishra, A., Alahari, K., Jawahar, C.V.: Top-down and bottom-up cues for scene text recognition. In: Proceedings CVPR, pp. 2687–2694 (2012)
26. Shi, C., Wang, C., Xiao, B., Zhang, Y., Gao, S., Zhang, Z.: Scene text recognition using part-based tree-structured character detection. In: Proceedings CVPR, pp. 2961–2968 (2013)
27. Shi, C., Wang, C., Xiao, B., Gao, S., Hu, J.: End-to-end scene text recognition using tree-structured models. Pattern Recognit. **47**(9), 2853–2866 (2014)
28. Shi, C., Wang, C., Xiao, B., Gao, S., Hu, J.: Scene text recognition using structure-guided character detection and linguistic knowledge. IEEE Trans. Circuits Syst. Video Technol. **24**(7), 1235–1250 (2014)
29. Zhu, X., Ramanan, D.: Face detection, pose estimation, and landmark localization in the wild. In: Proceedings CVPR, pp. 2879–2886 (2012)
30. Zhang, D., Wang, D.-H., Wang, H.: Scene text recognition using sparse coding based features. In: Proceedings ICIP, pp. 1066–1070 (2014)
31. Neumann, L., Matas, J.: Scene text localization and recognition with oriented stroke detection. In: Proceedings ICCV, pp. 97–104 (2013)
32. Su, B., Lu, S.: Accurate scene text recognition based on recurrent neural network. In: Cremers, D., Reid, I., Saito, H., Yang, M.-H. (eds.) ACCV 2014. LNCS, vol. 9003, pp. 35–48. Springer, Heidelberg (2015)
33. Bissacco, A., Cummins, M., Netzer, Y., Neven, H.: PhotoOCR: reading text in uncontrolled conditions. In: Proceedings ICCV, pp. 785–792 (2013)
34. Juang, B.-H., Chou, W., Lee, C.-H.: Minimum classification error rate methods for speech recognition. IEEE Trans. Speech Audio Process. **5**(3), 257–265 (1997)
35. Goel, V., Mishra, A., Alahari, K., Jawahar, C.V.: Whole is greater than sum of parts: recognizing scene text words. In: Proceedings ICDAR, pp. 398–402 (2013)
36. Neumann, L., Matas, J.: Real-time scene text localization and recognition. In: Proceedings CVPR, pp. 3538–3545 (2012)
37. Yildirim, G., Achanta, R., Susstrunk, S.: Text recognition in natural images using multiclass hough forests. In: Proceedings of International Joint Conference on Computer Vision, Imaging and Computer Graphics Theory and Applications (2013)
38. Feild, J.L., Learned-Miller, E.G.: Improving open-vocabulary scene text recognition. In: Proceedings ICDAR, pp. 604–608 (2013)
39. Novikova, T., Barinova, O., Kohli, P., Lempitsky, V.: Large-lexicon attribute-consistent text recognition in natural images. In: Fitzgibbon, A., Lazebnik, S., Perona, P., Sato, Y., Schmid, C. (eds.) ECCV 2012, Part VI. LNCS, vol. 7577, pp. 752–765. Springer, Heidelberg (2012)
40. Weinman, J.J., Butler, Z., Knoll, D., Feild, J.L.: Toward integrated scene text reading. IEEE Trans. Pattern Anal. Mach. Intell. **36**(2), 375–387 (2014)

Segmentation of Intra-retinal Layers in 3D Optic Nerve Head Images

Chuang Wang[1]([✉]), Yaxing Wang[2], Djibril Kaba[1], Haogang Zhu[3], You Lv[4],
Zidong Wang[1], Xiaohui Liu[1], and Yongmin Li[1]

[1] Department of Computer Science, Brunel University London, Uxbridge, UK
Chuang.Wang@brunel.ac.uk
[2] Tongren Hospital, Beijing, China
[3] Moorfields Eye Hospital NHS Foundation Trust, London, UK
[4] School of Computer and Engineering,
Nanjing University of Science and Technology, Nanjing, China

Abstract. Spectral-Domain Optical Coherence Tomography (SD-OCT)
is a non-invasive imaging modality, which provides retinal structures with
unprecedented detail in 3D. In this paper, we propose an automated
segmentation method to detect intra-retinal layers in SD-OCT images
around optic nerve head acquired from a high resolution RTVue-100 SD-
OCT (Optovue, Fremont, CA, USA). This method starts by removing all
the OCT imaging artifacts including the speckle noise and enhancing the
contrast between layers using the 3D nonlinear anisotropic. Afterwards,
we combine the level set method, k-means and MRF method to segment
three intra-retinal layers around optical nerve head. The segmentation
results show that our method can effectively delineate the surfaces of
the retinal tissues in the noisy 3D optic nerve head images. The signed
and unsigned significant differences between the segmentation results
and the ground truth over optic nerve head B-scans are 1.01 ± 1.13 and
1.93 ± 2.21.

1 Introduction

Optical Coherence Tomography (OCT) is a powerful biomedical tissue-imaging
modality, which can provide wealthy information, such as structure information,
blood flow, elastic parameters, change of polarization state and molecular content
[9]. Therefore, this imaging tool has been increasingly useful in diagnosing eye
diseases, such as glaucoma, diabetic retinopathy and age-related macular degen-
eration. These diseases are known to be the most common causes of blindness
in the developed countries according to the World Heath Organization (WHO)
survey [15]. In order to help ophthalmologists to perform more accurately and
efficiently the diagnosis of eye diseases, several medical image processing techniques are applied to extract some useful information from OCT data, such as
retinal layers, retinal vessels, retinal lesions, optic nerve head, optic cup and
neuroretinal rim. In this work, we focus on the intra-retinal layer segmentation
of 3D retinal images obtained from around the macular and the optic disc head.

© Springer International Publishing Switzerland 2015
Y.-J. Zhang (Ed.): ICIG 2015, Part III, LNCS 9219, pp. 321–332, 2015.
DOI: 10.1007/978-3-319-21969-1_28

There are two main reasons for intra-retinal layer segmentation [7]. First, the morphology and thickness of each intra-retinal layer are important indicators for assessing the presence of ocular disease. For example, the thickness of the nerve fiber layer is an important indicator of glaucoma. Second, intra-retinal layer segmentation improves the understanding of the pathophysiology of the systemic diseases. For instance, the damage of the nerve fiber layer can provide the indication of brain damages [7].

However, it is time consuming or even impossible for ophthalmologist to manually label each layers, specifically for the macular images with the complicated 3D layer structures. Therefore, a reliable automated method for layer segmentation is attractive in computer aided-diagnosis. 3D OCT layer segmentation is a challenging problem, and there has been significant effort in this area over the last decade. A number of different approaches are developed to do the segmentation, however, no typical segmentation method can work equally well on different 3D retinal images collected from different imaging modalities.

For most of the existing 3D segmentation approaches, a typical two-step process is adopted. The first step is de-noising to remove the speckle noises and enhance the contrast between layers (usually with 3D anisotropic diffusion method, 3D median filter, 3D Gaussian filter or 3D wavelet transform). The second step is to segment the layers according to the characteristics of the images, such as shapes, textures or intensities.

Snake based methods [11] attempt to minimize the energy of a sum of internal and external energy of the current contour. These methods work well on images with high contrast, high gradient and smooth boundary between the layers. However, the performance is adversely affected by the blood vessel shadows, other morphological features of the retinal, or irregular layer shapes. Zhu et al. [20] proposed a Floatingcanvas method to segment 3D intra-retinal layers from 3D optic nerve head images. This method can produce relatively smooth layer surface, however, it is sensitive to the low gradient between layers. Yazdanpanah et al. [18] proposed an active contour method, incorporating with circular shape prior information, to segment intra-retinal layer from 3D OCT image. This method can effectively overcome the affects of the blood vessel shadows and other morphological features of the retinal, however it cannot work well on images with irregular layer shapes.

Pattern recognition based techniques perform the layer segmentation by using boundary classifier, which is used to assign each voxel to layer boundary and non boundary. The classifier is obtained through a learning process supervised by reference layer boundaries. Fuller et al. [5] designed a multi-resolution hierarchical support vector machines (SVMs) to segment OCT retinal layer. Compared to other methods, the segmentation accuracy is slightly lower with 6 pixels of line difference and 8 % of the thickness difference. A column classification algorithm was proposed by Michael et al. [1] to segment the intra-retinal layers from 3D optic nerve head images. Lang et al. [12] trained a random forest classifier to segment retinal layers from macular images. However, the performance of the pattern recognition based techniques are highly relayed on training sets.

Graph based methods are aimed to find the global minimum cut of the segmentation graph, which is constructed with regional term and boundary term. Garvin [6] proposed a 3D graph search method by constructing geometric graph with edge and regional information and five intra-retinal layers were successfully segmented. This method was extended in [4], which combined graph theory and dynamic programming to segment the intra-retinal layers and eight retinal layer boundaries were located. Although these methods provide good segmentation accuracy, they can not segment all layer boundaries simultaneously and have slow processing speed. Lee et al. [13] proposed a parallel graph search method to overcome these limitations. Besides, a fast multi scale 3-D graph algorithm was developed to segment the intra-retinal surfaces for 3D optic nerve head images by Lee et al. [14]. Kafieh et al. [10] proposed the coarse grained diffusion maps relying on regional image texture without requiring edge based image information and ten layers were segmented accurately. However, this method has high computational complexity and does not work well for abnormal images.

In this paper, we propose an automatic approaches to segmenting intra-retinal layers from optic nerve head images. Markov Random Field (MRF) and level set method are used to segment retinal layers for 3D optic nerve head images. Firstly, the nonlinear anisotropic diffusion approach is applied to denoise the optic nerve head images and enhance the contrast between intra-retinal layers. Then, level set method is used to segment the retinal layer area. After that, the initial segmentation is obtained by using the k-means method. Because of the inhomogeneity and blood vessel shadows, the k-means method cannot segment all layers well. Therefore, MRF method is used to improve the initial segmentation through iteration until it converges or reaches the maximum iteration.

This paper is organised as follows. A detailed description of the proposed method for 3D OCT optic nerve head images is presented in Sect. 2. The experimental results are shown in Sect. 3. Finally, conclusions are drawn in Sect. 4.

2   Optic Nerve Head Intra-retinal Layer Segmentation

Figure 1 shows the process of layer segmentation for 3D optic nerve head images. The intra-retinal layers for optic nerve head images are segmented by two major steps: preprocessing step and layer segmentation step. During the preprocessing step, the nonlinear anisotropic diffusion approach is applied to 3D optic nerve head images to remove speckle noise and enhance the contrast between retinal layers and background. Intra-retinal layers are segmented by two major steps: preprocessing step and layer segmentation step. At the second step, four intra-retinal layers are segmented by using the combination methods, which include level set method, K-means cluster and MRF.

2.1   Preprocessing

During the OCT imaging of the retinal, the speckle noise is generated simultaneously. The conventional anisotropic diffusion approach (Perona-Malik) [8]

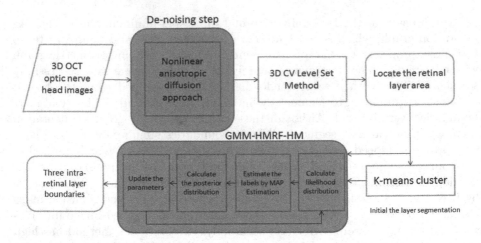

Fig. 1. Block diagram of retinal layers segmentation process for 3D optic nerve head images.

is used to remove the speckle noise and sharpen the boundaries of the retinal layers. The nonlinear anisotropic diffusion filter is defined as:

$$\frac{\partial}{\partial I(\bar{x}, t)} = div[c(\bar{x}, t)\nabla I(\bar{x}, t)] \tag{1}$$

where the vector $\bar{x}$ represents (x, y, z) and t is the process ordering parameter. $I(\bar{x}, t)$ is macular voxel intensity. $c(\bar{x}, t)$ is the diffusion strength control function, which is depended on the magnitude of the gradient of the voxel intensity. The function of $c(\bar{x}, t)$ is:

$$c(\bar{x}, t) = exp(-\frac{|\nabla I(\bar{x}, t)|^2}{\kappa}) \tag{2}$$

where κ is a constant variable chosen according to the noise level and edge strength. Finally, the voxel intensities are updated by the following formulate:

$$I(t + \triangle t) = I(t) + \triangle t \frac{\partial}{\partial t} I(t) \tag{3}$$

2.2 Vitreous and Choroid Boundaries Segmentation

The level set method has been extensively applied to image segmentation area. There are two major classes of the level set method: region-based models and edge-based models. The edge-based models use local edge information to direct active contour to the object boundaries, while the region-based models use a certain descriptor to identify each region of interest to guide the active contour to the desired boundary. In this study, the classical region based Chan-Vese model [3] is used to locate the boundaries of vitreous and choroid layer from

3D optic nerve head images because it works well when there is large gradient between retinal tissues and background.

The energy function of the Chan-Vese method is defined as:

$$E(\phi) = \lambda_1 \int_{outside(C)} (I(X) - c_1)^2 dX + \\ \lambda_2 \int_{inside(C)} (I(X) - c_2)^2 dX + \nu \int_{\Omega} |\nabla H(\phi(X))| dX \qquad (4)$$

where λ_1, λ_2 are constant parameters determined by the user, ν is set to zero. In addition, outside(C) and inside(C) indicate the region outside and inside the contour C, respectively, and c_1 and c_2 are the average image intensity of outside(C) and inside(C). ϕ is defined as a signed distance function (SDF) that is valued as positive inside C, negative outside C, and equal to zero on C. The regularization term Heaviside function H and the average intensities c_1 and c_2 are formulated as:

$$H(\phi(X)) = \frac{1}{2}(1 + \frac{2}{\pi} \arctan(\frac{X}{\epsilon})) \qquad (5)$$

$$c_1 = \frac{\int_{\Omega} I(X)H(\phi(X))dX}{\int_{\Omega} H(\phi(X))dX} \qquad c_2 = \frac{\int_{\Omega} I(X)(1-H(\phi(X)))dX}{\int_{\Omega} (1-H(\phi(X)))dX} \qquad (6)$$

In calculus of variations [2], minimizing the energy functional of $E(\phi)$ with respect to ϕ by using gradient decent method:

$$\frac{\partial \phi}{\partial t} = -\frac{\partial E(\phi)}{\partial \phi} \qquad (7)$$

where $\frac{\partial E(\phi)}{\partial \phi}$ is the *Gâteaux* derivative [2] of the energy function $E(\phi)$. The equation of (4) is derived by using Euler-Lagrange equation [16], which gives us the gradient flow as follow:

$$\frac{\partial \phi}{\partial t} = -\{\lambda_1(I(X) - c_1)^2 - \lambda_2(I(X) - c_2)^2\}H(\phi(X)) \qquad (8)$$

2.3   RNFL and RPE Layers Segmentation

After locating the boundaries of the vitreous and choroid layers, we define a region that includes all the layers. In order to reduce the computation load and increase the speed of the segmentation, we cut the retinal area out alone the top and bottom layer boundaries. The K-means cluster is used to initialize the shrinked data I_s into k classes $S = \{S_1, S_2, ..., S_k\}$:

$$X = \arg\min_S \sum_{i=1}^{k} \sum_{I_s(p) \in S_i} \|I_s(p) - \mu_i\|^2 \qquad (9)$$

where μ_i is the mean intensity in S_i.

However, the k-means cluster fails to accurately locate all the layers due to the blood vessel shadows and intensity inhomogeneities. Therefore, MRF is applied to update the initial input X through iteration until it converges or reaches the maximum iteration. There are four main steps of this method: first we calculate the likelihood distribution according the initialization information; then we estimate the labels using MAP method; after that, the posterior distribution is calculated and the parameter set is updated.

The MRF has been first introduced to segment Brain MR images [19]. Given a 3D image $Y = (y_1, ..., y_i, ..., y_N)$, where N is the total number of voxels and each y_i is a grey level voxel intensity, and $X = (x_1, ..., x_i, ...x_N)$ $(x_i \in L)$ is corresponding initial label of each voxel of the image. For example $L = \{0, 1\}$, the image is segmented into two regions. The RNFL and RPE layers are segmented by using MRF method. Here, we set $L = \{0, 1, 2, 3\}$.

EM algorithm is used to estimate the parameter set $\Theta = \{\theta_l | l \in L\}$. It is assumed that the voxel intensity y_i follows the gaussian mixture model with g components parameters θ_i given the label x_i:

$$P(y_i|x_i) = G_{mix}(y_i; \theta_i) \tag{10}$$

Based on the conditional independence assumption of y, the joint liked probability can be expressed as:

$$P(Y|X) = \prod_{i=0}^{N} P(y_i|x_i) = \prod_{i=0}^{N} G_{mix}(y_i; \theta_i) \tag{11}$$

Start: The initial GMM with g components parameter set Θ^0 is learned from the labels X and image data Y. The parameters can be expressed as:

$$\theta_l = (\mu_{l,1}, \sigma_{l,1}, \omega_{l,1}), ..., (\mu_{l,g}, \sigma_{l,g}, \omega_{l,g}) \tag{12}$$

And the weighted probability of the GMM is:

$$\begin{aligned} G_{mix}(y; \theta_l) &= \sum_{c=1}^{g} \omega_{l,c} G(y; \mu_{l,c}, \sigma_{l,c}) \\ &= \sum_{c=1}^{g} \frac{1}{\sqrt{2\pi\sigma_{l,c}^2}} \exp(-\frac{(y-\mu_{l,c})^2}{2\sigma_{l,c}^2}) \end{aligned} \tag{13}$$

E-step: At the tth iteration, we can obtain the parameters Θ^t, and the conditional expectation can be deduced as:

$$\begin{aligned} Q(\Theta|\Theta^t) &= E\left[\ln P(X, Y|\Theta)|Y, \Theta^t\right] \\ &= \sum_{X \in L} P(X|Y, \Theta^t) \ln P(X, Y|\Theta) \end{aligned} \tag{14}$$

where L is the set of all possible labels, and $P(X, Y|\Theta)$ can be rewritten as:

$$P(X, Y|\Theta) = P(X|Y)P(Y|\Theta) \tag{15}$$

M-step: Next parameter set Θ^{t+1} is estimated through maximizing $Q(\Theta|\Theta^t)$:

$$\Theta^{t+1} = \arg\max_{\Theta} Q(\Theta|\Theta^t) \tag{16}$$

The next let $\Theta^{t+1} \to \Theta^t$, and repeat from E-step.

It is assumed that the prior probability can be written as:

$$P(X) = \frac{1}{Z} \exp(-U(X)) \tag{17}$$

where $U(X)$ is the prior energy function. We also assume that:

$$P(Y|X, \Theta) = \prod_i P(y_i|x_i, \theta_{x_i}) = \prod_i G_{mix}(y_i; \theta_{x_i})$$
$$= \frac{1}{Z'} \exp(-U(Y|X)) \tag{18}$$

Under these assumptions, the MRF Algorithm [17] is given below:

1. Initialise the parameter set Θ^0.
2. Calculate the likelihood distribution $P^t(y_i|x_i, \theta_{x_i})$.
3. Estimate the labels by MAP estimation using the current parameter Θ^t:

$$X^{(t)} = \underset{X \in L}{\arg \max} \{P(Y|X, \Theta^{(t)})P(X)\}$$
$$= \underset{X \in L}{\arg \min} \{U(Y|X, \Theta^{(t)}) + U(X)\} \tag{19}$$

Given X and Θ, the likelihood energy (also called unitary potential) is

$$U(Y|X, \Theta) = \sum_{i=1}^{N} U(y_i|x_i, \Theta) = \sum_{i=1}^{N} [\frac{(y_i - \mu_{x_i})^2}{2\sigma_{x_i}^2} + \ln \sigma_{x_i}] \tag{20}$$

The prior energy function $U(X)$ is defined as:

$$U(X) = \sum_{c \in C} V_c(X) \tag{21}$$

where $V_c(X)$ is the clique potential and C is the set of all possible cliques. For 3D image, we assume that one voxel has at most 32-neighborhood. The clique potential is defined as:

$$V_c(x_i, x_j) = \beta(1 - I_{x_i, x_j}) \tag{22}$$

where β is a constant variable coefficient set to $1/6$. The function I_{x_i, x_j} is:

$$I_{x_i, x_j} = \begin{cases} 1, & if \ x_i = x_j \\ 0, & if \ x_i \neq x_j \end{cases} \tag{23}$$

Firstly, the initial estimation X^0 is calculated from the previous loop of the EM algorithm. Then, an iterative algorithm is developed to estimate the X^{k+1} provided X^k until $U(Y|X, \Theta) + U(X)$ converges or reaches the maximum k.

4. Calculate the posterior distribution for all $l \in L$ and voxels y_i using Bayesian rule:

$$P^t(l|y_i) = \frac{G_{mix}(y_i; \theta_l)P(l|x_{N_i}^t)}{P^t(y_i)} \tag{24}$$

Table 1. Signed and unsigned mean and SD difference between the ground truth and the proposed segmentation results for the four surfaces, respectively.

Surface	Signed difference (mean l± SD)	Unsigned difference (mean ± SD)
1	-0.42 ± 0.65	0.83 ± 0.79
2	1.01 ± 1.13	1.43 ± 1.98
3	0.51 ± 1.14	1.02 ± 1.62
4	-0.9 ± 1.53	1.93 ± 2.21

where the conditional probability $P(l|x^t_{N_i})$:

$$P(l|x^t_{N_i}) = \frac{1}{Z} \exp(- \sum_{j \in N_i} V_c(l, x^t_j)) \tag{25}$$

$x^t_{N_i}$ is the neighborhood configuration of x^t_i, and the intensity distribution function is:

$$P^t(y_i) = P(y_i|\theta^t) = \sum_{l \in L} G_{mix}(y_i, \theta_l) P(l|x^t_{N_i}) \tag{26}$$

5. Update the parameters by using $P(l|x^t_{N_i})$

$$\mu_l^{(t+1)} = \frac{\sum_i P^t(y_i) y_i}{\sum_i P^t(y_i)}$$
$$(\sigma_l^{(t+1)})^2 = \frac{\sum_i P^t(y_i)(y_i - \mu_l^{(t+1)})^2}{\sum_i P^t(y_i)} \tag{27}$$

3   Experiments

We tested the proposed method on SD-OCT optic nerve head images obtained with RTVue-100 SD-OCT (Optovue, Fremont, CA, USA) in Moorfileds Eye Hospital. The age of the enrolled subjects ranged from 20 to 85 years. This imaging modalities protocols have been widely used to diagnose the glaucoma diseases, which provide 3D image with 16 bits per pixel and 101 B-scans, 513 A-scans, 768 pixels in depth. Our methods successfully segmented the 4 intra-retinal surfaces of all the 3D optical nerve head images without any segmentation failures. The signed and unsigned mean and standard deviation (SD) difference between the ground truth and the proposed segmentation results of the four surfaces are given in Table 1. In terms of the signed and unsigned differences, the first surface gives the best performance (-0.42 ± 0.65) and (0.83 ± 0.79), respectively.

Figure 2 shows two examples of three intra-retinal layers segmented results from a 3D OCT optic nerve head image which the layer 1 is retinal nerve fiber layer, layer 2 includes Ganglion Cell Layer, Inner Plexiform Layer, Inner Nuclear Layer and Outer Nuclear Layer (GCL, IPL, INL and ONL), layer 3 is retinal pigment epithelium layer. Figure 2(a) shows the 60th B-scan, which includes the optic disc region. Three examples of 3D OCT optic nerve head image layer

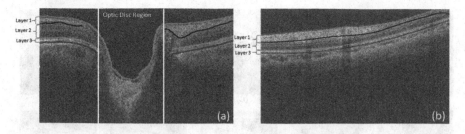

Fig. 2. Illustration of three intra-retinal layers segmented results of two cross-sectional B-scans from a 3D OCT optic nerve head image. (a) the 60th B-scan, which includes the optic disc region, (b) the 10th B-scan. Layer 1: retinal nerve fiber layer (RNFL), Layer 2 includes Ganglion Cell Layer, Inner Plexiform Layer, Inner Nuclear Layer and Outer Nuclear Layer (GCL, IPL, INL and ONL), Layer 3: retinal pigment epithelium layer (RPE).

segmented results are demonstrated in Fig. 3. In Fig. 3, four segmented layer surfaces are illustrated in 3D, and the shape of the surfaces are hypothesised to be related with eye diseases. Figure 4 illustrates the segmented results of 10 example B-scans from a segmented 3D optic nerve head image. Looking at these segmented segmentation results, our method can efficiently and accurately detect each layer of the retina in the 3D retinal images around the optic nerve head.

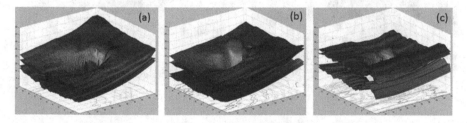

Fig. 3. Three examples of 3D OCT optic nerve head image layers segmentation results. Four segmented layer surfaces of 3 different 3D images are visualised in 3D. The shape of the surfaces are hypothesised to be related with eye diseases.

The RNFL thickness map is useful in discriminating for glaucomatous eyes from normal eyes. Therefore, the RNFL layer thickness map is generated after the segmentation of different retinal layers. With the thickness map of RNFL, we can distinguish the glaucomatous patient from the normal subjects. Figure 5 shows two examples of the thickness map of RNFL of a healthy subject and a glaucomatous patient. In Fig. 5(a), we can observe a thick retinal nerve fiber layer, while Fig. 5(b) displays a thin retinal nerve fiber layer.

The proposed approaches are implemented on MATLAB R2011b, and the average computation time of our algorithm is 208.45 s for a 3D optic never head image on Intel (R) Core(TM) i5-2500 CPU, clock of 3.3 GHz, and 8G RAM memory.

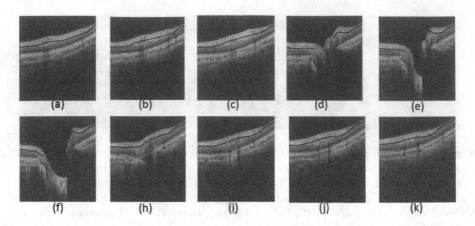

Fig. 4. Ten B-scan segmentation results from an example 3D segmented optic nerve head image, (a)-(k) are 10th, 20th, 30th, 40th, 50th, 60th, 70th, 80th, 90th, 100th B-scans, respectively. According to the segmentation results on B-scans from the 3D retinal images around the optic nerve head, the efficiency and accuracy of our method are shown.

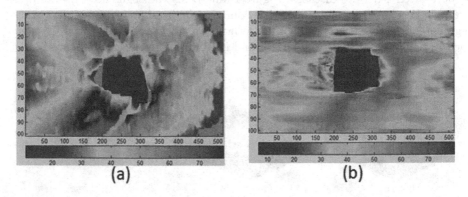

Fig. 5. The thickness maps of retinal nerve fiber layer (RNFL) from two 3D optic nerve head image examples. The RNFL thickness map is useful in discriminating for glaucomatous eyes from normal eyes. (a) a healthy subject (b) a glaucomatous patient.

4   Conclusions and Discussions

In this paper, an automated hybrid retinal layer segmentation method is presented for 3D optic nerve head images. This method was implemented with a typical two-staged process: de-noising step and segmentation step. The nonlinear anisotropic diffusion approach is used to filter the speckle noise and enhance the contrast between the layers as a preprocessing step.

A novel hybrid intra-retinal layer segmentation method for 3D optic nerve head images has been presented. This method combines the CV model based level set, k-means cluster and the Gaussian mixture model based Markov Random

Field. The segmentation results show that our approach can detect four surfaces accurately for 3D optic nerve head images.

It seems that the segmentation process is too complicated to involve three different methods, namely the level set method, k-means cluster and MRF. However, it is difficult or even impossible to segment all the layers simultaneously by using a single method because it requires larger computation memory and longer computation time for a high volume of 3D images. Although methods such as sub-sampling are applied to reduce the volume size, some important information may lose. Conversely, a better segmentation with less computation is obtained by using our method. More specifically, the CV model based level set method first segments the volume of retinal area, the k-means cluster method initialises the volume data into k regions, and the MRF method updates the initialization to overcome the artifacts such the blood vessel shadow and variation of the image intensity.

Acknowledgments. The authors would like to thank Quan Wang for providing the source of the MRF method.

References

1. Abràmoff, M.D., Lee, K., Niemeijer, M., Alward, W.L., Greenlee, E.C., Garvin, M.K., Sonka, M., Kwon, Y.H.: Automated segmentation of the cup and rim from spectral domain oct of the optic nerve head. Invest. Ophthalmol. Vis. Sci. **50**(12), 5778–5784 (2009)
2. Aubert, G., Kornprobst, P.: Mathematical Problems in Image Processing: Partial Differential Equations and the Calculus of Variations, vol. 147. Springer, Heidelberg (2006)
3. Chan, T.F., Vese, L.A.: Active contours without edges. IEEE Trans. Image Process. **10**(2), 266–277 (2001)
4. Chiu, S.J., Li, X.T., Nicholas, P., Toth, C.A., Izatt, J.A., Farsiu, S.: Automatic segmentation of seven retinal layers in sdoct images congruent with expert manual segmentation. Opt. Express **18**(18), 19413–19428 (2010)
5. Fuller, A.R., Zawadzki, R.J., Choi, S., Wiley, D.F., Werner, J.S., Hamann, B.: Segmentation of three-dimensional retinal image data. IEEE Trans. Vis. Comput. Graph. **13**(6), 1719–1726 (2007)
6. Garvin, M.K., Abràmoff, M.D., Kardon, R., Russell, S.R., Wu, X., Sonka, M.: Intraretinal layer segmentation of macular optical coherence tomography images using optimal 3-D graph search. IEEE Trans. Med. Imag. **27**(10), 1495–1505 (2008)
7. Garvin, M.K., Abràmoff, M.D., Wu, X., Russell, S.R., Burns, T.L., Sonka, M.: Automated 3-D intraretinal layer segmentation of macular spectral-domain optical coherence tomography images. IEEE Trans. Med. Imag. **28**(9), 1436–1447 (2009)
8. Gerig, G., Kubler, O., Kikinis, R., Jolesz, F.A.: Nonlinear anisotropic filtering of MRI data. IEEE Trans. Med. Imag. **11**(2), 221–232 (1992)
9. Huang, D., Swanson, E.A., Lin, C.P., Schuman, J.S., Stinson, W.G., Chang, W., Hee, M.R., Flotte, T., Gregory, K., Puliafito, C.A., et al.: Optical coherence tomography. Science **254**(5035), 1178–1181 (1991)

10. Kafieh, R., Rabbani, H., Abramoff, M.D., Sonka, M.: Intra-retinal layer segmentation of 3D optical coherence tomography using coarse grained diffusion map. Med. Image Anal. **17**(8), 907–928 (2013)
11. Kass, M., Witkin, A., Terzopoulos, D.: Snakes: active contour models. Int. J. Comput. Vis. **1**(4), 321–331 (1988)
12. Lang, A., Carass, A., Hauser, M., Sotirchos, E.S., Calabresi, P.A., Ying, H.S., Prince, J.L.: Retinal layer segmentation of macular oct images using boundary classification. Biomed. Opt. Express **4**(7), 1133–1152 (2013)
13. Lee, K., Abràmoff, M.D., Garvin, M.K., Sonka, M.: Parallel graph search: application to intraretinal layer segmentation of 3-D macular oct scans. In: SPIE Medical Imaging, p. 83141H (2012)
14. Lee, K., Niemeijer, M., Garvin, M.K., Kwon, Y.H., Sonka, M., Abràmoff, M.D.: Segmentation of the optic disc in 3-D oct scans of the optic nerve head. IEEE Trans. Med. Imag. **29**(1), 159–168 (2010)
15. Organization, W.H.: Coding Instructions for the WHO/PBL Eye Examination Record (version iii). WHO, Geneva (1988)
16. Smith, B., Saad, A., Hamarneh, G., Möller, T.: Recovery of dynamic pet regions via simultaenous segmentation and deconvolution. In: Analysis of Functional Medical Image Data, pp. 33–40 (2008)
17. Wang, Q.: GMM-based hidden markov random field for color image and 3D volume segmentation. arXiv preprint arXiv:1212.4527 (2012)
18. Yazdanpanah, A., Hamarneh, G., Smith, B.R., Sarunic, M.V.: Segmentation of intra-retinal layers from optical coherence tomography images using an active contour approach. IEEE Trans. Med. Imag. **30**(2), 484–496 (2011)
19. Zhang, Y., Brady, M., Smith, S.: Segmentation of brain MR images through a hidden markov random field model and the expectation-maximization algorithm. IEEE Trans. Med. Imag. **20**(1), 45–57 (2001)
20. Zhu, H., Crabb, D.P., Schlottmann, P.G., Ho, T., Garway-Heath, D.F.: Floating-canvas: quantification of 3D retinal structures from spectral-domain optical coherence tomography. Opt. Express **18**(24), 24595–24610 (2010)

Simple, Accurate, and Robust Nonparametric Blind Super-Resolution

Wen-Ze Shao$^{(\boxtimes)}$ and Michael Elad

Department of Computer Science, Technion-Israel Institute of Technology,
Haifa, Israel
shaowenze1010@163.com, elad@cs.technion.ac.il

Abstract. This paper proposes a simple, accurate, and robust approach to single image blind super-resolution (SR). This task is formulated as a functional to be minimized with respect to both an intermediate super-resolved image and a *non- parametric* blur-kernel. The proposed method includes a convolution consistency constraint which uses a non-blind learning-based SR result to better guide the estimation process. Another key component is the bi-ℓ_0-ℓ_2-norm regularization placed on the super-resolved, sharp image and the blur-kernel, which is shown to be quite beneficial for accurate blur-kernel estimation. The numerical optimization is implemented by coupling the splitting augmented Lagrangian and the conjugate gradient. With the pre-estimated blur-kernel, the final SR image is reconstructed using a simple TV-based non-blind SR method. The new method is demonstrated to achieve better performance than Michaeli and Irani [2] in both terms of the kernel estimation accuracy and image SR quality.

Keywords: Super-resolution · Blur-kernel estimation · Nonparametric · Dictionary learning · Blind deblurring

1 Introduction

Since the seminal work by Freeman and Pasztor [3] and Baker and Kanade [4], single image super-resolution (SR) has drawn a considerable attention. A careful inspection of the literature in this area finds that existing approaches, either reconstruction-based or learning-based, focus on developing advanced image priors, however mostly ignoring the need to estimate the blur-kernel. Two recent comprehensive surveys on SR, covering work up to 2012 [5] and 2013 [33], testify that SR methods generally resort to the assumption of a known blur-kernel, both in the single image and the multi-image SR regimes. More specifically, in the context of multi-image SR, most methods assume a squared Gaussian kernel with a suitable standard deviation δ, e.g., 3×3 with $\delta = 0.4$ [6], 5×5 with $\delta = 1$ [7], and so on. As for single image non-blind SR, we mention few commonly used options: bicubic low-pass filter (implemented by Matlab's default function *imresize*) [8–13, 21, 34, 35], 7×7 Gaussian kernel with $\delta = 1.6$ [13], 3×3 Gaussian kernel with $\delta = 0.55$ [14], and a simple pixel averaging kernel [15].

Interestingly, a related critical study on single image SR performance is presented in [1]. The authors have examined the effect of two components in single image SR,

© Springer International Publishing Switzerland 2015
Y.-J. Zhang (Ed.): ICIG 2015, Part III, LNCS 9219, pp. 333–348, 2015.
DOI: 10.1007/978-3-319-21969-1_29

i.e., the choice of the image prior and the availability of an accurate blur model. Their conclusion, based on both the empirical and theoretical analysis, is that the influence of an accurate blur-kernel is significantly larger than that of an advanced image prior. Furthermore, [1] shows that "an accurate reconstruction constraint[1] combined with a simple gradient regularization achieves SR results almost as good as those of state-of-the-art algorithms with sophisticated image priors".

Only few works have addressed the estimation of an accurate blur model within the single image SR reconstruction process. Among few such contributions that attempt to estimate the kernel, a parametric model is usually assumed, and the Gaussian is a common choice, e.g., [16, 17, 36]. However, as the assumption does not coincide with the actual blur model, e.g., combination of out-of-focus and camera shake, we will naturally get low-quality SR results.

This paper focuses on the general single image *nonparametric* blind SR problem. The work reported in [18] is such an example, and actually it does present a nonparametric kernel estimation method for blind SR and blind deblurring in a unified framework. However, it is restricting its treatment to single-mode blur-kernels. In addition, [18] does not originate from a rigorous optimization principle, but rather builds on the detection and prediction of step edges as an important clue for the blur-kernel estimation. Another noteworthy and very relevant work is the one by Michaeli and Irani [2]. They exploit an inherent recurrence property of small natural image patches across different scales, and make use of the MAP_k-based estimation procedure [19] for recovering the kernel. Note that, the effectiveness of [2] largely relies on the found nearest neighbors to the query low-res patches in the input blurred, low-res image. We should also note that, in both [18] and [2] an ℓ_2-norm-based kernel gradient regularization is imposed for promoting kernel smoothness.

Surprisingly, in spite of the similarity, it seems there exists a big gap between blind SR and blind image deblurring. The attention given to nonparametric blind SR is very small, while the counterpart blind deblurring problem is very popular and extensively treated. Indeed, a considerable headway has been made since Fergus et al.'s influential work [20] on camera shake removal. An extra down-sampling operator in the observation model is the only difference between the two tasks, as both are highly ill-posed problems, which admit possibly infinite solutions. A naturally raised hope is to find a unified and rigorous treatment for both problems, via exploiting appropriate common priors on the image and the blur-kernel.

Our contribution in this paper is the proposal of a simple, yet quite effective framework for general nonparametric blind SR, which aims to serve as an empirical answer towards fulfilling the above hope. Specifically, a new optimization functional is proposed for single image nonparametric blind SR. The blind deconvolution emerges naturally as a special case of our formulation. In the new approach, the first key component is harnessing a state-of-the-art non-blind dictionary-based SR method, generating a super-resolved but blurred image which is used later to constrain the blind SR.

---

[1] I.e., knowing the blur kernel.

The second component of the new functional is exploiting the bi-ℓ_0-ℓ_2-norm regularization, which was previously developed in [31] and imposed on the sharp image and the blur-kernel for blind motion deblurring.[2] We demonstrate that this unnatural prior along with a convolution consistency constraint, based on the super-resolved but blur- red image, serve quite well for the task of accurate and robust nonparametric blind SR. This suggests that appropriate unnatural priors, especially on the images, are effective for both blind SR and blind deblurring. In fact, it has become a common belief in the blind deblurring community that [22, 25–27, 31] unnatural image priors are more essential than a natural one, be it a simple gradient-based or a complex learning-based prior.

We solve the new optimization functional in an alternatingly iterative manner, estimating the blur-kernel and the intermediate super-resolved, sharp image by coupling the splitting augmented Lagrangian (SAL) and the conjugate gradient (CG). With the pre-estimated blur-kernel, we generate the final high-res image using a simpler reconstruction-based non-blind SR method [38], regularized by the natural hyper-Laplacian image prior [31, 32, 37]. Comparing our results against the ones by [2] with both synthetic and realistic low-res images, our method is demonstrated to achieve quite comparative and even better performance in both terms of the blur-kernel estimation accuracy and image super-resolution quality.

The rest of the paper is organized as follows. Section 2 details the motivation and formulation of the proposed nonparametric blind SR approach, along with an illustrative example for a closer look at the new method. In Sect. 3, the numerical scheme with related implementation details for the optimization functional is presented. Section 4 provides the blind SR results by the proposed approach and [2], with both synthetic and realistic low-res images. Section 5 finally concludes the paper.

2 The Proposed Approach

In this section we formulate the proposed approach as a *maximum* a posteriori (MAP) based optimization functional. Let $\mathbf{o}$ be the low-res image of size $N_1 \times N_2$, and let $\mathbf{u}$ be the corresponding high-res image of size $sN_1 \times sN_2$, with $s > 1$ an up-sampling integer factor. The relation between $\mathbf{o}$ and $\mathbf{u}$ can be expressed in two ways:

$$\mathbf{o} = \mathbf{DKu} + \mathbf{n} \tag{1}$$

$$\mathbf{o} = \mathbf{DUk} + \mathbf{n} \tag{2}$$

where $\mathbf{U}$ and $\mathbf{K}$ are assumed to be the BCCB[3] convolution matrices corresponding to vectorized versions of the high-res image $\mathbf{u}$ and the blur-kernel $\mathbf{k}$, and $\mathbf{D}$ represents a down-sampling matrix. In implementation, image boundaries are smoothed in order to

---

[2] In [31] the bi-ℓ_0-ℓ_2-norm regularization is shown to achieve state-of-the-art kernel estimation performance. Due to this reason as well as the similarity between blind deblurring and blind SR, we extend the bi-ℓ_0-ℓ_2-norm regularization for the nonparametric blind SR problem.

[3] BCCB: block-circulant with circulant blocks.

prevent border artifacts. Our task is to estimate $\mathbf{u}$ and $\mathbf{k}$ given only the low-res image $\mathbf{o}$ and the up-sampling factor s.

In the non-blind SR setting, the work reported in [1] suggests that a simpler image gradient-based prior (e.g., the hyper-Laplacian image prior [32, 37]) can perform nearly as good as advanced learning-based SR models. In such a case, the restoration of $\mathbf{u}$ is obtained by

$$\hat{\mathbf{u}} = \arg\min_{\mathbf{u}} \lambda \|\mathbf{DKu} - \mathbf{o}\|_2^2 + \sum_j \rho((\nabla \mathbf{u})_j), \tag{3}$$

where ρ is defined as $\rho(z) = |z|^\alpha$ with $0 \ll \alpha \le 1$ leading to a sparseness-promoting prior, $\nabla = (\nabla_h; \nabla_v)$ with ∇_h, ∇_v denoting the 1st-order difference operators in the horizontal and vertical directions, respectively, and λ is a positive trade-off parameter. In this paper, the fast non-blind SR method [38] based on the total variation prior (TV; $\alpha = 1$) is used for final SR image reconstruction. Nevertheless, the blind case is more challenging, and a new perspective is required to the choice of image and kernel priors for handling the nonparametric blind image SR.

2.1 Motivation and MAP Formulation

It is clear from (1) and (2) that the blur-kernel information is hidden in the observed low-res image. Intuitively, the accuracy of the blur-kernel estimation heavily relies on the quality of its counterpart high-res image that is reconstructed alongside with it. In blind deconvolution, it is generally agreed [19, 22] that commonly used natural image priors are likely to fail in recovering the true blur-kernel, as these priors prefer a blurred image over a sharp one. This applies not only to the simple ℓ_α-norm-based sparse prior ($0 \ll \alpha \le 1$), but also the more complex learning-based Fields of Experts [23] as well as its extension [24], and so on. As a consequence, unnatural sparse image priors are more advocated recently in the blind deblurring literature [22, 25–27, 31].

Due to the close resemblance between blind image SR and the simpler blind deconvolution problem, and the fact that SR is more ill-posed, the same rationale is expected to hold for both problems, implying that we should use a "more extreme" prior for the high-res image. We note, however, that this refers to the first phase of blind image SR, i.e., the stage of blur-kernel estimation. Such an unnatural prior would lead to salient edges free of staircase artifacts which in turn are highly effective as core clues to blur-kernel estimation. It is natural that this would sacrifice some weak details in the high-res image, but as we validate hereafter, more precise and robust blur-kernel estimation can be achieved this way.

Prior to introducing our advocated image and kernel priors for the blind image SR task, we discuss another term to be incorporated into our MAP formulation. We assume the availability of an off-the-shelf fast learning-based SR method that is tuned to a simple and narrow bicubic blur. In this paper three candidate methods are considered, including: Neighborhood Embedding (NE) [21], Joint Sparse Coding (JSC) [10], and Anchored Neighbor Regression (ANR) [11]. Because the bicubic low-pass filter does not coincide with most realistic SR scenarios, such an algorithm generally generates a super-resolved but blurred image, denotes as $\tilde{\mathbf{u}}$. The relation between $\tilde{\mathbf{u}}$ and the un-known high-res image $\mathbf{u}$ can be roughly formulated as $\mathbf{Ku} \approx \tilde{\mathbf{u}}$. Therefore, we simply force a convolution consistency constraint to our MAP formulation, which results in an optimization problem of the form

$$\min_{\mathbf{u},\mathbf{k}} \lambda \|\mathbf{DKu} - \mathbf{o}\|_2^2 + R_0(\mathbf{u},\mathbf{k}) + \eta \, \|\mathbf{Ku} - \tilde{\mathbf{u}}\|_2^2, \qquad (4)$$

where η is a positive trade-off tuning parameter, and $\mathscr{R}_0(\mathbf{u},\mathbf{k})$ is the image and kernel prior to be depicted in Subsect. 2.2. We set $\lambda = 0.01, \eta = 100$ for all the experiments in this paper. We emphasize that the convolution consistency constraint has greatly helped in decreasing unpleasant jagged artifacts in the intermediate super-resolved, sharp image $\mathbf{u}$, driving the overall minimization procedure to a better blur-kernel estimation.

2.2 Bi-l_0-l_2-Norm Regularization for Nonparametric Blind SR

The unnatural image priors that have been proven effective in blind deconvolution are those that approximate the ℓ_0-norm in various ways [22, 25–27]. Instead of struggling with an approximation to the ℓ_0-norm, in this paper, just like in [31], our strategy is to regularize the MAP expression by a direct bi-ℓ_0-ℓ_2-norm regularization, applied to both the image and the blur-kernel. Concretely, the regularization is defined as

$$\mathscr{R}_0(\mathbf{u},\mathbf{k}) = \alpha_{\mathbf{u}}(\|\nabla\mathbf{u}\|_0 + \frac{\beta_{\mathbf{u}}}{\alpha_{\mathbf{u}}}\|\nabla\mathbf{u}\|_2^2) + \alpha_{\mathbf{k}}(\|\mathbf{k}\|_0 + \frac{\beta_{\mathbf{k}}}{\alpha_{\mathbf{k}}}\|\mathbf{k}\|_2^2), \qquad (5)$$

where $\alpha_{\mathbf{u}}, \beta_{\mathbf{u}}, \alpha_{\mathbf{k}}, \beta_{\mathbf{k}}$ are some positive parameters to be provided.

In Eq. (5), the first two terms correspond to the ℓ_0-ℓ_2-norm-based image regularization. The underlying rationale is the desire to get a super-resolved, sharp image with salient edges from the original high-res image, which have governed the primary blurring effect, while also to force smoothness along prominent edges and inside homogenous regions. It is natural that such a sharp image is more reliable for recovering the true support of the desired blur-kernel than the ones with unpleasant staircase and jagged artifacts, requiring a kernel with a larger support to achieve the same amount of blurring effect. According to the parameter settings, a larger weight is placed on the ℓ_2-norm of $\nabla\mathbf{u}$ than its ℓ_0-norm, reflecting the importance of removing staircase artifacts for smoothness in the kernel estimation process.

Similarly, the latter two terms in (5) correspond to the ℓ_0-ℓ_2-norm regularization for the blur-kernel. We note that the kernel regularization does not assume any parametric model, and hence it is applicable to diverse scenarios of blind SR. For scenarios such as motion and out-of focus blur, the rationale of the kernel regularization roots in the sparsity of those kernels as well as their smoothness. Compared against the ℓ_0-ℓ_2-norm image regularization, the ℓ_0-ℓ_2-norm kernel regularization plays a refining role in sparsification of the blur-kernel, hence leading to an improved estimation precision. The ℓ_0-norm part penalizes possible strong and moderate isolated components in the blur-kernel, and the ℓ_2-norm part suppresses possible faint kernel noise, just as practiced recently in the context of blind motion deblurring in [26]. We should note that beyond the commonly used ℓ_2-norm regularization, there are a few blind deblurring methods that use ℓ_1-norm as well, e.g. [20, 25].

Now, we turn to discuss the choice of appropriate regularization parameters in Eq. (5). Take the ℓ_0-ℓ_2-norm-based image regularization for example. If $\alpha_{\mathbf{u}}, \beta_{\mathbf{u}}$ are set too small throughout iterations, the regularization effect of sparsity promotion will be so minor that the estimated image would be too blurred, thus leading to poor quality estimated blur-kernels. On the contrary, if $\alpha_{\mathbf{u}}, \beta_{\mathbf{u}}$ are set too large, the intermediate sharp image will turn to too "cartooned", which generally has fairly less accurate edge structures accompanied by unpleasant staircase artifacts in the homogeneous regions, thus degrading the kernel estimation precision. To alleviate this problem, a continuation strategy is applied to the bi-ℓ_0-ℓ_2-norm regularization so as to achieve a compromise. Specifically, assume that current estimates of the sharp image and the kernel are $\mathbf{u}_i$ and $\mathbf{k}_i$. The next estimate, $\mathbf{u}_{i+1}, \mathbf{k}_{i+1}$, are obtained by solving a modified minimization problem of (4), i.e.,

$$(\mathbf{u}_{i+1}, \mathbf{k}_{i+1}) = \arg \min_{\mathbf{u}, \mathbf{k}} \lambda ||\mathbf{DKu} - \mathbf{o}||_2^2 + \mathscr{R}_1^i(\mathbf{u}, \mathbf{k}) + \eta ||\mathbf{Ku} - \tilde{\mathbf{u}}||_2^2, \qquad (6)$$

where $\mathscr{R}_1^i(\mathbf{u}, \mathbf{k})$ is given by

$$\mathscr{R}_1^i(\mathbf{u}, \mathbf{k}) = c_{\mathbf{u}}^i \cdot \alpha_{\mathbf{u}}(||\nabla \mathbf{u}||_0 + \tfrac{\beta_{\mathbf{u}}}{\alpha_{\mathbf{u}}}||\nabla \mathbf{u}||_2^2) + c_{\mathbf{k}}^i \cdot \alpha_{\mathbf{k}}(||\mathbf{k}||_0 + \tfrac{\beta_{\mathbf{k}}}{\alpha_{\mathbf{k}}}||\mathbf{k}||_2^2), \qquad (7)$$

where $c_{\mathbf{u}}, c_{\mathbf{k}}$ are the continuation factors, which are respectively set as $2/3$, $4/5$, and $c_{\mathbf{u}}^i$ denotes $c_{\mathbf{u}}$ to the power of i^4; as for the regularization parameters $\alpha_{\mathbf{u}}, \beta_{\mathbf{u}}, \alpha_{\mathbf{k}}, \beta_{\mathbf{k}}$, they are uniformly set as $\alpha_{\mathbf{u}} = 1$, $\beta_{\mathbf{u}} = 10$, $\alpha_{\mathbf{k}} = 0.2$, $\beta_{\mathbf{k}} = 1$ for all the experiments in this paper. With this continuation strategy, the regularization effect is diminishing as we iterate, which leads to more and more accurate salient edges in a progressive manner, and is shown quite beneficial for improving the blur-kernel estimation precision.

We will demonstrate hereafter that the proposed regularization (7) plays a vital role in achieving high estimation accuracy for the blur-kernel, and an ℓ_0-norm-based image prior alone is not sufficient for serving this task.

2.3   A Closer Look at the Proposed Approach

To get a better insight for the proposed regularization on the sharp image and the blur-kernel, an illustrative example is provided in this subsection, relying on the numerical scheme to be presented in Sect. 3. Equation (7) is analyzed in a term-by-term way with three of its representative reduced versions studied, i.e.,

$$\mathscr{R}_2^i(\mathbf{u}, \mathbf{k}) = c_{\mathbf{u}}^i \cdot \alpha_{\mathbf{u}}(||\nabla \mathbf{u}||_0) + c_{\mathbf{k}}^i \cdot \alpha_{\mathbf{k}}(||\mathbf{k}||_0 + \tfrac{\beta_{\mathbf{k}}}{\alpha_{\mathbf{k}}}||\mathbf{k}||_2^2), \qquad (8)$$

---

[4] The same meaning applies to $c_{\mathbf{k}}^i$.

$$\mathscr{R}_3^i(\mathbf{u}, \mathbf{k}) = c_{\mathbf{u}}^i \cdot \alpha_{\mathbf{u}}(\|\nabla \mathbf{u}\|_0) + c_{\mathbf{k}}^i \cdot \beta_{\mathbf{k}}(\|\mathbf{k}\|_2^2), \tag{9}$$

$$\mathscr{R}_4^i(\mathbf{u}, \mathbf{k}) = c_{\mathbf{u}}^i \cdot \alpha_{\mathbf{u}}(\|\nabla \mathbf{u}\|_0). \tag{10}$$

Naturally, several other reduced versions of Eq. (7) can be tried as well; we select (8)–(10)[5] just for the convenience of presentation and illustration. With the given parameter values in Subsect. 2.2, we demonstrate that the success of Eq. (7) depends on the involvement of all the parts in the regularization term. In addition, the superiority of the continuation strategy as explained above is validated. Actually, a similar analysis has been made in the context of blind motion deblurring [31], demonstrating well the effectiveness of the bi-ℓ_0-ℓ_2-norm regularization.

In Fig. 1, a low-res version of the benchmark high-res image Lena is provided, that is blurred by a 7×7 Gaussian kernel with $\delta = 1.5$ and down-sampled by a factor 2. We note that other blur-kernel types are tried in Sect. 4. Since we are blind to the kernel size, we just assume it to be 31×31. The SSD metric (Sum of Squared Difference) [19] is utilized to quantify the error between the estimated blur-kernel and its counterpart

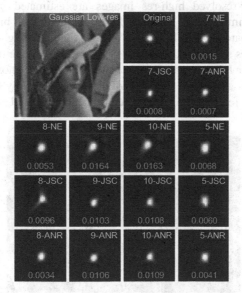

Fig. 1. An illustrative example of the bi-ℓ_0-ℓ_2-norm regularization for nonparametric blur-kernel estimation in single image blind SR. This figure shows the two times interpolated low-res image Lena (Nearest Neighbor), the ground truth blur-kernel, and the estimated ones using regularizations (7)-(10) with NE, JSC, ANR for generating the reference image $\tilde{\mathbf{u}}$. The parts denoted by 5-NE/JSC/ANR correspond to the full scheme without continuation.

---

[5] We should note that we have also selected a uniform set of parameter values for each of the formulations (8), (9) and (10), respectively, in order to optimize the obtained blind SR performance on a series of experiments. However, it was found that these alternative are still inferior to (7), just similar to the observation made in blind motion deblurring [31].

ground truth. For every regularization option, i.e., Equations (7)–(10), we test each of the three non-blind SR approaches, NE, JSC, ANR, for generating $\tilde{u}$. We also test the overall scheme without the continuation – this is denoted in the figure as 5-NE, 5-JSC, and 5-ANR.

Clearly, the regularization by Eq. (7) achieves the highest estimation accuracy compared to its degenerated versions. Take ANR for example: the SSD corresponding to 7-ANR is 0.0008, while those of 8-ANR, 9-ANR, 10-ANR and 5-ANR are 0.0034, 0.0106, 0.0109, and 0.0041, respectively. It is visually clear that the kernel of 5-ANR has a larger support than that of 7-ANR, validating the negative effect of the naive ℓ_0-norm without continuation on the kernel estimation. Also, from the result of 10-ANR we deduce that the ℓ_0-norm-based prior (with continuation) alone, is not sufficient. As incorporating other regularization terms into Eq. (10), particularly the ℓ_0-norm-based kernel prior and the ℓ_2-norm-based image prior, higher estimation precision can be achieved because of the sparsification on the blur-kernel and the smoothness along dominant edges and inside homogenous regions of the image. Lastly, we note that it is crucial to incorporate the convolution consistency constraint based on an off-the-shelf non-blind SR method: when η is set to 0 while other parameters in (6) are unaltered, the SSD of the estimated kernel increases to 0.0057.

In Fig. 2, super-resolved high-res images are estimated using learning-based non-blind SR algorithms [10, 11, 21], based on both the default bicubic low-pass filter and the kernels estimated by 7-NE, 7-JSC, 7-ANR shown in Fig. 1. It is clear that the super-resolved images shown in the second column of Fig. 2 are of much better visual perception and higher PSNR (peak signal-to-noise ratio) than those shown in the first column. We note that ANR [11] (29.5092 dB) performs slightly better than JSC [10] (29.3787 dB) when fed with our estimated blur-kernels, and both approaches are

Fig. 2. Super-resolved images. First column: non-blind results using the NE [21], JSC [10] and ANR [11] algorithms with the default bicubic blur-kernel. Second column: blind results using [10, 11, 21] with blur-kernels estimated from the proposed method respectively based on 7-NE, 7-JSC, and 7-ANR. Third column: blind results using the TV-based SR approach [38] with the estimated kernels.

superior to NE [21] (28.92858 dB), which accords with the experimental results in [11] that assume the known blur-kernels. It is also interesting to note that the TV-based SR method [38] (i.e., the third column in Fig. 2), along with our estimated blur-kernels, achieves better performance than all the candidate non-blind SR methods [10, 11, 21], among which the proposed 7-ANR+ [38] ranks the best (29.7531 dB). Recall the claim in [1] that an accurate reconstruction constraint plus a simpler ℓ_α-norm-based sparse image prior is almost as good as state-of-the-art approaches with sophisticated image priors. This aligns well with the results shown here. In Sect. 4, we utilize [38] for the final non-blind SR image reconstruction.

3 Numerical Algorithm

We now discuss the numerical aspect of minimizing the non-convex and non-smooth functional (6). Because of the involved ℓ_0-norm, the optimization task is generally NP-hard. We do not attempt to provide a rigorous theoretical analysis on the existence of a global minimizer of (6) or make a claim regarding the convergence of the proposed numerical scheme. We do note, however, that there are few encouraging attempts that shed some theoretical light on problems of related structure to the one posed here (see [28, 29]). Nevertheless, considering the blind nature of our problem, the focus here is on a practical numerical algorithm.

3.1 Alternating Minimization

We formulate the blur-kernel estimation in (6) as an alternating ℓ_0-ℓ_2-regularized least-squares problem with respect to **u** and **k**. Given the blur-kernel $\mathbf{k}_i$, the super-resolved, sharp image **u** is estimated via

$$\mathbf{u}_{i+1} = \arg\min_{\mathbf{u}} \alpha_{\mathbf{u}}||\nabla\mathbf{u}||_0 + \beta_{\mathbf{u}}||\nabla\mathbf{u}||_2^2 + \frac{\lambda}{c_{\mathbf{u}}^i}||\mathbf{DK}_i\mathbf{u} - \mathbf{o}||_2^2 + \frac{\eta}{c_{\mathbf{u}}^i}||\mathbf{K}_i\mathbf{u} - \tilde{\mathbf{u}}||_2^2. \quad (11)$$

Turning to estimating the blur-kernel $\mathbf{k}_{i+1}$ given the image $\mathbf{u}_{i+1}$, our empirical experimentation suggests that this task is better performed when implemented in the image derivative domain. Thus, $\mathbf{k}_{i+1}$ is estimated via

$$\mathbf{k}_{i+1} = \arg\min_{\mathbf{k}} \alpha_{\mathbf{k}}||\mathbf{k}||_0 + \beta_{\mathbf{k}}||\mathbf{k}||_2^2$$
$$+ \sum_{d\in\Lambda} \left\{ \frac{\lambda}{c_{\mathbf{k}}^i}||\mathbf{D}(\mathbf{U}_{i+1})_d\mathbf{k} - \mathbf{o}_d||_2^2 + \frac{\eta}{c_{\mathbf{k}}^i}||(\mathbf{U}_{i+1})_d\mathbf{k} - \tilde{\mathbf{u}}_d||_2^2 \right\}, \quad (12)$$

subject to the constraint set $\mathcal{C} = \{\mathbf{k} \geq 0, ||\mathbf{k}||_1 = 1\}$, since a blur-kernel should be non-negative as well as normalized. In Eq. (12), $(\mathbf{U}_{i+1})_d$ represents the convolution matrix corresponding to the image gradient $(\mathbf{u}_{i+1})_d = \nabla_d\mathbf{u}_{i+1}$, $\mathbf{o}_d = \nabla_d\mathbf{o}$, $\tilde{\mathbf{u}}_d = \nabla_d\tilde{\mathbf{u}}$.

Both (11) and (12) can be solved in the same manner as in [30, 31] based on the splitting augmented Lagrangian (SAL) approach. The augmented Lagrangian penalty parameters for (11) and (12) are set as $\gamma_{\mathbf{u}} = 100$, $\gamma_{\mathbf{k}} = 1 \times 10^6$, respectively. Note that, due to the involved down-sampling operator, we use the CG method to calculate each iterative estimate of $\mathbf{u}$ or $\mathbf{k}$. In the CG, the error tolerance and the maximum number of iterations are set respectively as $1e^{-5}$ and 15.

3.2   Multi-scale Implementation

In order to make the proposed approach adaptive to large-scale blur-kernels as well as to reduce the risk of getting stuck in poor local minima when solving (11) and (12), a multi-scale strategy is exploited. For clarity, the pseudo-code of multi-scale implementation of the proposed approach is summarized as Algorithm 1.

In each scale, the low-res image $\mathbf{o}$ and the super-resolved, but blurred image $\tilde{\mathbf{u}}$ are down-sampled two times accordingly as inputs to (11) and (12). In the finest scale the inputs are the original $\mathbf{o}$ and $\tilde{\mathbf{u}}$ themselves. The initial image for each scale is simply set as the down-sampled version of $\tilde{\mathbf{u}}$, and the initial blur-kernel is set as the bicubic up-sampled kernel produced in the coarser scale (in the coarsest scale it is simply set as a Dirac pulse).

Algorithm 1. Alternating minimization for nonparametric blind SR

1: **Input.** Images $\mathbf{o}$, $\tilde{\mathbf{u}}$, down-sampled images $\mathbf{o}_s$ and $\tilde{\mathbf{u}}_s$ in coarser scales $s < 4$, and $\mathbf{o}_4 = \mathbf{o}$, $\tilde{\mathbf{u}}_4 = \tilde{\mathbf{u}}$.

2: **Initialization.** $s = 1$, $i = 0$, $\mathbf{u}_0 = \tilde{\mathbf{u}}_1$, $\mathbf{k}_0 = $ Dirac pulse.

3: **While** $s \le 4$, do

    4: **While** $i < 10$, do

        5: • Solve (11) for $\mathbf{u}_{i+1}$ with 10 iterations of SAL;

        6: • Solve (12) for $\mathbf{k}_{i+1}$ with 10 iterations of SAL;

    7: **End**

    8: • $i = 0$;

    9: • Set $\mathbf{k}_0$ by upsampling $\mathbf{k}_{10}$ with projection onto C for the $(s+1)^{\text{th}}$ scale;

    10: • Set $\mathbf{u}_0$ by $\tilde{\mathbf{u}}_s$ for the $(s+1)^{\text{th}}$ scale;

    11: **End**

13: **Output :** $\hat{\mathbf{k}}$.

14: **Non-blind SR:** Super-resolve the final high-res image $\hat{\mathbf{u}}$ using the TV-based SR method [38] with the estimated kernel $\hat{\mathbf{k}}$.

---

4   Experimental Results

This section validates the benefit of the proposed approach using both synthetic and realistic low-res images.[6] The non-blind SR method ANR [11] is chosen for conducting the blur-kernel estimation in all the experiments. We make comparisons between our approach and the recent state-of-the-art nonparametric blind SR method reported in [2].

---

[6] Experiments reported in this paper are performed with MATLAB v7.0 on a computer with an Intel i7-4600 M CPU (2.90 GHz) and 8 GB memory.

Fig. 3. Test images from the Berkeley segmentation dataset used for quantitative evaluation of each nonparametric blind SR method. Left to right, top to bottom: (a)–(j).

It is noted that the estimated blur-kernels corresponding to [2] were prepared by Tomer Michaeli who is the first author of [2]. Due to this comparison, and the fact that the work in [2] loses its stability for large kernels,[7] we restrict the size of the kernel to 19×19. In spite of this limitation, we will try both 19×19 and 31×31 as the input kernel sizes to our proposed approach, just to verify its robustness against the kernel size.

The first group of experiments is conducted using ten test images from the Berkeley Segmentation Dataset, as shown in Fig. 3. Each one is blurred respectively by a 7×7, 11×11, and 19×19 Gaussian kernel with $\delta = 2.5$, 3 times down-sampled, and degraded by a white Gaussian noise with noise level equal to 1. Both the image PSNR and the kernel SSD are used for quantitative comparison between our method and [2]. Table 1 presents the kernel SSD (scaled by 1/100), and Table 2 provides the PSNR scores of correspondingly super-resolved images by the non-blind TV-based SR approach [38] with the kernels estimated in Table 1. From the experimental results, our method in both kernel sizes, i.e., 19×19, 31×31, achieves better performance than [2] in both the kernel SSD and the image PSNR. We also see that, as opposed to the sensitivity of the method in [2], our proposed method is robust with respect to the input kernel size.

Figure 4 shows SR results for a synthetically blurred image, with a severe motion blur. This example demonstrates well the robustness of the proposed approach to the kernel type, while either the non-blind ANR [11] or the blind method [2] completely fails in achieving acceptable SR performance. Figures 5 and 6 present blind SR results on two realistic images (downloaded from the Internet). The image in Fig. 5 is

---

[7] In [2] blur-kernels are typically solved with size 9×9, 11×11 or 13×13 for various blind SR problems.

Table 1. SSD of the blur-kernels estimated by [2] and our method. "Ours.1" corresponds to our method with an input kernel size of 19 × 19, and "Ours.2" corresponds to the size 31 × 31.

True size	$\times 10^{-2}$	a	b	c	d	e	f	g	h	i	j	Mean
7 × 7	[2]	0.97	0.47	1.06	0.77	1.28	0.83	1.13	1.08	1.46	0.26	**0.93**
	Ours.1	0.22	0.13	0.22	0.20	0.22	0.19	0.22	0.21	0.17	0.15	**0.19**
	Ours.2	0.23	0.14	0.25	0.15	0.27	0.17	0.23	0.22	0.18	0.13	**0.20**
11 × 11	[2]	0.29	0.18	0.42	0.32	0.70	0.56	0.87	0.41	0.62	0.10	**0.45**
	Ours.1	0.13	0.02	0.10	0.07	0.08	0.07	0.11	0.15	0.05	0.04	**0.08**
	Ours.2	0.11	0.04	0.09	0.08	0.07	0.05	0.07	0.13	0.05	0.03	**0.09**
19 × 19	[2]	0.22	0.15	0.38	0.26	0.63	0.30	0.83	0.35	0.55	0.09	**0.38**
	Ours.1	0.11	0.03	0.09	0.07	0.08	0.07	0.14	0.16	0.07	0.04	**0.09**
	Ours.2	0.09	0.05	0.11	0.08	0.07	0.06	0.13	0.14	0.08	0.03	**0.08**

Table 2. PSNR of correspondingly super-resolved images by the non-blind TV-based SR approach [38] with the estimated kernels in Table 1

True size	dB	a	b	c	d	e	f	g	h	i	j	Mean
7 × 7	[2]	21.0	25.8	22.7	23.0	21.1	25.6	21.2	22.9	22.4	27.7	**23.3**
	Ours.1	24.9	27.9	24.0	30.6	23.4	27.7	22.6	25.0	25.8	29.1	**26.1**
	Ours.2	24.9	27.8	24.2	30.5	22.7	27.7	22.1	25.1	25.7	28.8	**26.0**
11 × 11	[2]	21.7	25.9	22.7	23.5	20.6	25.5	21.1	23.3	22.5	27.7	**23.5**
	Ours.1	24.6	27.9	24.3	30.1	23.7	27.5	22.8	25.0	25.6	29.0	**26.1**
	Ours.2	24.6	27.7	24.3	30.0	23.7	27.5	22.6	25.0	25.6	28.9	**26.0**
19 × 19	[2]	21.7	26.1	22.6	23.8	20.7	25.2	21.1	23.4	22.6	27.8	**23.5**
	Ours.1	24.6	27.9	24.4	30.2	23.8	27.5	22.8	24.9	25.6	28.9	**26.1**
	Ours.2	24.6	27.6	24.4	30.2	23.8	27.5	22.7	25.0	25.6	28.9	**26.0**

somewhat a mixture of motion and Gaussian blur. We see that both our method and [2] produce reasonable SR results, while ours is of relatively higher quality; the faces in the super-resolved image with our estimated kernels can be better recognized to a great degree. As for Fig. 6, our method also produces a visually more pleasant SR image,

Fig. 4. SR with synthetic low-res Hollywood (×2). Left to right: non-blind ANR [11]; [2] + [38] (size 19 × 19); Ours.1 + [38] (size 19 × 19); Ours.2 + [38] (size 31 × 31).

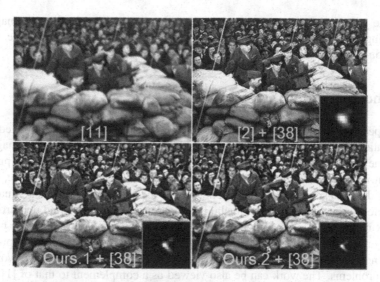

Fig. 5. SR with low-res Crowd (×2). Top left: non-blind ANR [11]; Top right: [2] + [38] (size 19 × 19); Bottom left: Ours.1 + [38] (size 19 × 19); Bottom right: Ours.2 + [38] (size 31 × 31).

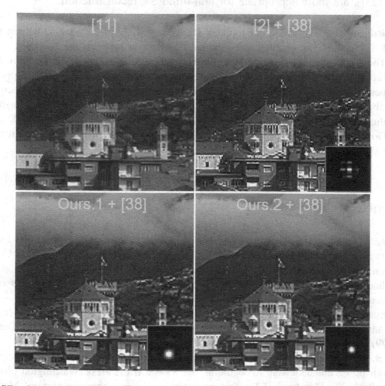

Fig. 6. SR with low-res building (×4). Top left: non-blind ANR [11]; Top right: [2] + [38] (size 19 × 19); Bottom left: Ours.1 + [38] (size 19 × 19); Bottom right: Ours.2 + [38] (size 31 × 31).

while the jagged and ringing artifacts can be clearly observed in the SR image corresponding to [2], which produces an unreasonable blur-kernel. Please see the SR images on a computer screen for better perception.

5   Conclusions and Discussions

This paper presents a new method for nonparametric blind SR, formulated as an optimization functional regularized by a bi-ℓ_0-ℓ_2-norm of both the image and blur-kernel. Compared with the state-of-the-art method reported in [2], the proposed approach is shown to achieve quite comparative and even better performance, in both terms of the blur-kernel estimation accuracy and the super-resolved image quality.

An elegant benefit of the new method is its relevance for both blind deblurring and blind SR reconstruction, treating both problems in a unified way. Indeed, the bi-ℓ_0-ℓ_2-norm regularization, primarily deployed in [31] for blind motion deblurring, proves its effectiveness here as well, and hence serves as the bridge between the two works and the two problems. The work can be also viewed as a complement to that of [1] in providing empirical support to the following two claims: (*i*) blind SR prefers appropriate unnatural image priors for accurate blur-kernel estimation; and (*ii*) a natural prior, no matter be it simple (e.g., ℓ_α-norm-based sparse prior [32]) or advanced (e.g., Fields of Experts [23]), are more appropriate for non-blind SR reconstruction.

Acknowledgements. We would like to thank Dr. Tomer Michaeli for his kind help in running the blind SR method [2], enabling the reported comparison between the proposed approach and [2]. The first author is thankful to Prof. Zhi-Hui Wei, Prof. Yi-Zhong Ma, Dr. Min Wu, and Mr. Ya-Tao Zhang for their kind supports in the past years. This work was partially supported by the European Research Council under EU's 7th Framework Program, ERC Grant agreement no. 320649, the Google Faculty Research Award, the Intel Collaborative Research Institute for Computational Intelligence, and the Natural Science Foundation (NSF) of China (61402239), the NSF of Government of Jiangsu Province (BK20130868), and the NSF for Jiangsu Institutions (13KJB510022).

References

1. Efrat, N., Glasner, D., Apartsin, A., Nadler, B., Levin, A.: Accurate blur models vs. image priors in single image super-resolution. In: Proceedings of IEEE Conference on Computer Vision, pp. 2832–2839. IEEE Press, Washington (2013)
2. Michaeli, T., Irani, M.: Nonparametric blind super-resolution. In: Proceedings of IEEE Conference on Computer Vision, pp. 945–952. IEEE Press, Washington (2013)
3. Freeman, W.T., Pasztor, E.C.: Learning to estimate scenes from images. In: Proceedings of Advances in Neural Information Processing Systems, pp. 775–781. MIT Press, Cambridge (1999)
4. Baker, S., Kanade, T.: Hallucinating faces. In: Proceedings of IEEE Conference on Automatic Face and Gesture Recognition, pp. 83–88. IEEE Press, Washington (2000)
5. Nasrollahi, K., Moeslund, T.B.: Super-resolution: a comprehensive survey. Mach. Vis. Appl. **25**, 1423–1468 (2014)

6. Mudenagudi, U., Singla, R., Kalra, P.K., Banerjee, S.: Super resolution using graph-cut. In: Narayanan, P.J., Nayar, S.K., Shum, H.-Y. (eds.) ACCV 2006. LNCS, vol. 3852, pp. 385–394. Springer, Heidelberg (2006)
7. Farsiu, S., Robinson, D., Elad, M., Milanfar, P.: Advances and challenges in super-resolution. Int. J. Imaging Syst. Technol. **14**, 47–57 (2004)
8. Yang, J., Wright, J., Huang, T., Ma, Y.: Image super-resolution via sparse representation. IEEE TIP **19**, 2861–2873 (2010)
9. Glasner, D., Bagon, S., Irani, M.: Super-resolution from a single image. In: Proceedings of IEEE International Conference on Computer Vision, pp. 349–356. IEEE Press, Washington (2009)
10. Zeyde, R., Elad, M., Protter, M.: On single image scale-up using sparse-representations. In: Boissonnat, J.-D., Chenin, P., Cohen, A., Gout, C., Lyche, T., Mazure, M.-L., Schumaker, L. (eds.) Curves and Surfaces 2011. LNCS, vol. 6920, pp. 711–730. Springer, Heidelberg (2012)
11. Timofte, R., Smet, V.D., Gool, L.V.: Anchored neighborhood regression for fast exampled-based super-resolution. In: Proceedings of IEEE International Conference on Computer Vision, pp. 1920–1927. IEEE Press, Washington (2013)
12. Dong, C., Loy, C.C., He, K., Tang, X.: Learning a deep convolutional network for image super-resolution. In: Fleet, D., Pajdla, T., Schiele, B., Tuytelaars, T. (eds.) ECCV 2014, Part IV. LNCS, vol. 8692, pp. 184–199. Springer, Heidelberg (2014)
13. Peleg, T., Elad, M.: A statistical prediction model based on sparse representations for single image super-resolution. IEEE TIP **23**, 2569–2582 (2014)
14. Yang, J., Lin, Z., Cohen, S.: Fast image super-resolution based on in-place example regression. In: Proceedings of IEEE Conference on CVPR, pp. 1059–1066. IEEE Press, Washington (2013)
15. Fattal, R.: Image upsampling via imposed edge statistics. In: ACM Transactions on Graphics, vol. 26, Article No. 95 (2007)
16. Begin, I., Ferrie, F.R.: PSF recovery from examples for blind super-resolution. In: Proceedings of IEEE Conference on Image Processing, pp. 421–424. IEEE Press, Washington (2007)
17. Wang, Q., Tang, X., Shum, H.: Patch based blind image super resolution. In: Proceedings of IEEE Conference on Computer Vision, pp. 709–716. IEEE Press, Washington (2005)
18. Joshi, N., Szeliski, R., Kriegman, D.J.: PSF estimation using sharp edge prediction. In: Proceedings of IEEE Conference on CVPR, pp. 1–8. IEEE Press, Washington (2008)
19. Levin, A., Weiss, Y., Durand, F., Freeman, W.T.: Understanding blind deconvolution algorithms. IEEE PAMI **33**, 2354–2367 (2011)
20. Fergus, R., Singh, B., Hertzmann, A., Roweis, S.T., Freeman, W.T.: Removing camera shake from a single photograph. ACM Trans. Graph. **25**, 787–794 (2006)
21. Chang, H., Yeung, D.-Y., Xiong, Y.: Super-resolution through neighbor embedding. In: Proceedings of IEEE International Conference on Computer Vision, pp. 275–282. IEEE Press, Washington (2004)
22. Wipf, D.P., Zhang, H.: Revisiting bayesian blind deconvolution. J. Mach. Learn. Res. **15**, 3595–3634 (2014)
23. Roth, S., Black, M.J.: Fields of experts. Int. J. Comput. Vis. **82**, 205–229 (2009)
24. Weiss, Y., Freeman, W.T.: What makes a good model of natural images? In: Proceedings of IEEE Conference on CVPR, pp. 1–8. IEEE Press, Washington (2007)
25. Krishnan, D., Tay, T., Fergus, R.: Blind deconvolution using a normalized sparsity measure. In: Proceedings of IEEE Conference on CVPR, pp. 233–240. IEEE Press, Washington (2011)

26. Xu, L., Zheng, S., Jia, J.: Unnatural L_0 sparse representation for natural image deblurring. In: Proceedings of IEEE Conference on CVPR, pp. 1107–1114. IEEE Press, Washington (2013)

27. Babacan, S.D., Molina, R., Do, M.N., Katsaggelos, A.K.: Bayesian blind deconvolution with general sparse image priors. In: Fitzgibbon, A., Lazebnik, S., Perona, P., Sato, Y., Schmid, C. (eds.) ECCV 2012, Part VI. LNCS, vol. 7577, pp. 341–355. Springer, Heidelberg (2012)

28. Blumensath, T., Davies, M.E.: Iterative hard thresholding for compressed sensing. Appl. Comput. Harmonic Anal. **27**, 265–274 (2009)

29. Storath, M., Weinmann, A., Demaret, L.: Jump-sparse and sparse recovery using potts functionals. IEEE Sig. Process. **62**, 3654–3666 (2014)

30. Shao, W.-Z., Deng, H.-S., Wei, Z.-H.: The magic of split augmented Lagrangians applied to K-frame-based ℓ_0-ℓ_2 minimization image restoration. SIViP **8**, 975–983 (2014)

31. Shao, W.-Z., Li, H.-B., Elad, M.: Bi-ℓ_0-ℓ_2-norm regularization for blind motion deblurring. arxiv.org/ftp/arxiv/papers/1408/1408.4712.pdf (2014)

32. Levin, A., Fergus, R., Durand, F., Freeman, W.T.: Image and depth from a conventional camera with a coded aperture. In: ACM Transactions on Graphics, vol. 26, Article No. 70 (2007)

33. Yang, C.-Y., Ma, C., Yang, M.-H.: Single-image super-resolution: a benchmark. In: Fleet, D., Pajdla, T., Schiele, B., Tuytelaars, T. (eds.) ECCV 2014, Part IV. LNCS, vol. 8692, pp. 372–386. Springer, Heidelberg (2014)

34. Timofte, R., Smet, V.D., Gool, L.V.: A+: adjusted anchored neighborhood regression for fast super- resolution. In: Proceedings of Asian Conference on Computer Vision, pp. 111–126 (2014)

35. Yang, J., Wang, Z., Lin, Z., Cohen, S., Huang, T.: Coupled dictionary training for image super-resolution. IEEE Trans. Image Process. **21**, 3467–3478 (2012)

36. He, Y., Yap, K.H., Chen, L., Chau, L.P.: A soft MAP framework for blind super-resolution image reconstruction. Image Vis. Comput. **27**, 364–373 (2009)

37. Krishnan, D., Fergus, R.: Fast image deconvolution using hyper-Laplacian priors. In: Proceedings of Advances in Neural Information Processing Systems, pp. 1033–1041. MIT Press, Cambridge (2009)

38. Marquina, A., Osher, S.J.: Image super-resolution by TV-regularization and Bregman iteration. J. Sci. Comput. **37**, 367–382 (2008)

Simulation of Interaction Between Fluid and Deformable Bodies

Ka-Hou Chan[1,2], Wen Wu[1]([✉]), and Wei Ke[2]

[1] Department of Computer and Information Science,
Faculty of Science and Technology,
University of Macau, Macau, China
wenwu@umac.mo

[2] School of Public Administration, Macao Polytechnic Institute, Macau, China

Abstract. Based on the Smoothed Particle Hydrodynamics (SPH) and Finite Element Method (FEM) model, we propose a method for real-time simulation of fluid with deformable bodies. The two-way coupling method for the fluid with deformable bodies is processed by the ray-traced collision detection method instead of the ghost particles. Using the forward ray-tracing method for both velocity and position, different normal and tangential conditions can be realized even for the cloth-like thin solids. The coupling forces are calculated based on the conservation of momentum and kinetic energy. In order to take full advantage of the computational power in modern GPUs, we implement our method in NVIDIA CUDA and OptiX. The simulation results are analyzed and discussed to show the efficiency of our method.

Keywords: Smoothed Particle Hydrodynamics · Finite Element Method · Ray-tracing · Two-way coupling · Conservation of momentum

1 Introduction

Physics-based simulation has been widely used in virtual reality applications, such as computer games, virtual surgeries and visual effects in movies. However, the computational burden is very high in the physics-based simulations which involve the interaction of an amount of objects with realistic motion.

Many researchers have presented methods of modeling physical behaviors of a single object, and achieved good results. Studies have then been started to focus on simulating the interaction of multiple objects. Such a simulation often includes multiple objects with complex geometries and different forms of interactions. Therefore, techniques to accelerate the simulation are required. Simulations of interaction systems with high complexity come with higher computational costs, which limit the scale and accuracy with which the models can be simulated. One way to solve this issue is to explore and exploit the computational power of specialized hardware, such as Graphics Processing Unit (GPU). By using the parallelism of GPUs, it is possible to create and develop novel solutions

© Springer International Publishing Switzerland 2015
Y.-J. Zhang (Ed.): ICIG 2015, Part III, LNCS 9219, pp. 349–359, 2015.
DOI: 10.1007/978-3-319-21969-1_30

that better suit specific problems. In particular, the real-time simulations of interaction systems can be obtained by dividing and computing multiple parts in parallel, thus achieving much greater performance.

In this paper, a real-time simulation method for fluid interacting with deformable bodies is proposed. In our method, the behaviors of the liquid and the soft objects are simulated based on the Smoothed Particle Hydrodynamics (SPH) and the co-rotated Finite Element Method (FEM), respectively. A novel method is proposed to efficiently and robustly compute the coupling forces during the interaction of the fluid and the deformable bodies without the complex coupling handling of the fluid-deformable bodies.

The overall simulation performance is accelerated by the GPU. We use the NVIDIA CUDA to exploit the power inherent in the modern GPU. CUDA contains modularized components which can ease the development of GPU-based simulations. Moreover, a coupling-force analyzing method according to physical laws is presented. Our contributions can be summarized as follows:

– A scheme of the ray-traced collision detection method is proposed and implemented on OptiX. No additional auxiliary particles are required in processing the interaction. Therefore, it can reduce the workload and make the simulation more stable.
– Bases on the conservation of momentum and kinetic energy, a novel method to compute the coupling forces between fluid and deformable bodies is proposed.
– The parallel algorithms of the two-way coupling simulation of the fluid and deformable bodies are presented by NVIDIA CUDA and OptiX on GPU.

2   Related Work

In the two-way coupling of the fluid-deformable bodies simulation, the actual forces that exerted on the solid body have been considered and simulated. In [1] and [7], the ghost particles were generated to process the interaction between the solid and fluid particles. The coupling force was computed after comparing the interactions between those particles. Although the ghost particles can easily solve many collision problems, it is hard to generate the ghost particles properly when the topological structure is quite complex. This method usually gives rise to the problem of particle stacking around the fluid surfaces. In [5], Müller et al. still had to allocate the properties of the generated particles, which were used in the exchange of momentum, from the mesh-based models. Yang et al. [9] proposed a coupling method which can handle the perfectly inelastic or perfectly elastic cases, and non-slip collision or free to slip cases. Furthermore, the properties of generated particles were finally retrieved back to the mesh-based model. Recently, Parker et al. [6] introduced the collision detection which was implemented by the ray-tracing method on GPU. It provides more reliable information about the colliding particles and related solid meshes for the coupling computation.

3   Method

Our method is summarized as follows:

Simulation of the Behaviors Respectively. To simulate the dynamic behaviors of the fluid and soft object by the SPH and FEM models, respectively. The dynamic behaviors are updated based on the result of the last time-step without considering the interaction between the fluid and deformable bodies.

Collision Detection in Both Frameworks. To apply ray-traced collision detection to each fluid particle and deformable body surface based on the current position.

Position and Penetration Handling. To combine the internal states with the external conditions in order to update the positions of the particles and deformable body surfaces, and to avoid the penetration occurred in forward checking.

Interaction of Coupling Velocities. To compute the two-way coupling velocities according to the conservation of momentum and kinetic energy about the inelastic collision and slip friction motions.

Rendering and Preparation. To render the fluid and soft bodies based on the current position and to prepare for the computation of the next iteration.

3.1   Fluid Simulation by SPH

In the SPH method, the fluid is represented by a finite number of sampled particles. The Navier-Stokes equation for incompressible fluid can be simplified as follows,

$$\nabla v = 0 \tag{1}$$

$$\rho a = \rho \left(\frac{\partial v}{\partial t} + v \cdot \nabla v \right) = -\nabla p + \mu \nabla^2 v + f \tag{2}$$

where ρ is the density, v is the velocity, p is the internal pressure and μ is the viscosity coefficient. The fluid properties can be expressed by discrete particles as follows,

$$A_i = \sum_j A_j \frac{m_j}{\rho_j} \omega \left(\| r_i - r_j \|, h \right) \tag{3}$$

where A_i is the attribute of particle i, such as mass, density and force, r is the current position, j indicates the index of all the neighboring particles within the support domain h of particle i, and $\omega \left(\| r_i - r_j \|, h \right)$ is the smoothing kernel for the fluid simulator. The support domain h is a spherical space with an effective radius of the smoothing length. Commonly, these kernel functions have a "bell curve" shape and certain kernels offer better results in liquid simulation [2,3].

3.2 Deformable Body by FEM

In Finite Element Method (FEM), the complex continuum is meshed into a set of volume tetrahedrons which are connected by a topological map. The internal elastic force in each element can be calculated by

$$f_e = K_e \left(x - p \right) \tag{4}$$

where x is the current node position and p is the original node position of each tetrahedron, and K_e is the stiffness matrix. Considering the performance and robustness for the nonlinear FEM, the co-rotated FEM [4] was utilized in our method. The global force can be calculated as follows,

$$f_e = R_e K_e \left(R_e^T x - p \right) \tag{5}$$

where R_e is the orthogonal rotation matrix which can be obtained by Gram-Schmidt method. Furthermore, if the original state of the deformable body is static and the topological structure is unchanged during the simulation, K_e can be pre-computed initially.

3.3 Penetration Handling

The forward ray-tracing method can accurately find the intersection point. Each particle emits a ray from its current position along its velocity direction. If a particle collides with a triangle, the distance between this particle and the nearest intersection point can be easily computed. Therefore, we can effectively avoid the penetration which depends on the displacement and the collision distance as follows,

$$p_i^{+\Delta t} = p_i + \min \left(v_i \Delta t, \frac{v_i}{\|v_i\|} dis_i \right) \tag{6}$$

where p_i is the position of particle i, dis_i is the distance between particle i and the nearest colliding point.

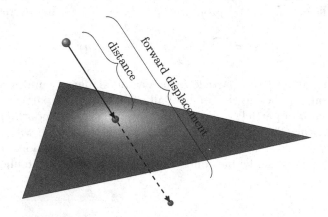

Fig. 1. Update the particle position to avoid penetration.

As shown in Fig. 1, after the forward tracing, the current yellow particle has moved to the red position. By comparing its forward displacement to the nearest colliding distance, the penetration can be avoided by replacing the red position with the green position. The coupling velocity at the green position is calculated.

4   Inelastic Collision

For incompressible fluid, the pressure force is proportional to the particle density. Since a higher fluid density often occurs around the body boundary, it results in the hydraulic pressure that may affect the body motion. According to the conservation of momentum law, the total momentum in the whole physical system is constant and the mass of the fluid particles in SPH doesn't change. Thus, the energy transfer between all boundary faces and colliding particles can be calculated as follows,

$$E_{face}^{+\Delta t} + E_{particle}^{+\Delta t} = E_{face} + E_{particle} \tag{7}$$

where E_{face} and $E_{particle}$ are the momentum of the face and momentum of the corresponding colliding particles, respectively. We obtain E_{face} as follows,

$$E_{face} = m_{face} v_{face} \tag{8}$$

where $m_{face} = average\{m_i\}$ and $v_{face} = average\{v_i\}$, i is the index of the nodes connecting to the corresponding face. And, we obtain $E_{particle}$ as follows,

$$E_{particle} = \Sigma_K m_k v_k \tag{9}$$

where K is the number of particles that have collided with the triangular faces, and k is the index of the collided particle in the current coupling time step,

4.1   Elastic and Shearing Effects

In order to model the boundary conditions, which are essential to implement the elastic and shear effects, the coupling velocity should be projected to the normal and tangential direction as $v_{normal} = n(v \cdot n)$ and $v_{tangent} = v - v_{normal}$ at first, here n is the normal vector of the intersection face. According to [9], the coefficients of the restitution and slip can be determined by

$$C_{restitution} = -\frac{\Delta v_{normal}^{+\Delta t}}{\Delta v_{normal}} \tag{10}$$

$$C_{slip} = \frac{\Delta v_{tangent}^{+\Delta t}}{\Delta v_{tangent}} \tag{11}$$

where Δv_{normal} and $\Delta v_{tengent}$ are the normal and tangential velocity of Δv, respectively. In general, a triangle face may collide with more than one particle at the same time, so Δv can be obtained by

$$\Delta v = v_{face} - v_{particle} = v_{face} - \frac{\Sigma_K m_k v_k}{\Sigma_K m_k} \tag{12}$$

Various boundary conditions including perfect elastic and free slip effects can be simulated by controlling the coefficients of the restitution and slip in the range of [0.0, 1.0].

4.2 Energy Transfer

The velocity of the colliding face can be obtained as follows,

$$v_{face}^{+\Delta t} = \frac{E_{face} + E_{particle} - C\left(M_{particle}v_{face} - E_{particle}\right)}{m_{face} + M_{particle}} \tag{13}$$

where $M_{particle} = \Sigma_K m_k$ is the total mass of the colliding particles, and $v_{face}^{+\Delta t}$ is the intermediate velocity which must be redistributed to the related nodes. Since one particle cannot collide with more than one triangular face at a time, the velocity of the colliding particles can be calculated by

$$v_i^{+\Delta t} = \frac{E_i + E_{face} - C\left(m_{face}v_i - E_{face}\right)}{m_i + m_{face}}, i = 1, 2 \ldots k \tag{14}$$

where m_i, v_i and E_i are the mass, velocity and momentum of particle i, respectively. C is $C_{restitution}$ or C_{slip} corresponding to the normal or tangential direction in Eqs. 13 and 14. Thus, the final coupling velocity of all colliding objects is $v = v_{normal} + v_{tangent}$.

4.3 Colliding Particle Searching

Each surface triangle may collide with more than one SPH particle at a time during the coupling interaction. In order to efficiently searching the colliding particles on each face, two index arrays were used to search the colliding particles of the face.

As shown in Fig. 2, one array stores the index of the face which is collided by particles. Another array stores the sorted index of the particles relevant to the corresponding faces. A parallel radix sorting algorithm was employed, and the sorting performance is $O\left(n \log n\right)$. Based on these two arrays, the first index and the number of colliding particles per face can be obtained.

5   Implementation and Experimental Results

The proposed method has been implemented on the PC with Intel(R) Xeon(R) CPU X5647 @ 2.93 GHz, 12.0 GB memory and NVIDIA Quadro 6000. The SPH, FEM and the coupling method were implemented by CUDA 6.5. The ray-traced collision detection was implemented by OptiX on GPU. The fluid was rendered by the screen space fluid rendering method [8];

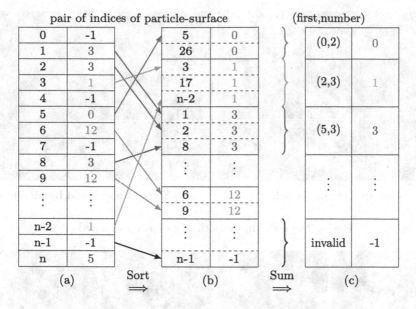

Fig. 2. Flow chart of searching the colliding particles.

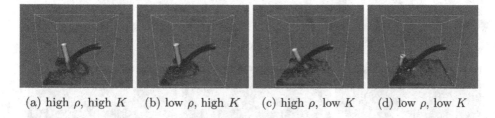

(a) high ρ, high K (b) low ρ, high K (c) high ρ, low K (d) low ρ, low K

Fig. 3. The liquid is poured on to soft tubes with different density and stiffness.

5.1 Experimental Results and Discussion

We tested our method by several scenarios.

As shown in Fig. 3, the fluid interacts with a soft tube in the box, in Fig. 3a and b, the tube has the high stiffness. The interactive force by fluid did not significantly change the shape of the tube. In Fig. 3c and d, a large deformation can be observed because of the low stiffness of the tube. Moreover, the tube with low density in Fig. 3b and d is pushed to the side by the spray liquid. The experimental results show that our method can naturally handle the energy transfer between both materials without additional conditions.

As shown in Fig. 4, the liquid is poured onto the cloth. The deformation of the cloth was simulated by FEM not the Mass-Spring System. This experiment has shown that the penetration can be successfully avoided by our proposed method in cloth-liked object during the interaction.

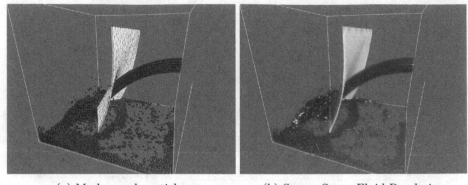

(a) Meshes and particles   (b) Screen Space Fluid Rendering

Fig. 4. The coupling of cloth-like object and liquid.

(a) $t = 3.0s$ (b) $t = 9.0s$ (c) $t = 12.0s$ (d) $t = 15.0s$

Fig. 5. The liquid is poured into a soft cup.

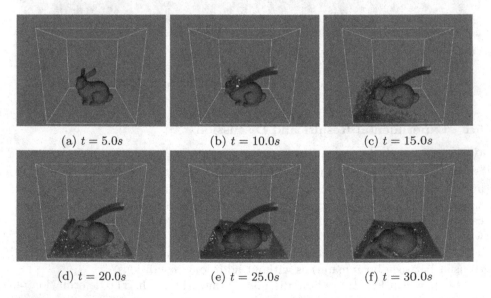

(a) $t = 5.0s$ (b) $t = 10.0s$ (c) $t = 15.0s$

(d) $t = 20.0s$ (e) $t = 25.0s$ (f) $t = 30.0s$

Fig. 6. The liquid is poured onto a soft bunny with high density and low stiffness.

As shown in Fig. 5, the cup has obvious deformed while the liquid exerting pressure on it. It can be handled robustly with co-rotated FEM model, and these SPH particles can be stable staying inside this cup.

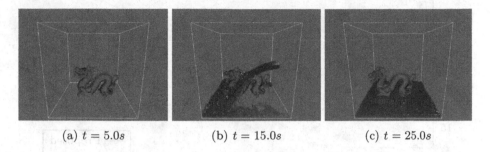

(a) $t = 5.0s$ (b) $t = 15.0s$ (c) $t = 25.0s$

Fig. 7. The liquid is poured onto a soft dragon.

As shown in Figs. 5, 6 and 7, the fluid interacting with the large deformable objects can be simulated in real time. The results show that our method can be used in the fluid interaction with highly complex and mesh-based large deformable bodies. The time performance of the experimental results is shown in Table 1.

Table 1. Time performance.

Soft object	Number of		Paralleled		Ray-tracing
	Elements	Particles	FEM (ms)	SPH (ms)	Coupling (ms)
Cloth	1.9k	65535	11.5	17.9	8.0
Cup	2.1k		11.9		8.1
Tube	6.4k		12.0		8.3
Bunny	22.0k		25.6		26.6
Dragon	34.2k		36.4		41.8

5.2 Comparison

The comparison of our method and the methods using the boundary particles in [5,9] is shown in Fig. 8. Compared with [9], a speedup of nearly $10\% \sim 15\%$ can be reached. It also shows that our performance is quite similar to [5], but our method can avoid the penetration effectively.

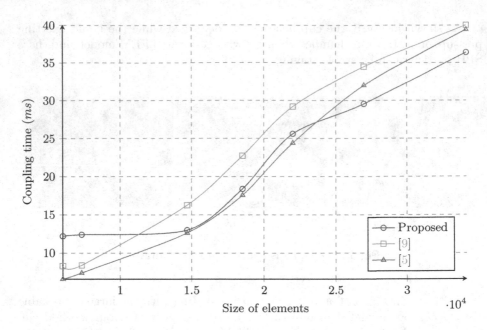

Fig. 8. The comparison of our method and the methods using the boundary particles in [5,9].

6   Conclusion and Future Work

We have presented a novel coupling method for simulating a wide variety of fluid-deformable body interaction. The ray-traced collision detection method has been presented to handle the interaction of the fluid particles and deformable models. Furthermore, the particle-face collecting and coupling energy transfer methods have been introduced. The experimental results showed that our method can reach nearly 10% ~ 15% faster than the coupling method by the boundary particles.

However, one of the main limitations of our approach is that the fluid penetration may occur if the large deformation is involved, since the precision of the calculation by CUDA is not high enough to detect some very close collisions. It may cause some data loss or unstable coupling during the interaction. In order to avoid this problem, either a smaller time-step or a more suitable constraint is required. It is also interesting to extend our method to simulate the interactions with multiple types of fluid.

Acknowledgment. This work was supported by the Research Grants of University of Macau MYRG150(Y1-L2)/FST11/WW, MYRG202(Y1-L4)/FST11/WEH, MYRG2014-00139-FST, and the FDCT project 043/2009/A2.

References

1. Akinci, N., Cornelis, J., Akinci, G., Teschner, M.: Coupling elastic solids with smoothed particle hydrodynamics fluids. Comput. Anim. Virtual Worlds **24**(3–4), 195–203 (2013)
2. Joldes, G.R., Wittek, A., Miller, K.: Real-time nonlinear finite element computations on GPU-application to neurosurgical simulation. Comput. Meth. Appl. Mech. Eng. **199**(49), 3305–3314 (2010)
3. Müller, M., Charypar, D., Gross, M.: Particle-based fluid simulation for interactive applications. In: Proceedings of the 2003 ACM SIGGRAPH/Eurographics Symposium on Computer Animation. Eurographics Association, pp. 154–159 (2003)
4. Müller, M., Dorsey, J., McMillan, L., Jagnow, R., Cutler, B.: Stable -time deformations. In: Proceedings of the 2002 ACM SIGGRAPH/Eurographics Symposium on Computer Animation, pp. 49–54. ACM (2002)
5. Müller, M., Schirm, S., Teschner, M., Heidelberger, B., Gross, M.: Interaction of fluids with deformable solids. Comput. Anim. Virtual Worlds **15**(3–4), 159–171 (2004)
6. Parker, S.G., Bigler, J., Dietrich, A., Friedrich, H., Hoberock, J., Luebke, D., McAllister, D., McGuire, M., Morley, K., Robison, A., et al.: Optix: a general purpose ray tracing engine. ACM Trans. Graph. (TOG) **29**(4), Article No. 66 (2010)
7. Schechter, H., Bridson, R.: Ghost SPH for animating water. ACM Trans. Graph. (TOG) **31**(4), Article No. 61 (2012)
8. van der Laan, W.J., Green, S., Sainz, M.: Screen space fluid rendering with curvature flow. In: Proceedings of the 2009 Symposium on Interactive 3D Graphics and Games, pp. 91–98. ACM (2009)
9. Yang, L., Li, S., Hao, A., Qin, H.: Realtime two-way coupling of meshless fluids and nonlinear FEM. Comput. Graph. Forum **31**(7), 2037–2046 (2012)

Single Image Dehazing Based on Visual-Physical Model

Wang Lin[✉], Bi Du-Yan, Li Quan-He, and He Lin-Yuan

Aeronautics and Astronautics Engineering College, Air Force Engineering
University, Xi'an 710038, China
WangLinsoco@163.com

Abstract. In this paper, we propose a novel model, combining the physical model and the visual model (visual-physical model), to describe the formation of a haze image. We describe the physical process of degraded image based on incorporation of optical imaging physical model and visual cognitive process, enriching the degradation factor. The variational approach is employed to eliminate the atmospheric light, then estimate transmission map via the median filter. We can recover the scene radiance based on MRF model, and use contrast limited adaptive histogram equalization to correct colors after defogging. Experimental results demonstrate that the proposed model can be applied efficiently to outdoor haze images.

Keywords: Haze removal · Visual-physical model · Variational approach · Markov random field · Contrast limited adaptive histogram equalization

1 Introduction

Different weather conditions such as haze, fog, smoke, rain, or snow will cause complex visual effects of spatial or temporal domains in images [1]. Such artifacts may significantly degrade the performances of outdoor vision systems relying on image feature extraction [2] or visual attention modeling [3], such as event detection, object detection, tracking, and recognition, scene analysis and classification, image indexing and retrieval. Removal of weather effects has recently received much attention, such as removals of haze, rain, and snow from image.

In this paper, we focus on haze removal from a single image. Based on the fact that haze is dependent on the unknown depth, dehazing is therefore a challenging problem. Furthermore, if the available input is only one single hazy image, the problem is under-constrained and more challenging. Hence, most traditional dehazing approaches [4] have been proposed based on using multiple hazy images as input or additional prior knowledge. Polarization-based methods [5] were proposed to remove the haze effects through two or more images taken with different degrees of polarization. In [6], more constraints obtained from multiple images of the same scene under different weather conditions were employed for haze removal. Nevertheless, taking multiple input images of the same scene is usually impractical in several real applications. Single image haze removal [7] has recently received much attention. In [29], He et al. obtained depth image of scenes and removed haze effect relying on the dark channel

© Springer International Publishing Switzerland 2015
Y.-J. Zhang (Ed.): ICIG 2015, Part III, LNCS 9219, pp. 360–368, 2015.
DOI: 10.1007/978-3-319-21969-1_31

prior. In [30], Fattal removed the scattered light to restore haze-free color images using an uncorrelation principle, but the algorithm cannot handle gray level haze images.

In this paper, inspired by the Retinex model [8, 9], Atmospheric Transmission Function (ATF) [10], and Monochromic Atmospheric Scattering Model (MASM) [11], we propose a novel model called the visual-physical model. Based on this new model, we propose to estimate the atmospheric light via the variational approach. We can then recover the scene radiance using MRF method, estimate the transmission map and refining it via the median filter. As a result, high-quality haze-free images can be recovered.

2 Visual-Physical Model

The VPM can be widely used to describe the formation of a hazy image $I(x)$, where x is the pixel index, is shown as:

$$I(x) = c(x)L(x) + d(x)L(x) \tag{1}$$

where $I(x)$ is the observed intensity, $c(x)$ is the scene radiance (the original haze-free image to be recovered) [19], $L(x)$ is the global atmospheric light, and $d(x)$ is the atmospheric scattering rate.

Obviously, when $d(x) = 0$, VPM can be used to describe the condition of complex illumination. When there are haze in atmosphere, $d(x) > 0$, VPM can be used to describe the haze degraded image and the image with both haze degradation and complex light degradation [12, 13]. In addition, the atmospheric light $L(x)$ is local smooth, and in this paper, we assume that the atmospheric scattering rate $d(x)$ does not have a local smoothing properties. So, when $|d(x_0) - d(x)| > > 0, x \in N_0(x_0)$, x_0 is the additive noise that cause interference, VPM can also describe the noise.

2.1 Eliminate the Atmospheric Light

The VPM can be described as follows:

$$I = cL + dL = (c + d)L = I'L \tag{2}$$

Based on the variational approach, we propose to estimate the atmospheric light via Kimmel algorithm [14, 20].

As a consequence, it can be written as:

$$\min \quad Q[l] = \int_\Omega (|\nabla l|^2 + \alpha(l - i)^2 + \beta|\nabla(l - i)|^2)d\Omega \tag{3}$$
$$s.t. \quad l \geq i \quad and \quad \langle \nabla l, \vec{n} \rangle = 0 \ on \ \partial\Omega$$

where $l = \log L$, $i = \log I$, Ω is the domain of definition of the image, Ω is edge of the image. α, β are two punishment parameter. $\vec{n}$ is the normal vector of the edge. $|\nabla l|^2$ is a bound term to keep the smoothness of the atmospheric light. $|l - i|^2$ is another bound term to keep the similarity of the atmospheric light and the input image [27]. The last bound term $|\nabla(l - i)|^2$ is to keep the smoothness of $(c + d)$.

With Kimmel's method [14], I' can be obtained.

2.2   Recovering the Scene Radiance

When I' is known, if we can get the evaluation of atmospheric scattering rate d', we can recover the scene radiance from the foggy image by maximizing the posterior probability [15]. d' can be estimated via dark channel prior based on median filter in order to preserve both edges and corners [21].

$$d'(x) = \text{med}_{\Omega_x}\left\{1 - \min_{c \in \{R,G,B\}}\{I'_c(x)\}\right\} \tag{4}$$

where Ω_x is a local patch centered at x, c denotes one of the three color channels $(R, G \text{ or } B)$ in the RGB (red, blue, and green) color space, and $I'_c(x)$ denotes the color channel c of $I'(x)$ [22]. Function med() is median filter function. The noise point which satisfied the equation $|d(x_0) - d(x)| > > 0, x \in N_0(x_0)$ will be filtrated [23].

By using the Bayes rule, this probability can be written as:

$$p(c|d', I') \propto p(I'|d', c)p(c|d') \tag{5}$$

where $p(I'|d', c)$ is the data likelihood and $p(c|d')$ is the prior on the unknown c. In practice, the log-likelihood is minimized instead of the maximization over the probability density function [24]. The energy derived from (5) using log-likelihood is:

$$E(c|d', I') = E(I'|d', c) + E(c|d') \tag{6}$$

The energy is thus the sum of two terms: the data and prior terms [28]. Data term $E(I'|d', c)$ can be denoted as E_{data_c}. And prior term $E(c|d')$ can be denoted as E_{prior_c}.

By definition, the data term is the log-likelihood of the noise probability on the intensity. As a consequence, it can be written as:

$$E_{data\_c} = \sum_{x \in X} f\left(\frac{|I'_x - c_x - d'_x|}{\sigma}\right) \tag{7}$$

where X is the set of image pixels and $f()$ is a function related to the distribution of the intensity noise with scale σ. In practice, a Gaussian distribution is usually used [25].

The prior term enforces the smoothness of the restored image by penalizing large difference of intensity between neighboring pixels [26]. It can be written as:

$$E_{prior\_c} = \xi \sum_{x \in X}(1 - d'_x)\sum_{y \in N(x)} g(|c_x - c_y|) \tag{8}$$

Where ξ is a factor weighting the strength of the prior on the data term, $N(x)$ is the set of relative positions of pixel neighbors, and $g()$ is a function related to the gradient distribution of the scene radiance. In practice, the identity function for $g()$ gives satisfactory results. $(1 - d'_x)$ is an exponential decay, without this decay, the effect of the data term becomes less and less important as haze density increases, compared to the prior term, and the result is over smoothed at high haze density [15]. To avoid this effect, the exponential decay is introduced in the prior term.

The energy function as (6) can be described as MRF model:

$$U(x) = \sum_{\{i\} \in C_1} V_1(x_i) + \sum_{\{i,j\} \in C_2} V_2(x_i, x_j) \tag{9}$$

In this paper, we use α-expand algorithm [16, 17] to get the optimal result of the energy function.

We adjust the image colors via contrast limited adaptive histogram equalization (CLAHE) [18] in this paper.

3 Experimental Results

To demonstrate the practicability and performance of the proposed Visual-Physical model, we evaluate the performance of the various outdoor images with and without applying the proposed dehazing method as a preprocessing step, in Sect. 3.1. Then, in Sect. 3.2, we compare our method with He's [29] and Fattal's [30] methods.

3.1 Experiments on Different Haze Image

As shown in Fig. 1, top of Fig. 1 shows the input image. The second line of Fig. 1 shows the atmospheric scattering rate image. The third line of Fig. 1 shows the atmospheric light image. The bottom of Fig. 1 shows the scene radiance image. The proposed algorithm can successfully restore degraded contrast and color of images.

Figure 1 shows the scenes recovered by the same restoration algorithm derived from visual-physical model with different input image. Obviously, the scene recovered by our method has good quality and visibility. In the red rectangle in Fig. 1d1, we can obtain that our method can well deal with large scene depth image. In the red rectangle in Fig. 1d2, we can obtain that our method can well retain edges. In the red rectangle in Fig. 1d3, we can obtain that our method can well recover texture.

Figure 1d1 shows dehazed image of city scene. Figure 1a1 has a relatively low contrast and appears gray. We produced a better result in Fig. 1d1, where the fog area has clearly been weakened. At the same time, the color of the building has been restored and the whole image is brighter. Figure 1d2 shows the result of close scene image and Fig. 1d3 shows the result of natural scene. We can also obtain that our method can well enhance the contrast of image and restore the color of scene.

a1   a2   a3
imput haze image

b1   b2   b3
atmospheric scattering rate image

c1   c2   c3
atmospheric light image

d1   d2   d3
scene radiance image

Fig. 1. Haze removal using our method. a1, a2, a3 are input haze image. d1, d2, d3, are image after haze removal by our approach.

3.2   Comparison Experiment

Figures 2, 3, and 4 shows the comparison of three methods, where it can be observed that the proposed method can unveil the details and recover vivid color information, but often over saturated in some regions.

Figures 2, 3, and 4 shows a comparison between results obtained by He's [29], Fattal's [30] and our algorithm. Figures 2C, 3C, and 4C show the results obtained by He's method [29], which can retain most of the details while its color is not consistent with the original one, but will introduce false contour on some edges. Figures 2D, 3D, and 4D show the results obtained by Fattal's method [30], this approach cannot well handle heavy haze images and may be failed in the cases that the assumption which surface shading are locally uncorrelated is broken.

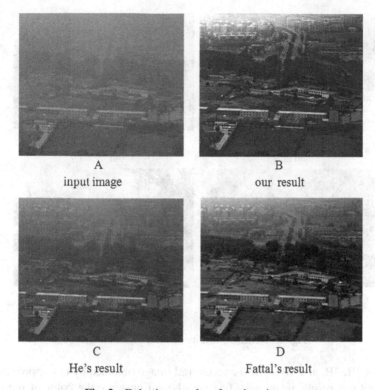

Fig. 2. Dehazing results of outdoor image.

Fig. 3. Dehazing results of indoor scene image.

<table>
<tr><td>A
input image</td><td>B
our result</td></tr>
<tr><td>C
He's result</td><td>D
Fattal's result</td></tr>
</table>

Fig. 4. Dehazing results of road scene image.

Figures 2B, 3B, and 4B show the recovered image obtained by our approach. It can be seen that our results retain very fine details and preserve the color of the original scene. But in some large depth scene regions, the recovered image is too bright. And it contains some white block effects on those regions.

Additionally, Table 1 shows the entropy, PSNR and variance of He's [29], Fattal's [30] and our method. The entropy and variance denote the quantity of information of image. The better recovered image has higher value of entropy and variance. The PSNR denotes the integrality of image structure information.

Based on Table 1, the proposed method can restore the naturalness of original image, enhance the contrast of image, and recover the details.

Table 1. Subjective evaluation results of He's, Fattal's and the proposed methods

	Entropy	PSNR	Variance
Our result	6.1796	18.2017	95.6163
He. K	5.7912	17.9681	89.3237
Fattal	4.6568	13.2778	113.9225

4 Conclusions

In this paper, we proposed an effective and efficient model to describe the haze image. Based on this visual-physical model, we can eliminate the atmospheric light via variational approach, estimate transmission map via the median filter, recover scene radiance via MRF model and correct colors via CLAHE. The proposed method is especially good performance for nature scene. It enhances the contrast of objects but will be over saturated in some regions.

References

1. Narasimhan, S.G., Nayar, S.K.: Vision and the atmosphere. Int. J. Comput. Vis. **48**(3), 233–254 (2002)
2. Maji, S., Berg, A.C., Malik, J.: Classification using intersection kernel support vector machines is efficient. In: Proceedings of IEEE Conference on Computer Vision and Pattern Recognition, pp. 1–8. Anchorage, Alaska, USA (2008)
3. Itti, L., Koch, C., Niebur, E.: A model of saliency-based visual attention for rapid scene analysis. IEEE Trans. Pattern Anal. Mach. Intell. **20**(11), 1254–1259 (1998)
4. Narasimhan, S.G., Nayar, S.K.: Interactive deweathering of an image using physical models. In: Proceedings of IEEE Workshop Color and Photometric Methods in Computer Vision (2003)
5. Schechner, Y.Y., Narasimhan, S.G., Nayar, S.K.: Instant dehazing of images using polarization. In: Proceedings of IEEE Conference on Computer Vision and Pattern Recognition, pp. 325–332. Kauai, Hawaii, USA (2001)
6. Nayar, S.K., Narasimhan, S.G.: Vision in bad weather. In: Proceedings of IEEE International Conference on Computer Vision, pp. 820–827. Kerkyra, Greece (1999)
7. Tan, R.: Visibility in bad weather from a single image. In: Proceedings of IEEE Conference on Computer Vision and Pattern Recognition, pp. 1–8. Anchorage, Alaska, USA (2008)
8. Xiao, J., Hays, J., Ehinger, K.A., Oliva, A., Torralba, A.: Sun database: large-scale scene recognition from abbey to zoo. In: CVPR, pp. 3485–3492. IEEE (2010)
9. Saxena, A., Sun, M., Ng, A.Y.: Make3D: learning 3D scene structure from a single still image. PAMI **31**(5), 824–840 (2009)
10. Adelson, E.H.: Lightness perception and lightness illusion. In: Gazzaniga, M. (ed.) The New Cognitive Neurosciences, 2nd edn, pp. 339–351. MIT Press, Cambridge (2000)
11. Narasimhan, S.G., Nayar, S.K.: Vision and the atmosphere. Int. J. Comput. Vis. **48**(3), 55–232 (2002)
12. Matlin, E., Milanfar, P.: Removal of haze and noise from a single image. In: Proceedings of SPIE Conference on Computational Imaging. SPIE, California, USA (2012)
13. Buades, A., Coll, B., Morel, J.: A non-local algorithm for image denoising. In: Proceedings of IEEE International Conference on Computer Vision and Pattern Recognition, pp. 60–65. IEEE, San Diego, USA (2005)
14. Kimmel, R., Elad, M., Shaked, D., et al.: A variational framework for retinex. Comput. Vis. **52**(1), 7–23 (2003)
15. Caraffa, L., Philippe, J.: Markov random field model for single image defogging. In: Proceedings of 2013 IEEE Intelligent Vehicles Symposium (IV), pp. 994–999. IEEE, Gold Coast, Australia (2013)
16. Boykov, Y., Veksler, O., Zabih, R.: Fast approximation energy minimization via graph cuts. IEEE Trans. PAMI **23**(11), 1222–1239 (2001)
17. Gupta, A., Efros, A.A., Hebert, M.: Blocks world revisited: image understanding using qualitative geometry and mechanics. In: Daniilidis, K., Maragos, P., Paragios, N. (eds.) ECCV 2010, Part IV. LNCS, vol. 6314, pp. 482–496. Springer, Heidelberg (2010)
18. Treibitz, T., Schechner, Y.Y.: Polarization: beneficial for visibility enhancement. In: Proceedings of IEEE International Conference on Computer Vision and Pattern Recognition, 525–532 (2009)

19. Chen, Z., Wong, K.Y.K., Matsushita, Y., Zhu, X., Liu, M.: Self-calibrating depth from refraction. In: ICCV, pp. 635–642 (2011)
20. Liu, B., Gould, S., Koller, D.: Single image depth estimation from predicted semantic labels. In: CVPR, pp. 1253–1260. IEEE (2010)
21. Oswald, M.R. Toppe, E., Cremers, D.: Fast and globally optimal single view reconstruction of curved objects. In: CVPR, pp. 534–541 (2012)
22. Tighe, J., Lazebnik, S.: Finding things: image parsing with regions and per-exemplar detectors. In: CVPR, pp. 3001–3008. June 2013
23. Yeh, C.H., Kang, L.W., Lin, C.Y.: Efficient image/video dehazing through haze density analysis based on pixel-based dark channel prior. In: 2012 International Conference on Information Security and Intelligence Control (ISIC), pp. 238–241 (2012)
24. Zhou, C., Cossairt, O., Nayar, S.: Depth from diffusion. In: CVPR, pp. 1110–1117. IEEE (2010)
25. Mittal, A., Moorthy, A.K., Bovik, A.C.: No-reference image quality assessment in the spatial domain. IEEE Trans. Image Process. 21(12), 4695–4708 (2013)
26. Mittal, A., Soundararajan, R., Bovik, A.C.: Making a "completely blind" image quality analyzer. IEEE Signal Process. Lett. 20(3), 209–212 (2013)
27. Kristofor, B.G., Dung, T.V., Truong, Q.N.: An investigation of dehazing effects on image and video coding. IEEE TIP 21(2), 662–673 (2012)
28. Ancuti, C.O., Ancuti, C., Hermans, C., Bekaert, P.: A fast semi-inverse approach to detect and remove the haze from a single image. In: Kimmel, R., Klette, R., Sugimoto, A. (eds.) ACCV 2010, Part II. LNCS, vol. 6493, pp. 501–514. Springer, Heidelberg (2011)
29. He, K.M., Sun, J., Tang, X.O.: Single image haze removal using dark channel prior. In: Proceedings of IEEE Conference on Computer Vision and Pattern Recognition, pp. 1956–1963. Miami (2009)
30. Fattal, R.: Single image dehazing. ACM Trans. Graph. 27, 1–9 (2008)

Single Image Super Resolution Algorithm with a New Dictionary Learning Technique K-Eigen Decomposition

Yingyue Zhou[✉], Hongbin Zang, Su Xu, and Hongying Zhang

Special Environment Robot Technology Key Laboratory of Sichuan Province,
School of Information Engineering,
Southwest University of Science and Technology,
Mianyang 621010, Sichuan, People's Republic of China
zhouyingyue@swust.edu.cn

Abstract. In this paper, we propose an algorithm to improve some important details of sparse representation based image super resolution (SR) framework. Firstly, a new dictionary learning technique K-Eigen decomposition (K-EIG) is proposed. It improves the classical K-SVD algorithm in dictionary atom updating. K-EIG accelerates the learning process and keeps the similar performance of the learned dictionary. Secondly, image patch classification and edge patches extension are integrated into the SR framework. Two over-complete dictionary-pairs are trained based on K-EIG. In reconstruction, the input low resolution (LR) image is split into patches and each one is classified. The patch type decides which dictionary-pair is chosen. Then the sparse representation coefficient of the LR signal is inferred and the corresponding high resolution (HR) patch can be reconstructed. Experimental results prove that our algorithm can obtain competitive SR performance when compared with some classical methods. Besides, the time-consuming of dictionary-pair learning is lower.

Keywords: Image super-resolution · Sparse representation · Dictionary learning

1 Introduction

Super resolution (SR) image reconstruction refers to a signal processing approach to obtain a high resolution (HR) image from observed single or multiple low resolution (LR) image(s) [1]. For the single image SR reconstruction problem, simple interpolation methods like "bilinear" or "bicubic" interpolation cannot do a good job because only the neighbor pixels are used to estimate the missing information. The enlarged image is blurry especially in the regions existing edges and textures. Some researchers [2, 3] merged the natural image priors into the traditional interpolation methods and generated the image with sharper edges. But these methods are unstable and sometimes easy to produce artifacts. Another kind of methods employs the machine learning techniques which are very popular nowadays. Freeman et al. [4, 5] first proposed this idea and named it as "example-based super-resolution". They estimated the missing details with the help of abundant example-pairs extracted from an external training set.

© Springer International Publishing Switzerland 2015
Y.-J. Zhang (Ed.): ICIG 2015, Part III, LNCS 9219, pp. 369–381, 2015.
DOI: 10.1007/978-3-319-21969-1_32

The algorithm attempts to learn the co-occurrence prior between LR and HR image patches. Then the prior is used in SR reconstruction. Example-based SR method breaks through the bottleneck of the conventional SR methods and generates more distinct image. Inspired by the manifold learning, neighbor embedding for SR was proposed [6]. In this method, multiple examples can contribute simultaneously to the generation of each HR image patch. In 2008, Yang et al. [7] employed "sparse coding" to represent an image patch sparsely over an example set. Moreover, the connection between LR and HR example is replaced by the same sparse representation coefficient over the LR or HR example set. Then, Wang [8] and Yang [9] successively used a pair of learned compact over-complete dictionary to replace the two huge example sets. This change speeds up the process of sparse coding greatly. However, it is very time-consuming to learn the over-complete dictionary-pair. So, some researchers try to accelerate the learning process [10–12]. In recent years, Dong et al. [13] proposed a nonlocal centralized sparse representation technique and Peleg et al. [14] presented a statistical prediction model based on sparse representations, which all generates the better SR images.

Here, we propose a fast dictionary learning technique K-Eigen Decomposition (K-EIG) and employ it into the sparse representation based SR framework. In addition, we merge the classification of image patches and the extension of edge patches skillfully into the whole algorithm to promote the quality of the SR images. The outline of this paper is as follows. In Sect. 2, we analyze the essence of the sparse representation based image SR methods. Then, the details of our proposed algorithm are presented in Sect. 3. In Sect. 4, we show the simulations and results. Conclusion is given in Sect. 5.

2 Reviews and Analysis

Let I_l be the given LR image and I_h be the corresponding HR image which needs to be estimated. Usually, the degradation model can be written as:

$$I_l = (I_h * f) \downarrow s, \tag{1}$$

where f is a blurring kernel, $*$ is the convolution operation and $\downarrow s$ means down-sampling with a factor s. In addition to the prior degradation model, an external training set TS containing various HR images T_h can be used. The objective of the example-based image SR methods is to predict the missing details in I_l by "borrowing" information from some similar examples in TS [15] and then reconstruct I_h. Next, we make an analysis from the following three aspects for the essence of sparse representation based image SR methods. Meanwhile, some representative prior work is also reviewed.

The first aspect is how to build the link between LR and HR image patches based on TS through learning. The link is a learned prior for SR reconstruction. With the degradation model, the LR version T_l for each T_h can be formed by $T_l = (T_h * f) \downarrow s$. For the sampling convenience, T_l is enlarged to be with the same size of T_h by interpolation. Then, a number of image patch-pairs (Tp_l, Tp_h) are sampled from every image-pair (T_l, T_h), representing the LR and HR version of the same region respectively. In the sparse representation based image SR methods, an effective link is through the common sparse representation coefficient [7–10]. Specifically speaking, a Tp_l can be represented by a sparse vector over a LR over-complete dictionary D_l and at the same time the corresponding Tp_h owns the same sparse vector over a HR dictionary D_h. Therefore, a key problem is how to construct the over-complete dictionary-pair (D_l, D_h) to meet the requirement. The second aspect is how to express the LR and HR image patches. In [5], the authors pointed out that the highest spatial-frequency components of the LR image are most important in predicting the extra details. Usually, there are three ways to get them, the high-pass filter [4, 5, 10], the image primitives [15, 16] and the low-order derivatives [6, 9]. For each LR image patch, a signal vector v_l can be formed from its highest spatial-frequency components. For a HR image patch, its mean value or LR version is often subtracted and then v_h is formed. These signal vector-pairs (v_l, v_h) represent the raw image patch-pairs. The third aspect is how to reconstruct I_h from I_l. Usually, the input I_l is scaled-up to the size of I_h by interpolation. Since the SR scheme works on the patches, I_l is broken into patches in advance. Then, the signal vector v_l of each patch Ip_l is calculated and its sparse representation vector α is inferred over D_l. Depending on the link learned in training, a HR version $\hat{I}p_h$ can be estimated. Through the rational combination such as averaging the multiple estimated values for each pixel, a HR image can be obtained.

3 The Details of Our Proposed SR Method

3.1 A New Dictionary Learning Algorithm K-EIG

Assume that the given set of signal examples is $Y = \{y_i\}_{i=1}^{M}$. $y_i(y_i \in \mathbb{R}^n)$ is a signal example and M is the number of signal examples. According to the theory of signal sparse representation [17], each y_i can be represented approximately by a sparse vector $\alpha_i(\alpha_i \in \mathbb{R}^L)$ over an over-complete dictionary D, $D \in \mathbb{R}^{n \times L}(L > n)$. Let A be a sparse vector set $A = \{\alpha_i\}_{i=1}^{M}$. Note that Y and A can be also treated as the matrices. Then, the problem of dictionary learning can be described as:

$$\min_{D,A}\{||Y - DA||_F^2\} \ s.t. \ \forall i, \ ||\alpha_i||_0 \leq T_0, \tag{2}$$

where $|| \alpha_i ||_0$ stands for the count of nonzero entries in α_i, T_0 is the maximum allowed number of nonzero entries in α_i. By now K-SVD [12] is the most prevalent dictionary learning algorithm [18–20]. It alternates between sparse coding of signal vectors and updating the dictionary atoms to get the solution. The creativity of K-SVD is that it updates one column in D at a time. All columns in D except one atom d_k is fixed. Besides, the kth row in A, denoted as α_T^k, is also put in question. So, the penalty term can be rewritten as:

$$||Y - DA||_F^2 = ||(Y - \sum_{j \neq k} d_j \alpha_T^j) - d_k \alpha_T^k||_F^2 = ||E_k - d_k \alpha_T^k||_F^2. \tag{3}$$

E_k stands for the representation error matrix based on the current D and A when d_k is removed. Note that some signal examples do not use d_k, so E_k should be restricted as E_k^R by choosing only the related columns. In order to use E_k^R to find the unknown $\tilde{d}_k$ and $\tilde{\alpha}_T^k$ for minimizing $||E_k^R - d_k\alpha_T^k||_F^2$, the singular value decomposition (SVD) of E_k^R is employed:

$$E_k^R = \mathbf{U}\mathbf{S}\mathbf{V}^T, \quad \tilde{d}_k = \mathbf{U}(:,1), \quad \tilde{\alpha}_T^k = \mathbf{V}^T(:,1) \times \mathbf{S}(1,1). \tag{4}$$

After updating dictionary atoms one by one, a new D can be obtained. Then, go back to the stage of sparse coding. A satisfactory dictionary fitting Y can be generated after several alternations. Unfortunately, the operation of E_k^R's SVD is time-consuming since the column number of E_k^R is usually large. It causes the high computational cost. Rubinstein et al. [11] offered an approximate K-SVD (AK-SVD) algorithm to accelerate K-SVD. However, it sacrifices the performance of the learned dictionary to promote the training speed. Next, we propose a new algorithm K-EIG to accelerate the learning process and try to keep the similar performance of the learned dictionary. The details of derivation are as follows.

For the convenience of derivation, the target function $||E_k^R - d_k\alpha_T^k||_F^2$ is denoted as $||E - d\alpha||_F^2$. Then, we expand $|| \cdot ||_F^2$:

$$
\begin{aligned}
fu &= ||E - d\alpha||_F^2 = \sum_j \sum_i (d(i)\alpha(j) - E(i,j))^2 \\
&= \sum_j \sum_i (d(i)^2\alpha(j)^2 - 2d(i)\alpha(j)E(i,j) + E(i,j)^2). \\
&= \sum_j [(\sum_i d(i)^2)\alpha(j)^2 - 2(\sum_i d(i)E(i,j))\alpha(j) + \sum_i E(i,j)^2].
\end{aligned}
\tag{5}
$$

Note that $\sum_i d(i)^2 = 1$. Besides, we can ignore $\sum_i E(i,j)^2$ because it can be treated as a constant. Therefore, fu turns to:

$$fu = \sum_j [\alpha(j)^2 - 2(\sum_i d(i)E(i,j))\alpha(j)]. \tag{6}$$

The formula in $[\cdot]$ can be considered as a form of quadratic equation about $\alpha(j)$. So, the minimum value of fu is reached at the bottom of the quadratic curve when $\alpha(j) = \sum_i d(i)E(i,j)$. And now:

$$fu = -\sum_j (\sum_i d(i)E(i,j))^2. \tag{7}$$

Thus $\alpha(j)$ is eliminated from fu and we can solve d directly under the normalization constraint with the help of Lagrange multiplier method. The Lagrange function is:

$$Lf = -\sum_j \left(\sum_i d(i)E(i,j)\right)^2 + \lambda\left(\sum_i d(i)^2 - 1\right). \tag{8}$$

Let $\partial Lf/\partial d(m) = 0$ where $d(m)$ is the mth element in d. Then we can obtain:

$$\partial Lf/\partial d(m) = -\sum_j \left(\sum_i d(i)E(i,j)\right)E(m,j) + \lambda d(m) = 0$$
$$\Rightarrow \sum_i d(i) \sum_j E(i,j)E(m,j) - \lambda d(m) = 0, \quad m = 1, 2, \ldots, n. \tag{9}$$

Let R be the autocorrelation matrix of E, i.e. $R = E \cdot E^T$. So, $\sum_j E(i,j)E(m,j) = R(i,m)$. Then, Eq. (9) turns to:

$$\sum_i R(i,m)d(i) - \lambda d(m) = 0, \ m = 1, 2, \ldots, n$$
$$\Rightarrow R(:,m)^T d = \lambda d(m), \ m = 1, 2, \ldots, n \Rightarrow R^T d = \lambda d. \tag{10}$$

Obviously, the solution of the above problem can be obtained by calculating the eigenvector of R^T. We choose the eigenvector corresponding to the largest eigenvalue as the optimal solution of the problem. Then, use $\alpha = d^T E$ to get α. Thus, we replace the implementation of E's SVD with R^T's eigen-decomposition and name the whole algorithm as K-Eigen decomposition. Compared with K-SVD, the advantage of K-EIG is computational simplicity. The reason is as follows. In K-SVD, the object of SVD is the matrix E_k^R with the size $n \times M_k$, where M_k represents the number of signals using d_k. Usually, M_k is related to the total number of input signals M. With the increasing of M, the column number of E_k^R is larger. It results in poor computational efficiency due to the slow implementation of E_k^R's SVD. Whereas, K-EIG implements eigen-decomposition of R^T. R^T is a square matrix of size $n \times n$. It is much smaller than E_k^R since $n \ll M_k$. So, the implementation of R^T's eigen-decomposition is much faster. It makes K-EIG more time-saving.

As described in Sect. 2, based on the signal vector-pairs (v_l, v_h) sampled from (T_l, T_h), we train the dictionary-pair (D_l, D_h) to satisfy the following formula:

$$\begin{cases} \min_{D_l, \alpha} \| v_l^{(i)} - D_l \cdot \alpha^{(i)} \|_2^2 \ s.t. \ \| \alpha^{(i)} \|_0 \leq T_0 \\ \min_{D_h, \alpha} \| v_h^{(i)} - D_h \cdot \alpha^{(i)} \|_2^2 \ s.t. \ \| \alpha^{(i)} \|_0 \leq T_0 \end{cases}, \quad \forall i \in \{1, 2, \ldots, M\}. \tag{11}$$

In order to get (D_l, D_h), we first generate D_l based on $\{v_l^{(1)}, v_l^{(2)}, \ldots, v_l^{(M)}\}$ by solving:

$$\boldsymbol{D}_l, \{\boldsymbol{\alpha}^{(i)}\} = \arg\min_{\boldsymbol{D}_l, \{\boldsymbol{\alpha}^{(i)}\}} \sum_{i=1}^{M} \parallel \boldsymbol{v}_l^{(i)} - \boldsymbol{D}_l \cdot \boldsymbol{\alpha}^{(i)} \parallel_2^2, \; s.t. \; \parallel \boldsymbol{\alpha}^{(i)} \parallel_0 \; \leq T_0, \quad \forall i \in \{1, 2, \ldots, M\}.$$

(12)

K-EIG can serve the above problem and we get $\boldsymbol{D}_l$ and $\{\boldsymbol{\alpha}^{(i)}\}$. Then, $\{\boldsymbol{\alpha}^{(i)}\}$ and $\{\boldsymbol{v}_h^{(1)}, \boldsymbol{v}_h^{(2)}, \ldots, \boldsymbol{v}_h^{(M)}\}$ both guide the computation of $\boldsymbol{D}_h$ directly as the way in [10]. Let $\boldsymbol{V}_h = [\boldsymbol{v}_h^{(1)}, \boldsymbol{v}_h^{(2)}, \ldots, \boldsymbol{v}_h^{(M)}]$ and $\boldsymbol{A} = [\boldsymbol{\alpha}^{(1)}, \boldsymbol{\alpha}^{(2)}, \ldots, \boldsymbol{\alpha}^{(M)}]$, then $\boldsymbol{D}_h$ can be obtained by $\boldsymbol{D}_h = \boldsymbol{V}_h \cdot \boldsymbol{A}^T \cdot (\boldsymbol{A}\boldsymbol{A}^T)^{-1}$. Now, $(\boldsymbol{D}_l, \boldsymbol{D}_h)$ can meet the requirement of common sparse representation coefficient. Compared with the joint dictionary training method used in [9], the direct dictionary-pair construction method employing K-EIG is fast and effective.

3.2   Sparse Representation Based SR Framework with Example Classification and Extension

Considering the types of image patches, we do an important work before training. That is classification for the sampled image patches. Each patch-pair $(\boldsymbol{Tp}_l, \boldsymbol{Tp}_h)$ will be put into a classifier and then marked by a label "smooth" or "edge". We employ the sorted quadrant median vector (SQMV) scheme proposed in [21] to classify every $\boldsymbol{Tp}_h$. SQMV is a simple but efficient tool to recognize an image patch belonging to uniform region or edge region. Then, the set of example-pairs is separated into two parts, "smooth" set and "edge" set. In order to increase the number of "edge" patch-pairs before learning, we rotate each HR image $\boldsymbol{T}_h$ by three different angles (90°, 180° and 270°) and three different images are formed. Then, we can generate more "edge" patch-pairs. For "smooth" class, there is no need to increase the patch number. Based on the two sets of signal vector-pairs, two different dictionary-pairs $(\boldsymbol{D}_l^{smooth}, \boldsymbol{D}_h^{smooth})$ and $(\boldsymbol{D}_l^{edge}, \boldsymbol{D}_h^{edge})$ are constructed respectively.

In reconstruction, the input LR image $\boldsymbol{I}_l$ is first interpolated to the objective size and then broken into lots of overlapped patches $\boldsymbol{Ip}_l$ with the size of $w \times w$. For each $\boldsymbol{Ip}_l$, we use the first-order combining second-order derivatives to represent it and form a signal vector $\boldsymbol{v}_l$. Through labeling $\boldsymbol{Ip}_l$ by SQMV scheme, we choose the appropriate dictionary-pair $(\boldsymbol{D}_l^{smooth}, \boldsymbol{D}_h^{smooth})$ or $(\boldsymbol{D}_l^{edge}, \boldsymbol{D}_h^{edge})$ for SR. A key problem is to infer the sparse representation vector of $\boldsymbol{v}_l$ over $\boldsymbol{D}_l$ by $\hat{\boldsymbol{\alpha}} = \arg\min_{\boldsymbol{\alpha}} \parallel \boldsymbol{v}_l - \boldsymbol{D}_l \cdot \boldsymbol{\alpha} \parallel_2^2 \; s.t. \; \parallel \boldsymbol{\alpha} \parallel_0 \; \leq T_0$. Orthogonal matching pursuit (OMP) [22] or convex relaxation techniques [17] can be used to solve the problem. After getting $\hat{\boldsymbol{\alpha}}$ for $\boldsymbol{Ip}_l$, we can reconstruct its HR version by $\hat{\boldsymbol{Ip}}_h = \boldsymbol{Ip}_l + reshape(\boldsymbol{D}_h \cdot \hat{\boldsymbol{\alpha}})$ where $reshape(\cdot)$ means rearranging a vector to a patch. By the simple "averaging" of these overlapped $\hat{\boldsymbol{Ip}}_h$, we get the estimated HR image $\hat{\boldsymbol{I}}_h$. Besides, to satisfy the degradation model, we add an operation of "backprojection" [9] to modify $\hat{\boldsymbol{I}}_h$ and generate the last $\hat{\boldsymbol{I}}_h$.

4 Simulations and Results

4.1 Testing the Performance of K-EIG

We test the performance of K-EIG by a synthetic experiment and compare it with other typical dictionary learning algorithms. A random matrix D_g of size 20×50 is generated with i.i.d uniformly distributed entries. Each column is normalized to a unit ℓ_2-norm. Then a number of data signals $\{y_i\}_{i=1}^M$ of dimension 20 are produced. Each signal is created by a linear combination of three different atoms in D_g, with uniformly distributed i.i.d coefficients in random and independent locations. Then, K-SVD [12], AK-SVD [11] and K-EIG are implemented respectively to obtain three recovered dictionaries D_r based on $\{y_i\}_{i=1}^M$ and then we observe which D_r is closest to D_g. Authors can see [12] for more details about success ratio computation. In order to test the robustness of algorithm, white Gaussian noise with varying signal-to-noise ratio (SNR) is added to $\{y_i\}_{i=1}^M$. Let $M = 1500$ and $T_0 = 3$. Set the number of alternate iteration by 30. The results of atom recovery performance are shown in Table 1. We see that K-SVD obtains the best performance under any SNR situation. The average success ratio of K-EIG is very close to K-SVD. AK-SVD is inferior to the other two algorithms. Besides, we compare the running speed of the three algorithms. We change the input signal number from $M = 1000$ to $M = 96000$ with interval of 5000 and keep the other parameters unchanged. The running platform is MATLAB 2009 and the computer is equipped with 2.60 GHZ Inter (R) Core(TM) i5 CPU & 4.0 GB memory. Figure 1 shows the time consuming curve. We see that the computation time of K-SVD rises rapidly with the increasing of input signals number. On the contrary, the time consuming of K-EIG and AK-SVD always keeps a low level even in the situation of large M.

Table 1. Comparison of several dictionary learning algorithms in average success ratio of atom recovery

SNR (dB)	K-SVD	AK-SVD	K-EIG
20	92.68 %	91.48 %	92.64 %
15	89.24 %	88.36 %	88.72 %
10	86.44 %	83.28 %	85.92 %
8	70.08 %	66.60 %	69.32 %

4.2 Testing Image SR Performance

In our SR experiments, we use a training set TS containing some HR natural images such as flowers, architectures, animals and human faces. In simulation, we assume that the degradation model $I_l = (I_h * f) \downarrow s$ is operated by the "bicubic filter" with a zoom factor $1/s$. During training, we extract about 8×10^4 image patch-pairs to be the training examples for each class. The patch size is 5×5. The column number of D_l or D_h is set by 1000. The number of alternate iteration of K-EIG is set by 40. Five color images are chosen as the test images. They are "lena", "child", "flower", "building", and "zebra". Then, five corresponding LR images are generated by the known

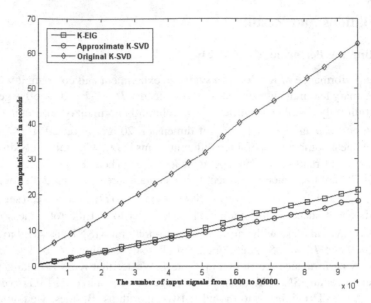

Fig. 1. Time consuming curve of three dictionary learning algorithms

degradation model. Our task is to reconstruct the HR versions of these LR images. As the way in other literatures, we just apply our SR algorithm to the illuminance channel (Y). The other channels (Cb, Cr) are processed by bicubic interpolation simply. Several representative and related image SR methods are also implemented for comparison purpose. They are "bicubic interpolation", "neighbor embedding [6]", "Yang's method [9]" and "Zeyde's method [10]". We choose the peak signal-to-noise ratio (PSNR) and the mean structure similarity index measure (MSSIM) [23] as the performance indexes to measure the quality of the reconstructed image.

We show the quantitative SR results in Tables 2 and 3 in case of $s = 2$ and $s = 3$. Clearly, our proposed method achieves the highest PSNRs and MSSIMs for all the test

Table 2. PSNRs (MSSIMs) results of reconstructed images with $s = 2$

Image	$s = 2$				
	Bicubic interpolation	Neigbor embedding	Yang's	Zeyde's	Our algorithm
Lena	35.41 (0.9297)	34.78 (0.9169)	37.24 (0.9436)	36.86 (0.9411)	37.56 (0.9457)
Child	37.06 (0.9513)	35.73 (0.9345)	38.37 (0.9629)	38.07 (0.9606)	38.64 (0.9659)
Flower	30.42 (0.8985)	29.81 (0.8764)	32.55 (0.9301)	32.11 (0.9249)	32.92 (0.9339)
Building	28.81 (0.8525)	27.92 (0.8233)	30.22 (0.8886)	29.91 (0.8817)	30.57 (0.8918)
Zebra	30.68 (0.9084)	29.80 (0.8774)	33.33 (0.9410)	32.86 (0.9352)	33.66 (0.9440)

Table 3. PSNRs (MSSIMs) results of reconstructed images with $s = 3$

Image	$s = 3$				
	Bicubic interpolation	Neigbor embedding	Yang's	Zeyde's	Our algorithm
Lena	32.11 (0.8798)	31.52 (0.8592)	33.57 (0.8997)	33.42 (0.8973)	33.63 (0.9009)
Child	33.94 (0.9042)	32.73 (0.8760)	34.97 (0.9206)	34.98 (0.9195)	35.18 (0.9225)
Flower	27.32 (0.8027)	26.71 (0.7644)	28.62 (0.8427)	28.50 (0.8388)	28.66 (0.8440)
Building	26.14 (0.7518)	25.54 (0.7208)	26.77 (0.7839)	26.73 (0.7788)	26.85 (0.7861)
Zebra	26.69 (0.7946)	25.57 (0.7383)	28.49 (0.8445)	28.50 (0.8390)	28.78 (0.8484)

images. In order to compare the reconstruction results visually, we present the estimated HR images by nearest interpolation, bicubic interpolation, neighbor embedding, Yang's, Zeyde's and our method in case of $s = 3$ in Figs. 2 and 3. Meanwhile, some details are magnified to clearly display the subtle difference. From them, we see that bicubic interpolation eliminates the sawtooth appearance in the images obtained by

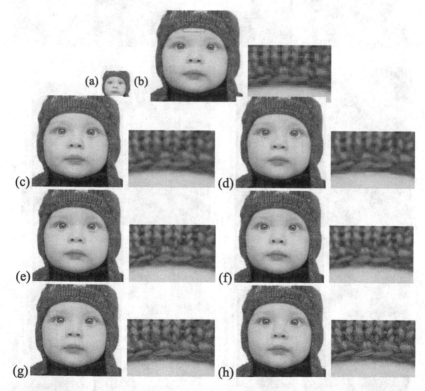

Fig. 2. (a) Input LR 'child' image, (b) estimated HR 'child' by nearest interpolation, (c) estimated HR 'child' by bicubic interpolation, (d) estimated HR 'child' by neigbor embedding, (e) estimated HR 'child' by Yang's method, (f) estimated HR 'child' by Zeyde's, (g) estimated HR 'child' by our method, (h) original 'child' image.

Fig. 3. (a) Input LR 'building' image, (b) estimated HR 'building' by nearest interpolation, (c) estimated HR 'building' by bicubic interpolation, (d) estimated HR 'building' by neigbor embedding, (e) estimated HR 'building' by Yang's method, (f) estimated HR 'building' by Zeyde's, (g) estimated HR 'building' by our method, (h) original 'building' image.

nearest interpolation, but it generates the blurred edges. Neighbor embedding is easy to produce some artifacts. For example, in the part between hat and face in Fig. 2(d), we can observe the discontinuous. Sparse representation based methods generate clearer HR images. Among them, our algorithm obtains the best results which are closest to the original HR images, thanks to the integration of patch classification and edge patches extension into the SR framework. In Fig. 3, we can see obviously that the lattice in Fig. 3(g) is reconstructed better than Fig. 3(b) and (f).

4.3   Testing the Time Performance of Dictionary-Pair Construction

Here, we compare the time performance of the three dictionary-pair construction methods (Yang's, Zeyde's and ours). The platform and computer configuration are the same as description in Sect. 4.1. The CPU running time is presented in Table 4. Obviously, our and Zeyde's method are much faster than Yang's method. Our method is slightly slower than Zeyde's one because our training process includes patch-classification, edge-patches extension and learning of two dictionary-pairs. It is worthy of spending more several minutes to obtain better dictionary-pair.

Table 4. Time comparison of three dictionary-pair constructing methods

Method	Time consuming (in s)
Yang's	10007
Zeyde's	238
Ours	411

5   Conclusion

In this paper, we propose a sparse representation based single image super resolution algorithm with a new dictionary learning technique K-EIG. Our proposed K-EIG is an improved algorithm based on the classical K-SVD algorithm. It replaces the implementation of SVD about the representation error matrix with eigen-decomposition about its autocorrelation matrix. This change overcomes the drawback that the operation of SVD is time-consuming in case of the large number of training examples. We employ a direct dictionary-pair construction method based on K-EIG to accelerate the whole training process. Besides, considering the types of image patches and the number of edge examples, patch classification and edge patches extension are integrated rationally into the SR framework. Extensive experimental results show that our SR algorithm generates better SR images compared with some classical or related methods.

Acknowledgment. This research is supported by the National Natural Science Foundation of China (Grant No.61401379), the General Project of Educational Commission of Sichuan Province in China (Grant No.14ZB0107), the Doctoral Research Fund of Southwest University of

Science and Technology in China (Grant No.13zx7148) and the Key Project of Educational Commission of Sichuan Province in China (Grant No.11ZA130).

References

1. Park, S.C., Park, M.K., Kang, M.G.: Super-resolution image reconstruction: a technical overview. IEEE Signal Process. Mag. **20**(3), 21–36 (2003)
2. Sun, J., Xu, Z., Shum, H.: Image super-resolution using gradient profile prior. In: Proceedings of IEEE Conference on Computer Vision and Pattern Recognition, pp. 1–8 (2008)
3. Dai, S., Han, M., Xu, W.: SoftCuts: a soft edge smoothness prior for color image super-resolution. IEEE Trans. Image Process. **18**(5), 969–981 (2009)
4. Freeman, W.T., Pasztor, E.C., Carmichael, O.T.: Learning low-level vision. Int. J. Comput. Vis. **40**(1), 25–47 (2000)
5. Freeman, W.T., Jones, T.R., Pasztor, E.C.: Example-Based super-resolution. IEEE Comput. Graphics Appl. **22**(2), 56–65 (2002)
6. Chang, H., Yeung, D.Y., Xiong, Y.: Super-resolution through neighbor embedding. In: Proceedings of IEEE Conference on Computer Vision and Pattern Recognition, pp. 275–282 (2004)
7. Yang, J., Wright, J., Huang, T., et al.: Image super-resolution as sparse representation of raw image patches. In: Proceedings of IEEE Conference on Computer Vision and Pattern Recognition, pp. 1–8 (2008)
8. Wang, J., Zhu, S., Gong, Y.: Resolution enhancement based on learning the sparse association of image patches. Pattern Recogn. Lett. **31**(1), 1–10 (2010)
9. Yang, J., Wright, J., Huang, T., et al.: Image super-resolution via sparse representation. IEEE Trans. Image Process. **19**(11), 1–8 (2010)
10. Zeyde, R., Elad, M., Protter, M.: On single image scale-up using sparse-representations. In: Boissonnat, J.-D., Chenin, P., Cohen, A., Gout, C., Lyche, T., Mazure, M.-L., Schumaker, L. (eds.) Curves and Surfaces. Lecture Notes in Computer Science, vol. 6920, pp. 711–730. Springer, Heidelberg (2010)
11. Rubinstein, R., Zibulevsky, M., Elad, M.: Efficient implementation of the K-SVD algorithm using batch orthogonal matching pursuit. Technical report, Technion-Israel Institute of Technology (2008)
12. Aharon, M., Elad, M., Bruckstein, A.: K-SVD: an algorithm for designing overcomplete dictionaries for sparse representation. IEEE Trans. Signal Process. **54**(11), 4311–4322 (2006)
13. Dong, W., Zhang, L., Lukac, R., Shi, G.: Nonlocal centralized sparse representation for image restoration. IEEE Trans. Image Process. **22**(4), 1382–1394 (2013)
14. Peleg, T., Elad, M.: A statistical prediction model based on sparse representations for single image super-resolution. IEEE Trans. Image Process. **23**(7), 3085–3098 (2014)
15. Fan, W., Yeung, D.Y.: Image hallucination using neighbor embedding over visual primitive manifolds. In: Proceedings of IEEE Conference on Computer Vision Pattern Recognition (2007)
16. Li, H., Xiong, H., Qian L.: Image super-resolution with sparse representation prior on primitives. In: Proceedings of Visual Communications and Image Processing (2010)
17. Elad, M.: Sparse and Redundant Representations From Theory to Applications in Signal and Image Processing. Springer, New York (2010)

18. Elad, M., Aharon, M.: Image denoising via sparse and redundant representations over learned dictionaries. IEEE Trans. Image Process. **15**(12), 3736–3745 (2006)
19. Zhou, Y., Ye, Z., Xiao, Y.: A restoration algorithm for images contaminated by mixed Gaussian plus random-valued impulse noise. J. Vis. Commun. Image Represent. **24**(3), 283–294 (2013)
20. Bao, G., Ye, Z., Xu, X., et al.: A compressed sensing approach to blind separation of speech mixture based on a two-layer sparsity mode. IEEE Trans. Audio Speech Lang. Process. **21**(5), 899–906 (2013)
21. Lin, C.H., Tsai, J.S., Chiu, C.T.: Switching bilateral filter with a texture/noise detector for universal noise removal. IEEE Trans. Image Process. **19**(9), 2307–2320 (2010)
22. Tropp, J.A.: Greed is good: algorithmic results for sparse approximation. IEEE Trans. Inf. Theory **50**, 2231–2242 (2004)
23. Wang, Z., Bovik, A.C., Sheikh, H.R., et al.: Image quality assessment: from error visibility to structural similarity. IEEE Trans. Image Process. **13**(4), 600–612 (2004)

Single Remote Sensing Image Haze Removal Based on Spatial and Spectral Self-Adaptive Model

Quan Yuan[✉], Huanfeng Shen, and Huifang Li

School of Resource and Environmental Sciences, Wuhan University, Wuhan,
People's Republic of China
1127905893@qq.com

Abstract. Remote sensing images are extensively applied in various fields, however, they usually suffer from haze pollution, which always leads to low contrast and color distortion. In this paper, we propose a novel and effective spatial and spectral self-adaptive haze removal model for remote sensing images. Our research is based on the dark channel prior, meanwhile, we ameliorate the prior in two aspects as follow: first, to remove uneven haze in remote sensing images, we modify the original constant ω to a matrix, and the value of ω changes with density of haze, so the processing intensity varies as haze density changes. Second, the dark channel prior has severe color distortion when dealing with bright landforms, to solve this problem, we separate these bright areas automatically from other landforms and handle them alone. Experimental results reveal that our proposed model is able to remove uneven haze and keep good color consistency when dealing with bright landforms. Both visual effect and quantitative assessment demonstrate that the proposed algorithm is effective.

Keywords: Remote sensing · Image dehazing · Dark channel prior · Self-adaptive

1 Introduction

Remote sensing images with high spatial resolution and abundant information have played a significant role in both civil and military fields in recent years. However, the observed images are taken at a considerable distance from surface of the earth, not all of the electromagnetic can reach the sensor after it passes through the atmospheric layer. Consequently, these images are usually vulnerable to climate effects [1, 2] and atmospheric conditions, such as cloud and haze.

In this paper, we mainly address remote sensing images degraded by haze, which indicate two distinguished features: first, regions polluted by haze have low contrast; second, these regions often suffer from color distortion to a certain extent. The haze removal processing targets at two features above as well, in other words, to promote the contrast and recover the true color in hazy regions.

Nevertheless, haze removal is a challenging task since the polluted regions contain both the information of haze and ground features [3]. Which results in that the information of ground features may be changed when haze is removal. Fortunately, in recent

© Springer International Publishing Switzerland 2015
Y.-J. Zhang (Ed.): ICIG 2015, Part III, LNCS 9219, pp. 382–392, 2015.
DOI: 10.1007/978-3-319-21969-1_33

years, removing haze from remote sensing images has attracted an increasing attention, and a number of researches have been undertaken. Here is a brief summery.

Richter [4] developed a haze removal method using haze transition (haze-free to haze) regions. The algorithm separates cloud, hazy and clear regions by matching the histogram of the clear regions to the hazy part, then a haze boundary region is introduced to generate a smoother transition from clear regions to haze.

The dark object subtraction (DOS) method [5] is a typical image-based atmospheric correction method, we can acquire a satisfactory haze-removal image by taking advantage of the darkest pixel in a homogeneous hazy image. However, this method fails to process images in which haze is non-uniform.

Zhang et al. [6] put forward a haze optimized transformation (HOT) to characterize the spatial distribution in Landsat TM/ETM+ images, then DOS based on HOT is applied to remove haze [7]. But the effect of HOT method relies on the selected hazy and haze-free regions to a great extent, it usually takes several times to acquire an ideal result.

He et al. [8] proposed the dark channel prior based on the statistic of 5000 outdoor haze-free images: in most of the non-sky patches, at least one color channel has some pixels whose intensity are very low and close to zero. Combined with the haze image model, the effect of this approach is very impressive. But this method will bring about two problems when applied to remote sensing images: first, the visual effect of dehazed image is not appealing when processing remote sensing images with uneven haze. Second, when the scene objects are inherently similar to the atmospheric light [8], such as bright bare soil, the dark channel prior will lead to severe color distortion.

In this paper, we put forward a fast and efficient spatial and spectral self-adaptive haze removal method to remove haze in remote sensing images. Experimental results demonstrate that our method not only can successfully dealing with images with uneven haze, but also may keep good color consistency in bight areas.

The remaining letter is organized as follows. In Sect. 2, the haze image model and dark channel prior are introduced in detail. In Sect. 3, a detailed description of our method is given. In Sect. 4, experimental results and a comparison with He and HOT are shown. Finally, conclusions are drawn in Sect. 5.

2 Background

2.1 The Haze Image Model

In computer graphics and computer vision, the haze image model, widely used to describe the formation of a haze image is [8–12]:

$$I(x) = J(x)t(x) + A[1 - t(x)] \tag{1}$$

Where I stands for the observed intensity, J is the scene radiance, A stands for the atmospheric light of the whole image, t is the medium transmission coefficient, standing for the portion of the light that is not scattered and reaches the imaging instrument.

In general, the haze image model indicates that the observed image is composed by two sections: the scene radiance and the global atmospheric light, and their proportion is t and $(1 - t)$ respectively. The term $A(1 - t)$ is called airlight [8, 11, 13, 14], and the term $(J*t)$ is called the direct attenuation [8, 11, 14].

For Eq. (1), in order to remove the haze in the image, it's necessary to recover the scene radiance J from the hazy image J. However, without knowing the value of A and t, it's obviously an ill-posed problem since only I is given. Therefore, A and t need to be estimated if we want to recover J. Once A and t is obtained, we may calculate the scene radiance J in the following formula:

$$J(x) = \frac{I(x) - A}{t(x)} + A \tag{2}$$

2.2   The Dark Channel Prior Method

A. Dark Channel Prior

In order to recover the scene radiance J in Eq. (1), the dark channel prior method proposed by He et al. [8] may estimate A and t relatively accurate, which has been a milestone in this research field until now. A brief introduction is presented next.

The dark channel prior is a statistic rule based on the observation on outdoor haze-free images: in most of non-sky patches in an outdoor image, at least one color channel has some pixels whose intensity are very low and close to zero [8]. Equivalently, in haze-free images the minimum intensity of such a patch is close to zero.

The conception of dark channel of an arbitrary image is formally defined as follows:

$$J^{dark}(x) = \min_{y \in \Omega(x)} \left[\min_{c \in \{r,g,b\}} J^c(y) \right] \tag{3}$$

Where $\Omega(x)$ is the local neighbor of pixel x, and J^c is one of the RGB channels. The dark channel $J^{dark}(x)$ in a haze-free image is tend to zero, which is called the dark channel prior (Fig. 1).

$$J^{dark} \rightarrow 0 \tag{4}$$

(a)   (b)   (c)

Fig. 1. Calculation of a dark channel. (a) An arbitrary image J. (b) Calculating the minimum of (r, g, b) values of each pixel. (c) The dark channel of J. The patch size of Ω is 15 × 15 (Color figure online).

To verify the theory, the author randomly select 5000 outdoor haze-free images and resize their size at 500*500 pixels. Then, the dark channels are computed using a patch size 15*15. It turns out that 75 % of the dark channels are 0, while 86 % are blow 16. Figure 2 shows the detailed distribution of the pixel intensity of dark channels.

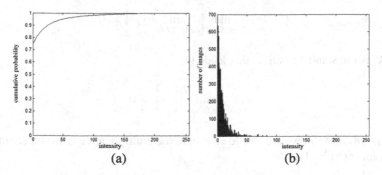

(a)   (b)

Fig. 2. Statistic results of the dark channels. (a) Cumulative distribution. (b) Histogram of the average intensity of each dark channel.

B. Estimate the Atmospheric Light A

The atmospheric light A stands for the most haze-opaque region in whole image, He et al. [8] estimated A based on the dark channel, and two major steps are expounded below in detail:

Firstly, picking up the top 0.1 % brightest pixels in the dark channel prior, these pixels are usually regarded as the most haze-opaque region.

Then, among the extracted 0.1 % pixels, the pixels with highest intensity in the input image are selected as the atmospheric light A.

It is necessary to declare that the atmospheric light may not be the brightest pixels in the whole image.

C. Estimate the Transmission $t(x)$

In Eq. (1), we assume that atmospheric light A is given, then the haze image model can be normalized by dividing A on both sides. Therefore, the normalized haze image model in each color channel can be rewritten as:

$$\frac{I^c(x)}{A^c} = \frac{J^c(x)}{A^c} * t(x) + 1 - t(x) \tag{5}$$

Furthermore, He assumed that the transmission $t'(x)$ in a local patch $\Omega(x)$ is invariable, and then calculated the dark channel on both sides of (5) by taking the minimum operation:

$$\min_{CE(r,g,b)}\left[\min_{y\in\Omega(x)}\frac{I^c(y)}{A^c}\right] = t'(x)\times\min_{CE(r,g,b)}\left[\min_{y\in\Omega(x)}\frac{I^c(y)}{A^c}\right] + [1-t'(x)] \tag{6}$$

According to the dark channel prior, the dark channel of a local patch is close to zero:

$$J^{dark}(x) = \min_{y\in\Omega(x)}\left[\min_{c\in\{r,d,b\}}J^c(y)\right] = 0 \tag{7}$$

As A^c is constantly positive, this leads to:

$$\min_{c\in(r,g,b)}\left[\min_{y\in\Omega(x)}\frac{J^c(y)}{A^c}\right] = 0 \tag{8}$$

Putting (8) into (6), we are able to eliminate the multiplicative term and estimate the transmission $t'(x)$ by Eq. (9):

$$t'(x) = 1 - \min_{c\in(r,g,b)}\left[\min_{y\in\Omega(x)}\frac{J^c(y)}{A^c}\right] = 0 \tag{9}$$

However, the image tends to be unnatural if we remove the haze thoroughly [8], to solve this problem, the author introduce a constant parameter $\omega = 0.95$ into (9):

$$t'(x) = 1 - \omega * \min_{c\in(r,g,b)}\left[\min_{y\in\Omega(x)}\frac{I^c(y)}{A^c}\right] \tag{10}$$

D. Recover the Scene Radiance $J(x)$

The transmission estimated by (10) in the last subsection is not accurate enough and may result in discontinuity even though no abrupt discontinuities occur in the image [8]. Therefore, to avoid block artifacts, a guided filter [15] is used to refine the transmission estimated in the last subsection. The filter kernel is explicitly expressed as:

$$W_{ij}(I) = \frac{1}{|w|^2}\sum_{k:(i,j)\in w_k}\left(1 + \frac{(I_i-\mu_k)+(I_j-\mu_k)}{\sigma_k^2+\epsilon}\right) \tag{11}$$

Where I stands for the guidance image, w_k is a window centered at the pixel k, $|w|$ is the number of pixels in the window w_k, σ_k^2 and μ_k stand for the variance and mean of I correspondingly, ϵ is a regularization parameter. And the original hazy image is guidance image in this letter.

Since the atmospheric light A and the refined transmission $t(x)$ can be estimated from the dark channel prior method, the scene radiance $J(x)$ is able to be recovered from the hazy image according to Eq. (2).

3 Spatial and Spectral Self-Adaptive Haze Removal Model

3.1 Spectral Adaptive: Processing Intensity Varies with Haze Density

When applying dark channel prior to remote sensing images with uneven haze, the effect is not ideal. As is showed in the picture below, thin haze is removed with effect while dense haze is not removed totally.

In original paper we notice that He applied a constant parameter $\omega = 0.95$ to reduce the unnatural distortion of the dehazed image. By assigning different values to ω, we found that different processing intensities are performed. Furthermore, the processing intensity increases as the value of ω grows (Fig. 3).

Fig. 3. Haze removal extent varies with ω. (a) Original hazy image. (b) $\omega = 1$. (c) $\omega = 0.8$. (d) $\omega = 0.6$.

In the next step, we modify the constant ω to a matrix ω. The value of ω varies from 0 to 1. Moreover, the value of ω grows as the density of haze in the corresponding region increases. By taking advantage of this matrix ω, we can apply different processing intensities to regions of different haze densities and remove the inhomogeneous haze in an image successfully.

3.2 Spatial Adaptive: Separate Different Landforms

He discovered that when dealing with scene objects inherently similar to the atmospheric light, such as sky regions in outdoor images, the dark channel prior is invalid and always leads to color distortion. Similar to sky regions in outdoor images, the bright bare soil in remote sensing images resembles the atmospheric light too. From

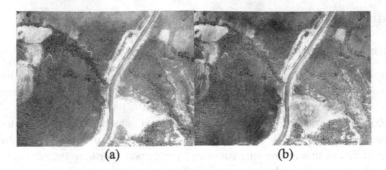

(a)   (b)

Fig. 4. Color distortion after haze removal with original dark channel prior (a) input image (b) haze removal with dark channel prior (Color figure online)

Fig. 4, we may find that after being processed by dark channel prior, these bright regions tend to be unnatural darker than they should be.

The reason why this phenomenon occurs is that unlike other landforms, such as vegetation and river, which often tend to indicate a low intensity in one of RGB channels, bare lands are inclined to have a higher intensity in all of RGB channels, which is similar to the spectral features of dense haze. So after haze removal operation with dark channel prior method, one of RGB channels in these bright regions are forced to be zero, and eventually they appear to be unnaturally darker, which is apparently incorrect.

Therefore, these bright ground features should be separated to other landforms and then processed alone. In this case, these regions may become more visually natural after haze removal.

After reduplicative statistics and verification, we found a judgment condition (12) to separate bright landforms to other ground features, experimental results demonstrate this judgment is effective and stable for aerial images. And in remote sensing images with near-infrared band, we can classify different landforms with NDVI and NDWI indexes, which are extensively applied to extract vegetation and water from remote sensing images.

$$\frac{G + B - 2 * R}{R - 0.5 * B} \leq 1.1 \tag{12}$$

At last, we perform different processing intensities to different landforms by assign ω different values. In general, the processing intensity of bright landforms is weaker than that of other landforms, such as vegetation and water.

4   Experimental Results and Analysis

To demonstrate the effectiveness of our algorithm, we manually select several aerial remote sensing images and do experiments on these images. The proposed method is implemented on a PC with 3.4 GHZ Intel Core i3 Processor using Visual C++ 6.0 in Window 7 environment. And the recovered images are visually appealing.

Figures 5 and 6 are comparisons between results recovered by He's original dark channel prior [8], HOT [5], and our algorithm. From two comparisons, we may notice that the original dark channel prior cannot completely remove dense haze in the image, at the same time, the bright bare lands suffer from color distortion and become unnatural darker after haze removal. HOT method is able to remove all haze, however, the dehazed image suffers from slight color distortion, and the resolution of the image decreases compared with the original image. In addition, the effect of HOT method relies on the selected regions of interest to a great extent, it usually takes several times to acquire the ideal result. The proposed method can not only remove the non-uniform haze in the image, but also can increase the contrast and restore the true color in hazy regions. And the image is visually appealing after haze removal operation.

Besides subjective visual effect, we also assess the experimental results with quantitative evaluation. In this paper, we adopt entropy [16] and average gradient as evaluation criteria. Entropy reflects the abundance of information in an image, meanwhile, average gradient is another significant evaluation criterion, and the higher the

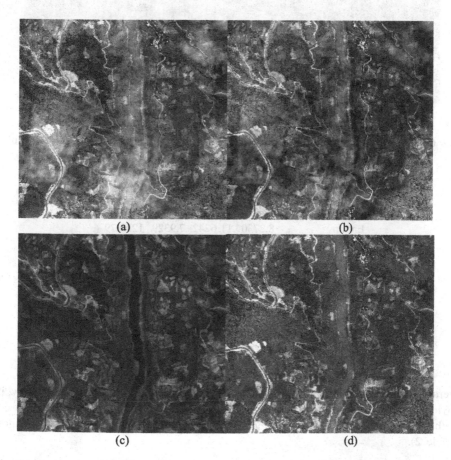

(a)   (b)

(c)   (d)

Fig. 5. Haze removal. (a) Input hazy image. (b) He's result. (c) HOT's result. (d) Our result (Color figure online).

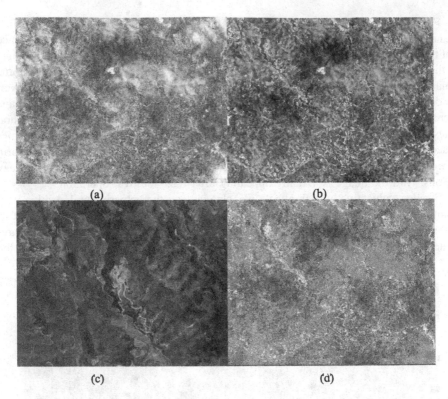

Fig. 6. Haze removal. (a) Input hazy image. (b) He's result. (c) HOT's result. (d) Our result.

Table 1. Quantitative evaluation of various methods in Fig. 5

	Input	He's	HOT	Ours
Entropy	8.2730	11.6242	7.9329	12.8879
Average gradient	5.3321	5.6170	2.1085	5.7715

Table 2. Quantitative evaluation of various methods in Fig. 6

	Input	He's	HOT	Ours
Entropy	7.9472	9.4329	7.6690	11.1066
Average gradient	5.7188	6.7236	2.3346	7.9650

average gradient of an image is, the clearer the image is. Judging from Table 1 below, it obvious that both entropy and average gradient have the highest value in our proposed method. It proves that our method can recover clearer and more natural images (Table 2).

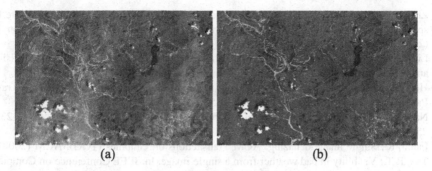

Fig. 7. Haze removal for ZY1-02C image. (a) Input hazy image. (b) Our result.

In addition, we are able to remove haze from remote sensing images with near-infrared band as well. Taking a ZY1-02C image for example, we can remove uneven haze in the image and keep good color consistency (Fig. 7).

5 Conclusion

In this paper, an efficient method is put forward to remove haze in remote sensing images, compared with the previous methods, our method has two main advantages: first, by modifying the original constant ω to a matrix, we can successfully remove non-uniform haze in remote sensing images. Second, our method is able to avoid severe color distortion and recover natural color in bright regions. Experiments indicate that the proposed method can archive appealing haze-free images in both visual effects and quantitative evaluation. Additionally, our proposed method, however, still causes slight color distortion [17, 18], a solution to this problem will be our future research direction.

References

1. Long, J., Shi, Z., Tang, W., Zhang, C.: Single remote sensing image dehazing. IEEE Geosci. Remote Sens. Lett. **11**(1), 59–63 (2014)
2. Wen, X., Yang, X. (eds.): Haze removal from the visible bands of CBERS remote sensing data. In: International Conference on Industrial and Information Systems, IIS 2009. IEEE (2009)
3. Shen, H., Li, H., Qian, Y., Zhang, L., Yuan, Q.: An effective thin cloud removal procedure for visible remote sensing images. ISPRS J. Photogram. Remote Sens. **96**, 224–235 (2014)
4. Richter, R.: Atmospheric correction of satellite data with haze removal including a haze/clear transition region. Comput. Geosci. **22**(6), 675–681 (1996)
5. Zhang, Y., Guindon, B.: Quantitative assessment of a haze suppression methodology for satellite imagery: effect on land cover classification performance. IEEE Trans. Geosci. Remote Sens. **41**(5), 1082–1089 (2003)

6. Zhang, Y., Guindon, B., Cihlar, J.: An image transform to characterize and compensate for spatial variations in thin cloud contamination of landsat images. Remote Sens. Environ. **82** (2), 173–187 (2002)
7. Li, H., Zhang, L., Shen, H., Li, P.: A variational gradient-based fusion method for visible and SWIR imagery. Photogram. Eng. Remote Sens. **78**(9), 947–958 (2012)
8. He, K., Sun, J., Tang, X.: Single image haze removal using dark channel prior. IEEE Trans. Pattern Anal. Mach. Intell. **33**(12), 2341–2353 (2011)
9. Narasimhan, S.G., Nayar, S.K.: Vision and the atmosphere. Int. J. Comput. Vis. **48**(3), 233–254 (2002)
10. Fattal, R.: Single image dehazing. ACM Transactions on Graphics (TOG). ACM (2008)
11. Tan, R.T.: Visibility in bad weather from a single image. In: IEEE Conference on Computer Vision and Pattern Recognition, CVPR 2008. IEEE (2008)
12. Narasimhan, S.G., Nayar, S.K.: Chromatic framework for vision in bad weather. In: Proceedings IEEE Conference on Computer Vision and Pattern Recognition, 2000. IEEE (2000)
13. Koschmieder, H.: Theorie der horizontalen Sichtweite II: Kontrast und Sichtweite. Beitr. Phys. freien Atmos. XII, **171** (1925)
14. Lan, X., Zhang, L., Shen, H., Yuan, Q., Li, H.: Single image haze removal considering sensor blur and noise. EURASIP J. Adv. Sig. Process. **2013**(1), 1–13 (2013)
15. He, K., Sun, J., Tang, X.: Guided image filtering. In: Daniilidis, K., Maragos, P., Paragios, N. (eds.) ECCV 2010, Part I. LNCS, vol. 6311, pp. 1–14. Springer, Heidelberg (2010)
16. Kapur, J.N., Kesavan, H.K.: Entropy Optimization Principles With Applications. Academic Press, New York (1992)
17. Lu, H., Li, Y., Zhang, L., Serikawa, S.: Contrast enhancement for images in turbid water. JOSA A. **32**(5), 886–893 (2015)
18. Serikawa, S., Lu, H.: Underwater image dehazing using joint trilateral filter. Comput. Electr. Eng. **40**(1), 41–50 (2014)

Small Infrared Target Detection
Based on Low-Rank Representation

Min Li[1], Yu-Jie He[1(✉)], and JinLi Zhang[1,2]

[1] Xi'an Research Institute of Hi-Tech, Xian 710025, China
{clwn,ksy5201314}@163.com,
jlz_007@sina.com
[2] Department of Information Engineering,
Engineering University of CAPF, Xian 710086, China

Abstract. How to achieve the correct detection result for the infrared small targets is the important and challenging issue in infrared applications. In this paper, a small infrared target detection method based on low-rank representation is proposed, which used the low-rank representation (LRR) to decomposed infrared image to background component and target component, then the detection task could be finished through threshold processing. In different experimental conditions, the results show that our method based on low-rank representation not only has higher detection performance but also reduce the false alarm rate effectively.

Keywords: Low-rank representation · Infrared image decomposition · Small infrared target detection

1 Introduction

Infrared small target detection is always one of the key techniques of the infrared guidance system and a hotspot research for military applications. On one hand, the small targets are usually submerged in the background clutter and the heavy noise with low SNR because of the transmitting and scattering of the atmospheric with long observation distance. On the other hand, the targets in images appear as a dim point which make the targets have no obvious feature and texture information useful. therefore, these two factors make the infrared small target detection more difficult [1].

Up to now, the methods of the infrared target detection can be classified into two categories [2]: detection based on single-frame and detection based on sequential frames. Considering the sequential detection methods are processed based on the prior information of the target and background, which would cause the methods cannot reach satisfactory performance because the information are hardly obtained in military application, the single-frame detection algorithms have attracted a lot of attentions of researchers who have proposed various single-frame detection methods which can be divided into three classes: background suppressing methods [3–5], target singularity analysis methods [6, 7], and some method using machine learning theory [8, 9].

Recently, based on the original data is drawn from several low-rank subspaces, low-rank representation(LRR) [10] was proposed for subspace segmentation or recovery,

© Springer International Publishing Switzerland 2015
Y.-J. Zhang (Ed.): ICIG 2015, Part III, LNCS 9219, pp. 393–401, 2015.
DOI: 10.1007/978-3-319-21969-1_34

which can decompose the data matrix into the clean matrix described by the self-expressive dictionary with low-rank coefficients and the sparse noise. Considering the underlying structure revealing and background modeling ability of low-rank representation with large errors or outliers, we propose a small infrared target detection method based on low-rank representation in this paper. This method decomposes the infrared image to target component and noise component on the basis of low-rank decomposition and background modeling. So the proposed method have better detection performance compared to the baseline algorithms as the experiments results shown.

2 Low-Rank Representation

Considering the given observation matrix $X \in R^{m \times n}$ was generated from a low-rank matrix $X_0 \in R^{m \times n}$ with some of its entries corrupted by an additive error $E \in R^{m \times n}$, the original data X_0 can be recovered by the following regularized rank minimization problem which is adopted by the established robust principal component analysis (RPCA) method [11]

$$\min_{Z,E} \ \text{rank}(X_0) + \lambda \|E\|_l, \ s.t. X = X_0 + E \tag{1}$$

Where λ is a parameter and $\|\bullet\|_l$ indicates a certain regularization strategy, such as the squared Frobenius norm $\|\bullet\|_F$ used for modeling specify the Gaussian disturbance, the l_0 norm $\|\bullet\|_0$ adopted for characterizing the random corruptions, and the $l_{2,0}$ norm $\|\bullet\|_{2,0}$ used to deal with sample specific corruptions and outliers. Based on the RPCA which assumes that the underlying data structure is a single low-rank subspace, the IPI model was proposed to small infrared target detection in [12]. However, considering the data is usually drawn from a union of multiple subspaces in most cases. The formula of low-rank representation is as follows:

$$\min_{Z,E} rank(Z) + \lambda \|E\|_l, \ s.t. X = AZ + E \tag{2}$$

where A is a dictionary that linearly spans the union of subspaces. The minimize Z^* indicates the lowest-rank representation of data X with respect to a dictionary A. Apparently, Eq. (2) is a highly non-convex optimization problem, but we can relax it by solving the convex problem:

$$\min_{Z,E} \|Z\|_* + \lambda \|E\|_l, \ s.t. X = AZ + E \tag{3}$$

where $\|\bullet\|_*$ denotes the nuclear norm of a matrix (i.e., the sum of its singular values).

When $A = I$, LRR degenerates to RPCA which can be seen as a special case of LRR model, an appropriate A can ensure that the LRR can reveal the true underlying data structure. Usually, the observation data X is chosen to be the dictionary. So, Eq. (3) becomes:

$$\min_{Z,E}\|Z\|_* + \lambda\|E\|_l, s.t. X = XZ + E \tag{4}$$

In order to adopt the augmented Lagrange multiplier method to solve the problem, We Introduce one auxiliary variables and convert Eq. (4) to the following equivalent formula:

$$\min_{Z,E,J}\|J\|_* + \lambda\|E\|_l \ s.t. X = XZ + E, J = Z \tag{5}$$

which equals to solving the following augmented Lagrange function:

$$L = \|J\|_* + \lambda\|E\|_l + tr\left[Y_1^T(X - XZ - E)\right] + tr\left[Y_2^T(Z - J)\right]$$
$$+ \frac{\mu}{2}(\|X - XZ - E\|_F^2 + \|Z - J\|_F^2) \tag{6}$$

Where Y_1 and Y_2 are Lagrange multipliers and $\mu > 0$ is a penalty parameter. By fixing the other variables, the Eq. (6) can be solved with respect to J, Z and E respectively and then updating the multipliers. We can employ the different regular strategies to noise for different applications. The solution steps are following as Algorithm 1 in the case of $l_{2,1}$ norm:

Algorithm 1: Solving Eq. (6) by inexact augmented Lagrange multiplier algorithms

---

Input: data matrix X, parameters λ

Initialize: $Z = J = 0, E = 0 Y_1 = Y_2 = 0, \ \mu = 10^{-6}, \ \mu_{max} = 10^{10}, \ \rho = 1.2$

Output: Z, E

While not converged do

1. Fix the others and update J by

$$J = \arg\min \ \frac{1}{\mu}\|J\|_* + \frac{1}{2}\|J - (Z + Y_2/\mu)\|_F^2$$

2. Fix the others and update E by

$$E = \arg\min \ \frac{\lambda}{\mu}\|E\|_{2,1} + \frac{1}{2}\|E - (X - XZ + Y_1/\mu)\|_F^2$$

3. Fix the others and update Z by

$$Z = (I + X^T X)^{-1}[X^T X - X^T E + J + (X^T Y_1 - Y_2)/\mu]$$

4. Update three Lagrange multipliers

$$Y_1 = Y_1 + \mu(X - XZ - E), \ Y_2 = Y_2 + \mu(Z - J)$$

5. Update the parameter μ

$$\mu = \min(\rho\mu, \mu_{max})$$

Check the convergence conditions

$$\|X - XZ - E\|_\infty < \varepsilon, \ \|Z - J\|_\infty < \varepsilon$$

End while

The step 1 and 2 of the Algorithm 1 which are convex problems both have closed form solutions. The step 1 can be solved by the following lemma:

Lemma 1 [13]: For the matrix $Y \in R^{n \times d}$ and $\mu > 0$, the problem as following has the only analysis solution.

$$\arg \min_{M \in R^{n \times d}} \mu \|M\|_* + \frac{1}{2} \|M - Y\|_F^2$$

Its solution can be described by singular value thresholding operator.

$$SVT_\mu(Y) = U \operatorname{diag}[(\sigma - \mu)_+] V^T \tag{7}$$

$$(\sigma - \mu)_+ = \begin{cases} \sigma - \mu & \sigma > \mu \\ 0 & otherwise \end{cases}$$

$U \in R^{n \times r}$, $V \in R^{d \times r}$ and $\sigma = (\sigma_1, \sigma_2, \sigma_3 \ldots \sigma_r) \in R^{r \times 1}$ can be achieved by singular value decomposition of matrix Y, $Y = U \sum V^T$ and $\sum = diag(\sigma)$.

The step 2 can be solved by lemma 2:

Lemma 2: Let $Q = [q_1, q_2, \ldots, q_i, \ldots]$ be a given matrix. If the optimal solution to

$$\min \lambda \|W\|_{2,1} + \frac{1}{2} \|W - Q\|_F^2$$

is W^*, then the i-th column of W^* is

$$W^*(:, i) = \begin{cases} \frac{\|q_i\| - \lambda}{\|q_i\|} q_i & if \lambda < \|q_i\| \\ 0 & otherwise \end{cases} \tag{8}$$

3 LRR Based Small Target Detection

An infrared image can be viewed as a combination of two components such as background, target. The background of the infrared image is transitions slowly which also has the property of non-local self-correlation, and the target is small with respect to the whole image. Thus we consider the background as low-rank matrix and the target as sparse matrix. Meanwhile, the small target is often located in heterogeneous background which causes the background data coming from multi-subspace. Thus, we decompose the original infrared image into two components images by using the LRR model, then the target location is determined by thresholding the target image. The whole method of small target detection based on LRR is depicted as Fig. 1 and the steps of the detection method are as follows:

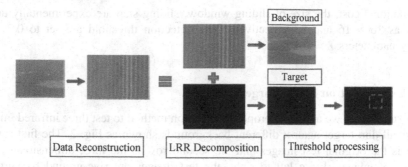

Fig. 1. Diagram of the small detection method based on LRR

(1) Image Data Reconstruction. we need to reconstruct the original image data $X \in R^{m \times n}$ to the matrix $\tilde{X} \in R^{k^2 \times w}$ by using a sliding window $k \times k$, which could increase the similarity of image blocks and reduce the rank of image data, from top and left to down and right with sliding steps s, and each sub-block extracting by the sliding window was vectorized as a column of matrix $\tilde{X}$, where w is the number of the sub-blocks.

(2) Image Decomposing. By solving Eq. (6), the original infrared image X can be decomposed into background and target by using LRR model with the reconstructed image data $\tilde{X}$ as input.

(3) Locating the Target. After obtaining the background component AZ, we could locate the target by the following steps: first, we calculate the target component by $T = \tilde{X} - AZ$. Then, T is inverse transformed to get the real target image $\tilde{T}$. Because the sliding step is usually less than the size of the window, the same position pixel in the final target image have different values from the adjacent sub-blocks, so we adopt the calculation of $v = median(x)$, where x is the different values from different sub-blocks having equally location. Finally, the target image $\tilde{T}$ can be located by threshold processing. If $\rho M \leq \tilde{T}(x, y)$, we see (x, y) as a target point, where M is the maximum value of $\tilde{T}$ and ρ is the threshold.

4   Experiments and Analysis

To evaluate the target detection performance, two groups of experimental are designed: The first group is single target detection experiments, three real images with different background are decomposed and the detection results are obtained directly using the proposed method; The second group of experiments is for the infrared sequences with some synthetic targets. We embed the small synthetic targets, generated from five real targets, into the images chosen from four real sequences. Then the detection performance is quantitatively evaluated by using some objective evaluation criteria such as local SNR, detection probability and false-alarm rate. We also test the conventional single-frame detection methods for comparison such as TDLMS, Top-Hat, Max-Median. In these two groups of experiment, based on the consideration of computational cost, the size of sliding window, sliding step are experimentally determined as 16×16 and 8, respectively. The detection threshold are set to 0.7. The penalty parameters $\lambda = 0.12$.

4.1   Experiment on Single Target Detection

In this subsection, we apply the proposed detection method to test three infrared images with small dim target against different backgrounds shown as Fig. 2. The first row of Fig. 2 is the original test images and the second row is the three-dimensional mesh surfaces of images. From left to right, the test images are rive-ground background image with size 128×128, coast background with size 200×256, sea-sky background image with size 200×256. The target detection experimental results on these three images by our method are shown in Fig. 3. From this figure, we can see the original infrared image are effectively decomposed into three different components such as the background component image shown in Fig. 3(b) and target component image show in Fig. 3(c). The Fig. 3(d) shows the three-dimensional (3-D) mesh surfaces of the target component image. The results of detection indicate that our method can accomplish the task of target detection effectively not only for the dim point targets but also for the porphyritic target like the target in Fig. 2(c) through separating the target component from other elements.

4.2   Experiment on Infrared Sequences with Multiple Target

In order to verify the performance of the proposed method more objectively, multi-targets detection experiments on four sequences are done in this subsection. We synthesized the test database by embedding the multi-targets into several background

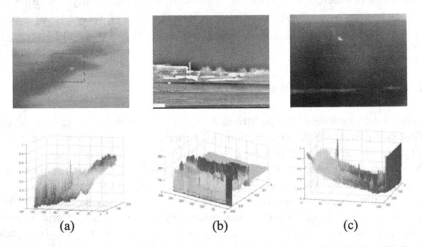

      (a)   (b)   (c)

Fig. 2. Infrared images with small dim targets against different backgrounds (a) land background (b) coast background (c) sea sky background

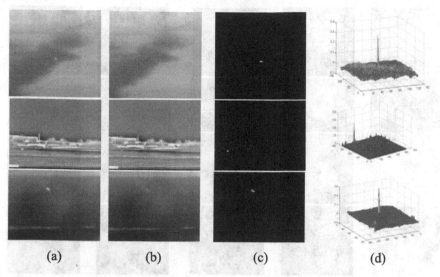

Fig. 3. Image decomposition results obtained by proposed algorithm (a) original image (b) background data (c) target component (d) 3-d mesh of target component

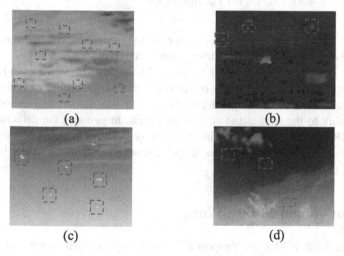

Fig. 4. The representative images for 4 groups of synthetic image (a) seq.1 (b) seq.2 (c) seq.3 (d) seq.4

images chosen from four real sequences using the method in [12]. As shown in Fig. 4, we can see that the contrast between target and background is very low in the seq.1 and seq.4, especially in the seq.4 the distant targets almost can not be observed. In the seq.2, there are road and building targets except for tank and aircraft targets with big size. And we compare our method with several typical algorithms, such as Max-Median, Top-Hat, TDLMS.

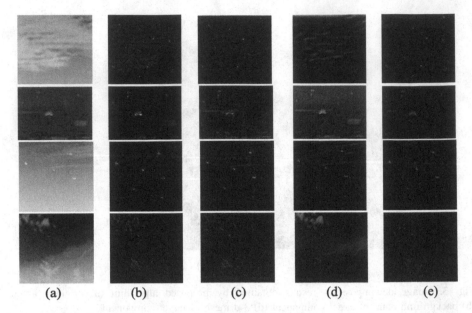

Fig. 5. The results of different methods (a) the representative images for 4 groups of synthetic image (b) max-median (c) top-hat (d) TDLMS (e) LRR

Figure 5 gives the comparisons between the proposed method and baseline methods. we can see that seq.1 has strong cloud clutter and several targets location are in the clouds and sky junction. From the second row, the proposed method can detect not only four flight targets in the sky but also the tank target on the road correctly and eliminate the road and building effectively, which illustrates our method also has detection ability to the spot target with large pixels. In general, the detection method based on LRR has less clutter and noise residual for different backgrounds compared to the other baseline methods with the target enhanced and more using information preserved at the same time.

5   Conclusion and Future Work

Based on the LRR model, we proposed a small target detection method which can transform the detection task into separation process of background and target components by solving the LRR in this paper. The results of two groups of experiments have validated that the proposed method has better detection performance compared to the conventional baseline methods. In the future work, the research attempt is to add the model of target into our method which could make the method have better ability of distinguishing between the target and noise.

Conferences

1. Zheng, C., Li, H.: Small infrared target detection based on harmonic and sparse matrix decomposition. Opt. Eng. **52**(6), 066401 (2013). (1-10)
2. Gao, C.Q., Zhang, T.Q., et al.: Small infrared target detection using sparse ring representation. IEEE Trans. Aerosp. Electron. Syst. Mag. **27**(3), 21–30 (2012)
3. Zeng, M., Li, J., Peng, Z.: The design of top-hat morphological filter and application to infrared target detection. Infrared Phys. Technol. **48**(1), 67–76 (2006)
4. Wang, P., Tian, J., Gao, C.: Infrared small target detection using directional highpass filters based on LS-SVM. Electron. Lett. **45**(3), 156–158 (2009)
5. Cao, Y., Liu, R.M., Yang, J.: Small target detection using two-dimensional least mean square (TDLMS) filter based on neighborhood analysis. Int. J. Infrared Millim. Waves **29**(2), 188–200 (2008)
6. Zheng, C., Li, H.: Method of infrared target detection based on the characteristic analysis of the local grey level. Infrared Laser Eng. **33**(4), 362–365 (2004)
7. Deshpande, S., et al.: Max-mean and max-median filters for detection of small targets. In Proceedings Signal and Data Processing of Small Targets, vol. 3809, pp. 74–83. SPIE, Denver, CO (1999)
8. Hu, T., et al.: Infrared small target detection based on saliency and principle component analysis. J. Infrared Millim. Waves **29**(4), 303–306 (2010)
9. Cao, Y., Liu, R., Yang, J.: Infrared small target detection using PPCA. Int. J. Infrared Millim. Waves **29**(4), 385–395 (2008)
10. Liu, G.C., Lin, Z.C., Yu, Y: Robust subspace segmentation by low-rank representation. In: Proceedings of ICML, pp. 663–670 (2010)
11. Liu, G., Lin, Z., Yan, S., et al.: Robust recovery of subspace structures by low-rank representation. IEEE Trans. Pattern Anal. Mach. Intell. **35**(1), 171–184 (2013)
12. Gao, C.Q., Meng, D.Y., et al.: Infrared patch-image model for small target detection in a single image. IEEE Tans. Image Proc. **22**(12), 4996–5009 (2013)
13. Cai, J.F., Candes, E.J., Shen, Z.W.: A singular value thresholding algorithm for matrix completion. SIAM J. Optim. **20**(4), 1956–1982 (2008)

Sophisticated Tracking Framework
with Combined Detector

Gwangmin Choe[1,2], Tianjiang Wang[1(✉)], Qi Feng[1], Chunhwa Choe[2],
Sokmin Han[2], and Hun Kim[2]

[1] School of Computer Science and Technology,
Huazhong University of Science and Technology,
Wuhan 430074, People's Republic of China
cca2005@foxmail.com, {tjwang,qfeng}@hust.edu.cn
[2] Kim Il Sung University, Pyongyang, Democratic People's Republic of Korea
hunkim64@163.com

Abstract. This paper proposes a combined detector containing the background subtraction and the object appearance model-based detector. This is used to solve such problems as linking, overlapping, false object detecting etc. Then, we give a non-linear multi-mode tracker with the combined detector to solve such problems as sudden appearance changes and long-lasting occlusions, etc. Finally, we test our proposed person tracking framework in multi-object tracking scenario. Experimental results demonstrate that our proposed approaches have promising discriminative capability in comparison with other ones.

Keywords: Detector · Tracker · Model of object appearance · Background subtraction · Shadow removal · Combined detector · Non-linear multi-mode tracker · Particle filter · Person re-identification

1 Introduction

Modeling an object appearance in tracking are mainly classified to two approaches: static and adaptive. Static models is proposed in the context of using assumption that the object appearance change is limited and known [1]. From this assumption, it is clear that unexpected changes of the object appearance can not be tracked. Adaptive methods are proposed to address this drawback, which update the object model during tracking [2]. These approaches assume that every update is correct. Under this underlying assumption, error of the model accumulated over time and drift are caused by every incorrect update. The drift problem has been addressed by introduction of so called visual constraints [3]. Even though this approach demonstrated increased robustness and accuracy, its performance was tested only on videos where the object was in the field of view. In scenarios where an object moves in and out of the frame, object re-detection is essential. Object detection have been extensively studied

---

T. Wang – He is currently a Professor with the School of Computer Science, Huazhong University of Science and Technology, Wuhan, China.

© Springer International Publishing Switzerland 2015
Y.-J. Zhang (Ed.): ICIG 2015, Part III, LNCS 9219, pp. 402–409, 2015.
DOI: 10.1007/978-3-319-21969-1_35

[4] and a range of ready-to-use object detectors are available [5] which enable tracking-by-detection. Apart from expensive off-line training, the disadvantage of tracking-by-detection is that all objects have the same model and therefore the identities can not be distinguished. An object tracking algorithm that splits the object model into three parts with different lifespan, is proposed to solve this problem [6]. This makes the tracker suitable for low-frame rate videos but the longest period the face can disappear from the camera view is limited. Another class of approaches for face tracking was developed as part of automatic character annotation in video [7]. These systems can handle the scenario considered in this paper, but they have been designed for off-line processing and adaptation for real-time tracking is not straightforward.

An approach called Tracking-Learning-Detection (TLD) has been designed for long-term tracking of arbitrary objects in unconstrained environments [8]. Learning part of TLD was analyzed in [9]. The object was tracked and simultaneously learned in order to build a detector that supports the tracker once it fails. The detector was build upon the information from the first frame as well as the information provided by the tracker. Apart from this, the detector was build upon the information from the gray-scale distribution, i.e. the model of object appearance. This means that, given a moving object, these approaches discard the information from the motion of object, i.e. the variation of foreground. These approaches, therefore, may result in tracking an object far away from the location with the real variation of foreground. Beside this problem, shadow removal was not considered in this detector. Also, the tracker can not guarantee the non-linear multi-mode tracking, i.e. this can not very well adapt to sudden appearance changes, long-lasting occlusions etc.

This work has three major contributions. First, a combined detector containing the background subtraction and the object appearance model-based detector is proposed to solve such problems as linking, overlapping, false object detecting etc. Second, a non-linear multi-mode tracker with the combined detector is used to solve such problems as sudden appearance changes and long-lasting occlusions, etc. The non-linear multi-mode tracker is chosen as the particle filter with spline resampling and global transition proposed in [12]. Also, a person re-identification is used to numbering person in the context of multi-target tracking.

2 The Proposed Method

In this section, we propose first a combined detector containing the background subtraction and the object appearance model-based detector. Then we give a non-linear multi-mode tracker with the combined detector.

2.1 Combined Detector

Background Subtraction. Background subtraction involves calculating a reference image, subtracting each new frame from this image and thresholding the result. What results is a binary segmentation of the image which highlights regions of non-stationary objects. Here, a color or gray-scale video frame is compared with a background model to determine whether individual pixels are part of the background or the foreground.

Given a series of either gray-scale or color video frames, methods based on background mixture model compute the foreground mask using Gaussian mixture models (GMM). In our framework, the adaptive background mixture model is used to compute the foreground mask. This method allows system learn faster and more accurately as well as adapt effectively to changing environments.

Shadow Removal Based on Level-Thresholding. The strategy of our proposed person tracking framework is to:perform first the shadow removal using a strong threshold even if foreground pixels are also removed simultaneously, then implement shadow removal using a weakness threshold in bounded local regions. The first step prevents background pixels retained by the shadow removal. Some parts foreground pixels will still lost when the only combination of the above two filters, and the lost pixels tend to be the contact parts among outlines. The main reasons result in losing foreground pixels are that the texture of background is unobvious and current pixels are in the penumbra. The second step guarantees regain of foreground pixels lost in the first step. In first step, the intensity ratio between the background and the current frame is calculated by Eq. (1), then the pixel is a shadow when it meets the formula Eq. (2).

$$
\begin{cases}
E_r(i,j) = \dfrac{\min(B_r(i,j), Cur_r(i,j))}{\max(B_r(i,j), Cur_r(i,j))} \\[2ex]
E_g(i,j) = \dfrac{\min(B_g(i,j), Cur_g(i,j))}{\max(B_g(i,j), Cur_g(i,j))} \\[2ex]
E_b(i,j) = \dfrac{\min(B_b(i,j), Cur_b(i,j))}{\max(B_b(i,j), Cur_b(i,j))}
\end{cases}
\tag{1}
$$

$$
M(i,j) = \begin{cases} 1, & E_r(i,j) < T_1 \ and \ E_g(i,j) < T_1 \ and \ E_b(i,j) < T_1 \\ 0, & otherwise \end{cases}
\tag{2}
$$

where $E_r(i,j)$, $E_g(i,j)$ and $E_b(i,j)$ are the intensity ratio images or the difference images for three channels; $B_r(i,j)$, $B_g(i,j)$ and $B_b(i,j)$ are background images; $Cur_r(i,j)$, $Cur_g(i,j)$ and $Cur_b(i,j)$ are current frames; $M(i,j)$ is the binary mask; T_1 is the threshold for the first level of shadow removal. In the binary mask, pixels with a value of 1 correspond to the foreground, and pixels with a value of 0 correspond to the background. Then, morphological operations on the resulting binary mask are performed to remove noisy pixels and to fill the holes in the remaining blobs. In second step, a weakness threshold is used to implement shadow removal in bounded local regions and recovery foreground pixels lost in the first step.

$$
M(i_b, j_b) = \begin{cases} 1, & E_r(i_b, j_b) < T_2 \ and \ E_g(i_b, j_b) < T_2 \ and \ E_b(i_b, j_b) < T_2 \\ 0, & otherwise \end{cases}
\tag{3}
$$

where T_2 is the threshold for the second level of shadow removal, and i_b and j_b are pixel coordinates in bounded local regions. Then, morphological operations on this binary mask are performed to remove noisy pixels and to fill the holes in the remaining blobs.

Combined Detector with the Object Appearance Model-Based Detector. This part detects people in an input image using the Histogram of Oriented Gradient (HOG) features and a trained Support Vector Machine (SVM) classifier, and detects unoccluded people in an upright position.

Local object appearance and shape can often be characterized rather well by the distribution of local intensity gradients or edge directions, even without precise knowledge of the corresponding gradient or edge positions. This is implemented by dividing the image window into small spatial regions, for each region accumulating a local 1-D histogram of gradient directions or edge orientations over the pixels of the region. The representation is formed by the combined histogram entries. For better invariance to illumination, shadowing, etc., contrast-normalizing is also used for the local responses before using them. This can be done by accumulating a measure of local histogram "energy" over somewhat larger spatial regions ("blocks") and using the results to normalize all of the cells in the block. We will refer to the normalized descriptor blocks as Histogram of Oriented Gradient (HOG) descriptors. Human detection chain is given by tiling the detection window with a dense (in fact, overlapping) grid of HOG descriptors and by using the combined feature vector in a SVM based window classifier. One-class SVM has been widely used for outlier detection. Only positive samples are used in training. The basic idea of one-class SVM is to use a hypersphere to describe data in the feature space and put most of the data into the hypersphere. The problem is formulated into an objective function as follows:

$$\min_{\mathcal{R}\in\mathbb{R},\xi\in\mathbb{R}^l,c\in F} R^2 + \frac{1}{vl}\sum_i \xi_i, \tag{4}$$

$$\|\varPhi(X_i) - c\|^2 \leq R^2 + \xi_i, \forall i \in \{1, ..., l\} : \xi_i \geq 0 \tag{5}$$

where $\varPhi(X_i)$ is the multi-dimensional feature vector of training sample X_i, l is the number of training samples, R and c are the radius and center of the hypersphere, and $v \in [0, 1]$ is a trade-off parameter. The goal of optimizing the objective function is to keep the hypersphere as small as possible and include most of the training data. The optimization problem can be solved in a dual form by QP optimization methods, and the decision function is:

$$f(X) = R^2 - \|\varPhi(X_i) - c\|^2, \tag{6}$$

where $\|\varPhi(X_i) - c\|^2 = k(X, X) - 2\sum_i \alpha_i k(X_i, X) + \sum_{i,j} \alpha_i \alpha_j k(X_i, X_j)$, and α_i and α_j are the parameters for each constraint in the dual problem. In our task, we use the radius basis function (RBF) $k(X, Y) = \exp\{-\|X - Y\|^2/2\sigma^2\}$ as kernel in one-class SVM to deal with high-dimensional, non-linear, multi-mode distributions. The decision function of kernel one-class SVM can well capture the density and modality of feature distribution.

The model is specified as either 128×64 or 96×48, whose size is the image size used for training indicated by the pixel dimensions. The images used to train the models include background pixels around the person. Therefore, the actual size of a detected person is smaller than the training image size.

$$M(i,j) = \begin{cases} 1, & if \, person \, is \, detected \\ 0, & otherwise \end{cases} \tag{7}$$

where $M(i,j)$ is the binary mask. Then, morphological operations on the resulting binary mask are performed to remove noisy pixels.

2.2 Non-linear Multi-mode Tracker with Combined Detector

Many trackers were build upon the model of object appearance. This means that, given a moving object, these detectors discard the information from the motion of object, i.e. the variation of foreground. Therefore, this may result in tracking an object far away from the location with the real variation of foreground. Our detector combines the information from the gray-scale distribution with the variation of foreground. This makes the tracker to search an object at the place consistent with the location where exists the real variation of foreground. This approach compares the result of PF(Particle Filter) with one of background subtraction, after PF implemented. That is, after PF implemented, this re-checks if object detected by background subtraction exists in the place as object region estimated by PF or how much they are overlapping. If existed or overlapped, the result of PF will be corrected to one of background subtraction, and if not, there will be two proposals. If the confidence of PF result is not sufficient, then it will be canceled completely, and if not, a new object region will be added to the result of background subtraction to compensate error of background subtraction. In fact, when object is overlapped seriously, real object region may be considered as background region from incompleteness of person detector. These regions will be just recovered by object appearance model-based detector.

$$M(i,j) = \begin{cases} 1, & if \, the \, large \, confidence, \, existed \, or \, overlapped \\ 0, & otherwise \end{cases} \tag{8}$$

where $M(i,j)$ is the binary mask.

Finally, PF is implemented around extended regions of each bounding boxes obtained by background subtraction, i.e. size of each extended region is lager than ones bounded by background subtraction. All coordinates for PF are calculated as relative coordinates for each extended regions.

3   Experimental Results

We evaluate the performance of our proposed tracking framework. Our experiment should be aimed at the relative evaluation for our proposed approaches themselves in relation with the previous approach. The sophisticated feature descriptor, of course, may be used to this tracking scenario to obtain high accuracy of tracking. However, our experiment should be aimed at the relative evaluation for our proposed tracking framework in relation with previous approaches. Therefore, these experiments do not use other feature descriptors. We test our proposed approach and the previous approach in several challenging image sequences.

The performance evaluation includes two parts. The first part contains the evaluation for the performance of our proposed tracking framework in image sequences given a single example of a specific object. The second part compares the performance of our proposed tracking framework with one of the previous framework in the context of tracking multiple object.

All experiments are conducted on an Intel® Core(TM) i5 2.40 GHz PC with 4 GB memory(1.32 GHz). The real image sequences are available at http:// www.ces.clemson.edu/~stb/research/headtracker and under MATLAB(2013a) directory.

The first set of experiments is implemented in a popularly used real video sequence containing 500 frames with resolution of 128 × 96 pixels, respectively. Figure 1 show the comparison of tracking results in real color video, the absolute error for every frame and the error histograms for two approaches, respectively. Red box indicates the result of our approach, and blue for the TLD. The experiment results show our proposed approach has also a robust performance for real video sequences. As a result, the tracker based on proposed approaches shows the most satisfactory performance among two trackers.

Fig. 1. Comparison of tracking result on real color video; Red box indicates the result of our approach, and blue for the TLD; Shown are frames 0, 3, 22, 98(top); 117, 126, 135, 188(middle); and 427, 457, 471, 500(bottom) (Color figure online).

Next, the second set of experiments is implemented in a color image sequence containing motion of multiple object. This video sequence contains 480 × 360-pixel color images. This video contain such variations as model distortion, occlusion, appearance of multi-objects and noise etc. The purpose of this experiment

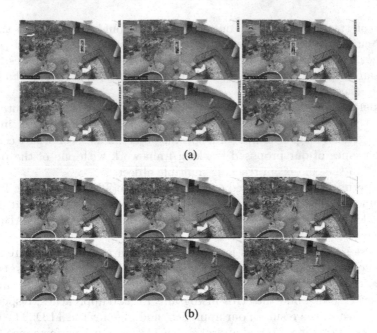

Fig. 2. Comparison of tracking result on color video with motion of multiple object; TLD(a) and our proposed approach(b); Shown are frames 30, 43, 45(top); and 48, 54, 65(bottom) (Color figure online).

is to evaluate the robustness of our proposed approach under the configuration of multiple object tracking. The result of this experiment is shown in Fig. 2. It can be seen clear that our tracking framework has better performance for occlusion and multiple object tracking than TLD.

All the above experimental results prove that our proposed tracking framework is more robust and accurate compared with the other approaches. The other important thing we want to emphasize here is that our approach may also obtain competitive tracking results on other image datasets.

4   Conclusion

In this paper, we first proposed the combined detector containing the background subtraction and the object appearance model-based detector. This was used to solve such problems as linking, overlapping, false object detecting etc. Then, the non-linear multi-mode tracker with the combined detector was proposed to solve such problems as sudden appearance changes and long-lasting occlusions, etc. Finally, we tested our proposed person tracking framework in single-object and multi-object tracking scenario. Future work should be aimed at extending our proposed tracking approaches to connecting with more sophisticated feature descriptors and similarity measures such as the geogram [13], SOG [14] and AIBS [15].

Acknowledgments. This research is founded by the grant of The Key Technology Research of Multi-Camera Cooperative Awareness and Data Fusion for Smart Community in Wuhan City No. 2014010202010110.

References

1. Isard, M., Blake, A.: Condensation - conditional density propagation for visual tracking. IJCV **29**(1), 5–28 (1998)
2. Lim, J., Ross, D., Lin, R.S., Yang, M.H.: Incremental learning for visual tracking. In: NIPS (2005)
3. Kim, M., Kumar, S., Pavlovic, V., Rowley, H.: Face tracking and recognition with visual constraints in real-world videos. In: CVPR (2008)
4. Viola, P., Jones, M.: Rapid object detection using a boosted cascade of simple features. In: CVPR (2001)
5. Kalal, Z., Matas, J., Mikolajczyk, K.: Weighted sampling for large-scale boosting. In: BMVC (2008)
6. Li, Y., Ai, H., Yamashita, T., Lao, S., Kawade, M.: Tracking in low frame rate video: a cascade particle filter with discriminative observers of different lifespans. In: CVPR (2007)
7. Everingham, M., Sivic, J., Zisserman, A.: Taking the bite out of automated naming of characters in TV video. IVC **27**, 545–559 (2009)
8. Kalal, Z., Matas, J., Mikolajczyk, K.: Online learning of robust object detectors during unstable tracking. In: OLCV (2009)
9. Kalal, Z., Matas, J., Mikolajczyk, K.: P-N Learning: bootstrapping binary classifiers by structural constraints. In: CVPR (2010)
10. Zhao, W., Chellappa, R., Phillips, P.J., Rosenfeld, A.: Face recognition: a literature survey. CSUR **35**(4), 399–458 (2003)
11. Lucas, B.D., Kanade, T.: An iterative image registration technique with an application to stereo vision. IJCAI **81**, 674–679 (1981)
12. Choe, G., et al.: Visual tracking based on particle filter with spline resampling. Multimedia Tools Appl. (2014). doi:10.1007/s11042-014-1960-z
13. Choe, G., et al.: Moving object tracking based on geogram. Multimedia Tools Appl. (2014). doi:10.1007/s11042-014-2150-8
14. Gong, L., Wang, T., Liu, F., Chen, G.: A Lie group based spatiogram similarity measure. In: ICME (2009)
15. Choe, G., et al.: An advanced association of particle filtering and kernel based object tracking. Multimedia Tools Appl. (2014). doi:10.1007/s11042-014-1993-3
16. Choe, G., et al.: Particle filter with spline resampling and global transition model. IET Comput. Vision **9**(2), 184–197 (2015)

Sparse Representation-Based Deformation Model for Atlas-Based Segmentation of Liver CT Images

Changfa Shi[1], Jinke Wang[2(✉)], and Yuanzhi Cheng[1]

[1] School of Computer Science and Technology,
Harbin Institute of Technology, Harbin, China
[2] Department of Software Engineering,
Harbin University of Science and Technology, Rongcheng, China
jkwang@hitwh.edu.cn

Abstract. Liver segmentation in computed tomography (CT) images is a fundamental step for various computer-assisted clinical applications. However, automatic liver segmentation from CT images is still a challenging task. In this paper, we propose a novel non-parametric sparse representation-based deformation model (SRDM) for atlas-based liver segmentation framework using nonrigid registration based on free-form deformations (FFDs) model. Specifically, during atlas-based segmentation procedure, our proposed SRDM provides a regularization for the resulting deformation that maps the atlas to the space of the target image, constraining it to be a sparse linear combination of existing training deformations in a deformation repository. We evaluated our proposed method based on a set of 30 contrast-enhanced abdominal CT images, resulting in superior performance when compared to state-of-the-art atlas-based segmentation methods.

Keywords: Liver segmentation · Atlas-based segmentation · Statistical deformation model · Sparse representation

1 Introduction

Segmentation of the liver tissue in computed tomography (CT) images is a fundamental step for various clinical applications, such as computer-assisted liver cancer diagnosis and surgical planning. However, automatic liver segmentation from CT images is still a challenging task, because of large shape variability, adjacent organs with similar intensity values, and the presence of tumors.

In the literature, a variety of methods have been proposed for liver segmentation [3,4]. Of these, one promising method is the atlas-based segmentation [7], where the prior knowledge about the liver tissue existence probability is incorporated. An atlas is typically consists of two parts: atlas intensity image and its corresponding atlas label image. After the atlas intensity image is warped to the space of the target image, the atlas label image is propagated to the target

© Springer International Publishing Switzerland 2015
Y.-J. Zhang (Ed.): ICIG 2015, Part III, LNCS 9219, pp. 410–419, 2015.
DOI: 10.1007/978-3-319-21969-1_36

image using the resulting transformation and defined as the final segmentation result. Therefore, the main source of error for atlas-based segmentation comes from the employed registration method. To largely avoid these registration errors caused by the large variability of soft tissue (e.g., liver), statistical deformation models (SDMs) [8] is proposed to regularize the resulting transformation that maps the atlas to the space of the target image, constraining it to be within principal subspace of plausible transformation learned from the training images. However, SDMs are parametric models assuming normal distribution of data and only account for small dense Gaussian noise.

In this paper, inspired by the recently proposed Sparse Shape Composition (SSC) shape prior modeling method [13], we propose a novel non-parametric sparse representation-based deformation model (SRDM) for atlas-based liver segmentation framework using nonrigid registration based on free-form deformations (FFDs) model [9]. Specifically, during atlas-based segmentation procedure, our proposed SRDM provides a regularization for the resulting deformation that maps the atlas to the space of the target image, constraining it to be a sparse linear combination of existing training deformations in a deformation repository. Because the sparse gross errors are explicitly modeled in our method, it is robust against both small dense Gaussian noise and sparse gross registration errors. We applied our proposed method to segment the liver tissue based on a set of 30 contrast-enhanced abdominal CT images.

2   Background

In this section, we briefly describe the main idea of nonrigid registration using free-form deformations (FFDs) and statistical deformation models (SDMs), we refer the readers to [8,9] for more details.

2.1   Nonrigid Registration Using Free-Form Deformations

Free-form deformations (FFDs) model based on B-splines [9] is a popular spline-based transformation model for nonrigid image registration. The main idea of FFDs is to deform a rectangular grid placed on the reference image by manipulating an underlying B-spline control points. The optimal transformation $\mathbf{T}$ is found by minimizing the following cost function:

$$C = C_{similarity}(I_{target}, \mathbf{T}(I_{source})) + \lambda C_{smooth}(\mathbf{T}), \tag{1}$$

which consists of two competing terms: image similarity (e.g., normalized mutual information (NMI) [10]) and transformation smoothness. The minimization problem can be iteratively solved by using gradient descent technique.

2.2   Statistical Deformation Models

Unlike the concept of statistical shape models (SSMs), in statistical deformation models (SDMs) [8], principal component analysis (PCA) is applied to the control points which form compact parameterization of the B-spline based FFDs rather than to the anatomical landmarks. Assume that we have a reference image I_r and a set of k training data $\{I_i \mid i = 1, 2, ..., k\}$. We can derive a set of k corresponding B-spline based FFDs $\{FFD_i \mid i = 1, 2, ..., k\}$, which map the liver structure of the reference image I_r to that of all other training data I_i, and each FFD_i is represented by a control point vector $\mathbf{C}_i = (x_1, y_1, z_1, ..., x_{n_p}, y_{n_p}, z_{n_p})^T$ with n_p underlying mesh of 3-D control points that parameterize the FFDs. We define the corresponding covariance matrix as: $\mathbf{S} = \frac{1}{k-1} \sum_{i=1}^{k} (\mathbf{C}_i - \bar{\mathbf{C}})(\mathbf{C}_i - \bar{\mathbf{C}})^T$, where $\bar{\mathbf{C}}$ is the mean control point vector (i.e., average deformation field) of all subjects: $\bar{\mathbf{C}} = \frac{1}{k}\sum_{i=1}^{k} \mathbf{C}_i$. Then the statistical deformation model (SDM) can be built by an eigen-decomposition on the covariance matrix $\mathbf{S}$:

$$\mathbf{S} = \mathbf{U}\mathbf{D}\mathbf{U}^T, \tag{2}$$

where columns of matrix of $\mathbf{U}$ form the principal modes of variation ϕ_m (eigenvectors), and diagonal entries of $\mathbf{D}$ are their respective variances λ_m (eigenvalues). Any valid deformation field of liver structure thus can be approximated by a linear combination of the first c modes of variation:

$$\mathbf{C} = \bar{\mathbf{C}} + \sum_{m=1}^{c} b_m \phi_m, \tag{3}$$

where $c = \min\{t \mid \sum_{i=1}^{t} \lambda_t / \sum_{i=1}^{k-1} \lambda_t > 0.98\}$, and b_m is the deformation parameter constrained to the interval $b_m \in \left[-3\sqrt{\lambda_m}, 3\sqrt{\lambda_m}\right]$.

3   Methods

In this section, we describe our proposed non-parametric sparse representation-based deformation model (SRDM) for atlas-based liver segmentation framework. Figure 1 shows the proposed segmentation framework, including training and testing phases.

In training phase, the liver atlas and our proposed SRDM which is employed as the deformation prior model are learned (Sect. 3.1). In testing phase, the atlas-based method is used to segment the liver tissue in the target image, where the learned deformation prior model (i.e., SRDM) is employed to regularize the deformation that maps the atlas to the space of the target image (Sect. 3.2).

3.1   Sparse Representation-Based Deformation Model

Before we can actually learn our proposed SRDM from training images, we need to construct the liver atlas first.

Construction of Liver Atlas. For the construction of liver atlas, we employ an iterative procedure to avoid bias towards particular anatomy of the selected reference image.

Let $\{I_i \mid i = 1, ..., K\}$ be the $K = 20$ preprocessed training images with corresponding label image $\{L_i \mid i = 1, ..., K\}$. One image with a mean liver shape is selected from the training data (I_1 in our study) as the initial template image. All other images are affinely mapped and resampled to this image. To avoid bias towards the chosen template image, we used the Minimal Deformation Target (MDT) strategy [11] to derive the initial average template. We define the mean deformation of I_1 when nonrigidly mapped to all other training images as: $\bar{T}_1 = \frac{1}{K-1} \sum_{j \neq 1} T_{1j}$. Then the MDT template for image I_1 is defined as: $MDT_1 = \bar{T}_1(I_1)$.

Ideally, MDT_1 can be directly employed as the final liver atlas. However, because the registration algorithm is topology preserving, MDT_1 is still biased towards the shape of the selected initial template image I_1 [11]. Therefore, we define MDT_1 as the initial average template, and all other training images are nonrigidly mapped and resampled to this image in an iterative fashion with a maximum iteration of 3. The FFD model based on B-splines is employed to perform all the nonrigid registration in this step.

Using this procedure, we obtain a set of K aligned training images $\{I_i' \mid i = 1, ..., K\}$ with corresponding label image $\{L_i' \mid i = 1, ..., K\}$. The liver atlas $(\bar{I}, \bar{L})$ can thus be defined as the average of the aligned data:

$$\bar{I} \leftarrow \frac{1}{K} \sum_{i=1}^{K} I_i', \quad \bar{L} \leftarrow \frac{1}{K} \sum_{i=1}^{K} L_i'. \tag{4}$$

Sparse Representation-Based Deformation Model. Once the liver atlas $(\bar{I}, \bar{L})$ is derived, we can build our proposed non-parametric sparse representation-based deformation model (SRDM).

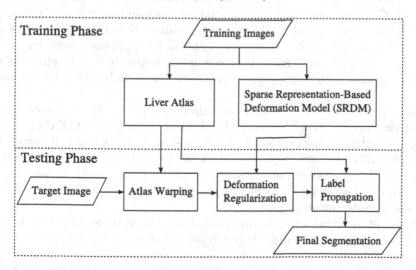

Fig. 1. The main workflow of our proposed liver segmentation framework, which consists of training and testing phases.

We first derive the training deformation data by nonrigidly registering the liver atlas to all the training images $\{I_i \mid i = 1, ..., K\}$, which are preprocessed by affinely registering and resampling to I_1. The FFD model based on B-splines is also employed to perform the nonrigid registration. Through this procedure, we derive a set of K training deformations, which are represented by the control point vectors of the B-splines that parameterize the FFDs: $\{\mathbf{C}_i \mid i = 1, 2, ..., K\}$.

Sparse Shape Composition (SSC) [13] is a sparse representation-based shape prior modeling method that implicitly incorporates the shape priors on-the-fly to overcome the main issues of traditional shape prior modeling method. Inspired by this method, we propose a novel non-parametric sparse representation-based deformation model (SRDM) to deal with registration errors caused by the large variability of liver tissue. Based on two sparsity properties of the input deformation (i.e., the input deformation can be approximately represented by a sparse linear combination of existing training deformations in a deformation repository; the input deformation may include sparse gross errors), we can cast the deformation modeling as the following sparse optimization problem:

$$(\hat{\mathbf{x}}, \hat{\mathbf{e}}) = \arg\min_{\mathbf{x}, \mathbf{e}} \|\mathbf{c} - \mathbf{D}\mathbf{x} - \mathbf{e}\|_2^2 + \lambda_1 \|\mathbf{x}\|_1 + \lambda_2 \|\mathbf{e}\|_1, \qquad (5)$$

where $\mathbf{c} \in \mathbb{R}^{3N}$ (N is the number of B-spline control points) is an input deformation to be refined, $\mathbf{D} = [\mathbf{C}_1, \mathbf{C}_2, ..., \mathbf{C}_K] \in \mathbb{R}^{3N \times K}$ is the deformation repository (i.e., the dictionary) that includes K training deformations $\mathbf{C}_i$, $\mathbf{x} \in \mathbb{R}^K$ denotes the coefficients of linear combination, $\mathbf{e} \in \mathbb{R}^{3N}$ represents the sparse gross errors, $\|\mathbf{v}\|_1 = \sum_i |v_i|$ is the ℓ_1-norm of $\mathbf{v}$ that induces sparsity, $\|\mathbf{v}\|_2$ is the Euclidean norm of $\mathbf{v}$, λ_1 and λ_2 are positive parameters that control the sparsity of $\mathbf{x}$ and $\mathbf{e}$ respectively. Then the input deformation $\mathbf{c}$ is refined as $\hat{\mathbf{c}} = \mathbf{D}\hat{\mathbf{x}}$.

Equation 5 is the sparse minimization problem of our proposed SRDM. Because of the sparsity-inducing property of the ℓ_1-norm, the solution of this optimization problem will be the sparsest, meaning that most entries in $\hat{\mathbf{x}}$ and $\hat{\mathbf{e}}$ will be zero. We employ $\mathbf{e}$ and the ℓ_2-norm to explicitly model the sparse gross errors and the small dense Gaussian noise, respectively. Therefore, SRDM is robust against both large sparse registration errors and small dense Gaussian noise.

Among numerous optimization algorithms proposed in the literature [1], we employ the Fast Iterative Shrinkage Thresholding Algorithm (FISTA) [2] to solve the sparse optimization problem in Eq. 5, due to its efficiency and robustness. The global rate of convergence of FISTA is $O(1/k^2)$, where k is the iteration counter [2]. For a more detailed description of the FISTA method, we refer the reader to [2]. Also it has been shown that stable recovery of both $\mathbf{x}$ and $\mathbf{e}$ in Eq. 5 can be guaranteed [12].

During atlas-based segmentation procedure, our proposed SRDM provides a regularization for the resulting deformation $\mathbf{c}$ that maps the atlas to the space of the target image, constraining the resulting deformation to be a sparse linear combination of existing training deformations learned from the training data in a deformation repository.

3.2   Atlas-Based Liver Segmentation Framework

After the liver atlas and SRDM are learned, we employ atlas-based method to segment the liver tissue, which is mainly based on nonrigid registration from the atlas to the target image.

Given a target image I_{new} to be segmented, which is preprocessed by affinely registering and resampling to I_1, the atlas intensity image $\bar{I}$ is nonrigidly warped to the space of preprocessed I_{new} using FFD model based on B-splines. Then the found deformation $\mathbf{c}$ that maps the atlas intensity image to the space of the target image is regularized by the learned SRDM deformation prior model according to Eq. 5. Finally, the atlas label image $\bar{L}$ is deformed by using the regularized deformation $\hat{\mathbf{c}} = \mathbf{D}\hat{\mathbf{x}}$ instead of the original deformation $\mathbf{c}$, and we derive the finally propagated atlas label image $\bar{L}'$. The final liver segmentation L_{new} is then extracted by thresholding the propagated atlas label image $\bar{L}'$ using Otsu's method, followed by removing unconnected components and filling small holes via the closing operator.

4   Results

To quantify the accuracy and performance of our proposed method, we have tested it on a set of 30 contrast-enhanced abdominal CT images. 20 CT images with corresponding ground truth, coming from the public database SLIVER07-Train (http://www.sliver07.org), were used for training models. These 20 images have varied in-plane resolution between 0.58 mm and 0.81 mm and slice thickness between 0.7 mm and 5.0 mm. The remaining 10 CT images from our clinical partner with corresponding expert segmentations were used for testing the accuracy of our proposed method. These 10 images have varied in-plane resolution between 0.58 mm and 0.67 mm, and a slice thickness of 1.0 mm. Most of the datasets in this study are pathological, including tumors, metastases and cysts.

We compared the segmentation results with the ground truth by using the average symmetric surface distance (ASD) metric, which is defined as the average distance between the surfaces of two segmentation results. The ASD is given in millimeters, and smaller value means more accurate segmentation result. We refer the readers to [4] for the detailed definition of the ASD metric.

Our method were implemented in C++ on Linux platform, and tested on a PC with a 2.5 GHz Intel quad-core processor. The source code is available at http://github.com/ivanshih/SRDM. We used the elastix package (http://elastix.isi.uu.nl) [5] to perform both affine and FFD model-based nonrigid registration between atlas and all the input images by maximization of the normalized mutual information (NMI) [10]. In the nonrigid registration procedure, we employed three resolution levels and the spacing of the underlying B-spline control points in the finest resolution level is set to 10 mm. We employed the FISTA implemented in the open source optimization toolbox SPAMS (http://spams-devel.gforge.inria.fr) [6] to solve the sparse optimization problems in Eq. 5.

In our implementation, the parameters used in the liver segmentation framework were the same for all the test data. We set $\lambda_1 = 60$ (sparsity parameter

Table 1. The mean and standard deviation of the generalization ability of the two different deformation prior modeling methods based on the SLIVER07-Train database.

	SDM	SRDM
Generality Measurement [mm]	2.31±0.45	2.19±0.44

for $\mathbf{x}$ in Eq. 5) and $\lambda_2 = 0.2$ (sparsity parameter for $\mathbf{e}$ in Eq. 5). We also compared our proposed SRDM model with the closely related statistical deformation model (SDM) [8]. In our implementation of SDM, 98 % of the total deformation variance in the datasets is captured by the used modes of variation.

4.1   Generalization Ability of the SRDM

We first evaluate the performance of our proposed SRDM based on the training data using the generalization ability measure.

The generalization ability quantifies the capability of the model to represent unknown deformations of the same object class. It can be measured by performing a series of leave-one-out tests on the training set, where the difference between the omitted training deformation $\mathbf{C}_i$ and the reconstructed deformation $\mathbf{C}_i^*$ of $\mathbf{C}_i$ is measured. The final result is defined as the average over the complete set of tests. To quantify the difference between two corresponding deformations, we employed the root-mean-square deviation (RMSD) based metrics. The generalization ability can be defined as:

$$\mathcal{G} = \frac{1}{K} \sum_{i=1}^{K} \sqrt{\frac{\|\mathbf{C}_i^* - \mathbf{C}_i\|^2}{3N}}, \tag{6}$$

where N is the number of B-spline control points. And smaller value of the generalization ability indicates better deformation modeling method.

We also compared our model with the SDM deformation prior model. Table 1 shows the quantitative comparisons of the generalization ability based on the SLIVER07-Train database. Compared with SDM, our proposed SRDM achieves a better generalization ability with a smaller variance.

4.2   Liver Segmentation from CT Images

To demonstrate the effectiveness of our proposed SRDM, we applied it to the application of segmenting the liver tissue in CT Images. Specifically, SRDM was used to regularize the resulting deformation $\mathbf{c}$ that mapped the atlas to the space of the target image during the atlas-based segmentation procedure. We also compared our model with two closely related methods: traditional unregularized FFD model and SDM regularized model. To make a fair comparison, the same atlas-based liver segmentation framework is employed in all compared methods. Only the deformation prior modeling method used to refine the resulting deformation $\mathbf{c}$ is different.

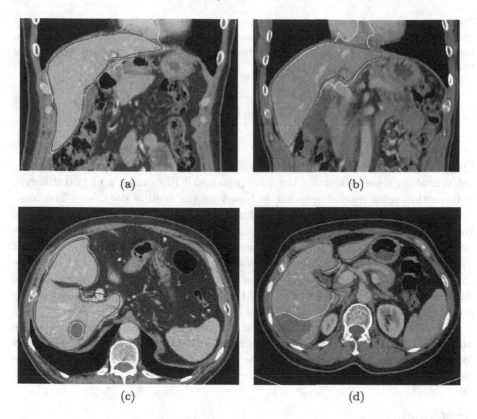

(a)   (b)

(c)   (d)

Fig. 2. Visual comparisons of liver segmentation results between unregularized FFD model and our proposed SRDM deformation prior method in two difficult cases: adjacent organ (i.e., the heart) has similar intensity values as the live tissue (first row); and the livers contain large tumors (second row). Each figure shows one case. The red contour shows the ground truth, the yellow and blue contours show the results of the unregularized FFD model and our method, respectively.

Qualitative Results: Figures 2a and b compare the segmentation results between unregularized FFD model and our method in difficult cases where adjacent organ (i.e., the heart) has similar intensity values as the live tissue. The unregularized FFD model based method over-segments the live tissue and includes part of the heart with similar intensity values, while our method successfully excludes these regions. Figures 2c and d compare the segmentation results between unregularized FFD model and our method in difficult cases where the livers contain large tumors. The unregularized FFD model cannot restore regions containing large tumors, while our method successfully preserves and reconstructs these regions. The reason is that in our method, these segmentation errors of the unregularized FFD model are explicitly modeled and reconstructed as the sparse gross errors. Therefore, these experimental results demonstrate that our method is robust in overcoming both over- and under-segmentation.

Table 2. Quantitative comparisons of liver segmentation results between the unregularized FFD model and two different deformation prior modeling methods based on the testing database. The measure is represented as mean and standard deviation of the overall datasets.

	FFD	SDM	SRDM
ASD [mm]	2.17±0.70	1.91±0.58	**1.72±0.47**

Quantitative Results: Table 2 shows the quantitative comparisons of liver segmentation results between the unregularized FFD model and two different deformation prior modeling methods based on the testing database. The measure is represented as mean and standard deviation of the overall datasets. Of these compared methods, our method achieves the best accuracy and the smallest variances according to the ASD metric, indicating the robustness of our method against registration errors caused by the large variability of liver tissue. In particular, the mean ASD of our method is 1.72 mm. The mean ASD of the unregularized FFD model and SDM based method are 0.45 mm and nearly 0.2 mm higher than that of our method, respectively.

These experiments demonstrate that our proposed method is more accurate and robust than the other two methods in segmenting the liver tissue, especially for difficult cases where adjacent organs have similar intensity values as the live tissue and the livers contain large tumors.

5   Conclusion

In this paper, we have presented a novel non-parametric sparse representation-based deformation model (SRDM) for atlas-based liver segmentation framework. To deal with registration errors caused by the large variability of liver tissue, our proposed SRDM provides a regularization for the resulting deformation that maps the atlas to the space of the target image. We evaluated our proposed method for liver segmentation based on a set of 30 contrast-enhanced abdominal CT images and achieved promising results, especially for difficult cases where adjacent organs have similar intensity values as the live tissue and the livers contain large tumors. Comparison with unregularized FFD model and SDM shows the superior performance of our proposed method.

In the future, we plan to employ more training data to learn the atlas and SRDM, which we believe will further improve the segmentation accuracy.

Acknowledgments. This work was supported by the Scientific Research Fund of Heilongjiang Provincial Education Department (No.12541164).

References

1. Bach, F., Jenatton, R., Mairal, J., Obozinski, G.: Convex optimization with sparsity-inducing norms. In: Sra, S., Nowozin, S., Wright, S.J. (eds.) Optimization for Machine Learning. Neural Information Processing Series, pp. 19–54. MIT Press, MIT Press (2011). Chapter 2
2. Beck, A., Teboulle, M.: A fast iterative shrinkage-thresholding algorithm for linear inverse problems. SIAM J. Imaging Sci. **2**(1), 183–202 (2009)
3. Campadelli, P., Casiraghi, E., Esposito, A.: Liver segmentation from computed tomography scans: a survey and a new algorithm. Artif. Intell. Med. **45**(2), 185–196 (2009)
4. Heimann, T., van Ginneken, B., Styner, M., Arzhaeva, Y., Aurich, V., Bauer, C., Beck, A., Becker, C., Beichel, R., Bekes, G., Bello, F., Binnig, G.K., Bischof, H., Bornik, A., Cashman, P., Chi, Y., Cordova, A., Dawant, B.M., Fidrich, M., Furst, J.D., Furukawa, D., Grenacher, L., Hornegger, J., Kainmüller, D., Kitney, R., Kobatake, H., Lamecker, H., Lange, T., Lee, J., Lennon, B., Li, R., Li, S., Meinzer, H.P., Németh, G., Raicu, D.S., Rau, A., van Rikxoort, E.M., Rousson, M., Ruskó, L., Saddi, K.A., Schmidt, G., Seghers, D., Shimizu, A., Slagmolen, P., Sorantin, E., Soza, G., Susomboon, R., Waite, J.M., Wimmer, A., Wolf, I.: Comparison and evaluation of methods for liver segmentation from CT datasets. IEEE Trans. Med. Imaging **28**(8), 1251–1265 (2009)
5. Klein, S., Staring, M., Murphy, K., Viergever, M.A., Pluim, J.P.W.: Elastix: a toolbox for intensity-based medical image registration. IEEE Trans. Med. Imaging **29**(1), 196–205 (2010)
6. Mairal, J., Bach, F., Ponce, J., Sapiro, G.: Online learning for matrix factorization and sparse coding. J. Mach. Learn. Res. **11**, 19–60 (2010)
7. Park, H., Bland, P.H., Meyer, C.R.: Construction of an abdominal probabilistic atlas and its application in segmentation. IEEE Trans. Med. Imaging **22**(4), 483–492 (2003)
8. Rueckert, D., Frangi, A.F., Schnabel, J.A.: Automatic construction of 3D statistical deformation models of the brain using non-rigid registration. IEEE Trans. Med. Imaging **22**(8), 1014–1025 (2003)
9. Rueckert, D., Sonoda, L.I., Hayes, C., Hill, D.L.G., Leach, M.O., Hawkes, D.J.: Non-rigid registration using free-form deformations: application to breast MR images. IEEE Trans. Med. Imaging **18**(8), 712–721 (1999)
10. Studholme, C., Hill, D.L.G., Hawkes, D.J.: An overlap invariant entropy measure of 3D medical image alignment. Pattern Recogn. **32**(1), 71–86 (1999)
11. Wang, Q., Seghers, D., D'Agostino, E., Maes, F., Vandermeulen, D., Suetens, P., Hammers, A.: Construction and validation of mean shape atlas templates for atlas-based brain image segmentation. In: Christensen, G.E., Sonka, M. (eds.) IPMI 2005. LNCS, vol. 3565, pp. 689–700. Springer, Heidelberg (2005)
12. Wright, J., Ma, Y.: Dense error correction via ℓ^1-minimization. IEEE Trans. Inf. Theory **56**(7), 3540–3560 (2010)
13. Zhang, S., Zhan, Y., Dewan, M., Huang, J., Metaxas, D.N., Zhou, X.S.: Towards robust and effective shape modeling: sparse shape composition. Med. Image Anal. **16**(1), 265–277 (2012)

Survey of Astronomical Image Processing Methods

Hai Jing Zhu, Bo Chong Han, and Bo Qiu[(✉)]

School of Electronic and Information Engineering,
Hebei University of Technology, Tianjin, China
sfighter@126.com

Abstract. The image processing is becoming a key issue in astronomical data analysis. This paper introduces the algorithms and methods applied in astronomical image processing from different aspects. The paper first shows methods of lossless compression of astronomical images, like the pyramidal median transform, segment-based DPCM and 5/3 integer wavelet transform. Secondly it shows the algorithms of astronomical image segmentation, edge detection and de-noising. Finally, many different methods of image recovery and restoration are introduced briefly. We summarize a number of recent achievements on astronomical image processing in this survey, and list the recent published papers.

Keywords: Astronomical image · Image compression · Image restoration · Survey

1 Introduction

With the development of astronomy, image processing has become more and more important and played a key role for astronomical research.

Raw astronomical images usually contain noises and blurs, so that they cannot be used in analysis and research directly. And under the enhancement of quality, the size of astronomical image grows up. As a result, it is difficult to store and transmit these large image files. Consequently, image processing in astronomy such as compression, denoising, segmentation and restoration is required.

In this paper we give a general review of astronomical image processing methods. Our review starts from Sect. 2 with image compression problems. In Sect. 3 we consider the issue of image segmentation and edge detection. In Sect. 4 the deblurring and denoising filtering methods are reviewed. The algorithms of image restoration are described in Sect. 5. We will review a range of important results in astronomical image processing, and a central theme about how these methods and algorithms are put forward and how they work.

2 Astronomical Image Compression

With the development of technology, image has been becoming a more and more critical medium of information. However, when we begin to study astronomical images, we find that the high-quality images are always with a large size and carry large

© Springer International Publishing Switzerland 2015
Y.-J. Zhang (Ed.): ICIG 2015, Part III, LNCS 9219, pp. 420–429, 2015.
DOI: 10.1007/978-3-319-21969-1_37

databases. So it is interesting for the data providers and users to make use of the most effective image compression techniques.

Image compression is required in many fields like medicine, remote sensing and astronomy. Compression reduces the storage media costs and the network bandwidth needed to transmit the files to users. Image compression also reduces a number of bytes of data that are transferred to or from local disks during data analysis operations. In [8], we know the extensive literature on astronomical image compression can be divided into 2 main categories: loss compression, in which some of the information (ideally only noise) is discarded, and lossless compression techniques where all the information is preserved so that the original data can be exactly reconstructed. Lossless compression by definition preserves all the information in the images and is often preferred or required in situations where the data provider must be certain that no information is lost. In this paper we just focus on lossless compression.

Traditional methods of lossless compression like Huffman coding, arithmetic coding, dictionary based LZW encoding, bit plane coding and the run length encoding widely used in different situations. The Huffman coding method based on statistical properties of image is used in star image where the most areas are stable; while the bit-plane coding method is more available in images with many details or with a high resolution, for instance the photographs of the sun.

The wavelet transform is also extensively used to astronomical image compression. In [5], it presents an algorithm based on the wavelet transformation which can achieve image compression with or without information loss, as well as compression of specific interesting image regions. The paper focuses on the compression encoding technique after wavelet transformation, when finished the analysis of frequency band the critical parameters are extracted to transmit so that this algorithm can obtain a good result of image information with a least data. According to the fluctuations in network bandwidth the algorithm timely adjusts the compression rate. The astronomical image information will be effectively transmitted for remote observation in time.

In [8], the author uses a relatively new compressed image format that is based on the FITS tiled-image compression convention. The current implementation of this convention in the CFITSIO library supports 4 lossless compression algorithms: Rice, Hcompress, PLIO and GZIP. The article introduces the main features of each of the algorithms. It should be noted that the GZIP algorithm has a users electable parameter for fine tuning the tradeoff between speed and compression ratio. Also the effect of noise on lossless image compression is discussed and a comparison on different compression algorithms is made. In this paper the author has performed a detailed evaluation of various lossless compression techniques on a large sample of astronomical images that are representative of the types of images from many sky survey projects. Using optimal compression methods on such images can make a large difference in the amount of disk space and network bandwidth needed to analyze, archive, and reconstruct the images.

In [11], the paper describes the basis theoretical of image compression, given a detailed description of the implementation principle of Huffman coding, LZW coding and predictive coding. Then it introduces the wavelet transform theory, expounds the second generation of integer wavelet transform theory and implementation steps based on lifting scheme, compares these technologies with experimental methods, and points out that an important prospects for hybrid coding. The characteristics of astronomical images are analyzed and summarized: large, special, formatted, high-gray and noisy. In order to solve the high-gray problem, this paper uses gray image stretching technology to achieve astronomical images display. After analyzing the experiment results of predicting and IWT, this paper proposes a new sub-block DPCM and integer wavelet transform using in astronomical image lossless compression algorithm. And it has done a comprehensive exposition of the algorithm, then the importance of astronomical images sub-block is discussed in detail, while the DPCM prediction strategy is selected by experiments, and the (5, 3) wavelet is selected being symmetric extension of the wavelet transform boundary approach. The predicting and IWT algorithm applied in astronomical images is especially emphasized.

In [6], the paper presents a new lossless image compression method in order to solve the increasingly outstanding issue of storing massive astronomical image data in devices of limited storage space and low bandwidths [3]. In [1], the author uses integer 5/3 wavelet transformation with the combination of DPCM to achieve a lossless compression of image, however, the compression ratio is not so good since the Haar wavelet has a weak ability of redundancy removing. In [4], the authors combine DPCM with IWT and get a lossless compression of medical images with a higher compression ratio, but, when the picture is extra large this method will arouse a diffusion of prediction error. In [7], the loss and lossless image compression methods are improved by using EZW, but the algorithms are too complex to achieve hardware implementation. In the method presented in [6] a large astronomical image is segmented first, then successively coded with the Differential Pulse Code Modulation, 5/3 Integer Wavelet Transformation, and Huffman algorithm. The author briefly outlines the approach of the lossless compression, and discusses the details of the principle of the method and the implementation of the relevant algorithms. The experiment indicates that the compression ratio of out method is higher than those of the Linux tar command, PKZip, WinZip, and WinRar, respectively; the compression ratio is also much faster than the software's WinZip and WinRar. In addition, this algorithm has a parallel structure and is easy for hardware implementation.

3   Image Segmentation and Edge Detection

In astronomy, researchers aren't commonly interested in all the information in an image when they are studying on it; on the contrary, they often pay more attention to some regions of an image, which are generally called foreground. So it is very important to delete unnecessary data when memorizing and transmitting huge data [12]. One extensively used approach is, according to the characteristics of astronomical images astronomers make edge detection by using LOG (Laplacian of the Gaussian) operator in order to find out the outline of foreground, then segment the foreground.

In [12] a view finding technology based on digital image processing method is introduced, which finds out where the interested region is and segment it by using LOG operator. Noticed that astronomical images are mostly with single foreground and pure background, there is large contract ratio between foreground and background and the edge of image is sharp so that the LOG operator can be efficient to detect the edge and segment the background.

In astronomical image segmentation and edge detection, to meet the needs of high-speed and real-time is especially important. The paper [13] presents a method based on pipelining, using FPGA to build a SOC. Through design and verification it shows the method can achieve high speed, multi-channel and clock synchronization in astronomical image segmentation.

The paper [14] introduces four edge detection algorithms. They are different algorithms based on local hybrid filter de-noising model, sparse de-noising, least squares support vector machine, and the sparse representation de-noising model. In addition, the proposed algorithms are comparable, and their advantages and disadvantages in the SAR image edge detection are analyzed in order to facilitate further research.

In the sky, the stars' magnitudes vary a lot, so there are a lot of faint stars as shown in the star chart. When the distance between the imaging system and the target is big enough to a certain extent, the size of the target in the image is very small, may accounting for only a few, or even, a pixel. Meanwhile, the energy due to the attenuation caused by long-distance transmission, the star source signal intensity is relatively low with respect to the noise. Under such conditions, to detect the moving point target has important applications in guidance, astronomical observations, remote sensing and other disciplines.

(1) In the case of low SNR, it is not a small problem to detect moving point targets. For detecting moving point targets, in order to avoid the exhaustive search for the three-dimensional image sequences to detect moving targets, researchers have explored a number of ways, including 'a matched filter method' (1983, Reed), which uses matched filter theory applied to the three-dimensional image processing sequence, where the moving point target detection problem is transformed into a three-dimensional transform domain to find the optimal (matched) filter problem. And besides of this, there are dynamic programming method, Hove transform optimal projection method, sequential hypothesis testing, neural networks and other methods.

(2) With the development of photonics technology, astronomy and navigation technology has been improved in celestial navigation system for automatic generation of artificial sight detection technology, which is becoming increasingly important. It has become a powerful tool to improve the accuracy. Astral detection unit is a key part of celestial navigation system, which directly detects the position of the stars in the field of star tracking and direct astronomical positioning. Gray distribution feature uses satellite target point by sub-pixel positioning algorithm to determine the position of the target image. Sub-pixel positioning algorithms which can be used here are: centroid, weighted centroid method, Gaussian surface fitting method, and parabolic fitting method.

(3) In [15–17], star pattern recognition algorithms are introduced. Star sensor key algorithm, is to establish the relationship between the stars in star map and satellite image points according to the inertia coordinate system, in order to gain information about the location of the reference star. Star pattern recognition is a more mature star sensor algorithm to get the star map of each reference star magnitude, location coordinates and other information through the star identification.

Currently star pattern recognition algorithm can be applied in practical engineering, to the principle of a simple, easy to implement to identify triangles majority. Though there are some flaws in triangle recognition algorithms, domestic and foreign researchers are still improving it to achieve high recognition hit rate.

Figure 1 shows astronomical positioning triangle: O is the station, Z is the zenith, P is the north celestial pole. Guide device is based on the visual axis in the geocentric inertial coordinate system, given astronomical latitude and longitude respectively. By location triangle, horizontal photoelectric measuring system can work properly.

By the star pattern recognition to determine the star map of the star image after correspondence with the stars, it can be based on the principle of pinhole imaging model. Pinhole imaging model is shown in Fig. 2.

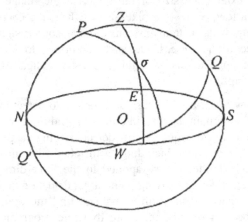

Fig. 1. Positioning the triangle diagram of astronomy

4   Denoising

In astronomical research, the images are often obtained by CCD (Charge-Coupled Device). Those images are normally affected by all kinds of noises during acquisition and transmission. And due to the interference of cosmic rays, some 'salt noises' can systematically introduce into CCD images during their acquisition. It is necessary to study how to reduce the noises effectively and how to realize the star searching and centering.

In [18], a ROAD (Rank-Ordered Absolute Difference) algorithm used to remove impulse noises and stellar-searching in CCD image is systematically introduced. The ROAD statistical values quantify how different in intensity the particular pixels are from their most similar neighbors. The noise removal filter based on a simple statistic to detect impulse pixels is to effectively remove noise from an image while keeping its features intact.

In [19], the author proposes a new parametric imaging technique which improves the resolution and sensitivity by enhancing the MVDR parametric imaging and

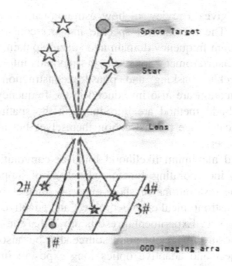

Fig. 2. Schematic model of pinhole imaging

introducing better power estimates based on least squares. Simulations demonstrate that the approach has higher resolution, and performs better in noisy situations.

In [14], several de-noising models based on the multi-scale geometric transformation have been proposed for the imaging features of SAR image, including the cycle spinning de-noising model based on Wavelet Contourlet transform, Gaussian mixture de-noising model based on the complex Contourlet transform, de-noising model based on local hybrid filter, and so on.

5   Restoration and Reconstruction

In most applications, the acquired images represent a degraded version of the original scene for instance astronomical imaging (e.g., using ground based imaging systems or extraterrestrial observations of the earth and the planets). The degradation can be due to the atmospheric turbulence, the relative motion between the camera and the scene, and the finite resolution of the acquisition instrument. So image restoration is a key issue in astronomy. However image restoration is a well-known, ill-posed inverse problem which requires regularization.

5.1   Reconstruction from Speckle Image

Because of atmospheric turbulence, the performance of high resolution imaging of large optical instruments is severely limited. Speckle imaging is one of the ways to eliminate atmospheric blurring based on recording series of images with short exposure to freeze the turbulence to obtain restoration image for reconstruction. Recently speckle image reconstruction has been shown great power to help binary star system in related reports.

In [25], the paper gives a review of how astronomical images are reconstructed from speckle images. The methods of speckle image reconstruction are described, including methods in both frequency domain and spatial domain. In the frequency part of the article, speckle interferometer for retrieving modulus information is introduced. Knox-Thompson, speckle masking and phase reconstruction from modulus for retrieving phase information are also introduced in the frequency part. LWH method and iterative shift-and-add method are introduced in the spatial part. Not only the methods of astronomical image reconstruction themselves but also their applications are presented in the paper.

In [26], a modified maximum likelihood blind de-convolution algorithm is proposed in this paper by incorporating dynamic shrinkage of support region. The algorithm is applied to the restorations of short exposure images of astronomical point source star, images of astronomical extended object and adaptive optics long exposure images of point source star. Experimental results prove that the algorithm works well not only for short exposure images of point source star, but also for images of astronomical extended object and adaptive optics long exposure images. The PSNR of reconstruction images is raised by over 10 %. The novelty of this algorithm is that the support region of astronomical object can be contracted adaptively according to the threshold in reconstruction iterations.

In [27], the author surveys image reconstruction methods aimed at speckle images and methods to simulate the speckle images. Then the author tests typical reconstruction methods and introduces those methods in his dissertation. On the other hand a reconstruction method based on Kalman filter and containing physical constraints is proposed and tested with both simulated and real data. While to contrast with it the Kalman filter based reconstruction method without physical constraints is also illustrated. The Kalman filter based reconstruction with physical constraints shows positive prospect.

5.2   Blind Deconvolution Methods

In astronomy, image resolution and contrast will be decreased because of the complexity of imaging conditions. When we observe an astronomical object from the surface of the earth, its emitted or reflected light has to invariably pass through the atmosphere, which yields a blurry observed image. De-blurring images of an observed celestial body is therefore a fundamental problem in astronomy. This problem is compounded by the fact that the blur is not only unknown, but also is continually changing in time as well as spatially due to refraction-index fluctuations caused by atmospheric turbulence. So image restoration has being a study focus in image processing. Existing image restoration algorithms, such as Wiener filtering, builds on the known point spread function. However, point spread function is often unknown in practice because imaging conditions are unknown, like the relative motion between camera and objects and atmospheric disturbance. Therefore, the research on blind de-convolution and blind restoration is very necessary in theory and practice.

The all-pervasive presence of noise is what makes de-convolution particularly difficult. The paper 'De-convolution in Astronomy: a Review' gives a review of different de-convolution methods in recent 10 years. The diversity of resulting algorithms reflects different ways of estimating the true signal under various idealizations of its properties. Different ways of approaching signal recovery are based on different instrumental noise models, whether the astronomical objects are point-like or extended, and indeed on the computational resources available to the analysts. It presents a number of results in the survey of image restoration.

In the paper [34], a blind de-convolution approach based on the maximum-likelihood estimation technique with real optical band limitation constraint is presented for removing the effect of atmospheric turbulence on this class images through the minimization of the convolution error function by using the conjugation gradient optimization algorithm. As a result, the object function and the point spread function could be estimated from a few record images at the same time by the blind de-convolution algorithm. According to the principle of Fourier optics, the relationship between the telescope optical system parameters and the image band constraint in the frequency domain is formulated during the image processing transformation between the spatial domain and the frequency domain.

The convergence property of multi-frame blind de-convolution applied to improve the resolution of astronomical image is influenced by initial object estimate, constraint conditions and photon noise. In the paper [36], a method of determining band limitation of the point-spread function from the optical imaging system parameters is proposed, in which the initial object estimate of blind de-convolution algorithm is formed by using Knox-Thompson method to reconstruct object phase from short-exposure images. A novel method, which is used to decrease photon noise, edge effects and ringing of restoration images, is developed. An improved multi-frame blind de-convolution algorithm with a strict constrained optimization method of the expectation-maximization based on maximum likelihood estimation is presented. The restored images in experiment show that the proposed multi-frame blind de-convolution algorithm is valid for overcoming effects of atmospheric turbulence and photon noise, improving the resolution of real observed astronomical images, and capable of partly removing the diffraction effect of optical system on restored images.

5.3   Restoration Based on Maximum-Likelihood Algorithm

Traditional image restoration algorithms always deal with Gaussian noise, however, the real astronomical images are polluted by Gaussian and Poisson mixed noise. Therefore, the paper [28] introduces a imaging model of Poisson-Gaussian distribution, makes an effective approximation to the Maximum Likelihood (ML) algorithm based on the mixed model, and proposes a modified ML algorithm based on Poisson-Gaussian mixed noise to avoid the sensitivity to noise and the dependence to the original estimation of PSF. Experimental results show that the algorithm works well, and the robustness is well.

In [29], the effective approximation model based on Maximum-likelihood (ML) function proposed by Benvenuto is analyzed for astronomy image restoration, then a new image restoration algorithm with convergence faster than that of traditional ML method is proposed in which PSF known a prior is not required. The turbulence PSF is estimated from observed blur images to make the PSF estimation in accordance with an imaging environment. By incorporating adaptive estimation of PSF into ML restoration, an enhanced ML algorithm is presented. Additionally, the PSF is updated successively during iteration. The ML restoration and de-noising are performed alternatively in iteration. The results show that the proposed algorithm works much better than ML does. In conclusion, the algorithm allows the iterative process in ML algorithm to converge stably and the image quality to be improved. Experiment results show that the presented method can be used routinely in astronomical image restoration.

6 Conclusion

In this study we give a review of the astronomical image processing methods and sort them into different aspects. In this field, it has a lot of special issues, as well as the common issues in image processing field. They may influence each other.

References

1. Tian, J., Liu, B., Liu, J.: The information entropy preserved coder of still image by integer haar wavelet transforms and sub block DPCM. J. China Inst. Commun. **11**, 29–34 (2000)
2. Li, Z., Zhou, W.: The application of the digital image compression technique to astronomy. Prog. Astron. **14**, 259–261 (1996)
3. Zhao, L., Tian, Y., Sha, Y., Li, J.: Lossless compression of medical images by combining integer wavelet transform with DPCM. J. Northeast. Univ. (Nat. Sci.) **10**, 1454–1457 (2007)
4. Wu, D., Wang, J., Zhang, H.: Research of hyper-spectral image lossless compressing technology based on DPCM between spectra and IWT. Acta Photonica Sin. **1**, 156–159 (2008)
5. Ye, H., Dong, S.: Satellite cloud imagery compression based on wavelet transform. Comput. Eng. Sci. **10**, 60–65 (2004)
6. Guifu, Z., Hui, D., Feng, W., Kaifan, J.: Study of a lossless compression method of astronomical images using segment-based DPCM and 5 /3 integer wavelet transformations. Astron. Res. Technol. **1**, 73–80 (2011)
7. Li, L., Dai, H.B., Xu, J.: The study of the application of image compression based on wavelet transformation in astronomical remote observation. Astron. Res. Technol. **4**, 380–384 (2008)
8. Pence, W.D., Seaman, R., White, R.L.: Lossless astronomical image compression and the effects of noise. Publ. Astron. Soc. Pac. **121**, 414–427 (2009)
9. Haixia, C.: The research of lossless compression arithmetic based on integer wavelet transform's still image. Xi'an University of Science and Technology, Xi'an (2008)
10. Shengxue, Q.: Satellite image processing algorithm research and its corresponding hardware implementation. Beijing University of Posts and Telecommunications, Beijing (2007)
11. Guifu, Z.: Research and realization of lossless compression methods of astronomical image. Kunming University of Science and Technology, Kunming (2009)
12. Meng, K., Jin, S.-Z., Wang, B., Wang, Y.: Viewfinding technology in astronomic images. Res. Comput. Appl. **72–73**, 101 (2003)
13. Fei, W., Tang, Q., Liu, P., Cai, H.: Implementation of high-speed astronomical image segmentation based on pipelining. Sci. Technol. Eng. **22**, 5433–5436 (2010)
14. Shuaiqi, L.: The processing algorithm study for remote sensing images based on multi-scale geometric transformation. Beijing Jiaotong University, Beijing (2013)

15. Bo, Z.: Independent study day hierarchical star identification algorithm based on star sensor. Graduate School of Chinese Academy of Sciences (Changchun Institute of Optics and Precision Instruments and physical), Changchun (2004)

16. Lei, Z., Xin, H., Zhonghui, W.: Other fast-sky autonomous star identification. Optics and Precis. Eng. **17**(4), 909–915 (2009)

17. Zhang, S.D., Wang, Y., Sun, H.: Triangulation and radial basis function neural network in star pattern recognition. Optics Precis. Eng. **20**(2), 395–402 (2012)

18. Wenzhong, X.: Design and implementation of denoising and star-searching in ccd astronomical images. Jinan University, Guangzhou (2007)

19. Ben-David, C., Leshem, A.: Parametric high resolution techniques for radio astronomical imaging. IEEE J. Sel. Top. Sig. Proc. **2**, 670–684 (2008). Bar-Ilan University, Ramat Gan

20. Yubao, C.: Research of infrared weak-target detection based on mathematical morphology, pp. 322–326, Hefei (2006)

21. Han, J., Zhang, Y., Chen, Z.: Real time detection algorithm of weak targets in astronomical images. Opto-Electron. Eng. **12**, 1–4 (2005)

22. Jingchang, A.: Research on automated processing and target detection of astronomical. Information Shandong University, Jinan (2011)

23. Chantas, G.K., Galatsanos, N.P., Likas, A.C.: Bayesian restoration using a new nonstationary edge-preserving image prior Giannis K. Chantas. IEEE Trans. Image Process. **15**(10), 2987–2997 (2006)

24. Babacan, S.D., Molina, R., Katsaggelos, A.K.: Parameter estimation in tv image restoration using variational distribution approximation. IEEE Trans. Image Process. **17**(3), 326–339 (2008)

25. Huo, Z., Zhou, J.: Methods of astronomical image reconstruction from speckle image. Prog. Astron. **1**, 72–90 (2010)

26. Geng, Z., Wang, Z.: Modified high definition reconstruction algorithm of astronomical speckle images. Optics Precis. Eng. **7**, 1151–1156 (2007)

27. Zhuoxi, H.: Research on astronomical image reconstruction from speckle image. Tsinghua University, Beijing (2010)

28. Wei, X., Geng, Z., Song, X., Wang, L., Tang, C.: Modified maximum likelihood algorithm based on Poisson-Gaussian mixed noise. Comput. Eng. **1**, 222–224 (2012)

29. Geng, Z., Wei, X., Shen, C.: Astronomical image restoration based on maximum-likelihood incorporated parameter estimation. Optics Precis. Eng. **11**, 2943–2950 (2013)

30. Vega, M., Mateos, J., Molina, R., Katsaggelos, A.K.: Astronomical image restoration using variational methods and model combination. Stat. Methodol. **9**, 19–31 (2011)

31. Zhao, J., Wu, Y., Jin, J., Qiao, B., Wang, B., Wang, Z., Ma, X.: Image restoration based on real time wave-front information.Optics Precis. Eng. **6**, 1350–1356 (2012)

32. Zhu, W., Sui, C., Tang, Y., Shen, X., Hu, J.: Application of restoration technology to blurred images in astronomical image processing. Infrared (Mon.) **3**, 6–10 (2005)

33. Jichao, J., Baojun, Z., Fenfang, T., Juan, L.: Astronomical image enhancement algorithm based on regional image restoration. Chin. J. Sci. Instrum. **7**, 1455–1461 (2011)

34. Bertero, M., Boccacci, P.: Image restoration methods for the large binocular telescope (LBT). Astron. Astrophys. **3**, 1–15 (2000)

35. Luo, L., Wang, L., Cheng, W., Shen, M.: Approaches to convergence enhancement of multiframe blind deconvolution of astronomical images. Acta Phys. Sin. **12**, 6708–6713 (2006)

36. Luo, L., Fan, M., Shen, M.: Blind deconvolution of astronomical images with band limitation determined by optical system parameters. Acta Astron. Sin. **3**, 374–382 (2007)

Synthesis of High Dynamic Range Image Based on Logarithm Intensity Mapping Function

Shaojun Zhang, Sheng Zhang$^{(\boxtimes)}$, Hailong Cheng, and Chuan Jiang

Key Laboratory of Advanced Sensor and Integrated System,
Tsinghua University, Shenzhen, China
zhangsjl3@mails.tsinghua.edu.cn,
zhangsh@sz.tsinghua.edu.cn,
619545841@mail.qq.com, dtrs_007@163.com

Abstract. Nature light has a dynamic range beyond the modern camera can capture. So lots of commercial software applies techniques to reconstruct high dynamic range (HDR) image from low dynamic range (LDR) images. One of the popular methods is to recover the radiance of scene from LDR stacks [2]. However it needs to know the exact exposure time of LDR images and costs much time to solve the camera response function. These defects make it impossible to be built in hardware or real time systems. In this paper, we propose a new technique to synthesize HDR image based on the *intensity mapping function* (IMF). We first solve the IMF based on *cross-histogram map,* and then synthesize the pixel values from LDRs as if they have the same exposure time. We test our technique on several demos and get satisfying results with good visual quality in bright and dark scenes. Besides, because our method costs less time than the 'software' method, it is more suitable for further hardware application.

Keywords: Intensity mapping function · Spatially varying pixel exposure · High dynamic range image · Contrast-preserving tone-mapping operator

1 Introduction

Nowadays, high dynamic range (HDR) image technology draws lots of attention from researchers and groups all around the world. The real scenes in the nature often have a range of light variance much broader than 255, thus causing the conventional cameras not able to capture the whole range in only a single shot. Scenes including both bright reflection and dark shadows are always difficult for photographers to capture. So, kinds of software develop the post-processing methods to synthesize HDR images for those photographers.

Promoted by the prosperity of HDR imaging, lots of commercial software and image signal processing (ISP) hardware develop the function to get HDR images. Among them, 'software' methods always recover the HDR scene radiances from a stack of low dynamic range images (LDRs) exposed at different periods. For example, [1, 2] solves *camera response function* (CRF) first, and then weights and sums the LDRs together, [3] fuses different LDRs together utilizing some characters such as

© Springer International Publishing Switzerland 2015
Y.-J. Zhang (Ed.): ICIG 2015, Part III, LNCS 9219, pp. 430–443, 2015.
DOI: 10.1007/978-3-319-21969-1_38

contrast, saturation and exposure time, [4] averages float LDR pixel values by specially designed weighting function, [6] takes an original image with high resolution but low dynamic range as input, and generates an output image with extended dynamic range by applying the trade-off between the image resolution and the dynamic range, [14] develops a linear relation between with two LDRs and then fuse them together to a HDR one based on the linear function and [16] uses the gradient information of the visible regions and recovers the saturated regions by the energy minimization approach. However, always limited by time cost and delays, 'ISP' methods are less than 'software' methods and need specially design. One of them first gets the exposure ratio k by dividing the high exposure time by low exposure time as $k = e_1/e_2$, and then multiplies the low exposed pixels by the exposure ratio. The whole synthesis equation can be written as $X_{HDR} = X_{low}*k + X_{high}$. However, this method has some drawbacks, such as bad fidelity and low brightness.

In this paper, we propose an algorithm to synthesize HDR image based on the *logarithm intensity mapping function* (IMF), which denotes the relation between intensity values of same pixel location from LDRs. We first calibrate the logarithm IMF curve using least square method and then get HDR image by weighting and summing the mapped intensities from LDRs. To eliminate ghosting of HDR and avoid aligning LDR images, we capture different exposed images using *spatially varying pixel exposures* (SVEs) in one shot. Thus, we develop a low-computational-cost and ISP-suited method to synthesize HDR image. To illustrate the main method, the rest parts of our paper are organized as follows. In Sect. 2, the basic theories of HDR imaging are introduced such as camera response function, intensity mapping function, SVE and cross-histogram. Section 3 outlines theoretical framework of our main algorithm including the solving of IMF and the designing of weighting function. The experiment results are presented in Sect. 4 and the further discussions are included in Sect. 5.

2 Basic Knowledge of High Dynamic Imaging Work

In work [2, 10], the acquisition model of camera has been proposed. Given the scene radiance L, the irradiance E reach into the camera can be derived by $E = epL$, where e is the exposure and p is an optical factor. The exposure e can be further expressed as $e = (\pi d^2)t$, where t is the exposure time and d is the aperture size. Then, the pixel value X of image and irradiance E are related by the non-linear *camera response function* (CRF) f expressed as:

$$X = f(E) \tag{1}$$

And works [2, 4] hold the point view that obtaining the HDR image is a matter of recovering scene radiance E from the intensity values X by reverse response function g:

$$g = f^{-1} \tag{2}$$

Finally, the obtained HDR pixel value X_i is expressed as follows in [2, 4].

$$X_i = \frac{\sum_j w(i,j)E(i,j)}{\sum_j w(i,j)} \tag{3}$$

In the above equation, $w(i, j)$ is a weighting function, i is the index of pixel and j is the index of differently exposed image.

To solve out the reverse camera response function g, kinds of methods are utilized. The primary method makes use of uniformly illuminated chart with known reflectance patches and computes the function g based on the relationship between illumination and intensity value. However this method appears inconvenient for most situations. So, chart-free methods are introduced such as sampling and fitting [2], solving *intensity mapping function* (IMF) τ instead [5] and so on. These CRF-based methods are practical when built in software, but hardly applicable to real time system due to its huge computational cost and time delay.

To establish our method, IMF τ is deployed instead of function g. In two differently exposed LDR images, the intensity value in the corresponding pixel location can be paired together as (X_1, X_2), where X_1 is from low exposure and X_2 denotes is from high exposure. The number of these pairs is expressed as $J(X_1, X_2)$ and shown in the figure called *cross-histogram* (see Fig. 2). And function τ well describes the relation between values X_1, and X_2. In [5], it has the expression as

$$X_2 = \tau(X_1). \tag{4}$$

Some important properties of IMF τ are as follows from [5]:

- $\tau(0) = 0$
- τ monotonically increases
- $X <= \tau(X)$
- $\lim_{n \to \infty} \tau^{-n}(X) = 0$

As explained in [5], due to quantization and saturation of the pixel value, the cross-histogram curve may seem not so smooth and monotonic increasing as the theory describes. So it introduces accumulative histogram function and obtains the IMF τ. Different with algorithm from [5], we assume IMF have a logarithm formation and propose a fitting algorithm to calibrate the intensity mapping function after a partition of cross-histogram. Further on, we develop a weighting function and utilize it with IMF to construct HDR image. In the end, we test our algorithm on computer and get satisfying HDR image. The detail algorithm will be included in the following chapters and we will show that our algorithm is a better alterative suiting real-time ISP hardware system.

3   Algorithm to Construct HDR Image

We divide our method into several sections. Section 3.1 introduces our technology to get LDRs. Section 3.2 includes the algorithm to solving the intensity mapping function from the cross-histogram. The methods to synthesis HDR image based on the IMF is shown in Sect. 3.3. Section 3.4 takes a tone-mapping strategy to show HDR image on LDR screen.

3.1   Acquisition of Spatially Varying Pixel Exposures

Spatially varying pixel exposure (SVE) has been introduced by many CMOS systems and used in differently-exposed frames acquisition. To obtain SVEs, optical masks with spatially varying transmittance are put adjacent to the CMOS sensor (see Fig. 1a). And different number of pixels in one pattern can be applied in different CMOS systems. The optical masks control the amount of light transmits through them and producing differently exposed frames in one shot [8, 9]. With SVEs, we easily acquire the different exposed images. And thanks to the short duration of one shot, the effect of object motion and scene motion can be eliminated and thus avoid the global alignment before synthesis. Here, we make use of SVE masks with two different-exposed pixels in one pattern and obtain two frames, one long exposure and one short exposure, in one shot (see Fig. 1b).

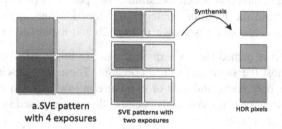

a.SVE pattern with 4 exposures   SVE patterns with two exposures   HDR pixels

Fig. 1. SVE pattern with 4 exposures is shown on the left (marked as Fig. 1a). The right one (marked as Fig. 1b) shows the procedure of synthesis of HDR pixels with 2 exposures.

3.2   Recovery of Intensity Mapping Function

The Grossberg's Algorithm. The cross-histogram of two different exposures contains all information to construct the intensity mapping function as proved in [5]. The function τ can be derived from the image's cumulative histogram called $H(x)$ which denotes the number of pixels with value between 0 and x. Given the continuous histogram function $h(x)$ which indicates the number of pixels with intensity value x, $H(x)$ can be solved by:

$$H(X) = \int_0^X h(u)du \tag{5}$$

Actually the histogram function $h(x)$ is discrete, so the above integration needs to be turned to accumulation. After the accumulation, the corresponding pixel values X_1 and X_2 from the same pixel location of two images have the following relation as (6) shows. It implies the numbers of pixels with smaller values than them is exactly the same [5].

$$H_1(X_1) = H_2(X_2) \tag{6}$$

And from IMF, we get $X_2 = \tau(X_1)$. Then, substituting it into (6) yields

$$H_1(X_1) = H_2(\tau(X_1)) \tag{7}$$

Supposing X is arbitrary value from the low exposure, IMF τ can be derived from reverse function of H as follows.

$$\tau(X) = H_2^{-1}(H_1(X)) \tag{8}$$

The Partitioning and Fitting Algorithm. We first partition the cross-histogram into different parts and propose to calibrate the logarithm IMF in some of the parts. In [14], it illustrates a linear *J-function* which has similar sub-parts and properties with parts of IMF. Here we extend the partition strategy of J-function and apply it to our IMF. Partition of the cross-histogram is shown in Fig. 2b and explanations are as follows.

- Part I. This part is named the *low exposed zone*. In this zone, the pixels' abscissa values are almost the same and near a constant. These low abscissa values mean they are in the dark scene and lack of exposure in low exposed image. However, their ordinate values are not constants because they are exposed in a long period in the high exposed image.
- Part II. We name this part the *appropriate exposed zone*. In this part, the abscissa value and ordinate value are both variables. Because this part of both images expose appropriately and the pixels here contains most information of the scene.
- Part III. We call this part the *noise zone*. In this part, the pixel values are disperse from the 'main curve' due to the photoelectron noise and intensity quantization.
- Part IV. We name this part the *over exposed zone*. Pixels in this part have the same ordinate values nearly 255. However, because exposed appropriately in low exposed image, the abscissa values are less than saturation.

We see that the low-exposed zone and over-exposed zone both loss some information from the scene. In reality, when exposed at a short period, the dark scene can't be recognized, and when exposed at long period, the bright scene may show saturation and noising. The aim of HDR imaging is to include these dark and bright parts in one image by recover the intensity values from other zones. In one sense, the pixel values

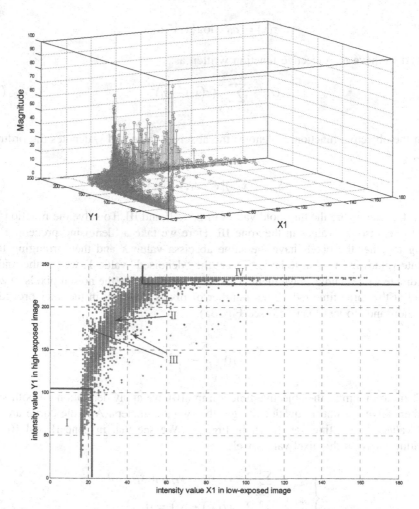

Fig. 2. Cross-histogram maps are shown. The top one (marked as Fig. 1a) is a 3D histogram, in which the Z-coordinate denotes the number of pixels have value *(X1, X2)* respectively. The bottom one (marked as Fig. 2b) is a 2D cross-histogram which has been partition into 4 parts.

from zone I and IV are not reliable due to noise, so we chose zone II and III to recover the intensity mapping function. Different from [14], we extend the noise zone and then use a denoising method to make the data useful in this area.

Because all the values are discrete in the cross-histogram image, so we apply a fitting strategy to calibrate the curve that best satisfy the IMF in a least square error sense. And to recover the function means recovering a finite number of pixel values that satisfy $X_2 = \tau(X_1)$ in the range of (0, 255). To achieve it, we assume the IMF has a logarithm formation and solve the least squares problem in zone II and III. Here, we give the form of the function that

$$\tau(x) = a_0 * \log(x) + a_1 \tag{9}$$

And we have the objective function written as:

$$O = \sum_{(x_i,y_i) \in S} (\tau(x_i) - y_i)^2 \tag{10}$$

In the objective function, x_i denotes the abscissa value and y_i denotes the ordinate value.

$$S = \{(x, y)|x \geq \varepsilon_1, y \leq \varepsilon_2\} \tag{11}$$

In it, ε_1 and ε_2 are the threshold values of zone II and III. To solve the function, we need to denoise the values in the zone III. Here we take a 'denoising procedure' by getting together the pixels have the same abscissa value X and then arranging their ordinate values from small to large. To get the "denoised" value Y, we get the middle 10 ordinate values and average them. This way, we eliminate the noised pixels in zone III and at the same time reduce the number of pixels involved in the later procedure from thousands to less than 255 (see Fig. 3a).

$$Y = \frac{1}{10} \sum_{i \in \{i|x_i=X\}} y_i \tag{12}$$

Then, to minimize the objective function in (10), we apply derivation on both sides and then solve the linear equations to get the two parameters. And the curve and the pixel values after fitting are shown in Fig. 3b. We see that in zone II and III, the logarithm curve fit the pixel values well.

$$\begin{cases} \frac{\partial O}{\partial a_0} = \sum_{(x_i,y_i)} 2 * (\tau(x_i) - y_i) \log(x_i) = 0 \\ \frac{\partial O}{\partial a_1} = \sum_{(x_i,y_i)} 2 * (\tau(x_i) - y_i) = 0 \end{cases} \tag{13}$$

3.3   HDR Imaging Based on the Intensity Mapping Function

After the recovery of IMF, we apply a weighting algorithm to the dark and bright scene in LDR images and synthesize the different exposures together to HDR image. As we know, the low exposure includes the information of saturated scene and the high exposure includes the information of dark scene, so we proposed to fuse these parts together based on the intensity mapping function. In [14], it proposed the zone I, II and III of high exposure contain the needed information of scene and try to fuse the zone IV of low exposure to high exposure linearly.

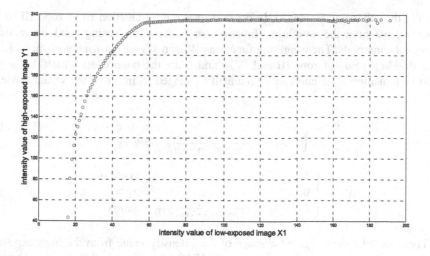

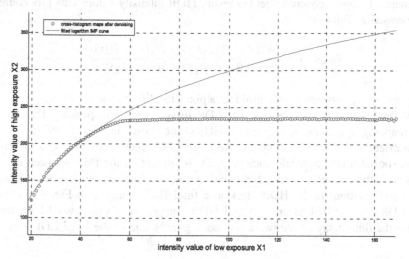

Fig. 3. Cross-histogram maps after denosing are shown. The top one (marked as Fig. 3a) shows the relation between pixels in two LDR images. The bottom one (marked as Fig. 3b) shows a logarithm IMF line after fitting (red continues line) and cross-histogram (blue circles) (Color figure online).

Here, we first map the zone IV from low exposure to the high exposure by substituting the pixel values to IMF. Given the intensity value of low exposure X_{low}, we have the value after mapping written as:

$$X'_{low} = \tau(x_{low}) \tag{14}$$

Second, we develop a weighting function to fuse the different zone together. In the low exposure, the information in zone IV is weighted 1, while information in other zones is weighted 0. In the high exposure, information in zone I, II and III are weighted

1, while the other is weighted 0. In order to make the transition from zone III to IV smoother, we give the weighting function an S-shape increasing (and decreasing) between the intervals. The weighting functions W_1 and W_2 are shown below, in which ξ is the dividing value of zone III and IV. ε and α are the parameters which define the width of transition zone and can be manually changed to improve the visual sense.

$$W_1 = \begin{cases} 0 & x_1 < \xi - \varepsilon \\ 1 & x_1 > \xi + \varepsilon \\ \frac{x_1 - \xi + \varepsilon}{2*\varepsilon} * \frac{1}{1 + \alpha*(\exp(-(x-\xi))/2)} & others \end{cases} \tag{15}$$

$$W_2 = \begin{cases} 1 & x_2 < \xi - \varepsilon \\ 0 & x_2 > \xi + \varepsilon \\ 1 - \frac{x_2 - \xi + \varepsilon}{2*\varepsilon} * \frac{1}{1 + \alpha*(\exp(-(x-\xi))/2)} & others \end{cases} \tag{16}$$

Then, we take the weighted average of the intensity value from the high exposure and "mapped" low exposure to get the result, HDR intensity value. This procedure can be expressed as follows:

$$X_{HDR}(i,j) = \frac{W_1(x_1'(i,j))x'(i,j) + W_2(x_2(i,j))x_2(i.j)}{W_1(x_1'(i,j)) + W_2(x_2(i,j))} \tag{17}$$

By the above procedures, we build up a pixel level synthesis algorithm to construct a HDR image from different SVEs. The LDR images and corresponding HDR images (tone-mapping operators are applied on HDRs) are shown in Figs. 5 and 6.

To extend our algorithm to synthesize more LDR images, we would like to choose a mid-exposed image as a reference map. Then, we obtain the IMF between the LDR stacks with the reference respectively and synthesize high dynamic stacks. Last, we weight and accumulate the HDR stack to a final HDR image (see Fig. 4). Although more LDRs are needed to get satisfied HDR image, we choose two LDRs for use because the time delay of hardware increases greatly due to the large LDR stack.

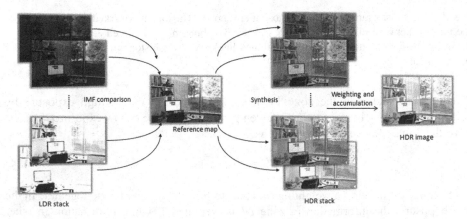

Fig. 4. The overall procedure of dealing with more pictures is shown in this figure.

3.4   A Contrast-Preserving Tone-Mapping Operator

The aim of tone-mapping is to preserve contrast, brightness and details of a HDR image which is shown on a typical 255-intensity-level screen [11]. Here we use a global contrast-preserving mapping operator to reduce the intensity levels to 255.

First we normalize the pixel intensity from $(0, X_{max})$ to $(0, 1)$ by applying the equation:

$$X_f \frac{X_i}{X_{\max}} \tag{18}$$

After normalization, the pixel values all become float numbers. Then we take a few steps to apply the multipeak histogram equalization operator from [12] to enhance the contrast while compress the intensity value.

The algorithm in [12] detects N breakpoints $\{d_1, d_2 \ldots d_N\}$ and $N + 1$ peaks of the histogram. Then the histogram B is divided into $N + 1$ subsections based on the breakpoints which can be expressed as:

$$B = B_1 \cup B_2 \cup \ldots \cup B_{N+1} \tag{19}$$

For each B_j, the probability density function can be written as follows [15], where i denotes the index of peak and j denotes the index of intensity level:

$$p_i(j) = \frac{X_f(j)}{\sum\limits_{d_i \leq j < d_{i+1}} X_f(j)} \tag{20}$$

Then the histogram equalization process is applied separately to each of the peaks of histogram. The cumulative intensity function is written as follows:

$$C_i(k) = \sum_{j=d_i}^{k} p_i(j) \tag{21}$$

After the multipeak histogram equalization, the intensity levels of each peak are spread out between the breakpoints. Lastly, we extend the range of intensity value from $(0, 1)$ to $(0, 255)$. This way, we can preserve the contrast and compress the intensity levels.

4   Experiment Results

We test our algorithm on variety of scenes and then compare the HDR images with results from method of [2] and [6]. The respective low dynamic stacks are taken in different exposure time while other settings of camera are kept static during a shot.

In Fig. 5 the 'office' pictures which are taken under different exposures are shown in the first line. The low exposed image has dark areas in indoor scene like the book

Fig. 5. Four images show scenes of offices. In the first line is LDR images. In the second line is HDR image and details got by our algorithm. The contrast HDR images with details resulted from 'software' method [2] and [6] are shown in the third and fourth line.

Fig. 6. These images show scenes of castles. In the first line is LDR images. In the second line is HDR image and details got by our algorithm. The contrast HDR images with details resulted from 'software' method [2] and [6] are shown in the third and last line.

shelf and desk, while the high exposed image has saturated areas in the outdoor scene such as the tree and road. Shown in the second line, our HDR image has appropriately recovered missing information in LDRs. To contrast with the HDR image from our algorithm, the third line and fourth line show the 'software' results from [2] and [6]. Figure 6 shows another stack of images which include castles in bright light. In the first line are two LDRs, the second line is our HDR image while the third and last line are the 'software' results. In all our and [2] 's HDR images, the missing areas clearly reappear and remain high contrast. However, some images based on [6] 's method reappear with high quality, while some other images with excessive bright parts may have an even brighter appearance due to the summation of the intensity without any distinguish with pixels, and thus cause losing of some information.

The experiment results suggest that our HDR images can keep good or even better visual quality than those 'software' results. In fact, our method needs not to know the exact exposure time of the LDR stacks and thus becomes more convenient to photographers. Another advantage is the low time cost, mostly because our technology needs not to resolve the camera response function, which is always the most time-costly part. (In fact, the method from [6] has similar running time as ours, but it trades the quality of HDR picture (see Figs. 5 and 6's details) for fast speed. So we didn't satisfy with the method even the running time is short.) We simulate both algorithm on the same computer and show the running time in Table 1. (We run the MATLAB code of our own and from [2] respectively.) Table 1 demonstrates different size of images varies greatly in the computational time. To construct a better HDR image with more texture and higher contrast, higher-resolution LDR images are needed. Totally, our IMF-based method shows a time-cost superiority towards 'software' method. Thus, our algorithm is expected to be more suitable to build in the graphic hardware in the future. In addition, it makes capturing of HDR videos possible with an ordinary camera.

Table 1. Computational time of our algorithm and 'software' methods.

Size(w*h)	Time cost of our algorithm	Time cost of 'software' method from [2] (s)	Time cost of method from [6] (s)
903*600	1.32	2.11	1.43
1024*685	1.84	3.82	1.68
4368*2912	20.75	60.38	23.30

5   Conclusion and Discussion

HDR imaging has been a popular subject in the machine vision field in the past years. Lots of software techniques have been proposed to synthesize HDR image using a bracket of low dynamic exposures. However, most of them need to resolve the over-determined camera response function and thus cost a lot of time. So we propose to synthesize HDR images based on the intensity mapping function. And then we apply a contrast-preserving tone-mapping operator to turn the intensity level range to (0, 255).

Totally, our algorithm shows advantages of less computational cost to the 'software' methods and thus more suitable to be built in real-time ISP hardware.

In the future work, we would like to develop better denoising algorithm which can eliminate unreliable pixels and increase HDR's SNR in the dark and saturated areas. Also, we would like to investigate different tone-mapping techniques to maintain better texture and more details.

References

1. Mei, Y., Qiu, G.: Recovering high dynamic range radiance maps from photographs revisited: a simple and important fix. In: 2013 Seventh International Conference on Image and Graphics (2013)
2. Debevec, P.E., Malik, J.: Recovering high dynamic range radiance maps from photographs (1997)
3. Mertens, T., Kautz, J., Van Reeth, F.: Exposure fusion-a simple and practical alternative to high dynamic rang photography. Comput. Graph. Forum 28(1), 161–171 (2009)
4. Mann, S., Picard, R.W.: On being 'Undigital' with digital cameras: extending dynamic range by combining differently exposed pictures. In: 48th Annual Conference, Cambridge (1995)
5. Grossberg, M.D., Nayar, S.K.: Determining the camera response from images: what is knowable. IEEE Trans. Pattern Anal. Mach. Intell. 25(11), 1455–1467 (2003)
6. Lin, H.-Y., Huang, J.-W.: Extended dynamic range imaging: a spatial down sampling approach. In: IEEE International Conference on Systems, Man, and Cybernetics, San Diego, CA, USA, 5–8 October 2014
7. Sakaue, S, Tamura, A., Nakayama, M., Maruno, S.: Adaptive gamma processing of the video cameras for the expansion of the dynamic range. In: IEEE Manuscript Received, 12 June 1995
8. Hirakawa, K., Simon, P.M.: Single-shot high dynamic range imaging with conventional camera hardware. In: IEEE International Conference on Computer Vision (2011)
9. Aguerrebere, C., Almansa, A., Gousseau, Y.: Single shot high dynamic range imaging using piecewise linear estimators
10. Aguerrebere, C., Delon, J., Gousseau, Y., Muse, P.: Study of the digital camera acquisition process and statistical modeling of the sensor raw data (2013)
11. Qian, T.L., Shafie, S., Saripan, M.I.: A local tone mapping operator for high dynamic range images. In: IEEE (2011)
12. Wongsritong, K., Kittayaruasiriwat, K., Cheevasuvit, F., Dejhan, K., Somboonkaew, A.: Contrast enhancement using multipeak equalization with brightness preserving. In: IEEE (1998)
13. Vytla, L., Hassan, F., Carletta, J.E.: A real-time implementation of gradient domain high dynamic range compression using a local poisson. Solver. J. Real-Time Image Proc. 8, 153–167 (2013)
14. Shen, G.-Q.: Wide dynamic range algorithm design based on the image signal processor. In: Dissertation for the Master Degree in Engineering, Harbin Institute of Technology (2012)
15. Ooi, C.H., Kong, S.P.: Bi-histogram equalization with a plateau limit for digital image enhancement. IEEE Trans. Consum. Electron. 55(4), 2072–2080 (2009)
16. Cho, W.-H., Ki-Sang, H.: Extending dynamic range of two color images under different exposures. In: International Conference on Pattern Recognition (ICPR) (2005)

Temporal Domain Group Sparse Representation Based Cloud Removal for Remote Sensing Images

Xinghua Li[1], Huanfeng Shen[1,2(✉)], Huifang Li[1],
and Qiangqiang Yuan[3]

[1] School of Resource and Environmental Sciences,
Wuhan University, Wuhan, China
{lixinghua5540,shenhf,huifangli}@whu.edu.cn
[2] Collaborative Innovation Center of Geospatial Technology,
Wuhan University, Wuhan, China
[3] School of Geodesy and Geomatics, Wuhan University, Wuhan, China
yqiang86@gmail.com

Abstract. The reconstruction of the missing information of optical remote sensing images contaminated by unwanted cloud has attracted a great deal of attention. However, in practice, cloud removal is a challenging problem. In this paper, we propose to reconstruct the missing information by temporal domain group sparse representation. With the help of temporal normalization, the temporal complementation of multitemporal remote sensing images is strengthened. The group sparse representation, which seeks similar patches from the temporal domain, is then applied to recover the missing information. The experiments demonstrated that the proposed method is both quantitatively and qualitatively effective.

Keywords: Cloud removal · Group sparse representation · Image reconstruction · Passive remote sensing · Remote sensing images · Temporal domain

1 Introduction

Since remote sensing observation is multi-scale, multispectral, multitemporal, and low-cost, it has become one of the most frequently used and most powerful approaches to understanding and investigating the earth. However, with regard to passive remote sensing instruments, the information acquisition of the underlying surface is inevitably occluded when they are subject to a cloudy atmosphere. For example, on average, at any one time, approximately 35 % of the global land surface is obscured by clouds [1], and in some individual countries, the cloud cover rate can be much higher. When clouds are not the research focus, they are detrimental. In order to better investigate our planet, research into cloud removal for remote sensing images is of great importance.

Cloud removal can be particularly difficult when there is a large area of cloud cover. In such a situation, the spatial domain based methods (e.g., partial differential equation based [2], maximum a posteriori based [3]), and the spectral domain based

© Springer International Publishing Switzerland 2015
Y.-J. Zhang (Ed.): ICIG 2015, Part III, LNCS 9219, pp. 444–452, 2015.
DOI: 10.1007/978-3-319-21969-1_39

methods (e.g., quantitative image restoration [4], robust M-estimator multiregression [5]) are often ineffective. As a result, the temporal domain based methods have become more popular in the research community. Temporal replacement is the most simple and basic type of temporal domain based method, and it can be classified into direct and indirect replacement. In terms of direct replacement, the cloud-contaminated pixels are replaced by their counterparts from another time, but the time interval must be sufficiently short that the temporal difference can be ignored. The representative methods include image mosaicing [6], the maximum value composite (MAC) technique [7], and optimal pixel selection [1]. In contrast, when the temporal difference is great, indirect replacement is required. Unlike direct replacement, a transformation is needed to reduce the temporal difference. Temporal fitting [8], for example, belongs to this kind of approach. In brief, temporal replacement is simple and widely used; however, it ignores the local changes with time.

Temporal replacement is usually suitable for a short time series of remote sensing images; in contrast, when the time series is long, more effective methods are required. The most noteworthy are the temporal filter methods, in which the two most common and classical methods (sliding window filter) are the best index slope extraction (BISE) method [9] and the adaptive Savitzky-Golay (SG) filter [10]. In addition, the function-based curve fitting methods are also effective, e.g., the asymmetric Gaussian (AG) approach [11]. The third type of filter method is the frequency filter, such as the famous harmonic analysis of time series (HANTS) method [12]. To some degree, a long time series is a double-edged sword, from which the temporal filter methods both benefit and are impaired.

In addition to the above methods, in consideration of the advantage over signal representation, sparse representation based methods have been the subject of much attention in the field of missing information reconstruction. The basic idea of sparse representation is to represent the signal by a linear combination of a few elements from a dictionary, in which the elements are called atoms. Lorenzi et al. [13] proposed to reconstruct the cloud-contaminated region by two geo-registered images from different periods, under a compressive sensing perspective, and the results were promising. Li et al. [14] then proposed multitemporal dictionary learning to further utilize the temporal complementation in a longer time series. Recently, Li et al. [15] made a comparison between spectral complementation and temporal complementation in the framework of sparse representation, and the authors concluded that the results are generally better when spectral complementation is available. In general, the aforementioned sparse representation methods can obtain good results; however, as Zhang et al. [16] noted, these methods just make use of the local sparsity while ignoring the nonlocal similarity [17]. In order to make better use of the temporal sparsity and nonlocal similarity, we propose temporal group sparse representation to reconstruct the missing information of optical remote sensing images.

The rest of this paper is organized as follows. Section 2 introduces the proposed group sparse representation algorithm, which is followed by the validated experiments in Sect. 3. Section 4 concludes the paper.

2 Algorithm

In this section, the proposed algorithm is introduced. It includes three main parts: temporal normalization and permutation, temporal similar patch search, and temporal group sparse representation.

2.1 Temporal Normalization and Permutation

Suppose that T multitemporal remote sensing images $\{I_t\}_{t=1}^T \in \mathbb{R}^{m \times n}$ are geo-registered. For brevity, we first assume that each image I_t is two-dimensional. Specifically, I_1 is contaminated by clouds, and the corresponding area is denoted by Ω, and the rest of the area (cloud-free) is denoted by $\overline{\Omega}$. For the other $\{I_t\}_{t=2}^T$, the area of each image is also divided into Ω and $\overline{\Omega}$, as I_1 is. Hereafter, I_1 is called the target image (cloud-contaminated) and $\{I_t\}_{t=2}^T$ are the reference images (cloud-free). As the shooting times are different, differences exist between the target image and the reference images. To reduce the differences, temporal normalization is adopted. We assume that the reference images are linearly correlated to the target image. The linear relationships can then be obtained by their shared good region $\overline{\Omega}$. Finally, based on the derived linear relationships, the reference images are temporally normalized. Mathematically, the linear relationships are modeled by:

$$I_1\left(\overline{\Omega}\right) = a_t I_t\left(\overline{\Omega}\right) + b_t, \quad t = 2, 3, \cdots, T \tag{1}$$

where $I_t\left(\overline{\Omega}\right)$ denotes the pixels in region $\overline{\Omega}$ of I_t, and a_t and b_t are the normalized parameters. With a least-squares solver, each pair of a_t and b_t are easily obtained. Subsequently, $\{I_t\}_{t=2}^T$ are normalized by:

$$I_t^n\left(\overline{\Omega} \cup \Omega\right) = a_t I_t\left(\overline{\Omega} \cup \Omega\right) + b_t, \quad t = 2, 3, \ldots, T \tag{2}$$

where I_t^n represents the normalized reference images.

To better utilize the temporal correlation between the target and reference images, we resort to temporal permutation. As shown in Fig. 1, after temporal normalization, the same rows from different images will be grouped together chronologically. This approach is also beneficial to the temporal similar patch search, which is introduced in Sect. 2.2. If the images themselves are multispectral, the normalization and permutation is undertaken according to their corresponding spectral bands, as in the previous process.

2.2 Temporal Similar Patch Search

The most notable characteristic of temporal group sparse representation is the grouping of the similar patches. The similar patches represent the so-called nonlocal similarity. In this section, we describe how to search for the similar patches. After the temporal

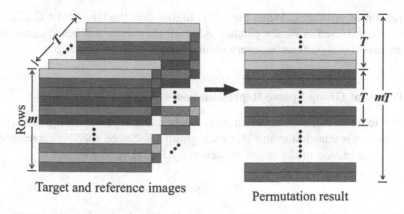

Target and reference images   Permutation result

Fig. 1. Temporal permutation.

permutation, the result is denoted by a column-stacked $x \in \mathbb{R}^{mnT}$. Let $x_k \in \mathbb{R}^B$ denote the extracted patch from x with the size of $\sqrt{B} \times \sqrt{B}$ at position k, and $k = 1, 2, \ldots, N$, where N is the total patch number. We let

$$x_k = P_k(x) \tag{3}$$

where $P_k(\bullet)$ represents the operator which extracts the k-th patch, and we let it be a vector. Correspondingly, $P_k^-(\bullet)$ means to put back the vector into its original patch position in the image domain.

The similarity criteria between vectors include the Euclidean distance, the cosine distance, the correlation coefficients (CCs), and so on. Based on our experiments, the CC is better than most other similarity criteria. As a result, the similar patches are determined according to the CC. The higher the CC, the more similar to the reference patch the current patch is. Taking x_i and x_j as an example, their CCs are calculated by:

$$CC_{i,j} = \frac{\sum_B \left(x_i - \mu_{x_i} \right) \left(x_j - \mu_{x_j} \right)}{\sqrt{\sum_B \left(x_i - \mu_{x_i} \right)^2} \sqrt{\sum_B \left(x_j - \mu_{x_j} \right)^2}} \tag{4}$$

where $CC_{i,j}$ denotes the CCs of x_i and x_j, and $\sum_B (\bullet)$ represents the sum of the B elements. Here, we reiterate that x is also contaminated by clouds. If we directly select similar patches, the wrong patches may be merged. In this situation, simple interpolation of the corrupted pixels makes a difference. Since the cloud-contaminated region is usually large, spatial domain interpolation using the corrupted image itself will obtain a poor result. Therefore, we resort to temporal interpolation. No matter how large the cloud region is, the nearest-neighbor interpolation is effective. This is also the reason that we undertake the temporal permutation described in Sect. 2.1.

In order to reduce the computational complexity, we do not search for the similar patches to x_k in the whole of x. Instead, the similar patches to x_k are searched for in the neighborhood of position k. When the CC is higher than the threshold $CC_{threshold}$, the patches are considered as similar patches. After all the similar patches to x_k are found, x_{G_k} is obtained by concatenating every similar vector column by column.

2.3 Temporal Group Sparse Representation

According to Sect. 2.2, we know that each patch x_k corresponds to a group x_{G_k}. The group sparse representation means that each group x_{G_k} can be sparsely represented by the linear combination of the atoms of dictionary D_{G_k} [16]. We let

$$x_{G_k} = P_{G_k}(x) \tag{5}$$

Similarly, $P_{G_k}^{-}(\bullet)$ is the inverse operation of $P_{G_k}(\bullet)$. As in [16], the group sparse representation is expressed as:

$$x = D_G \circ \alpha_G = \sum_{k=1}^{N} P_{G_k}^{-}(D_{G_k}\alpha_{G_k}) \left/ \sum_{k=1}^{N} P_{G_k}^{-}(E_{D_k\alpha_k}) \right. \tag{6}$$

where $E_{D_k\alpha_k}$ means the same size as $D_{G_k}\alpha_{G_k}$ with all ones, and $(\bullet)./(\bullet)$ represents the element-wise division. In fact, this equation means the average of all the overlapped patches according to their overlapped times. Given the group dictionary D_{G_k}, reconstructing the missing information is to solve:

$$\arg\min_{\alpha_G} \|M(x - D_G \circ \alpha_G)\|_2^2 + \lambda\|\alpha_G\|_0 \tag{7}$$

where M is a diagonal matrix with diagonal elements consisting of 0 and 1, with 0 representing the missing position, λ is the regularized parameter, and $\|\bullet\|_0$ and $\|\bullet\|_2$ denote the ℓ_0 and ℓ_2 norms, respectively. Since (7) is NP-hard, it is substituted by the convex version:

$$\arg\min_{\alpha_G} \|M(x - D_G \circ \alpha_G)\|_2^2 + \lambda\|\alpha_G\|_1 \tag{8}$$

where $\|\bullet\|_1$ denotes the ℓ_1 norm. According to [16], Eq. (8) is equivalent to:

$$\arg\min_{\alpha_{G_k}} \left\|\alpha_{G_k} - \gamma_{r_{G_k}}\right\|_2^2 + \tau\|\alpha_{G_k}\|_0 \tag{9}$$

where $\gamma_{r_{G_k}}$ is the singular value of the residual matrix r_{G_k}, and τ is the new regularized parameter. This can be solved based on either the hard or soft threshold.

3 Experiments

To validate the effectiveness of the proposed temporal domain group sparse representation (TDGSR), we undertook both simulated and real data cloud removal experiments based on Moderate Resolution Imaging Spectroradiometer (MODIS) images. In the two experiments, the data were both the 250-m resolution reflectance product of MODIS L1B, and the images were cropped to the size of 400 × 400 from the geo-registered images. For brevity, only one reference image was used in each experiment. For the simulated experiment, the image to be reconstructed was acquired by Terra MODIS on November 2, 2013 (some pixels of which were artificially removed), and the reference image was acquired by Aqua MODIS on November 4, 2013, in the same geographical area. For the real data experiment, the cloud-contaminated image was acquired by Terra MODIS on December 27, 2008, and the reference image was acquired by Terra MODIS on December 18, 2008. Additionally, the parameters were set as follows: patch size $\sqrt{B} = 4$, $CC_{threshold} = 0.85$, and τ is an adaptive parameter to the number of similar patches.

3.1 Simulated Experiment

In the simulated experiment, the artificially corrupted image was reconstructed by direct replacement of the reference image, MT-KSVD [14], and the proposed TDGSR, respectively. Figure 2 shows the reconstruction results of the different algorithms. From the visual effect, the direct replacement [Fig. 2(c)] obtained the worst result, which

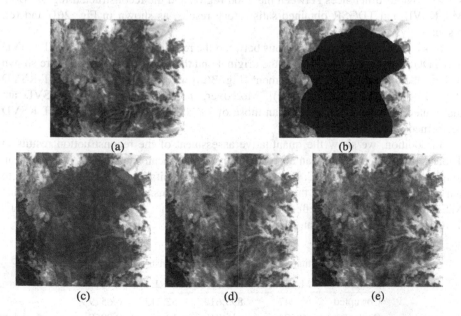

Fig. 2. Reconstruction results of the different methods. (a) Original image. (b) Corrupted image. (c) Reconstruction result using direct replacement of the reference image. (d) Reconstruction result using MT-KSVD. (e) Reconstruction result using the proposed TDGSR.

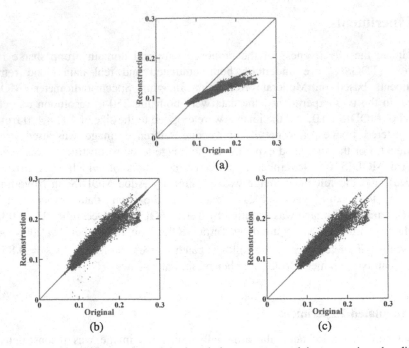

Fig. 3. Scatter plots between the original and the reconstructed images using the different algorithms. (a) Direct replacement. (b) MT-KSVD. (c) TDGSR.

shows obvious differences between the good region and the reconstructed region. Both MT-KSVD and TDGSR obtained satisfactory results, as shown in Fig. 2(d) and (e), respectively.

Since the difference is not obvious between the reconstruction results of MT-KSVD and TDGSR, scatter plots between the original and the reconstructed images are shown in Fig. 3. As before, direct replacement [Fig. 3(a)] was less effective than MT-KSVD [Fig. 3(b)] and TDGSR [Fig. 3(c)]. Moreover, the scatter plots of MT-KSVD are distributed a bit more discretely than those of TDGSR, which means that MT-KSVD performed worse than TDGSR.

In addition, we show the quantitative assessment of the reconstruction results in Table 1 by the metrics of mean absolute error (MAE), mean square error (MSE), mean relative error (MRE), and CC. Because of the length limitation, we refer the readers to our previous paper [14] for their calculation expressions. Table 1 demonstrates that MT-KSVD and TDGSR effectively reconstructed the missing information, and TDGSR performed better than MT-KSVD.

Table 1. Quantitative assessment of the reconstruction results.

Method	MAE / 10^{-3}	MSE / 10^{-5}	MRE / %	CC
Corrupted	66.947	895.612	52.213	0.6579
Replacement	18.594	116.812	13.973	0.9058
MT-KSVD	4.690	6.512	3.676	0.9851
TDGSR	4.381	6.112	3.468	0.9858

3.2 Real Data Experiment

In order to verify the cloud removal effect for real remote sensing images, we also conducted a real data experiment. As in the simulated experiment, obvious differences exist between the good part and the reconstructed part of the cloudy area in the result of direct replacement. Both MT-KSVD and TDGSR effectively reconstructed the missing information obscured by clouds, and again performed better than direct replacement (Fig. 4).

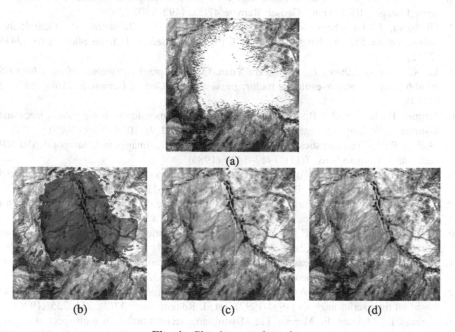

(a)

(b)   (c)   (d)

Fig. 4. Cloud removal results.

4 Conclusions

This paper has proposed a cloud removal algorithm for remote sensing images, using group sparse representation in the temporal domain. The main idea is to make use of the temporal sparsity and nonlocal similarity in the multitemporal images. Temporal correlation is utilized in the reconstruction process of the missing information. In order to make better sense of the temporal correlation, temporal normalization and permutation are also adopted. Simulated and real data experiments both confirmed that the proposed method is an effective approach.

Acknowledgements. This work was supported by the National Natural Science Foundation of China (NSFC) under Grant Nos. 41422108 and 41401396, the Postdoctoral Science Foundation of China under Grant No. 2014M552083, and the Fundamental Research Funds for the Central Universities of China under Grant No. 2014205020201. The authors would also like to thank the anonymous reviewers.

References

1. Lin, C.-H., Lai, K.-H., Chen, Z.-B., Chen, J.-Y.: Patch-based information reconstruction of cloud-contaminated multitemporal images. IEEE Trans. Geosci. Remote **52**(1), 163–174 (2014)
2. Barcelos, C., Batista, M.A.: Image inpainting and denoising by nonlinear partial differential equations. In: 16th Brazilian Symposium on Computer Graphics and Image Processing (SIBGRAPI), pp. 287–293. Sao Carlos, Brazil (2003)
3. Shen, H., Zhang, L.: A MAP-based algorithm for destriping and inpainting of remotely sensed images. IEEE Trans. Geosci. Remote **47**(5), 1492–1502 (2009)
4. Gladkova, I., Grossberg, M.D., Shahriar, F., Bonev, G., Romanov, P.: Quantitative restoration for MODIS band 6 on aqua. IEEE Trans. Geosci. Remote **50**(6), 2409–2416 (2012)
5. Li, X., Shen, H., Zhang, L., Zhang, H., Yuan, Q.: Dead pixel completion of aqua MODIS band 6 using a robust m-estimator multiregression. IEEE Geosci. Remote S. **11**(4), 768–772 (2014)
6. Helmer, E., Ruefenacht, B.: Cloud-free satellite image mosaics with regression trees and histogram matching. Photogramm. Eng. Remote Sens. **71**(9), 1079–1089 (2005)
7. Holben, B.N.: Characteristics of maximum-value composite images from temporal AVHRR data. Int. J. Remote Sens. **7**(11), 1417–1434 (1986)
8. Zhang, J., Clayton, M.K., Townsend, P.A.: Functional concurrent linear regression model for spatial images. J. Agric. Biol. Environ. S. **16**(1), 105–130 (2011)
9. Viovy, N., Arino, O., Belward, A.S.: The best index slope extraction (BISE): a method for reducing noise in NDVI time-series. Int. J. Remote Sens. **13**(8), 1585–1590 (1992)
10. Savitzky, A., Golay, M.J.E.: Smoothing and differentiation of data by simplified least squares procedures. Anal. Chem. **36**(8), 1627–1639 (1964)
11. Jönsson, P., Eklundh, L.: Seasonality extraction by function fitting to time-series of satellite sensor data. IEEE Trans. Geosci. Remote **40**(8), 1824–1832 (2002)
12. Verhoef, W., Menenti, M., Azzali, S.: Cover a colour composite of NOAA-AVHRR-NDVI based on time series analysis (1981-1992). Int. J. Remote Sens. **17**(2), 231–235 (1996)
13. Lorenzi, L., Melgani, F., Mercier, G.: Missing-area reconstruction in multispectral images under a compressive sensing perspective. IEEE Trans. Geosci. Remote **51**(7), 3998–4008 (2013)
14. Li, X., Shen, H., Zhang, L., Zhang, H., Yuan, Q., Yang, G.: Recovering quantitative remote sensing products contaminated by thick clouds and shadows using multitemporal dictionary learning. IEEE Trans. Geosci. Remote **52**(11), 7086–7098 (2014)
15. Li, X., Shen, H., Zhang, L., Li, H.: Sparse-based reconstruction of missing information in remote sensing images from spectral/temporal complementary information. ISPRS J. Photogramm. doi: 10.1016/j.isprsjprs.2015.03.009
16. Zhang, J., Zhao, D., Gao, W.: Group-based sparse representation for image restoration. IEEE Trans. Image Process. **23**(8), 3336–3351 (2014)
17. Buades, A., Coll, B., Morel, J.M.: A non-local algorithm for image denoising. In: IEEE Computer Society Conference on Computer Vision and Pattern Recognition (CVPR), pp. 60–65, San Diego, USA (2005)

Text to Head Motion Synthesis
for Chinese Sign Language Avatar

Wenjing He[1,2]($\boxtimes$), Junfa Liu[1], and Yiqiang Chen[1]

[1] Institute of Computing Technology, Chinese Academy of Sciences, Beijing, China
hewenjing@ict.ac.cn
[2] University of Chinese Academy of Sciences, Beijing, China

Abstract. Head movement is an essential constituent of Chinese Sign Language (CSL), which helps to complete the definition of signing gestures and to assist in sending messages. Adding head motions into signing animations benefits for both the reality and the intelligibility. By analyzing the head motions both defined in words of CSL and captured from large motion data of a real signer performance, this paper proposes a quintuple for formalized head movement description. A Text To Head Motion (TTHM) synthesis model is established to perform a low-level semantic mapping from words to head gestures. Experimental results verify that improvement is achieved both in naturalness rating and understandability of signing animations after synthesizing with head motions.

Keywords: Signing avatar · Chinese Sign Language · Head motion

1 Introduction

Chinese Sign Language (CSL) is the primary manner of communications for most deaf people in China. Several researches provided deaf people with signing avatar to get access to the society by CSL animations [1,2]. However, the performance of these applications is barely satisfactory. Too much attention paid on hand gesture generation makes animations always hard to understand. Actually, deaf people use facial expression and head motions to express meanings in real signing performance, which helps to give feedbacks and engage human-to-human communications. According to the linguistical research, head motion can signal both the grammar and prosody structure of utterance through signing [3]. Adding head poses into signing animations is a natural way to help the computer-animated avatar look lifelike and enhance the understandability of the animated presentations. By analyzing the head motion defined in Chinese Sign Language [4] and exploring head motion features extracted from real signing data, we propose a quintuple which describes the attributes affecting head movement in signing performance. The proposed text to head motion (TTHM) model initially performs

Y. Chen—This work was supported by a grant from National Natural Science Foundation of China (61173066).

a primary analysis of the utterance text to determine its semantic, pragmatic head gesture, which translates the textual features into quintuple parameters. Then the quintuple has been transcribed into motion parameters which can be processed by the animation engine. At last, the animation synthesis platform fulfills the synchronous generation of hand and head gestures.

2   Head Motion Quintuple in Chinese Sign Language

To figure out the feature of head motion in Chinese Sign Language, we analyzed the head motion defined in the book of CSL. Firstly, we sort the head movements defined in the book according to textual description, which can be described into four aspects as follows, head motion type, motion direction, range of movement, and repetition of activity. According to the statistics, most of the descriptions do not indicate the direction. Although over half of the definitions give the description of amplitude, no quantitative range of movement has been narrated. And two thirds of the head movement definition do not give the exact times of repetition of the motion. In short, the head motion definitions in the book are too rough to synthesize by computer graphic technologies. Then the investigation of functional head movements was conducted on real signer data. For real signing data collection, we employed a native sign language teacher to perform 12 fairy stories. We labeled the head motion with both types and functions. In general, nine kinds of head motions and ten kinds of functions were labeled in the signing data. The emphasis, positive, negative is as the same as functions discussed in [5]. We explored two other accompany head motions of sign language. A spatial-reference means the usage of points around signer representing entities under discussion [6]. Head moves accordingly with hand gestures can be labeled as an action-cooperation. Except defined head motions, however, it is impossible to make a conclusion that a word has a correspondence with a certain head movement when serving as a specific function. Grammar information provides us some indication that signer emphasizes the subject with nodding. And predicate verbs are often accompanied by action-cooperation head motions. In addition, the words that express directional information have a high correlation with specific head movements, such as the signer turns left when signing "left". Generally, most of data were signed in the moderate speed and amplitude. Changes occurred when expressing emphasis in a slower speed and surprise in a larger range and so on. And it is worth noting that most of the labeled head motions were timing and scope constrained by the accompanying words. Keeping still or lengthening the head pose usually occurred at the last sign of a clause or a sentence.

According to the analysis above, a parametric descriptor of head motion lists as follows.

$$head =< BU, A, R, S, P > \tag{1}$$

where BU represents the basic uniform of head motion. Nine kinds of head movements, that are *nod, shake, dazzle, raising, lowering, left/right_turn, left/right_tilt,* are presented in the value set. *forward* and *backward* leads to displacement of the torso, which will be discussed in the future. A defines the degree of amplitude, which in the book is always narrated as "slight". Here we expand its value set to three levels, *slight, neutral, strong* according to the rotation range around each axis [7]. R is the times of repetition, S describes the absolute time of the head motion, three values *slow, neutral, fast* indicate the speed of the movement. P is the rhythm parameter, which indicates the prosody attributes of the head motion. Its value influences the shape of the head motion trajectory. For example, a *Hold* will remain the motion for a few frames to represent a pause or a turn during signing.

3 TTHM Synthesis Model

The TTHM synthesis model maps from words or functions to head movements, the framework is shown in Fig. 1, we will detail these processing steps in the following sections.

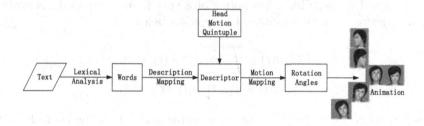

Fig. 1. The TTHM synthesis framework.

3.1 Lexical Analysis

Input sentences firstly are parsed into individual words, then the gesture data can be selected from an animation database according to the word. The synthesis platform later synthesize an animation of a virtual human character based on the word sequences. For our head motion generation, the results of lexical analysis help to locate the word that either defines a head movement or has a functional head motion.

3.2 Description Mapping

The description mapping takes word parsed by the previous phase as input and maps it to a certain head motion quintuple. Noting that not every word maps to a head movement. For the words that are defined with head motion, the textual description varies among words and most of the definitions do not specify the direction of movements. Under the guidance of an experienced signer, we mapped the motion defined in the book to the nine kinds of movements mentioned above. In general, the rest of attributes that the definition hasn't specified the value are all set the neutral value.

For the functional head motion, head motions need to be determined manually. The attributes setting follows the same neutral strategy without specification. However, one can change the speed or amplitude to realize different functions. A gesture data sequence accompanying with head motion descriptors is generated to synthesize animations.

3.3 Motion Mapping

The motion mapping translates the head motion quintuple into variables which can be processed by the animation engine. In our sign language synthesis platform, these variables are rotation angles. In general, the scope and the timing of linguistic head movements is linguistically constrained to the manual sign they accompany [3]. Under the length of the accompany hand gesture, we adopted an optimal control based head motion trajectory synthesis approach [8]. Each kind of basic head motion defines several key points, then the optimization of the trajectory can be formally written as a cost function which embeds into an optimal control model. Given key points of a specific head motion, an optimal motion trajectory can be computed by equation below.

$$F(z, u, t) = \int_{t_0}^{t_f} h(z(t), u(t), t)\, dt$$

$$s.t. \quad \dot{z}(t) = f(z(t), u(t), t)$$

(2)

where $z(t) = [q(t), \dot{q}(t), \ddot{q}(t)]^T$ is the state vector and $u(t)$ is the control vector. $q(t)$ is the head motion rotation angles to be solved. The system subjects to start and end conditions $z(t_0) = z_0$, $z(t_f) = z_f$. The trajectories of angles have been computed with respect to the minimum angle jerk:

$$F_{AJ} = \frac{1}{2} \int_{t_0}^{t_f} \dddot{q}^T(t)\, \dddot{q}(t)\, dt$$

(3)

where $\dddot{q}(t)$ is the third derivation of joints' angles which makes up the control vector $u(t)$. The *amplitude* can be used to set the start and end conditions to change the range of the head motion. The *speed* is used to vary the number of frames to realize different scale of velocity. Other parameters can be set accordingly to provide variations in head motion generation.

3.4 Animation Synthesis

After motion mapping, the textual head motion description has been transcribed into parameterized motion trajectory. The animation engine takes these rotation angles as input to drive the movement of the virtual agent. And the animation engine generates hand animation synchronously with head motion.

4   Experiment

Experiments in this paper focuses on the effect of the head movements after adding to the animation sequences. Three trials had been conducted to test the influence of head movements on the naturalness and comprehensibility of an animation performance. For each of the random selected five sentences, we generated two animations of virtual human performance. One animation showed the head movements generated by the rules of our system. For the other animation, hand gestures without head motion had been generated.

We firstly divided the recruited 20 participants into two groups to grade the naturalness of synthesized animations. One group was assigned animations with head motion and the other without head movement. They were asked to rate the naturalness of the performances with a scale from 1 to 5. The higher the score is, more natural the animation looks. Table 1 shows the results of this experiment. "HM" is short for head motion. Overall, the grades of the proposed approach demonstrate that our method performs better. However, there is no significant difference between the two approaches. One possible explanation could be related to discontinuity between adjacent head movements. For instance, there were two successive slight right-tilt head movements in the third sample sentence. The short transition period caused the distortion of the motion. What's more, only few of the words in the sentences were generated with head motion weakened the continuity of animations. For our future work, heuristics are needed to prevent inordinate amounts of head switching, or overly repetitive activations of the same motion. Considering the action-cooperation head motion, a study of relationship between hand and head gestures may achieve automatical non-defined head motion prediction and improve the naturalness further.

Table 1. Naturalness ratings.

	1	2	3	4	5	Ave
Without HM	2.56	3.21	2.84	3.13	3.50	3.04
With HM	4.13	3.01	4.37	3.65	4.55	3.94

For the comprehension task, the participants setting was the same as naturalness rating. The test composed of two parts. Lexical test examined the effect of head movement to distinguish signs that resembled in hand gestures but had nuances in head motion definition. Figure 2 shows an example that the upper sign is "sleep" and the lower sign is "face". We can see that if there were no head movement in the upper sign, these two words are hard to differentiate. The lexical test selected five sets of sign word, and each set was made up of two sign words. Participants were asked to match the animation to a specific word, while the words were prepared in advance for each set including some other disturbance terms. Table 2 shows the average correct recognition rate of every set, word in bold of each set defines head movement in the book. Great improvement has been achieved in sign words discrimination with head motion.

Fig. 2. Signing animation of "sleep" (upper) and "face" (lower)

Table 2. Lexical discrimination test results.

Sets	Words	Without HM	With HM
1	**Modesty**,abdomen	0.38	0.60
2	**sleep**,face	0.60	0.91
3	**aware**,head	0.75	0.95
4	**affirm**,you	0.63	0.68
5	**coy**,eye	0.38	0.77

Sentential test verified the assistance of head movement in semantic expression. Participants were asked to answer five questions drew from animations used in naturalness tests. Figure 3 shows the result of sentential comprehension tasks. Compared to animations without head motion, the correct answering rate of animation with head motion is much higher. Especially, head movement helps to indicate the negative information. For instance, the head-shake in the fourth sentence assisted participants in ticking off the right answer that "she don't care about others' ridicule". However, the rate of uncertainty ("other" in the figure) remains high in both the proposed animations and animations without head movements. One reason may explain that the animation signed by virtual human is not understandable for participants. Changes in speed, appropriate pause in signing help to signal the structure of sentences and leave response time to process information. A further study of prosodic head movement synthesis is needed to improve the sentential comprehensibility.

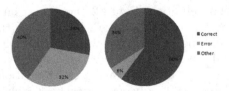

Fig. 3. Comparison of comprehensibility between animations without head motion (left) and with head motion (right)

5   Conclusion

Head movement plays an important role in sign language, and it also has a great effect on the lifelike signing animation generation. A formalized head motion descriptor is needed to feed the animation engine to animate the virtual head. By analyzing the head motion accompanying hand gesture both defined in the book of CSL and extracted from real signing performance, we propose a head movement description quintuple and realize the TTHM synthesis model. Experimental results show that the animations integrated with head motion rate higher in naturalness. However, the comprehensibility test is not as significant as expected. It achieves better to distinguish the words that are resemble in hand gestures but have differences in head movement. The manual description mapping weakens the usability of the animation engine. A more intelligent way of description mapping is the next step of this work. As discussed above, our future work focuses on enhancing further both the naturalness and understandability of signing animations. Attention will be paid to study the correlation between hand and head gesture to generate realistic animation. And the prosody structure will also be investigated to improve the expressiveness of animations.

References

1. Wang, Z., Gao, W.: A method to synthesize Chinese Sign Language based on virtual human technologies. J. Softw. **13**, 2051–2056 (2002)
2. Yan, Q., Chen, Y., Liu, J.: Gesture synthesis based on virtual newscaster for broadcast TV news programes. J. Comput. Res. Dev. **46**, 1893–1899 (2009)
3. Pfau, R., Quer, J.: Nonmanuals: Their Prosodic and Grammatical Roles, Sign Language. Cambridge University Press, Cambridge (2010)
4. The Chinese Association of the Deaf: Chinese Sign Language. HuaXia, Beijing (2003)
5. Heylen, D.: Challenges ahead: head movement and other social in conversations. In: Joint Symposioum on virtual Social Agents, pp. 45–52 (2005)
6. Huenerfauth, M., Pengfei, L.: Effect of spatial reference and verb inflection on the usability of sign language animations. Univ. Access Inf. Soc. **11**, 169–184 (2012)
7. Kocoń, M.: Idle motion synthesis of human head and face in virtual reality environment. In: Ma, M., Oliveira, M.F., Petersen, S., Hauge, J.B. (eds.) SGDA 2013. LNCS, vol. 8101, pp. 299–306. Springer, Heidelberg (2013)
8. Stein, T., Simonidis, C., Seemann, W., Schwameder, H.: A computational model of human movement coordination. In: 33rd Annual German Conference on AI, pp. 23–32, Karlsruhe, Germany, 21–24 September (2010)

The Real-Time Vision System for Fabric Defect Detection with Combined Approach

Pengfei Li[✉], Zhuo Zhao, Lei Zhang, Hongwei Zhang, and Junfeng Jing

School of Electronic and Information, Xi'an Polytechnic University,
Xi'an 710048, China
zz725@126.com, jingjunfeng0718@sina.com

Abstract. A real-time machine vision detection system based on computer for fabric defect detection is presented in this paper. Hardware platform and software algorithm are the two main parts included in it. In hardware platform, image acquisition subsystem and transmission operated synchronously to achieve synchronization between motion and acquisition through the encoder and video capture card. Moreover, double-buffer technique with an alternative acquisition mode is applied to make the system more real-time. Each defect detection algorithm is regarded as a single detection unit which is integrated in the software system. Then different detection units are employed at different fabrics and defects to gain better detection efficacy. It could be concluded that the proposed system provides a lower cost, higher performance and more excellent expansibility solution for enterprises via the variety of experiments.

Keywords: Machine vision · Defect detection · Automatic visual inspection · Fabric

1 Introduction

Matters to the economic benefits, it is crucial for every enterprise to have quality control and product testing in textile industry. The existence of defects will drop 45 % to 60 % on the value of fabric according to the statistical data [2], which has a great effect on its market competitiveness. Actually, defect detection is the main task of product quality checking for the textile enterprises. Although with low efficiency, poor accuracy, high missing rate and human factors, human vision inspection has occupied the dominant position in practical production [8], which will no longer meets the need of modern textile industry. It is reported that the detection rate will be lower than 60 % while an experienced inspector detecting a batch of 2 m-width cloth at the speed of 30 m/s [3]. Vision exhausted, human sight damaged and exponential decline of detection rate will be caused after continuous human vision inspecting. It will be a trend that human vision inspection method is doomed to be eliminated, so a low cost, high performance and real-time detection system is urgently demanded. In recent years, many researches

© Springer International Publishing Switzerland 2015
Y.-J. Zhang (Ed.): ICIG 2015, Part III, LNCS 9219, pp. 460–473, 2015.
DOI: 10.1007/978-3-319-21969-1_41

for automatic fabric defect detection have been done at domestic and abroad. Most of them can be classified into four classes including structure based, statistics based, model based and spectral analyze based [9]. Many algorithms are considered as classical methods in image processing field such as Fast Fourier Transform, Gabor filter [10], gray level co-occurrence matrix and Wavelet transform [6,7]. However, these methods are unavailable to various target objects and most of them are only validated at a simulation environment without applying to industrial situations. In addition, these algorithms are fruitless for the research achievements to solve the practical problems because of their relatively poor efficiency and real time in the industry.

In this paper, machine vision detection system based on Personal Computer (PC) is presented for fabric detection with low cost, high accuracy (0.264 mm/pixel) and good real time. For selection of standard components, transmission and image acquisition subsystem are possesses with great scalability in whole system. Each algorithm is taken as a single detection unit integrated in software system. Furthermore, the import of double-buffer [3] alternative acquisition technique, image mosaic [4], database and report printing will greatly strengthen real time and input-output abilities of the system. Finally, software system and hardware platform are combined through a feature-rich graphical user interface, which brings much convenience.

The paper is constructed as follow: Sect. 2 shows the system hardware platform in details. Section 3 introduces core detection methods including Otsu method (Otsu), Golden image subtraction method (GIS), and then a graphical user interface is designed. Section 4 gives performance tests and experiment results, including detection effects, precision and real time.

2 Hardware Platform

The hardware platform of Machine vision detection system is mainly contains three aspects, mechanical frame, transmission and image acquisition subsystem. The interaction between proposed system and looms could be come true, which brings full automatic production. The design of whole system is shown in Fig. 1. Besides, transmission and image acquisition subsystem play essential roles in the detection system.

2.1 Transmission

Transmission is made up of shafts, motors, transducers and encoder. Several driven shafts and three driving shafts that are driven by motors in transmission. When the system is running in a high speed, the phenomenon of fabric shaking will leads to poor acquisition quality in practical application. To solve the problem, driven shafts are installed as a structure of shaft group, then tension of fabric is enlarged on shafts and fabric shaking is eliminated in detection area.

Fig. 1. Mechanical structure of system

Transmission in machine vision detection system is operated as followings:

(1) Through 485 bus, commands are transmitted from computer to transducers in modbus protocol.
(2) Motors are driven by transducers when the commands have been received.
(3) The rolling shafts driven by motors makes testing fabric running.
(4) Pulse signal generated from encoder that is driven by shafts, which will be external trigger signal for synchronous acquisition.

2.2   Image Acquisition

Image acquisition subsystem is a critical part in the whole system, which affects the performance of detection. Line scan cameras, video capture card, illuminant and a high performance computer are involved in image acquisition.

The procedure of image acquisition could be executed in four steps:

(1) Encoder driven by a shaft outputs external trigger signal to PCI video capture card.
(2) From I/O port, video capture card receives external trigger signal and controls the CCD cameras exposuring, collecting a row of image (2048 pixels) via camera link ports.
(3) After running step 1 and step 2, object image is collected in form of row by row until it reaches 500 rows and a frame (2048 × 500) is captured.
(4) Video capture card sends the image data to RAM through PCI port in computer and displays it on VGA monitor.

The image acquisition subsystem is shown in .

To capture high quality image of target object, E2V SM2-CL series line scan CDD cameras are selected. Their line scan frequency reaches to 28 KHz. The camera has a high resolution of 2048 pixels and equips a camera link port with

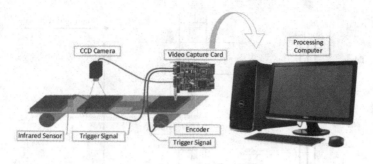

Fig. 2. Image acquisition subsystem

the data rate of 60 Mb/s, which meets the need of image acquisition at a high speed and resolution.

As for Automated optical inspection equipment, the quality of image acquisition is relevant to illuminant. The LED matrix illuminant is chosen to provide system lighting for the reason of long life, energy saving, uniform stability and lasting operation. The incident light and transmitted light are integrated in the system in practical application. The incident light is introduced to enhance fabric surface texture and defects. While transmitted light is installed below the target object to stand out background defects.

The video capture card and computer play key roles in section of image acquisition and processing. For the need of image acquisition, Bitflow Inc Neon-CL series video capture card is selected because of its advanced data processing ability, high speed camera link ports, PCI data exchange interface and rich external I/O ports. Owing to the design of duo-core FPGA and DSP structure, video capture card has acquisition speed of 85 MHz 24 bit, which supports the real-time performance. In addition, synchronization between image acquisition subsystem and transmission is another job of video capture card.

Concurrent working strategy of multi-camera is introduced to adapt to wide scale detecting situation. Cameras are installed at same distance, receiving a same external trigger signal and outputting synchronous images. In Fig. 3, the coordinate of detection area is built with X axis for running direction and Y axis for width direction. The scan area of each camera could have its own coordinate which has the same X axis and offset Y axis. With the help of coordinate system, defects locating could be achievable, then combined with image mosaic algorithm, all scan images fuse together and build up full scale detection.

3 Detection Algorithm

In proposed system, machine vision detection algorithm has mach effect on the detection performance. The precision and running speed will be key factors in researching to detection algorithms for the need of practical applications in industrial field. As for the current research in fabric field, its not an easy thing to find up a detection algorithm to deal with various fabrics and defects in

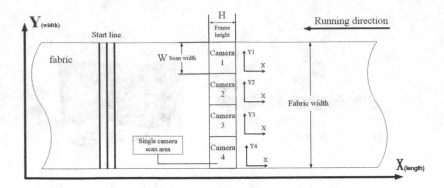

Fig. 3. Coverage of multi-camera scanning

practical production. The combination of multi-algorithm is proposed in fabric defect detection. Every detection algorithm is regarded as a detection unit in the software system and then different algorithms exert their advantages to different target fabric, which makes the system stronger and smarter. Figure 4 gives the model of detection method.

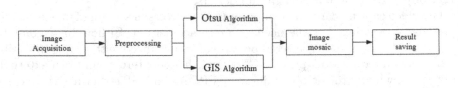

Fig. 4. Model of detection method

To realize the real-time system, operational efficiency and time consumption are strictly demanded in the design of algorithms. Imagining, three line scan CCD cameras are selected to give a 1500 mm-width cloth a full scale scan with its running speed of 80 m/min. Furthermore, the defects with the size of 1 mm × 1 mm on fabric surface are required to be detected. Calculation period should strictly limited in a third period of single cycle acquisition. That is to say, three images (resolution 0.264 mm/pixel) with the size of 2048 × 500 must be processed within a period of capturing a frame in detecting task. The parallel working mode in double-buffer alternative acquisition technique is shown in Fig. 5. The data in Buffer A is being processed after acquisition and Buffer B captures the image data at the same time. It would be cycles in this way. Compared with the serial data processing mode of single buffer, double-buffer alternative acquisition technique has doubled the running efficiency of the system that enhances the real time in data processing.

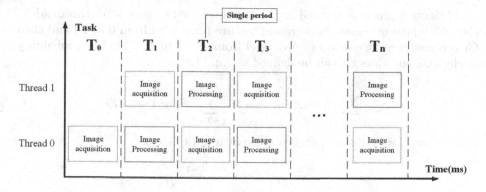

Fig. 5. Double-buffer alternative working mode

3.1   Otsu Algorithm

As a method of maximum variance between the two classes, Otsu algorithm divides test image into two classes including foreground and background [11]. In this system, background can be seen as image texture and foreground represents surface defects. A suitable threshold T is gained from algorithm to give defects segmentation, then fabric defects and background texture will be decoupled.

Owing to the principle, Otsu algorithm has a feature of high speed and shorter detection period which is most suitable for the fast fabric detection. Figure 6 shows the procedure of algorithm.

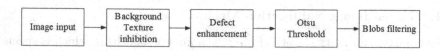

Fig. 6. Procedure of Otsu algorithm

Assuming the test fabric image has L gray levels, the pixels in level q have an amount of n_q and the total of pixels in the image can be expressed as $n = n_0 + n_1 + \ldots + n_{L-1}$. In the condition of uniform quantization, gray level probability P_q is given in Eq. (1). $\omega(K)$ and $\mu(K)$ represent gray probability cumulative value and mean value of pixels below the K gray level as shown in Eqs. (2) and (3):

$$P_q = \frac{n_q}{n} \tag{1}$$

$$\omega(K) = \sum_{q=0}^{K} P_q , \quad \omega(L-1) = 1 \tag{2}$$

$$\mu(K) = \frac{\sum_{q=0}^{K} q P_q}{\omega} \qquad K = 0,1,...,L-1; \tag{3}$$

If the test image is divided into two classes by the gray level threshold T, class C_0 represents image background texture (gray level from 0 to T) and class C_1 represents surface defects (gray level from $T + 1$ to $L - 1$). The probability of class C_0 and class C_1 can be defined as Eq. (4):

$$\omega_0 = \sum_{q=0}^{T} P_q = \omega(T) \ , \quad \omega_1 = \sum_{q=T+1}^{L-1} P_q = 1 - \omega(T) \tag{4}$$

The mean values of two classes are shown in Eq. (5) :

$$\mu_0 = \frac{\sum_{q=0}^{T} qP_q}{\omega_0} \ , \quad \mu_1 = \frac{\sum_{q=T+1}^{L-1} qP_q}{\omega_1} \tag{5}$$

The average gray value of whole image can be expressed as Eq. (6):

$$\mu = \mu_0\omega_0 + \mu_1\omega_1 \tag{6}$$

$$\sigma_B^2 = \omega_0(\mu_0 - \mu)^2 + \omega_1(\mu_1 - \mu)^2 \tag{7}$$

where, when the variance σ_B^2 between two classes reaches its maximum value, the corresponding threshold T selected from gray level $[0, L - 1]$ is the perfect segmentation threshold of Otsu algorithm. The image will be given a binary processing by threshold T.

3.2   Golden Image Subtraction Method

Golden image subtraction method (GIS) is a kind of algorithm which is specialized in the defects on fabric with repeating patterns, such as grey cloth, plaid cloth and other cloth with the same pattern [5].

Preprocessing, defect detection and post processing are the three main sections in algorithm procedure. First of all, Preprocessing is necessary after the image acquisition. The use of Gaussian smoothing is to eliminate image background texture and random noise, then histogram equalization is to enhance the defects; Secondly, defects are segmented from test image by a proper threshold that is gained from training algorithm on the reference image; Finally, the detection results from GIS algorithm are dealt with median filtering, which could eliminate the noise.

GIS algorithm is based on the theory of graphic subtraction as shown in Fig. 7. With the theory, defects could be segmented from test images through the subtraction between golden template image and the sub image that is intercepted from test image of same size. The energy of GIS is defined as Eq. (8):

$$R = (r_{xy}) = \frac{1}{mn} \sum_{i=1}^{m} \sum_{j=1}^{n} |g_{ij} - h_{ij}| \tag{8}$$

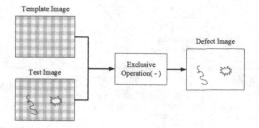

Fig. 7. The theoretical foundation of GIS algorithm

where $x = 1, ..., M - m + 1$, $y = 1, ..., N - n + 1$. The golden template image G is extracted from reference image with the size of $m \times n$ that should be at least bigger than the smallest repeating pattern on test image. While the sub image $H_{xy} = H_{xy}(i, j)$ extracted from the test image has the same size with G. R in a piece of area can be defined as the mean of absolute value between G and H. The execution steps of GIS algorithm are shown as follow:

(1) Extract golden template image G with the size of $m \times n$ from reference image.
(2) According to Eq. (8), the GIS energy of a pixel can be achieved by calculating the mean of absolute value between G (golden template image) and H (extracted sub image from test image). As show in Fig. 8, from the 1-st pixel to the $(M - m + 1)$-th pixel in first row and from the 1-st row to the $(N - n + 1)$-th row, GIS energy matrix with the size of $(M - m + 1) \times (N - n + 1)$ is created.
(3) As output from GIS detection, GIS energy matrix R will be returned.
(4) Every element from GIS energy matrix of test image will be compared with the threshold T. When the element value is bigger than T, it will be set as 1. On the opposite, it will be 0. Then binary image with the size of $(M - m + 1) \times (N - n + 1)$ can be gotten. Owing to repeating pattern and no defects, the reference image has uniform values in GIS energy matrix. Defects have obvious difference from normal areas in test image and energy is happened to jump beyond the threshold. The threshold T can be defined as the maximum value of reference image GIS energy matrix.

In Post processing, result generated from GIS thresholding has been mixed with white noise and random noise, which can't be the final result of detection. It should be filtered to reduce the effect of noise and improve the accuracy of detection. Through validation, the introduction of median filtering has a best effect on noise smoothing and final detection result will be given in Sect. 4.

3.3 Graphical User Interface

To validate proposed algorithm, both completed software system and well designed graphical user interface are to be developed. Meanwhile, their development could put the detection system into practical use. Software of proposed

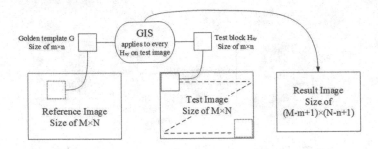

Fig. 8. The execution mechanism of algorithm

machine vision detection system is exploited with C++ programming language at Windows 7 32 bit operation system and development to detection algorithm involved in C++ library, OpenCV and video capture card software development kit. Graphical user interface is built in visual C++ MFC development environment. In Fig. 9, framework of machine vision software system is given.

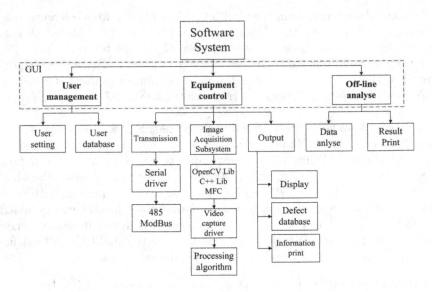

Fig. 9. Software system

As shown in Fig. 9, software in machine vision detection system mainly consists of three sections.

(1) Module of user management contains many functions such as adding users, user delete, system login and authority management.
(2) As shown in Fig. 10, system controlling module has realized the real-time online detection. Users could handle the whole system including transmission, image acquisition and image processing. Furthermore, operation status,

captured image and detecting results could also be shown in graphical user interface during detection to accomplish the purpose of interaction between human and machine.

In menu or toolbar at the top, many control functions including direction control, speed control, printer control, etc. are offered to user. Captured image and detection result are real-time shown in median area. Operation status of the system could be found at the bottom, which one could know how fast is the system running or how many defects detected.

After automatic detection, all defects information during detection such as positions, types and saving paths will be written in database, and then saved data is available to the functions of print, analysis and other further works.

(3) Module of data analysis and statistic respectively provides user a function of offline data analyze and statistic to defects information during the production.

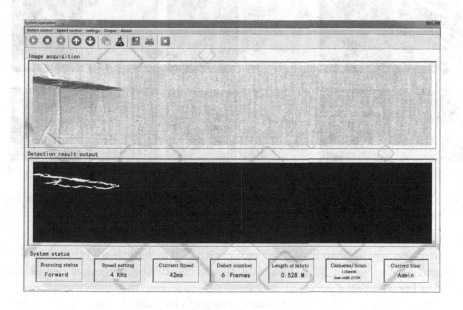

Fig. 10. Graphical user interface

4   Results and Discussion

Hit rate, fault rate [1], detection precision, real time and other performances of machine vision detection system would be tested in this section. Through the offline-online experiments, hit rate and fault rate could be validated. In the tests to real time and running speed, time consumption of single period detection is taken as benchmark here. All the proposed tests are running at a situation of indoor, ambient temperature and natural light.

4.1   Algorithm Effectiveness

At first, Offline tests to detection algorithm would be executed and all test defect sample images are from textile surface defects reference benchmark database of Technische Universit at Hamburg-Harburg University in Germany. About fifty defect test images with the size of 256×256 and 52 defect free reference images are selected. Among the samples, there are 13 kinds of fabric texture and 9 kinds of common defect are covered. The detection results of partial selected sample images are shown in Fig. 11.

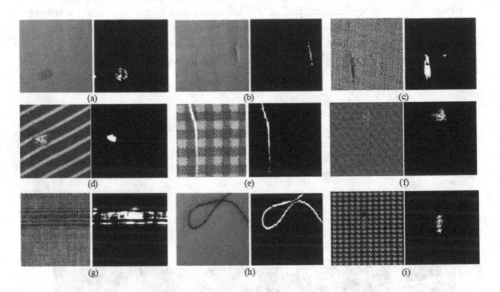

Fig. 11. Offline test results (a) oil print (b) scratch (c) small hole (d) big hole (e) broken end (f) knots (g) weft broken (h) thread (i) netting multiple

In online test, a batch of grey cloth with 500 m length and 1 m width is detected at a speed of 30 m/min, and then some of the detection results are given in Fig. 12.

The offline-online experiment results are given in Table 1. The hit rate (HR), missing rate (MR) and fault rate (FR) are given in Eqs. (9), (10) and (11), respectively.

$$HR = \frac{detected\ number}{whole\ number\ of\ defects} \times 100\% \qquad (9)$$

$$MR = 1 - HR \qquad (10)$$

$$FR = \frac{fault\ number}{detected\ number} \times 100\% \qquad (11)$$

It can be seen that many different kinds of fabric defects could be better detected.

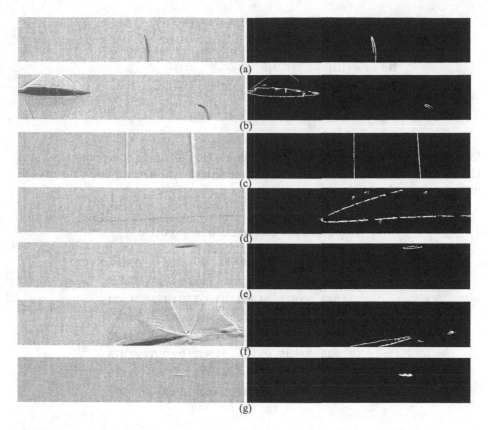

Fig. 12. Online detection results (a) oil print (b) hole (c) crease (d) thread (e) scratch (f) suture (g) neppiness

4.2 Performance Verification

The computer is in charge of controlling and processing, so system performance has close relevance to computer hardware. The computer hardware configuration is: CPU i7-4790 3.6GHz, RAM 8G DDR3, GPU Nvidia GTX745. Resolution of captured image has reached 0.264 mm per pixel owing to the installation and debugging to the image acquisition subsystem. It can be seen that every piece of area with the size of 1 mm × 1 mm on fabric surface will be covered with 16 pixels. It is easy for the system to detect defects of 1 mm level. The line scan CDD cameras with resolution of 2048 pixels are selected in the proposed system of which the output images have a height of 500 rows as a frame. That is to say, the output image with the size of 2048 × 500 from a single camera need to be processed. A camera has a scan width of 540 mm (0.264 mm/pixel × 2048 pixels). With the help of good scalability of system, one can add hardware equipment to realize full scale scan according to the project.

Two cameras are selected to give detection to a batch of cloth with the width of 1m. Time consumption of single period calculation is taken as test benchmark

Table 1. Detection rate

	Offline detection	Online detection
Hit rate (HR)	0.946	0.903
Fault rate (FR)	0.047	0.062
Missing rate (MR)	0.054	0.097

for system real-time verification. Table 2 shows that all kinds of defect image have their processing time recorded in online test and each five experiment results are as a group to obtain the average.

Table 2. Time consumption of algorithm

Image index	Time consumption (ms)					Average (ms)
a	25.875	24.994	25.217	25.003	24.847	25.187
b	33.533	35.611	34.132	33.857	34.493	34.324
c	27.552	25.895	27.396	26.476	26.604	26.784
d	23.330	26.586	23.768	24.985	24.262	24.586
e	23.235	22.745	22.311	21.843	22.255	22.478
f	31.588	30.253	29.564	31.115	28.903	30.285
g	19.821	21.036	19.532	20.628	19.335	20.071

It can be concluded from experiment results that proposed detection method has a shorter running time within the period of capturing single frame and fulfils the requirement of real time, which makes sure the maximum running speed of system beyond 80 m/min.

5   Conclusion

Machine vision detection system is presented for fabric defect on Personal Computer platform. The system has many advantages than other embedded platforms in terms of lower cost and stronger scalability. Furthermore, it could cooperate with other textile equipment like loom or detection machine, which makes the production automatically. Good scalability of hardware helps the system competent for various target objects. However, traditional single detection algorithm is more and more difficult to distinguish a variety of fabrics and defects. A single algorithm is regarded as a detection unit for one certain defect in the software system, which means the more schemes integrated in, the more kinds of defects can be detected. The proposed method, integrating Otsu and GIS, is different from theoretical research with real time, high detection rate and practical application. Combined with the double-buffer alternative acquisition technique, the detection scheme would be more efficient. Graphical user interface provides an easy way to handle and puts the system into practical use. With the help of image acquisition subsystem, system resolution reaches 0.264 mm per pixel, which could be precise enough to distinguish the defects of 1 mm level. The maximum detection speed is 80 m/min with detection rate beyond 90 % by various online-offline experiments.

Acknowledgments. The authors gratefully thank the Scientific Research Program Funded by Natural Science Foundation of China (61301276), Xian Polytechnic University Young Scholar Backbone Supporting Plan, Discipline Construction Funds of Xian Polytechnic University (107090811). Project supported by the Xi'an Polytechnic University Scientific Research Foundation for doctors (BS1416).

References

1. Schneider, D., Holtermann, T., Merhof, D.: A traverse inspection system for high precision visual on-loom fabric defect detection. Mach. Vis. Appl. **25**(6), 1585–1599 (2014)
2. Stojanovic, R.: Real-time vision-based system for textile fabric inspection. Real-Time Imaging **7**(6), 507–518 (2001)
3. Cho, C.-S., Chung, B.-M.: Development of real-time vision-based fabric inspection system. IEEE Trans. Ind. Electron. **52**(4), 1073–1079 (2005)
4. Sari-Sarraf, H.: Vision system for on-loom fabric inspection. IEEE Trans. Ind. Appl. **35**(6), 1252–1259 (1999)
5. Ngan, H.Y.T., et al.: Wavelet based methods on patterned fabric defect detection. Pattern Recogn. **38**(4), 559–576 (2005)
6. Jing, J., Hang, L.: Combined fabric defects detection approach and quadtree decomposition. J. Ind. Text. **41**(4), 331–344 (2012)
7. Wang, J.-W.: Singular value decomposition combined with wavelet transform for LCD defect detection. Electron. Lett. **48**(5), 266–267 (2012)
8. Chandra, J.K., Datta, A.K.: Detection of defects in fabrics using subimage-based singular value decomposition. J. Text. Inst. **104**(3), 295–304 (2013)
9. Mahajan, P.M., Kolhe, S.R., Patil, P.M.: A review of automatic fabric defect detection techniques. Adv. Comput. Res. **1**(2), 18–29 (2009)
10. Kumar, A., Pang, G.: Defect detection in textured materials using gabor filters. IEEE Trans. Ind. Appl. **38**(2), 425–440 (2002)
11. Xue, J.-H., Titterington, D.M.: Tests and Otsu's methods for image thresholding. IEEE Trans. Image Process. **20**(8), 2392–2396 (2011)

The Research of Long Time Occlusion Problem Based on Object Permanence

Xiang-Dan Hou[✉] and Ming-Jing Zhang

Department of Computer Science and Engineering,
Hebei University of Technology, Tianjin, China
hxd@scse.hebut.edu.cn

Abstract. In the video surveillance system, due to the complicated background, the targets in the movement process often appear some or full of occlusion. How to detect occlusions, handle of issues efficiently, especially in the event of long time occlusion. Accurate target identification and tracking is the key indicators to evaluate the robustness of a target tracking algorithm. This paper deals with long time occlusions based on the concept of "object permanence" in psychology. This paper proposes a method based on "object permanence" algorithm to solve the identification and tracking problems after long time occlusions. The experimental results show that this algorithm can effectively solve the occlusion problem.

Keywords: Object permanence · Long time occlusion · Target tracking

1 Introduction

In the research field of computer vision, target tracking technology combines advanced achievements of image processing, artificial intelligence and pattern recognition. It has important practical value and broad development prospects in military target tracking, traffic monitoring, industrial production monitoring and many other fields [1]. However, since the complexity and the diversity of the target features and external environments, target tracking has been a challenging task. A robust target tracking algorithm must be able to resolve all the difficulties encountered during tracking process, such as rotation, size changes, illumination changes, and occlusion is the most difficult one [2].

The occlusion problem is very common in the process of target tracking. General can be divided into the following three types [3]:

(1) According to the occlusion type: self-occlusion; other objects occlusion; occlusion between targets;
(2) According to the degree of occlusion: partial occlusion; total occlusion;
(3) According to the time of occlusion: short time occlusion; long time occlusion.

Science and Technology Fund Project of Hebei Provincial Transportation Department(Y-2012023).

Y.-J. Zhang (Ed.): ICIG 2015, Part III, LNCS 9219, pp. 474–482, 2015.
DOI: 10.1007/978-3-319-21969-1_42

The occlusion process can be divided into the following three stages [4]:

(1) Target into the occlusion state, this process lost some or all of the target information;
(2) Target holds the occlusion state, target information keeps the state of loss;
(3) Target leaves the occlusion state, target information is gradual recovery.

The target information is not stable or even lost during tracking process caused by occlusion. The key to tracking algorithm is to get enough target information and determine the location of the target. When the target appeared two times, the method can accurately identify the target. Thus, when occlusion occurs, how can we use the remaining target information continue to track is an important basis for the evaluation of a target tracking algorithm [5]. This paper deals with long time occlusion of the target tracking based on the "object permanence" method. It has achieved good tracking effect for long time occlusion.

2 Tracking Algorithm in Occlusion

In order to solve the occlusion problem, domestic and foreign researchers have done a lot of research. They have put forward many effective algorithms, which achieved better results in certain situations. These algorithms can be divided into five categories: (1) Center weighted matching region; (2) sub-block matching; (3) the trajectory prediction; (4) Bayesian theory; (5) multi-algorithm fusion.

A typical center-weighted algorithm is mean-shift algorithm [6]. Mean-shift algorithm is a non-parametric pattern matching algorithm based on kernel density estimation. This algorithm describes the color of the target distribution through the establishment of weighted histogram. It requires large amount of calculation and delays for application of real-time monitoring system.

Matching algorithm based on sub-block main idea is that the entire target area is divided into several sub-blocks and tracked separately [7]. This algorithm requires accurate matching of target sub-blocks. But in the case of severe or total occlusion, this algorithm can't find enough sub-block information and may cause the target lost.

Trajectory prediction is the use of target motion information, such as position, velocity, acceleration, etc. to predict the target position in the next frame.

Trajectory prediction refers to uses the motion information, such as position, velocity, acceleration, to predict the target position in the next frame. Kalman filter algorithm [8] is a classic predictive estimation algorithm. It is often applied to target tracking, especially the trajectory prediction in occlusion. But this trajectory prediction is mainly applied to linear motion, does not apply to non-linear movement, or non-Gaussian assumption of dynamic systems.

Bayesian filter theory, models tracking problem into a Bayesian posterior probability distribution maximization problem. The core idea is to use some discrete random sampling points (particles) to approximate the probability density function of the state variables [9]. The algorithm can solve partial occlusion, short-term occlusion and analogue interference and other complex issues.

For occluded target, using a single tracking algorithm is often difficult to achieve perfect results, especially for the case of server occlusion. Therefore, the researchers consider integration of multiple algorithms to enhance the robustness of the algorithm. Paper [10] combines the Mean-shift algorithm, Sift algorithm and Kalman filter. It has a good tracking performance for the complex situation of distortion, occlusion, rotation, but the time complexity of the algorithm is high.

Aiming at the shortcomings of the above algorithms, this paper put forward the research of solving long time occlusion problem based on "object permanence". This algorithm does not need to know prior knowledge of the target's color, size, location and other characteristics, so that it has good flexibility and applicability.

2.1 The Principle of Object Permanence

Object permanence refers to the understanding of the objective world [11, 12] "Even if the eyes can't see, the objects also remain". Simple said is the object still exists after leaving the eye-sight. Applied to the occlusion problem refers to a complete occluded object will appear near the occluder.

2.2 Object Modeling

In the process of target tracking, effectively extract prospects information is the key to successful tracking. But the reality is, the complex background, constantly changing illumination, silhouette interference bring a great deal of difficulties for foreground object extraction [13]. To solve this problem, we need a way to dynamically establish and maintain a simple, common object models [14], and timely updates. Therefore, we use the foreground object extraction method based on background subtraction Gaussian mixture model, and use the ellipses approximate target contours.

For later convenience, definitions are as follows:

Contour ellipse $e = (c_x, c_y, \alpha, \beta, \theta)$. The (c_x, c_y) is the coordinates of the center point of the ellipse, which is the coordinates of the central position of the object. α, β, respectively, represent a major axis and a minor axis, θ represents the angle of the ellipse in the two-dimensional plane.

Foreground pixel $p = (x, y)$. The (x, y) represents the coordinates of the current pixel.

The space distance between the foreground pixels and the ellipse:

$$D(p, e) = \sqrt{\vec{v} * \vec{v}} \tag{1}$$

$$\vec{v} = \begin{bmatrix} \cos(\theta) & -\sin(\theta) \\ \sin(\theta) & \cos(\theta) \end{bmatrix} \left(\frac{x - c_x}{\alpha}, \frac{y - c_y}{\beta} \right)^T \tag{2}$$

3   The Application of Object Permanence for Long Time Occlusion

In the experiments, we assume that the camera is stationary. First, input video image sequence and use background subtraction method to separate foreground and background pixels. We can get different foreground pixels blobs. Then, obtain the relationship between the targets and foreground pixels blobs. Next, analysis the occlusion relationship based on "object permanence". Finally, update the object models and predict the targets positions.

3.1   The Relationship Between the Foreground Pixel and Object

The position relationship between the targets maybe independent of each other or exist occlusion. When each target motion is independent, it's easy to mark. But when interactions occur between moving targets, the problem of foreground pixels belonging to needs a reasonable allocation. Therefore, the foreground pixels are marked as follows:

Target pixels set inside the ellipse:

$$I(e) = \{p|D(p,e) \leq 1\} \tag{3}$$

Assume that in a period of time, obtaining M foreground pixel blobs $b_j (1 \leq j \leq M)$, tracking to N targets $e_i (1 \leq i \leq N)$. In case of occlusion, especially when full occlusion, a foreground blob may contain more than one target, but a target will not be recognized as several blobs, so M ≤ N. At this time, a foreground blob may relate to multiple targets. The relationship between the blobs and the foreground pixels can be found in the following four conditions, as shown in Fig. 1.

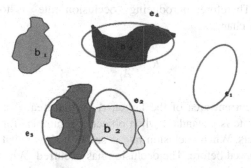

Fig. 1. The relationship between foreground pixel blobs and targets

(1) A foreground pixel blob doesn't relate to any target

$$\forall e_i, b \cap I(e_i) = \Phi \tag{4}$$

The formula (4) shows that the existing targets are not relate to the blob. Therefore, it is a new target appears in the video screen. Just like b_1.

(2) A target object is not relate to any foreground pixel blobs

$$\left(\cup_{j=1}^{M} b_j \right) \cap I(e) = \Phi \tag{5}$$

The formula (5) shows that the targets sets don't contain any detected pixels inside the blob. Therefore the target has disappeared, like e_1.

(3) A target associates with only one blob. As target e_4 and blob b_3.

(4) A blob associates with multi-targets. As target e_2 and blob e_3. They both scramble for the pixels in blob b_2 at the same time.

3.2   The Judgment of Occlusion Types Based on Object Permanence

In the occlusion problem, even in a simple partial occlusion situation, the relationship between targets and blobs is not just one to one. In order to solve the problem of missing and error tracking caused by occlusion, this paper based on "Object permanence" analyses the occlusion-ship between targets.

In the process of occlusion, target tracking relies on the spatial distribution information and appearance model information of targets. When two targets belong to different blobs, two objects began to scramble for the same blob of pixels, following the gradual process of occlusion. As shelter target, the original pixels have no obvious changes, still be marked for the objects. But the occluded target's number of pixels is gradually reduced. On account of the reduction of pixels is accompanied by the occlusion occurring. Therefore, introducing "occlusion rate" is to the quantitative characterization of the changes.

$$R_i = \frac{A_i}{A_i'} \tag{6}$$

A_i represents the current area of the target, A_i' is the area of a target before the occlusion. Occlusion rate is a standard when object e_i scrambles for the same blob of pixels with other objects. When occlusion rate is small, it shows that this target area is less than the area observed before. The occlusion has occurred. When occlusion rate is less than a certain threshold value, the target is completely occluded. At this time, the object e_i has disappeared.

$$R_i \leq T \tag{7}$$

Through the experimental tests, the threshold set to 35 % (T), can achieve good effect of distinction. When T is close to 0 %, which means a contour color of mis-classification will make the occluded target appearances again. It is a false judgment.

In fact, occlusion process is not only to determine whether the occlusion occurred, but also need to judge the shelter. The occlusion of two objects is evident. But for multiple objects occlusion, shelter judgment is very complicated. When multiple objects take place occlusion, the shelter should be located near the occluded target, and just occupy a partial of occluded target.

Among the many shelters, for each possible one, which occupies the largest part of occluded pixels, is considered to be the ultimate shelter. On the principle of "object permanence", before occluded targets appearing, we assume that the shelter completely covered the occlude targets, and they move together. When the occluded targets appear again near its shelter, the two objects separated gradually. The occluded pixels will reconstruct the target and displayed on the monitor screen.

3.3 Linear Prediction

The above mentioned method is based on the spatial distribution relationship between objects and blobs. It also can predict trajectories according to the position of target contour ellipse linear equation [15]. The judgments of targets need to mark the contour of different colors and central algorithm tags. Therefore, accurate tracking of a target need to ensure the same contour color, labels, accurate positioning in the entire process of tracking.

4 The Results and Analysis

An ideal multi-target tracking algorithm evaluation should include the following four aspects:

(1) It can accurately detect the position of each target;
(2) It can keep continuous tracking of the target;
(3) Each target corresponds to a unique ID;
(4) It has certain robustness to occlusion.

In order to verify the effectiveness of the proposed algorithm, we test respectively for outdoor, indoor, single pedestrians, multi pedestrians and standard video library CAVIAR pedestrian motion video. In this experiment, we use the windows 7 operating system as the platform, use the C++ language coding and testing in the visual studio 2008 editor. The hardware platform is the Intel core i5 CPU, 2.9 GHz, 2 GB memory.

Figure 2 is a single outdoor movement. It is the results for the pedestrian was full occlude by a tree after a period of time. The target disappeared for 102 frames. Figure 3 is the outdoor single movement process. It is tracking results of the target after a long time occlusion by a large vehicle. Figure 3(b) shows the target re-emerges after disappearing of 241 frames. This program can accurately identify the original target after long time occlusion.

Figure 4 shows the tracking results of opposite interior movement of totally occlusion after for some time. Figure 4(b) frame 498: two targets in the first encounter.

| (a) Frame 169 | (b) Frame 264 | (c) Frame 407 |

Fig. 2. Pedestrian occlude by a tree

| (a) Frame 154 | (b) Frame 498 | (c) Frame 537 |

Fig. 3. Pedestrian occlude by a large vehicle

| (a) Frame 154 | (b) Frame 498 | (c) Frame 537 |

Fig. 4. The opposite interior movement

| (a) Frame 426 | (b) Frame 457 | (c) Frame 469 |

Fig. 5. Meet_Walk_Split

Table 1. Statistics results

Tracking algorithm	Target acquisition	Accurate rate		Error rate		
		No occlusion	With occlusion	Loss rate	Misjudgment rate	False matching rate
Mean shift	Manual	62 %	10 %	13 %	15 %	7 %
Object permanence	Auto	79 %	75 %	2 %	4 %	2 %

Target 0 is full occluded by target 1. Then target 0 disappears for 85 frames. Figure 4(c) shows the correct tracking results of the two targets after separation.

Figure 5 is the tracking results of "Meet_Walk_Split" in video standard video library CAVIAR. The results indicate that the algorithm can track the three people accurately after they met. Figure 5(b) shows the 457th frame, target 2 fully occludes target 3. They walked together for 10 frames and then separated. The recognition effect of this algorithm is shown in Fig. 5(c).

Table 1 shows the statistical average track of time, accuracy rate, error rate and other information of the results. Experimental results show that the algorithm is simple, high efficiency, and realizes real-time tracking multiple targets. In the target tracking process, this algorithm has advantages such as lower error matching rate. It has better solution of long time occlusion, error tracking of similar targets and illumination mutation problem.

5 Conclusion

This paper presents an algorithm based on "object permanence" to solve the occlusion in a longer time and larger space scope. The method can accurately track targets in and out of the monitor screen. In the process of tracking, it can dynamically build the appearance and motion model of the targets. The algorithm successfully uses object permanence to solve occlusion. The experimental results have shown the superiority of the proposed algorithm in solving the problem of target matching after long time occlusion. It can be used in indoor, outdoor surveillance, video capture, and has a wide range of application.

Acknowledgements. Express my heart thanks to teachers and students who give me help in this research.

References

1. Zhang, H., Hu, S., Yang, G.: Video object tracking based on appearance models learning. J. Comput. Res. Dev. **52**, 177–190 (2015)
2. Peng, B.: Research on Occlusion in Image Sequence Tracking. Xidian University, Xidian (2014)

3. Zheng, K., Huang, W., Zhang, Z.: Occlusion handling in moving object tracking system. Comput. Eng. Des. **11**, 2816–2818 (2009)
4. Xue, C., Zhu, M., Liu, C.-X.: Review of tracking algorithms under occlusions. Chin. Opt. **2**, 388–393 (2008)
5. Ouyang, N., You, J.-H., Mo, J.-W., Zhang, T.: Tracking multiple objects in occlusions. Appl. Res. Comput. **27**, 1984–1986 (2010)
6. Ning, J., Zhang, L., Zhang, D., et al.: Scale and orientation adaptive mean shift tracking. Comput. Vis. IET **6**, 52–61 (2012)
7. Sun, Y.-Y., He, X.-H., Song, H.-Y.: A block-matching image registration algorithm for video super-resolution reconstruction. Acta Autom. Sin. **37**, 37–43 (2011)
8. Du, C., Liu, W.-N., Liu, L.: Target tracking algorithm based on kalman filter and particle filter. Chin. J. Liq. Cryst. Disp. **26**, 384–389 (2011)
9. Xia, S.-Z., Liu, H.-W., Jiu, B.: A method of relay of tracking based on bayesian theory. J. Electron. Inf. Technol. **33**, 652–658 (2011)
10. Chen, A.H., Meng, B., Zhu, M.: Multi-pattern fusion algorithm for target tracking. Opt. Precis. Eng. **17**, 185–190 (2009)
11. Zhang, C-F., Lin, Y-H.: Discussion of piaget object permanence. Psychol. Explor. **4**, 11–15 (1988)
12. Zeng, Q., Dong, Q., Tao, S.: The research object of the permanent mechanism for the development of infant. Acta Psychol. Sin. **4**, 394–399 (1997)
13. Lu, H., Li, H.-S., Fei, S.-J., Li, W.-C.: Adaptive method for tracking mobile object in occlusion. Comput. Eng. Des. **33**, 2343–2346 (2012)
14. Li, J.-Y., Xu, L.-Y.: A multi-target tracking algorithm combined with occlusion segmentation. Telecommun. Eng. **2**, 172–176 (2013)
15. Chen, X.-H, Zhu, S.-H.: Moving objects detection algorithm based on visual attention mechanism and gaussian mixture model. In: 2011 International Conference on Signal, Image Processing and Applications, vol. 21 (2011)

The Segmentation Interventricular Septum from MR Images

Qian Zheng[1], Zhentai Lu[2(✉)], Minghui Zhang[2], Shengli Song[1],
Huan Ma[1], Lujuan Deng[1], Zhifeng Zhang[1(✉)], Qianjin Feng[2],
and Wufan Chen[2]

[1] Zhengzhou University of Light Industry, Zhengzhou, China
zhangzhifeng@zzuli.edu.cn
[2] Southern Medical University, Guangzhou, China
luzhentai@163.com

Abstract. We present a fully automated method to segment the interventricular septum from cardiac MR images in this paper. By introducing the circular Hough transformation our model can automatically detect the contours of left ventricle as circles used as the initialization. The interior and exterior energies are weighted by the entropy, which improves the robust of the evolving curve. Local neighborhood information is used to evolve the level set function, which can reduce the impact of the heterogeneous grays inside of regions and improve the segmentation accuracy. The adaptive window size is utilized to reduce the sensitivity to initialization rather than a fixed window size. The Gaussian kernel is used to not only ensure the smoothness and stability of the level set function, but also eliminate the traditional Euclidean length term and re-initialization. Finally, we segment the septum automatically by the classical segmentation methods combined with anatomical location information. Extensive experiments indicate that the superior performance of the proposed method over the state-of-the-art methods in terms of both good robustness and high efficiency.

Keywords: Septum · Entropy · Local neighborhood information · Adaptive window · Gaussian function

1 Introduction

Active contour models (ACMs) have been widely used for automatic image segmentation and object tracking. According to the type of adopted image features, the existing active contour models can be broadly divided into edge-driven models [1–4] and region-driven models [5–7]. The chan–vese (CV) model [5] is a classical active contour model depended on the assumption of intensity homogeneity. Using the global information of the image, the CV model can extract the contour that has an unobvious change of gradient in the image. Therefore, the CV model can obtain a good result even if the image has weak object boundaries. However, due to intensity inhomogeneity and complex construction in cardiac MR images, the CV model cannot accurately detect the boundary of the object in such types of images.

© Springer International Publishing Switzerland 2015
Y.-J. Zhang (Ed.): ICIG 2015, Part III, LNCS 9219, pp. 483–490, 2015.
DOI: 10.1007/978-3-319-21969-1_43

To segment images with intensity heterogeneity, Li et al. [8] proposed the local binary fitting (LBF) model which is able to utilize image information in local regions. A kernel function was introduced to define a local binary fitting energy in a variational formulation, and the local intensity information can be embedded into region-based active contour model. LBF model has better performance than CV model in segmentation accuracy. Nevertheless, the LBF model is susceptible to the initial contour placement and the configuration of controlling parameters due to the limitation of the localized energy.

Lonkton and Tannenbaum [9] presented a novel framework based on the localizing region-based active contours to segment objects with heterogeneous feature profiles. This method takes the local image information into account, and has resulted in significant improvement in accuracy for segmenting heterogeneous images. The limitations of this model are its sensitive to the initialization and the window size of the local region.

In this paper, we aim to develop a novel method for segmenting the septum. In the automatic segment the LV step, we present a robust adaptive Gaussian regularizing CV model using the entropy and local neighborhood information for automatically segmenting the LV from cardiac MR images, namely ASLV. First, the circular Hough transformation (CHT) is used to locate the epicardial and endocardial contours of the left ventricle (LV) as the initialization. Second, the interior and exterior energies in traditional cost function are weighted by the entropies of interior and exterior regions, so that the homogeneity proportions of the interior and exterior regions are adjusted adaptively and avoid to the optimal configuration of controlling parameters. Third, local region energies were computed over neighborhoods of points close to the curve. The local neighborhood information (LNI) will lead to sensitivity to the initialization. The adaptive window size is used to reduce the sensitivity to initialization rather than a fixed window size. Fourth, the Gaussian regularizing is used to not only keep the level set function smooth and stable, but also remove the traditional Euclidean length term and re-initialization. In the automatic segment the septum step, we utilize the threshold segmentation method to extract the septum automatically by the usage of the segmented LV. Qualitative and quantitative evaluations were carried out on the real medical images of clinical patients in terms of accuracy and robustness properties. The encouraging results show that the present method can segment the septum from the cardiac images exactly and efficiently.

2   Methodology

2.1   GREVLCV Model

In the previous work, we have proposed a GREVLCV [10] to segment the LV. Let $I(z)$ denote a given image defined on domain Ω and a closed curve C is considered as the zero level set of a signed distance function ϕ, i.e., $C = \{x|\phi(x) = 0\}$, which divides the image into object $\phi(\Omega_i) > 0$ and background $\phi(\Omega_o) < 0$. The energy function expressed by level set function ϕ is

$$\varepsilon(\phi) = v \int_{\Omega} H(\phi)dz + \int_{\Omega} \delta(\phi) \int_{\Omega} F_j(\phi)dxdz \tag{1}$$

$F_j(\phi)$ is the "fitting" term of the energy function in

$$F_j(\phi) = E_i^j(\phi)\left|I(x) - u_j\right|^2 H(\phi) + E_o^j(\phi)\left|I(x) - v_j\right|^2 (1 - H(\phi)) \tag{2}$$

where v are the fixed parameters, and the $E_i^j(\phi)$ and $E_o^j(\phi)$ is the entropy of interior/exterior region in the neighborhood centered pixel j. u_j and v_j are the averages of $I(j)$ inside and outside C in the local neighborhood centered pixel, respectively, can be written as

$$u_j = \frac{\int_{\Omega_j} I(x)H(\phi(x))dx}{\int_{\Omega_j} H(\phi(x))dx}, \ v_j = \frac{\int_{\Omega_j} I(x)(1 - H(\phi(x)))dx}{\int_{\Omega_j} (1 - H(\phi(x)))dx} \tag{3}$$

Minimizing the above energy function by using the steepest descent method, we obtain the following variational formulation

$$\frac{\partial \phi(z)}{\partial t} = \delta(\phi(z))\left[-v - \int_{\Omega} \nabla_{\phi}F_j(\phi(x))dx\right] \tag{4}$$

where $\nabla_{\phi}F_j(\phi) = \delta(\phi)(E_i^j(\phi)\left|I(x) - u_j\right|^2 - E_o^j(\phi)\left|I(x) - v_j\right|^2)$.

2.2 Adaptive Window of Local Energy of Points Along the Curve

Due to intensity inhomogeneity and complex construction in the medical images, the CV model will fail to provide accurate segmentation results. Figure 1 illustrates the considerable challenge in medical image segmentation. It is obvious that both of the intensity distributions of the foreground and the background vary sharply, so it is difficult for the CV to find appropriate constants to fit the foreground and the background. Moreover, the foreground and background share the similar intensity. The heterogeneity of regions and the presence of nearby structures of similar intensity affect the curve evolution, leading to the detection of false boundaries.

To solve the above problems, the information of the local regions inside and outside the curve in neighborhoods of points near the evolving curve is utilized in GRELCV model. To optimize the internal energy of the image, each point is considered separately and moved to minimize the energy computed in its neighborhood (Fig. 2(a)). The irregular contour is the evolving curve and the square is the neighborhood of a point near the curve. Arrows point to the local regions inside and outside the contour in the neighborhood. The energy optimization is then conducted by fitting a model to each local region. Directly use local neighborhood information (LNI) may lead to sensitive to the initial model. Additionally, we must give preference to the size of the neighborhood window in experiments. We instead the fixed window size by an adaptive window, which is estimated by the local entropy of the neighborhood.

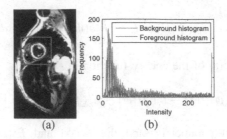

(a)   (b)

Fig. 1. The challenge in the segmentation. (a) The background and foreground. (b) The histograms of the background and foreground.

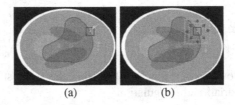

(a)   (b)

Fig. 2. The challenge in the segmentation. (a) The background and foreground. (b) The histograms of the background and foreground.

The evolving curve cannot move to minimize the energy computed in the homogeneous region. Thereby, if the entropy of the region is very small, this region is homogeneous and we will increase the size of the window. As shown in Fig. 2(b), the blue rectangle is the initial and the bigger green rectangle is the adaptive neighborhood window, the blue arrow point to the expanding direction of the window. Instead of selecting a single parameter of the size of the neighborhood window, we calculate a local window size for each point on the curve adaptively. For simplify, in the automatic segment the LV step, the robust adaptive Gaussian regularizing CV model using the entropy and local neighborhood information for segmenting the LV from cardiac MR images automatically, namely ASLV.

2.3   The Extraction of the Nearest and Biggest Connected Region

Suppose that the right blood pool extraction is similar to the segmentation of the object which is pointed by the red arrow, as shown in Fig. 3(a). We assume that the circle has been delineated, and the center has been detected (b). First, the image is turned into a binary image segmented by the threshold, which is determined by the mean value of the circle (c). Second, we labeled the image by the connected component. Third, we plot a square of three radius of the circle (d) and compute the ratio, which is the pixels of the connected components corresponded to the pixels of the connected components in the red rectangle region (e). Fourth, the connected component corresponded to the largest ratio is extracted (f). Last, we draw lines from the center (g), and find the two lines which intersect the extracted region at only one point. The two lines are called start line and end line as shown in (h).

Figure 4 shows some typical images and the septum extraction process. By analyzing the relation blood pool of the right ventricular and LV, the septum is extracted automatically.

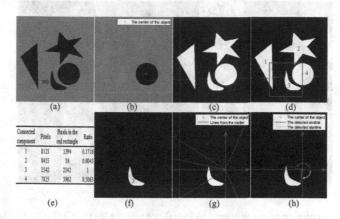

Fig. 3. The example of the extraction of the nearest and biggest connected region. (a) The synthetic image. (b) The segmented circle. (c) Threshold segmentation. (d) The labeled connected components. (e) The ratio of the pixels of the connected components corresponded to the pixels of the connected components in the red rectangle region. (f) The connected components corresponded to the largest ratio. (g) The example of some lines from the center. (h) The start line and the end line (Color figure online).

3 Experiments

MR images of the cardiac were performed at 1.5 T with the protocol name of cardiac T2 Star DB 650, at the department of Orthopedics, Royal Brompton Hospital, London, UK, and were collected from 2006 to 2009. The final data set comprised of 117*8 images of 117 patients (60 male/57 female). The patients' ages ranged from 11 to 51 years old. Patients were placed supine in the MR scanner and T2 Star DB images were performed with the following parameters: pixel spacing = 1.5625 mm, slice thickness = 10 mm, and image matrix size of 256 pixels × 160 pixels. For quantitative analysis of the algorithm, we compared the automatic segmentation results to the Gold Standard. The Gold Standard is the 2D slice a randomly selected 2D slice within the septum that was segmented by 4 independent medical experts. The medical experts were performed using specially designed software and saved for validating the performance of the proposed method. The trained radiologist ensured that the segmented images covered the interventricular septum.

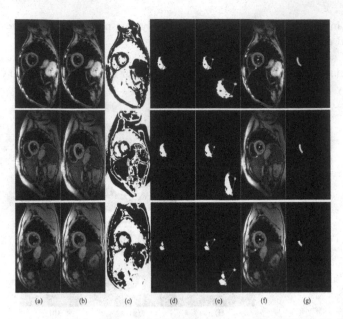

Fig. 4. The segmentation of the septum. (a) Initial contour set by the CHT. (b) The segmentation by the present method (red) and the ellipse-fitting (green). (c) Threshold segmentation. (d) The right ventricle. (e) The start line (yellow) and end line (red). (f) The image and the segmentation result. (g) The segmentation of the septum (Color figure online).

The segmentation of the septum is important to assess the myocardial iron loading in cardiac MR images. We present a method to automatically segment the septum (ASS). Figure 4 shows the segmentation of the septum. Figure 4(b) is the segmentation of the endocardium and epicardium of the left ventricle by the present method. Due to the smoothness of the myocardium, we use two separate ellipses to fit the endocardium and epicardium segmentation results (as shown in green color line). With the usage of the segmented endocardium, the image is separated into two regions by the threshold that is determined by the mean value of the region in the endocardium, as shown in Fig. 4(c). We find the right ventricle that is biggest and nearest region to the LV (as shown in Fig. 4(d)). The center of the LV region is as a point, and the radiation from the point is done and we find the two lines which intersects the region of the extracted right ventricle at only one point (as shown in Fig. 4(e)). Then, the septum is segmented, as shown in Fig. 4(f) and (g).

We segment the LV by ASLV and NCV method, and segment the septum by the usage of the two methods respectively. To compare the automatic segmentation of the septum, we show in Fig. 5 the Dice values, scaled to a range of the same size (0.35). Our method is more noticeable than the NCV.

A quick look at the Dice similarity measures can be done also using a boxplot, see Fig. 6. Note that there is substantially more variability in the ratings of our method than in the NCV method. The t-test is 2. 9468e-09, and our method is better than NCV.

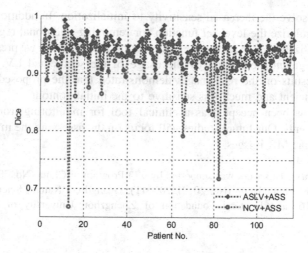

Fig. 5. The Dice values for the 117 patients segmented by ASLV + ASS and NCV + ASS method.

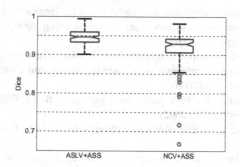

Fig. 6. Boxplot representation of Dice values for the 117 patients segmented by ASLV + ASS and NCV + ASS method

4 Conclusions

The black-blood T2* has been shown to be effective by yielding high contrast images, providing superior myocardial border definition, and largely reducing blood signal contamination from the myocardium. We have presented an adjustable automatically parameters model for black-blood cardiac images. By introducing the CHT, the present method can detect the endocardium and epicardium of the left ventricle automatically. Traditional CV model is unsuitable for medical segmentation as it has two difficulties such as parameters setting and affluence from heterogeneity intensities. For the first difficulty, we utilize entropy distances to weight the energies of inside and outside the contour. For the second one, we bring in the local neighborhood information to reduce the effect of inhomogeneity inside regions. Instead of selecting the fixed neighborhood window size in NCV, we calculated the local window size for each point on the curve adaptively and solve the increased sensitivity to initialization. In addition, we use the Gaussian to regularize the level set function for removing traditional regularized term and the re-initialization, also reduce the computation time. Finally, we present a method to automatic segment the septum by the usage of the segmented LV. Encouraging experimental results on the real images demonstrated that the proposed algorithm is very robust, efficient and much less sensitive to the initial contour.

MRI-T2* has been accepted as a clinical tool for monitoring iron overload in thalassemia patients. Our future studies will focus on the assessing the myocardial iron loading in cardiac MR images.

Acknowledgments. This work was supported by 973 Program of China (No. 2010CB732500), Guangzhou Science Foundation (No. 2012J2200041), Guangdong Natural Science Foundation (2014A030313316) and Doctoral Foundation of Zhengzhou University of Light Industry (2014BSJJ080).

References

1. Kass, M., et al.: Snakes: active contour models. Int. J. Comput. Vis. **1**, 321–331 (1988)
2. Zhu, G., et al.: Boundary-based image segmentation using binary level set method. Opt. Eng. **46**,050501–050501-3 (2007)
3. Li, C., et al.: Level set evolution without re-initialization: a new variational formulation. In: IEEE Computer Society Conference on Computer Vision and Pattern Recognition, 2005, CVPR 2005, pp. 430–436 (2005)
4. Vasilevskiy, A., Siddiqi, K.: Flux maximizing geometric flows. IEEE Trans. Pattern Anal. Mach. Intell. **24**, 1565–1578 (2002)
5. Chan, T.F., Vese, L.A.: Active contours without edges. IEEE Trans. Image Process. **10**, 266–277 (2001)
6. Lie, J., et al.: A binary level set model and some applications to Mumford-Shah image segmentation. IEEE Trans. Image Process. **15**, 1171–1181 (2006)
7. Zhang, K., et al.: Active contours driven by local image fitting energy. Pattern Recogn. **43**, 1199–1206 (2010)
8. Li, C., et al.: Implicit active contours driven by local binary fitting energy. In: IEEE Conference on Computer Vision and Pattern Recognition, 2007, CVPR 2007, pp. 1–7 (2007)
9. Lankton, S., Tannenbaum, A.: Localizing region-based active contours. IEEE Trans. Image Process. **17**, 2029–2039 (2008)
10. Zheng, Q., et al.: Gaussian regularizing CV model using entropy and neighborhood information. In: World Congress on Medical Physics and Biomedical Engineering May 26-31, 2012, pp. pp. 1832–1835, Beijing, China (2013)

Two-Stage Learning to Robust Visual Track via CNNs

Dan Hu[1,2(✉)], Xingshe Zhou[1], Xiaohao Yu[3], and Zhiqiang Hou[2]

[1] School of Computer Science,
Northwestern Polytechnical University, Xi'an, China
plahudan@mail.nwpu.edu.cn
[2] Information and Navigation College,
Air Force Engineering University,
Xi'an, China
[3] General Research Institute,
Equipment Academy of Air Force, Beijing, China

Abstract. Convolutional Neural Networks (CNN) are an alternative type of deep neural network that can be used to model local correlations and reduce translation variations, which have demonstrated great performance in some computer vision areas except the visual tracking due to the lack of training data. In this paper, we explore applying a two-stage learning CNN as a generic feature extractor offline pretrained with a large auxiliary dataset and then transfer its rich feature hierarchies to the robust visual tracking task. Instead of traditional neuron models in CNNs, we introduce a strategy to use ReLU for training acceleration. Empirical comparisons prove our CNN based tracker outperforms several state-of-the-art methods on an open tracking benchmark.

Keywords: Visual tracking · Deep learning · Convolutional neural network

1 Introduction

Visual tracking is a fundamental problem in computer vision with a wide range of applications, such as video surveillance for security, intelligent transportation system, and human-computer interface. Although existing applied visual tracking techniques in well-controlled environments, the challenging requirements for practical applications is how to long-term track continuously changed target, which is triggered by the harsh nature, including partial occlusion, illumination change, shape deformation, background interfering, etc. The key point to resolve the above problem is how to improve the robustness of visual tracking algorithm [1].

Unfortunately, in most existing trackers, even those reporting satisfactory results, features are manually defined and combined [2, 3], which may not be good enough for robust tracking, due to the limitations of prior knowledge about the object and the complex environments. Recently, deep learning, which are machine learning algorithms inspired by brains, based on learning multiple levels of representation, have gained significant attention thanks to their success on automatic feature extraction via multi-layer nonlinear transformations, especially in computer vision [4], speech recognition [5] and natural language processing [6].

© Springer International Publishing Switzerland 2015
Y.-J. Zhang (Ed.): ICIG 2015, Part III, LNCS 9219, pp. 491–498, 2015.
DOI: 10.1007/978-3-319-21969-1_44

However, the application of deep learning in visual tracking is less explored. The reason is, in the case of visual tracking, we typically have only very few positive instances extracted from the first video frame for training (in fact mostly we only have one single labeled example), which makes the direct applying of the deep learning approaches infeasible.

In this work, we attempt to train a two-stage Convolutional Neural Network (CNN) [7] as a generic image feature extractor by a purely supervised learning, that is offline pretrained and then transfer its rich feature hierarchies into online tracking to overcome this problem. Our proposed method is similar in spirit to DLT [8], the first work on applying deep neural networks that is a Stacked Denoising Autoencoder (SDAE) [9], to visual tracking, and has reported encouraging results, but there are some key differences that are worth noting:

1. Fully-connected deep learning models, such as SDAE used in DLT, ignore the topology and correlation of 2D images as need to learn weights separately for every location. However, CNNs use convolution and weights sharing technique to capture better local and repetitive similarity in images with much fewer connections and parameters. So our model is easier to train.
2. Shifts or distortions may cause the position of object to vary, which desires the model to incorporate translation invariance, that could be captured by weights sharing and pooling mechanisms much more efficiently in CNNs. So our algorithm demonstrates better performance in some scenes with occlusion and illumination changes.
3. To make training faster, we use ReLU function and a very efficient GPU implementation of the convolution operation.

We evaluate our proposed algorithm through quantitative and qualitative comparisons with DLT and other state-of-the-art trackers on an open tracking benchmark, which manifests the promising substantial improvements over the other trackers.

The rest of this paper is organized as follows: Sect. 2 describes our CNN model. Section 3 presents the details of the CNN tracking algorithm. Section 4 shows promising comparative results and Sect. 5 summarizes the conclusion.

2   Our Model

The architecture of our network is depicted in Fig. 2. Below, we first describe some novel or unusual feature of our network's architecture.

2.1   Rectified Linear Units

Instead of using the standard way to model a neuron's output f as a function of its input x with sigmoid function $f(x) = (1 + e^{-x})^{-1}$ or $f(x) = \tanh(x)$, we refer to neurons with nonlinearity as Rectified Linear Units (ReLUs), that is non-saturating nonlinearity function $f(x) = \max(0, x)$ introduced by Nair and Hinton [10], in terms of reducing training time with gradient descent. Deep convolutional neural networks with ReLUs train several times faster than their equivalents with tanh units, as demonstrated in Fig. 1, which shows the number of iterations required to reach 25 % training error on the CIFAR-10 dataset for a particular four-layer convolutional network [4]. From this plot, it can be seen that networks with ReLUs consistently learn about 6 times faster than equivalents with traditional neurons, which would have a great influence on the performance of large models trained on large dataset. Thus, in this work, we employ ReLU function to our CNN neurons.

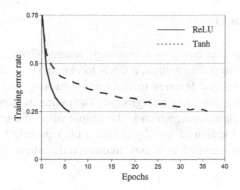

Fig. 1. Comparison of the number of iterations required to reach 25 % training error in a CNN with ReLU and Tanh function [4].

2.2 Our CNN Model

Now we are ready to describe the overall architecture of our own CNN which would be constructed as a generic feature extractor and then be transfered its rich feature hierarchies into our online tracking framework.

As depicted in Fig. 2, our CNN contains two convolutional layers, corresponding ReLUs as activation function and max-pooling operators. The input to the CNN's visible layer is locally normalized 32×32 image patches. The first convolutional layer filters the input image with 10 kernels of size 11×11, and the second convolutional layer takes as input the output of the first convolutional layer and filters it with 16 kernels of size 5×5. All these kernels scan each image in the previous layer with different weight vectors, and the max-pooling operators over the local neighborhoods reduce the resolution from the feature maps derived by the former convolution operators. The fully-connected layer is connected to all neurons in the previous layer, and the output of the full-connected layer is fed to a 256-way softmax which produces a distribution over the 256 class labels. Thus, the number of neurons in the network's remaining layers is given by $(32 \times 32) - (22 \times 22 \times 10) - (11 \times 11 \times 10) - (7 \times 7 \times 160) - (4 \times 4 \times 160) - (1024) - (256)$.

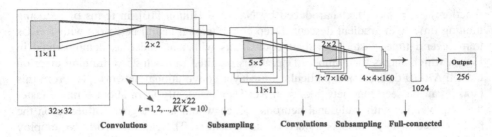

Fig. 2. Architecture of our CNN.

3   Our CNN Tracker

Now we present our tracker based on a two-stage learned CNN. In the first place, we employ a large dataset to offline pretrain a CNN to extract rich feature hierarchies, and then we transfer the learned features to the online tracking tasks to distinguish the tracked object from its surrounding background. The online tracking process will select the region with the highest score, which is the output of a softmax classifier on top of the CNN, as the new location of the object based on a particle filter framework. The whole CNN model is finetuned in a lazy manner only when significant appearance change happens.

3.1   Learning Stage 1: Offline Pretraining

In this work, we use Tiny Images [11], which is a dataset of 79 million unique 32×32 color images gathered from the Internet. Each image is loosely labeled with one of 75,062 English nouns, which covers all visual object classes. Despite their low resolution, it is still possible to recognize most of the objects and scenes. Meanwhile, the dataset contains more copious and abundant amount of images which have related objects in similar spatial arrangements. In [12], the authors experimentally probe that pretraining with such training data, would benefit and lead to a large improvement in detection performance. All of these motivate our choice of these low resolution images which can effectively reduce computational complexity.

We randomly sample 1 million images from this dataset with 256 classes as the inputs of our CNN model to pretrain it to be a generic feature extractor. We did not pre-process the images in any other way, except for scaling the raw pixels to the range [0, 1] linearly.

3.2   Learning Stage 2: Online Tracking and Update

Inspired by the work of Wang et al. [8], our visual tracking algorithm is also carried out based on a particle filter framework, which is a sequential Monte Carlo importance sampling method for estimating the latent state variables of a dynamical system based on a sequence of observations.

In the first frame, the object to track has been provided by the bounding box. Then the object region and the surrounding regions are regarded as positive sample and negative samples, correspondingly, which are used to fine-tune the CNN to adapt to the appearance of object in the first frame. When a new video frame arrives, the confidence for each particle is made by the network's softmax by making a simple forward pass through the network.

Instead of updating the CNN model at each frame, which would be computationally expensive, we propose to update the CNN in a lazy manner, only when the maximum confidence of all particles in a frame is below a predefined threshold, which indicates significant appearance change of the object being tracked occurs. This method accelerates our tracking algorithm exceedingly on the reason that the appearance of the object is not always changing in adjacent frames, our CNN model can remain discriminant until significant appearance change happens.

4 Experiments

4.1 Experimental Setup

(1) Evaluation Dataset: We evaluate the performance of our proposed method on a recently released benchmark [13], which is the largest open dataset consisting of 50 fully annotated sequences and attributes, to facilitate tracking evaluation. These attributes are defined by the factors that affect tracking performance, such as occlusion, fast motion, and illumination variation. We compare our CNN tracker with some state-of-art trackers, including DLT [8], MIL [14], IVT [15], CT [16], and VTD [17].

(2) Evaluation Metrics: Performances are measured by tracking success rate (TSR) and tracking precision (TP). Tracking success rate is calculated by the percentage of frames in which the overlapping ratio between the estimated location and the ground truth against the entire union box is larger than 50 %. Tracking precision is defined as the Euclidean distance between the center of bounding box and the ground truth in pixels.

(3) Implementation Details: We run our algorithm in Matlab on a desktop PC with a 3.2 GHz i5 quad core CPU and a NVIDIA GTX750 GPU, by invoking the Matlab parallel computing toolbox to accelerate the computation. We use the contrastive divergence algorithm with momentum for optimization. We start with learning rate of 0.1 with momentum 0.5 and increase it to 0.9 after 5 epochs. We train about 20 epochs in total with the batch size to 100. The threshold for online fine-tuning the whole network is set to 0.8. The particle filter uses 1000 particles in a search window twice to the area of bounding box around the estimated location in last frame. We also run the DLT code[1] on our platform. The results of other trackers are obtained from [13].

---

[1] http://winsty.net/dlt.html.

4.2 Experiment Comparison

Performances of the 6 tracker over 8 video sequences are summarized in Table 1, the best results are highlighted in bold font. It's clearly observed that our proposed method achieves the best results compared with other trackers on 5 video sequences. For the other 3 video sequences, ours is also among the best three methods, and all results outperform DLT. The key to this success is the translation invariance gained by weights sharing and pooling mechanisms, which make our algorithm demonstrates better performance in some scenes with occlusion and illumination changes.

Table 1. The performance comparison of our proposed method and the other visual trackers. The results are shown in the order of TSR/TP.

	Woman	David	Shaking	Trellis	Girl	Singer1	Bolt	David3
Ours	**83.1/7.5**	73.8/6.0	70.9/7.2	**96.4/3.0**	83.7/2.9	**100/2.7**	40.3/85.8	**69.3/50.9**
DLT	67.1/9.4	66.1/7.1	35.4/11.5	93.6/3.3	73.5/4.0	100/3.3	2.3/388.1	33.3/104.8
MIL	12.2/123.7	17.7/13.1	26.0/28.6	25.9/71.7	29.4/13.7	10.3/26.0	1.1/393.5	68.3/29.7
IVT	21.5/111.2	**92.0/3.9**	1.1/138.4	44.3/44.7	18.6/22.5	96.3/7.9	1.4/397.0	63.5/52.0
CT	16.0/109.6	25.3/15.3	92.3/10.9	23.0/80.4	17.8/18.9	10.3/16.8	0.6/363.8	34.9/88.7
VTD	17.1/133.6	49.4/27.1	**99.2/5.2**	30.1/81.3	-/-	99.4/3.4	**55.7/14**	-/-

Thanks to the GPU and ReLU which accelerate our CNN training, our tracker achieve an average frame rate of 19.6 fps on our platform, as shown in Table 2, which is sufficient for many real-time applications.

Table 2. Running time on 8 video sequences (fps)

Woman	David	Shaking	Trellis	Girl	Singer1	Bolt	David3	Average
25.73	20.08	19.26	23.50	16.85	18.73	14.67	18.17	19.62

Figure 3 shows some key frames with bounding boxes reported by all 6 trackers for each of the 8 video sequences, which present our tolerance to occlusions, pose and illumination changes.

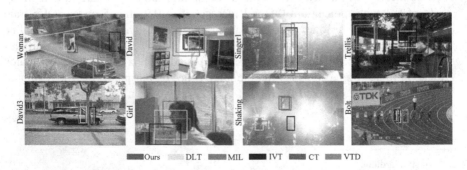

Fig. 3. Comparison of 7 trackers on several key frames of 8 video sequences.

The woman and david3 sequence are challenging for severe occlusions and pose changes. Our tracker doesn't drift for woman whilst most other trackers fail or drift at about frame 550. For david3, our tracker rarely misses the target completely expect full occlusion. The girl, david, shaking, singer1 and trellis are all arduous since drastical pose changes in addition to illumination vary for the last three. For singer1 and trellis, our method can track the object accurately along the entire sequence. For girl, most trackers drift at about frame 86, while our method can track the girl even after the girl turns. For david, all trackers drift or even fail to different degrees except for IVT, our tracker yield the second best results. For shaking, VTD and CT give satisfactory results, followed by ours which is much better than DLT. The Bolt is challenging for the severe deformation, most trackers fail or drift in early frames, and our results yield the second best result followed by VTD.

Our tracker shows the promising performance for most video sequences. The empirical comparisons suggest the outstanding future for the application of deep learning in visual tracking. Furthermore, our results can be improved simply by waiting for faster GPUs and bigger datasets to become available.

5 Conclusion

We have proposed a novel two-stage learning method for visual tracking based on Convolutional Neural Networks. To realize this approach, we first train a CNN model using an auxiliary Tiny Images dataset to learning generic image feature representation. Then we transfer it to a particle filter online tracking framework, which predicts the new location with highest confidence using the output of our CNN. Our CNN model was finetuned only when significant appearance change occurs. Empirical comparisons demonstrate that CNN based tracker achieves encouraging results and CNN has better capability than SDAE in visual tracking application.

Acknowledgements. The authors would like to thank the editors for their time and effort. This research was supported by the National Natural Science Foundation of China (61472391, 61403414)

References

1. Yang, H., Shao, L., Zheng, F., Wang, L., Song, Z.: Recent advances and trends in visual tracking: a review. Neurocomputing **74**(18), 3823–3831 (2011)
2. Adam, A., Rivlin, E., Shimshoni, I.: Robust fragments-based tracking using the integral histogram. In: IEEE Conference on Computer Vision and Pattern Recognition, CVPR (2006)
3. Hare, S., Saffari, A., Torr, P.H.: Struck: structured output tracking with kernels. In: IEEE International Conference on Computer Vision, ICCV (2011)
4. Krizhevsky, A., Sutskever, I., Hinton, G.E.: Imagenet classification with deep convolutional neural networks. In: Annual Conference on Neural Information Processing Systems, NIPS (2012)

5. Sainath, T.N., Kingsbury, B., Saon, G., Soltau, H., Mohamed, A.R., Dahl, G., Ramabhadran, B.: Deep convolutional neural networks for large-scale speech tasks. Neural Networks **64**, 39–48 (2015)
6. Socher, R., Liu, C., Ng, A.: Parsing natural scenes and natural language with recursive neural networks. In: International Conference on Machine Learning, ICML (2011)
7. LeCun, Y., Bengio, Y.: Convolutional networks for images, speech, and time-series. In: Arbib, M.A. (ed.) Handbook of Brain Theory and Neural Networks. MIT Press, Cambridge (1995)
8. Wang, N., Yeung, D.Y.: Learning a deep compact image representation for visual tracking. In: Annual Conference on Neural Information Processing Systems, NIPS (2013)
9. Vincent, P., Larochelle, H., Lajoie, I., Bengio, Y., Manzagol, P.A.: Stacked denoising autoencoders: learning useful representations in a deep network with a local denoising criterion. J. Mach. Learn. Res. **11**, 3371–3408 (2010)
10. Nair, V., Hinton, G.E.: Rectified linear units improve restricted boltzmann machines. In: International Conference on Machine Learning, ICML (2010)
11. Torralba, A., Fergus, R., Freeman, W.T.: 80 million tiny images: a large data set for nonparametric object and scene recognition. IEEE Trans. Pattern Anal. Mach. Intell. **30**(11), 1958–1970 (2008)
12. Agrawl, P., Girshick, R., Malik, J.: Analyzing the performance of multilayer neural networks for object recognition. In: European Conference on Computer Vision, ECCV (2014)
13. Wu, Y., Lim, J., Yang, M.: Online object tracking: a benchmark. In: IEEE Conference on Computer Vision and Pattern Recognition, CVPR (2013)
14. Babenko, B., Yang, M., Belongie, S.: Robust object tracking with online multiple instance learning. IEEE Trans. Pattern Anal. Mach. Intell. **33**(8), 1619–1632 (2011)
15. Ross, D., Lim, J., Lin, R., Yang, M.: Incremental learning for robust visual tracking. Int. J. Comput. Vis. **77**(1), 125–141 (2008)
16. Zhang, K., Zhang, L., Yang, M.-H.: Real-time compressive tracking. In: European Conference on Computer Vision, ECCV (2012)
17. Kwon, J., Lee, K.: Visual tracking decomposition. In: IEEE Conference on Computer Vision and Pattern Recognition, CVPR (2010)

Undersampled Dynamic MRI Reconstruction by Double Sparse Spatiotemporal Dictionary

Juerong Wu[1,2], Dongxiao Li[1,2(⊠)], Xiaotian Qiao[1],
Lianghao Wang[1,2], and Ming Zhang[1,2]

[1] Department of Information Science and Electronic Engineering,
Zhejiang University, Hangzhou 310027, China
lidx@zju.edu.cn
[2] Zhejiang Provincial Key Laboratory of Information Network Technology,
Hangzhou 310027, China

Abstract. Dynamic magnetic resonance imaging (dMRI) is widely used in human motion organ and functional imaging. But it requires reducing the imaging time to obtain high spatial and temporal resolution. This paper proposes a double sparse spatiotemporal dictionary model for compressed sensing reconstruction of dMRI from undersampled data. The model extends the ordinary 2-D dictionary to 3-D spatiotemporal dictionary by sparse representation of both the signals and dictionary atoms. Specifically, the first level sparse representation of dictionary atoms is learned with K-SVD algorithm. The second level sparse representation of spatiotemporal patches is obtained by OMP algorithm. An alternate iterative optimization is applied to solve the problem. Experiment results demonstrate that comparing with the state of the art method k-t FOCUSS and single level dictionary learning – DLMRI, the proposed method performs better in removing aliasing artifacts and in capturing temporal variations as well.

Keywords: Dynamic magnetic resonance imaging (dMRI) · Compressed sensing (CS) · Double sparse spatiotemporal dictionary

1 Introduction

Dynamic magnetic resonance imaging (dMRI) plays an important role in clinical diagnoses, such as cardiac cine, perfusion and functional MRI. In order to capture the subtle changes in vivo, high spatial and temporal resolution is required in dMRI. But due to physical and physiological constraints, the motion during the full data acquisition process for one frame cannot be neglected, which leads to a loss of data consistency. To reduce the scan time, a range of techniques has been proposed, such as parallel imaging, fast-scan trajectory (spiral, radial) and randomly under sampling of k-space data [1]. However, they all led to ill-posed inverse problems of reconstruction since they do not satisfy the Nyquist sampling theorem.

The recent theory of compressed sensing (CS) aims to reconstruct signals and images from significantly fewer measurements and is thus suitable for dMRI

© Springer International Publishing Switzerland 2015
Y.-J. Zhang (Ed.): ICIG 2015, Part III, LNCS 9219, pp. 499–509, 2015.
DOI: 10.1007/978-3-319-21969-1_45

reconstruction [2]. For example, k-t FOCUSS [3] successfully employed the compressed sensing theory for cardiac imaging applications by transforming the time varying image using Fourier transform along the spatial direction and residual encoding along the temporal direction. According to whether the reconstruction is processed in a transform domain or directly in the image domain, CS can be divided into two categories. The former has to find a sparse transform domain, such as DCT, wavelet [4], whichever meets the appropriate structure and fast numerical calculation demands. It is of low computational complexity but not flexible enough for the complex structure of images. The latter constructs a dictionary learned directly in image domain [5], and provides more flexible representation. However, its high degree of freedom demands a large amount of computation, which limits the practical size of the dictionary.

To deal with the existing problems mentioned above, we propose a new dictionary model that is flexible and of low complexity in computation. This work is inspired by the double sparse dictionary model proposed by Rubinstein et al. [6] which showed good performance in image denoising [7]. In under sampled MRI, the reconstruction quality mainly suffered from aliasing artifacts and image noise. And the temporal and spatial correlations in dynamic MRI make it very suitable to use a two-level dictionary. On the other hand, a lot of work has been done and demonstrated that dictionaries based on the image patch can preserve more local details than the global dictionaries [8–10].

A patch-based double sparse spatiotemporal DL model was developed in our work for under sampled dMRI reconstruction. First, the reconstructed image sequence is divided into overlapping patches along both spatial and temporal directions. Then we used a double sparse model to deal with the huge number of 3-D patches. Specifically, the first level sparse representation of dictionary atoms is trained using the K-SVD algorithm [11], which generalized the K-means clustering process and has been widely used in dictionary update stage. The second level sparse representation of spatiotemporal patches is obtained by orthogonal matching pursuit (OMP) algorithm [12], which is a greedy stepwise least squares sparse-coding algorithm. Last, alternate iterative optimization is applied to obtain the optimal sparse representation in two levels.

The rest of this paper is organized as follows. In Sect. 2, the basics of DL and double sparse dictionary model are briefly described. In Sect. 3, we will describe the proposed double sparse spatiotemporal DL model in detail. And alternate iterative optimization is used to solve the dMRI reconstruction problem. Section 4 presents the experiment results on cardiac cine imaging. We conclude our work in Sect. 5 and discuss future directions.

2   Related Work

Dictionary Learning (DL) focuses on building a suitable dictionary that provides efficient sparse representations for a class of signals [5]. Mathematically, given a set of signals $X = \{x_i\}_{i=1}^{N}$, DL aims to solve the following problem:

$$\min_{D,A}\|X - DA\|_F \ s.t \ \|\alpha_i\|_0 \leq K, \ \forall i \tag{1}$$

where $\|\bullet\|_F$ denotes the Frobenius norm, $\|\bullet\|_0$ is the l_0 norm, $\|\bullet\|_2$ is the l_2 norm, D stands for the overcomplete dictionary, $A = [\alpha_1, \alpha_2, \ldots, \alpha_N]$, α_i is the sparse representation of x_i over D, and K is the sparse constraint.

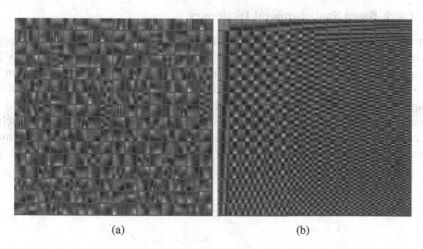

(a)   (b)

Fig. 1. (a) The trained dictionary atoms (8×8 image patches). (b) 2-D DCT dictionary.

The double sparse dictionary model suggests that not only each signal can be represented as a sparse combination of atoms in the dictionary, but each atom of the dictionary has itself a sparse representation over some base dictionary [6]. Figure 1(a) shows an example of the first level overcomplete dictionary atoms. As we can see, these atoms are similar and regular patches, and can be efficiently represented by sparse coefficients with the second level DCT dictionary in Fig. 1(b). The double sparse dictionary is therefore expressed as

$$D = \Phi B \tag{2}$$

where B is the atom representation matrix, assumed to be sparse. Examples of base dictionary Φ include the discrete cosine transform (DCT) dictionary and Wavelet dictionaries. They are analytic dictionaries which have efficient implementations and strong structures.

Specifically, double sparse DL aims to solve the optimization problem

$$\min_{B,A} \sum_{ij} \|X - \Phi BA\|_F \quad s.t. \ \forall i \ \ \|\alpha_i\|_0 \leq K$$

$$s.t. \ \forall j \ \ \|\beta_j\|_0 \leq L, \|\Phi \beta_j\|_2 = 1 \tag{3}$$

with K as the sparse constraint of signals and L as the sparse constraint of dictionary atoms. Note that in this formulation, the atom normalization constraint is commonly added for convenience.

3 The Proposed Method

3.1 Patch-Based Spatiotemporal Dictionary

To sparsely represent static images using DL, an image is divided into overlapping patches since patch based dictionaries can capture local image features effectively [8]. In dynamic MRI, we can also reconstruct the image sequence frame by frame in the same manner. But high coherence exhibits in temporal direction as well, which enables a sparse representation in both spatial and temporal domains [13]. We captured the consecutive patches in temporal direction as three dimensional spatiotemporal patches.

Let R_{ijk} be the operator that extracts a spatiotemporal patch x_{ijk} from dMRI image sequence X, which is located at (i,j,k) and with a predefined size of (n_f, n_p, n_t). The corresponding DL problem is modeled as

$$\min_{B,A} \sum_{ijk} \left\| \mathbf{R}_{ijk} X - \Phi BA \right\|_F$$

$$s.t. \ \left\| \alpha_{ijk} \right\|_0 \leq K, \tag{4}$$

$$\left\| \beta_{ijk} \right\|_0 \leq L, \ \left\| \Phi \beta_{ijk} \right\|_2 = 1, \ \forall i,j,k$$

Here, A and B denotes the set containing all α_{ijk} and β_{ijk} respectively. The base dictionary Φ is the Kronecker product of three 1-D DCT dictionaries. Assuming Φ_0 is the DCT dictionary of 1-D signals, the 3-D spatiotemporal DCT dictionary is $\Phi = \Phi_0 \otimes \Phi_0 \otimes \Phi_0$. Generalizations to higher dimensions are straightforward to derive in the same way. So the two-level dictionary is more suitable for high dimensional reconstruction in MRI.

For the dMRI image sequence, a straightforward method is to build a single dictionary over all the frames, but it is only suitable for short period image sequence. The spatial structures and temporal variations would significantly change over a long period, thus calls for temporal dependent dictionaries. Specifically, we extracted a sub image sequence X_Ω to construct the corresponding dictionary $\mathbf{D}_\Omega$ for this period. It reduces the dictionary size and adapts to the change of spatial structures and temporal variations.

3.2 Dynamic MRI Reconstruction

The problem formulation for dynamic MRI reconstruction based on double sparse dictionary learning needs to consider the following characteristics. First, it should be able to enforce the sparsity of the patches of the reconstructed image sequence in an adaptive dictionary and the sparsity of this dictionary's atoms in a base dictionary. Then, It should also be able to reduce the artifacts typically seen in the zero-filled (filled with zeros in the missing undersampled k-space data) Fourier reconstruction. At the same time, it should produce a reconstruction that is consistent with the acquired k-space data. Thus, based on the above double sparse spatiotemporal DL model, we formulate the dMRI reconstruction problem as follows:

$$\min_{X,B,A} \sum_{ijk} \left\| R_{ijk}X - \Phi BA \right\|_F + \lambda \left\| F_u X - \Upsilon \right\|_F$$

$$s.t. \ \left\| \alpha_{ijk} \right\|_0 \leq K,$$

$$\left\| \beta_{ijk} \right\|_0 \leq L, \ \left\| \Phi \beta_{ijk} \right\|_2 = 1, \ \forall i,j,k$$

(5)

where Y is the undersampled k-space data of X, F_u denotes the corresponding Fourier encoding matrix. The first term in the cost function corresponds to the quality of the double sparse representation of spatiotemporal patches with base dictionary Φ. The second term in the cost enforces data fidelity in k-space, since the k-space measurements may be inaccurate and with noise. The weight λ in the formulation is a tuning parameter, which depends on the measurement noise.

We used an alternating optimization procedure to solve the problem. First, X is assumed fixed, the sparse representation B of dictionary atoms and sparse representation A of signals are jointly learned. The K-SVD algorithm [11] is used to learn the dictionary D. Since the base dictionary Φ is set as 3-D DCT dictionary, the K-SVD algorithm mainly get the sparse representation B. Once the dictionary is learnt, the orthogonal matching pursuit (OMP) algorithm is used to find the sparse coding A [12]. Then, the double sparse representation A and B are fixed, and X is updated to satisfy data consistency. The least squares solution satisfies the normal equation

$$\left(\sum_{ijk} R_{ijk}^H R_{ijk} + \lambda F_u^H F_u \right) X = \sum_{ijk} R_{ijk}^H \Phi B \alpha_{ijk} + \lambda F_u^H \Upsilon$$

(6)

The superscript H denotes the Hermitian transpose operation. $F_u^H \Upsilon$ is the zero-filled reconstruction of the measured data. Solving (6) directly is impractical because it involves the inverse operation of a huge matrix. $F_u^H F_u$ is a Q × Q matrix and typically Q may be 256 × 256. We do some simplifications according to the properties of some parameters. The term $\sum_{ijk} R_{ijk}^H R_{ijk}$ is a diagonal matrix, equal to ηI, where η is a scaling factor equal to the size of patch ($n_f \times n_p \times n_t$). And the huge matrix is converted to $FF_u^H F_u F^H$, which is also a diagonal matrix with ones and zeroes [8]. We define the "patch averaged result", which means each pixel value obtained by averaging contribution of patches that cover it

$$x_p = \frac{\sum_{ijk} R_{ijk}^H \Phi B \alpha_{ijk}}{\eta}$$

(7)

Then we transform from image space to Fourier space and use the sampled subset of k-space to replace corresponding points. That ensures the reconstruction result is consistent with the undersampled k-space data. Finally, the reconstruction X is obtained by Inverse Fast Fourier Transform.

$$x = x_p + \left(\frac{\lambda}{\lambda + 1} \right) \mathbf{F}_u^H (y - \mathbf{F}_u x_p) \tag{8}$$

Algorithm 1 shows the pseudo code. The algorithm is initialized with a zero-filled Fourier reconstruction, $\mathbf{F}_u^H \mathbf{Y}$. The stopping criterion of the algorithm is that a predefined maximum iteration number is reached.

Algorithm 1

Input: Y - undersampled k-space measurements

   n_f, n_p, n_t - patch sizes

   K - sparse constraint of signals
   L - sparse constraint of dictionary atoms
   J - maximum iterations

Output: X – reconstructed dMRI image sequence

Initialization: $X_0 = \mathbf{F}_u^H \mathbf{Y}$, Φ =3-D DCT dictionary

Iteration:

   1) Learn the sparse representation B from patches of X using K-SVD algorithm.

   2) Compute α_{ijk} for all patches using OMP.

   3) Compute the patch averaged result x_p of each pixel (7).

   4) Update X using (8).

---

4   Experimental Results

We used two sets of dynamic cardiac cine data to validate the proposed method. The sizes of data sets are $256 \times 256 \times 25$ [3] and $190 \times 90 \times 70$ [14] (#PE × #FE × frame) respectively. Sampling schemes used in the experiment is Cartesian sampling with random phase encodes. The central part of the k-space is fully sampled with eight PE lines. The undersampling factor (the number of the fully sampled data points to that of the undersampled data point) in this experiment is 4. The sampling masks and cardiac cine image sequences are shown in Fig. 2.

The performances of the proposed method were evaluated in two ways. First, we compared the results with the state of the art method in dMRI reconstruction - k-t FOCUSS [3]. In k-t FOCUSS, a motion estimation/compensation (ME/MC) approach was proposed to exploit the correlation between the frames using motion vectors

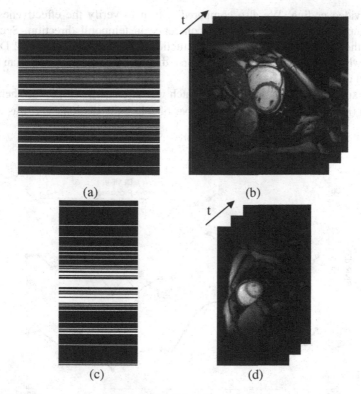

Fig. 2. (a) Sampling mask in k-space with 4 fold undersampling of dataset 1. (b) The reference dMRI image sequence of the cardiac cine in dataset 1. (c) Sampling mask of dataset 2. (d) The reference dMRI image sequence in dataset 2.

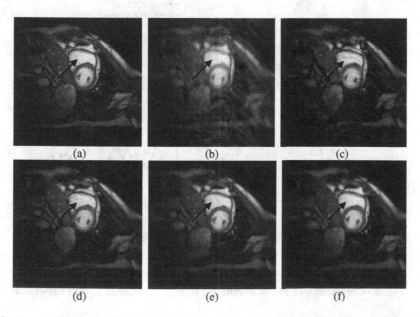

Fig. 3. Reconstructions of the fifteenth frame in dataset1. (a) Ground truth, (b) zero-filled, (c) k-t FOCUSS, (d) k-t FOCUSS with ME/MC, (e) DLMRI, (f) proposed method

similar to video coding. We also compared with it to verify the effectiveness of the proposed model in capturing the high coherence in temporal direction. Second, we compared the results with DLMRI reconstruction frame by frame using 2-D patches [8], to see whether the two level double sparse dictionary performs better than ordinary single level dictionary.

In the experiments, the size of the 3D patch was $(n_f, n_p, n_t) = (6, 6, 6)$. Then the size of an atom (η) was 216 and the atom number of 3-D DCT dictionary Φ was also 216.

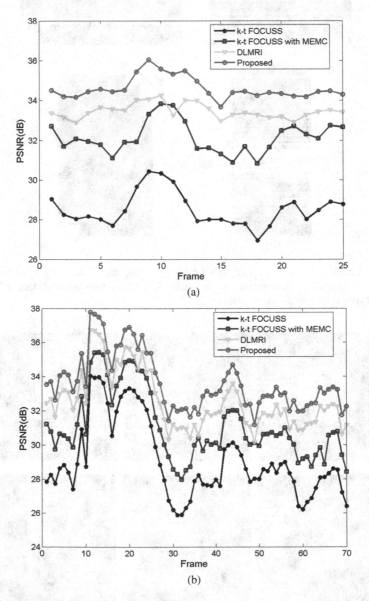

Fig. 4. Comparison of PSNR in different frames. (a) Dataset 1. (b) Dataset 2.

We worked with maximum overlap of 3D spatiotemporal patch (the stride between corresponding pixel locations in adjacent image patches was 1). The sparse constraint of signals was set as $K = 0.15 \times P \approx 32$ [8]. The sparse constraint of dictionary atoms L was 6. The maximum iterations J was 10. The relevant parameters in the 2-D DLMRI reconstruction experiment used the same setting for comparison.

Figure 3 shows the reconstruction results of the fifteenth frame in dataset 1. The zero-filled reconstruction is badly blurred with artifacts. And the artifacts are also typically seen in k-t FOCUSS result. Although the quality of image is improved with ME/MC approach. But as the arrows indicate the details, the proposed method and DLMRI behave better in removing aliasing artifacts. It means that the patch-based dictionary learning method preserve more local detail than other optimization methods such as k-t FOCUSS.

The quality of the reconstruction is quantified using PSNR, the ratio of the peak intensity value of the reference to the mean-squared error (MSE) relative to the reference image. Figure 4 shows that the proposed method achieves a highest PSNR for all frames in both two datasets. This proves that with the double sparse design and high coherence in temporal direction, we had a better dictionary in dMRI reconstruction than 2-D MRI dictionary in the quality of image reconstruction. Otherwise, the two-level dictionary is easier to be extended to high dimensional reconstruction while get the same or even better reconstruction quality than single level dictionary.

In Fig. 5, we illustrated the temporal variation at a fixed position in the frequency encoding direction [15]. It can be observed that even zero-filled method captures main motion feature, but it is very blurry and lost some local contrasts. As the arrows point, the proposed method preserves more key motion details while others lost some temporal variations.

Figure 6 shows the reconstructions of the 43th frame by different methods and corresponding temporal profiles in dataset 2. Also, the proposed method behaved better in removing aliasing artifacts and preserved more key motion details in temporal profiles than other methods.

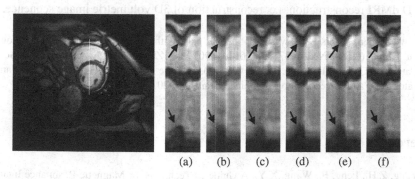

Fig. 5. Comparison of temporal profiles in dataset 1. (a) full sampled, (b) zero-filled, (c) k-t FOCUSS, (d) k-t FOCUSS with ME/MC, (e) DLMRI, (f) proposed method

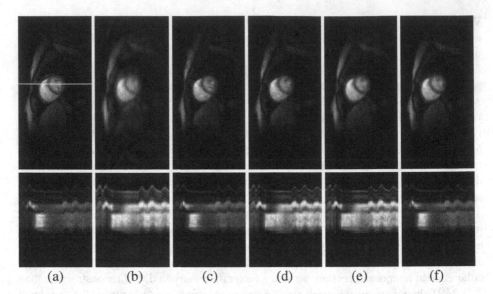

(a)   (b)   (c)   (d)   (e)   (f)

Fig. 6. Comparison of reconstructions of the 43th frame and temporal profiles in dataset 2. (a) full sampled, (b) zero-filled, (c) k-t FOCUSS, (d) k-t FOCUSS with ME/MC, (e) DLMRI, (f) proposed method

5 Conclusion

This paper proposed a patch-based double sparse DL model for dMRI reconstruction. This method combines the double sparse model and high coherence in spatial and temporal domains to train a 3-D dictionary, which is able to capture local structure spatially and temporally. The experimental results show that our method performs better in removing aliasing artifacts compared with k-t FOCUSS, a state of the art method in dMRI. And for the single level dictionary learning - DLMRI, the proposed method is easier to be extended to high dimensional space. In the future work, we would like to extend the model for 4-D dMRI reconstruction, i.e. reconstruction of 3D volumetric image sequence.

Acknowledgment. This work was supported in part by the National Natural Science Foundation of China (Grant No. 61271338, 61401390), the Zhejiang Provincial Natural Science Foundation of China (Grant No. LQ14F010005), and the Open Projects Program of National Laboratory of Pattern Recognition of China (Grant No. 201306308).

References

1. Yang, Z.H., Feng, F., Wang, X.Y.: A Guide to Technique of Magnetic Resonance Imaging: Criterion of Examination, Clinical Strategy and Application of New Techniques. People's Military Medical Press, Beijing (2007)
2. Gamper, U., Boesiger, P., Kozerke, S.: Compressed sensing in dynamic MRI. J. Magn. Reson. Med. **59**(2), 365–373 (2008)

3. Jung, H., Sung, K., Nayak, K.S.: k-t FOCUSS: a general compressed sensing framework for high resolution dynamic MRI. J. Magn. Reson. Med. **61**(1), 103–116 (2009)
4. Lustig, M., Donoho, D., Pauly, J.M.: Sparse MRI: the application of compressed sensing for rapid MR imaging. J. Magn. Reson. Med. **58**(6), 1182–1195 (2007)
5. Tosic, I., Pascal, F.: Dictionary learning. J. Signal Process. Mag. **28**(2), 27–38 (2011)
6. Rubinstein, R., Zibulevsky, M., Elad, M.: Double sparsity: learning sparse dictionaries for sparse signal approximation. IEEE Trans. Signal Process. **58**(3), 1553–1564 (2010)
7. Liang, R., Zhao, Z., Li, S.: Image denoising using learned dictionary based on double sparsity model. In: 2011 4th International Congress on Image and Signal Processing (CISP), vol. 2, pp. 691–695. IEEE (2011)
8. Ravishankar, S., Bresler, Y.: MR image reconstruction from highly undersampled k-space data by dictionary learning. IEEE Trans. Med. Imaging **30**(5), 1028–1041 (2011)
9. Wang, Y., Ying, L.: Compressed sensing dynamic cardiac cine MRI using learned spatiotemporal dictionary. IEEE Trans. Biomed. Eng. **61**(4), 1109–1120 (2014)
10. Awate, S.P., DiBella, E.V.R.: Spatiotemporal dictionary learning for undersampled dynamic MRI reconstruction via joint frame-based and dictionary-based sparsity. In: 2012 9th IEEE International Symposium on Biomedical Imaging (ISBI), pp. 318–321. IEEE (2012)
11. Aharon, M., Elad, M., Bruckstein, A.: K-SVD: an algorithm for designing overcomplete dictionaries for sparse representation. IEEE Trans. Signal Process. **54**(11), 4311–4322 (2006)
12. Pati, Y.C., Rezaiifar, R., Krishnaprasad, P.S.: Orthogonal matching pursuit: Recursive function approximation with applications to wavelet decomposition. In: Signals, Systems and Computers, pp. 40-44 (1993)
13. Wang, Y., Zhou, Y., Ying, L.: Undersampled dynamic magnetic resonance imaging using patch-based spatiotemporal dictionaries. In: 2013 IEEE 10th International Symposium on Biomedical Imaging (ISBI), pp. 294–297. IEEE (2013)
14. Lingala, S.G., Jacob, M.: Blind compressive sensing dynamic MRI. IEEE Trans. Med. Imaging **32**(6), 1132–1145 (2013)
15. Wang, Y., Ying, L.: Compressed sensing dynamic cardiac cine MRI using learned spatiotemporal dictionary. IEEE Trans. Biomed. Eng. **61**(4), 1109–1120 (2014)

Underwater Image Devignetting and Colour Correction

Yujie Li[1], Huimin Lu[1,2,3(✉)], and Seiichi Serikawa[1]

[1] Kyushu Institute of Technology, Kitakyushu, Japan
luhuimin@ieee.org
[2] Shanghai Jiaotong University, Shanghai, China
[3] Tongji University, Shanghai, China

Abstract. This paper describes a novel method to recover underwater images by devignetting and colour correction. Scattering and colour distortion are two major problems of degradation for underwater imaging. Scattering is caused by large suspended particles. Colour distortion corresponds to the varying degrees of attenuation encountered by light traveling in water with different wavelengths, rendering ambient underwater environments dominated by a bluish tone. To this end, we propose a novel underwater imaging model, which is much closer to the light propagation model in underwater environment. We remove the noise by dual-tree complex wavelet transform. Then, solve the non-uniform illumination of artificial lights by devignetting. Finally, we recover the image colour through camera spectral responses. The corrected images are characterized by reduced noised level, better exposedness of the dark regions, improved global contrast while the finest details and edges preserving.

Keywords: Underwater imaging · Inherent optical properties · Image devignetting · Colour correction

1 Introduction

Underwater exploration of the seafloor is used for various scientific reasons, such as assessing the biological environment, mineral exploration, and taking population census. The problem of mitigating sea mines is challenging and multifaceted. Ocean mines may be located on the seafloor in the water column. Recently, two deficiencies in mine counter measures are mentioned by researchers. First, the problem of mine hunting is one of the most important and difficult problems. Second, the key technologies for mine and mine-like objects recognition are not solving. To this end, in the last decade, most unmanned systems were developed for supporting underwater mining. The goal in developing automation for underwater mine detection is automatically determine the mine location and recognize the mine-like objects instead of the human. There are two stages of mine hunting operations. One is search-classify-map (SCM), which is intended to locate all sufficiently mine-like objects in a given operational area. The other is reacquire-and-identify (RI), which is to distinguish the mines or non-mines and prosecutes them accordingly [1].

© Springer International Publishing Switzerland 2015
Y.-J. Zhang (Ed.): ICIG 2015, Part III, LNCS 9219, pp. 510–521, 2015.
DOI: 10.1007/978-3-319-21969-1_46

Although the underwater objects detection technology makes a great progress, the recognition of underwater objects also remains a major issue in recent days. Challenges associated with obtaining visibility of objects have been difficult to overcome due to the physical properties of the medium. Different from the common images, underwater images suffer from poor visibility due to the medium scattering and light distortion. First of all, capture images underwater is difficult, mostly due to attenuation caused by light that is reflected from a surface and is deflected and scattered by particles, and absorption substantially reduces the light energy. The random attenuation of the light is mainly cause of the haze appearance while the fraction of the light scattered back from the water along the sight considerable degrades the scene contrast. In particular, the objects at a distance of more than 10 meters are almost indistinguishable while the colours are faded due to the characteristic wavelengths are cut according to the water depth . Moreover, as the artificial light is employed, there usually leave a distinctive footprint of the light beam on the seafloor.

There have been many techniques to restore and enhance the underwater images. Y.Y. Schechner et al. [2] exploited the polarization dehazing method to compensate for visibility degradation. Combining point spread function and a modulation transfer function to reduce the blurring effect by Hou et al. [3]. Although the aforementioned approaches can enhance the image contrast, these methods have demonstrated several drawbacks that reduce their practical applicability. First, the equipment of imaging is difficult in practice (e.g. range-gated laser imaging system, which is hardly applied in practice). Second, multiple input images are required, which is difficult to capture by hardware. Third, they cannot solve the colour distortion very well.

In this paper, we introduce a novel approach that is able to enhance underwater images based on single image to overcome the drawbacks of the above methods. We propose a new guided median filter instead of the soft matting to solve the alpha mattes more efficiently. In short summary, our technical contributions are in threefold: first, the proposed guided median filter can perform as an edge-preserving smoothing operator like the popular bilateral filter, but has better behavior near the edges. Second, the devignetting method has a fast and non-approximate constant-time algorithm, whose computational complexity is independent of the filtering kernel size. Third, the proposed colour correction method is effectively in underwater image enhancement.

The organization of this paper is as follows. In Sect. 2, underwater imaging model will be discussed. And we will demonstrate an image enhancement system on Sect. 3. We apply the enhancement model in underwater optical images in Sect. 4. Finally, a conclusion is presented in Sect. 5.

2   Underwater Imaging Model

In the optical model [4], the acquired image can be modelled as being composed of two components. One is the direct transmission of light from the object, and the other is the transmission due to scattering by the particles of the medium. Mathematically, it can be written as

$$I(x) = J(x)t(x) + (1 - t(x))A \tag{1}$$

where I is the achieved image. J is the scene radiance or haze-free image, t is the transmission along the cone of vision, and $t(x) = e^{-\beta d(x)}$, β is the attenuation coefficient of the medium, $d(x)$ is the distance between the camera and the object, A is the veiling colour constant and $x = (x, y)$ is a pixel. The optical model assumes linear correlation between the reflected light and the distance between the object and observer.

The light propagation model is slightly different underwater environment. In the underwater optical imaging model, absorption plays an important role in image degrading. Furthermore, unlike scattering, the absorption coefficient is different for each colour channel, being the highest for red and lowest for blue in seawater. These leads to achieve the following simplified hazy image formation model:

$$I(x) = J(x)e^{-(\beta_s+\beta_a)d(x)} + (1 - e^{-\beta_s d(x)})A \tag{2}$$

where β_s is the scattering coefficient and β_a is the absorption coefficient of light. The effects of haze are highly correlated with the range of the underwater scene. In this paper, we simplify the situation as at a certain water depth, the transmission t is defined only by the distance between camera and scene (see Fig. 1).

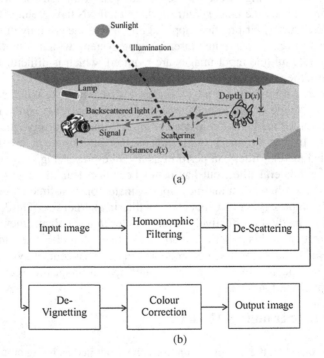

(a)

(b)

Fig. 1. Underwater optical imaging model; (a) underwater imaging model; (b) underwater imaging reconstruction pipeline.

3   Underwater Image Processing

Homomorphic Filtering. The homomorphic filter is used to correct non-uniform illumination and to enhance contrast of the image. Assume the captured image is a function of the product of the illumination and the reflectance as

$$f(x, y) = i(x, y)r(x, y) \tag{3}$$

where $f(x,y)$ is the captured image, $i(x,y)$ is the illumination multiplicative factor, and $r(x,y)$ is the reflectance function. Taking the logarithm to achieve,

$$\ln(f(x, y)) = \ln(i(x, y)) + \ln(r(x, y)) \tag{4}$$

Compute FFT of the Eq. (4),

$$F(w_x, w_y) = I(w_x, w_y) + R(w_x, w_y) \tag{5}$$

Then, utilize the High-pass Filters to the coefficients of FFT. And after inverse-FFT, we can get the filtered images. The processed images also contains some noise, in the next subsection, we use the DTC-wavelet transform based denoising method [5].

Transmission Estimation. After denoising, we use the de-scattering method to remove the haze in turbidity particles. According to recent researches, we found that the red colour channel is attenuated at a much higher rate than the green or blue channel. We further assume that the transmission in the water is constant. We denote the patch's transmission as. Take the maximum intensity of the red colour channel to compare with the maximum intensity of the green and blue colour channels. We define the dark channel $J_{dark}(x)$ for the underwater image $J(x)$ as,

$$J_{dark}(x) = \min_{c \in \{r,g,b\}} (\min_{y \in \Omega(x)} J_c(x)) \tag{6}$$

where $J_c(x)$ refers to a pixel x in colour channel $c \in \{r\}$ in the observed image, and Ω refers to a patch in the image. The dark channel is mainly caused by three factors, shadows, colourful objects or surfaces and dark objects or surfaces.

Here, take the min operation in the local patch on the haze imaging Eq. (1), we assume the transmission as:

$$\min(I_c(x)) = \tilde{t}_c(x) \min_{y \in \Omega(x)} (J_c(x)) + (1 - \tilde{t}(x))A_c \tag{7}$$

Since A_c is the homogeneous background light and the above equation perform one more min operation among all three colour channels as follows:

$$\min_c \min_{y \in \Omega(x)} (\frac{I_c(x)}{A_c}) = \tilde{t}_c(x) \min_c (\min_{y \in \Omega(x)} (\frac{J_c(x)}{A_c})) + (1 - \tilde{t}(x)) \tag{8}$$

In Ref, let us set $V(x) = A_c(1-t(x))$ as the transmission veil, $W = \min_c(I_c(x))$ is the min colour components of $I(x)$. We have $0 \leq V(x) \leq W(x)$. For grayscale image, $W = I$. Utilize the guided trigonometric bilateral filter (GTBF), which will be discussed in the next subsection. We compute the $T(x) = \text{median}(x) - GTBF_\Omega(|W - \text{median}(x)|)$. And then, we can acquire the by $V(x) = \max\{\min[wT(x), W(x)], 0\}$, here w is the parameter in $(0,1)$. Finally, the transmission of each patch can be written as,

$$\tilde{t}(x) = 1 - \frac{V(x)}{A_c} \tag{9}$$

The background A_c is usually assumed to be the pixel intensity with the highest brightness value in an image. However, in practice, this simple assumption often renders erroneous results due to the presence of self-luminous organisms. So, in this paper, we compute the brightest pixel value among all local min corresponds to the background light A_c as follows:

$$A_c = \max_{x \in I} \min_{y \in \Omega(x)} I_c(y) \tag{10}$$

where $I_c(y)$ is the local colour components of $I(x)$ in each patch.

Guided Median Filtering Refinement. In the above subsection, we roughly estimated the camera-object distance $d(x)$. This distance depth contains mosaic effects and produces less accurately. Consequently, we need to use the proposed weighted guided median filter to reduce the mosaicking. In this section, we introduce our constant time algorithm for weighted guided median filter.

The traditional median filter [10] has been considered as an effective way of removing "outliers". The traditional median filter usually leads to morphological arti-facts like rounding sharp corners. To address this problem, the weighted median filter has been proposed. The weighted median filter is defined as

$$h(\mathbf{x}, i) = \sum_{y \in N(\mathbf{x})} W(\mathbf{x}, \mathbf{y})\delta(V(\mathbf{y}) - i) \tag{11}$$

where $W(\mathbf{x}, \mathbf{y})$ corresponds to the weight assigned to a pixel $\mathbf{y}$ inside a local region centered at pixel x, the weight $W(\mathbf{x}, \mathbf{y})$ depends on the image d that can be different from V. $N(\mathbf{x})$ is a local window near pixel $\mathbf{x}$. i is the discrete bin index, and δ is the Kronecker delta function, δ is 1 when the argument is 0, and is 0 otherwise.

Then the compute the refined depth map by weighted guided median filter is defined as:

$$I_x^{WG} = \frac{\sum_{y \in N(x)} f_S(x, y) f_R(I_x, I_y) I_y W_y}{\sum_{y \in N(x)} f_S(x, y) f_R(I_x, I_y) W_y} \tag{12}$$

where y is a pixel in the neighborhood $N(x)$ of pixel x. Note that kernels other than Gaussian kernels are not excluded.

$$f_S(x, y) = v(x - y) = \frac{1}{2}e^{-\frac{(x-y)(x-y)}{2\sigma_D^2}} \tag{13}$$

where x and y denote pixel spatial positions. The spatial scale is set by σ_D. The range filter weights pixels based on the photometric difference,

$$f_R(I_x, I_y) = w(f(x) - f(y)) = \frac{1}{2}e^{-\frac{(f(x)-f(y))(f(x)-f(y))}{2\sigma_R^2}} \tag{14}$$

where $f(\cdot)$ is image tonal values. The degree of tonal filter is set by σ_R. W_y is the weight map, which is defined as:

$$W_y = \sum_{y \in N(x)} f_s(y, q) f_R(y, q) e^{-(\|I_y - I_q\|_2)/2\sigma_R} \tag{15}$$

where q is the coordinate of support pixel centered around pixel y. The final refined depth map is produced by:

$$h(\tilde{d}(x), i) = \sum_{y \in N(x)} I_x^{WG}(d(x), x)\delta(V(x) - i) \tag{16}$$

This filters images, preserving edges and filters noise based on a dimensionality reduction strategy, having high quality results, while achieving significant speedups over existing techniques.

Recovering the Scene Radiance. With the transmission depth map, we can recover the scene radiance according to Eq. (1). We restrict the transmission $t(x)$ to a lower bound t_0, which means that a small certain amount of haze are preserved in very dense haze regions. The final scene radiance $J(x)$ is written as,

$$J(x) = \frac{I_c(x) - A_c}{\max(t(x), t_0)} + A_c \tag{17}$$

Typically, we choose $t_0 = 0.1$. The recovered image may be too dark.

Devignetting. In the underwater environment, we must use artificial light for imaging. However, it will cause the vignetting effect. In Ref. [6], K. Sooknanan et al. proposed a multi-frame vignetting correction model for removing the vignetting phenomenon which involves estimating the light source footprint on the seafloor. This artificial light correction can well done, however, it cost large time for computing. So, in this paper, we intend to introduce a signal frame-based vignette removal method. Given the fact that we are interested in the overall effect of light attenuation through the system and not all of the image formation details, we have derived an effective degradation model, $Z(r, \theta)$ as follows,

$$Z(r, \theta) = O(r, \theta)V(r) \tag{18}$$

where Z is the image with vignetting, O is the vignetting-free image, and V is the vignetting function. Our goal is to find the optimal vignetting function V that minimizes asymmetry of the radial gradient distribution. By taking the log of Eq. (26), we get

$$\ln(Z(r, \theta) = \ln O(r, \theta) + \ln V(r) \tag{19}$$

Let $\mathbf{Z} = \ln Z$, $\mathbf{O} = \ln O$, and $\mathbf{V} = \ln V$. We denote the radial gradients of $\mathbf{Z}$, $\mathbf{O}$, and $\mathbf{V}$ for each pixel (r, θ) by $R_r^Z(r, \theta)$, $R_r^O(r, \theta)$, $R_r^V(r, \theta)$. Then,

$$R_r^Z(r, \theta) = R_r^O(r, \theta) + R_r^V(r, \theta) \tag{20}$$

Given an image $\mathbf{Z}$ with vignetting, we find a maximum a posterior (MAP) solution to $\mathbf{V}$. Taking Bayes rule, we get,

$$\mathbf{V} = \arg \max_{\mathbf{V}} P(\mathbf{V}|\mathbf{Z}) \sim \arg \max_{\mathbf{V}} P(\mathbf{Z}|\mathbf{V})P(\mathbf{V}) \tag{21}$$

Considering the vignetting function at discrete, evenly sampled radii: $(\mathbf{V}(r_t), r_t \in S_r)$, where $S_r = \{r_0, r_1, \ldots, r_{n-1}\}$. Each pixel (r, θ) is associated with the sector in it resides, and sector width is δr. The vignetting function is in general smooth, therefore, we obtain,

$$P(\mathbf{V}) = e^{-\lambda_s \sum_{r_t \in S_r} V''(r_t)^2} \tag{22}$$

where λs is chosen to compensate for the noise level in the image, and $\mathbf{V}''(r_t)$ is approximated as

$$V''(r_t) = \frac{V(r_{t-1}) - 2V(r_t) + V(r_{t+1})}{(\delta r)^2} \tag{23}$$

Using the sparsity prior method on the vignetting-free image $\mathbf{O}$,

$$P(\mathbf{Z}|\mathbf{V}) = P(R_r^O) = e^{-|R_r^O|^\alpha}, < 1 \tag{24}$$

Substituting Eq. (32) and Eq. (28), we have

$$P(\mathbf{Z}|\mathbf{V}) = e^{-\sum_{(r,\theta)} |R_r^Z(r,\theta) - R_r^V(r)|^\alpha} \tag{25}$$

The overall energy function $P(\mathbf{Z}|\mathbf{V})P(\mathbf{V})$ can be written as

$$E = \sum_{(r,\theta)} |R_r^Z(r, \theta) - R_r^V(r)|^\alpha + \lambda_s \sum_{r_t \in s_r} V''(r_t)^2 \tag{26}$$

Through minimize E, we can estimate the $\mathbf{V}(r_t)$. Then, we use the IRLS technique for estimating the vignetting function.

Spectral Properties-Based Colour Correction. We take the chromatic transfer function τ for weighting the light from the surface to a given depth of objects as

$$\tau_\lambda = \frac{E_\lambda^{surface}}{E_\lambda^{object}} \tag{27}$$

where the transfer function τ at wavelength λ is derived from the irradiance of the surface $E_\lambda^{surface}$ by the irradiance of the object E_λ^{object}. According to the spectral response of RGB camera, we convert the transfer function to RGB domain:

$$\tau_{RGB} = \sum_{}^{k} \tau_\lambda \cdot C_b(\lambda) \tag{28}$$

where the weighted RGB transfer function is τ_{RGB}, $C_b(\lambda)$ is the underwater spectral characteristic function of colour band b, $b \in \{r,g,b\}$. k is the number of discrete bands of the camera spectral characteristic function.

Finally, the corrected image is gathered from the weighted RGB transfer function by

$$J_\lambda(x) = \hat{J}_\lambda(x) \cdot \tau_{RGB} \tag{29}$$

where $J_\lambda(x)$ and $\hat{J}_\lambda(x)$ are respectively the colour corrected and uncorrected images.

4   Experimental Results and Discussions

The performance of the proposed algorithm is evaluated both analytically and experimentally by utilizing ground-truth colour patches. Both results demonstrate that the proposed algorithm has superior haze removal effects and colour balancing capabilities of the proposed method over the others. In the experiment, we compare our method with Fattal's model [7], He's model [8], and Xiao's model [9]. Here, we select the best parameters for each model. The computer used is equipped with Windows XP and an Intel Core 2 (2.0 GHz) with 1 GB RAM. The size of the images is 345 × 292 pixels.

In the first experiment, we simulate the mine detection system in the darkroom of our laboratory (see Fig. 2). We take OLYMPUS STYLUS TG-2 15 m/50ft underwater camera for capture images [13]. The distance between light-camera and the objects is 3 meters. The size of the images is 640 × 480 pixels. We take the artificial light as an auxiliary light source. As a fixed light source, it caused uneven distribution of light. Because the light is absorbed in water, the imaging array of the camera captured a distorted video frame, see Fig. 2(a). Figure 2(b) shows the denoised image, electrical noise and additional noise are removed. After estimation, we use single frame vignetting method to remove artificial light. And the dehazing method is proposed to eliminate the haze in the image. After that, the contrast of Fig. 2(d) is obviously than Fig. 2(c). The obtained image is also too dark. So, αACE is used to enhancement the image. And finally, the sharp-based recognition method is used to distiguish the objects. Fig. 3 shows the results of devignetting by different methods.

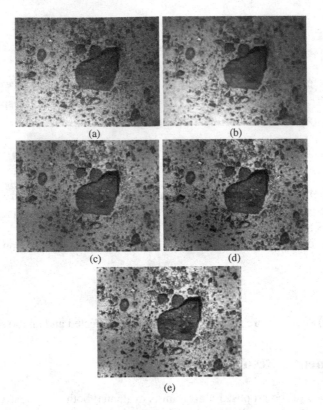

(a)   (b)

(c)   (d)

(e)

Fig. 2. Simulation of objects detection in water tank; (a) Captured video frame; (b) denoised image; (c) de-vignetting; (d) GMF dehazing; (e) colour correction.

In addition to the visual analysis mentioned above, we conducted quantitative analysis, mainly from the perspective of statistics and the statistical parameters for the images (see Table 1). This analysis includes Peak Signal to Noise Ratio (PSNR) [11], Quality mean-opinion-score (Q-MOS) [6], and Structural Similarity (SSIM) [12].

Table 1. Comparative analysis of different de-scattering methods.

Methods	PSNR	Q-MOS	SSIM	CPU time [s]
Fattal	11.21	46.11	0.4225	20.61
He	16.94	88.45	0.6992	10.66
Xiao	24.63	92.38	0.8030	5.21
Ours	29.87	94.58	0.8963	5.46

Let x_i and y_i be the i-th pixel in the original image A and the distorted image B, respectively. The *MSE* and *PSNR* between the two images are given by

$$MSE = \frac{1}{N} \sum_{i=1}^{N} (x_i - y_i)^2, \tag{30}$$

$$PSNR = 10 \log_{10} \left(\frac{L^2}{MSE} \right) \tag{31}$$

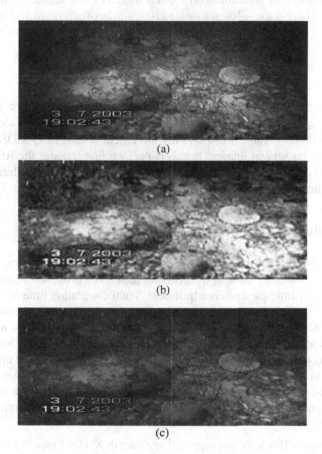

(a)

(b)

(c)

Fig. 3. Results of different devignetting methods; (a) input image; (b) histogram equation; (c) our method.

where, PSNR means the peak signal to noise ratio (values are over 0, the higher the best).

Reference proposed a multi-scale SSIM method for image quality assessment. Input image A and B, let μ_A, μ_B, and σ_{AB} respectively as the mean of A, the mean of B, the covariance of image A and image B. The parameters of relative importance α, β, γ are equal to 1. The SSIM is given as follow:

$$SSIM(\mathrm{x}, \mathrm{y}) = \frac{(2\mu_A\mu_B + C_1)(2\sigma_{AB} + C_2)}{(\mu_A^2 + \mu_B^2 + C_1)(\mu_A^2 + \mu_B^2 + C_2)} \tag{32}$$

where C_1, C_2 are the small constants. SSIM is named as structural similarity (values are between 0 (worst) to 1 (best)).

The objective quality predictions do not map directly to the subjective mean opinion scores (MOS). There is a non-linear mapping function between subjective and objective predictions. In a novel logistic function to account for such a mapping is proposed,

$$Q - MOS = \frac{100}{1 + \exp(q_1(Q + q_2))} \tag{33}$$

where, Q is the multi-band pooling that produced the strongest correction with the LIVE database. q_1 and q_2 represent the different observers. The Q-MOS value is between 0 (worst) to 100(best). Table 1 displays the numerical results of Q-MOS, PSNR and SSIM measured on several images. In this paper, we first transfer the RGB image to gray image, and then take the mathematical indexes for evaluating the different methods. The results indicate that our approach works well for haze removal.

5 Conclusions

This work has shown that it is possible to enhance degraded video sequences from seabed observation systems using the image processing ideas. The proposed algorithm is automatic and requires little parameters adjustment. Total computing time of our system is about 10 s. We proposed a simple prior based on the difference in attenuation among the different colour channels, which inspire us to estimate the transmission map. Another contribution is to compensate the transmission by guided median filters, which not only has the benefits of edge-preserving and noise removing, but also speed up the computational cost. Meanwhile, the proposed underwater image colourization method can recover the underwater distorted images well than the state-of-the-art methods. The artificial light correction method can eliminate the non-uniform illumination very well.

Acknowledgments. This work was supported by Grant in Aid for Research Fellows of Japan Society for the Promotion of Science (No.13J10713), Grant in Aid for Foreigner Research Fellows of Japan Society for the Promotion of Science (No.15F15077), Open Research Fund of State Key Laboratory of Marine Geology in Tongji University (MGK1407), and Open Research Fund of State Key Laboratory of Ocean Engineering in Shanghai Jiaotong University (OEK1315).

References

1. Stack, J.: Automation for underwater mine recognition: current trends and future strategy. Proc. SPIE **80170K**, 1–21 (2011)
2. Schechner, Y.Y., Averbuch, Y.: Regularized image recovery in scattering media. IEEE Trans. Pattern Anal. **29**(9), 1655–1660 (2007)

3. Hou, W., Gray, D.J., Weidemann, A.D., Fournier, G.R., Forand, J.L.: Automated underwater image restoration and retrieval of related optical properties. In: Proceedings of International Symposium. of Geoscience and Remote Sensing, pp. 1889–1892 (2007)
4. Narasimhan, S.G., Nayar, S.K.: Vision and the atmosphere. Int. J. Comput. Vis. **48**(3), 233–254 (2002)
5. Selesnick, I.W., Baraniuk, R.G., Kingsbury, N.G.: The dual-tree complex wavelet transform. IEEE Signal Process. Mag. **22**(6), 123–151 (2005)
6. Sooknanan, K., Kokaram, A., Corrigan, D., et al.: Improving underwater visibility using vignetting correction. Proc. SPIE **8305**, 83050M-1–83050M-8 (2012)
7. Fattal, R.: Single image dehazin. In: SIGGRAPH, pp. 1–9 (2008)
8. He, K., Sun, J., Tang, X.: Single image haze removal using dark channel prior. IEEE Trans. Pattern Anal. **33**(12), 2341–2353 (2011)
9. Xiao, C., Gan, J.: Fast image dehazing using guided joint bilateral filter. Visual Comput. **28**(6–8), 713–721 (2012)
10. Lu, H., Li, Y., Serikawa, S.: Underwater image enhancement using guided trigonometric bilateral filter and fast automation color correction. In: Proceedings of International Conference on Image Processing, pp. 3412–3416 (2013)
11. Wang, Z., Bovik, A.C., Sheikh, H.R., Simoncelli, E.P.: Image quality assessment: from error visibility to structural similarity. IEEE Trans. Image Process. **13**(4), 600–612 (2004)
12. Zheng, Y., Lin, S., Kang, S.B., Xiao, R., Gee, J.C., Kambhamettu, C.: Single-image vignetting correction from gradient distribution symmetries. IEEE Trans. Pattern Anal. **35**(6), 1480–1494 (2013)
13. Lu, H., Li, Y., Zhang, L., Serikawa, S.: Contrast enhancement for images in turbid water. J. Opt. Soc. Am. **32**(5), 886–893 (2015)

Video Based Face Tracking and Animation

Changwei Luo[1], Jun Yu[1], Zhigang Zheng[1],
Bin Cai[2], Lingyun Yu[1], and Zengfu Wang[1,2]([✉])

[1] Department of Automation,
University of Science and Technology of China, Hefei, China
luocw@mail.ustc.edu.cn
[2] Institute of Intelligent Machines,
Chinese Academy of Sciences, Hefei, China
zfwang@ustc.edu.cn

Abstract. We propose a system for video based face tracking and animation. With a single video camera, our system can accurately track the facial feature points of a user, and transfer the tracked facial motions to the avatar's face. We use constrained local model (CLM) to track the feature points. The original CLM only makes use of local texture and performs an exhaustive local search around the current estimate of feature points. This often leads to local minima. To overcome this problem, we incorporate the global texture into CLM. The improved CLM not only gives discriminative capability to each feature point, but also gives good match to the whole texture. After obtaining the 2D positions of the feature points, we estimate blendshape coefficients based on a set of user-specific 3D key shapes. Finally, facial animations are created using blendshape interpolation. Experiments demonstrate the effectiveness of our system.

Keywords: Face tracking · Facial animation · Local texture · Global texture

1 Introduction

Generating 3D facial animation from a video is useful in many applications. Taking video games for an example, instead of using a keyboard or a mouse, the players can control the facial expression of a virtual hero by performing desired facial actions in front of a camera. This would greatly increase the interest of the game players. Besides, video conference has become an efficient means to achieve collaboration over long distances. However, there are several disadvantages for video conference. A crucial disadvantage is the lack of anonymity. Unlike text or voice based conversational systems, video conference systems will immediately reveal a person's face. This is unacceptable for many applications where anonymity is required. An attractive solution for this problem is using avatars or virtual faces.

Various methods have been proposed for creating avatar animation from videos [1–5]. Although these methods have different acquisition systems and

© Springer International Publishing Switzerland 2015
Y.-J. Zhang (Ed.): ICIG 2015, Part III, LNCS 9219, pp. 522–533, 2015.
DOI: 10.1007/978-3-319-21969-1_47

Fig. 1. Two examples of CLM fitting. The images are from Multi-PIE database [6]

processing pipelines, they share many fundamental principles. In [2,3], stereo cameras are used for facial performance capture. These systems require careful calibration and are not easy to use. In this paper, we focus on video based facial animation using a single camera.

Synthesizing video based facial animation require accurate face tracking. In [7], optical flow is applied for facial feature tracking. Tracking by optical flow is unreliable especially for less salient landmarks. Geometric priors as well other constraints are often incorporated to prevent drifts [8,9]. The active appearance model (AAM) is popular for face tracking [10,11]. However, the tracking accuracy is insufficient. Compared with AAM, the constrained local model (CLM) [12] has shown good performance for face tracking. CLM outperforms AAM in that it is discriminative and generalize well to unseen texture variation. It also offers greater invariance to illumination variation. In [13], the displaced dynamic expression (DDE) model is proposed for real-time face tracking. Although the DDE model has shown good performance, the training of a DDE model is tedious.

In our system, CLM is used to track the feature points in a video. The original CLM [12] only makes use of local texture and performs an exhaustive local search around the current estimate of feature points. This often leads to local minima. To improve the tracking accuracy, we incorporate the global texture of AAM into CLM. The improved CLM not only gives discriminative capability to each landmark, but also gives good match to the whole texture. Our method effectively incorporates shape prior, local texture and global texture.

After obtaining the 2D positions of the feature points, we estimate blendshape coefficients based on a set of user-specific 3D key shapes. The 3D key shapes are automatically generated based on the user's face model and the target face model. Finally, facial animations are created using blendshape interpolation.

2   Facial Tracking

Given the video of a person's face, we use constrained local model [12] to track the feature points. For face images with neutral facial expressions, the accuracy of CLM fitting is relatively high. However, for face images with various facial expressions, CLM is not able to accurately locate all the feature points. This is the case especially for feature points on the lip contours (see Fig. 1). The reason is that the texture around the lips exhibits large variations. The local detectors (i.e., the patch experts) of CLM fail to discriminate these feature points. To improve the tracking accuracy, we add global texture of AAM to CLM.

2.1 Constrained Local Model

The CLM consists of a shape model and set of patch experts. The shape model describes the rigid and non-rigid shape variations. A face shape is defined on a set of feature points (landmarks), and is represented by a vector $s = (x_1, x_2, \cdots, x_v)^T$. s contains the coordinates of v feature points, $x_i = (x_i, y_i)$ is the 2D location of the ith feature point. The shape s can be expressed as a linear combination of mean shape s_0 and n orthonormal bases s_i,

$$s = s_0 + \sum_{i=1}^{n} s_i p_i \tag{1}$$

where $p = [p_1, p_2, ..., p_n]$ are the shape parameters. The feature point x_i of shape s is then placed in the image frame by applying a 2D similarity transform $F(x_i; q)$.

$$F(x_i, q) = \begin{bmatrix} q_1 & -q_2 \\ q_2 & q_1 \end{bmatrix} \begin{bmatrix} x_i \\ y_i \end{bmatrix} + \begin{bmatrix} q_x \\ q_y \end{bmatrix} \tag{2}$$

where $q = [q_1, q_2, q_x, q_y]$ are the pose parameters.

For a CLM with v feature points, there are also v patch experts, each corresponding to a feature point. The ith patch expert is used to calculate the probability of alignment for the ith feature point $p(l_i = 1 | x_i, I)$.

$$p(l_i | x_i, I) = \frac{1}{1 + \exp\{\rho \cdot C_i(x_i; I) + \varepsilon\}} \tag{3}$$

where I denotes the input image. $l_i \in \{1, -1\}$ is a discrete random variable denoting whether the ith feature point is aligned or misaligned. The constants ρ and ε are learned through cross-validation [12]. $C_i(x_i; I)$ is the output of a classifier. Here we use the linear support vector machine (SVM).

$$C_i(x_i; I) = w_i^T \cdot \psi(x_i) + b_i \tag{4}$$

where w_i^T and b_i are the weights and biases of the SVM classifier, $\psi(x_i; I)$ is an image patch centered at x_i.

By performing an exhaustive local search within the search window Ψ_i, we obtain a response map for each feature point. Each response map is approximated by a Gaussian distribution $N(x_i; u_i, \Sigma_i)$, u_i and Σ_i are the mean and covariance of the Gaussian distribution, respectively. u_i can be chosen as the locations with maximum response in the response map, and

$$\Sigma_i = \sum_{x \in \Psi_i} \frac{p(l_i = 1 | x, I)}{\sum_{y \in \Psi_i} p(l_i = 1 | y, I)} (x - \mu_i)(x - \mu_i)^T \tag{5}$$

The parameters p and q of CLM are solved by minimizing the following objective function [12,14]:

$$Q_{clm} = \frac{1}{2} \cdot ||p||^2_{\Lambda^{-1}} + \frac{1}{2} \cdot \sum_{i=1}^{v} ||F(x_i; q) - u_i||^2_{\Sigma_i^{-1}} \qquad (6)$$

2.2 Combining Global Texture of AAM

The texture of AAM is defined within the mean shape s_0, and is also called shape normalized texture. Figure 2 shows the process of generating shape normalized texture. To reduce the space of texture variation and the computation load, only only part of the global texture is used (see Fig. 2(d)).

Texture variation is modeled by the linear combination of mean texture A_0 and m orthonormal vectors A_i.

$$A(x) = A_0(x) + \sum_{i=1}^{m} c_i A_i(x) \qquad (7)$$

where $c = [c_1, c_2, ..., c_m]$ is the texture parameters.

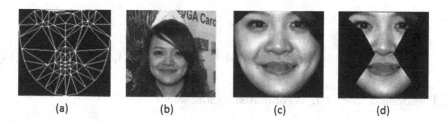

(a)　　　　　　(b)　　　　　　(c)　　　　　　(d)

Fig. 2. The process of generating shape normalized texture. (a) The mean shape. (b) An example facial image. (c) Shape normalized texture. (d) Only the texture around the lips and the eyes is used

To combine the texture of AAM into CLM, we define an improved objective function of CLM as follows:

$$Q = (1 - \omega_a)Q_{clm} + \omega_a K \cdot Q_{aam} \qquad (8)$$

where

$$Q_{aam} = \frac{1}{2}||A_0(x) + \sum_{i=1}^{m} c_i A_i(x) - I(W(x; p, q))||^2 \qquad (9)$$

K is a scaling factor that makes Q_{aam} and Q_{clm} commensurate. ω_a is a weight that balances Q_{aam} and Q_{clm}. $W(x; p, q)$ is the piecewise affine warp function.

The objective function (8) is minimized using Gauss-Newton gradient descent method. Give the initial estimate of p, we iteratively solve for increments to the parameter Δp, and then update $p \leftarrow p + \Delta p$.

$$\Delta p = -H^{-1} \cdot \frac{\partial Q}{\partial p} \tag{10}$$

where H is the Hessian matrix, $\frac{\partial Q}{\partial p}$ is the derivative of Q with respect to p.

$$\frac{\partial Q}{\partial p} = (1 - \omega_a) \frac{\partial Q_{clm}}{\partial p} + \omega_a K \cdot \frac{\partial Q_{aam}}{\partial p} \tag{11}$$

For the Q_{clm} term, we have

$$\frac{\partial Q_{clm}}{\partial p} = \Lambda^{-1} p + \sum_{i=1}^{v} J_i^T \Sigma^{-1} (F(x_i; q) - u_i) \tag{12}$$

where $J_i = \frac{\partial F(x_i; q)}{\partial p^T}$. For the Q_{amm} term, we have

$$\frac{\partial Q_{aam}}{\partial p} = SD \cdot [I(W(x; p, q)) - A_0(x)] \tag{13}$$

$SD = [SD_1, SD_2, ..., SD_n]^T$, and

$$SD_j = \nabla I \frac{\partial W}{\partial p_j} - \sum_{i=1}^{m} [A_i^T(x) \cdot \nabla I \frac{\partial W}{\partial p_j}] \cdot A_i(x) \tag{14}$$

The Hessian matrix H is computed as follows,

$$H = (1 - \omega_a) H_c + \omega_a K \cdot H_a \tag{15}$$

where

$$H_a = SD \cdot (SD)^T \tag{16}$$

$$H_c = \Lambda^{-1} + \sum_{i=1}^{v} J_i^T \Sigma_i^{-1} J_i \tag{17}$$

The initial estimate of p can be obtained by using the results of CLM fitting. We solve for q using a similar procedure.

2.3   Adaptive Control of Weight

The weight ω_a on the Q_{aam} term should be controlled appropriately to ensure better performance. In the early iterations, the value of Q_{aam} is usually very large. The Q_{aam} term should have little influence. In the later iterations, the search points are closer to the true landmark points and the Q_{aam} term becomes much smaller, the weight on Q_{aam} should be increased. Therefore, we use the following function to adaptively control the weight:

$$\omega_a^{(i)} = \exp(-a \cdot (\frac{Q_{aam}^{(i-1)}}{Q_0})^2) \tag{18}$$

where a is a constant. $\omega_a^{(i)}$ is the weight for the ith iteration ($i = 1, 2, 3, ...$). $Q_{aam}^{(i-1)}$ is valuated at the ith iteration. Q_0 corresponds to the initial estimation, and $Q_{aam}^{(0)} = Q_0$. Thus, once $\omega_a^{(1)}$ is known, a can be determined as follows,

$$a = -\ln \omega_a^{(1)} \tag{19}$$

3   Facial Animation

We create facial animation using a blendshape model. In our system, 39 blendshapes are used. $b = [b_1, b_2, ..., b_{39}]$ is the blendshape coefficient vector. To synthesize facial animation, the tracked facial motions need to be transformed to blendshape coefficients.

Since the face geometry of the target face model is usually different from that of the user, blendshapes of the target face model can not be directly fitted to the tracked feature points.

To accurately estimate the blendshape coefficients, blendshapes of the target character need to be adapted to a specific user. In [4], the user-specific blendshapes are generated based on a pre-built bilinear face model. Building the bilinear face model is expensive. In this paper, we estimate the blendshape coefficients based on a set of user-specific 3D key shapes.

Firstly, we capture a frontal neutral facial image of the user, and locate v ($v = 66$) feature points. Given the x,y-coordinates of the v feature points, we recover their z-coordinates using the method of [15]. The x, y, z-coordinates of these feature points are concatenated to form a 3D base shape K_0 for a specific user. The feature points are triangulated to create a mesh. The mesh is also referred as the user's face model. Next, we select v ($v = 66$) feature vertexes on the target face model. These feature vertexes are also triangulated according to the feature points. Finally, the deformations of the feature vertexes can be transferred to feature points by means of deformation transfer [16], and 39 3D key shapes $K = [K_1, ..., K_{39}]$ are obtained. Figure 3 shows an example of generated user's face model and the 3D key shapes.

Based on the 3D key shapes and the tracked facial shape s, blendshape coefficients are calculated by fitting the 3D key shapes to s [17]. Using a weak-perspective camera model, the fitting procedure is minimizing the following energy,

$$E = \sum_{i=1}^{v} \left\| \sigma R \cdot (K_0 + \sum_{j=1}^{39} b_j K_j)^{(i)} + T - s^{(i)} \right\|^2 \tag{20}$$

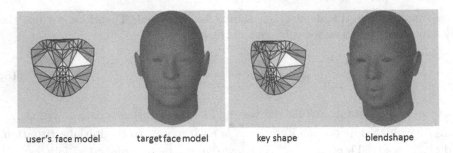

Fig. 3. From left to right: the user's face model, the target face model, an example of generated 3D key shapes, the corresponding blendshape

where σ is a scaling factor, R is the first two rows of a 3D rotation matrix and T is a translation vector. $s^{(i)}$ is the 2D position of the ith feature point in s.

Similar to [4], an animation prior is added to the fitting procedure to enhance temporal coherence. Given the blendshape coefficient vectors for h previous frames $B_h = [b^{-1}, b^{-2}, \cdots, b^{-h}]$, we combine B_h with the current frame's weight vector b into a single vector (b, B_h). The probability distribution of (b, B_h) is modeled with a Gaussian mixture model $N(b, B_h)$. The Gaussian mixture model is trained using pre-generated animation frames [18].

Finally, we estimate the blendshape coefficients b via

$$\arg\min \ E - \omega_1 \ln N(b, B_h) \tag{21}$$

where ω_1 is a constant. In our experiments, $\omega_1 = 0.5$, $h = 2$. We use an iterative two-step approach to solve the pose parameters (σ, R and T) and the blendshape coefficients b. Firstly, we fix the blendshape coefficients and solve for the pose parameters using Levenberg-Marquardt algorithm [19]. Secondly, we fix the pose parameters and solve for the blendshape coefficients using the gradient projection algorithm based on BFGS solver [20].

4   Experiments

Our system is implemented in C++ and parallelized using OpenMP. The openCV library is used for image processing. In our experiments, we first evaluate the fitting performance of the improved CLM. Then we show some generated animations.

Training. More than 800 frontal facial images are used to train our model. The improved CLM requires training a shape model, a set of patch experts. It also requires training a texture model. The shape model and the texture model are obtained by principal component analysis. The patch experts are set to (11×11)-pixels in size, and trained using positive examples and negative examples. Positive examples are obtained from the images patches centered at the true feature points, while negative examples are obtained by sampling patches shifted away from the ground truth.

Figure 4 shows an example of the response maps obtained from the trained patch experts. We can see that the response map centered at the eye corner has good discriminative ability. The response map centered at the mouth corner has multiple peaks. This makes the local detector difficult to find the ground truth feature point. By incorporating global texture into CLM, it is possible to accurately locate the feature points as more texture information is provided. To handle large head rotations, we also built two models for left and right profile images.

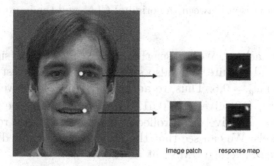

Image patch   response map

Fig. 4. An example of the response maps obtained from the trained patch experts

Determining the Weight ω_a. The weight ω_a for the global texture is determined experimentally. Firstly, we set ω_a to 0, 0.1, 0.2,...,0.9, 1.0. In each case, we evaluate the fitting accuracy using 180 testing images. The fitting accuracy is measured by the root mean square error (RMSE) between the search shape and the manually labeled shape. The RMSE is calculated for each testing image, and then the average RMSE is calculated on all testing images. Figure 5 shows the

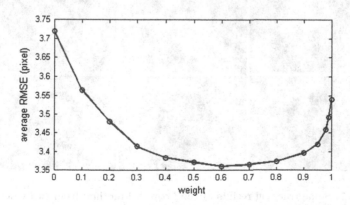

Fig. 5. The average RMSE for different values of ω_a.

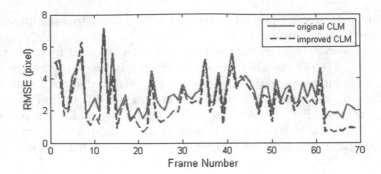

Fig. 6. Comparison between the original CLM and the improved CLM.

average RMSE at each ω_a. We can see that the RMSE reduces significantly after incorporating global texture. It is also shown that the smallest average RMSE is 3.36 pixels with $\omega_a = 0.6$. Thus, to adaptively control the weight, we can set $\omega_a^{(1)}$ to 0.6, and Eq. (19) gives $a = 0.51$. Then we evaluate the fitting accuracy for the case where adaptively controlled weight is used. The resulting average RMSE is 3.22 pixels. We can see that the adaptively controlled weight leads to a further decrease of average RMSE at about 4.17 %.

Tracking. We have also evaluated the performance of the improve CLM on FGNet talking face video (http://www-prima.inrialpes.fr/FGnet/data/01-TalkingFace/talking_face.html). The results are shown in Fig. 6. It is shown that the fitting error of the improved CLM is much smaller than that of original CLM [12]. Figure 7 shows some selected tracking results from FGNet talking face video and another video.

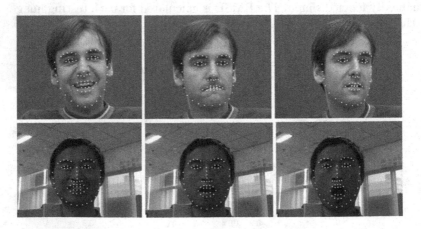

Fig. 7. Some tracking results of the proposed method from two videos.

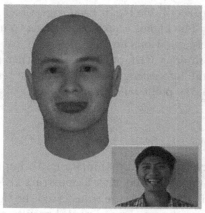

Fig. 8. Face tracking and animation for different users.

Animation. In the setup stage, a frontal facial image with neutral expression is captured for the user. Based on this image, the system automatically generates a set of user-specific 3D key shapes. At run time, facial features are tracked using the improved CLM. To speed up the tracking process, the weight ω_a can stop updating after one or two iterations. The tracked feature points are then used to compute blendshape coefficients. Our system runs at about 6 fps. Figure 8 shows the results of two users controlling and animating the facial expressions of an avatar. It is shown that the animations are quite realistic.

User Study. A user study is carried out to evaluate our system. Several animations are first generated from original facial video files using our system. The animations are then presented to 20 human subjects. The subjects are generally not connected with the topic. For each animation, the subjects are asked

Table 1. Questions in the questionnaire and the mean score for the subjective test

Questions	Mean score
1. Do the facial movements of the avatar look natural and realistic?	8.2
2. Do you recognize the avatar's facial expressions?	7.6
3. To what extent do the synthesized facial movements follow those in the original videos?	7.8

Table 2. General impression of our system from a few tested subjects

1. The system is very interesting.
2. I fell comfortable while interacting with the avatar. The avatar looks alive.
3. Sometimes the movements of eyes and lips are not well transferred to the avatar.
4. Except human avatars, non-human avatars should be added to the system.

to answer previously prepared questions (see Table 1). In these questions, the score is graded on the scale from 10 to 1. The higher score corresponds to more positive answers. The mean scores for these questions are also shown in Table 1.

In addition, the subjects are asked to interact with our system and then give the general impression of our system. Some interesting remarks from the tested subjects are shown in Table 2. These remarks point out our next goals.

5 Conclusion

We describe a system for video based face tracking and animation. To improve the tracking accuracy, global texture is incorporated into a constrained local model. To create facial animation, tracked face motions are transferred the target face based on a set of user-specific 3D key shapes. Experimental results show that the proposed system is effective for creating video based facial animation.

Acknowledgements. This work was supported by National Natural Science Foundation of China (61472393).

References

1. Rhee, T., Hwang, Y., Kim, J., Kim, C.: Real-time facial animation from live video tracking. In: Proceedings of the 2011 ACM SIGGRAPH/Eurographics Symposium on Computer Animation (2011)
2. Zhang, L., Snavely, N., Curless, B., Seitz, S.: Spacetime faces: high resolution capture for modeling and animation. ACM Trans. Graph. **23**(3), 548–558 (2004)
3. Jiang, J., Zeng, M., Liang, B., Liu, X.: High quality binocular facial performance capture from partially blurred image sequence. In: IEEE International Conference on Computer-Aided Design and Computer Graphics (CAD/Graphics), pp. 196–203 (2013)
4. Cao, C., Weng, Y., Lin, S., Zhou, K.: 3D shape regression for real-time facial animation. ACM Trans. Graph. **32**(4), 41:1–41:10 (2013). Article No. 41
5. Luo, C., Yu, J., Wang, Z.: Synthesizing performance-driven facial animation. Acta Automatica Sinica **40**(10), 2245–2252 (2014)
6. Gross, R., Matthews, I., Cohn, J., Kanade, T., Baker, S.: Multi-pie. Image Vis. Comput. **28**(5), 807–813 (2010)
7. Chai, J., Xiao, J., Hodgins, J.: Vision-based control of 3D facial animation. In: Eurographics/SIGGRAPH Symposium on Computer Animation (2003)
8. Decarlo, D., Metaxas, D.: Optical flow constraints on deformable models with applications to face tracking. Int. J. Comput. Vis. **38**(2), 99–127 (2000)
9. Zhang, W., Wang, Q., Tang, X.: Real time feature based 3-D deformable face tracking. In: Forsyth, D., Torr, P., Zisserman, A. (eds.) ECCV 2008, Part II. LNCS, vol. 5303, pp. 720–732. Springer, Heidelberg (2008)
10. Chen, Y., Yu, F., Ai, C.: Sequential active appearance model based on online instance learning. IEEE Sig. Process. Lett. **20**(6), 567–570 (2013)
11. Gao, X., Su, Y., Li, X., Tao, D.: A review of active appearance models. IEEE Trans. Sys. Man Cyber. Part C **40**, 145–158 (2010)

12. Wang, Y., Lucey, S., Cohn, J.: Enforcing convexity for improved alignment with constrained local models. In: Proceedings of the IEEE Computer Society Conference on Computer Vision and Pattern Recognition, pp. 1–8 (2008)
13. Cao, C., Hou, Q., Zhou, K.: Displaced dynamic expression regression for real-time facial tracking and animation. ACM Trans. Graph. **33**(4), 43:1–43:10 (2014). Article No. 43
14. Saragih, J., Lucey, S., Cohn, J.: Deformable model fitting by regularized landmark mean-shift. Int. J. Comput. Vis. **91**(2), 200–215 (2011)
15. Saragih, J., Lucey, S., Cohn, J.: Real-time avatar animation from a single image. In: IEEE International Conference on Automatic Face and Gesture Recognition, pp. 117–124 (2011)
16. Summer, R., Popovic, J.: Deformation transfer for triangle meshes. ACM Trans. Graph. **22**(3), 399–405 (2004)
17. Chuang, E., Bregler, C.: performance driven facial animation using blendshape interpolation. Technical report, Stanford University (2002)
18. Weise, T., Bouaziz, S., Li, H., Pauly, M.: Realtime performance-based facial animation. In: Proceedings SIGGRAPH (2011)
19. More, J.: The levenberg-marquardt algorithm: implementation and theory. In: Watson, G.A. (ed.) Numerical Analysis. Lecture Notes in Mathematics, vol. 630, pp. 105–116. Springer, Heidelberg (1978)
20. Byrd, R., Lu, P., Nocedal, J., Zhu, C.: A limited-memory algorithm for bound constrained optimization. SIAM J. Sci. Comput. **16**, 1190–1208 (1995)

Video Stabilization via Piecewise Linear L1 Optimization for Airship Earth Observation

Xiaozhou Xu[1](✉), Jing Yu[2], and Weidong Sun[1]

[1] State Key Labratory of Intelligent Technology and Systems,
Tsinghua National Labratory for Information Science and Technology,
Department of Electronic Engineering, Tsinghua University, Beijing 100084, China
peter63598@126.com, wdsun@tsinghua.edu.cn
[2] College of Computer Science and Technology, Beijing University of Technology,
Beijing 100124, China
yujing@tsinghua.edu.cn

Abstract. Video stabilization has been gaining in importance in earth observation and video surveillance on boarded of airship platforms. As the airship platforms have obvious low-frequency vibration caused by wind and the unstable attitude may also lead to geometric distortion in the video streams, and most of the traditional methods are designed for casual handheld devices which cannot effectively handle those kinds of problems, a new video stabilization method for airship earth observation is proposed. In this method, a modified camera path planning method based on piecewise linear L1 optimization is given under the specific motion properties of airship platform and the needs of geometric correction for each frame, and the camera path reconstruction is carried out with vision based motion estimation and sparse GPS and attitude data. The effectiveness of our method is confirmed by quantitative experiments over a variety of video streams.

Keywords: Airship earth observation · Video stabilization · Geometric correction · Path planning · Piecewise linear L1 optimization

1 Introduction

Airships are more and more widely used in both civilian and military fields, such as earth observation, rescue operation and activity surveillance. Earth observation is one of the most useful applications of airship platforms, which generates much interest in video stabilization for the fact that airship platforms are strongly wiggled by the wind and its attitude is also unstable. But the traditional video stabilization methods designed for casual handheld devices are unable to effectively remove the low-frequency wobble of the video frames caused by the wind, and geometric correction cannot be applied at the same time for each frame which is a common need for airship earth observation.

Generally, as one of the post-processes of digital videos, video stabilization includes three main steps: (1) camera motion estimation; (2) smooth camera path planning; (3) applying per-frame warps to produce stabilized video frames.

© Springer International Publishing Switzerland 2015
Y.-J. Zhang (Ed.): ICIG 2015, Part III, LNCS 9219, pp. 534–544, 2015.
DOI: 10.1007/978-3-319-21969-1_48

For the camera motion estimation, traditional video stabilization methods use global parametric transforms like affine model or other 2D models [1]. These 2D video stabilization methods use transformation parameters as translations and rotations instead of recovering camera's real 3D path and orientation, so they do not perform effectively for airship earth observation. Recently, many new techniques are proposed for the reconstruction of scene and camera path. 3D camera trajectories are used to estimate "content-preserving" warps to original video frames [2–4] and converting first-person videos to hyper-lapse videos [2]. But, these kind of 3D video stabilization methods usually apply Structure from Motion (SfM) to estimate camera's path which is computational complex and less robust.

As to path planning method, linear smoothing models like gauss filter [1] and spline fitting model are widely used. Grundmann et al. optimized the original path with L1 norm which results in polynomial approximation result [6].

In our method, considering the specific low-frequency vibration problem in the airship earth observation, camera's position and orientation path are reconstructed using piecewise linear L1 optimization and vision based estimation, which makes full use of the platform's GPS and attitude data. And then, a video image warp method is given using the above path planning results, in order to producing a stable and geometric corrected video streams.

The rest of the paper is organized as follows. Since our method is designed for airship platforms, we first introduce the specific optimization objectives for airship earth observation, and then discuss about the modified position and orientation path planning method based on piecewise linear L1 optimization. Secondly, we introduce the method of camera's path and orientation reconstruction using sensor data. Thirdly, the method for projecting, image warp and fusion combined with geometric correction will be given. Finally, the effectiveness of our method will be confirmed through some quantitative experiments.

2 Path Planning Based on Piecewise Linear L1 Optimization

Instead of handheld devices which may cause high-frequency jitter into the video streams, airship platforms suffer from low-frequency vibration (less than 5 Hz) caused by the wind and their own inertia which make the platform to roll and pitch. Then the airships may yaw and the videos could seem deviate from its original camera path, have a geometric distortion and combine with visible wiggle of the scenes in video streams. Since video stabilization is to satisfy conflicting objective, we formulate the path planning as an optimization method with the following 4 objectives:

1. **Approximation.** The optimal position and orientation of the camera should near the original one, so the field of view of the stabilized video streams could remain large enough.
2. **Motor Pattern Recovery.** Airships move in a straight line until next remote control given signal. Path planning based on airship's motor pattern benefits both to visual comfort and future applications like earth observation or target tracking.
3. **Smoothness.** The optimal path should be smooth in both position and orientation.

4. **Geometric Correction.** The optical axis of camera should remain vertical to avoid image distortion, and the optimal orientation should remain no pitch and roll.

Most previous video stabilization methods employ path planning algorithm [1–5, 9] and many of the latest works apply L1 optimization. Such as, Grundmann et al. optimized the original path with L1 optimization which results in polynomial approximation result [6]. However, these methods don't perform well due to the specific motion properties of airship platform and the specific requirements for earth observation. Considering the 4 conditions above, a new piecewise linear L1 optimization path planning method is proposed in this paper.

2.1 Optimization Objectives for the Path Planning

Let $\{P_t = (x_t, y_t, z_t), f_t = (\theta_t, \phi_t, \psi_t)\}$ be the set of input camera positions and orientations of a video with n frames, and let $\{P_t^{out}, f_t^{out}\}$ be the desired output camera positions and orientations in which (x, y, z) stand for the position of camera in ground frame and (θ, ϕ, ψ) stand for the airship platform's Euler angles yaw, roll and pitch.

So the approximation objectives of positions and orientations are stated mathematically as penalty terms:

$$E_{approx-p} = \sum_t \left\| P_t^{out} - P_t \right\|^2 \tag{1}$$

$$E_{approx-f} = \sum_t \left\| f_t^{out} - f_t \right\|^2 \tag{2}$$

Then the image geometric correction objective demands the optimal orientation remain no pitch and roll. So in our smoothed orientation, roll (around x-axis) and pitch (around y-axis) remain 0.

Different from the needs of handheld devices and first-person video camera platforms, the swings of the scenes in video streams not only influence visual comfortableness but also not benefit earth observation related works like mapping, visual interpretation and so on. As the ideal path of an airship platform is a straight line until next remote control signal is given, the optimal path should always be piecewise linear. So, the smoothness and motor pattern recovery objectives can be included in the same penalty term, because an L1 norm constraint is applied to the second-order deviation of the path:

$$E_{smooth-p} = \sum_{t=2}^{n-1} \left| p_{t-1}^{out} - 2p_t^{out} + p_{t+1}^{out} \right| \tag{3}$$

$$E_{smooth-f} = \sum_{t=2}^{n-1} \left| \theta_{t-1}^{out} - 2\theta_t^{out} + \theta_{t+1}^{out} \right| \tag{4}$$

where, n is the length of video frames. Then, the weighted sum of these objectives gives our combined optimization objective:

$$E = \mu_1 E_{approx-p} + \mu_2 E_{smooth-p} + \mu_3 E_{approx-f} + \mu_4 E_{smooth-f} \qquad (5)$$

where $\mu_1, \mu_2, \mu_3, \mu_4$ are balancing coefficients.

2.2 Modified Path Planning Based on Piecewise Linear L1 Optimization

From Eq. 5 we can obviously find out that positions and orientations can be optimized separately. Then we divide the optimization objective of Eq. 5 into two objectives so that the optimization of the positions sequence P_t does not depend on the orientations sequence f_t. Since the objective of geometric correction makes sure that the output roll and pitch keep 0, so the two reduced objectives now become:

$$E_p = \sum_t \left\| P_t^{out} - P_t \right\|^2 + \lambda_1 \sum_{t=2}^{n-1} \left| p_{t-1}^{out} - 2p_t^{out} + p_{t+1}^{out} \right| \qquad (6)$$

$$E_f = \sum_t \left\| \theta_t^{out} - \theta_t \right\|^2 + \lambda_2 \sum_{t=2}^{n-1} \left| \theta_{t-1}^{out} - 2\theta_t^{out} + \theta_{t+1}^{out} \right| \qquad (7)$$

where λ is a nonnegative parameter used to control the trade-off between smoothness and the size of the residual.

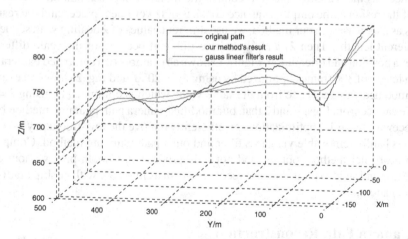

Fig. 1. Path planning result of a sequence of positions with 300 frames optimized by using linear filter and piecewise linear L1 optimization with $\lambda_1 = 2000$.

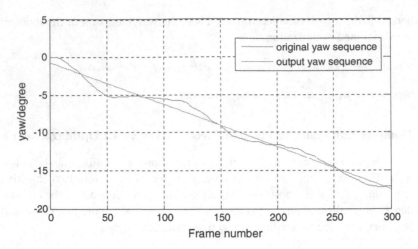

Fig. 2. Orientation planning result of a sequence of yaw degree with 300 frames optimized by using piecewise linear L1 optimization with $\lambda_2 = 50$.

Since these two objectives share the same formation, in this section we optimize them using the same method. The objective of Eq. 6 is closely related to L1 trend filtering [10], which minimize the second-order derivation in L1 norm, therefore results in a series of linear angles. The optimization target function follows variation on H-P filtering which is a widely used trend filter and is also well studied in [6].

Since λ is the parameter used to control the trade-off between smoothness and the size of the residual, the output sequence consists of fewer linear pieces and the residual grows as λ increases. In our method, we use different values of λ dealing with sequences of different lengths. Then λ_1 and λ_2 are also different because of the scale difference between position and orientation. Figure 1 shows an example of a smoothed camera path with a length of 300 frames optimized by using $\lambda_1 = 2000$, and Fig. 2 shows an example of a smoothed yaw sequence from the same video which is optimized by using $\lambda_2 = 50$.

We can see from Figs. 1 and 2 that, our modified camera path planning method based on piecewise linear L1 optimization can efficiently remove the low-frequency vibration which is hardly removable via gauss filter and other path planning method. Comparing with linear filter method, our method not only produces a smooth path without over-smoothing and sudden turns, but also recovers a path fitting more with airship platform's motion pattern.

3 Camera Path Reconstruction

In Sect. 2, we have introduced our path planning method mainly considering of airship platform's four optimization objectives using platform's position and orientation path. In this section, we will introduce our position and orientation path reconstruction using vision based motion estimation and sparse GPS and attitude data.

3.1 Vision Based Motion Estimation

We define the coordinates in the inertia frame with a tilde as $\tilde{q} \in R^3$ and the coordinates in the camera frame using the same letter without a tilde as $q \in R^3$. And we assume the optical axis of the camera coincides with the vertical axis of the camera frame and we describe the position and orientation of the camera at time t by $(p_t, R_t) \in SE(3)$, which $SE(3)$ is the special Euclidean group. Assume we have some coplanar feature points $\{\tilde{q}_j\}_{j=1}^{m} \in P$, where P denotes the plane which means the ground surface. Figure 3 shows the geometric relationship between camera frame and inertia frame. For a fixed point on ground, the coordinates in the inertial frame $\tilde{q}$ and q_i in camera frame i are related by:

$$\tilde{q} = R_i q_i + p_i \tag{8}$$

If $(p_{i-1}, R_{i-1}), (p_i, R_i) \in SE(3)$ are the statuses of camera frames i-1 and i, so for $j = 1, \ldots m$, we have:

$$q_i^j = R_i^T R_{i-1} q_{i-1}^j - R_i^T (p_i - p_{i-1}) \tag{9}$$

where q_{i-1}^j, q_i^j are the coordinates of the fixed points $\tilde{q}_j$ in camera frames i-1 and i. Let n_i denotes the unit normal vector of plane P in camera frame i, so we have:

$$\frac{1}{d_i} n_i^T q_i^j = 1, j = 1, \ldots, m \tag{10}$$

where d_i denotes the distance between camera and the plane P of frame i. Substitution Eq. 10 into Eq. 9, we have:

$$q_i^j = A q_{i-1}^j \tag{11}$$

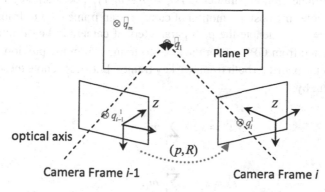

Fig. 3. Geometry of camera frame related to ground plane

We call the matrix:

$$A = R_i^T R_{i-1} - \frac{1}{d_{i-1}} R_i^T (p_i - p_{i-1}) n_{i-1}^T \tag{12}$$

as the planar essential matrix for it contains all the motion parameters (p, R) and all the structure parameters (n, d).

It turns out that $A_L = \xi A$ for $\xi \in R$ where A_L is the perspective transform matrix between neighboring frames and the middle singular value of the matrix A is equal to 1. To recover all the position and orientation path $\{(p_t, R_t)\}$ and structure parameters $\{(n_t, d_t)\}$, we need to do more SVD analysis which is introduced in [7] and iterate from frame 1 to n. Then we can recover orientations of Euler angles $\{f_t = (\theta_t, \phi_t, \psi_t)\}$ from matrices set $\{R_t\}$. And using the prior knowledge of the distance d_1 from camera to plane P in frame 1, we can recover $\{d_t\}$ by iterations of $d_i = d_{i-1} / \det(A)$ which is well introduced in [8].

In the application of airship video stabilization, the flight height of airship platform is usually more than 500 meters, so if the buildings on ground are not too high which could be assured in suburb area, the error of Eq. 10 is less than 1 %. And the higher the airship flies, the more accurate this model's result will be. This estimation method is confirmed reliable under a variety of experimental videos.

3.2   Accumulated Error Suppression

Since homographies tend of overfit and outliers may not be completely rejected, accumulated error of path estimation is inevitable. The accumulated error of path reconstruction will cause image wobble in stabilized video because of the error of motion compensation. Grundmann et al. using mixed transform estimation between two key frames but it cannot be able to dealing with real camera path [6].

In this paper, a method using sparse data from GPS and attitude sensor to suppress accumulated error of path reconstruction is proposed. The interval of the input data is about 2 s, as shown in Table 1. As we apply the same method to both position and orientation path, so in this section we only introduce the detailed method dealing with the position path. If we have $k = 50$ frames for every two key frames, then we have a series of inter-frame motion parameters $\{m_i = p_i - p_{i-1}\}_{i=1}^{k}$ between key frames 0 and 1, where m_i denotes the position motion of camera from frame $i - 1$ to frame i. And let $s_0 = p_{\text{key}-0}, s_1 = p_{\text{key}-1}$ denote the path parameters of camera at key frame 0 and key frame 1 calculated from GPS sensor data. As to frame t from the previous key frame, we can recover the path data both from two key frames. Let s_t^0, s_t^1 denote these two results and we get them by:

$$s_t^0 = s_0 + \sum_{i=1}^{t} m_i \tag{13}$$

$$s_t^1 = s_1 - \sum_{i=t+1}^{k} m_i. \tag{14}$$

Table 1. An example set of GPS and attitude data

Time h:m:s	Longitude degree	Latitude degree	Height m	Roll degree	Pitch degree	Yaw degree
15:01:40	107.2540304	29.7495648	716.372	−8.3	−10.8	242.1
15:01:42	107.2539269	29.7491639	717.436	−2.6	−10.4	150.9
15:01:54	107.2543448	29.7488933	721.668	1.4	−1.5	112.1
15:01:56	107.2548677	29.7487718	723.134	−0.2	−2.3	98.5
15:01:58	107.2554071	29.7487358	723.915	0.3	0.6	92.1

Then we get final path estimation of p_t using weighted sum of s_t^0 and s_t^1:

$$p_t = \frac{k-t}{k}s_t^0 + \frac{t}{k}s_t^1 \tag{15}$$

We apply this method to both position and orientation path, so we can have a path reconstruction result with accumulated error suppression.

3.3 Perspective Transformation Estimation

In Sect. 3.1, a method of SVD analysis with inter-frame perspective transform matrix is introduced. However, robustness demands good outlier rejection. To balance the computational complexity and robustness, RANSAC method ends when the matched feature points agree with the estimated model up to a threshold distance.

4 Video Retargeting and Image Fusion

The last step is retargeting video frames with the smoothed camera position and orientation path given in the previous section and producing a stable video. From path reconstruction and planning method, a smooth position and orientation path of camera frame is given. If the camera path reconstruction result is $\{P_t = (x_t, y_t, z_t), f_t = (\theta_t, \phi_t, \psi_t)\}$ and the smoothed camera path result is $\{P_t^{out}, f_t^{out} = (\theta_t^{out}, 0, 0)\}$, clearly the new frames in stabilized video could be rendered by projection model with camera motion compensation.

(a) Projected image with missing area   (b) New stitched image

Fig. 4. A result of Image Fusion. Stitch the projected image with missing area (a) with neighboring key frames to produce new stitched image (b).

Learning from Sect. 3.1, the projection transform matrix for frame t would be:

$$A_L = k[R_t^T R R_t - \frac{1}{d_t} R_t^T R^T (p_t^{out} - p_t) n_t^T] \tag{16}$$

where the rotation matrix of compensation could be directly got from orientation compensative vector $(\theta_t^{out}, -\phi_t, -\psi_t)$ and the term k confirms the matrix normalized. Our experiments show the projection transform matrix A_L is sensitive to the normal vector n_t and we apply gauss filter to these vectors' orientations with a small kernel length which helps increasing our method's robustness.

The projected new frames are irregular, and we assume the field of view of the output video is user-supplied and in our experiment we set it to 85 % of the field of view of the input video. Most of the output images after cutting with the supplied output field of view are without invalid pixels and usable. But images in video streams with sudden turns of camera will lost too many pixels after projection with the compensative transform. So image stitching and fusion is a necessary step for those frames.

In our method, we use neighboring key frames to stitch with the unusable frame. For those missing pixels in frame t, we track those pixels with motion compensation in neighboring key frames. Since the interval of two key frames is about 2 s, the miss area of the output frame can always be found. As to stitching these two images, we apply traditional weighted sum algorithm around the stitching seam. An example of completion of miss area by fusion with neighboring key frames is shown in Fig. 4.

5   Result and Evaluation

To evaluate the performance of our proposed method, a variety of experiments are conducted on quantitative videos.

Our method is evaluated under a variety of video streams taken in Chongqing and Qinghai at heights of more than 500 meters by Canon DSLR with resolution reduced to 576*720, consisting scenes like rivers, towns, roads and so on. In Fig. 5, one video stabilization result is shown. In this figure, top row shows the original input image sequence and the second row shows the stabilized sequence of our proposed method. The yellow arrows in this figure stand for the motion vectors of one frame towards another after 0.5 s. We can see from Fig. 5 that, our proposed method can effectively reduce both high-frequency jitter and low-frequency wobble of the video streams, and produce stable videos without geometric distortion.

Considering the evaluation of stabilized video, two quantitative indexes are given in this paper: FOV loss E_{approx} and video smoothness $E_{smoothness}$. FOV loss is represented by path approximation penalty term stated in Eqs. 1 and 2, and smoothness is represented by the second-order derivation of the smoothed camera path stated in Eqs. 3 and 4 which are the smaller the better. These two indexes change when λ in path planning method changes. The curves between E_{approx} and $E_{smoothness}$ of two different path planning methods are shown in Fig. 6. The figure is evaluated under experiments on more than 20 video streams each with 300 frames, and the result

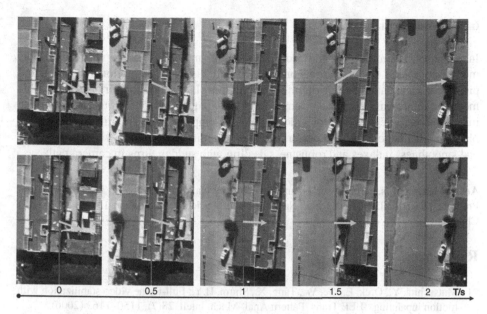

Fig. 5. Result of video stabilization. First row shows the input sequence within 2 s, and second row shows the stabilized sequence with projection and stitching. The yellow arrows stand for the motion vectors of one frame towards another after 0.5 s.

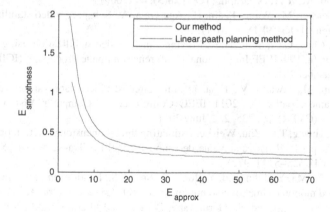

Fig. 6. Relations of the two quantitative indexes stand for FOV loss and video smoothness of two different path planning methods.

shows that the stabilization quality of our proposed method performs about 20 % better than traditional gauss linear filter.

And comparing with linear filter in Fig. 1, we can clearly see linear filter tends of over-smoothing and its result has sudden turns of path. Our path planning method can not only remove the low-frequency vibration of platform's camera, path but also recover the airship platform's motion pattern with piecewise linear optimal path.

6 Conclusion

In this paper, we introduce a new video stabilization method for airship platforms. This method completes camera path reconstruction with vision based motion estimation and piecewise linear path planning optimized for airship platforms with four objectives. This method can not only effectively remove the low-frequency wobble but also complete image geometric correction for video streams. Compared with traditional linear path planning method, our method performs better regarding to stabilized video's FOV loss and smoothness indexes and robustness dealing with sudden turns in camera path.

Acknowledgements. This work is supported by the National Science & Technology Pillar Program (No.2012BAH31B01) and National Nature Science Foundation (No.61171117) of China.

References

1. Matsushita, Y., Ofek, E., Ge, W., Tang, X., Shum, H.Y.: Full-frame video stabilization with motion inpainting. IEEE Trans. Pattern Anal. Mach. Intell. **28**(7), 1150–1163 (2006)
2. Kopf, J., Cohen, M.F., Szeliski, R.: First-person hyper-lapse videos. ACM Trans. Graph. (TOG) **33**(4), 78 (2014)
3. Liu, F., Gleicher, M., Jin, H., Agarwala, A.: Content-preserving warps for 3D video stabilization. ACM Trans. Graph. (TOG) **28**(3), 44 (2009)
4. Liu, F., Gleicher, M., Wang, J., Jin, H., Agarwala, A.: Subspace video stabilization. ACM Trans. Graph. (TOG) **30**(1), 4 (2011)
5. Hsu, Y.F., Chou, C.C., Shih, M.Y.: Moving camera video stabilization using homography consistency. In: 19th IEEE International Conference on Image Processing (ICIP), pp. 2761–2764, September 2012
6. Grundmann, M., Kwatra, V., Essa, I.: Auto-directed video stabilization with robust L1 optimal camera paths. In: 2011 IEEE Conference on Computer Vision and Pattern Recognition (CVPR), pp. 225–232, June 2011
7. Tsai, R.Y., Huang, T.S., Zhu, Wei-Le: Estimating three-dimensional motion parameters of a rigid planar patch, II: singular value decomposition. IEEE Trans. Acoust. Speech Signal Process. **30**(4), 525–534 (1982)
8. Shakernia, O., Ma, Y., John Koo, Y., John, T., Sastry, S.: Landing an unmanned air vehicle: vision based motion estimation and nonlinear control. Asian J. Control **1**, 128–145 (1999)
9. Kim, S.-J., Koh, K., Boyd, S., Gorinevsky, D.: L1 trend filtering. SIAM Rev. Prob. Tech. Sect. **51**(2), 339–360 (2009)
10. Oreifej, O., Li, Xin, Shah, M.: Simultaneous Video Stabilization and Moving Object Detection in Turbulence. IEEE Trans. Pattern Anal. Mach. Intell. **35**(2), 450–462 (2013)

Automated Procedural Generation of Urban Environments Using Open Data for City Visualisation

David Tully[1], Abdennour El Rhalibi[1(✉)], Zhigeng Pan[2],
Christopher Carter[1], and Sud Sudirman[1]

[1] School of Computing and Mathematical Sciences, Liverpool John Moores University,
Liverpool, UK
dtully@2008.ljmu.ac.uk,
{A.Elrhalibi,c.j.carter,S.Sudirman}@ljmu.ac.uk
[2] Digital Media and HCI Research Center, Hangzhou Normal University,
Hangzhou, People's Republic of China
zgpan@hznu.edu.cn

Abstract. Ever increasing populations are putting considerable strain on the critical infrastructures of our towns, cities, and countries. The interconnecting and interdependent components of these man-made living procedures and protocols give-way in unforeseen, unplanned situations. Having the ability to visualise these interconnecting entities and the interaction they have on one another is critical for future city planners. We propose a novel framework called Project Vision Support that provides an automated visualisation of real world open data maps for the creation of procedurally generated urban environments. This framework can then be used to implement planning and scheduling algorithms for the orchestrated task of emergency services for crisis management response.

Keywords: Critical infrastructure protection · Games technology · Visualisation · Open data · Procedural content generation

1 Introduction

The term *Critical Infrastructure* (CI) is primarily associated with facilities which are critical for the functioning of our society and economy. Examples of such facilities are electrical power systems, gas distribution systems, financial services, telecommunication systems, emergency services, etc. These universal services power and support practically every activity that modern society does. We, both as individuals or organisations, intrinsically rely on these universal services in our daily lives. Such services are implicitly assumed on a day-to-day basis and are therefore required to be both reliable and trustworthy. In times of crisis the resilience and reliability of these services becomes even more crucial.

According to the latest report that we are aware of, in the US alone there are 560,104 critical infrastructures. This consists of 28,600 networked Federal Deposit Insurance Corporation institutions, 2 million miles of gas pipeline, 2,800 power plants (with

© Springer International Publishing Switzerland 2015
Y.-J. Zhang (Ed.): ICIG 2015, Part III, LNCS 9219, pp. 545–551, 2015.
DOI: 10.1007/978-3-319-21969-1_49

300,000 production sites providing assets), 104 nuclear power plants, 80,000 dams, 60,000 chemical plants, 87,000 food-processing plants, and 1,600 water-treatment plants [1]. These figures are expected to have increased in the last decade since that report was published. These infrastructures have interconnections and interdependencies towards one another. For example, if resources are not delivered to power plants then electricity cannot be generated. These cascading effects can have devastating consequences if not planned for. If the electricity is not generated, the supply of power to water processing and pumping stations will stop, thusly major communities will be without power and without clean drinking water. Power outages caused by unforeseen cascading effects has struck the USA spanning many decades. In 1965, 30 million people went without power for half a day. In 1971, 1977, and 2003 there were widespread power outages throughout parts of the northeast and Midwestern areas of the USA and spanning into parts of southern Canada. In 2012, hurricane Sandy disabled power supplies from high winds and flooding.

In the UK, on March 29th 2004, a fire broke out in a tunnel 30 feet under the streets of Manchester. This tunnel was designed and built in the cold war era and are housing multiple telecommunication cables. Approximately 130,000 fixed telephone lines were affected by the fire. This caused a more devastating cascading effect as communications to emergency services were completely halted. The incident was estimated to have cost the local business, community and government £22 million pounds worth of damaged over the 5-day disaster [2].

The ability to visualise and predict cascading effects in modern urban environments, especially big cities such as London and New York will not only be extremely helpful to crisis managers but also to city planners for accurate decision making. Early work on disaster support frameworks for disaster management has been created by Michalowski et al. called *NEGOPLAN,* a rule-based model of sequential decision-making [3]. Michalowski states that there are four phases in disaster support decision making. The first is mitigation phase, which aims to reduce the risk to property, assets, and human life. The second is preparedness phase which contains a set of actions closest to the onset of a disaster aimed at minimising the damage and enhancing disaster response operations. The third is response phase, a coordinated response to contain disasters to prevent further fallout and finally the recovery and reconstruction phase – planned actions to minimise further fallout and reconstructing a normal functioning system.

In this paper we propose a framework called *Project Vision Support* (PVS) to model and visualise cascading effects resulting from the interconnections, interdependencies, and interactions between critical infrastructures. This framework can provide more detailed decision making criteria for crisis managers and be used for accurate automated planning and scheduling of emergency services in the event of a disaster. An initial prototype of this framework has been developed and used to visualise urban environments of an area on OpenStreetMap (OSM) [4] website and it has received many positive feedbacks from professionals and academics.

While critical infrastructure protection research has received a healthy attention from researchers in the past decade, to the best of our knowledge, there are not many research proposals in this field that make use of a combination of visualisation, planning, scheduling, artificial learning, prediction, and games technology. We believe the combination of these areas can greatly improve the quality of the decisions made by crisis managers. We will start our discussion with a review on related projects.

2 Review of Related Projects

The SAVE (Sustainability Assessment Visualisation and Enhancement) project visualises the interactions between society, environment, and economics, as well as the future possible consequences of the current behaviours through mathematical modelling of materials used in construction [5]. The simulation uses the analytic network process (ANP) methodology, a network built of elements, each having individual attributes (numerical interaction values with the world), and creates a *super matrix* containing initial judgements of these attribute values, and then using a pair-wise comparison against a *fundamental scale* (basically a table of judgments of the priority of the elements) to create a *comparison matrix* which is used to create the *eigenvectors* of each element. The *eigenvectors* are combined with the *super matrix* to create an *unweighted super matrix* which is then calculated with a final pair-wise matrix representing the interactions of the clusters of elements and the *eigenvectors* to give the final *weighted matrix*. This becomes the measurable priorities of the sustainability factors corresponding to objects in a real world. This matrix can be applied to objects in a virtual world through shader programs to visualise the colour changes. We would like to create something similar to this mathematical matrix representation of vulnerabilities in our framework to show areas which are subject to flooding or potential fire hazards.

ALLADIN (Autonomous Learning Agents for Decentralised Data and Information) is a project for the automated decision making of agents, particularly emergency service representations. The project has 3 main subcategories: Situational Awareness; RoboCup Rescue; and Evacuation. We would like to build upon the 2D representations of the project by applying the concepts and algorithms into the 3rd dimension.

3 Project Vision Support Framework

The Project Vision Support framework that we are developing combines the role of visualisation, planning, scheduling, artificial learning, prediction, and games technology in the critical infrastructure protection. The rationale of our approach is as follows:

Visualisation is an important factor in understanding the interdependencies between critical infrastructures. As detailed in [6], there are four types of interdependencies between infrastructures namely Physical, Geographical, Cyber and Logical. The first two are particularly important. Physical interdependencies consist of one infrastructures input being the output of another. If upset is caused to the output of an infrastructure which is used by other infrastructures, the cascading effects can ripple through the interconnections, snow-balling and causing unforeseen issues and further upsets. Geographical interdependencies relates to the locations of assets; be it personnel, server farms, access points etc. For example, a water mill is reliant on the flowing water of a river. If the water flow stops, then the internal infrastructure of the water mill will stall. Knowing the information of the surrounding geographical details will be critical for the accurate modelling and decision making of evacuation plans, also, supply and demand constraints between infrastructures. These interdependencies can be represented as a 3D visualisation of an area.

Furthermore, 3D visualisation can also be used to represent Population Mobility. Population Mobility models are especially interesting to our research and framework because it is the modelling of how entities move and interact within urban environments. This model has been used for the modelling electric power grids and wireless communications. We can use this model for traffic flow modelling and evacuation modelling with multiple transportation systems. Osogami et al. of IBM, model transportation systems in two categories: *microscopic* modelling tracks the individual details of vehicles such as location, and is often the most detailed description of traffic modelling but this addition of parameters means more computations; *macroscopic* is concerned with tracking the speed and flow of traffic but does not allow the study of minute changes in the traffic model [7]. We can apply these modelling types to all entities and parameters of our virtual world, to the fire resistance of materials for buildings, to the evacuation of humans in transport systems.

Planning, scheduling, artificial learning and prediction play an important role in critical infrastructure protection. They can be thought of as being completely separate or comprehensively entwined. Planning concerns itself with finding a sequence of actions for an initial state to a goal state. With planning, a difficulty is solving general purpose planning problems because of the complexity of inferring what a general problem is, and how it can be broken down into smaller problems and then converting these to commands to be executed. It is much easier to develop ad hoc techniques to solve particular problems [8]. Multiple algorithms and descriptive languages have been created to encapsulate planning: STRIPS, planning domain definition language (PDDL), action description language (ADL), a behaviour language (ABL) [9], Finite State Machines (FSM), Rule Based Systems (RBS), and many others. El-Rhalibi et al. evaluate the performance of multiple planning algorithms for use for digital interactive storytelling (DIS): Graphplan; SatPlan; Heuristic Search Planner (HSP); LPG-TD; Fast-Forward (FF); Metric-FF; Marvin; JSHOP2 [10]. They conclude that JSHOP2 produced the fastest solution in their test bed of a small story of medium complexity, in 0.021 s, with FF (0.023 s), Metric-FF (0.036 s) and Marvin (0.040 s) being very close in terms of speed. We believe a crisis situation is a story, a start, middle, and an end. We intend to build on top of the PDDL for more accurate descriptions of our specific domain of emergency services interactions. Scheduling is similar to planning but is concerned with creating a time dependent sequence, and this is where we feel the constraint satisfaction entwines with scheduling. For an action to trigger, pre checks must be done (will that calculation finish on time?). Orkin [11] states the benefits of goal oriented action planning (GOAP), and presents his modular regressive GOAP, built from the structure of PDDL, and has given great results for the automated planning of non-player characters (NPC) in commercial multi-million dollar games. He states regressive GOAP maps well to NPCs of games and also maps prioritisation of actions if multiple solutions are found to problems. The decoupling of the goals and actions allows for sharing of behaviours, thusly designers only need to write an action once and it is available for all types of agents. Orkin states their planner calculates accurate plans in real-time which is particularly interesting because the simulation we plan to create will be within a highly dynamic scene. We intend to include this type of hierarchical approach to planning in our framework for agents representing emergency services.

We have developed a prototype of the Project Vision Support framework to show the potentials of our approach. The prototype runs on Windows based machines and is programmed using the C# language utilising the Microsoft XNA framework with additional extension methods and classes. Addition libraries such as Awesomium [12] which allows integration of web platforms into.Net applications such as: Javascript, PHP, SQL, HTML5, and web access, and the Nuclex framework [13], an open source set assemble libraries which take care of low level code features such as multithreading and 3D text rendering, have been added, resulting in a procedurally generated 3D world harvesting real-world map data obtained from OSM website. Although the integration of map data is not streamlined, and multiple steps must be taken to include the files into the project solution in Visual Studio 2013, we believe the use of the Awesomium libraries will alleviate this pre-compiled multi-step process.

OSM is an open licensed world mapping project using local volunteers to map their surrounding areas, as well as input from GPS data and other donated services and sources. This community driven project can be kept up to date with their already implemented web and desktop mapping programs by anyone with a web connection and a supporting computer. To counter act the use of amateur mappers, OSM has created quality assurance tools to help created a better quality of OSM data. OSM has been used in academic and commercial projects in hundreds of websites and mobile applications and other devices.

Data from OSM is in XML format. It has four main elements: *Node* (a point on the Earth's surface using longitude and latitude values); *Way* (an order list of *nodes*, if the first *node* if the same as the last *node* in the list then this creates a boundary, such as the edges of a house); *Relations*; and *Tag* (extra information describing the node or way such as *Tag = Home*). The OSM XML document is serialised into class objects using the XSD tool. The loaded XML document is sorted and stored in lists of separate types obtained from the *Tag* attribute: buildings; government buildings; hospital boundaries; police boundaries; amenities; and roads of varying types (highways, residential, paths etc.).

During run time, a procedural content generation (PCG) technique is used to create 3D models from the information extracted from OSM. The technique is algorithmic and requires minimal or zero manual input. It works by extruding the 2D GPS data to create 3D models that represent the different buildings in the area. PCG has been used for making every aspect of a complete scene in a 3D game with varying accuracy. Figure 1 shows the prototype of the procedurally generated scene around the Liverpool Women Hospital. The visualisation runs at 47.78 frames per second on average and use 822,000 Kb of system memory. The image shows the hospital highlighted in red and educational areas highlighted in green. The buildings are created by extruding planes from the points within a *way* list, one by one, and used a triangulation algorithm for the creation of the rooftops. The roads are generated in a similar fashion, but needs to be extended with interpolation algorithms to create smooth curving roads.

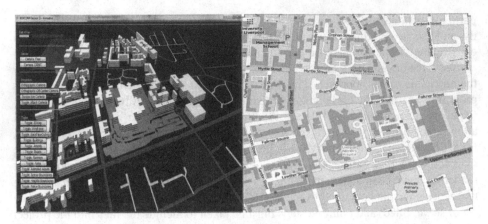

Fig. 1. (Left) Highlighted procedurally generated Liverpool's women's hospital and (Right) the 2D image obtained from OSM web portal of the same scene

4   Summary and Future Work

We have presented initial components which we intended to combine into a consolidated framework for helping and advising correct decision making for crisis managers. We have also presented an initial prototype capable of generating relatively realistic user selected environment from the global mapping service OSM. Further improvements to the prototype are planned as the research progresses.

On the user interface side, we intend to improve the frame rate and reduce the memory usage by means of culling techniques and advanced shaders. We plan to visualise the heuristic pathfinding solutions coupled with constraints such as road width, direction, and traffic density for accurate and realistic pathfinding plans for emergency services. This is made possible because the road network is built of nodes and they are compatible with the A-star pathfinding method.

Modelling the interconnections between entities and infrastructures and representing the visualisation with games technology has been accomplished with the GlassBox Engine [14]. The data-driven simulation integrates simulation units which act as representations of input/output infrastructures such as factories. Each unit has resources such as coal and when active produces power and pollution. The simulation rules trigger animation effect presenting a one to one representation of cause and effect. Addition modular components can be added to extend the functionality of the simulation unit. The units are tailoring to representing: economic loops, residential environments, industrial units, and commercial outlets. The engine is designed to contain tens of thousands of agents which carry the resources used and produced by the simulation units along directed paths. The agents trigger simulation rules when they arrive at their destination, manipulating data and visualising cause and effect. From observations of the simulations, the direction the agent takes is random choice, and the resource allocations are on a first come first serve basis. A issue with the simulation is the size of the map and the cube like nature of the resource and road network layout. We would like to build upon: the resource allocation techniques of agents for the prioritisation of constrained assets; the details of the map using real-world data as well as the scale of map representation.

The Project Vision Support framework that we are proposing is unique in a sense that there are not many existing work in critical infrastructure protection field that make use of a combination of visualisation, planning, scheduling, artificial learning, prediction, and games technology. Thus by doing so, we can greatly improve the quality of the decisions made by crisis managers.

Acknowledgments. This research is co-supported by the NSF key project with grant no (61332017) and the National project with grant no (2013BAH24F00).

References

1. Miller, A.: Trends in process control systems security. Secur. Priv. **3**(5), 57–60 (2005)
2. BCS, IT Now - Protecting Critical Infrastructure, IT Now - Summer, pp. 32–33 (2014). http://www.bcs.org/content/conWebDoc/53064
3. Michalowski, W., Kersten, G., Koperczak, Z., Szpakowicz, S.: Disaster management with NEGOPLAN. Expert Syst. Appl. **2**(2–3), 107–120 (1991)
4. OpenStreetMap.com (2014). http://www.openstreetmap.org/#map=0/-85/-142. Accessed 25 May 2015
5. Falconer, R.E., Isaacs, J., Blackwood, D.J., Gilmour, D.: Enhancing urban sustainability using 3D visualisation. Proc. ICE-Urban Des. Plan. **164**(3), 163–173 (2011)
6. Rinaldi, S.: Modeling and simulating critical infrastructures and their interdependencies. In: Proceedings of the 37th Annual Hawaii International Conference on System Sciences (2004)
7. Osogami, T., Imamichi, T., Mizuta, H., Suzumura, T., Ide, T.: Toward simulating entire cities with behavioral models of traffic. IBM J. Res. Dev. **57**(5), 6:1–6:10 (2013)
8. Barták, R., Salido, M., Rossi, F.: Constraint satisfaction techniques in planning and scheduling. J. Intell. Manuf. **21**(1), 1–12 (2010)
9. Mateas, M., Stern, A.: A behavior language for story-based believable agents. IEEE Intell. Syst. **17**(4), 39–47 (2002)
10. El Rhalibi, A., Goudoulakis, E.; Merabti, M.: DIS planning algorithms evaluation. In: 2012 Consumer Communication Networking Conference (CCNC), pp. 492–496. IEEE (2012)
11. Orkin, J.: Symbolic representation of game world state: Toward real-time planning in games. In: AAAI Workshop Challenges Game AI (2004)
12. Awesomium HTML UI Engine. http://www.awesomium.com/. Accessed 25 May 2015
13. Nuclex Framework. https://nuclexframework.codeplex.com/. Accessed 25 May 2015
14. GlassBox Engine. http://www.ea.com/uk/sim-city/videos/glassbox-game-engine. Accessed 25 May 2015

Nonlocal and Nonlinear
Model in Image Editing Technique

Yanxia Bao[1,2]([✉]), Yang Shen[1,2], and Xinting Wang[1,2]

[1] Engineering and Design School, Lishui University,
Lishui, People's Republic of China
754389598@qq.com
[2] Digital Media and HCI Research Center,
Hangzhou Normal University, Hangzhou, People's Republic of China

Abstract. One of the most important problems in image editing applications is how to preserve the important structure of image.Local linear model is widely applied to image editing application such as image filter, alpha matting. It preserves the local linear structure in image which describes the local feature of image.

In this paper, we propose the nonlocal nonlinear model in image editing method. In the nonlocal area of image, nonlinear structure is extracted from images by least square method and kernel trick.Different from local linear model, nonlocal nonlinear model can represent the nonlinear structure in nonlocal area of image. It can be widely applied to image denoising, image upsampling, alpha matting. Results show our model is effective.

Keywords: Image editing · Image upsampling · Kernel methods

1 Introduction

Image editing is an important research area in computer vision and image processing technique. In recent years, local linear model is widely applied to image editing applications such as image filter,alpha matting. For example, closed form matting assumes the alpha value in local area of image satisfy the local linear model. Guided filter assumes the output of filter is the linear form of pixels in guidance image. All those methods assume the pixels in local neighbor area of image can be represented by linear form.

However, if the local linear model fails in special conditions, the application could not achieve perfect results. In this paper, we expand the local linear model to nonlocal nonlinear model. Different from the general local linear model defined on gray of pixels, nonlocal nonlinear model is defined on the nonlocal feature of

Y. Bao—Project supported by the Zhejiang Provincial Natural Science Foundation of China (No. LY13F020019), and is co-supported by the NSF key project with grant no (61332017) and the National project with grant no (2013BAH24F00).

Y.-J. Zhang (Ed.): ICIG 2015, Part III, LNCS 9219, pp. 552–561, 2015.
DOI: 10.1007/978-3-319-21969-1_50

image, and assume that the feature of image in each nonlocal area satisfy the nonlinear model, which can be seen as the extension of local linear model.

In the further discussion, many applications is introduced based on nonlocal nonlinear model, such as image filter and image upsampling and alpha matting. With the nonlocal nonlinear model, we show that our method can achieve better results. Our method can be widely applied to image denoising [1], upsamping [2], alpha matting [3–5]. Results show our filter is effective.

2 Related Work

Image editing is the important technique in image processing, including alpha matting, image filter, etc. In recent years, local linear model is widely applied to image editing application to get the optimizational results. It is one of the most important assumptions in the image editing method.

Levin et al. [6] proposed a new colorization method by using the local linear model, they assume the color in each small neighbor area satisfy the linear structure. This idea was expanded to alpha matting. Levin et al. [7] assume that the alpha value satisfy the local linear model in each small neighbor area. However, when alpha value do not satisfy the local linear model, closed form matting could not get effective results. In the area that foreground and background color is hard to propagate, local model also fail to work. Different from Levin's work [7], we assume the alpha value satisfy the nonlinear model in K nearest neighbor(KNN). Compared with old method, our nonlocal model achieves more effective results.

Image filter is widely applied to image editing application. Early image filters focus on how to maintain the edge of image such as bilateral filter [8]. Current image filter techniques aim to maintaining the important structure of image such as edges. Geodesic filter [9] maintains the edge structure of image by preserving the geodesic distance. Adaptive filter [10,11] proposed a realtime high dimension filter based on adaptive manifolds. All those works focus on how to implement a high efficient filter and preserve the edge structure.

The edges can also be looked as a kind of local structure in image. We think an effective filter should preserve the local structure of image which reflect the relationship of neighbor pixels. He et al. [12] proposed guided filter based on guidance image.In this paper, we expand the guided filter by using the non-local nonlinear model instead of local linear model, and preserve the nonlocal nonlinear structure in target image.

By the local nonlinear model, we also propose a new image upsampling method. Different from traditional upsampling method such as Bicubic interpolation, our method is based on fitting, assume each neighbor area in image satisfy the nonlinear structure, so we can learn the nonlinear structure from low resolution image, and interpolate the subpixels by nonlinear structure. This method is not sensitive to noise and achieve smooth results. Experiment results show our method is effective.

3   Alpha Matting with Nonlocal and Nonlinear Learning Model

In local linear model of alpha matting,the following linear equation is assumed in local neighbor of each pixels.

$$\alpha_i = X^T \beta_1 + \beta_2 \tag{1}$$

where X is the data vector of gray value of pixels in each local area.

Similar with the learning based matting [13] and KNN matting [5]. The nonlinear model is used instead of local linear model. Nonlocal area model is used instead of local area model.

We assume the *alpha* value in KNN neighbor satisfy the following nonlinear equation. Each pixels in KNN tree is defined by five dimension vector:(r, g, b, x, y).x, y is the spatial position of pixels in image. In each KNN neighbor, the alpha value of pixel i satisfy the following nonlinear equation:

$$\alpha_i = f(x_i) = \Phi(X)^T . \beta \tag{2}$$

where $\Phi(X)$ is the date vector of nonlinear functions $\Phi(x)$, x is the r, g, b channels of pixels in KNN neighbor of pixel i. Formula 2 can be seen as the expansion form of formula 1,

The coefficient β can be solved by following formula:

$$argmin \| \alpha_i - \Phi(X_i) . \begin{bmatrix} \beta_1 \\ \beta_2 \end{bmatrix} \|^2 + \lambda \begin{bmatrix} \beta_1 \\ \beta_2 \end{bmatrix}^2 \tag{3}$$

$$\begin{bmatrix} \beta_1 \\ \beta_2 \end{bmatrix} = \Phi(X_i) . (\Phi(X_i) \Phi(X_i)^T + \lambda I)^{-1} \alpha_i \tag{4}$$

Substituting the β to formula 2. The formula 1 can be expanded to following equation:

$$f(x_i) = \Phi(x)^T . \beta$$
$$= (\Phi(X_i)^T . \Phi(X_i) + \lambda I_m)^{-1} \Phi(X_i) . \Phi(x_i) . f(X_i) \tag{5}$$

Notice that the formula 5 is decided by the inner product of two data vectors kernel functions $K(x_1, x_2)$ is used to represent the inner product by kernel trick.

$$K_i(X_i, X_i) = \Phi(X_i)^T . \Phi(X_i) K_i(x_i, x_j) = \Phi(x_i) . \Phi(x_j) \tag{6}$$

$K_i(X_i, X_i)$ is the matrix represented by following formula:

$$K_i(X_i, X_i) = \begin{bmatrix} k(x'_{\tau 1}, x'_{\tau 1}) & \cdots & k(x'_{\tau 1}, x'_{\tau m}) \\ \cdots & \cdots & \cdots \\ k(x'_{\tau m}, x'_{\tau 1}) & \cdots & k(x'_{\tau m}, x'_{\tau m}) \end{bmatrix} \tag{7}$$

where $k(x_i, x_j)$ is the kernel function in machine learning.

$$\alpha_i = f(x_i)$$
$$= (K_i + \lambda_r I)^{-1} k_i).f(X_i) \qquad (8)$$
$$= \kappa(x_i).f(X_i) = \kappa(x_i).\overline{\alpha_i}$$

Formula 8 provides the linear relation between the α_i and the alpha value of neighbor pixels. It leads to the closed form solution for alpha matting. Since the Gaussian kernel always get hard edges [5] in alpha matting, the polynomial kernel is used instead of gaussian kernel which can get smooth results in alpha matte. Compared with closed form matting and KNN matting, Fig. 1 show that our method can get better results.

In Fig. 1, closed form matting could not eliminate the characters in background with local model, which details are shown in Fig. 2. KNN matting [5] and CMM matting [14] eliminated the characters, but do not eliminate the noise around the hair with linear model. Our method is nonlinear and nonlocal, it get the better alpha matte in Fig. 2d and f.

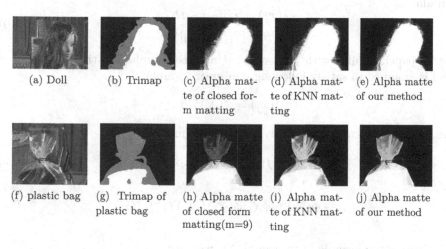

(a) Doll　(b) Trimap　(c) Alpha matte of closed form matting　(d) Alpha matte of KNN matting　(e) Alpha matte of our method

(f) plastic bag　(g) Trimap of plastic bag　(h) Alpha matte of closed form matting(m=9)　(i) Alpha matte of KNN matting　(j) Alpha matte of our method

Fig. 1. Alpha matting by nonlocal and nonlinear model.

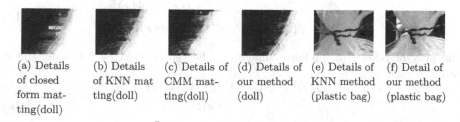

(a) Details of closed form matting(doll)　(b) Details of KNN matting(doll)　(c) Details of CMM matting(doll)　(d) Details of our method (doll)　(e) Details of KNN method (plastic bag)　(f) Detail of our method (plastic bag)

Fig. 2. The details of alpha matte by different method.

4 Learning Based Filter with Nonlinear Model

In this section, the learning based filter is defined by nonlinear model. For a giving image I, the filtering output at pixel i is the weighted average of local neighbor pixels in image I, which is represented by following formula:

$$I'_i = F_i.\dot{I}_i \tag{9}$$

$\dot{I}_i$ is the data vector of pixels around the pixel i, F_i is the weight vector of the filter, which should be designed to maintain the feature of image. In this paper, the weight F_i is solved by learning from guidance image.

Let the feature of pixel i in guidance image be represented by d dimension vector x_i. The feature can be represented by (R, G, B) channels of pixels. For the pixel $i \in \Omega_i$, and $\Omega_i = [\tau_1, \tau_2, \tau_3...\tau_m]$ include the m neighbor pixels around the i. X_i is the $m * d$ matrix which describe the features of pixels in Ω_i. We denote $X_i = [x_{\tau_1}, x_{\tau_2}, x_{\tau_3}...x_{\tau_m}]$.

Let the gray of pixel i be $f(x_i)$, guided filter assume the $f(x_j)$ in Ω_i of guidance image satisfy the local linear model, which is represented by following formula:

$$f(x_j) = x_j.\beta, j \in \Omega_i$$
$$\beta = [\beta_1, \beta_2...\beta_d]^T \tag{10}$$

In this paper, similar with nonlocal and nonlinear alpha matting, the gray of pixel is assumed to satisfy following nonlinear formula:

$$f(x_j) = \Phi(X)^T.\beta \tag{11}$$

The coefficient β can be solved by least square method:

$$\beta = \arg min\|f(X_i) - \Phi(X_i).\beta\|^2 + \gamma\|\beta\|^2 \tag{12}$$

$$\beta = \Phi(X_i).(\Phi(X_i)\Phi(X_i)^T + \lambda I)^{-1}.f(x_i) \tag{13}$$

Substituting the formula 13 to formula 11, we have

$$f(x_i) = \Phi(x)^T.\beta$$
$$= (\Phi(X_i)^T.\Phi(X_i) + \lambda_r I_m)^{-1}\Phi(X_i).\Phi(x_i).f(X_i) \tag{14}$$

The gray of pixel i in guidance image can be represented by following linear form:

$$f(x_i) = (K_i + \lambda_r I_m^{-1})k_i.f(X_i)$$
$$= \kappa(x_i).f(X_i) \tag{15}$$
$$\kappa(x_i) = (K_i + \lambda_r I_m^{-1})k_i$$

where $\kappa(x_i)$ is the vector which describes the local structure of guidance image.

Assuming the local structure of input image is similar with that of guidance image, the output of filter can be represented by following formula:

$$I_i^{t'} = \kappa(x_i).\dot{I}_i^t \tag{16}$$

where $\dot{I}_i^t$ is the data vector of pixels around the pixel i in the input image, and $\kappa(x_i)$ is the structure coefficient learned from guidance image.

We apply our nonlinear model to all windows which contain the pixel i in the input image. In each different windows we can get the different output of pixel i. the simple strategy is to average all the different value in different windows ω_k.

Let $f(x_i, x_j)$ be the j_{th} data in data vector $\kappa(x_i)$. The weight of filter in formula 9 can be represented by following formula:

$$F_i^j = \sum_{(i,j)\in\omega_k} (f(x_i, x_j)), \forall i \in \omega_k \tag{17}$$

4.1   Guided Filter and the Learning Based Filter

In learning based filter, the feature of image can be represented by different forms. Let the feature be defined by $x' = [I, 1]$. I is the gray of pixels. By assuming the linear model is satisfied in each small windows, formula 11 can be substituted by following formula:

$$I = x^T \beta_1 + \beta_2 = x^T \begin{bmatrix} \beta_1 \\ \beta_2 \end{bmatrix} \tag{18}$$

So we can get following formula by least square problem:

$$\begin{bmatrix} \beta_1 \\ \beta_2 \end{bmatrix} = \arg min \| I_i - X_i. \begin{bmatrix} \beta_1 \\ \beta_2 \end{bmatrix} \|^2 + \gamma \begin{bmatrix} \beta_1 \\ 0 \end{bmatrix}^2$$

$$X_i = \begin{bmatrix} I_1 & 1 \\ I_2 & 1 \\ ... \\ I_m & 1 \end{bmatrix} \tag{19}$$

Notice that the formula 18 is the local linear model represented in [7, 12]. Formula 18 is the same as that in guided filter, so guided filter can be seemed as the special case of learning based filter.

However, our method is quite different from guided filter. Guided filter is based on local linear model, the learning based filter is based on learning and can be expanded to nonlinear model and nonlocal model, it can not only be defined on gray of pixels, but also be defined on feature of image.

In Fig. 4, we show the results of different filters. It is clear that our method and guided filter get better results. Without guidance image, adaptive manifold filter could not preserve the edge with heavy noise. Domain interpolation filter also could not eliminate the noise when the noise is heavy. Because our method

Fig. 3. The image with noises and the guidance image

learn the nonlinear structure from guidance image, our filter can get good results even with heavy noise. Comparing with polynomial kernel, gaussian kernel is effective in maintaining the edge, we find that learning based filter can maintain the texture and edge very well (Fig. 3).

5   Image Upsampling by Learning

From previous section, we know that our method can extract the nonlinear structure from nonlocal area of image. This nonlinear structure can help us to upsample the image.

Let the gray of pixel i be represented by $f(x_i)$. Different from that of alpha matting, x_i is the x and y coordinates of pixel i in image. X_i is the $2*m$ matrix,each row in X_i contains the coordinate of a pixel around the pixel i.

Assuming the pixels i in local area of low resolution image satisfy $f(x_i) = \Phi(X_i)^T.\beta$, then $f(x)$ can be learned by local nonlinear model in low resolution image. Similar with that in alpha matting and learning based filter, with the known pixels in X_i, $f(x_i)$ can be solved by following formula:

$$f(x_i) = (K_i + \lambda_r I)^{-1} k_i.f(X_i) \tag{20}$$

$$K_i = \begin{bmatrix} k(x'_{\tau 1}, x'_{\tau 1}) & ... & k(x'_{\tau 1}, x'_{\tau m}) \\ ... & ... & ... \\ k(x'_{\tau m}, x'_{\tau 1}) & ... & k(x'_{\tau m}, x'_{\tau m}) \end{bmatrix} \tag{21}$$

We use gaussian kernel function. It is defined by following formula.

$$k(x, y) = \gamma.exp(-\|x - y\|^2) \tag{22}$$

where $\|x - y\|^2$ is the Euclidean distance of two pixels x, y. In low resolution image, X_i is the data vector of pixels with integer coordinates in small windows. To upsample the image, we only need to calculate the gray of pixels in fractional coordinates. Since the pixels in X_i is known, the gray of pixels in fractional coordinates can be easy to calculate by formula 20.

(a) Adaptive man- (b) Domain inter- (c) Learning based (d) Guided filer
ifold filter   polation filter   filer

Fig. 4. Image denoising with guidance image.

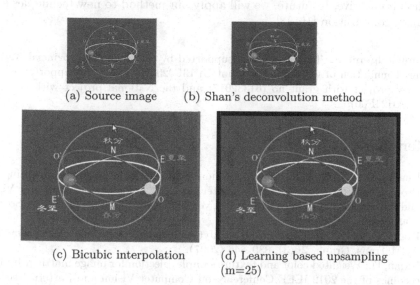

(a) Source image   (b) Shan's deconvolution method

(c) Bicubic interpolation   (d) Learning based upsampling
                                    (m=25)

Fig. 5. Image upsampling by learning filter.

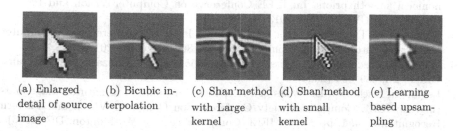

(a) Enlarged   (b) Bicubic in-   (c) Shan'method   (d) Shan'method   (e) Learning
detail of source terpolation   with Large   with small   based upsam-
image   kernel   kernel   pling

Fig. 6. The details of upsampling image.

In figure 6, we show the details of different upsampling methods. In Fig. 6b, Bicubic interpolation could not get smooth results around the arrow. The noise around the arrow is amplified by interpolation. Shan's method is based on deconvolution. Large kernel in Fig. 6c leads to ring artifacts. Small kernel produces noises around arrow in Fig. 6d. Learning based upsampling method learns the linear information including edges from low solution image. It achieves smooth results, which are better than other methods (Fig. 5).

6   Conclusion

In this paper, a new image editing is proposed based on learning. This method can be applied to image denoising and image upsampling. Results show that the method is effective. In future, we will apply our method to new techniques such as image composition [15–18]

Acknowledgement. This research is supported by the Zhejiang Provincial Natural Science Foundation of China, under grant LY13F020019, and is co-supported by the NSF key project with grant no (61332017) and the National project with grant no (2013BAH24F00).

References

1. Buades, A., Coll, B., Morel, J.-M.: A non-local algorithm for image denoising. In: Proceedings of the 2005 IEEE Computer Society Conference on Computer Vision and Pattern Recognition (CVPR 2005), vol. 02, pp. 60–65. IEEE Computer Society, Washington, DC (2005)
2. Kopf, J., Cohen, M.F., Lischinski, D., Uyttendaele, M.: Joint bilateral upsampling. ACM Trans. Graph. **26**(3), 839–846 (2007)
3. Rajan, D.: Weighted color and texture sample selection for image matting. In: Proceedings of the 2012 IEEE Conference on Computer Vision and Pattern Recognition (CVPR 2012), pp. 718–725. IEEE Computer Society, Washington, DC (2012)
4. Chen, X., Zhou, D., Zhou, S.Z., Zhao, Q., Tan, P.: Image matting with local and nonlocal smooth priors. In: IEEE Conference on Computer Vision and Pattern Recognition (CVPR), June 2013
5. Chen, Q., Li, D., Tang, C.-K.: Knn matting. In: IEEE Conference on Computer Vision and Pattern Recognition (CVPR), pp. 869–876, June 2012
6. Dani, A.L., Lischinski, D., Weiss, Y.: Colorization using optimization. ACM Trans. Graph. **23**, 689–694 (2004)
7. Levin, A., Lischinski, D., Weiss, Y.: A closed form solution to natural image matting. In: IEEE Computer Society Conference on Computer Vision and Pattern Recognition, vol. 1, pp. 61–68. IEEE Computer Society, Washington, DC (2006)
8. Tomasi, C., Manduchi, R.: Bilateral filtering for gray and color images. In: Proceedings of the Sixth International Conference on Computer Vision, ICCV 1998, pp. 839-846. IEEE Computer Society, Washington, DC (1998)
9. Criminisi, A., Sharp, T., Rother, C., P'erez, P.: Geodesic image and video editing. ACM Trans. Graph. **29**(5), 134:1–134:15 (2010)

10. Gastal, E.S.L., Oliveira, M.M.: Adaptive manifolds for real-time high-dimensional filtering. ACM Trans. Graph. **31**(4), 33:1–33:13 (2012)
11. Gastal, E.S.L., Oliveira, M.M.: Domain transform for edge-aware image and video processing. ACM Trans. Graph. **30**(4), 69:1–69:12 (2011)
12. He, K., Sun, J., Tang, X.: Guided image filtering. In: Daniilidis, K., Maragos, P., Paragios, N. (eds.) ECCV 2010, Part I. LNCS, vol. 6311, pp. 1–14. Springer, Heidelberg (2010)
13. Zheng, Y., Kambhamettu, C.: Learning based digital matting. In: IEEE 12th International Conference on Computer Vision, ICCV 2009, Kyoto, Japan, pp. 889–896. IEEE, 27 September– 4 October 2009
14. Shi, Y., Au, O.C., Pang, J., Tang, K., Sun, W., Zhang, H., Zhu, W., Jia, L.: Color clustering matting. In: ICME, pp. 1–6. IEEE (2013)
15. Chen, X., Zou, D., Zhao, Q., Tan, P.: Manifold preserving edit propagation. ACM Trans. Graph. **31**(6), 132:1–132:7 (2012)
16. Wang, J.: Image matting with transductive inference. In: Gagalowicz, A., Philips, W. (eds.) MIRAGE 2011. LNCS, vol. 6930, pp. 239–250. Springer, Heidelberg (2011)
17. Shen, Y., Lin, X., Gao, Y., Sheng, B., Liu, Q.: Video composition by optimized 3D mean-value coordinates. Comput. Animat. Virtual Worlds **23**(3–4), 179–190 (2012)
18. Gao, Y., Chen, Z.H., Chen, M.G., Shen, Y.: An improved approach to the efficient construction of and search operations in motion graphs. Sci. China Inf. Sci. **55**(5), 1042–1051 (2012)

Mesh Extraction from a Regular Grid Structure Using Adjacency Matrix

David Tully[1], Abdennour El Rhalibi[1,2(✉)], Zhigeng Pan[2],
Christopher Carter[1], and Sud Sudirman[1]

[1] School of Computing and Mathematical Sciences, Liverpool John Moores
University, Liverpool, UK
dtully@2008.ljmu.ac.uk, {A.Elrhalibi, c.j.carter,
S.Sudirman}@ljmu.ac.uk
[2] Digital Media and HCI Research Center, Hangzhou Normal University,
Hangzhou, People's Republic of China
zgpan@hznu.edu.cn

Abstract. Crisis management is a modern phenomenon brought about by natural disasters and acts of terrorism. Building a modern crisis management response program needs a multi-disciplinary architecture and accurate, up-to-date, real-world data. The creation of virtual environments depicting critical infrastructure buildings and conduits between these highly interconnected man-made structures is a complex procedure. The crossover between games technology and use of real-world map data for real-world simulations is becoming more common with the advancements of computer hardware and software, and the accuracy of real-world map data. However, there are many problems with using real-world map data for simulation due to the large potential of missing and error prone data involved in this big data. Within this work we use three types of data sets; Ordnance Survey data, LiDAR data, and OpenStreetMap data to provide accurate map and 3D environment information for crisis management systems. Combining these large data-sets can reduce errors and retrieve missing data for use within a modern game engine for visualization analysis. We propose a novel technique for data extraction using adjacency matrices for custom model generation corresponding to real-world structures such as landscapes, buildings, road systems, area boundaries, or a combination of these at different resolutions.

Keywords: Crisis management · Adjacency matrix · Computer games · Visualization

1 Introduction

For the creation of a modern crisis management tool to aid crisis managers, as proposed by [1], needs accurate up-to-date data and advanced visualization techniques for the interacting and displaying of large complex layering of multiple data-sets to the crisis manager. A modern visualization system depicting up-to-date, accurate information is needed when dealing with large interconnected real-world scenes. For example, the first responders of a crisis event would be helped if they had a 3D visualization of the

© Springer International Publishing Switzerland 2015
Y.-J. Zhang (Ed.): ICIG 2015, Part III, LNCS 9219, pp. 562–572, 2015.
DOI: 10.1007/978-3-319-21969-1_51

infrastructures surrounding the affected area such as buildings and especially the conduits connecting a highly dense area [2–5]. Having a system which can combine multiple data-sets and produce accurate terraformed scenes for crisis managers to interact and understand unseen scenarios and landscapes is critical for making the best possible plans to solve the crisis. The use of a modern computer game engine can provide high level API's for the generation of large, highly realistic visualized real-world scenes. The use of this hardware and software is relatively cheap in current time, and destined to become even cheaper. In contrast, the availability of accurate real-world data is often extremely expensive and difficult to obtain. Combining games technology and real-world large data-sets is a difficult task in itself, due to the large differences between the data-sets and the choices of hardware and software available. Another issue is the high level of training needed to use this hardware and software. Generating large realistic scene within virtual environments needs custom algorithms to produce scenes which can run at a minimum of 30 frames-per-second. Triangulation techniques such as Delaunay triangulation has been used to reduce the potential vertex and triangle generation in models in computer games, thus reducing calculations. Using adjacency matrices and uniform 2D grids of accurate data, we can remove the use of complex triangulation algorithms to reduce highly dense shaped objects.

Within this paper we discuss procedures needed to produce accurate complete data-sets for the extraction of custom model meshes obtained by the use of adjacency matrices with use with uniform 2D grids. This technique combines 3 data-sets; Ordnance Survey data UK, LiDAR data, and OpenStreetMap.Org data.

The structure of the paper is as follows: In Sect. 2, we discuss the concept of crisis management. In Sect. 3 we present some of the data we use in our approach based on Ordnance Survey and LiDAR data. In Sect. 4, we introduce the map data we use based on OpenStreetMap data. In Sect. 5, we discuss the Interpolation and combination of data-sets. In Sect. 6, we introduce our technique based on artefact extraction using adjacency matrices. In Sect. 7, we present the effect and accuracy of different interpolation techniques of on our extraction approach when changing the resolution of the map data. In section we conclude the paper.

2 Crisis Management

Critical infrastructures surround our daily lives; be it transportation, financial transactions, water, gas, electricity, the internet. They are the backbone to our way of life. If upset is caused to one of these highly interconnected infrastructures, it can have unpredictable disastrous consequences which can cascade through all connected infrastructures. A train carrying hazardous materials crashed in 2001 in the USA [6]. The cascading effects consisted of multiple fires, a burst water pipe which flooded local streets which in turn short circuited local electricity supplies, preventing the use of local communication systems such as telephones. 1200 homes were affected for many days.

Having a modern crisis management tool capable of displaying connections and visualize highly accurate real world urban environments with minimal errors within data-sets can provide crisis managers with specific in sites into unfamiliar territory. Our techniques proposed can allow the extraction of specific map data which can then be used in a layered fashion allowing the user to see; landscapes, buildings, road systems, area boundaries, or a combination of these at different resolutions.

3 Ordnance Survey and LiDAR Data

Ordnance survey (OS) data is acquired through the UK government web portals. The data in use by our procedures represents height points on the terrain of the UK. Each point is contained in text file. Each file covers 10 km^2 containing 200^2 points which are 50 m apart. This large distance in sampling data provides large potential for increased errors rates and missing artefacts from scenes. Light detection and ranging (LiDAR) tries to improve this by sampling height data obtained by projecting light beams from a low flying plane and records the time the light beam takes to bounce from the ground to the plane. This creates height points accurate to within 5 to 15 cm margin of error. LiDAR data is provided in two formats; digital-terrain-model and digital-surface- model. LiDAR has trouble reflecting off water and penetrating bio-material such as trees and shrubberies which introduces error. Another issue with LiDAR is the expense of obtaining accurate data and the large amount of data produced. An estimated 113.2 terabytes of storage needed to store a complete set of 4 spatial resolutions of LiDAR maps; 2 m, 1 m, 0.5 m, and 0.25 m sampling points, covering the UK. Interpolation techniques can be utilized to up sample data to generate missing data points but will introduce small amounts of error. An added benefit of this will be lower storage facilities will be needed. The maps produced can be used by a modern game engine to create accurate terraformed landscapes. Within this work we propose a novel mesh extraction technique for the extraction of artefacts regular complete data sets. The large data-sets of real-world data is a difficult challenge for a multiple of reasons, be it data storage; LiDAR coverage for the UK in 4 spatial resolutions; 2 m, 1 m, 0.5 m 0.25 m point sampling. The data we use **has been** donated by Geomatics-group[1]. They process the raw data with multiple techniques to produce two separate models; the digital-terrain-model (DTM) and the digital-surface-model (DSM). A DTM is the terrain of a map not including structures such buildings, trees, pylons etc. while a DSM contains all assets of an environment. The DSM maps have a distinct problem of capturing movable objects such as birds which introduce high spike of error within a scene. This creates visually inaccurate scenes but also, if spatial analysis is performed on the DSM map, this can produce cascading errors within procedures.

4 OpenStreetMap Data

OpenStreetMap[2] (OSM) is a worldwide open source platform for mapping local areas. The user generated data is often more up-to-date than the likes of Google maps[3] which can be 4 years out of date for rural areas. This is a problem for generating accurate

---

[1] https://www.geomatics-group.co.uk.

[2] https://www.openstreetmap.org.

[3] https://www.google.co.uk/.

virtual scenes. OSM provides object types which specify the longitude and latitude locations of points on the Earth's surface. OSM contains 4 main types of object: *node* which represents a single location; *way* which represent an open or closed list of *nodes* which is used for building boundaries and road systems; *relation* which adds information between a multiple of *ways* or *nodes*; and *tag* which is a key-value object which states what the *node* or *way* represents. Using this data we have created large visualizations of real-world cities. Figure 1 shows our procedurally generated city of Manchester in UK covering 1,277 km^2 area.

Fig. 1. Left OpenStreetMap.Org screen shot of part of Manchester UK. Right procedurally generated navigable virtual scene of the complete Manchester OSM file 1,277 km^2

5 Interpolation and Combination of Data-Sets

To generate complete maps used for mesh extraction, complete data sets are needed. In this section we will cover problems which are common within these data-sets and procedures needed to reduce or remove these errors. For building mesh extraction we will be using the DSM maps of the LiDAR data-set. As stated this map type can have multiple errors within it, from flocks of birds producing large spikes of error data, to missing sections of data due to the light beams not being able to bounce off water or produce accurate readings through bio-material. Combining data from the DTM with the DSM maps can fill in missing data but if data is missing from the DTM map then data can be retrieved from a lower resolution map. The OS maps are the lowest resolution maps available. Interpolation must be done to produce a resolution according to the DTM/DSM map we are creating it for, in this case it will be OS map at 50 m resolution to LiDAR 2 m resolution. The use of multiple interpolation techniques to interpolate to a higher resolution is discussed in a later section.

Working with DSM maps which have missing data spanning a buildings edge is a special case for interpolation. Using OSM building boundary data, the edges of the buildings can be determined within the LiDAR maps. Using these boundaries we can interpolate or duplicate data contained within the boundary, or use a smoothing technique commonly found in image processing techniques [7]. If no data is within a boundary, because either data is missing from the LiDAR data or the LiDAR data is out of date, then this is process which is needed to be completed for future work.

It is needed to be stated that OSM provides longitude and latitude locations projected in EPSG:3857[4] schema. Working with GIS systems, this projection schema is not a problem, but combining it with the ordnance survey national grid reference scheme uses by OS and LiDAR data, is an issue due to their projection differences. However, tools are available to convert from one to another[5].

6 Artefact Extraction Using Adjacency Matrices

The DSM LiDAR maps contain all assets within an environment which are captured at data acquisition time, be it pylons, cars, birds, buildings, and other artefacts. A DTM map visualized within a modern game engine at the highest resolution of 0.25 m covering 1 km^2 contains 16 million vertices. The need of an extraction process is required to extract specific artefacts from a DSM to then use to place it on top of the DTM. If the DTM is visualized at the same resolution, this will use 16 million vertices, and plus the vertices added from the extraction process. The user can state at what resolution the DTM needs to be viewed at. There are many level of detail algorithms for large polygon reduction rates for use with large open scenes [8–10]. These algorithms reduce the polygon count but for intricate artefact structures such as churches, high detail is needed for realism and also spatial boundary analysis. Extracting mesh data for specific object, we can remove potential erroneous movable objects. Categorized map layers can be placed on top of the DTM to create a more accurate representation of real-world scenes which reduce model imperfections.

After maps have been preprocessed to check completeness, artefact extraction can take place. The following statements will focus on building extraction, but can be used for any boundary positions. Using OSM data to map the boundaries of buildings, we can use adjacency matrices to extract specific data points from the regular 2D grid of the LiDAR map. Adjacency matrices are multi-dimensional array stating the adjacency connections of objects[6].

The algorithm proceeds as follows:

Convert the building or artefact boundary points we wish to extract from OSM projection to OS national grid reference schema.

Create a 2D array of same width and height of the LiDAR map which will contain 0 s and 1 s populated by the next process.

Loop through all the points of the LiDAR map and if the point is contained within the boundary if the converted OSM artefact, then within the empty 2D array at the same index, insert a 1, else insert a 0. This will create a new array containing only 0 s, and 1 s containing only the LiDAR data points obtaining to that artefact.

The next process is to convert those points to a model mesh. This is done by looping through the 2D array of 0 s and 1 s.

For simplicity and explanation in accordance with the diagrams, we will depict the starting index of the 2D array as the top-left point of the map. This is how the data points are formulated with the LiDAR, which is confusing due to OS national grid reference starts at the bottom left of maps.

Looping through, the algorithm will check if each point is either a 0 or 1. If it is 1, then the adjacency matrices will be generated. Two matrices will be generated. The first matrix will contain the points to the left, to the bottom, and diagonally bottom left. The second will contain the right, bottom right, and bottom surrounding points. Figure 3 shows the adjacency matrices generated.

To generate triangle within the vertex array used within a game engine or model for a CAD drawing, we need to create a technique which can loop through points and decide to generate a triangle in a certain position and orientation as to always extract complete sets without missing potential points. This is a complex task. For example, given 4 vertices to make a polygon there are 2 ways to orientate the triangle. For the procedural extraction of points the triangles need to be orientated and positioned in a specific order as to eliminate future complications. Figure 2 shows the triangle orientations needed. The left side shows a purple triangle (top left) generated if the first matrix contains points top left, top right, bottom right. If only the bottom left, bottom right and top right then the yellow triangle will be generated. If all points are within the matrix then the purple triangle will be generated. See the right side of Fig. 2 for the configurations needed to generate the other triangles.

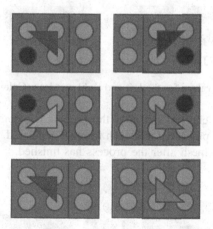

Fig. 2. Triangle orientation and placement

The matrices contain 0 s and 1 s which are converted to a binary sequence. The sequence will be ordered as stated in Fig. 3. Within the figure the binary sequence will be 0010 which equals 2.

Figure 4 shows the combinations of binary sequence values for matrices generated for the left and right matrices. The algorithm runs the value through an if-else statement to generate the corresponding triangles. For example, if the left matrix is equal to 11 or

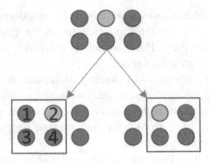

Fig. 3. Two adjacency matrices generated from specific point. Left matrix contains points to the left, bottom left, and bottom of the point. Right matrix contains points to the right, bottom right and bottom of the point.

15 then generate the purple triangle; else if the value is equal to 14 generate the yellow triangle. For the right matrix, if the value is equal to 13 or 15, generate the orange triangle, else if the value is equal to 7 then generate the green triangle.

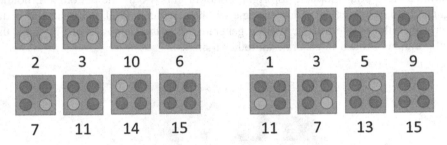

Fig. 4. Binary values for the left and right matrices (Color figure online).

Figure 5 shows the end product after the process has completed. The left image shows each point being processed and each triangle generated. The right image shows the complete polygonal mesh after the process has finished.

Fig. 5. Example of a complete map after matrix analysis and triangle generation. Left depicts the individual triangles after each process. Right is the end model mesh.

Fig. 6. Procedural city generation of part of New York Manhattan containing buildings, roads, and rail networks

Within each point being checked, if a triangle is generated, it needs to be added to a vertex array for use with creating the model, and also added to an index array. DirectX can rasterize triangle strips by adding each triangle to an array, but this is a huge performance cost, thus the addition of an index array can be used to offset the performance cost. For each point of each triangle, we can check whether it has been added to the vertex array already; if it has been added, then we extract the index value of the vertex in the array, and add that index value to the index array.

Figure 6 depicts a procedural city generation of part of New York Manhattan containing buildings, roads, and rail networks using map data and related OSM, and LiDAR data.

7   Interpolation Experiment Results

Interpolating from an OS map at 50 m resolution to 2 m resolution to match the LiDAR DTM resolution accurately is dependent on the interpolation technique used. The experiment consisted of an OS map at 50 m resolution and a benchmark LiDAR DTM map covering the same 1 km^2 location within the UK. The OS map covers 10 km^2 at 200^2 points, so a subset needs to be extracted to match the same area and coverage of the LiDAR DTM map which is 1 km^2 at 20^2 points. In contrast the LiDAR DTM 2 m resolution map is 1 km^2 at 500^2 points. After this preprocessing has taken place the OS subset map can be interpolated. The comparison will be to determine which interpolation technique introduces the most amount of error when interpolating. There are a multiple of reasons why we need to compare interpolation techniques. Using interpolation to interpolate from a low resolution map to a higher resolution means that less storage is needed. For example, interpolating from 20^2 to 500^2 points is a total of 400 points to 250000 points respectively; which is equivalent to 625 50 m resolution 1 km^2 maps. The calculations of the different interpolation techniques need to be considered. When speed if of the essence, interpolating huge data sets to from a low resolution to a high resolution will take time. When time is not an

Fig. 7. Blue line represent ease-out, orange line represents ease-in, and the red line represents ease-in-out (color figure online)

issue and visual accuracy is, then more complex computational interpolation techniques can be used.

The interpolation techniques we used for our experiments are: Linear, circular, cubic, sinusoidal, quadratic, catmull-rom, exponential, quartic, and quantic. The interpolation techniques were obtained from a tweening library.[7] A tweening library is a term used for calculating the values in-between two other values, and is often used for animations. The library contains functions for easing-in, easing-out, and ease-in-out, see Fig. 7.

The tweening library does not contain an API for the Catmull-Rom interpolation function. Catmull-Rom interpolation needs additional point data either side of the values being interpolated to generate the tangent angle for entering and exiting the interpolated values. For this, additional tangent points are needed which are extracted from the surrounding maps of the map being interpolated. This experiment has only worked with a map which has complete surrounding maps. To work with missing data values, multiple pre-processing techniques will have to be employed but this is left for future work and is not relevant for this type of experiment.

Table 1. Error rates after interpolation technique is applied to 50 m resolutions at 20^2 point map to generate a 2 m resolution at 500^2 point map

Interpolator	Interpolated point map mean average height	Benchmark point map mean average height	Error in metres
Quintic	37.73528	37.79643	0.06115
Quartic	37.73481	37.79643	0.06162
Exponential	37.73467	37.79643	0.06176
Catmull-Rom	37.73452	37.79643	0.06191
Quadratic	37.7342	37.79643	0.06223
Sinusoidal	37.73419	37.79643	0.06224
Cubic	37.73419	37.79643	0.06224
Circular	37.73406	37.79643	0.06237
Linear	37.73349	37.79643	0.06294

---

[7] http://xnatweener.codeplex.com/.

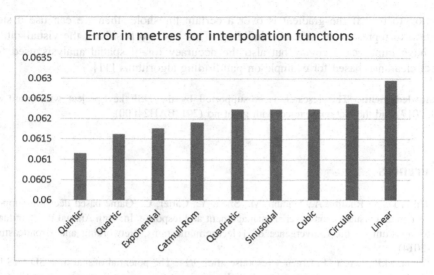

Fig. 8. Error in meters bar-chart for interpolation experiment

The error rates of the interpolation techniques are generated by first interpolating the 50 m 20^2 point maps to 2 m 500^2 point maps. The values are summed together and divided to find the mean average. This average is compared to the complete benchmark LiDAR DTM map which has had the same mean average calculated. The results are shown in Table 1 and Fig. 8. As Table 1 shows, the potential error for all interpolation techniques is 6 cm's. Linear interpolation introduces the most amount of error, where the quantic interpolation function produces the least amount of error, but the computations between the interpolation techniques are considerably different.

8   Conclusion

Within this paper we have presented a technique for a novel mesh extraction technique by iterating through regular complete 2D grids of real-world height map data to be visualized and utilized within a crisis management support system. The extracted meshes will be used in a layered hierarchy of map layers to view combinations of maps. We have also discussed interpolation techniques needed to interpolate from a low resolution to a high resolution point map. The interpolated maps are used for the process of inserting data into the missing data points of the high resolution LiDAR maps. The processes combined are a step closer to creating a tool set for a modern disaster support system.

In the future work, we plan to complete a comprehensive analysis of interpolation techniques used for interpolating low resolution map data to a higher resolution map, categorizing multiple maps containing different landscapes; water and land, land only, and maps with cliff faces. Using ease-in, ease-out, and ease-in-out interpolation functions need to be examined further to specify which function needs to be implemented at specific points. Using the gradient value between points, we can determine which function to use. If the gradient is over a certain threshold, then we can use a step function to represent the side of a building. This has two positives; the visualization will have improved accuracy but also the accuracy for of spatial analysis used for object clearance based for example on pathfinding algorithms [11].

Acknowledgments. This research is co-supported by the NSF key project with grant no (61332017) and the National project with grant no (2013BAH24F00).

References

1. Tully, D., El Rhalibi, A., Merabti, M., Shen, Y., Carter, C.: Game based decision support system and visualisation for crisis management and response. In: 15th Annual PostGraduate Symposium on the Convergence of Telecommunications, Networking and Broadcasting (2014)
2. Kwan, M.P., Lee, J.: Emergency response after 9/11: The potential of real-time 3D GIS for quick emergency response in micro-spatial environments. Comput. Environ. Urban Syst. **29** (2), 93–113 (2005)
3. Kopylec, J., D'Amico, A., Goodall, J.: Visualizing cascading failures in critical cyber infrastructures. In: Goetz, E., Shenoi, S. (eds.) Critical Infrastructure Protection. IFIP, vol. 253, pp. 351–364. (2008)
4. Rinaldi, S.: Modeling and simulating critical infrastructures and their interdependencies. In: Proceedings of the 37th Annual Hawaii International Conference on System Sciences 2004, pp. 1–8 (2004)
5. Scarlatos, P., Kaisar, E., Teegavarapu, R.: Modeling and simulation of catastrophic events affecting critical infrastructure systems. In: Proceedings of the 11th International Conference on Mathematical Methods and Computational Techniques in Electrical Engineering (MMACTEE 2009), pp. 334–346 (2009)
6. Dudenhoeffer, D., Hartley, S., Permann, M.: Critical infrastructure interdependency modeling: a survey of U.S. and international research. In: Report from U.S. Dep. Energy Natl. Lab. Oper. by Battelle Energy Alliance, August, 2006. doi:10.2172/911792
7. Bertalmio, M., Sapiro, G., Caselles, V., Ballester, C.: Image inpainting. In: 27th Annual Conference on Computer Graphics and Interactive Techniques, pp. 417–424 (2000)
8. Xia, J.C., El-Sana, J., Varshney, A.: Adaptive real-time level-of-detail based rendering for polygonal models. IEEE Trans. Vis. Comput. Graph. **3**(2), 171–181 (1997)
9. Lindstrom, P., Koller, D., Ribarsky, W., Hodges, L.F., Faust, N.: Real-Time, Continuous Level of Detail Rendering of Height Fields 1 Introduction 2 Related Work 3 Motivation
10. Hoppe, H.: Smooth view-dependent level-of-detail control and its application to terrain rendering. In: Proceedings of the Visualization 1998 (Cat. No. 98CB36276) (1998)
11. Harabor, D., Botea, A.: Hierarchical path planning for multi-size agents in heterogeneous environments. In: 2008 IEEE Symposium on Computational Intelligence and Games, CIG 2008, pp. 258–265 (2008)

Investigation on the Influence of Visual Attention on Image Memorability

Wulin Wang[1], Jiande Sun[1,2(✉)], Jing Li[3,4], Qiang Wu[1], and Ju Liu[1,2]

[1] School of Information Science and Engineering, Shandong University, Jinan 250100, China
{jd_sun,wuqiang,juliu}@sdu.edu.cn, wangwulin@hotmail.com
[2] The Hisense State Key Laboratory of Digital-Media Technology, Qingdao 266061, China
[3] School of Mechanical and Electrical Engineering, Shandong Management University,
Jinan 250100, China
lijingjdsun@hotmail.com
[4] School of Information Sicence and Engineering, Shandong Normal University, Jinan 250014,
Shandong, China

Abstract. The research of image memorability has received increasing attention recently. In this paper, the influence of the visual attention based features on image memorability is explored, which is different from most of the existing studies focusing on various appearance features. In this paper, the dataset used by Isola et al. are adopted. The visual saliency map of each image in the dataset is generated via the visual attention model. The corresponding object-saliency map is obtained by replacing each object with its average visual saliency. The global, local, and joint spatial histograms based on the object-saliency map are obtained and the relationship between visual attention and memorability is explored based on these visual attention based features. The experiments are carried out by using two existing visual attention models and demonstrate that these mentioned visual attention based features are more effective than the appearance features to predict the image memorability.

Keywords: Image memorability · Visual attention · Scene understanding · Support vector machine

1 Introduction

Recently the research of image memorability has attracted increasing interests. If the features that are able to predict the memorability of images can be figured out, it is possible to modify the memorability of an image, which is promising in lots of image-related applications.

Image memorability is considered as the probability of correctly being detected a repetition of the image. Isola et al. showed that memorability is a trait intrinsic to images across different viewers [5]. The main issue of measuring the image memorability is to find the features that can predict the memorability of images accurately. There have been lots of studies on image memorability. Argembeau et al. took happy and angry expressions of face images into account and studied the effects of emotion on the memory [1].

© Springer International Publishing Switzerland 2015
Y.-J. Zhang (Ed.): ICIG 2015, Part III, LNCS 9219, pp. 573–582, 2015.
DOI: 10.1007/978-3-319-21969-1_52

Bainbridge et al. exploited more features than facial expressions in the study of the memorability of face images [2]. Isola et al. investigated the memorability of generic images, which include ordinary people or scenery and proposed to predict the image memorability according to different features, labels and attributes [3–5]. Khosla et al. considered the memorability depended on the difference between the initial image representation and its internal degraded version [6]. They predicted the memorability via using a noisy memory process of encoding images in the memory. Kim et al. showed that Weighted Object Area (WOA) and Relative Area Rank (RAR) can predict the image memorability [7]. Though these above researches have shown exciting performance, they still have some limitations. Only the appearance features are utilized to characterize the images and no visual factors are considered.

In the procedure of perceptual cognition, appearance features are on the first step and they stimulate the vision. The appearance features do not connect to memory directly, though they are the main features used in image analysis and play an important role in image understanding. Visual attention is a mechanism of visual system to deal with the regions with different visual saliences selectively and it is the step connected to the memory directly. The visual attention features can transfer the information of visual stimuli to the memory. Therefore, it is reasonable that visual attention has positive influence on image memorability.

In this paper, an investigation on visual attention based image memorability prediction is carried out, in which the features based on visual attention are utilized to predict the memorability. Two existing visual attention models are used to demonstrate the effectiveness of visual attention on the image memorability. The experiments demonstrate that these visual attention based features are more effective than the appearance features in predicting image memorability. Section 2 introduces the algorithm proposed by Isola et al. in [5]. Two visual attention models used in this paper are introduced in Sect. 3. How to investigate the influence of visual attention on image memorability is described in Section. Section 5 shows the experiment results and Sect. 6 gives the conclusion.

2 Previous Work on Image Memorability

In 2013, Isola et al. measured the memorability scores of 2400 images including people and natural scenery via a Visual Memory Game in [5]. These images are randomly sampled from different scene categories of the SUN dataset [10]. The memorability score of an image is defined as the probability of participants correctly detecting a repetition of the image in their study and this score is treated as the ground truth. Isola et al. trained a support vector regression SVR to map features of images to memorability scores. One half of the images scored by one half of the participants are used as the training examples, and the remaining are used as the test examples. It is data-dependent. During training, grid search is performed to choose the optimal parameters for SVR.

The performance is usually quantified by the Spearman's rank correlation (ρ). ρ is used to measure the statistical correlation between two groups of variables, and its theoretical value is between -1 and 1. ρ is greater than zero means a monotonically increasing trend of the two, and ρ is less than zero means a monotonically decreasing trend. Here ρ is used to evaluate the correlation between the feature and the ground truth memorability score of a photo. If ρ is greater than zero and it is large, it indicates this feature is advisable to representing the image memorability.

Many possible traits about image memorability were investigated in [5], which included external factors, various image-based, object-based and semantic features of images. External factors included different observers, time delays, context and subjective judgments about whether the image was memorable. Results demonstrated that memorability is an intrinsic and stable trait of an image.

For the image-based features, the hue, intensity and saturation of an image are investigated. The value of ρ between each of them and memorability was close to zero, which implied that each of them was correlated weakly with memorability. The object-based features such as labelled object counts, labelled object areas and spatial histograms of object distribution are also investigated by the means of machine learning. The experimental results showed that object based features had positive effect on image memorability. The semantic features included scene category and other semantic attributes labelled by human users, i.e. spatial layout of the scene, location of famous place and appearance of people (e.g., clothing, race, gender, etc.). When SVRs were trained to map these attributes to memorability scores, the performance of ρ was large. It implied that semantic attributes were efficient to characterize the memorability of an image. Meanwhile, they studied various global and local features algorithmically extracted from an image, i.e. SIFT, HOG, GIST and so on.

The study of Isola et al. focuses on the influence of appearance features on image memorability, which represents the image from the view of visual stimuli. However, what affects the memory directly is the visual reaction to visual stimuli, that is, visual attention. Therefore, we try to investigate the influence of visual attention on image memorability from the point of visual reaction.

3   Visual Attention Models

3.1   Itti's Attention Model

Visual attention has been proved to play an important role in the fields of image content analysis and understanding. Visual attention modelling simulates the behavior of human visual system by automatically producing saliency map of the target image and then detects out the regions of interests from the image, which are attractive to viewers.

Itti et al. proposed the most classical model which combined three kinds of low level appearance features, i.e. color, intensity and orientation, to extract salient regions [8]. The contrast of pixel was defined as its saliency, so the saliency map was constructed by computing the contrast of a pixel to its surroundings. Usually the regions with strong contrast to their surroundings had a high degree of saliency, which attracted people's attention, while the ones with weak contrast tended to be ignored. It was proved that this approach could extract approximate salient regions.

3.2   Attention Model with Cross-Layer Fusion

The attention model with cross-layer fusion was proposed by Sun et al. [9]. It was an improvement for the classical Itti's attention model by combining the local and global saliency. It computed the contrast saliency of the global and local layers respectively and combined the two layer saliency to generate a weight model and then optimized the global saliency using the weight model as a feedback from local layer. The final visual saliency map was obtained by performing the morphological post-processing. Figure 1 shows the framework of this visual saliency model. It could detect out more accurate salient regions.

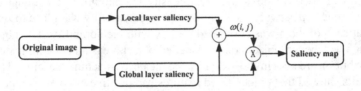

Fig. 1. The framework of the cross-layer visual attention model. The optimization on the weighting cross the global and local layers improves the performance of attention model on detect out the body and boundary of the salient regions.

4   Image Memorability Based on Visual Attention

In this paper, the global, local and joint spatial histograms based on visual attention are investigated to predict image memorability. Figure 2 shows the framework. All objects in the images including people and scenery are labelled. The visual saliency map of each image is obtained via two existing visual attention models. The object regions are replaced with the average visual saliency in it, and the corresponding object-saliency map is generated. The global, local and joint spatial histograms are calculated based on the generated map.

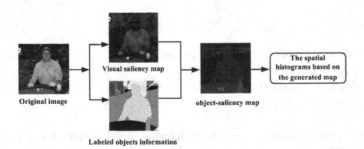

Fig. 2. The framework of image memorability prediction based on visual attention. Visual saliency provides the visual weights to emphasize the relationship between the vision and memory.

To investigate the role of these spatial histograms based on visual attention in predicting image memorability, a support vector regression is trained to map these features to memory scores in this paper. The ground truth memorability scores are regarded as labels. The experiment on 25 regression trials is performed and for each trial, both the images and participants are separated to two independent, random halves (same as [5]). Half of the images are sampled randomly from the 2222 images and their features are seen as training examples. Meanwhile, ground truth memorability scores corresponding to these examples are treated as training labels. The rest examples are used as test ones. During training, cross validation is performed to choose the optimal parameters for each SVR.

5 Experiments and Analysis

The dataset in [5], which consists of 2222 images selected from the SUN dataset in [10] are used in the experiments. The images are fully annotated with segmented object regions and are all resized to 256*256. A memorability score for each image is provided as the ground truth. Figure 3 shows three examples of experimental images. Figure 3(a) shows original images, and the visual saliency maps obtained by cross-layer based visual attention model are shown in Fig. 3(b). Figure 3(c) shows the object labelled maps, and Fig. 3(d) shows the object-saliency maps. It can be seen from Fig. 3 that the salient regions are captured well.

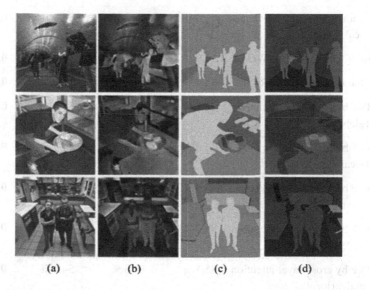

(a)	(b)	(c)	(d)

Fig. 3. (a) Example images, (b) visual saliency map, (c) objects labelled map and (d) object-saliency map. The difference between the visual and object saliency implies the influence of visual attention to memorability.

The performance is evaluated via Spearman's rank correlation (ρ). ρ is used to evaluate the correlation between the feature and the ground truth memorability score of an image. That ρ is greater than zero indicates the feature is advisable to representing the image memorability. The human consistency is set as $\rho = 0.75$ according to the study of [5], which is used as the upper bound in the performance of automatic methods, i.e., the ideal value. We evaluate the performance on 25 different training or testing splits of the data (the same splits as [5]) with an equal number of images for training and testing (i.e., 1111). The train splits are scored by one half of the participants and the test splits are scored by the other half of the participants. In addition, the performance can also be evaluated by average ground truth memorability over the images with the top N highest predicted memorability scores. The numerical comparison is listed in Table 1.

Table 1. Comparison between predictions and ground truth according to object based features, semantic features and SHVFs based on two attention models.

	T-20	T-100	B-20	ρ
Labelled object counts	82.4 %	79.0 %	55.2 %	0.44
Labelled object areas	84.3 %	82.3 %	53.5 %	0.48
Spatial histograms	85.1 %	82.3 %	52.7 %	0.48
Scene category	81.1 %	77.6 %	56.3 %	0.37
Combination of all global and local features	83.4 %	80.7 %	53.9 %	0.46
Spatial features in [7] (WOA)	84.9 %	82.2 %	51.2 %	**0.49**
Spatial features in [7] (RAR)	85.5 %	81.9 %	52.0 %	**0.50**
SHVF by Itti's attention model (global)	82.7 %	80.3 %	55.7 %	0.42
SHVF by Itti's attention model (local)	85.6 %	82.0 %	54.7 %	**0.48**
SHVF by Itti's attention model (joint)	**85.9 %**	82.3 %	54.5 %	**0.48**
SHVF by cross-layer attention model (global)	83.3 %	80.4 %	55.9 %	0.43
SHVF by cross-layer attention model (local)	85.5 %	82.3 %	54.1 %	**0.49**
SHVF by cross-layer attention model (joint)	**85.7 %**	**82.6 %**	53.1 %	**0.49**
Ideal value	86.9 %	84.3 %	39.6 %	0.75

Table 1 lists the comparisons on predictions and ground truth, where the predictions are obtained based on object based features, semantic features, combination of global and local features, spatial features in [7] and spatial histograms of visual features (SHVF) obtained by attention models respectively. The object-based features include labelled object counts, labelled object areas and spatial histograms. The semantic features refer to scene category. **T-20** and **T-100** denote the average ground truth memorability over the images with the top 20 and top 100 highest predicted memorability scores. **B-20** denotes the average ground truth memorability over the images with the top 20 lowest predicted memorability scores. In general, the value of Top 20 is about 81 %–85 % and ρ is 0.37–0.48 in [5].

In Table 1, T-20 obtained, by global, local and joint SHVF by two attention models is 85.9 %. It is 2.5 % higher than that obtained by the combination of all global and local features, 0.8 % higher than that obtained by object based features, i.e., spatial histograms and 4.8 % higher than that obtained by semantic features, i.e., scene category. T-100 obtained by global, local and joint SHVF by two attention models is 82.6 %. It is 1.9 %, 0.3 % and 5.0 % higher than that obtained by the combination of all global and local features, object based features and semantic features respectively. Moreover, local and joint SHVF are much closer to the ideal value than global SHVF and the other features. In addition, its highest Spearman's rank correlation ρ can reach 0.49, which is 0.03, 0.01 and 0.12 higher than the combination of all global and local features, object based features and semantic features and almost equal to that in [7]. It shows that the global, local and joint SHVF obtained by attention model are more effective in predicting image memorability. Especially the local SHVF is a little better than the global one due to the selective visual attention.

Figure 4 shows the comparison on ground truth and the predictions among labelled object counts, labelled object areas, spatial histograms, scene category and SHVFs by different attention models. The predicted memorability scores are sorted in descending order, which correspond to the sequence number 1–1111. In order to show the comparison clearly, only the top 100 numbers are shown in Fig. 4. The vertical axis corresponds to average ground truth memorability over the images with the top N highest predicted memorability scores. For instance, when N is equal to 100, the vertical axis corresponds to the average ground truth memorability over the images with the top 100 highest predicted memorability scores. From Fig. 4, it can be seen that when N is less than 100, the average ground truth memorability obtained by SHVF based on two attention models is higher than the others and much closer to the ideal value. It shows that visual attention based features can achieve better performance.

Figure 5 demonstrates the comparison on ground truth and the predictions between the combination of all global and local features and SHVF based on Itti's attention model. Compared to the combination of all global and local features, the performance achieved by local and joint SHVF by Itti's attention model are better. Especially when N is less than 20, the predicted memorability score is much closer to the ideal value. Although performance achieved by global spatial histograms are a little worse than those obtained by the combination of all global and local features, it can still imply that the features can be used to represent image. While the local and joint SHVF by Itti's attention model are proved to be more effective for representing image memorability.

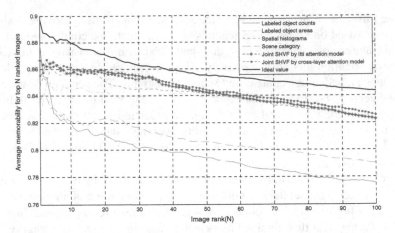

Fig. 4. Comparison between ground truth and predictions according to object based features, semantic features and SHVF based on two attention models. The prediction performance considering attention models is better than those without considering attention models.

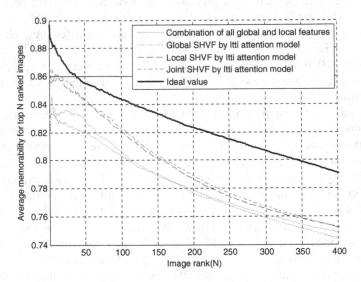

Fig. 5. Comparison between ground truth and predictions according to all global and local features and SHVF by Itti's attention model. The joint feature shows the reasonable better performance.

Figure 6 shows the comparison on the predictions and ground truth between the combination of all global and local features and SHVF based on cross-layer attention model. Figure 6 shows the similar comparison results as Fig. 5. It proves that the features based on visual attention are effective for representing image memorability.

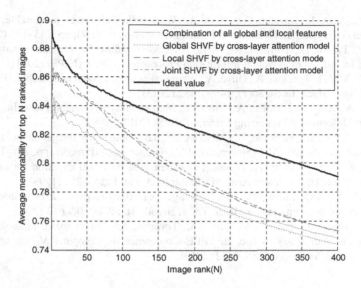

Fig. 6. Comparison between ground truth and the predictions according to all global and local features and SHVF by cross-layer based model. The joint feature shows the reasonable better performance.

6 Conclusions

In this paper, we investigate the influence of the features based on visual attention on image memorability via the spatial histograms of visual features (SHVF) obtained by two visual attention models. The comparison results show that the visual attention has positive influence on predicting image memorability. Moreover, local and joint visual features have better performance than global ones, which is a reasonable reflection of the important role of selective attention in visual system. Future work will investigate the relationship between image memorability and other visual attention related-measures such as spatial and temporal distribution of visual attention regions, the order and intensity of visual attention without the labels.

Acknowledgments. The work is supported by the Natural Science Foundation of Shandong Province (ZR2014FM012). The contact author is Jiande Sun (jd_sun@sdu.edu.cn).

References

1. D'Argembeau, A., Van der Linden, M., Comblain, C., Etienne, A.-M.: The effects of happy and angry expressions on identity and expression memory for unfamiliar faces. Cogn. Emot. **17**(4), 609–622 (2003)
2. Bainbridge, W., Isola, P., Blank, I., Oliva, A.: Establishing a database for studying human face photograph memory. In: Proceedings of the Cognitive Science Society (2012)

3. Isola, P., Xiao, J., Torralba, A., Oliva, A.: What makes an image memorable. In: IEEE Conference on Computer Vision and Pattern Recognition (CVPR), pp. 145–152 (2011)
4. Isola, P., Parikh, D., Torralba, A., Oliva, A.: Understanding the intrinsic memorability of images. In: Advances in Neural Information Processing Systems (NIPS) (2011)
5. Isola, P., Xiao, J., Torralba, A., Oliva, A.: What makes a photograph memorable. IEEE Trans. Pattern Anal. Mach. Intell. **36**(7), 1469–1482 (2013)
6. Khosla, A., Xiao, J., Torralba, A., Oliva, A.: Memorability of image regions. In: Advances in Neural Information Processing Systems (NIPS) (2012)
7. Kim, J., Yoon, S., Pavlovic, V.: Relative spatial features for image memorability. In: Proceedings of the 21st ACM International Conference on Multimedia, pp. 761–764 (2013)
8. Itti, L., Koch, C., Niebur, E.: A model of saliency-based visual attention for rapid scene analysis. IEEE Trans. Pattern Anal. Mach. Intell. **20**(11), 1254–1259 (1998)
9. Sun, J.D., Xie, J.C., Liu, J., Thomas, S.: Image adaptation and dynamic browsing based on two-layer saliency combination. IEEE Trans. Broadcast. **59**(4), 602–613 (2013)
10. Xiao, J., Hayes, J., Ehinger, K., Oliva, A., Torralba, A.: Sun database: large-scale scene recognition from abbey to zoo. In: IEEE Conference on Computer Vision and Pattern Recognition (CVPR), pp. 3485–3492 (2010)

Predicting and Visualising City Noise Levels to Support Tinnitus Sufferers

William Hurst[1], Graham Davis[2], Abdennour El Rhalibi[1(✉)],
David Tully[1], and Zhigeng Pan[3]

[1] School of Computing and Mathematical Sciences,
Liverpool John Moores University, Liverpool, UK
{W.Hurst,A.Elrhalibi}@ljmu.ac.uk,
d.tully@2008.ljmu.ac.uk
[2] WYG Environmental, Manchester, UK
graham.davis@wyg.com
[3] Digital Media and HCI Research Center,
Hangzhou Normal University, Hangzhou
People's Republic of China
zgpan@hznu.edu.cn

Abstract. On a daily basis, urban residents are unconsciously exposed to hazardous noise levels. This has a detrimental effect on the ear-drum, with symptoms often not apparent till later in life. The impact of harmful noises levels has a damaging impact on wellbeing. It is estimated that 10 million people suffer from damaged hearing in the UK alone, with 6.4 million of retirement age or above. With this number expected to increase significantly by 2031, the demand and cost for healthcare providers is expected to intensify. Tinnitus affects about 10 percent of the UK population, with the condition ranging from mild to severe. The effects can have psychological impact on the patient. Often communication becomes difficult, and the sufferer may also be unable to use a hearing aid due to buzzing, ringing or monotonous sounds in the ear. Action on Hearing Loss states that sufferers of hearing related illnesses are more likely to withdraw from social activities. Tinnitus sufferers are known to avoid noisy environments and busy urban areas, as exposure to excessive noise levels exacerbates the symptoms. In this paper, an approach for evaluating and predicting urban noise levels is put forward. The system performs a data classification process to identify and predict harmful noise areas at diverse periods. The goal is to provide Tinnitus sufferers with a real-time tool, which can be used as a guide to find quieter routes to work; identify harmful areas to avoid or predict when noise levels on certain roads will be dangerous to the ear-drum. Our system also performs a visualisation function, which overlays real-time noise levels onto an interactive 3D map.

Keywords: Hazardous noise levels · Data classification · Tinnitus · Visualisation · Hearing loss · Prediction · Real-Time

© Springer International Publishing Switzerland 2015
Y.-J. Zhang (Ed.): ICIG 2015, Part III, LNCS 9219, pp. 583–598, 2015.
DOI: 10.1007/978-3-319-21969-1_53

1   Introduction

Hearing loss in the elderly has a significant cost impact on the UK's National Health Service every year, where it is estimated that 10 million people suffer from damaged hearing [5]. This specifically covers 6.4 million who are retirement age or above and 3.7 million individuals of working age. It is estimated that by 2031 there will be 14.5 million people suffering from some form of hearing loss [5]. This will have a major cost bearing on the health service provision, more so than conditions such as diabetes or cataracts [5].

The current UK health and safety guideline state that, when exposed to a sound of 85 dB(A) or higher in the work place, the employee must wear some form of hearing protection. The European Control of Noise at Work Regulations, however, states that noise exposure of 80 dB(A) or higher should be counteracted with protective gear. We use the European guidelines for our research. The impact of harmful noise levels on an individual's hearing can differ. However, the more time spent exposed to a sound over 80db, the more damage is caused to the ear-drum. Tinnitus is a condition, for which, currently, there is no cure. The symptoms include buzzing, ringing or monotonous sounds in the ear, which are permanent and constant throughout the day and night. Action on Hearing Loss (formerly RNID) state that in 2011, 10 % of adults in the UK had some form of Tinnitus. The condition is brought about by damage to the ear drum and often caused by expose to frequent loud noises on a daily basis. Sufferers of Tinnitus find that the symptoms are exacerbated by regular exposure to loud noises encountered during their daily activities.

As our research shows, the level of noise in city centres and public places can have a significant impact on an individual's hearing. In this paper, an approach for assessing and predicting noises levels at specific urban locations during the day is presented. The system performs a data classification process to identify and predict harmful noise areas at diverse periods. The approach also visualises the noise levels in public places, such as city centres. The analysis is achieved by using machine learning classifiers to detect, and subsequently predict, trends in high noise levels at specific times of the day. A visualisation of the results allows the user to view the best times to avoid certain areas of a city through an interactive tool.

The rest of the paper is as follows. Section 2 presents a background and motivation behind the research. The dataset used in our research is detailed in Sect. 3 which includes an account of our system design and data classification techniques. Section 4 provides a discussion and account of the results. Section 5 presents an overview of the visualisation process for a real-time graphical display of the harmful levels in a city. The paper is concluded in Sect. 6, which provides a discussion on the work presented and details how the work will be taken further in the future.

2   Background

In the UK, in 2010, £1.34 was spent on care for each individual affected by hearing damage. This is significantly lower than the nation spends on diabetes (£21.21) and sight loss (£14.21) wellbeing. In Australia, it is estimated that the disease burden on the economy associated with hearing loss was $11.3 billion, during a study taken in 2005 [5]. The World Health Organisation anticipates that hearing loss will have an incremental drain on health care providers in the next 15 years. For example, it is projected that hearing damage will be the most common disease in the UK by 2031 [4]. There is a significant cost benefit to governments in the prevention of hearing damage. The aim of this project is to illustrate how noise levels in metropolitan areas impact hearing. A greater awareness of harmful sounds, and where and when they occur, may reduce the costs of health care and alleviate symptoms in conditions such as Tinnitus. By providing urban residents with detailed real-time noise maps, specific to their location, enables individuals to safeguard their hearing and be aware of the potential damage to the regular exposure to levels over 80 dBs in their daily lives.

2.1   Hearing Loss and Noise Prediction

The most common cause of hearing damage is age related. However, the cause can be prolonged exposure to sounds which are over 80 db(A). There are known to be four different levels of hearing loss:

(1) Mild hearing loss, where individuals have difficulty hearing outside the mean range of 25 to 39 decibels.
(2) Moderate hearing loss relates to individuals who find it difficult to follow speech and hear between 40 and 69 decibels.
(3) Severe hearing loss refers to individuals who require hearing aids and the use of sign language to communicate.
(4) Profound deafness, refers to individuals who are able to only hear 95 decibels or higher.

Hearing loss is a non-life-threatening condition and, for that reason, is often overlooked in a healthcare environment, particularly in developing markets [17]. This is enforced by the research put forward by Figueira et al., which details the creation of humanitarian apps, for audiometric hearing tests in affordable format [17]. The idea is to make hearing-loss healthcare more available in emerging markets by employing existing mobile technology. Their proposed App evaluates an individual's hearing ability through their mobile device and, subsequently, detects if the user has hearing damage. The project, however, is reliant on the availability of smart phones and the results have not been compared with an audiometer to test the successfulness of the project. Research, such as this, paves the way for making hearing loss treatment more widely available, particularly in emerging markets, however it does little towards the prevention of hearing-loss.

The system proposed in this paper consists of three topographies: intelligent noise evaluation; sound prediction and interactive visualisation. Noise visualisation is the ability to digitally record or assess sound and present a conception to a user. The conception of sounds provides an ideal way to communicate data which is invisible to the human eye and where the effects are not visible. The process can be made possible through use of an acoustic camera [19] to directly visualise sound in real-time.

Alternatively, class 1 integrating sound level meters can monitor specific noise levels and construct datasets, which can be used for post-analysis.

Noise level prediction focuses on intelligent forecasting down to the street level in an urban environment. No research has covered the use of intelligently predicting noise levels in urban areas or the generation of interactive noise maps as a guide to hearing-impairment sufferers. Current sound prediction models rely on forecasting through use of simple calculations to estimate future sound levels. This technique is employed when new transportation or development projects are planned. No systems present a real-time hour by hour visualisation to the street level.

2.2 Tinnitus

Tinnitus is a condition which results in the perception of monotonous sounds resonating in the ear. The resonances are the result of absence of corresponding external sounds. The condition is permanent and there is no cure and can be made worse by expose to frequent loud noises. For that reason, the condition requires management. The British Tinnitus Association estimated that around 10 % of the UK population have some form of Tinnitus; with a further 1 % having a condition which can affect their lifestyle [6]. It is a condition which is unseen and the level of suffering is only known by the patient as there are no visible symptoms. Having a strong form of Tinnitus is also linked to and can cause depression. Holmes et al. stated that in 2009, the level of depression is higher amongst sufferers of Tinnitus than it is in the general population [7]. Tinnitus can have psychological effects on the patient. Often communication becomes difficult, and the effects may also mean that the individual is unable to use a hearing aid as the buzzing, ringing or monotonous sounds in the ear are enhanced. Action on Hearing Loss state that sufferers of hearing loss are more likely to withdraw from social activities.

A specific goal, of the research put forward in this paper, is to aid with the prevention of Tinnitus and reduce its symptoms. This is achieved by providing an approach for sufferers to avoid exposure to excessive noise levels during the day. Frequent and prolonged encounters of loud noises in the daytime can trigger the ringing and buzzing sounds which are associated with Tinnitus and often last well into the evening and night.

2.3 Noise Visualisation

Data is not fixed and is a changing entity [1]. This is particularly true for sound data, which is dynamic and has a varied level of granularity. Creating sound visualisations for the hearing impaired is developing research area [8]. As technology advances, access to smart equipment has been made easier [9]. For example, Brophy et al., focus on the visualisation of loud sounds [9] in real-time to aid the hearing impaired visualise the environment around them. Their approach provides greater interactivity for an individual with a hearing impairment and the surroundings. The project works by capturing the environment using a camera when a loud sound is detected. The image is then displayed to the individual with the hearing impairment via the use of virtual reality glasses. Using visualisation techniques can help project unseen environmental characteristics in real-time. This is of particular benefit to sufferers of Tinnitus, and the reducing of hearing damage caused by urban noise. By providing a visual guide about noise levels down to individual street level, areas can be avoided if necessary.

In this paper, we present an approach and tool for the analysis, prediction and visualisation of noise data in public places. Specifically, the focus on the sound data sets from Leicester city centre in the UK. The dataset is provided by WYG Environmental.

2.4   Noise Assessment of an Urban Area

The approach put forward involves interacting with data to find hidden information and view if trends in noise patterns develop over time. The environmental noise monitoring was undertaken using Rion NL-52 class 1 integrating sound level meters to establish baseline ambient, background and specific source noise levels. Measurements were taken in accordance with BS 7445-1:2003 The Description and Measurement of Environmental Noise: Guide to Quantities and Procedures. The measurement equipment was checked against the appropriate calibrator at the beginning and end of the measurements, and no drift was observed. The following statistical parameters were recorded at a variety of logging periods, including: L_{Aeq}, L_{Amax}, L_{Amin}, L_{A10}, L_{A90} and linear L_{eq} values. All the values are sound pressure levels in dB (re: 2×10^{-5} Pa). Sound levels can be measured in frequency bands to provide detailed information about the spectral content of the noise. These measurements are usually undertaken in octave or third octave frequency bands. If these values are summed logarithmically, a single figure value can be calculated. This describes the total amount of acoustic energy measured but does not take any account of the ear's ability to hear certain frequencies more readily than others.

Instead, the dB(A) figure is used. This is found to relate better to the loudness of the sound heard. The dBA figure is obtained by subtracting an appropriate correction, which represents the variation in the ear's ability to hear different frequencies, from the individual octave or third octave band values, before summing them logarithmically. As a result, the dB(A) value provides a depiction of how loud a sound is in reality. The 'A' is used to state average, whereas 'C' would be the peak noise, i.e. dB(C). Consequently, the dataset includes 10 features, each is accounted below:

- L_{Aeq}: Sounds vary and fluctuate with time. Instead of having an instantaneous value to describe the noise event, an average of the total acoustic energy experienced over its duration provides a more accurate account. The LAeq, 07:00 – 23:00 for example, describes the equivalent continuous noise level over the 12 h period between 7 am and 11 pm. LAeq is calculated using the formula:

$$L_{Aeq} = SEL - 10Log(t) + 10Log(n)$$

T is Time and n is the amount of events within a given time. SEL is the sound level over one second. his would typically have the same energy content as the whole event.

- L_{Amin}: The quietest instantaneous noise level recorded, specifically the quietest 125 ms measured during any given period of time, is given the LAmin annotation.
- L_{Amax}: The L_{Amax} is the loudest instantaneous noise level. Again, this is usually the loudest 125 ms measured during a given time block.
- L_E: The L_E feature provides an assessment of impact sounds and blast noises, used for actions such as train passes. So that for a given number of passes an overall average can be calculated. It consists of the sound exposure level. The value represents the energy rate for the measurement range that is replaced by the energy value for one second. In other words, it is essentially a one second equivalent of the overall measurement.
- L_y: L_y is the peak 'C' weighted sound pressure level used for occupational noise assessments to determine requirements for hearing protection.
- LN1-5: LN1 to LN5 consist of the percentile levels (5th, 10th, 50th, 90th and 95th). The most common ones to use are 10th and 90th, referred to as LA10 and LA90.

A sample of this data captured is displayed in Table 1. The table shows a section of the data recorded for 5 of the features. The total dataset used for this research involves 2386 records or data with 10 features.

Table 1. Sample dataset (dB)

Record	Start time	Leq	LE	Lmax	Ly	LN1
1	11:31:19	69.0	93.8	79.8	101.8	77.1
2	11:36:19	69.9	94.7	92.0	111.3	78.6
3	11:41:19	69.3	94.1	84.3	100.1	82.3
4	11:46:19	69.9	94.7	82.2	99.3	78.0
5	11:51:19	68.8	93.6	81.4	103.9	77.8
6	11:56:19	67.7	92.5	83.6	102.2	76.3
7	12:01:19	80.0	104.8	102.1	110.8	93.1
8	12:06:19	71.3	96.1	85.2	100.8	82.6
9	12:11:19	70.8	95.6	82.6	100.0	80.0
10	12:16:19	67.5	92.3	83.6	95.8	74.4

3   Approach

Tinnitus sufferers often avoid going into public places as they fear their symptoms will be exacerbated by exposure to loud noises throughout the day [7]. The tool presented in this paper helps patients identify times of the day when it may be preferable to go outside. More specifically, it details areas they should avoid in order to ensure the symptoms are not triggered or made worse [8]. We also predict that the tool will be cost beneficial to governments. The aim is to help with the action on hearing loss by making people more aware of the damage which can be caused, unawares, in busy urban areas. The approach conducts the following steps.

(1) City noise collection as defined in Sect. 2.4.
(2) Noise data classification and noise level prediction: The focus is on the identification of trends in data and a detection of when the most harmful levels occur so that the information can be overlaid on a map. First a visualisation of the entire data set is presented using a scatter graph format. The idea is to display trends in data in occur and that noise levels have characteristics at different times of day. Secondly a classification process forms a predictive model to identify the noise models anticipated at specific times of the day.
(3) Sound visualisation: The third stage involves the development of a visualisation tool which provides an interactive guide to Tinnitus sufferers. The tool details which areas of a city should be avoided and suggest what times of day they should best go out in public. This involves two stages:
    a. Develop map interface of city or urban environment.
    b. Overlay results in real-time in an understandable and interactive format.

3.1 Data Examination

In this section a visualisation of the noise collection, which took place in Leicester city centre (UK) on 21/08/2013 to 29/08/2013, is presented. The visualisations show a scatter plot of the decibel levels throughout the 2386 rows of raw data. The idea is to demonstrate that visual trends in the data occur at regular intervals. Figure 1 displays an overview of the maximum noises levels recorded at five minute intervals over a period of 9 days.

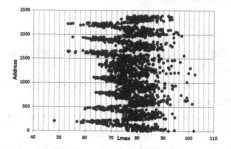
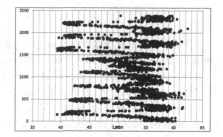

Fig. 1. L_{max} noise levels   **Fig. 2.** L_{min} noise levels

Noise levels are displayed along the x-axis while the reading labels are displayed along the y-axis. The numbers 0 to 2500 refer to each of the noise levels samples starting at 11:31:19 on Day 1 and ending at 18:16:19 on Day 9. The graph shows a clear repetitive trend in the data. Each-day has a similar spike in noise levels. This is caused by rush hour traffic at regular intervals. Similarly, in Fig. 2, a trend in the min noise levels over the 9 days is visible. There are identifiable times of day, which are regularly louder than other times of day. However, the main cluster on noise is around the 55 dB to 60 dB level.

The approach of this work lies in being able to predict nose levels and present the results in an interactive map. Increases in noise levels during rush hours are predictable, but the exact noise levels and the impacts on Tinnitus sufferers are unknown. Often subtle changes in noise levels can have a negative impact on the sufferer. This work also aims to present an approach for recognising the unexpected noise levels and identify if harmful noise levels occur outside of rush hour periods.

3.2 Case Study

Breaking down the graph into individual days we see identifiable trends in noise data. Figure 3 displays a scatter plot of the maximum noise level readings taken at a sampling rate of 5 min intervals over 24 h.

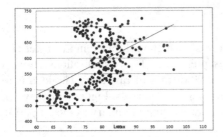

Fig. 3. L_{max} 24 noise levels over 24 Hours   **Fig. 4.** L_{min} noise levels over 24 Hours

Whereas, Fig. 4 displays a scatter plot of the minimum noise level readings taken, again at a sampling rate of 5 min intervals over 24 h.

A linear trend line is included in both Figs. 3 and 4 to show the linear division of the data samples recorded during the 24 h time blocks.

Figures 5 and 6 display the Max and Min noise levels over day 2. A similarity in the pattern of noise behaviour can be seen at comparable times of day.

However, it can be a challenge to identify these patterns by eye when the data set is considerably large and containing data from different areas of the city. For the reason the use of data classification techniques is adopted to identify the trends in noise levels. The results are used for the visualisation process. The results are used to show a projection of noise levels at specific times of day and allocate a warning level so that the users will know when to avoid the area and how great the risk is to their hearing.

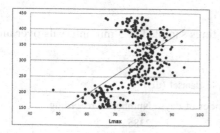

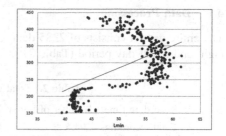

Fig. 5. L_{max} noise levels day 2   **Fig. 6.** L_{min} noise levels day 2

4 Data Classification

The methodology involves employing a selection of supervised learning to predict trends in the noise levels. Specifically, the classifiers used include: Uncorrelated Normal Density based Classifier (UDC), Quadratic Discriminant Classifier (QDC), Linear Discriminant Classifier (LDC), Decision Tree (TREEC), and Parzen Classifier (PARZENC).

Linear Discriminant Classifier (LDC), is a technique which works by sorting or dividing data into groups based on characteristics to create a classification [11]. A discriminant function is obtained by monotonic transformation of posterior probabilities [12]. In other words, it performs an ordered transformation of unknown quantities, which are separated by a linear vector. Quadratic Discriminant Classifier (QDC) works in a similar way to LDC by dividing the data into groups based on given characteristics. However, by using QDC the data is divided using a quadratic surface rather than a one-dimensional one. QDC makes no assumptions that covariance are alike. In other words, it assumes that the changing of two random variables will not be the same [13].

Uncorrelated Normal Density based Classifier (UDC) also operates comparably to the QDC classifier but computation of a quadratic classifier, between the classes in the dataset, is done by assuming normal densities with uncorrelated features. Quadratic Bayes takes decisions by assuming different normal distribution of data [14]. LDC, QDC and UDC are density based classifiers. Decision Tree (TREEC) is a classifier which uses decision rules to divide the classes of data [12]. It operates by using criterion functions (the sum of squared errors), stopping rules (criteria for appropriate number of splits in a decision tree) or pruning techniques (the removal of unwanted tree sections).

Using decision tree is a particularly ideal choice of classifier because it is well-known as one of the most effective supervised classification techniques [13]. Parzen Classifier (PARZENC) functions by including aspects of the training data when the classifier is built up. It is a non-linear classifier and it has the benefit that its parameters can be user supplied or optimised [12, 14].

4.1 Data Processing

The entire dataset consists of 2385 data recordings sampled at 5 min intervals over an eight and a half day period (Table 2).

Table 2. Total sample dataset (dB)

Recording time	Number of hours	Number of days	Number of recording
Total recordings	204.5	8.52	2385

The raw dataset was divided into different hours of the day. In the analysis, rush hours are compared against off peak travel times to show how different noise levels can be identified. 3 days are randomly selected from the dataset for the comparison. The dataset was then divided into on-peak and off-peak hours. Table 3 details the number of total on-peak and off peak recordings over the three random days selected for a case study.

Table 3. On-peak/off-peak recordings

Recording time	Number of hours	Number of days	Number of recording
On-peak	27	1.125	324
Off-peak	45	1.875	540
Totals	72	3	864

The data set for on-peak and off-peak is unbalanced, as the number of on-peak hours in the day is lower than off-peak. In this research, off-peak is defined as between 10 pm – 6am and 9 am to 4 pm. On-Peak is defined as between 6 am 9 am and 4 pm to 7 pm. Using this model, a balanced dataset for the classification process is developed. Table 4 displays the number of samples used for the classification process.

Table 4. Noise samples for classification

Recording time	Total hours	Time of recording	Number of recordings
On-peak	9	3:00–5:59	108
Off-peak	9	6:00–8:59	108
Total	18	——	216

4.2 Data Analysis

Similarly to Figs. 1, 2, 3, 4, 5 and 6, Fig. 7 displays a scatter plot of the off-peak and on-peak noise levels in Leicester city centre for two features selected from the dataset.

Off-peak is represented by blue crosses, while On-Peak is displayed as red dots. There is a clear visible difference in behaviour when comparing usage levels. The visualisation relates to two features, L_{max} and L_{min} noise levels. The values along the x-axis (feature 1) denote the maximum noise level for the On-Peak usage. The values along the y-axis refer to the maximum noise levels for Off-Peak. Both features cover a three day period.

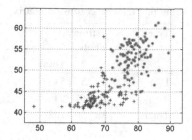

Fig. 7. Scatter plot of the off-peak and on-peak

Visualisation techniques may not always provide a straightforward approach to distinguishing between types of behaviour. The difference in noise levels between on-peak and off-peak hours may not always be easy to identify. Often the changes in behaviour may be subtle and a challenge to detect. The visualisations displays that there is cross-over between 65 dB and 80 dB, for example. However small the differences, the effects are felt by tinnitus sufferers [17].

For that reason, the approach put forward in this paper involves a machine learning classification technique to detect subtle trends in data and predict when noise patterns occur. A mathematical comparison enables detection and predicative model for identifying trends in noise levels in real-time. The results of the classification techniques used are displayed in Table 5. Each of the experiments were conducted 30 times in order to account for errors. This also enables consistency in the results [15, 16].

Table 5. Classification results

Classifiers	AUC (%)	Sensitivity	Specificity	Error
PolyC	94.44	0.9074	0.9259	0.0556
UDC	92.59	0.9259	0.9259	0.0741
KNNC	92.59	0.9259	0.9259	0.0741
ParzenC	92.59	0.9259	0.9259	0.0741
NaivebC	91.67	0.9074	0.9259	0.0833
LDC	90.74	0.9259	0.8889	0.0926
SVC	90.74	0.9074	0.9074	0.0926
TreeC	90.74	0.8704	0.9444	0.0926
QDC	89.81	0.9259	0.8704	0.1019

Overall, the classifiers were able to identify the difference between on-peak and off-peak hours which a high success rate. The results are provided by a confusion matrix evaluation. Table 6 displays a sample confusion matrix provided by the Naivebc classification results.

Table 6. Naivebc confusion matrix

True labels	Estimated labels		
	1	**2**	**Totals**
1	49	5	54
2	9	45	54
Totals	58	50	108

The confusion matrix determines the distribution of errors across all classes. The estimate of the classifier is calculated as the trace of the matrix divided by the total number of entries. Additionally, a confusion matrix provides the point where miss-classification occurs. In other words, it shows true positive (TP), false positive (FP), true negative (TN) and false negative (FN) values. Diagonal elements show the performance of the classifier, while off diagonal presents errors. In this case the matrix shows that the classifier detects 49 of 54 off-peak sounds accurately. 45 of 54 on-peak sounds are correct.

Figures 8, 9, 10 display a histogram distribution of the classification performance results. As Fig. 8 displays, there is a divide in the classifiers' performance, however, most are able to perform consistently, with four able to achieve between 92 % and 94.44 %.

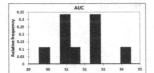 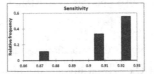 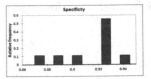

Fig. 8. AUC histogram   **Fig. 9.** Sensitivity histogram   **Fig. 10.** Specificity histogram

The results obtained support the findings that our methodology can be used to accurately classify and predict noise levels. In this case, off-peak and on-peak noise is identified accurately.

4.3   Discussion

In this section, a discussion on the classification results is presented. A visualisation of the High range (between 92.59 and 94.44 %); the medium range (90.74 % to 91.67 %) and the low level range (89 %) is presented. Figure 11 displays a visualisation of the results for the UDC classification (high level).

As in Fig. 7, off-peak is represented by blue crosses, while on-peak is displayed as red dots. The data is in the form of a banana set and separated into groups by likelihood contours. The data inside the contours is most likely to belong to the group. Figure 12, again shows the UDC classification, in this case in the form of a spherical set plot. The

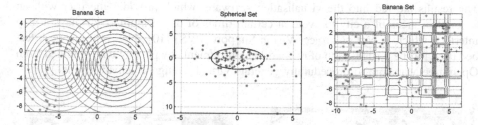

Fig. 11. UDC visualisation   **Fig. 12.** UDC sphere plot   **Fig. 13.** Naivebc banana set plot

graph shows how the classifier is able to accurately group 92.59 % of the data accurately, and separates the on-peak from the off-peak noise. Both graphs display how the classifier is able to sort the data mathematically.

Figure 13 displays a visualisation of the naivebc classifier (mid-level). Contour-lines, formed by the naivebc process, encase groups of data, which are assed to belong to either the on-peak or off-peak grouping. As before, off-peak is represented by blue crosses, while on-peak is displayed as red dots and the scatter plot is in the form of a banana set. The graph displays a visualisation of the AUC of the classifier's performance. 91.67 % of the data is grouped accurately, however misclassification can be identified by the red dots and blue crosses which are grouped incorrectly.

Figures 14 and 15 present a visualisation of the QDC classification process (low range). The linear and spherical line, generated by the QDC analysis, displays the division between the two sets of data.

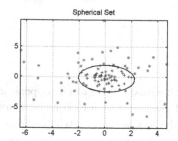

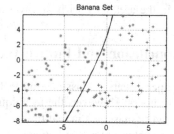

Fig. 14. QDC spherical plot   **Fig. 15.** QDC linear plot

As both graphs display, misclassification occurs and blue (off-peak) data can be seen outside of the spherical plot or on the incorrect side of the linear line (Fig. 15).

5 Data Visualisation

The classification process offers the approach for noise level analysis. The visualisation employs the use of a game engine to visualise the results. By means of this technique, an interface, which can present a directional sound map for the target user, is devised.

The results are fed into the visualisation software, which provides the user with an account of areas of a city to avoid at certain times of day. Figure 16 displays a map interface which is part of Project Vision Support (PVS) [10]. PVS is framework test bed used for the visualisation of real world environments by parsing data obtained from OpenStreetMap.com to procedurally generate virtual, navigable environments [10].

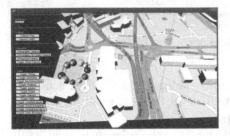

Fig. 16. Map interface   **Fig. 17.** Map interface leicester city centre (UK)

The image shows a map with spheres relating to sound levels. Each of the spheres relates to one of the features from our dataset. The size of the sphere is denoted by the levels of sound types in the area visualised. Figure 17 displays a map interface of Leicester city centre (UK). The conception functions by incorporating real-world map data incorporating map, which is converted in the data manager. Features, initially sent to a temporary data store are used to create feature vectors and train classifiers for the sound prediction. The results are then projected into the map.

The system provides a predictive function to allow users to view expected noise levels in the area they wish to travel to.

6   Conclusion and Future Work

This paper covers a classification technique for distinguishing between on-peak and off-peak hours. However, the techniques employed are a demonstration of how noise levels can be classified in real-time to present an analysis of where and when is the best time to travel or enter a certain area of the city. Tinnitus sufferers can simply choose to avoid leaving the house in peak times. However, our work provides a method for sufferers to be able to leave the house whenever they want by being able to identify in real-time when to avoid specific areas. In the future, we will extend this research to perform an evaluation of other areas such as motorways and different cities around the UK. We will use the data to both present visualisations of the noise patterns in cities and to show how noise pollution levels vary across different environments. We will incorporate further datasets such as holiday periods and weather patterns to create a more holistic noise level model. The future aim of the work will be to conduct a user case study assess the effectiveness of the app.

Acknowledgments. This research is co-supported by the NSF key project with grant no (61332017) and the National project with grant no (2013BAH24F00).

References

1. Fry, B.: Visualizing Data, 1st edn. O'Reilly Media, New York (2008). (28 December 2007). ISBN: 0596514557
2. Hurst, W., Merabti, M., Fergus, P.: Behavioural observation for critical infrastructure security support. In: 7th European Modelling Symposium on Mathematical Modelling and Computer Simulation, pp 36–41 (2013)
3. Hurst, W., Merabti, M., Holmes, S., Iram, S., Fergus, P.: Protecting Critical Infrastructures through Behavioural Observation. Inderscience Int. J. Crit. Infrastruct. **10**(2), 174–192 (2014)
4. Mathers., C.D., Loncar, D.: Updated projections of global mortality and burden of disease, 2002-2030: data sources, methods and results. In: WP on Evidence and Information for Policy World Health Organization (2006)
5. Action on Hearing Loss. www.actiononhearingloss.org.uk. Accessed May 2015
6. British Tinnitus Association (BTA) (2015). www.tinnitus.org.uk/,facts-and-figures. Accessed May 2015
7. Holmes, S., Padgham, N.: More than ringing in the ears: a review of tinnitus and its psychosocial impact. J. Clin. Nurs. **18**(21), 2927–2937 (2009)
8. RNID, What's That Noise? A profile of personal and professional experience of tinnitus in Northern Ireland. RNID, Belfast (2010)
9. Brophy, J.: The visual representation of sound for the hearing impaired, Senior Project Electrical Engineering Department. California Polytechnic State University, San Luis Obispo (2013)
10. Tully, D., El Rhalibi, A., Merabti, M., Shen, Y., Carter, C.: Game based decision support system and visualisation for crisis management and response. In: 15th Annual Post-Graduate Symposium on the Convergence of Telecommunications, Networking and Broadcasting, pp 283–288 (2014)
11. Kuncheva, E.: Combining Pattern Classifiers: Methods and Algorithms. JohnWiley and Sons, NewYork (2004)
12. Fergus, P., Cheung, P., Hussain, A., Al-Jumeily, D., Dobbins, C., Iram, S.: Prediction of preterm deliveries from EHG signals using machine learning. PLoS ONE **8**(10), e77154 (2013)
13. Duin, R.P., Juszczak, P., Paclik, P., Pakalska, P., De Ridder, D., Tax, D.M., Verzakov, S.: Matlab Toolbox for Pattern Recognition, 4th edn. Delft Pattern Recognition Research, The Netherlands (2007)
14. Lotte, F.: Study of Electroencephalographic Signal Processing and Classification Techniques towards the use of Brain-Computer Interfaces in Virtual Reality Applications (2009)
15. Salkind, N.J.: Statistics for People Who (Think They) Hate Statistics, 3rd edn. Sage Publications, London (2008)
16. Idowu, I., Fergus, P., Hussain, A., Dobbins, C., Al-Askar, H.: Advance Artificial Neural Network Classification Techniques Using EHG for Detecting Preterm Births
17. Figueira., S., Nguyen., K., Panditrao, S.: HearThat? - An app for diagnosing hearing loss. In: Global Humanitarian Technology Conference (GHTC) (2014)

18. Lang, J.: Assessment of noise impact on the urban environment, a study on noise prediction models. National Institute for Research on Heat and Noise Technology, Austria (1986)
19. Lumnitzer., E., Behun., M., Bilova, M.: Implementation of method for dynamic noise visualisation into educational process. In: 9th International Conference on Emerging eLearning Technologies and Applications (ICETA), pp 17–19 (2011)

Heart-Creates-Worlds: An Aesthetic Driven Fitness Training System

Lizhen Han[1], Mingmin Zhang[1(✉)],
Feng Tian[2], and Xinting Wang[3]

[1] State Key Lab of CAD and CG, Zhejiang University,
Hangzhou, Zhejiang, China
hlz-1@126.com, zmm@cad.zju.edu.cn
[2] School of Design, Engineering and Computing,
Bournemouth University, Bournemouth, UK
ftian@bournemouth.ac.uk
[3] DMI Research Center,
Hangzhou Normal University, Hangzhou, China
403258354@qq.com

Abstract. We present a novel fitness training system called Heart-Creates-Worlds (HCW) as a practical while pervasive solution to encourage effective daily physical activity. In this system, the aesthetic audiovisual effects of a virtual world are tightly associated with the user's real time heart rate, while the heart rate reflects the users' physiological and psychological state accordingly. By physically act on the control of the representation of the virtual world, users are being persuaded into traveling in a more aesthetically pleasing virtual surroundings than in the displeasure one, meanwhile, naturally fix themselves at the target fitness training zone. A pilot user study was conduct to evaluate the effectiveness and enjoyment of HCW. The results indicate that, this kind of aesthetic-driven fitness training system is helpful on encouraging regular physical performance with enough amounts.

Keywords: CHI · Aesthetic driven · Fitness training · Real time heart rate · System design

1 Introduction

In the high technology and digital age, lacking in activity become more seriously. The sedentary lifestyle is linked to many diseases, including diabetes and heart disease, as well as ailments such as obesity, which is becoming the major root cause of early death [1].

Computer systems which could engage people do more physical activity to improve health is important for pursuing better life in the digital age. Game-related exercising has been reported to increase presence and to motivate to exercise [2].

© Springer International Publishing Switzerland 2015
Y.-J. Zhang (Ed.): ICIG 2015, Part III, LNCS 9219, pp. 599–608, 2015.
DOI: 10.1007/978-3-319-21969-1_54

However, in the context of fitness training system design, encouraging regular performance with enough doses (i.e., amount of intensity, duration and frequency) is challenging for both the player and the designer. According to the updated recommendation [3], healthy adults need moderate-intensity aerobic physical activity for a minimum of 30 mins on five days each week, or vigorous-intensity aerobic activity for a minimum of 20 mins on three days each week, or the combinations of these two. This is the minimum dose to promote and maintain health, help people far away from over 25 diseases linked to physical inactivity and sedentary lifestyle [4]. Unfortunately, most of the public fail to meet the dose to reap these benefits [5].

In this study, we try to take up this challenge by introducing aesthetic as an incentive strategy for fitness training system design. As a promise of happiness, beauty has a positive strength. It naturally has the power of motivation on pursuing pleasure. It may cause resentment and dissatisfaction when not achieved. People seek for beauty instinctively. Based on this, an original aesthetic-driven fitness training system, Heart-Creates-Worlds (HCW), is implemented as a new way for encouraging regular physical activity.

2   Related Work

Exertion game or exergame is regarded as a possible solution of encouraging more physical activity in a video game play way [1]. A particular relevance one is Expresso bike [6]. Expresso bike is an exercise bike with a screen that shows one's biking through virtual environments. It attempts to make exercise more exciting with videogame-like simulation. The key feature is its competitive virtual riding courses, which can be updated by the company over the bike's built-in internet connection. Our prototype system of HCW take the same way of virtual cycling, the biggest difference is on the use of aesthetic as motivate strategy. On the whole, while challenging and exciting, in scientific aspect of proper done, exergames tend to course excess in exercise dose.

To encourage players to do regular exercises, some exergames aim to capture player's action, emotion or the physiological data such as heart rate to control the game play [7–9], or auto-adapt the game level for fair game play experiences [10–12]. Some try constraining player for more quantity and intensity by setting higher objectives or goals [13,14]. Others use competitions or award strategies to lure player spending more time [15].

Most of the approaches above adopt compulsive incentive strategies with constraints to attract and retain players. Through seemingly endless challenges, attractive stories, definite tasks, clear targets, excited competitions, honorary medals, etc., players are spurred to try their best to win. This may however leads to addiction which may bad for health. Faster is not always better for exercise. Meanwhile, although Sinclair et al. [16] advocate exergame should take the guidelines of ACSM (American College of Sports Medicine) [3] as a scientific guarantee of true health, very few exergames have actually abided it strictly.

3   Our Method: Heart-Creates-Worlds

3.1   Concept of the Method

Beauty presents a standard of comparison, and it can cause resentment and dissatisfaction when not achieved. Beauty naturally has the power of motivation on pursuing harmony and happiness, avoiding uncomfortable and unhappiness.

Ugliness is the opposite of beauty. It is a property of a person or thing that is unpleasant to look upon and results in a highly unfavorable evaluation. To be ugly is to be aesthetically unattractive, repulsive, or offensive [17].

The main idea of our method is to use beauty as an incentive strategy to designg fitness training system. We called it aesthetic driven method. It need to combine the user's aesthetical feelings of system representation with their body states and physical performance. By carefully design the user interface with meaningful context awareness, users will be stimulated to do the proper interaction by means of beauty seeking and ugly avoiding. Vice versa, a beautiful appearance of a virtual world may encourage more fitness interaction to hold the harmony of system between computer and human body.

3.2   Scientific Guidelines from Sports Medicine

Using target heart rate as a tool for exercise prescription is common. It represents the percentage difference between resting and MHR (maximum heart rate) added to the resting heart-rate [18]. The estimation of MHR has been a feature of exercise physiology and related applied sciences since the late 1930's. In this paper, we use the easiest and well-known formula, 220 minus age, to calculate MHR. One should figure out his/her target zone depending on his/her goal and fitness capacity.

Commonly there are 5 zones that are used as guidelines to train in.

1. Light Zone - 50 % to 60 % MHR.
2. The energy efficient or Recovery Zone - 60 % to 70 % MHR.
3. Aerobic Zone - 70 % to 80 % MHR.
4. Anaerobic Zone - 80 % to 90 % MHR.
5. The red line zone or VO2 Max zone - 90 % to 100 % MHR [19].

Each training zone has its subtle physiological effect to fitness enhance. According to ACSM, in order to maintain or improve cardio respiratory fitness, exercise must be performed in the range of 65 % to 90 % of a person's MHR. The aerobic zone of 70 % to 80 % MHR is generally considered as the best target zone for improving cardiovascular fitness and improving general health and fitness. In HCW, we set this moderate-intensity zone as our target training zone for instance.

We follow the ACSM physical activity guidelines in year of 2007 [3] and focus on 30 min of moderate-intensity physical activity five days a week for optimum benefits. This recommendation is for the average healthy adult to maintain health and reduce the risk for chronic disease. That means our exertion system design aimed to a relatively long term exercise benefit.

3.3   System Framework

As a low-cost while pervasive virtual fitness training system, HCW is composed of several components which are displayed in Fig. 1:

Fig. 1. System equipment

(a) Physical sensors for virtual cycling: a sensor embedded spinning indoor bike is employed to control an avatar to mimic the user's action. The speed and orientation data is collected for immersive virtual cycling.
(b) Heart rate data reading and recording: a set of wireless heart rate monitor (PolarWearLink+ W.I.N.D. transmitter and Polar WindLink) is installed to record and transmit the data of real-time heart rate. It is easy to wear and suitable for interactive performing.
(c) Signal processing: a porpular PC with P42.4 GHz CPU, 512 M memory, and a GeForce 5700LE video card is well done.
(d) Display terminal: a porpular monitor or a set of projector is worked.

From laboratory to technical exhibition, many users take participant in the test of HCW. The system has a stable running and easy to control. When a user rides the bike, his/her direction and speed are captured by the sensors. An avatar in the virtual environment will mimic his/her exercise according to the captured data. During exercise, the visual and aural effect of the virtual world of HCW changes accordingly to the user's exercise intensity and physical state.

3.4   System Description

In HCW, user's inner physical state is visualized into a 3D representation of desert landscape interactively. With the usage of 3D interface instead of 2D interface, we aimed to leave a chance to the user for virtual roaming and immersion.

a) From <50% to 50-60% HR Zone   b) In 60-70% HR Zone

c) In 75-80% HR Zone   d) In 80-85% HR Zone

e) From 80-85% to 85-90% HR Zone   f) From 85-90 to 90-100% HR Zone

Fig. 2. Overview of the key scenes of HCW. These scenes are generated interactively in real time and represent user's different physical state.

The physical exercise intensity affects the user's physiological data, especially the HR level, which are vividly visualized in the virtual world. The property of the scene's elements such as color, shape, size, value, orientation etc. is all meaningfully associated to players' physical state under the ordinary cognition. One can easily make his instinctive judgment on what state level his body belongs to and thus adjust his exercise intensity accordingly (shows in Fig. 2).

We mainly associate the HR zones with the states of a palm tree as a case. The heart rate based calorie burning is associated with the color tone of the leaf. We totally divide six zones from below 50 % up to 100 % MHR. The VO2 Max zone is very intense and burns the highest number of calories, we design an old type of palm tree with the warmest hue of red leafs to imply the highest body state level. The intensity range under 50 % of MHR is regarded have no use for health, so the tree corresponding to this range has the coolest hue of green leafs and the smallest size like a sapling. The aerobic zone as our target zone, get the best appearance of the palm tree which has the perfect green leafs and the proper size, which looks very strong and full of life energy. Others are analogized by this order. Finally we got eight models of palm trees corresponding to the six main HR zones from 50–100 % MHR.

As a necessary assistance, six intensity levels of the sky-light respectively correspond to the six main HR zones is set up too. That means the sky-light of the virtual scene is interactively changed from dimly early morning to bright high noon according to the player's exercise intensity. The sky-light will fall in dusk when the exercise time is enough and no longer respond to the player's physical effort. The palm tree also do not respond to the heart rate variation any more when exercise time is over.

At this step, we give an answer on how a user could recognize which level his exercise intensity is belongs to instantly, and the solution on when a user could stop his physical effort for time is enough. Beauty has done its special work by both on enriching the basic empty world and on distinguishing the beautiful appearance of palm trees.

4   System Evaluation

To evaluate the usability and feasibility of our method, we conducted two types bilot user study to testify the system of HCW. One is a short period public testing, another is a long term in-lab study.

4.1   Short Period Public Testing

The short period public testing is made on a provincial exposition of new science and technology. In this exhibition, our system catch the masses eyeballs and get a widely participation. More than 30 people take our test. From little school boy to retired aunts, nurse to worker, green hand to fitness expert, sorts of people show great interest in our work and happily to have a try (Fig. 3). We talk to each of them and ask for their feelings and advices. Almost all the participants give positive support and great agreement with this novel and useful exertion system type. The main advice of them is to enrich the scene and give some awards for the good job.

4.2   Long Term In-Lab Study

Participants. 12 graduate student (5 female and 7 male) aged from 24–26 with no knowledge of our research goals were invited and were divided into two groups equally. The two groups had the same average age. The six participants in group A do popular static virtual scene roaming as a baseline method. Others in group B play with HCW.

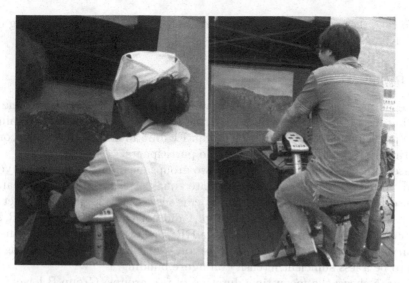

Fig. 3. Visitors on an exposition experience a previous version of HCW

Procedure. To do the study, we specially prepare another system as the contrast and baseline for HCW. This system is a simulation of the popular scene-roaming exertion game model. In this system, we make a copy of the game world of HCW and remove all the relationship between player's physiological data and the game element, the incentive strategy is also delete. We preset all the elements include all kinds' state of the palm trees, flowers and animals on a fixed road. The two game systems seem similar but totally different in their interactive effect and function realization. We call this system VsHCW temporarily for test.

Each group was asked to do their exercise separately on two sets of equipment in two rooms, totally five times in five days. Every participant does their task by turns each time. A five days exercise schedule is preset for all the participants. The schedule consists of three parts: 1. Warm-up (5 min of increasing intensity); 2. Cycling (20 min in moderate intensity); and 3. Cool-down (5 min return to pre-exercise intensity). We told the participants exercise in this program is benefit for their health, but not limit them to obey. We ask each participant do their exercise as free as their real will and we just want to collect the HR data and interested in their true attitude of daily exercise.

Participants of group A put on the heart rate monitor and roaming in the static virtual world of VsHCW. They cannot see their real-time HR data when performing, but they can get a trending line graph of the heart rate recording from a software names Polar ProTrainer 5 at the end. We collect their HR data recording every time.

Group B do exercise by play with HCW. Their HR data recording is also collected, and meanwhile, some system snapshot picture is gathered for consideration.

We take the two groups as comparison and collect their HR recording data for analyzing.

4.3   Results

From each participants' HR recording, we can get not only their real-time HR data, but also actual exercise duration time. Figure 4 shows the average value of all the participants HR data of each group. Figure 5 illustrate the mean score of total time duration of each group's whole participants.

Based on the equal mean age of 25, two groups mean HR of the main cycling period can be compared in an approximate equal level. From Fig. 4, we can see that use HCW, participants of group B can successfully keep their target HR zone in a moderate value of 79 %. Group A did not stay in the target HR zone of 70–80 % MHR, and fall into the lower HR zone of 60–70 %. This means use ordinary virtual roaming way has no use on exercise intensity controlling and tends to be a less sufficient intensity on figure building.

Figure 5 shows the mean time duration of two groups. Group B have a dramatic mean score in keeping exercise quantity. The HR recording displayed that

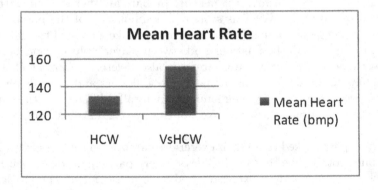

Fig. 4. Mean HR compared with two groups

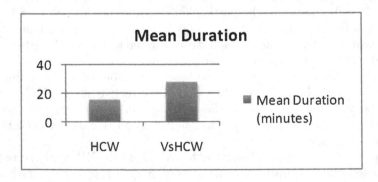

Fig. 5. Mean duration compared with two groups

after the third day, several participants in group A lost their patient in enough time exercising. Play with HCW looks useful and helpful to keep an enough exercise time in a relatively long term.

We have a conversation with each group separately after they have finished the test. Participants in group B seemed excited to express their feelings. *"I used to think doing daily exercise in half an hour is a hard work and a long times wasting. I never think it can be done in such an interesting way. It is a quite easy and pleasant thing to act with HCW." "Without HCW, I don't think I can stay in the target training zone. I often exercise in a less or exceed intensity before." "I love the beautiful scene I have building. I would like to gather the snapshots every day." "It is really amazing! I am traveling in a world creates by my heart!"* While participants in group A looked less of interest to talk about the system they have experienced. *"It is ordinary." "Wow, the scenes looks good, but a little boring." "The heart rate level? No, I don't know how to grasp it." "It is just a virtual roaming. I can hardly get any benefit from it for my body health."*

From the user study, we got a positive result of HCW. This give us great encourage on our research. Almost all the participants in group B support this new method on fitness training system design. Their main advice for this system is to enrich the scene maps and library of elements. That is what we plan to do after we testify the system's usability and effectiveness.

5 Conclusion

In this paper, we present a novel virtual system called HCW. HCW use a most pleasurable persuasive technology to engage health behavior change. We address an interesting position on improving the interaction of a virtual world full of personal biofeedback. This is meaningful in line with the increasing need for pleasure and engaging user experience with interactive systems.

This research is mainly about how to guide and engage users do daily physical activity in a most effcient and natural way via adaptive biofeedback interface and aesthetic context awareness. The system present here has been evaluated by a pilot user study and got encouraging results on effective physical activity and great satisfaction. We hope our work could give a new sight on designing fitness training system as well as the field of CHI.

Acknowledgments. This research is co-supported by the NSF key project with grant no (61332017), (61173124) and the National project with grant no (2013BAH24F00).

References

1. Whitehead, A., Johnston, H., Nixon, N., Welch, J.: Exergame effectiveness: what the numbers can tell us. In: 5th ACM SIGGRAPH Symposium on Video Games, pp. 55–62. ACM Press (2010)
2. Mokka, S., Vtnen, A., Heinil, J., Vlkkynen, P.: Fitness computer game with a bodily user interface. In: Second International Conference on Entertainment Computing, pp. 1–3. Carnegie Mellon University (2003)

3. Haskell, W.L., Lee, I., Pate, R.R., Powell, K.E., Blair, S.N., Franklin, B.A., Bauman, A.: Physical activity and public health: updated recommendation for adults from the American college of sports medicine and the american heart association. Circulation **116**(9), 1081 (2007)
4. Warburton, D., Charlesworth, S., Ivey, A., Nettlefold, L., Bredin, S.S.: A systematic review of the evidence for Canadas physical activity guidelines for adults. Int. J. Behav. Nutr. Phys. Act. **7**(1), 39 (2010)
5. Garriguet, D., Janssen, I., Craig, C.L., Clarke, J., Tremblay, M.S.: Physical activity of Canadian adults: accelerometer results from the 2007 to 2009 Canadian health measures survey, pp. 7–14. Statistics Canada, Ottawa (2011)
6. Expresso bike. http://ifholdings.com
7. Nacke, L.E., Kalyn, M., Lough, C., Mandryk, R.L.: Biofeedback game design: using direct and indirect physiological control to enhance game interaction. In: SIGCHI Conference on Human Factors in Computing Systems, pp. 103–112. ACM (2011)
8. Hamilton, I., Imperatore, G., Dunlop, M.D., Rowe, D., Hewitt, A.: Walk2Build: a GPS game for mobile exergaming with city visualization. In: 14th International Conference on Human-Computer Interaction with Mobile Devices and Services Companion, pp. 17–22. ACM (2012)
9. Lane, N.D., Lin, M., Mohammod, M., et al.: BeWell: sensing sleep, physical activities and social interactions to promote wellbeing. J. Mob. Netw. Appl. **19**(3), 345–359 (2014)
10. Park, T., Hwang, I., Lee, U., Lee, S.I., Yoo, C., Lee, Y., Song, J.: ExerLink: enabling pervasive social exergames with heterogeneous exercise devices. In: 10th International Conference on Mobile Systems, Applications, and Services, pp. 15–28. ACM (2012)
11. Buttussi, F., Chittaro, L., Ranon, R., Verona, A.: Adaptation of graphics and gameplay in fitness games by exploiting motion and physiological sensors. In: Butz, A., Fisher, B., Krüger, A., Olivier, P., Owada, S. (eds.) SG 2007. LNCS, vol. 4569, pp. 85–96. Springer, Heidelberg (2007)
12. Lamoth, C.J., Alingh, R., Caljouw, S.R.: Exergaming for elderly: effects of different types of game feedback on performance of a balance task. Stud. Health Technol. Inform. **181**, 103–107 (2012)
13. Masuko, S., Hoshino, J.: A fitness game reflecting heart rate. In: SIGCHI International Conference on Advances in Computer Entertainment Technology, pp. 53. ACM (2006)
14. Doyle, J., Kelly, D., Patterson, M., Caulfield, B.: The effects of visual feedback in therapeutic exergaming on motor task accuracy. In: Virtual Rehabilitation (ICVR), pp. 1–5. IEEE (2011)
15. Diakopoulos, N., Kivran-Swaine, F., Naaman, M.: Playable data: characterizing the design space of game-y infographics. In: SIGCHI Conference on Human Factors in Computing Systems, pp. 1717–1726. ACM (2011)
16. Sinclair, J., Hingston, P., Masek, M., Nosaka, K.K.: Using a virtual body to aid in exergaming system development. IEEE Comput. graph. Appl. **2**, 39–48 (2009)
17. Agnes, M.E.: Webster's New World College Dictionary, 3rd edn. Pocket Star Books, Riverside (1995)
18. Karvonen, J., Vuorimaa, T.: Heart rate and exercise intensity during sports activities practical application. Sports Med. **5**(5), 303–311 (1988)
19. Foster, C., Florhaug, J.A., Franklin, J., Gottschall, L., Hrovatin, L.A., Parker, S., Dodge, C.: A new approach to monitoring exercise training. J. Strength Cond. Res. **15**(1), 109–115 (2001)

Author Index

Printed in the United States
By Bookmasters